**Oryx Sourcebook Series
in Business and Management**

Government
Regulation
of Business
An Information
Sourcebook

Oryx Sourcebook Series in Business and Management

Oryx Sourcebook Series in Business and Management

Government Regulation of Business

An Information Sourcebook

by Robert Goehlert and Nels Gunderson
Paul Wasserman, Series Editor

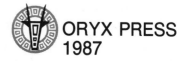

ORYX PRESS
1987

The rare Arabian Oryx is believed to have inspired the myth of the unicorn. This desert antelope became virtually extinct in the early 1960s. At that time several groups of international conservationists arranged to have 9 animals sent to the Phoenix Zoo to be the nucleus of a captive breeding herd. Today the Oryx population is over 400, and herds have been returned to reserves in Israel, Jordan, and Oman.

Library of Congress Cataloging-in-Publication Data

Goehlert, Robert, 1948–
    Government regulation of business.
    (Oryx sourcebook series in business and management) no.2

    Includes index.
    1. Trade regulation—United States—Bibliography.
I. Gunderson, Nels. II. Title. III. Series.
KF1600.A1G64   1987   016.34373'08   86-31177
ISBN 0-89774-261-3   016.3473038

Contents

Introduction

SCOPE

This bibliography is designed to assist librarians, researchers, government personnel and businesspeople interested in the government regulation of business and industry. For the most part, our focus is on government regulation of business at the national level, but we have also included some material that deals with regulation at the international, regional, state and local level. The bibliography includes citations drawn from a variety of fields, including business, economics, political science, law, history, public administration and the general social sciences.

Our aim in compiling this volume was to prepare a comprehensive bibliography on the government regulation of business, political deliberation, economic impact and the functions, organization and procedures of the major federal regulatory agencies. The bibliography includes books, articles, dissertations, essays, research reports and selected documents. As there is a wealth of documents dealing with regulation, we felt that it would be best to leave these out of the volume. One can identify documents by using a number of indexes which we have identified in the section on Reference Works.

Since the bibliography is intended primarily for an English-speaking audience, all the citations are to English-language works. In general, the time period covered by the bibliography extends primarily from 1945 to 1985. While most of the citations identified were published within the last forty years, there are some citations to earlier works, especially if they provide coverage for areas that have not been extensively researched. This is also true in the first section of the bibliography, the annotated section of key or core works on government regulation.

The chief criteria we used to determine which materials to include were that they be analytical, scholarly in nature and not merely descriptive. Consequently, the emphasis is on research monographs, articles from major journals and dissertations. Because of the enormous amount of descriptive material aimed at policymakers, we selectively included such materials in some categories, especially when there was little scholarly work done in those areas. Generally, we tended to include only materials that were commercially available and that could be found in academic libraries.

ARRANGEMENT

We have divided the bibliography into six major sections. The first section is a listing of key monographs on the government regulation of business. All of these entries are annotated. The next four sections include additional materials corresponding to the four subsections of the first section. The materials in these sections are largely journal articles and dissertations. The last section contains reference materials. These materials are broken down into nineteen subsections. All of the entries for reference works are annotated. We have also included a Subject Index, which includes more specific subjects and an Author Index and Title Index. The Subject Index includes material from Sections I through V. The Title Index is for the items cited in Section I, the Core Library Collection, and Section VI, Reference Works. The items in these two sections were selected as the most important titles on the topic of government regulation; they are also the items most referred to by title. All sections are indexed in the Author Index.

The arrangement of the bibliography reflects the nature of the literature. Most of the citations in the first four sections are theoretical and comparative in nature, while the fifth section contains materials on individual regulatory agencies. Consequently, this bibliography can be used to quickly find materials on either a particular topic or federal regulatory agencies.

COMPILATION

In compiling this bibliography, we checked a variety of sources. Primarily, we searched thirteen indexes: *Business Periodical Index, Business Index, Legal Resources Index, Index to Legal Periodicals, United States Political Science Documents, Social Sciences Index, Humanities Index, Public Affairs Information Service Bulletin, ABC Pol Sci, Writings on American History, America: History and Life, International Political Science Abstracts,* and *Sage Public Administration Abstracts.* For dissertations, we made an exhaustive key word search of *Comprehensive Dissertation Index.* For books and research reports, we checked *Books in Print, Cumulative Book Index, American Book Publishing Record, Public Affairs Information Service Bulletin,* as well as the holdings of the Indiana University Libraries.

The thirteen indexes were chosen to incorporate a variety of disciplines, including history, political science and law, as they provide the best coverage of government regulation. We hope that this bibliography will prove beneficial to researchers and students in the field of regulation. This bibliography is also intended to generate interest in the study of regulation by surveying what has been done and pointing out areas of neglected research.

Government Regulation of Business

I. Core Library Collection

ECONOMICS OF REGULATION

1. Adams, Walter, and Gray, Horace M. *Monopoly in America: The Government as Promoter.* New York: Macmillan, 1955. 221 p.
An examination of the relationship between the free market economy, the formation of monopolies and government regulation. Taxation, public utilities, defense procurement, and atomic energy are several of the important areas covered. Well documented and indexed.

2. Anderson, James E., ed. *Economic Regulatory Policies.* Lexington, MA: Lexington Books, 1976. 215 p.
A collection of noteworthy essays which examine trade regulation and economic issues. Consumerism, agriculture, labor relations and fiscal policy are several of the major topics covered within this work. Contributors include professors Lloyd Musolf, George Daly and Charles B. Hagan.

3. Anderson, Ronald A. *Government and Business.* 4th ed. Cincinnati, OH: South-Western, 1981. 420 p.
A text of constitutional and administrative law as applied to business and labor. Landmark Supreme Court cases and opinions by justices are included. An index of cases and a text of the U.S. Constitution are provided.

4. Aram, John D. *Managing Business and Public Policy: Concepts, Problems, and Cases.* Boston: Pitman, 1983. 583 p.
A textbook collection of business cases dealing with corporate management, environmental safety and government regulation. Cases are preceded by a brief summary from the author.

5. Asch, Peter, and Seneca, Rosalind. *Government and the Marketplace.* Chicago: Dryden Press, 1985. 492 p.
A textbook analysis of federal trade regulation. The rationale for government intervention and an assessment of current federal policies are discussed. Includes footnoted references and charts.

6. Backman, Jules., ed. *Business and the American Economy, 1776–2001.* New York: New York University Press, 1976. 196 p.
An edited work which examines the history, present state and future of the free market economy. The evolving role of business and the Federal Reserve's impact on the economy are surveyed from a historical perspective. Includes tables, charts and exhibits.

7. Baratz, Morton S. *The American Business System in Transition.* New York: Crowell, 1970. 101 p.
This book features a brief study of the free enterprise system's salient characteristics. The rise of industrial oligarchy and the consequential formation of social policy are explored.

8. Bardach, Eugene, and Kagan, Robert A. *Going by the Book: The Problem of Regulatory Unreasonableness.* Philadelphia, PA: Temple University Press, 1982. 375 p.

An analytic study of administrative law and regulatory enforcement. Issues ranging from mandatory corporate disclosure to the private regulation of industry are given in-depth treatment. Thoroughly researched and documented.

9. Bardach, Eugene, and Kagan, Robert A., eds. *Social Regulation: Strategies for Reform.* San Francisco, CA: Institute for Contemporary Studies, 1982. 420 p.

This edited volume surveys the issues of government regulation and social policy. Executive branch oversight and the development of effective forms of regulatory enforcement are studied. Regulatory strategy is also examined.

10. Baumol, William J. *Welfare Economics and the Theory of the State.* Cambridge, MA: Harvard University Press, 1965. 212 p.

This book explores the rationale for government intervention in a free market, capitalist state. Welfare policy, the theory of state, and the issue of unemployment equilibrium are considered in some depth. Economic competition and the pursuit of profit are other topics covered.

11. Baumol, William J., and Oates, Wallace E. *The Theory of Environmental Policy: Externalities, Public Outlays, and the Quality of Life.* Englewood Cliffs, NJ: Prentice-Hall, 1975. 272 p.

A detailed work which investigates factors affecting the enforcement and planning of environmental policy. Charts, equations and mathematical models are included to justify regulatory action. The interplay of market forces are analyzed from the point of view of a public administrator.

12. Beauchamp, Tom L. *Case Studies in Business, Society, and Ethics.* Englewood Cliffs, NJ: Prentice-Hall, 1983. 258 p.

A timely collection of case studies which focus on industry, trade and government relations. Issues of consumerism, health care, environmental regulation, and multinational corporate development are presented. Social and ethical considerations are emphasized.

13. Benton, Lewis R., ed. *Private Management and Public Policy: Reciprocal Impacts.* Lexington, MA: Lexington Books, 1980. 239 p.

A collection of essays covering a wide ranging number of public policy areas. The regulation of business, the economy and higher education are examined. Contributors include Oscar Dunn, Edward Mazze and Richard Weeks.

14. Berenbeim, Ronald. *Regulation: Its Impact on Decision Making.* New York: Conference Board, 1981. 48 p.

This book surveys the dynamics of government regulation and its effect on the corporate and managerial decision-making process. Nine areas of regulatory activity are hypothetically explored, including those of equal opportunity employment, occupational safety, the environment, cost accounting practices, and consumer protection. Tabular charts are used to illustrate the findings of the studies.

15. Bernstein, Marver H. *Regulating Business by Independent Commission.* Princeton, NJ: Princeton University Press, 1955. 306 p.

This excellent work traces the history of regulatory policy and practice from the late nineteenth century through the 1950s. The intellectual development, politics, process and enforcement of regulation are analyzed in some detail. The formation and evolution of regulatory commissions are surveyed.

16. Blair, John M. *Economic Concentration: Structure, Behavior and Public Policy.* New York: Harcourt Brace Jovanovich, 1972. 742 p.

A leading work which explores the extent and effect of an oligopolistic corporate economy upon market behavior, labor unions, managerial practices and innovation. Mergers, monopolies, public policy, pricing and the role of government in regulating business are other areas which receive excellent coverage. Appendices include a select list of noteworthy senate hearings and reports before the Subcommittee on Antitrust and Monopoly, Committee on the Judiciary.

17. Blair, Roger D., and Lanzillotti, Robert F., eds. *The Conglomerate Corporation: An Antitrust Law and Economics Symposium.* Cambridge, MA: Oelgeschlager, Gunn and Hain, 1981. 374 p.
This volume of collected essays focuses on the antitrust debate and its many ramifications. The effects of mergers and acquisitions on the free market system are surveyed. Well documented with tables, charts and supporting material.

18. Blough, Roger M. *The Washington Embrace of Business.* New York: Columbia University Press, 1975. 161 p.
A brief study which analyzes government regulation of industry from 1933 to the mid-1970s with special emphasis on the steel industry. President Kennedy's "jaw boning" of the steel industry in April 1962 is covered in some detail. Exhibits chronologically documenting the 1962 steel industry negotiations and events are included.

19. Bonbright, James C. *Public Utilities and the National Power Policies.* New York: Columbia University Press, 1940. 82 p.
A brief work which discusses government regulation of the utilities industry. The power policies of the Roosevelt administration and the rural electrification movement are among the topics covered. A list of further reading is provided.

20. Brown, Courtney C., ed. *The Creative Interface.* Washington, DC: The American University, Center for the Study of Private Enterprise, School of Business Administration, 1968–1973. 5 vols.
A multi-volume collection of lectures delivered at American University during the late 60s and early 70s. Topics on environmental protection, consumerism, private enterprise, international business and urban affairs, among others, are featured. Lecturers include such notable public figures as Edmund Muskie, Maurice Stans, Sol Linowitz and William Ruckelshaus.

21. Brozen, Yale. *Concentration, Mergers and Public Policy.* New York: Macmillan, 1982. 427 p.
This book covers in some detail the issues and theories of monopolistic corporate behavior. Market share, pricing competition and profitability are examined. Tables and charts are provided in most chapters.

22. Cargil, Thomas F., and Garcia, Gillian G. *Financial Deregulation and Monetary Control.* Stanford, CA: Hoover Institution Press, 1982. 154 p.
This noteworthy work focuses on the Depository Institution Deregulation and Monetary Control Act of 1980. The events leading to banking deregulation are traced as well as decontrol's subsequent impact on the financial system. Federal Reserve monetary policy is also studied. A bibliography is provided.

23. Carron, Andrew S., and MacAvoy, Paul W. *The Decline of Service in the Regulated Industries.* Washington, DC: American Enterprise Institute for Public Policy Research, 1981. 73 p.
A brief work which explores the causes and consequences of government regulation in the transportation, utility and telecommunications industries. The effects of regulation on service quality, profitability and productivity are emphasized. Tables and documentation are extensively provided.

24. Clay, Cassius M. *Regulation of Public Utilities: A Crucial Problem in Constitutional Government.* New York: Holt, 1932. 309 p.
This work considers the constitutionality of federal public utility regulation. States rights, the judicial review of commission decisions and the economic costs and benefits of utility regulation are among the issues examined. Includes legal references.

25. Cordes, Joseph J. *The Impact of Tax and Financial Regulatory Policies on Industrial Innovation.* Washington, DC: National Academy of Sciences, 1980. 34 p.
A brief book which explores the effect of tax and macroeconomic policies on the development of new products. Government regulation of capital markets and the taxation of personal income are studied. Footnotes and a bibliography are provided.

26. Corley, Robert N., and Black, Robert L. *The Legal Environment of Business.* 5th ed. New York: McGraw-Hill, 1981. 614 p.

This textbook provides a compendium of business, antitrust and administrative law. Labor practices, mergers and acquisitions, the court system, environmental affairs and consumer protection receive excellent coverage. The work includes a glossary of terms and a text of the U.S. Constitution.

27. Cotter, Cornelius P. *Government and Private Enterprise.* New York: Holt, Rinehart and Winston, 1960. 527 p.

An empirical study which surveys government regulation of business. Regulatory policies dating from the late nineteenth century through the 1950s are featured. Antitrust enforcement, utility rate regulation, the establishment of the FCC, FPC, and FTC as well as other important topics are considered. Brief bibliographies appear at the end of each chapter.

28. Cowing, Thomas G., and Stevenson, Rodney E., eds. *Productivity Measurement in Regulated Industries.* New York: Academic Press, 1981. 417 p.

This collection of papers examines the effect of regulation on several major sectors of the economy. The banking, utility, natural gas, trucking and telecommunication industries are studied in an attempt to determine how output and efficiency are influenced by government intervention. Includes tables, charts, indexes, and a bibliography.

29. Crew, Michael A. *Public Utility Economics.* New York: St. Martin's Press, 1979. 246 p.

A textbook analysis of the issues and theories associated with utility management and regulation. Peak-load pricing, energy conservation and the policy implications for electricity supply are among the topics explored. Includes a mathematical appendix, solutions to selected problems and bibliographic references.

30. Dewing, Arthur S.; Thorp, Willard L.; and Lyon, Leverett S. *Controlled and Competitive Enterprise.* New York: American Management Association, 1937. 27 p.

A brief collection of essays written in the 1930s which examine the public policy issues of regulatory control of a free market economy. The relationships between business and government are considered. A short question and answer session follows the first essay by Arthur S. Dewing.

31. Dimock, Marshall E. *Business and Government.* 3d ed. New York: Holt, 1957. 559 p.

This textbook focuses on the many facets of government regulation of private industry. The relationship between government and organized labor, agriculture, monopolies and banking are surveyed. Indexes of legal cases, names and subjects are provided.

32. Dominguez, George S. *Business, Government, and the Public Interest.* New York: AMACOM, 1976. 40 p.

A brief work which analyzes the federal bureaucratic structure and its relation to business enterprise. Legislation affecting business is examined. The author offers solutions designed to help make government policies more responsive to private industry.

33. Dunfee, Thomas W., and Gibson, Frank F. *Modern Business Law: An Introduction to Government and Business.* Columbus, OH: Grid, 1977. 329 p.

This textbook of legal cases covers the major areas of business law. The legal process, torts, ethics and fair employment practices, among other topics, are investigated. Appendices, as well as case and subject indexes, are included.

34. Dunlop, John T., ed. *Business and Public Policy.* Cambridge, MA: Harvard University Press, 1980. 118 p.

A brief collection of essays on government regulation, public policy and private enterprise. Contributors include such noteworthy public figures as George Shultz, Irving Shapiro and John T. Dunlop. Derek C. Bok, president of Harvard University, has written an introduction to the work.

35. Edwards, Corwin D. *Maintaining Competition: Requisites of a Governmental Policy.* New York: McGraw-Hill, 1949. 337 p.

A timely work which analyzes suitable government policies and programs designed to foster a free market system. The adverse effects of economic concentration and monopolies are studied. Antitrust administration is also explored.

36. Bells, Richard S. F. *The Political Crisis of the Enterprise System.* New York: Macmillan, 1980. 101 p.

A concise study which surveys some of the problems business faces in the industrial and developing nations. The author discusses corporate strategies, self-regulation, philanthropy, social responsibility and the business-government interface. The future survival of the free enterprise system is emphasized.

37. Fainsod, Merle; Gordon, Lincoln; and Palamountain, Joseph C. *Government and the American Economy.* 3d ed. New York: Norton, 1959. 996 p.

This thorough textbook examines major industrial and economic events from the 1800s through the mid-twentieth century. Railroad, utility, antitrust and securities regulation, among other topics, are explored. An excellent bibliography, table of cases and index appear within the work.

38. *The Federal Agenda, A Business View: Summary of a Conference Board Conference.* New York: The Conference Board, 1977. 15 p.

A brief examination by business leaders of the federal government's programs, priorities and policies. Unemployment, inflation, labor relations and the public's image of business are discussed. Remarks by leading executives Fletcher L. Byrom, Reginald H. Jones, Laurence Fenninger and Bert Lance, among others, are included.

39. Foster, J. Rhoads, et al., eds. *Boundaries between Competition and Economic Regulation.* Washington, DC: Institute for Study of Regulation, 1983. 332 p.

This edited work provides an excellent analysis of government regulation and regulatory reform. The effects of deregulation in the airline, telecommunications, and motor carrier industries are summarized by experts. Contributors include professors, chief executive officers and utility commissioners.

40. Fox, Eleanor M., and Halverson, James T., eds. *Industrial Concentration and the Market System: Legal, Economic, Social, and Political Perspectives.* Chicago: Section of Antitrust Law, American Bar Association, 1979. 311 p.

This edited volume includes essays by experts in law, business and economics. Antitrust, economic concentration, free market competition and corporate responsibility are several of the major areas studied. Yale Brozen, Alfred D. Chandler, Ira Millstein and Mark Green are among the numerous contributors. A substantial bibliography on industrial concentration is provided.

41. Friedman, Milton. *Tax Limitation, Inflation and the Role of Government.* Dallas, TX: Fisher Institute, 1978. 110 p.

A work which critically appraises the economic policies of the 60s and 70s. The tax code, inflation, unemployment and monetary policies are assessed. Friedman's theoretical differences with liberal economist John K. Galbraith are explicated.

42. Fritschler, A. Lee, and Ross, Bernard H. *Business Regulation and Government Decision-Making.* Cambridge, MA: Winthrop Publishers, 1980. 256 p.

An excellent book which surveys federal regulatory process and rule making procedure and its impact on corporations. An analysis of how government regulations are devised and implemented is included. Tables, illustrations and an appendix of Washington based organizations of interest to business executives are provided.

43. Fromm, Gary, ed. *Studies in Public Regulation.* Cambridge, MA: MIT Press, 1981. 393 p.

This noteworthy collection of essays examines regulatory policy in the insurance, railroad and telecommunications sectors of the economy. Government regulation of the national economy is also discussed in some detail. Contributors and commentators include distinguished experts Alfred E. Kahn, George J. Stigler, Sam Peltzman and Richard Levin, among others.

44. Galbraith, John K. *Economics and the Public Purpose.* New York: New American Library, 1975. 334 p.

A leading study of economic theory, reform and the free market system. The impact of technology, planning and price determination are examined. A summary of the dynamics of public policy formation and implementation is featured.

45. Goldberg, Walter H., ed. *Governments and Multinationals: The Policy of Control versus Autonomy.* Cambridge, MA: Oelgeschlager, Gunn and Hain, 1984. 343 p.

This book assesses the role of large corporations operating in foreign countries. The relationship between multinational firms and government industrial policies is studied. Numerous tables and charts are included.

46. *Government and the Regulation of Corporate and Individual Decisions in the Eighties.* Englewood Cliffs, NJ: Prentice-Hall, 1981. 119 p.

An analysis of current regulatory policy conducted by the President's Commission for a National Agenda for the Eighties. Conclusions, options and proposals are presented in an attempt to make public policy more responsive to the needs of business, the economy and society. Consumer and environmental protection, price controls, job discrimination, and industrial regulation are several of the major areas covered.

47. Graymer, LeRoy, and Thompson, Frederick, eds. *Reforming Social Regulation: Alternative Public Policy Strategies.* Beverly Hills, CA: Sage Publications, 1982. 288 p.

An edited collection of essays which surveys government regulation of the automobile industry and the economy in general. Deregulatory activity is also investigated. Alfred Kahn, Eugene Bardach and Roger G. Noll are among the distinguished contributors.

48. Green, Mark J., ed. *The Monopoly Makers: Ralph Nader's Study Group Report on Regulation and Competition.* New York: Grossman, 1973. 400 p.

This edited work explores how federal regulation has helped foster monopolistic practices. Several major areas of the private economy are considered including the communications, transportation and utility industries. Chapters are documented with supporting material.

49. Greenberg, Edward S. *Serving the Few: Corporate Capitalism and the Bias of Government Policy.* New York: Wiley, 1974. 275 p.

This book provides an analysis of the relationship between the federal government and big business. The distribution of income/benefits under corporate capitalism and the function of the "positive state" are presented. The administration of health care, the courts and government spending are used as examples to support the author's contentions.

50. Greer, Douglas F. *Industrial Organization and Public Policy.* 2d ed. New York: Macmillan, 1984. 693 p.

A textbook which examines the structure, conduct and performance of the modern corporate state. Government regulation, economic concentration, profit maximization, inflation and technological change are among the numerous areas covered. Subject, industry, company, author and case indexes are provided.

51. Haberer, Joseph. *Science and Technology Policy.* Lexington, MA: Lexington Books, 1977. 216 p.

This edited collection of essays explores the history, formation and future of the government's national science policy. Contributors include Jurgen Schmandt, Stewart Ferguson, Barry Bozeman and J. David Roessner, among others. Separate names and subject indexes are provided.

52. Hargrove, Ervin C. *The Missing Link: The Study of the Implementation of Social Policy.* Washington, DC: Urban Institute, 1977. 128 p.

A scholarly work which analyzes policy research and formation. The relationship between politics, government organizations and the implementation of policy is described. Footnoted references are provided.

53. Hawley, Ellis W. *The New Deal and the Problem of Monopoly; A Study in Economic Ambivalence.* Princeton, NJ: Princeton University Press, 1966. 525 p.

An excellent book which surveys the industrial programs and policies in effect during the great depression of the 1930s. The NRA, antitrust enforcement and the recession of 1937 are examined in some depth. New Deal economic planning strategies and considerations are stressed.

54. Heesterman, A. R. G. *Macro-Economic Market Regulation.* New York: Crane, Russak, 1974. 256 p.

This work analyzes the problems and established theories associated with managing national economies. Keynesianism, monetarism and the neo-classical model are studied. Supporting bibliographic references are provided.

55. Herman, Edward S. *Corporate Control, Corporate Power.* Cambridge: Cambridge University Press, 1981. 432 p.

An outstanding book which traces the evolution of power in the private sector of the economy from 1900 through the mid-1970s. Intercorporate linkages and the relationship between government and big business are assessed. Tables, figures and bibliographic citations are included.

56. Herring, E. Pendleton. *Public Administration and the Public Interest.* New York: McGraw-Hill, 1936. 416 p.

A study which explores the many factors influencing public policy formation and implementation. The relationship between independent regulatory commissions, special interest agencies and the public welfare is examined. The problems associated with strong bureaucracies and a democratically elected government are assessed.

57. Heslop, Alan, ed. *Business-Government Relation.* New York: New York University Press, 1976. 87 p.

This edited volume briefly explores the proper role the state should play in regulating the private economy. Government's relation to the economy and its responsibilities to society are also discussed. Contributors include such well-known figures as Herbert Stein, Milton Friedman, William F. Buckley, Jr. and Arthur J. Goldberg.

58. Hessen, Robert. *In Defense of the Corporation.* Stanford, CA: Hoover Institution Press, 1979. 133 p.

A brief work which refutes anti-corporate charges by Ralph Nader and other critics of big business. It also addresses issues and topics including those of shareholder victimization, corporate divestiture and corporate democracy. Well documented and indexed.

59. Jacobs, Donald P., ed. *Regulating Business: The Search for an Optimum.* San Francisco, CA: Institute for Contemporary Studies, 1979. 260 p.

This collection of essays surveys government regulatory policies in the financial, airline, energy and health care sectors of the economy. Contributors include professors Almarin Phillips, Paul MacAvoy and Richard J. Zeckhauser, among others. An index and bibliography are provided.

60. Jacoby, Neil H., ed. *The Business-Government Relationship: A Reassessment: Proceedings of a Seminar at the Graduate School of Management, The University of California, Los Angeles.* Palisades, CA: Goodyear, 1975. 184 p.

An excellent collection of papers which define and examine problems, models and policies of corporate/state relations. Murray Weidenbaum, Roger Noll, W. Michael Blumenthal and Daniel Bell are several of the noteworthy contributors. Antitrust policies, the social costs of government intervention and the potential of public policy research are topics presented.

61. Johnson, Arthur M. *Government-Business Relations: A Pragmatic Approach to the American Experience.* Columbus, OH: Merrill Books, 1965. 446 p.

This textbook analyzes the politics and process of industrial regulation by the state. Public policy issues such as government subsidies, protective tariffs and antitrust enforcement are covered. Study questions are provided following each chapter.

62. Johnson, Chalmers, ed. *The Industrial Policy Debate.* San Francisco, CA: ICS Press, 1984. 275 p.

An excellent collection of essays which examine the pros and cons of a national industrial policy. The efficacy of protectionism, tax preferences and industrial targeting are examined. Contributors include such noted authorities as Aaron Wildavsky, Murray Weidenbaum, Eugene Bardach and Paul Seabury.

63. Johnson, M. Bruce, ed. *The Attack on Corporate America: The Corporate Issues Sourcebook.* New York: McGraw-Hill, 1978. 348 p.

An edited work which critically examines the arguments commonly invoked against big business. Social responsibility, minority discrimination, pricing policies, planned obsolescence and corporate mergers are several of the timely issues considered by business and economic professors. A consolidated bibliography and a suggested list of additional readings are provided.

64. Kahn, Alfred E. *The Economics of Regulation: Principles and Institutions.* New York: Wiley, 1970. 352 p.

This major two-volume work surveys the regulatory process in the utility, transportation, natural gas and security brokerage industries. The relationship between monopoly and free market trade practices is analyzed. An excellent bibliography is included.

65. Kaysen, Carl, and Turner, Donald F. *Antitrust Policy.* Cambridge, MA: Harvard University Press, 1965. 345 p.

A work which surveys oligopolistic market structures and the public policy considerations associated with antitrust legislation. The author stresses the maintenance of desirable levels of economic performance, within an industry, as an alternative goal of antitrust policy. A methodological appendix of industries is provided.

66. Koontz, Harold, and Gable, Richard W. *Public Control of Economic Enterprise.* New York: McGraw-Hill, 1956. 851 p.

A thorough work which analyzes government regulation of business and industry. The regulation of the public utility, transportation and security industries is studied. Rationales for government economic planning and control are also examined.

67. Kugel, Yerachmiel, and Cohen, Neal P. *Government Regulation of Business Ethics: U.S. International Payoffs.* Dobbs Ferry, NY: Oceana Publications, 1981. 3 vols.

A compendium of those federal laws which regulate international business enterprise and corrupt business practice. Opinions rendered in relevant federal court cases are included.

68. Lamb, Robert, et al. *Business, Media and the Law: The Troubled Confluence.* New York: New York University Press, 1980. 137 p.

This brief work explores what steps business and industry must take to regain a better public image. The regulatory process and administrative law as applied to private enterprise are assessed. A bibliography is included.

69. Lane, Robert E. *The Regulation of Businessmen: Social Conditions of Government Economic Control.* Hamden, CT: Archon Books, 1966. 144 p.

A concise book which investigates the societal and economic implications of government regulatory policy. The institutional relationship between businessmen and bureaucrats is assessed. An excellent bibliography is included.

70. Larson, John A., ed. *The Regulated Businessman: Business and Government.* New York: Holt, Rinehart and Winston, 1966. 302 p.

An edited volume which summarizes government economic policy and control of the private sector. Analyses of antitrust enforcement, administrative law and defense industry policy are featured. Louis Banks, Lawrence Lessing and Richard A. Smith are several of the leading contributors.

71. Lee, R. Alton. *A History of Regulatory Taxation.* Lexington, KY: University of Kentucky, 1973. 228 p.

A historical account of how taxation has been used to control certain sectors of the private economy. The imposition of taxes on firearms, gambling and grain futures are examined. Includes an index to the legal cases cited within the work.

72. Leonard, William N. *Business Size, Market Power, and Public Policy.* New York: Crowell, 1969. 257 p.
A book which discusses, from an economic perspective, the elements of industrial organization, market behavior and public policy. Mergers, business competition and the relationship between business strategy and government policy are analyzed. Tables and figures are provided.

73. Leys, W. A. R., and Perry, C. M. *Philosophy and the Public Interest.* Chicago: Committee to Advance Original Work in Philosophy, 1959. 72 p.
A brief scholarly work which considers some of the fundamental questions associated with public policy formation. The role that taxation, self-regulation governmental expenditure and non-governmental political and religious organizations play in determining public policy is examined. An index to "the authors quoted" is provided.

74. Liebhafsky, Herbert H. *American Government and Business.* New York: Wiley, 1971. 587 p.
This interdisciplinary textbook surveys the philosophical, legal, political, economic and historical events which have led to current corporate regulatory policies. Explanations of administrative law, the Federal Reserve System, antitrust enforcement, and consumer protection are presented. Includes footnoted references and an index.

75. Lin, Steven A., ed. *Theory and Measurement of Economic Externalities.* New York: Academic Press, 1976. 265 p.
This scholarly work discusses analytical and empirical developments in the field of externalities. David A. Starrett, Lloyd S. Shapley, David F. Bradford and Hugh O. Nourse are among the economists contributing to this edited volume.

76. Lindblom, Charles E. *Politics and Markets.* New York: Basic Books, 1977. 403 p.
An interdisciplinary study which analyzes the dynamics of the private enterprise system and its relation to the democratic government. The communist economic system, corporate governance, policy formation and market economics are among the areas covered. Footnoted references are provided.

77. Lodge, George C. *The New American Ideology: How the Ideological Basis of Legitimate Authority in America Is Being Radically Transformed, the Profound Implications for Our Society in General and the Great Corporations in Particular.* New York: Knopf, 1975. 350 p.
A scholarly book which traces the history of economic theory and Lockean political thinking. Property rights, corporate legitimacy and the relationship between business and government are featured topics. The Japanese ideal of property rights and the individual's relationship with society is also examined.

78. Lund, Leonard. *Business Involvement with Local Government.* New York: Conference Board, 1977. 6 p.
A brief work which explores the results of a survey conducted by the Conference Board to assess corporate/company involvement with municipal government. Evaluations by city officials of the advice and leadership provided by company executives and employees are made available. A list of the major companies participating in the survey is provided.

79. Lusk, Harold F., et al. *Business Law and the Regulatory Environment: Concepts and Cases.* Homewood, IL: Richard Irwin, 1982. 1281 p.
This leading textbook summarizes the major tenets of corporate and business law. Contracts, securities, partnerships and the legal system are among the areas covered. The Uniform Commercial Code, Uniform Partnership Act and Model Business Corporation Act are included in the appendices of the work.

80. Lusterman, Seymour. *Managing Business-State Government Relations.* New York: Conference Board, 1983. 59 p.
A concise study which examines the relationship between state governments and companies/corporations. Current company practices and organizational arrangements in effect with state governments are surveyed. An appendix lists several corporate job descriptions of "state government relations managers."

81. MacAvoy, Paul W., et al. *Government Regulations of Business: Its Growth, Impact, and Future: Papers.* Washington, DC: Council on Trends and Perspective, Chamber of Commerce of the United States, 1979. 108 p.

This brief collection of essays explores the effects of regulation on the behavior of business. Business-government interaction, the deregulation of the aviation industry and the measurement of the costs of regulation are topics featured. Contributors include Robert Leone, Paul W. MacAvoy and Edwin T. Haefele.

82. McCraw, Thomas K. *Prophets of Regulation: Charles Francis Adams, Louis D. Brandeis, James M. Landis, Alfred E. Kahn.* Cambridge, MA: Belknap Press, 1984. 387 p.

Focusing on the lives and accomplishments of four leading government figures, this work surveys the evolution of regulatory policy. The establishment and early history of the FTC, SEC and ICC is discussed. Well documented with supporting material.

83. McGrath, Phyllis S. *Redefining Corporate-Federal Relations.* New York: Conference Board, 1979. 102 p.

An in-depth analysis of corporate practice and recent trends in business/government relations. Corporate political fund-raising, PACS, and the formation of an effective government relations program are several of the many topics explored. Charts, tables and an appendix of job descriptions of government relations and lobbying positions is provided.

84. McKenzie, Richard B. *Fugitive Industry: The Economics and Politics of Deindustrialization.* San Francisco, CA: Pacific Institute for Public Policy Research, 1984. 281 p.

This analytical work explores the causes and consequences of industrial relocation. Assessments of and proposed solutions to the problems associated with plant closings are studied. A bibliography is provided.

85. McKeage, Everett C. *Public Utility Regulatory Law: Regulatory Procedure and Judicial Review.* New York: Vantage, 1956. 107 p.

A work devoted to the study of utility regulation. The valuation of utility property, the role of regulatory commissions and the present impact of the Interstate Commerce Act on state authority are among the topics examined. Includes explanatory references.

86. MacRae, Duncan, and Wilde, James A. *Policy Analysis for Public Decisions.* North Scituate, MA: Duxbury Press, 1979. 325 p.

This introductory textbook explores the problems, models and considerations of systematic political analysis and decision making. Case studies supplement most chapters of the work. A bibliography and student exercises are included.

87. Malawer, Stuart S. *Federal Regulation of International Business: Annotated Source Book of Legislation, Regulations and Treaties.* Washington, DC: National Chamber Foundation, 1981. 4 vols.

A multi-volume compendium which lists explanations, by topic or statute, of laws and regulations.

88. Marcus, Alfred A. *The Adversary Economy: Business Responses to Changing Government Requirements.* Westport, CT: Quorum Books, 1983. 255 p.

This noteworthy work explores how business and industry have adapted to the proliferation of economic and social regulation during the last few decades. Compliance and "stonewalling" strategies are examined. Extensively documented with footnotes and a select bibliography.

89. Marketing Concepts, Inc. *The Study of American Opinion: Public Attitudes toward Emerging Issues, Business, Government, Labor, Professions, Institutions: 1978 Report.* Washington, DC: U.S. News and World Report, 1978. 348 p.

A survey which quantifies by category (i.e., income, age, occupation, political leaning, etc.) opinion in the United States. The perceived dependability of various professions and the level of consumer satisfaction are among the areas surveyed. A sample of the questionnaire is provided.

90. Markham, Jesse W. *Conglomerate Enterprise and Public Policy.* Boston: Division of Research, Graduate School of Business Administration, Harvard University, 1973. 218 p.

This work discusses the leading concerns associated with corporate mergers and acquisitions. An analysis of the structural impact of diversification, conglomerate management and market competition is included. The policy implications of the merger movement of the 1960s are also examined.

91. Miller, Arthur S. *The Modern Corporate State: Private Governments and the American Constitution.* Westport, CT: Greenwood Press, 1976. 269 p.

A work which analyzes the impact of giant corporations on our society. The history, present state and future of corporate power is surveyed. A critical examination of government's relationship with big business is the focus of several chapters.

92. Miller, James C., and Yandle, Bruce, eds. *Benefit-Cost Analyses of Social Regulation: Case Studies from the Council on Wage and Price Stability.* Washington, DC: American Enterprise Institute for Public Policy Research, 1979. 171 p.

A collection of essays which investigates the proliferation and consequences of regulatory policies and programs. Case studies involving product safety, consumer health, energy, international trade and the environment are studied. Contributors include economists Robert L. Greene, Thomas M. Lenard, Dianne R. Levine and Milton Z. Kafoglis.

93. Millstein, Ira M., and Katsh, Salem M. *The Limits of Corporate Power: Existing Constraints on the Exercise of Corporate Discretion.* New York: Macmillan, 1981. 265 p.

Focusing on government regulation of business, this work explores the tax systems, antitrust laws and equal opportunity employment programs. The influence of social values on the corporate decision-making process is surveyed. Extensive bibliographic references are included.

94. Mitchell, Bridger M., and Kleindorfer, Paul R., eds. *Regulated Industries and Public Enterprise: European and United States Perspectives.* Lexington, MA: Lexington Books, 1980. 289 p.

An edited collection of papers which assess regulatory policies in the air transportation, public utility and postal industries. Ingo Vogelsang, Walter Schulz, Roger Sherman and John C. Panzar are among this work's contributors.

95. Mitnick, Barry M. *The Political Economy of Regulation: Creating, Designing, and Removing Regulatory Forms.* New York: Columbia University Press, 1980. 506 p.

A major work devoted to the theory, process and study of regulatory policy. A description and analysis of the rationales for government are included. Tactics and strategies employed by industry in their relations with government regulatory agencies are explored.

96. Moskow, Michael H. *Strategic Planning in Business and Government.* New York: Committee for Economic Development, 1978. 86 p.

This concise work advocates transferring corporate strategic and operational planning technique to government agencies. Lessons federal bureaucracies can learn from private industry's systematic view of the decision-making process are considered. A case study appendix is provided.

97. Mueller, Dennis C. *Public Choice.* Cambridge: Cambridge University Press, 1979. 279 p.

This book examines the political science and public sector decision-making process through the application of economic theory. Social welfare functions, voter patterns, the two party political system, and normative political theories are discussed. A thorough bibliography is included.

98. Musolf, Lloyd D. *Mixed Enterprise.* Lexington, MA: Lexington Books, 1972. 172 p.

An outstanding work which focuses on joint ventures undertaken between governments and the private sector. The experiences of France, Italy, Japan, Mexico, Israel and Taiwan, among other countries, are surveyed. Supporting bibliographic references are provided for each chapter.

99. Nadel, Mark V. *Corporations and Political Accountability.* Lexington, MA: D. C. Heath, 1976. 265 p.

This analytical study proposes remedies and reforms designed to curb the concentration of corporate power. The relationship between public policy formation and business is examined. Regulatory politics, political elections, corporate lobbying and the issues associated with corporate accountability are assessed.

100. Nader, Ralph; Green, Mark; and Seligman, Joel. *Taming the Giant Corporation.* New York: Norton, 1976. 312 p.

A book which critically assesses the power of big business and its impact on society. A case for federal chartering of corporations is proposed, by the authors, to place checks on corporate influence and political power. Well documented with footnotes and bibliographic references.

101. Neal, Alfred C. *Business Power and Public Policy.* New York: Praeger, 1981. 163 p.

A noteworthy study which examines the role large companies play in influencing national economic planning. Corporate social responsibilities, cost-price behavior and the power of labor unions are among the areas explored. Former Secretary of Commerce Philip M. Klutznick provides a foreword to the book.

102. Needham, Douglas. *The Economics and Politics of Regulation: A Behavioral Approach.* Boston: Little, Brown, 1983. 482 p.

An excellent textbook examination of the regulatory process designed for upper level undergraduate and introductory graduate courses. The behavior of regulated firms and monopolies is studied. Includes footnoted references, tables and mathematical equations.

103. Olson, Mancur. *The Logic of Collective Action: Public Goods and the Theory of Groups.* Cambridge, MA: Harvard University Press, 1965. 176 p.

An excellent interdisciplinary examination of pressure group theory, class theory, trade unionism, economic freedom and organizational behavior. The author discusses, in some detail, special interest groups and Marxian class theory.

104. Peters, Charles, and Branch, Taylor, eds. *Blowing the Whistle: Dissent in the Public Interest.* New York: Praeger, 1972. 305 p.

This edited collection of essays explores waste, fraud and corruption in the Congress and bureaucracies of the United States government. Abuses of power in the Pentagon, Justice Department and Senate are examined. Contributors include journalists Jeffrey Record, Robert Benson, Adam Hochchild and Peter Gall.

105. Petersen, Harold C. *Business and Government.* New York: Harper and Row, 1981. 478 p.

A textbook compendium of the major legal issues facing administrators, executives and politicians who are responsible for managing the private and public sectors of the economy. Price regulation, antitrust policies, patents and incomes policies are among the topics featured within this work. Includes an index of legal cases.

106. Phillips, Almarin W., ed. *Promoting Competition in Regulated Markets.* Washington, DC: Brookings Institution, 1975. 397 p.

An edited work covering the various policy considerations associated with the regulation of business and industry. The regulatory policies governing the transportation, telecommunications, insurance, utility and financial sectors of the economy are analyzed. Contributors include George C. Eads, Leonard Weiss, Edwin M. Zimmerman and Dennis Smallwood.

107. Posner, Richard A. *Economic Analysis of Law.* Boston: Little, Brown, 1977. 572 p.

This textbook interpretation of business and economic law provides coverage of torts, contracts, antitrust, taxation and property rights among many other related legal areas. Suggested readings, problems and a table of cases are included.

108. Raphael, Jesse S. *Governmental Regulation of Business.* New York: Free Press, 1966. 260 p.

This work surveys regulatory policy from the turn of the century through the mid-1960s. Federal regulation of interstate commerce, business practices, securities, labor relations, and food and drugs are discussed. A table of court cases is provided.

109. Reagan, Michael D. *The Managed Economy.* New York: Oxford University Press, 1963. 288 p.

Advocating more effective control of the private sector, this work explains why the American economy no longer functions as the free market model of Adam Smith's time. The role of government and the private corporation is examined. Includes bibliographic notes and an index.

110. Redford, Emmette S. *Administration of National Economic Control.* New York: Macmillan, 1952. 403 p.

An excellent book which analyzes the tools and techniques of developing and implementing economic policy. Tax policies, interest group participation and the role that government agencies play in managing the economy are examined. The effectiveness of administrative control is also discussed.

111. Reisman, George. *The Government against the Economy.* Ottawa, IL: Caroline House, 1979. 207 p.

A critical assessment of government imposed price controls. An explanation of the principles and operations of a free market economy is presented. Bibliographic references are included.

112. Rhine, Shirley H. *The Impact of Regulations on U.S. Exports.* New York: Conference Board, 1981. 56 p.

A brief survey which ascertains which regulations and trade policies have hindered the growth of U.S. exports. Suggestions for stimulating exports and eliminating trade barriers are provided. Replete with supporting tables and charts.

113. Ripley, Randall B., et al. *Structure, Environment, and Policy Actions: Exploring a Model of Policy-Making.* Beverly Hills, CA: Sage Publications, 1973. 56 p.

This concise work summarizes, on a theoretical basis, some of the inherent problems associated with the formation and implementation of public policy. The study is supported by a longtitudinal trend analysis of policy actions undertaken. Statistical tables are provided.

114. Robinson, Louis, and Nugent, Rolf. *Regulations of the Small Loan Business.* New York: Russell Sage Foundation, 1935. 284 p.

A timely work which traces the history of lending and the development of small loan legislation. The organization of small loan offices and the question of the maximum rate of charge are among the topics considered. Replete with supporting tables and charts.

115. Rostow, Eugene V. *Planning for Freedom: The Public Law of American Capitalism.* New Haven, CT: Yale University Press, 1959. 437 p.

This work examines legal control of the national economy. Fiscal and monetary policy and regulation of the market is discussed. Appendices include a list of selected statutory provisions and statistical tables.

116. Russell, Milton R., ed. *Perspectives in Public Regulation: Essays on Political Economy.* Carbondale, IL: Southern Illinois University Press, 1973. 130 p.

An edited collection of essays which discuss regulatory policy in the utility and securities industries. Contributors include professors of business administration and the social sciences, as well as industry executives. Bibliographic references and an index are provided.

117. Samuels, Warren J., and Schmid, A. Allan. *Law and Economics: An Institutional Perspective.* Boston: Nijhoff, 1981. 268 p.
This edited collection of essays provides an analysis of economic regulation and theory. The interrelation between legal and economic processes is examined. Contributors include professors Warren J. Samuels, A. Allan Schmid, Josef M. Broder and James D. Shaffer.

118. Schmalensee, Richard. *The Control of Natural Monopolies.* Lexington, MA: Lexington Books, 1979. 178 p.
A work which reviews alternative corporate control strategies. The regulation of utility industries through taxation, rate structuring and adjustment formulas are explored. Includes a select bibliography.

119. Schnitzer, Martin. *Contemporary Government and Business Relations.* Chicago: Rand McNally, 1978. 572 p.
Focusing on government regulation of industry, this textbook reviews the development of federal policy from 1870 to the present. The impact of antitrust policy, consumer protectionism, environmental legislation and equal opportunity employment practices upon business is examined. Includes tables, charts and a glossary.

120. Schubert, Glendon. *The Public Interest.* New York: Free Press, 1960. 244 p.
This scholarly work examines the processes of public policy formation from the perspective of rationalist, idealist and realist political theories. A select bibliography is provided.

121. Schultze, Charles L. *The Public Use of Private Interest.* Washington, DC: Brookings Institution, 1977. 93 p.
A concise book which assesses the ineffectiveness of government regulation and intervention in the private sector of the economy. As an alternative, Schultze recommends incentives based on new tax and transfer policies as well as greater free market involvement. Footnoted references are provided.

122. Sethi, S. Prakash, and Swanson, Carl L., eds. *Private Enterprise and Public Purpose: An Understanding of the Role of Business in a Changing Social System.* New York: Wiley, 1981. 461 p.
An edited volume devoted to the study of the corporate community's relationship with government and society. Corporate ethics, governance and social responsibility are several of the many topics covered. Contributors include professors Gerald L. Cavanagh, Irving Kristol, Edwin M. Epstein, Christopher DeMuth and Allan Roth.

123. Sharp, Margaret. *The State, the Enterprise and the Individual.* London: Weidenfeld and Nicolson, 1973. 296 p.
A study concerned with the problems of applied microeconomics. Planning, corporate behavior, antitrust, cost benefit analysis and federally provided social services are among the topics discussed. Includes bibliographic references, tables and graphs.

124. Shepherd, William G. *Public Policies toward Business.* 7th ed. Homewood, IL: R. D. Irwin, 1985. 541 p.
A textbook which summarizes the fundamental considerations and concerns associated with government regulation of the private economy. Antitrust laws, mergers, pricing, trade barriers and deregulation are topics covered within this work. Case, name and subject indexes are provided.

125. Shepherd, William G. *The Treatment of Market Power: Antitrust, Regulation, and Public Enterprise.* New York: Columbia University Press, 1975. 326 p.
This scholarly work problematically investigates government economic policy and the free market economy. Industrial policies, conventional markets, policy instruments and an analysis of the financial sector are among the topics featured. Appendices and footnoted references are provided.

126. Shepherd, William G., and Gies, Thomas G., eds. *Regulation in Further Perspective: The Little Engine that Might.* Cambridge, MA: Balinger, 1974. 138 p.
An excellent work which addresses the timely problems of regulatory politics and policy implementation. Regulatory reform, the Averch-Johnson Hypothesis and utility regulation are several of the topics covered. Graphs, tables and footnotes are included.

127. Shipper, Frank, and Jennings, Marianne M. *Business Strategy for the Political Arena.* Westport, CT: Quorum Books, 1983. 177 p.
An excellent study which summarizes the current relationship between the federal government and business in the United States. The effects of political action committees, strategic political planning and judicial review are several of the topics surveyed from a business perspective. Appendices and a select bibliography are included.

128. Shonfield, Andrew. *In Defense of the Mixed Economy.* New York: Oxford University Press, 1984. 231 p.
This work considers how government policies and institutions can best serve the economic needs of society. Trends in Europe and the United States are explored. A discussion of corporate approaches to foreign and domestic government policy is featured.

129. Siegan, Bernard H. *Economic Liberties and the Constitution.* Chicago: University of Chicago Press, 1980. 383 p.
A history of the Court's role in interpreting regulation of the private sector. Due process, personal rights and the judicial abdication are several of the areas assessed. An index of cases and footnoted references are provided.

130. Siegan, Bernard H., ed. *Government, Regulation and the Economy.* Lexington, MA: Lexington Books, 1980. 146 p.
An edited collection of debates which focus on what role government should play in the private sector. Industrial regulation, energy policy, minimum wage law and public employee collective bargaining are among the issues discussed. Contributors include such notable public figures as John Kenneth Galbraith, Gary Hart, Stephen Solarz, Jake Garn and Howard Phillips.

131. Siegan, Bernard H., ed. *The Interaction of Economics and the Law.* Lexington, MA: Lexington Books, 1977. 171 p.
A collection of scholarly essays which analyze regulatory trade policies. Regulation of business, land use, foreign competition and the political economy are among the topics addressed. Herbert Stein, Harry Mame, Sam Peltzman and W. Allen Wallis are among the work's contributors.

132. Siegan, Bernard H., ed. *Regulation, Economics, and the Law.* Lexington, MA: Lexington Books, 1979. 123 p.
A series of debates which explore various economic and regulatory issues. Government regulation of energy, federal/state land use legislation, corporate social responsibility and national health insurance are among the issues debated. Contributors include Stewart Udall, Richard Lamm, Lester Breslow and Milton Friedman.

133. Smead, Elmer E. *Governmental Promotion and Regulation of Business.* New York: Appleton-Century-Crofts, 1969. 582 p.
A thorough book covering the many facets and considerations associated with public sector management of the private economy. Taxation, tariffs and antitrust enforcement are analyzed as well as government regulation of the media, railroads, airlines and the utility industry. Includes a table of legal cases.

134. Smith, Bruce L. R., ed. *The New Political Economy: The Public Use of the Private Sector.* New York: Halsted, Wiley, 1975. 344 p.
This edited work explores the relationships between government and various public and private institutions. Higher education, medicare, grants-in-aid, the military industrial complex and the regulation of the private economy are among the topics explored. Contributors include Michael D. Reagan, Paul M. Densen, David C. Warner and Martin Edmonds.

135. Smoot, Dan. *The Business End of Government.* Boston: Western Islands, 1973. 231 p.
A negative assessment of the federal government's attempt to regulate corporate activity and the health and safety of workers. The regulation of labor unions, antitrust enforcement and pollution control are cited as examples of government failure.

136. Sobel, Robert. *The Age of Giant Corporations; A Microeconomic History of American Business, 1914–1970.* Westport, CT: Greenwood Press, 1972. 257 p.
A historical account which surveys the activities of business, industry and corporate executives in the twentieth century. The relationship between political and industrial power is analyzed. Includes an excellent bibliography.

137. Solo, Robert A. *The Political Authority and the Market System.* Cincinnati, OH: South-Western, 1974. 418 p.
A historical analysis of the free enterprise system from 1800 through the mid-twentieth century. Antitrust policy, corporate mergers, the New Deal credo and the political economy are among the areas assessed. Government regulation of railroads, airlines and the communications industry is discussed.

138. Steiner, George A. *Business and Society.* 2d ed. New York: Random House, 1975. 610 p.
This textbook considers the balance between private enterprise, government and the public interest. Government regulation of business, labor union influence, corporate ethics and antitrust issues are among the areas covered. An in-depth bibliography is provided.

139. Steiner, George A. *Government's Role in Economic Life.* New York: McGraw-Hill, 1953. 440 p.
An outstanding work which focuses on federal regulation and control of the economy. Problems and issues associated with the formation and execution of public policy are assessed. The administrative machinery of government is examined. Includes tables, charts and diagrams.

140. Steiner, George A., and Steiner, John F. *Business, Government, and Society: A Managerial Perspective.* 3d ed. New York: Random House, 1980. 625 p.
A textbook which considers the underlying forces and relationships between corporations and the federal bureaucracy. Consumerism, pollution, business ethics, managerial ideologies and the social responsibilities of business are among the many topics examined. Includes an extensive bibliography.

141. Stokes, M. *Conquering Government Regulation: A Business Guide.* New York: McGraw-Hill, 1982. 272 p.
A practical work which instructs business executives on how to best deal with government agencies and regulations. The regulatory process, lobbying an agency, litigation and bureaucratic rule making are discussed in some detail. A table of cases is provided.

142. Stone, Harlan F. *Public Control of Business: Selected Opinions.* New York: Howell, Soskin, 1940. 324 p.
A classic work which assesses the role government should play in regulating the private economy. Public utility rate making, labor relations, competition and monopoly, and state regulation are among the topics featured.

143. Thayer, Frederick C. *Rebuilding America: The Case for Economic Regulation.* New York: Praeger, 1984. 168 p.
An analysis of how economic and trade policy can be used to achieve economic recovery and growth. The regulatory reforms undertaken during the 1970s are assessed. Includes policy recommendations.

144. Thompson, Fred., ed. *Regulatory Regimes in Conflict: Problems of Regulation in a Continental Perspective.* Lanham, MD: University Press of America, 1984. 157 p.
A brief work which compares the political economies of Canada, the U.S. and Europe. Airline deregulation, toxic waste and regulatory reform are among the other topics examined. A list of bibliographic references is included.

145. Tolchin, Susan J., and Tolchin, Martin. *Dismantling America. The Rush to Deregulate.* Boston: Houghton Mifflin, 1983. 323 p.
An excellent study of the federal government's current laissez-faire approach to business and industry. An analysis of the political and social implications of deregulation is provided. Includes a bibliography, footnoted references and a federal agency acronyms list.

146. Tollison, Robert D., ed. *The Political Economy of Antitrust.* Lexington, MA: Lexington Books, 1980. 147 p.
An edited work which analyzes the many issues associated with antitrust policy. The relationship between antitrust enforcement and the economy is discussed in detail. Among the contributors are professors Yale Brozen, Donald Dewey, Ernest Gellhorn and Thomas Morgan.

147. Waldmann, Raymond J. *Regulating International Business through Codes of Conduct.* Washington, DC: American Enterprise Institute for Public Policy Research, 1980. 139 p.
An excellent work which addresses some of the economic and foreign policy issues associated with multinational corporate enterprise. U.S. policy considerations, technology regulation and the role governments play in regulating corporate activity are examined. Appendices of international codes of conduct and a bibliography are provided.

148. Weidenbaum, Murray L. *Business, Government, and the Public.* 2d ed. Englewood Cliffs, NJ: Prentice-Hall, 1981. 336 p.
A textbook study of federal regulation of the private sector. Government regulation of job safety, consumer safety, environmental management and personnel practices are several of the areas assessed. An excellent bibliography is included.

149. Weidenbaum, Murray L. *The Costs of Government Regulation.* St. Louis, MO: Center for the Study of American Business, Washington University, 1977. 12 p.
This work briefly summarizes the negative effect federal regulatory policies have had on private enterprise. The difficulty of understanding and complying with government agency directives as well as the inflationary impact of certain regulations are among the topics addressed.

150. Weiss, Leonard W., and Klass, Michael W. *Case Studies in Regulation: Revolution and Reform.* Boston: Little, Brown, 1981. 301 p.
An edited textbook intended for college students on government control of business and industry. The effect of public policy on market competition, airline regulation, natural gas prices and the decontrol of oil prices is studied.

151. Weiss, Leonard W., and Strickland, Allyn D. *Regulation: A Case Approach.* 2d ed. New York: McGraw-Hill, 1982. 444 p.
Intended for college undergraduates, this work illustrates the dynamics of federal regulatory policy. Antitrust enforcement, economic and social regulation are among the general areas studied. A list of legal cases is included.

152. Wiebe, Robert H. *Businessmen and Reform.* Cambridge, MA: Harvard University Press, 1962. 283 p.
This noteworthy study explores how the progressive movement of the early twentieth century influenced business leaders. The impact of business and industry upon progressive politics is also assessed. Includes a bibliography and footnoted references.

153. Wilcox, Clair. *Public Policies toward Business.* 5th ed. Homewood, IL: R. D. Irwin, 1975. 766 p.
A comprehensive textbook survey of government regulatory policies designed for the upper college level. Antitrust enforcement, mergers, public policy formation and regulation of the financial sector are among the many areas analyzed. Indexes of cases, names and subjects are provided.

154. Williamson, Oliver E. *Markets and Hierarchies: Analysis and Antitrust Implications.* New York: Free Press, 1975. 286 p.
A work devoted to the study of monopoly, oligopoly and conglomerate market structures. Vertical corporate integration, organizational frameworks, market competition and public policy formation are among the various areas examined. An extensive bibliography is provided.

155. Winter, Ralph K. *Government and the Corporation.* Washington, DC: American Enterprise Institute for Public Policy Research, 1978. 73 p.
A discussion which advocates a hands-off public policy approach to the problem of industrial relocation. The author argues in favor of federal restrictions on state takeover statutes and contends the socioeconomic power of large corporations is overestimated.

156. Wolfson, Nicholas. *The Modern Corporation: Free Market versus Regulation.* New York: Free Press, 1984. 191 p.
A provocative book which assesses the role corporate sector influence plays in our society. The regulatory relationship between government and industry is discussed. Footnoted references are provided for each chapter.

POLITICS OF REGULATION

157. Abramson, Mark A. *The Funding of Social Knowledge Production and Application: A Survey of Federal Agencies.* Washington, DC: National Academy of Sciences, 1979. 487 p.
A study which describes the various activities funded by the federal government in the areas of social research and development. Each chapter is devoted to a specific agency of the government and its funding of social research. An index of agencies and an appendix of recently created federal commissions is provided.

158. American Bar Association, Commission on Law and the Economy. *Federal Regulation: Roads to Reform.* Washington, DC: The Association, 1979. 171 p.
A final ABA report consisting of proposals and recommendations designed to increase the effectiveness and efficiency of the regulatory process. A general analysis of government regulatory policy is presented. Includes footnotes, tables and an appendix of supporting documentation.

159. American Enterprise Institute for Public Policy Research. *Major Regulatory Initiatives during 1979: The Agencies, the Courts, and the Congress.* Washington, DC: The Institute, 1980. 46 p.
A brief analysis outlining the leading legal, economic, bureaucratic and political regulatory developments. The activities of independent agencies, executive branch agencies as well as court actions and congressional initiatives are summarized.

160. Anderson, James E. *The Emergence of the Modern Regulatory State.* Washington, DC: Public Affairs Press, 1962. 172 p.
A well-written historical study of government regulation of business and industry from 1887 to 1917. An examination of the ideas and thinking which influenced government's early attempts in regulating economic activity is presented. Footnoted references are provided for each chapter.

161. Arnold, R. Douglas. *Congress and the Bureaucracy: A Theory of Influence.* New Haven, CT: Yale University Press, 1979. 235 p.
An empirical study which explores the relationship between Congress and the federal bureaucracy. The work measures the responsiveness of administrative agencies to congressional pressure. Examples of geographic politics, coalition building, military employment patterns and awards of grants-in-aid are cited to illustrate the author's theories of political influence. Bibliographic references, appendices and tabular charts are included.

162. Asimow, Michael. *Advice to the Public from Federal Administrative Agencies.* New York: M. Bender, 1973. 206 p.
A report which explains where and how to seek advice within the federal bureaucracy. Agency practices and various informal processes in effect are ascertained. Procedures of most of the major federal bureaus are included.

163. Backman, Jules, ed. *Regulation and Deregulation.* Indianapolis, IN: Bobbs-Merrill, 1981. 174 p.
An examination, by leading economists and executives, of the dynamics of the federal regulatory infrastructure. Private sector competition, regulatory excess and the deregulation of the airline and banking industries are among the areas addressed. Contributors include Jules Backman, Dick Netzer, Yale Brozen and Murray Weidenbaum.

164. Balzano, Michael P. *Reorganizing the Federal Bureaucracy: The Rhetoric and the Reality.* Washington, DC: American Enterprise Institute for Public Policy Research, 1977. 43 p.
A brief work which examines recent attempts to restructure and simplify government agencies. The problems, controversy and politics encountered during the reorganization of several federal agencies are described.

165. Bedingfield, Robert E., et al. *Competition and Regulation—Some Economic Concepts.* Lexington, VA: Washington and Lee University, 1976. 154 p.
A collection of papers which assess various aspects of trade regulation. Research and development, intrastate telecommunication rate setting and railroad regulation are among the topics discussed. Includes tabular charts.

166. Belonzi, Arthur; D'Antonio, Arthur; and Helfand, Gary. *The Weary Watchdogs: Governmental Regulators in the Political Process.* Wayne, NJ: Avery Publishing Group, 1977. 221 p.
A study which evaluates government attempts to regulate the profit motive. The history and function of such federal agencies as the FTC, ICC, SEC, FDA and EPA are examined. A selected bibliography, footnoted references and a corporate/agency index are included.

167. Berry, Jeffrey M. *Lobbying for the People: The Political Behavior of Public Interest Groups.* Princeton, NJ: Princeton University Press, 1977. 331 p.
This noteworthy study analyzes the development, maintenance and legislative activities of advocacy organizations. Organizational resources, tactics and strategies of advocacy, and decision-making processes (with a public interest group) are several of the topics examined. Appendices and a bibliography are included.

168. Blachly, Frederick F., and Oatman, Miriam E. *Federal Regulatory Action and Control.* Washington, DC: Brookings Institution, 1940. 356 p.
This timely study analyzes the legal and administrative problems associated with government regulation of the economy. The various forms of federal administrative action, procedure and enforcement are ascertained. Includes supporting documentation.

169. Breyer, Stephen. *Regulation and its Reform.* Cambridge, MA: Harvard University Press, 1982. 472 p.
This work assesses the effects of federal regulatory policies and the justification for government intervention in the private sector. Regulatory reform, classical forms of regulation, rate making, and policy formation are several of the topics discussed. Appendices of regulatory agencies and administrative law are included.

170. Browne, William P. *Politics, Programs, and Bureaucrats.* Port Washington, NY: Kennikat Press, 1980. 180 p.
An insightful examination of the internal structure and function of federal agencies. Legislative politics, intergovernmental relations, bureaucratic conflict, rule making and the call for reorganization are among the topics addressed. Diagrams and bibliographic references are provided.

171. Campbell, Rita R. *Drug Lag: Federal Government Decision-Making.* Stanford, CA: Hoover Institution Press, 1976. 62 p.
A brief study of the Food and Drug Administration's regulatory procedures and their impact on the approval of new drugs. Includes a bibliography and footnotes.

172. Carey, William L. *Politics and the Regulatory Agencies.* New York: McGraw-Hill, 1967. 149 p.
An appraisal of congressional and White House influence upon the federal bureaucracy. The logistics of shepherding agency sponsored legislation through Congress is discussed. Includes footnoted references and an index.

173. Carter, William A., and Lindahl, Martin. *Corporate Concentration and Public Policy.* 3d ed. Englewood Cliffs, NJ: Prentice-Hall, 1959. 698 p.
This work analyzes antitrust regulation of large business. The steel, chemical, automobile and petroleum industries are among those studied. Includes footnoted references and tables with supporting data.

174. Clark, Timothy B.; Kosters, Marvin H.; and Miller, James C., eds. *Reforming Regulation.* Washington, DC: American Enterprise Institute for Public Policy Research, 1980. 161 p.
An excellent collection of speeches which address the issues and problems associated with deregulation and sunset legislation. The legislative veto, the budgets of regulatory agencies, cost-benefit analysis and reform initiatives are discussed. Paul W. MacAvoy, Edward M. Kennedy, Charles Percy, Irving Kristol and Lloyd Cutler are several of the distinguished contributors.

175. Common Cause. *Serving Two Masters: A Common Cause Study of Conflicts of Interest in the Executive Branch.* Washington, DC: Common Cause, 1976. 74 p.
An analysis which is critical of current regulations designed to prevent conflict of interest in the various offices, councils and agencies of the federal government. Common Cause recommendations, based on findings of widespread infractions, call for a total overhaul of regulations governing the executive bureaucracy.

176. Conant, Michael. *The Constitution and Capitalism.* St. Paul, MN: West, 1974. 306 p.
Intended for non-lawyers, this work introduces one to the Supreme Court's decision-making process. The Court's constitutional interpretation of taxation, corporate charters, federal regulation, paper currency and bankruptcy laws are summarized. A table of cases and an appendix of the U.S. Constitution is provided.

177. Craig, Barbara H. *The Legislative Veto: Congressional Control of Regulation.* Boulder, CO: Westview Press, 1984. 176 p.
An excellent analysis of regulatory politics in the U.S. Congress. The constitutional and political issues associated with controlling the bureaucracy are assessed.

178. Cushman, Robert E. *The Independent Regulatory Commissions.* New York: Oxford University Press, 1941. 780 p.
An in-depth study of federal administrative agencies. The histories of the ICC, FTC, FPC and the Federal Reserve Board, among other commissions, are featured. A table of cases and a "chart of facts" are provided.

179. Davis, Glenn, and Helfand, Gary. *The Uncertain Balance: Governmental Regulators in the Political Process.* Garden City Park, NY: Avery Publishing Group, 1984. 200 p.
An interdisciplinary textbook analysis of regulatory politics. The relationship between ideology and regulation is studied. The last section of the work explores specific federal agencies and their functions.

180. Davis, James W. *The National Executive Branch: An Introduction.* New York: Free Press, 1970. 228 p.
Intended primarily for college undergraduates, this text examines the structure and organization of those offices and councils which report directly to the President. Their functions, authority and relationship with Congress are several of the topics addressed. Footnoted references are included for each chapter.

181. Davis, Kenneth C. *Administrative Law and Government.* 2d ed. St. Paul, MN: West, 1975. 391 p.

A textbook which analyzes the governmental processes used to carry out legislative policies. The administrative process, primary jurisdiction, rules and rule making and fair informal procedure are several of the major topics examined in some detail. Includes a table of cases and appendices of the Administrative Procedure Acts.

182. Davis, Kenneth C. *Administrative Law Text.* St. Paul, MN: West, 1959. 617 p.

A textbook for law students devoted to the study of agency rule making, procedure and process. Administrative remedies, *res judicata, estoppel* and unreviewable administrative action are among the topics summarized. Includes a table of cases.

183. Demaris, Ovid. *Dirty Business: The Corporate-Political Money-Power Game.* New York: Harper's Magazine Press, 1974. 442 p.

A highly critical assessment of the relationship between the corporate sector, government and political parties. According to the author, corporate charity, political reform and energy crises ultimately perpetuate ineffectual laissez-faire economic policies. Includes footnoted references and tabular charts.

184. Dimock, Marshall E. *Law and Dynamic Administration.* New York: Praeger, 1980. 166 p.

A noteworthy study which examines government regulation of the private economy. The relationship between regulation, litigation and private sector productivity is explored. Includes a bibliography.

185. Dominguez, George S. *Government Relations: A Handbook for Developing and Conducting the Company Program.* New York: Wiley, 1982. 420 p.

A practical guide which summarizes, in some detail, the mechanics and structure of regulatory bureaucracy for business managers. Regulatory compliance, planning, litigation and public relations strategies are several of the concepts explored. Includes tables, an appendix and a brief bibliography.

186. Farris, Martin T., and Simpson, Roy J. *Public Utilities: Regulation, Management, and Ownership.* Boston: Houghton Mifflin, 1973. 355 p.

A textbook study of the public utility industry's role in the economy. Rate regulation, utility finance and the ecological and social problems of energy producing utilities are topics covered. Subject, case and name indexes are provided.

187. Ferguson, Allen R., ed. *Attacking Regulatory Problems: An Agenda for Research in the 1980s.* Cambridge, MA: Ballinger, 1981. 232 p.

This edited work surveys those areas where federal regulation can be improved and made more cost effective. Regulatory research, behavior, priorities and methods are assessed by leading experts. George C. Eads, Robert Dorfman, Charles Plott and David Harrison are among the work's contributors.

188. Fesler, James W. *The Independence of State Regulatory Agencies.* Chicago: Public Administration Service, 1942. 72 p.

A brief study which explores the possibility of restructuring independent state commissions with alternative organizational arrangements. State utility commissions, professional licensing boards, liquor control boards and labor departments are among the types of organizations critically examined.

189. Fiorina, Morris P. *Congress, Keystone of the Washington Establishment.* New Haven, CT: Yale University Press, 1977. 105 p.

A book which briefly analyzes the political network of insiders, officials and politicians in the nation's capital. The rise of the Washington establishment, political party realignment and the role of congressional staffs are examined. An appendix of government growth (spending and employment) during the last several decades is provided.

190. Freedman, James O. *Crisis and Legitimacy: The Administrative Process and American Government.* New York: Cambridge University Press, 1978. 324 p.

A scholarly work devoted to the study of agency administration and procedure. Agency performance, judicial review, the delegation of power and administrative law are among the topics covered. Includes footnoted references and a bibliography.

191. Freund, Ernest. *The Growth of American Administrative Law.* St. Louis, MO: Thomas Law Book Company, 1923. 190 p.
This collection of essays examines administrative process in the Federal Trade Commission, Interstate Commerce Commission and state public service commissions. Joseph E. Davies, John A. Kurtz and Charles Nagel are among the contributors to this work.

192. Freyer, Tony A. *Forums of Order: The Federal Courts and Business in American History.* Greenwich, CT: JAI Press, 1979. 187 p.
An excellent book which addresses the legal and historical ramifications of business regulation. The principle of paper negotiability, post-bellum legal developments, reform, and the *Swift v. Tyson* and Erie cases are examined. Replete with footnoted references and a selected bibliography.

193. Friendly, Henry J. *The Federal Administrative Agencies: The Need for Better Definition of Standards.* Cambridge, MA: Harvard University Press, 1962. 175 p.
A timely study devoted to the improvement of administrative adjudication. The successful regulatory criteria employed by the Interstate Commerce Commission, Federal Communications Commission and National Labor Relations Board are examined. Includes footnoted references.

194. Gatti, James F., ed. *The Limits of Government Regulation.* New York: Academic Press, 1981. 186 p.
This collection of essays denounces federal regulatory policies and programs. The cost, consequences and benefits of economic and social regulation are critically assessed. Essayists include Murray Weidenbaum, Thomas Sowell, Harry Bolwell, William Simon and Thomas Murphy.

195. Gawthrop, Louis C. *Administrative Politics and Social Change.* New York: St. Martin's Press, 1971. 117 p.
A scholarly account of executive branch administration and structure. Executive branch political/social strategy and analysis is explored. Footnoted references and a bibliography are provided.

196. Gellhorn, Ernest. *Administrative Law and Process in a Nutshell.* St. Paul, MN: West, 1974. 336 p.
This textbook provides an overview of executive agency procedures and processes. Agency jurisdiction, rules and rule making, the hearing process and judicial review are among the topics examined. Includes a table of cases.

197. Gellhorn, Walter. *Federal Administrative Proceedings.* Baltimore, MD: Johns Hopkins University Press, 1941. 150 p.
A timely study of the dynamics of bureaucratic procedure. The effect of lay elements on the administrative process are examined. Bibliographic references are provided.

198. Gellhorn, Walter. *Individual Freedom and Governmental Restraints.* Baton Rouge, LA: Louisiana State University Press, 1956. 215 p.
This work explores the consequences of public sector control of private economic activity. The issue of censorship is also addressed. Bibliographic footnotes are provided.

199. Gies, Thomas G., and Sichel, Werner, eds. *Deregulation: Appraisal before the Fact.* Ann Arbor, MI: Division of Research. Graduate School of Business Administration, University of Michigan, 1982. 163 p.
A collection of essays which address some of the key questions and concerns associated with regulatory reform. The deregulation of the securities, transportation and natural gas industries are analyzed. Contributors include Elizabeth E. Bailey, William G. Shepherd, Marcus Alexis and Harvey J. Levin.

200. Goldwater, Barry M. *The Coming Breakpoint.* New York: Macmillan, 1976. 184 p.
This provocative book denounces the consequences of bureaucratic proliferation and continued federal deficit spending. Concerns about bureaucratic boondoggles, labor's clout in government, individual freedom and the future of the social security system are expressed.

201. *Government Regulation.* Washington, DC: American Enterprise Institute for Public Policy Research, 1979. 56 p.

A brief work which summarizes those regulatory reform initiatives undertaken by Congress and the Carter White House during the late 1970s. The Culver, Eagleton and Schmitt Bills are among the bills analyzed.

202. Graham, George A., and Reining, Henry, eds. *Regulatory Administration: An Exploratory Study.* New York: Wiley, 1943. 254 p.

An edited textbook which examines government regulation of public health, utilities, railroads and working conditions. The location and use of authority in regulatory agencies is analyzed. Contributors include O. W. Wilson, William E. Mosher, Gaylord W. Anderson and Wilbur LaRoe.

203. Gramlich, Edward M. *Benefit-Cost Analysis of Government Programs.* Englewood Cliffs, NJ: Prentice-Hall, 1981. 273 p.

This work discusses how benefit-cost analyses of government programs are conducted. It is most useful for its discussion of how benefit-cost analysis is related to regulatory decisions.

204. Greene, James. *Regulatory Problems and Regulatory Reform: The Perceptions of Business.* New York: Conference Board, 1980. 50 p.

A study of the experiences business managers and executives have encountered in dealing with the federal bureaucracy. The problems of delay, overregulation and overlap are discussed. A glossary of agency acronyms and an appendix of executive responses are provided.

205. Haefele, Edwin T. *Representative Government and Environmental Management.* Baltimore, MD: Johns Hopkins University Press, 1973. 188 p.

A scholarly work which analyzes the political problems and public policy considerations associated with environmental regulation. The activities of the Potomac River Basin and San Francisco Bay Commissions are examined. Tables, appendices and figures are provided.

206. Harris, Joseph P. *Congressional Control of Administration.* Washington, DC: Brookings Institution, 1964. 306 p.

A study of efforts by Congress to exert control over administrative operations. The appropriations process, exercising legislative vetos and control of the federal budget are among the areas covered. Includes bibliographic and explanatory footnotes.

207. Heatherly, Charles L., ed. *Mandate for Leadership: Policy Management in a Conservative Administration.* Washington, DC: Heritage Foundation, 1981. 1093 p.

A lengthy volume of recommendations and proposals intended to influence and more clearly define the "conservative agenda" of President Reagan's first term. New policy directions to be undertaken in the cabinet departments and regulatory agencies are described. Jeffrey B. Gayner, David Winston, James E. Hinish, Jr., and Robert P. Hunter are among the contributors.

208. Henderson, Thomas A. *Congressional Oversight of Executive Agencies; A Story of the House Committee on Government Operations.* Gainesville, FL: University of Florida Press, 1970. 74 p.

This brief study examines the history and activities of the HCGO. The committee's resolution of bureaucratic conflict is studied. Footnotes and references are provided.

209. Herring, E. Pendleton. *Federal Commissioners: A Study of Their Careers and Qualifications.* Cambridge, MA: Harvard University Press, 1936. 151 p.

This timely book investigates the experience and educational background of top agency officials. The politics of appointment and the problem of tenure are explored. A bibliography, appendices and footnoted references are provided.

210. Holtzman, Abraham. *Legislative Liaison: Executive Leadership in Congress.* Chicago: Rand McNally, 1970. 308 p.

An excellent study of the relationship between Congress and the White House. The career backgrounds and duties of liaison officers are described. Includes name and subject indexes.

211. Hoos, Ida R. *Systems Analysis in Public Policy; A Critique.* Berkeley, CA: University of California Press, 1972. 259 p.
This study explores the origins, applications, uses and abuses of a quantitative systems approach to problem solving in the public sector. The theoretical perspective, techniques and applications of systems analysis are examined. Footnoted references included.

212. Horowitz, Donald L. *The Jurocracy: Government Lawyers, Agency Programs, and Activist Courts.* Lexington, MA: Lexington Books, 1977. 145 p.
This study explores the role attorneys and litigants play in the administrative process. The overlapping responsibilities of the judicial and administrative branches of government are noted. Tables, figures and bibliographic references are included.

213. Jaffe, Louis L. *Judicial Control of Administrative Action.* Boston: Little, Brown, 1965. 704 p.
A legal treatise on the growth of federal administrative process and power. Primary jurisdiction, judicial review, legislative power and sovereign immunity are among the related areas examined. A table of cases and an index are provided.

214. Jowell, Jeffrey L. *Law and Bureaucracy: Administrative Discretion and the Limits of Legal Action.* Port Washington, NY: Kennikat Press, 1975. 214 p.
An examination outlining the restrictions and environment administrative agencies work within. The politics of agency administration, bureaucratic control and advocacy group involvement are among the topics covered. Bibliographic references are included.

215. Karber, James W. *Challenges to Regulation: The Collected Speeches of James W. Karber.* Washington, DC: Public Utilities Reports, 1969. 69 p.
This brief booklet identifies some of the leading financial, economic and political problems associated with regulatory policy. Regulatory jurisdiction, economic competition and technological innovation are among the areas discussed.

216. Kaufman, Herbert. *Administrative Feedback: Monitoring Subordinates' Behavior.* Washington, DC: Brookings Institution, 1973. 83 p.
A brief study which analyzes the problems associated with administrative control within public sector organizations. Noncompliance by subordinates, negative motivation, restricted jurisdiction and a strategy for organizational improvement are several of the many topics addressed. Footnoted references are included.

217. Kaufman, Herbert. *Are Government Organizations Immortal?* Washington, DC: Brookings Institution, 1976. 79 p.
A thin work which considers the factors affecting a federal agency's continued existence. The birth, turnover and death of government organizations is studied. Includes footnotes, tables and charts.

218. Kaufman, Herbert. *Red Tape, Its Origins, Uses, and Abuses.* Washington, DC: Brookings Institution, 1977. 100 p.
A brief account summarizing the frustrations of bureaucratic regulation, procedure and process. Bibliographic references provided.

219. Keezer, Dexter M. *The Public Control of Business.* New York: Harper and Row, 1936. 267 p.
A work devoted to the study of government regulation of the private sector. The legislative and judicial logic of antitrust enforcement is examined. Includes an index of court cases cited.

220. Kirst, Michael W. *Government without Passing Laws.* Chapel Hill, NC: University of North Carolina Press, 1969. 167 p.
This study explores how Congress uses the appropriations process to control administrative agencies. Appropriation bills authorizing expenditures for HEW, Agriculture, USIA, Defense, Public Works and the State Department are examined. References to hearing and reports are provided.

221. Kohlmeier, Louis M. *The Regulators: Watchdog Agencies and the Public Interest.* New York: Harper and Row, 1969. 339 p.
A work devoted to the study of those laws, policies and programs which regulate private economic activity. The regulation of the energy, banking and broadcasting industries is discussed. Bibliographic references and an appendix of federal administrative agencies are provided.

222. Krislov, Samuel, and Rosenbloom, David H. *Representative Bureaucracy and the American Political System.* New York: Praeger, 1981. 208 p.
An excellent study of the relationship between democratic government and bureaucratic organizations. Bureaucratic representation through accountability and interaction with the public is assessed. Includes numerous footnoted references.

223. Landis, James M. *The Administrative Process.* New Haven, CT: Yale University Press, 1938. 160 p.
An examination of bureaucratic procedure and policy making. The relationship between administrative policies, the courts and the legislative branch of government is assessed. Includes footnoted references.

224. Lave, Lester B. *The Strategy of Social Regulation: Decision Frameworks for Policy.* Washington, DC: Brookings Institution, 1981. 166 p.
This work investigates the regulatory decision-making process and how it can be made more effective. The author demonstrates how systematic fact-gathering techniques and cost-benefit analysis can improve government regulation of food additives, contaminants, and occupational health and safety. An appendix and selected bibliography are provided.

225. Leiserson, Avery. *Administrative Regulation: A Study in Representation of Interests.* Chicago: University of Chicago Press, 1942. 292 p.
This book examines the relationship between special interest groups and administrative agencies. The legal aspects of interest group representation are discussed. Bibliographic and explanatory references are provided.

226. Library of Congress. Legislative Reference Service. *Separation of Powers and the Independent Agencies: Cases and Selected Readings.* Washington, DC: U.S. Government Printing Office, 1970. 1714 p.
An encyclopedic collection of writings which address the issue of administrative power and jurisdiction in a federalist system. Contributors include such distinguished figures as Oliver Wendell Holmes, Roscoe Pound, John Farlie, Louis Jaffe and John Dickinson. Includes footnoted references.

227. Lorch, Robert S. *Democratic Process and Administrative Law.* Detroit, MI: Wayne State University Press, 1980. 262 p.
A study which assesses the fairness and efficacy of administrative adjudication. The separation and delegation of power is discussed. Appendices of the original and revised Administrative Procedure Act are provided.

228. Lowi, Theodore L. *The End of Liberalism.* 2d ed. New York: Norton, 1979. 331 p.
A provocative study of liberal political philosophy and its decline in the United States. Pluralism, interest group politics, urban policy and juridical democracy are among the many topics examined. Includes explanatory and bibliographic references.

229. Macaulay, Hugh H., and Yandle, Bruce. *Environmental Use and the Market.* Lexington, MA: Lexington Books, 1977. 145 p.
This study explores the economic aspects of environmental policy and theory. The political question of who should pay for environmental clean-up costs is addressed. Includes appendices with supporting data and a bibliography.

230. MacAvoy, Paul W., ed. *The Crisis of the Regulatory Commissions: An Introduction to a Current Issue of Public Policy.* New York: Norton, 1970. 212 p.
An edited collection of essays which address the topic of industry regulation by commission. The transportation, broadcasting and natural gas industries are analyzed. Contributors include Felix Frankfurter, George Stigler, William Baumol and E. W. Kitch.

231. MacAvoy, Paul W., ed. *Unsettled Questions on Regulatory Reform.* Washington, DC: American Enterprise Institute for Public Policy Research, 1978. 33 p.
A very brief work outlining areas where deregulation and bureaucratic restructuring would be beneficial. Discussion participants include Lloyd Cutler, Roger Noll, Sam Peltzman and John E. Robson.

232. McCraw, Thomas K., ed. *Regulation in Perspective: Historical Essays.* Cambridge, MA: Harvard University Press, 1981. 246 p.
An edited collection of essays which examine economic and social policy from 1900 to 1930. The "new" social regulation is appraised from a historical and comparative perspective. Contributors include Morton Keller, Ellis Hawley, Samuel P. Hays and David Vogel. Bibliographic references are provided.

233. Machan, Tibor R., and Johnson, M. Bruce, eds. *Rights and Regulation: Ethical, Political, and Economic Issues.* Cambridge, MA: Ballinger, 1983. 309 p.
A collection of essays which examine some of the social, moral and practical concerns associated with government control of private enterprise. Regulatory due process, "intergenerational justice," statutory systems of regulation and workmen's compensation laws are among the areas covered. Contributors include professors Nicholas Rescher, Steven Kelman, Norman Karlin and Rolf Sartorius.

234. Mainzer, Lewis C. *Political Bureaucracy.* Glenview, IL: Scott, Foresman, 1973. 187 p.
An excellent analysis of public administration and adjudication. Administrative regulation, bureaucratic due procedure and the policy-administrative relationship are examined. Former Senator Edward Brooke of Massachusetts has provided an introduction to this book. Footnoted references and a bibliography are provided.

235. Martin, Donald L., and Schwartz, Warren F., eds. *Deregulating American Industry: Legal and Economic Problems.* Lexington, MA: Lexington Books, 1977. 120 p.
This edited work assesses some of the leading issues and concerns associated with trade regulation. Regulatory reform and the economic consequences of deregulation are discussed by professors of economics, law and business.

236. Meier, Kenneth J. *Regulation, Politics, Economics, and Bureaucracy.* New York: St. Martin's Press, 1985. 334 p.
This work explores the history and current state of government regulatory policy. Consumer protection, pollution control, antitrust policy and regulatory reform are among the many topics examined. Includes footnoted references, a table of court cases cited and an appendix of policy hypotheses.

237. Milbrath, Lester W. *The Washington Lobbyists.* Chicago: Rand McNally, 1963. 431 p.
An excellent study of the role special interest representatives play in the legislative and political arena. The lobbyist's impact upon policy and the decision-making process is examined. Tables, appendices and a bibliography are provided.

238. Miles, Robert, and Bhambri, Arvind. *The Regulatory Executives.* Beverly Hills, CA: Sage Publications, 1983. 215 p.
An exceptional study which examines the role agency administrators believe they should play in protecting the public interest. The differences in role perceptions, expectations, political philosophies and issue management strategies are presented. Footnoted references and charts are included.

239. Miller, Arthur S. *The Supreme Court and American Capitalism.* New York: Free Press, 1968. 259 p.
An essay exploring the relationship between the Supreme Court and the rise of the corporation. Constitutional doctrine and the consolidation of corporate power is analyzed. A table of cases and a brief list of further reading is provided.

240. Moore, W. S., ed. *Regulatory Reform: Highlights of a Conference on Government Regulation, Held in Washington, D.C. on 10–11 September 1975.* Washington, DC: American Enterprise Institute for Public Policy Research, 1976. 65 p.
A brief, edited account of a conference which assesses federal control of the private economy. Topics under discussion include the regulation of the energy, health care and transportation industries. Participants include Ralph Nader, Hubert Humphrey, Ronald Reagan, John Dingell and Carl Curtis.

241. Mosher, Frederick C. *The GAO: The Quest for Accountability in American Government.* Boulder, CO: Westview Press, 1979. 379 p.
An excellent history of the Government Accounting Office from its inception in the 1920s through the 1970s. The independence and role of the GAO is examined. A selected bibliography and tables are provided.

242. Nelson, Dalmas H. *Administrative Agencies of the USA, Their Decisions and Authority.* Detroit, MI: Wayne State University Press, 1964. 341 p.
A study of the power and scope of federal bureaucracy. Assessment, penalty, censorship, corporal, remissive and benefactory administrative orders are examined in some detail. An appendix, table of cases and footnoted references are provided.

243. Niskanen, William. *Bureaucracy and Representative Government.* Chicago: Aldine-Atherton, 1971. 241 p.
A comparative study of bureau behavior. A basic and variant model of bureaucratic behavior is presented. Charts and formulas are provided.

244. Noll, Roger G. *Reforming Regulation: An Evaluation of the Ash Council's Proposals.* Washington, DC: Brookings Institution, 1971. 116 p.
A brief acCount summarizing the council's report. The failures and theories of regulatory behavior are examined. Government regulation of the banking, energy, farming and food and drug industries is discussed by several noted experts.

245. Ornstein, Norman J., and Elder, Shirley. *Interest Groups, Lobbying and Policymaking.* Washington, DC: Congressional Quarterly Press, 1978. 245 p.
This concise volume surveys pressure group theories and strategies. Case studies dealing with clean air legislation and the B-1 bomber are presented. Includes a selected bibliography and footnoted references.

246. Owen, Bruce M., and Braeutigam, Ronald R. *The Regulation Game: Strategic Use of the Administrative Process.* Cambridge, MA: Ballinger, 1978. 271 p.
A guide to industry regulation and bureaucratic procedure. Regulation of the natural gas, real estate, cable television, transportation and telephone industries are examined. Includes footnoted references and a general bibliography.

247. Peters, Charles, and Nelson, Michael, eds. *The Culture of Bureaucracy.* New York: Holt, Rinehart and Winston, 1979. 278 p.
An edited collection of papers which examine the nature and characteristics of federal administrative agencies. The management and responsiveness of government bureaucracy is studied. James Fallows, Robert Samuelson, Walter Shapiro and Charles Peters are among the contributors to this work.

248. Pierce, L. C. *The Politics of Fiscal Policy Formation.* Pacific Palisades, CA: Goodyear, 1971. 255 p.
This excellent study examines the fiscal policymaking process of the federal government. The roles of the executive branch and the Congress in formulating fiscal policy are described. A selected bibliography and footnoted references are provided.

249. Poole, Robert W., ed. *Instead of Regulation: Alternatives to Federal Regulatory Agencies.* Lexington, MA: Lexington Books, 1982. 404 p.
An edited collection of essays which survey regulatory policies and agencies. The regulation of the airline, communication, securities, food and drug, and energy industries is discussed. George Hilton, Alan Reynolds, Robert S. Smith and George J. Benstin are among the economists and educators who have contributed to the work.

250. President's Advisory Council on Executive Organization. *A New Regulatory Framework: Report on Selected Independent Regulatory Agencies.* Washington, DC: U.S. Government Printing Office, 1971. 198 p.
A report which offers various recommendations on how the efficiency of federal administrative agencies can be improved. Proposals are also presented clarifying their role and mission. Includes a selected bibliography and appendices summarizing the council's findings.

251. Pressman, Jeffrey L., and Wildavsky, Aaron. *Implementation.* Berkeley, CA: University of California Press, 1973. 182 p.
A study of the federal government's attempt to revitalize Oakland, California, through the Economic Development Administration (EDA). Other business loan and health center programs are discussed. A bibliography and an EDA chronology are provided.

252. Quirk, Paul J., and Derthick, Martha. *The Politics of Deregulation.* Washington, DC: Brookings Institution, 1985. 265 p.
An analysis of how regulatory reforms designed to foster market competition are enacted. The lack of effective opposition to deregulation and the mobilization of congressional support for regulatory reform are topics examined. Includes tables and bibliographic references.

253. Reigel, Stanley A., and Owen, P. John. *Administrative Law: The Law of Government Agencies.* Ann Arbor, MI: Ann Arbor Science, 1982. 138 p.
A concise study of bureaucratic jurisdiction, rule making and power. Includes a glossary, table of cases and text citations to the Administrative Procedures Act.

254. Ripley, Randall B., and Franklin, Grace A. *Congress, the Bureaucracy, and Public Policy.* Homewood, IL: Dorsey Press, 1976. 193 p.
This textbook critically examines the relationship between the legislative and bureaucratic branches of government. The implementation of domestic, foreign and defense policy is explored. Includes figures, tables and bibliographic references.

255. Rourke, Francis E. *Bureaucracy, Politics, and Public Policy.* 2d ed. Boston: Little, Brown, 1976. 173 p.
An examination of the role bureaucracy plays in the policy decision-making process. The roots of bureaucratic power and the mobilization of political support are studied. A selected bibliography and footnoted references are provided.

256. Rourke, Francis E., ed. *Bureaucratic Power in National Politics: Readings.* 3d ed. Boston: Little, Brown, 1978. 199 p.
An exceptional collection of essays which assess the function, influence and nature of federal administrative agencies. The relationship between the executive branch of government, Congress and the bureaucracy is analyzed. Max Weber, Arthur M. Schlesinger, Herbert Kaufman and Richard Fenno are among this work's distinguished contributors.

257. Sabatier, Paul A., and Mazmanian, Daniel. *The Implementation of Regulatory Policy: A Framework of Analysis.* Davis, CA: Institute of Governmental Affairs, University of California, 1979. 52 p.
A brief research report summarizing the variables which influence the enforcement of policy. Recent efforts involving conceptual integration are noted. Includes bibliographic footnotes.

258. Salomon, Leon I. *The Independent Federal Regulatory Agencies.* New York: Wilson, 1959. 195 p.
An edited collection of essays which explore the history, politics and administrative processes of federal commissions. The SEC, ICC and FCC are among the agencies critically assessed. Marver Bernstein, Robert S. Rankin, Anthony Lewis, Louis Jaffe and William P. Rogers are among the work's contributors. A bibliography is included.

259. Schwartz, Bernard. *Administrative Law.* 2d ed. Boston: Little, Brown, 1984. 727 p.
A textbook study of agency rule making and bureaucratic due process. The delegation of power, fair hearing requirements and the availability of review are among the aspects of administrative procedure examined. Includes a table of cases and an appendix of the Federal Administrative Procedure Act.

260. Schwartz, Bernard. *The Professor and the Commissions.* New York: Knopf, 1959. 275 p.

An investigation of the background and politics of the Interstate Commerce Commission, Federal Communications Commission, Federal Power Commission, Federal Trade Commission. The influence, independence and review (by Congress) of these regulatory agencies are appraised.

261. Seidman, Harold. *Politics, Position, and Power: From the Positive to the Regulatory State.* 4th ed. New York: Oxford University Press, 1986. 367 p.

A depiction of the structural characteristics of the federal bureaucracy. The Nixon and Carter federal reorganization plans are among the topics covered. An excellent bibliography is provided.

262. Sperry, Roger L., et al. *GAO 1966–1981: An Administrative History.* Washington, DC: General Accounting Office, 1981. 274 p.

A work which traces the development of the Government Accounting Office. The legislative charter, management of the organization and the office's program planning are among the topics covered. An index and acronyms glossary are provided.

263. Stanbury, W. T. *Government Regulation: Scope, Growth, Process.* Brookfield, VT: Renouf, 1980. 267 p.

A collection of essays which examine regulatory policies in the United States and Canada. Economic and environmental regulation and regulatory reform are among the areas analyzed. Contributors include Robert D. Anderson, Fred Thompson, Margot Priest and W. T. Stanbury.

264. Stigler, George J. *The Citizen and the State: Essays on Regulation.* Chicago: University of Chicago Press, 1975. 209 p.

A critical analysis of regulation theory and government economic policy. The proper relationship between the economist and the state is examined. Bibliographic footnotes are provided.

265. Stone, Alan. *Regulation and Its Alternatives.* Washington, DC: Congressional Quarterly Press, 1982. 290 p.

An analytical study of regulatory process and reform. Market competition, equity, deregulation and the government's economic policy goals are several of the topics addressed. A brief research guide and bibliographic footnotes are provided.

266. Sutherland, J. W. *Administrative Decision-Making: Extending the Bounds of Rationality.* New York: Van Nostrand Reinhold, 1977. 315 p.

This textbook analyzes decision theory in public and private organizations. The structure of decision-making responsibilities, decision performance and management of the decision-making function are among the topics examined. Includes bibliographic references, charts and an appendix.

267. Szanton, Peter, ed. *Federal Reorganization: What Have We Learned?* Chatham, NJ: Chatham House, 1981. 170 p.

An assessment of the costs and benefits of federal agency restructuring. Criteria for judging the efficiency of government organizations and methods for implementing reorganization plans are presented. Contributors include Harold Seidman, Allen Schick, I. M. Destler and Alan L. Dean.

268. Thompson, Frederick, and Jones, L. R. *Regulatory Policy and Practices: Regulating Better and Regulating Less.* New York: Praeger, 1982. 253 p.

This work explores the need for economic regulatory reform. The politics, objectives, extent and analysis of regulation are the primary focus of the book. Tables, figures, indexes and an abbreviations list are provided.

269. Truman, David B. *The Governmental Process: Political Interests and Public Opinion.* 2d ed. New York: Knopf, 1971. 544 p.

A scholarly examination of political influence and the administrative process. The role judicial, legislative and electoral systems play in the political process are described. A bibliography and supplementary references are provided.

270. Tullock, Gordon. *The Politics of Bureaucracy.* Washington, DC: Public Affairs Press, 1965. 228 p.

A book which analyzes the relationship between administrative agencies, politicians and special interest groups. Parkinson's law, bureaucratic enforcement and the external checks placed upon bureaucracy are among the topics examined. James M. Buchanan has provided a foreword to the work.

271. Tussman, Joseph. *Obligation and the Body Politic.* New York: Oxford University Press, 1960. 144 p.

A brief essay in political philosophy which examines the democratic model of government. The social contract theory of politics is supported. Includes an appendix on "nature and politics."

272. Ullmann, John E. *The Prospects of American Industrial Recovery.* Westport, CT: Quorum Books, 1985. 244 p.

An analysis of how the arms race has adversely affected the economy. The trade gap, product innovation, resource allocation and military expenditures are discussed. Includes footnoted references and tabular charts.

273. Ueges, Joseph A., comp. *The Dimensions of Public Administration.* 2d ed. Boston: Holbrook Press, 1975. 611 p.

This collection of essays explores public policy, organizational dynamics, public personnel management and the budgetary process. Contributors include Herbert A. Simon, James I. Gibson, Arthur M. Schlesinger, Jr., Felix A. Nigro and Richard M. Nixon. Includes footnoted references and a readings list.

274. Wade, Henry W. R. *Towards Administrative Justice.* Ann Arbor, MI: University of Michigan Press, 1963. 138 p.

A comparative study of bureaucratic due process in the United States and Great Britain. The British tribunal system, independent U.S. federal agencies, the Administrative Procedure Act and the Franks Committee (British) are examined. A table of statutes and legal cases is provided.

275. Waller, John D., et al. *Monitoring for Government Agencies.* Washington, DC: Urban Institute, 1976. 170 p.

A practical guide designed to help public sector administrators determine the effectiveness of government programs. Procedures used in establishing monitoring procedures, collecting data, and utilizing information are examined. Tables, figures and an appendix are included.

276. Wallis, Wilson A. *An Overgoverned Society.* New York: Free Press, 1976. 292 p.

This work explores how the growth of regulatory bureaucracy has affected the economic and social welfare. The relationship between government policy, economic growth and prices is discussed. Includes bibliographic references.

277. Weiss, Carol H.,, and Barton, Allen H. *Making Bureaucracies Work.* Beverly Hills, CA: Sage Publications, 1980. 309 p.

An edited collection of papers which address the issue of bureaucratic and civil service reform. Congressional oversight, the public interest, bureaucratic decentralization and the public's perception of the federal government are topics discussed. Professors Dorothy Nelkin, Charles E. Lindbloom, David Cohen and D. Garth Taylor are among the contributors to this work.

278. Welborn, David M. *Governance of Federal Regulatory Agencies.* Knoxville, TN: University of Tennessee Press, 1977. 179 p.

An analysis of federal regulatory commissions, including the Civil Aeronautics Board, Federal Communications Commission, Federal Power Commission, Federal Trade Commission and the Securities and Exchange Commission. Administrative decision-making process and the dynamics of organizational structure are discussed. Tables, charts and a bibliography are provided.

279. White, Lawrence J. *Reforming Regulation: Processes and Problems.* Englewood Cliffs, NJ: Prentice-Hall, 1981. 244 p.

A book which analyzes economic and social regulation. Case study analysis and recommendations for improvement are provided. Includes footnoted references and tabular charts.

280. White, Michael. *Management Science in Federal Agencies: The Adoption and Diffusion of a Socio-Technical Innovation.* Lexington, MA: Lexington Books, 1975. 111 p.

A longitudinal and comparative field investigation of the activities of management scientists in government agencies. The development and adoption of a descriptive phase model of an organization is presented. A bibliography, footnotes and the interview questionnaire used to collect the study's data are included.

281. Whitman, Willson. *David Lilienthal: Public Servant in a Power Age.* New York: H. Holt, 1948. 245 p.

An official account of Lilienthal's work and political activities as chairman of the TVA.

282. Willoughby, William F. *Principles of Legislative Organization and Administration.* Washington, DC: Brookings Institution, 1934. 657 p.

This work examines the organization and operation of the government as a working institution. Includes analyses of government's legislative functions. Explanatory and bibliographic references are provided.

283. Wilson, James Q., ed. *The Politics of Regulation.* New York: Basic Books, 1980. 468 p.

This edited collection of essays explores the relationship between private sector power and the public interest. An analysis of government regulation of electrical utilities, airlines, the shipping industry and environmental standards is presented. Professors Paul J. Quirk, Douglas D. Anderson, Steven Kelman and James Q. Wilson are among the contributors to this work.

284. Woll, Peter. *Administrative Law, The Informal Process.* Berkeley, CA: University of California Press, 1963. 203 p.

A study which examines the process of administrative adjudication and rule making. Among the agencies analyzed are the IRS, FTC, NLRB and the SEC. Extensively footnoted.

285. Woll, Peter. *American Bureaucracy.* 2d ed. New York: Norton, 1977. 260 p.

This excellent work examines the growth, development and organization of federal administrative agencies. The relationship betwen the bureaucracy, the Presidency and the Congress is described. Includes footnoted references.

286. Wright, Deil S. *Understanding Intergovernmental Relations: Public Policy and Participants' Perspectives in Local, State, and National Governments.* North Scituate, MA: Duxbury Press, 1978. 410 p.

A textbook examination of government structure and finance. Federal aid to state and local governments, models of national-state-local relations, and public employment are among the topics covered. An appendix of commonly used terms and acronyms is provided.

287. Ziegler, Harmon L., and Baer, Michael A. *Lobbying: Interaction and Influence in American Legislatures.* Belmont, CA: Wadsworth, 1969. 209 p.

An excellent study of the role and importance of lobbying in the U.S. political system. The relationship between legislators and lobbists is discussed in some detail. Includes bibliographic and explanatory footnotes as well as supporting data.

REGULATORY ACTIVITIES

288. Aaker, David A., and Day, Georges, eds. *Consumerism: Search for the Consumer Interest.* New York: Free Press, 1982. 500 p.

An edited collection of essays by leading experts summarizing the current state of consumer affairs. Advertising, selling practices, warranties service, and government regulatory policy are among the topics covered. Includes discussion questions, footnoted references and an index.

289. Ackerman, Bruce A., et al. *The Uncertain Search for Environmental Quality.* New York: Free Press, 1974. 386 p.

A study of the decision-making process which led to the environmental clean-up of the Delaware River in the early 1970s. The technocratic model of scientific fact finding and public policy formation is described. A bibliography, and appendices of legal orders, regulations, clean-up cost estimates and interview data are provided.

290. Adams, Bruce, and Kavanagh-Baran, Kathryn. *Promise and Performance: Carter Builds a New Administration.* Lexington, MA: Lexington Books, 1979. 202 p.

A critical appraisal of the federal appointment process under Jimmy Carter. The selection of cabinet members, the White House staff, federal judges and the Vice Presidential candidate are appointments considered in this work. Includes tables and footnoted references.

291. Allen, Clark L. *Prices, Income and Public Policy.* 2d ed. New York: McGraw-Hill, 1959. 501 p.

A textbook analysis of the political and market economy. The demand for labor services, consumer demand, competitive pricing, antitrust policy and the elements of income theory are among the topics explored. An appendix of "fundamental quantitative relationships" is provided.

292. Anderson, Douglas D. *Regulatory Politics and Electric Utilities: A Case Study in Political Economy.* Boston: Auburn House, 1981. 191 p.

This work examines the politics of power utility regulation and rate structuring. The origins of state utility regulation in the early 1900s are analyzed. Includes bibliographic references.

293. Anderson, Frederick R., et al. *Environmental Improvement through Economic Incentives.* Baltimore, MD: Johns Hopkins University Press, 1977. 195 p.

This excellent work explores a number of alternative environmental control strategies intended to replace or complement direct administrative regulation. Money charge applications, environmental monitoring methods, resource allocation and the politics of charge setting are examined. Footnoted references are included.

294. Anderson, Thomas J. *Our Competitive System and Public Policy.* Cincinnati, OH: South-Western, 1958. 586 p.

A study of the impact legislative, judicial and bureaucratic actions have on the free market economy. Closed shop agreements, jurisdictional disputes and nonprice competition are among the topics examined. Includes extensive legal and legislative references.

295. Andrews, Richard N. L. *Environmental Policy and Administrative Change: Implementation of the National Environmental Policy Act.* Lexington, MA: Lexington Books, 1976. 230 p.

This book assesses the provisions, interpretation and enforcement of the NEPA. A legislative history of the act is presented. Professor Lynton K. Caldwell has written an informative foreword to the work. Tables and footnoted references are provided.

296. Arrow, Kenneth J., and Kalt, Joseph P. *Petroleum Price Regulation: Should We Decontrol?* Washington, DC: American Enterprise Institute for Public Policy Research, 1978. 47 p.

A critical analysis of the effects domestic crude oil price controls have upon the economy. Favoring decontrol, the authors conclude that it would benefit petroleum producers and result in more efficient allocation of scarce resources.

297. Ashford, Nicholas A. *Crisis in the Workplace: Occupational Disease and Injury.* Cambridge, MA: MIT Press, 1976. 588 p.

A report devoted to the study of the technical, legal, political and economic problems associated with enforcing health and safely standards. The widespread effects of occupational diseases and the difficulties of defining "health hazards" are among the topics covered. Includes an appendix of the 1970 OSHAct and footnoted references.

298. Axelrod, Regina S., ed. *Environment, Energy and Public Policy.* Lexington, MA: Lexington Books, 1981. 175 p.

This edited collection of essays explores the complex relationship between environmental concerns and the development of energy resources. Oil import policy, the role of local governments in determining energy policy and the desirability of nuclear power are among the issues raised. Contributors include professors Helen Ingram, Michael E. Kraft and Dankwart A. Rustow.

299. Bacow, Lawrence S., et al. *Social Regulation: Strategies for Reform.* New Brunswick, NJ: Transaction Books, 1982. 420 p.

A provocative work which considers the costs and benefits of health and safety regulation. Product safety, regulatory enforcement and liability law are among the topics discussed. George C. Eads, Michael Levin, Lawrence S. Bacow and Eugene Bardach are among the experts contributing to this volume.

300. Bain, Joe S. *Industrial Organization.* 2d ed. New York: Wiley, 1968. 678 p.

A textbook study of market structure and the regulation of business. Market performance, product differentiation, monopoly and economic policy are among the areas examined. Includes a supplementary readings list.

301. Balk, Walter L., and Shafritz, Jay M., eds. *Public Utility Productivity: Management and Measurement.* Albany, NY: New York State Department of Public Service, 1975. 256 p.

An examination by scholars and executives of comparative performance and productivity measurement in the utility industry. Methodological issues and managerial efficiency are among the topics discussed. Contributors and commentators include John W. Kendrick, Edward F. Renshaw, Peter C. Manus and Ralph E. Miller.

302. Baram, Michael S. *Alternatives to Regulation: Managing Risks to Health, Safety and the Environment.* Lexington, MA: Lexington Books, 1982. 155 p.

A book which assesses the need for regulatory restructuring. Common-law alternatives, self-regulation, liability laws and the influence of government policy are discussed. Includes bibliographic references.

303. Barnes, Irston R. *The Economics of Public Utility Regulation.* New York: Crofts, 1942. 952 p.

This classic work on the economics of public utilities is especially important as a historical record of research and thinking on the topic during the first half of this century.

304. Bauer, John. *Updating Public Utility Regulation: Assuring Fair Rates and Fair Returns.* Chicago: Public Administration Service, 1966. 234 p.

A work which addresses the issues associated with utility rate fixing by state appointed public service commissions. Precedent setting legal cases and utility rate standards are analyzed. Appendices, tables and explanatory notes are included.

305. Best, Arthur. *When Consumers Complain.* New York: Columbia University Press, 1981. 232 p.

A survey of common product defects and the resulting difficulties encountered by consumers. The prospects for improving the consumer complaint process are assessed. Includes footnoted references and an appendix of comparative consumer data.

306. Black, Stanley W.; King, Robert G.; and Conner, Glen. *The Banking System: A Preface to Public Interest Analysis.* Washington, DC: Public Interest Economics Center, 1975. 458 p.
> An excellent study of the regulation and structure of the banking industry. The function, performance and role of banking organizations are ascertained. Footnoted references and tables with supporting information are included.

307. Bonbright, James C. *The Art of Valuation.* Edited by Arlo Woolery. Lexington, MA: Lexington Books, 1978. 145 p.
> A dialogue between tax commissioners, business professors and assessors at a public utility conference. Capital structure, value as defined by statutes, work-in-progress financing and debt-equity ratios are among the many topics discussed. Footnoted references and appendices are provided.

308. Bonbright, James C. *Principles of Public Utility Rates.* New York: Columbia University Press, 1961. 433 p.
> A study of optimum and reasonable pricing standards in the power industry. Cost of service standards and the principles of rate making are examined. Includes a table of cases and bibliographic references.

309. Breed, Alice G. *The Change in Social Welfare from Deregulation: The Case of the Natural Gas Industry.* New York: Arno Press, 1979. 155 p.
> This work compares regulated and unregulated resource allocation and output. Includes economic equations, tabular charts and footnoted references.

310. Brill, Allan E. *The Right to Financial Privacy Act: A Compliance Guide for Financial Institutions.* Englewood Cliffs, NJ: Prentice-Hall, 1979. 239 p.
> A procedural manual designed to help financial institutions fulfill the requirements of the Right to Financial Privacy Act of 1978. Compliance information, flow charts, business forms and a copy of the statute are provided.

311. Buchan, Robert J., and Johnston, Christopher C. *Telecommunications Regulation and the Constitution.* Montreal, Quebec: Institute for Research on Public Policy, 1983. 276 p.
> This collection of papers assesses the effects of two regulatory proposals on the Canadian telecommunications industry. The possible impact of the proposals on telephone service quality and rates is analyzed. Appendices of the draft proposals are provided.

312. Burkhardt, R. *The Federal Aviation Administration.* New York: Praeger, 1967. 249 p.
> A history of the FAA from its inception in the mid-50s to 1966. The agency's organization, function, operations and international activities are described. An organizational chart and appendices of FAA budgets, area offices and administrators are provided.

313. Burns, E. M. *Social Economics for the 1970s: Programs for Social Security, Health and Manpower.* New York: Dunellen, 1970. 189 p.
> This volume discusses some of the new economic developments of the 1970s. It is particularly useful for its discussion of how social changes affect government regulatory activities.

314. Callies, David L. *Regulating Paradise: Land Use Controls in Hawaii.* Honolulu, HI: University of Hawaii Press, 1984. 245 p.
> This work surveys land use control at the local, state and federal levels in the Hawaiian islands. The determination of land use policy and an analysis of the land use management process are presented. An extensive bibliography is included.

315. Calvert, Thomas H. *Regulation of Commerce under the Federal Constitution.* Northport, NY: Thompson, 1907. 380 p.
> A study of the constitutional provisions which have an impact on government control of private enterprise. The regulatory powers of Congress and the states are ascertained. Includes footnoted references and a table of cases.

316. Capron, William M., ed. *Technological Change in Regulated Industries; Papers Prepared for a Conference of Experts, with an Introduction and Summary.* Washington, DC: Brookings Institution, 1971. 238 p.

This collection of essays assesses the effects of government regulation on industrial innovation. The regulation of the air transport, surface freight, communications and electrical power industries is discussed. William Hughes, Fred M. Westfield, Almarin Phillips and Roger G. Noll are among the work's contributors. Tables and figures provided.

317. Carron, Andrew S. *Transition to a Free Market: Deregulation of the Air Cargo Industry.* Washington, DC: Brookings Institution, 1981. 45 p.

An analysis of how the air freight industry has adapted to regulatory reform and decontrol. The author offers some basic rules designed to make the deregulatory process more manageable and less costly.

318. Caves, Richard E. *Air Transport and Its Regulators.* Cambridge, MA: Harvard University Press, 1962. 479 p.

A noteworthy study of the market structure, conduct and performance of the airline industry. The regulation of airline fares, competition and entry (into the industry) are discussed. Tables, references and supporting data are provided.

319. Caves, Richard E., and Roberts, Marc J., eds. *Regulating the Produce: Quality and Variety.* Cambridge, MA: Ballinger, 1974. 268 p.

This scholarly study examines the impact regulatory policy has on the quality control of goods and services. The home appliance, airline, television broadcasting and natural gas industries are analyzed. Includes bibliographic references.

320. Chase, Stuart. *Government in Business.* New York: Macmillian, 1935. 296 p.

A noteworthy work which examines public control of the private sector. "New Deal collectivism," big business and models of regulatory control are among the topics covered.

321. Cicchetti, Charles J., and Jurewitz, John L. *Studies in Electric Utility Regulation.* Cambridge, MA: Ballinger, 1975. 266 p.

A collection of essays which focus on the economic and policy issues associated with utility rate structures. Block pricing, energy demand forecasting, utility taxation and rate-of-return regulation are among the topics examined. Tables, charts and a brief bibliography are provided.

322. Crane, Dwight B. *The Effects of Banking Deregulation.* Washington, DC: Association of Reserve City Bankers, 1983. 109 p.

A brief study which summarizes recent changes in the financial services industry. The current competitive framework, structure and decontrol of the banking industry is examined. Includes tables of statistical data and footnoted references.

323. Crew, Michael A., ed. *Problems in Public-Utility Economics and Regulation.* Lexington, MA: Lexington Books, 1979. 177 p.

An analysis of utility rate-of-return and price structures. The economic efficiency of regulated and unregulated utility firms is examined. Includes footnoted references.

324. Crew, Michael A., ed. *Regulatory Reform and Public Utilities.* Lexington, MA: Lexington Books, 1982. 257 p.

An edited collection of essays which examine the pressures facing regulated utilities and their regulators. Industrial co-generation, electricity pricing and a cost-benefit analysis of local measured telephone service are among the topics addressed. Almarin Phillips, Paul L. Joskow, Michael Crew and John F. Stewart are among the economists contributing to this work.

325. Csikos-Nagy, Bela. *Towards a New Price Revolution.* Budapest, Hungary: Akademiai Kiado, 1979. 189 p.

This scholarly study examines micro and macro price structures and their impact upon the economy. Capitalist and socialist economies are studied. Includes supporting economic data and footnoted references.

326. Dales, J. H. *Pollution, Property and Prices.* Toronto, Ontario: University of Toronto Press, 1968. 111 p.
This work examines the problems of environmental pollution from the viewpoint of an economist interested in social problems. The relationship between law, economics and property rights is explored. A readings list is provided.

327. Derthick, Martha. *Policymaking for Social Security.* Washington, DC: Brookings Institution, 1979. 446 p.
A work which examines the successes and problems of the Social Security system from its inception in 1935 through the 1970s. An in-depth assessment of the politics, history and financing of the system is presented. Includes a legislative chronology.

328. Dewar, Margaret E., ed. *Industry Vitalization: Toward a National Industrial Policy.* New York: Pergamon Press, 1982. 252 p.
An edited collection of papers which consider what the relationship between the federal government and troubled industries should be. The industrial policies of Japan, Germany and Britain are surveyed. Joel S. Hirschhorn, Thomas P. Egan, W. Bruce Erickson and Vera Miller are among the contributors to this work.

329. Donieger, D. D. *The Law and Policy of Toxic Substances Control.* Baltimore, MD: Johns Hopkins University Press, 1978. 178 p.
This case study examines government attempts to control vinyl chloride and other hazardous substances. The approaches and statutory provisions used by federal agencies in regulating industrial polluters are noted. Extensively footnoted.

330. Dorfman, John. *A Consumer's Arsenal.* New York: Praeger, 1976. 270 p.
A helpful guide which explains consumer rights and redress procedures. State by state consumer protection information is provided. Section three of the book refers one to various government agencies for specific types of consumer problems.

331. Doron, Gideon. *The Smoking Paradox: Public Regulation in the Cigarette Industry.* Cambridge, MA: Abt Books, 1979. 141 p.
A provocative study of government attempts to discourage tobacco use. A historical survey of tobacco regulation and an empirical assessment of its effects are provided. Includes charts, figures and appendices with supporting data.

332. Dougherty, Thomas J. *Controlling the New Inflation.* Lexington, MA: Lexington Books, 1981. 171 p.
This excellent work examines government attempts to regulate wages and prices. The impact of the Kennedy, Nixon, Ford and Carter wage and price control policies are assessed. The effects of controls on the energy, housing and health care industries are discussed.

333. Douglas, George W., and Miller, James C. *Economic Regulation of Domestic Air Transportation: Theory and Policy.* Washington, DC: Brookings Institution, 1974. 211 p.
An analysis of airline competition and the Civil Aeronautic Board's role in regulating air carriers. An economic model of industry behavior (under regulation) is developed. Includes supporting tables, charts and bibliographic references.

334. Dunlap, Thomas R. *DDT: Scientists, Citizens, and Public Policy.* Madison, WI: University of Wisconsin Press, 1975. 318 p.
An excellent account of the controversy surrounding the use of DDT as an insecticide. The history of DDT's development and the opposition to its proliferation are examined. Appendices, footnotes and a bibliography are provided.

335. Elkouri, Frank. *Trade Regulation: Cases and Materials.* Englewood Cliffs, NJ: Prentice-Hall, 1957. 312 p.
A textbook analysis of antitrust laws, monopolies, mergers and unfair trade practice. Practical information on patents, copyrights and trademarks is also provided. Includes a table of cases and a general readings list.

336. Erickson, Myron L.; Dunfee, Thomas W.; and Gibson, Frank F. *Antitrust and Trade Regulation: Cases and Materials.* Columbus, OH: Grid, 1977. 430 p.
A textbook study of regulated industries, monopolies and administrative procedure. Problematic questions are provided at the end of each chapter.

337. Evans, Joel R. *Consumerism in the United States: An Inter-Industry Analysis.* New York: Praeger, 1980. 452 p.
An examination of the activities of the consumer movement in leading sectors of the economy. The clothing, appliance, banking, petroleum and drug industries are among those covered. Includes tables and numerous footnoted references.

338. *Expanding Economic Concepts of Regulation in Health, Postal and Tele-communications Services.* Edited by Charles F. Phillips. Lexington, VA: Washington and Lee University, 1977. 126 p.
An edited collection of essays which examine regulatory structure and policy. Telephone rate pricing and health care system cost controls are among the topics examined. Includes tables and explanatory references.

339. Feldman, Laurence P. *Consumer Protection: Problems and Prospects.* St. Paul, MN: West, 1980. 254 p.
A study of seller-consumer issues and the federal regulation of product safety. Consumer redress, the safety of food and drugs, truth-in-advertising practices and product warranties are among the many areas examined. An appendix listing consumer protection legislation from 1906 to 1980 is provided.

340. Ferguson, Allen R., and Leveen, E. Phillip. *The Benefits of Health and Safety Regulation.* Cambridge, MA: Ballinger, 1981. 270 p.
This edited volume consists of lectures and dialogue from a conference on social regulation. An assessment of health and safety regulation is featured. Professor James W. Vaupel, Allen R. Ferguson, George Eads and Professor David Harrison are among the conferees contributing to this work.

341. Fraser, Douglas A., and Byron, Fletcher L. *Failing Industries: The Role of Government.* Pittsburgh, PA: Carnegie-Mellon University Press, 1980. 60 p.
A brief discussion, by a top executive and a leading labor leader, on the efficacy of a national industrial policy and federal assistance to troubled industries. Tax policies, import restrictions and industrial productivity are among the topics addressed.

342. Friedlaender, Ann F., ed. *Approaches to Controlling Air Pollution.* Cambridge, MA: MIT Press, 1978. 465 p.
An edited collection of essays which assess the major factors influencing the enforcement of clean air regulation. Regulatory strategies, government policy and the costs of implementing the Clean Air Act are discussed. Professors Allen Kneese, Lester Lave, James E. Krier and William Drayton, Jr. are among the work's contributors.

343. Friedlaender, Ann F. *The Dilemma of Freight Transport Regulation.* Washington, DC: Brookings Institution, 1969. 216 p.
This study analyzes the problems associated with regulatory policy as applied to railroads and the trucking industry. Alternatives to present government policies and the relaxation of existing rules are discussed. Tables and charts with supporting data are provided.

344. Fuller, John G. *The Gentlemen Conspirators: The Story of the Price-Fixers in the Electrical Industry.* New York: Grove Press, 1962. 224 p.
A fascinating account of antitrust violations by top executives from Allis-Chalmers, General Electric and Pennsylvania Transformer during the late 1950s. Details and events surrounding this sensational legal case are described.

345. Funigiello, Phillip J. *Toward a National Power Policy: The New Deal and the Electric Utility Industry, 1933–1941.* Pittsburgh, PA: University of Pittsburgh Press, 1973. 296 p.
A study of the Roosevelt Administration's promotion of electrical power, New Deal utility policies, and the influence of the electric power industry during the 1930s. Includes footnoted references and an extensive bibliography.

346. Galbraith, John K. *A Theory of Price Control.* Cambridge, MA: Harvard University Press, 1952. 81 p.
A classic work which examines the economic concepts of market imperfections, disequilibrium and limited mobilization. A prewar view of price control as a tool of economic policy is presented. Includes explanatory references.

347. Gellhorn, Ernest, and Pierce, Richard J. *Regulated Industries in a Nutshell.* St. Paul, MN: West, 1982. 394 p.
A compendium of administrative law and business regulation intended for students, lawyers and government regulators. Price regulation, antitrust action, substantive due process and deregulation are several of the areas covered. Includes a table of legal cases.

348. Giebelhaus, August W. *Business and Government in the Oil Industry: A Case Study of Sun Oil, 1876–1945.* Greenwich, CT: JAI Press, 1980. 332 p.
This work explores the history and development of Sun Oil and the petroleum industry in general. The complex relationship between the oil industry and the federal government is examined. A selected bibliography, footnoted references and statistical tables are included.

349. Ginsburg, Douglas H., and Abernathy, William J., eds. *Government, Technology, and the Future of the Automobile.* New York: McGraw-Hill, 1980. 483 p.
An edited collection of essays which address the issue of government regulation of the automobile industry. The impact of current regulatory policy on innovation, fuel economy and automobile performance is discussed. Business professors, corporate executives, government administrators and journalists are among those who have contributed to this work. A selected bibliography is included.

350. Goldberg, Lawrence G., and White, Lawrence J., eds. *The Deregulation of the Banking and Securities Industries.* Lexington, MA: Lexington Books, 1979. 356 p.
This edited volume analyzes the current trend to decontrol financial markets. Interest rate deregulation, variable rate mortgages and the Glass-Stegall Act are several of the topics explored. Contributors include H. Michael Mann, Robert C. Hall, Lee A. Pickard and Almarin Phillips among others.

351. Goldberg, Victor P. *Consumer Choice, Imperfect Information and Public Policy.* Davis, CA: University of California, Institute of Governmental Affairs, 1973. 26 p.
A brief report which analyzes consumer information processing techniques. Insurance and welfare economics are examined from the perspective of a consumer.

352. Goodman, John C. *The Regulation of Medical Care: Is the Price Too High?* San Francisco, CA: Cato Institute, 1980. 135 p.
A provocative study which analyzes the impact of government involvement on the health care system. Medical insurance, nursing care, hospital administration and paramedicine are among the areas examined. Includes footnoted references and tables with supporting data.

353. Goodman, Robert. *The Last Entrepreneurs: America's Regional Wars for Jobs and Dollars.* New York: Simon and Schuster, 1979. 292 p.
An examination of regional economics, attempts by local government to attract new business and the problem of displaced workers. The impact of industrial (geographic) rotation, job creation and new technologies on the economy are studied. Bibliographic references are provided.

354. Gordon, Richard L. *Reforming the Regulation of Electric Utilities: Priorities for the 1980's.* Lexington, MA: Lexington Books, 1982. 311 p.
This analysis of utility regulatory policies summarizes the economic and political difficulties the electrical power industry currently faces. The impact of government regulation on power company investment and growth is examined. Charts with supporting data and an excellent bibliography are provided.

355. Gormley, William T. *The Politics of Public Utility Regulation.* Pittsburgh, PA: University of Pittsburgh Press, 1983. 271 p.
A timely study which focuses on the controversial issues associated with state regulation of power companies. State utility commissioners, company executives and consumer advocates discuss the complexities of the regulatory process. Reform proposals are offered, by the author, as possible alternatives to the present system.

356. Grabowski, Henry G. *The Regulation of Pharmaceuticals: Balancing the Benefits and Risks.* Washington, DC: American Enterprise Institute for Public Policy Research, 1983. 74 p.
This brief analysis of the drug industry explores the impact of FDA regulation on the discovery, safety and approval of new drugs. Includes footnoted references.

357. Green, Mark J., and Waitzman, Norman. *Business War on the Law: An Analysis of the Benefits of Federal Health/Safety Enforcement.* Washington, DC: Corporate Accountability Research Group, 1981. 211 p.
A critical study of Reagan administration efforts to deregulate business and industry. The authors quantify some of the benefits of government regulation. Includes footnoted references and an appendix of regulatory cost-benefit analysis.

358. Greer, Douglas F. *Business, Government and Society.* New York: Macmillan, 1983. 587 p.
A textbook study of economic and social regulation intended for undergraduates. Antitrust policy, equal employment opportunity and price controls are among the topics featured. Includes questions and exercises for each chapter.

359. Hall, George R.; Kolbe, Lawrence A.; and Read, James A. *The Cost of Capital, Estimating the Rate of Return for Public Utilities.* Cambridge, MA: MIT Press, 1984. 183 p.
A survey of the alternative means used by public utilities in determining consumer rates. Evaluative criteria, market-to-book ratios, equity capital estimation and factor analysis are among the concepts discussed. Includes appendices.

360. Hamilton, F. E., ed. *Industrial Change: Experience and Public Policy.* New York: Longman, 1978. 183 p.
An edited collection of essays which assess the influence of government regulation on industrial location and development in selected countries. Government policies in India, Britain, Nigeria, Poland, Germany and the United States are examined. John H. Cumberland, Kenneth Warren, John Rees and Peter R. Odell are among the contributors to this work.

361. Harris, Seymour. *Price and Related Controls in the United States.* New York: McGraw-Hill, 1945. 392 p.
An analysis of government regulation of the economy during war and peace time. The benefits, problems and inconsistencies of price control policies are examined. Includes graphs, footnoted references and tabular charts.

362. Hillman, Jordan J. *Competition and Railroad Price Discrimination: Legal Precedent and Economic Policy.* Evanston, IL: Transportation Center at Northwestern University, 1968. 164 p.
An excellent study of government regulatory policy toward railroads from 1887 to 1910. The role court rulings, the ICC and carrier competition played in determining rates is discussed. Includes subject and case indexes.

363. Hilton, George W. *The Transportation Act of 1958: A Decade of Experience.* Bloomington, IN: Indiana University Press, 1969. 262 p.
This work summarizes the origins and provisions of the 1958 act and evaluates its impact on railroads. The act's motor carrier provisions, loan guaranties and comity rule are studied. Includes appendices of the act and tables of railroad passenger deficits.

364. Hines, Lawrence G. *Environmental Issues: Population, Pollution, and Economics.* New York: Norton, 1973. 339 p.
An appraisal of the pressures placed on government to provide environmental protection. The role the public sector should play in controlling pollution in a free market economy is considered. Includes tables and exhibits.

365. Hunter, Beatrice T. *The Mirage of Safety: Food Additives and Federal Policy.* New York: Scriber's, 1975. 322 p.
A study which documents the FDA's laxity in effectively regulating the food industry's use of preservatives, dyes and antioxidants. The FDA is criticized for its inability to promptly restrict or ban the use of hazardous substances. An examination of the influence food industry lobbyists have on the outcome of the FDA examinations is also presented.

366. Hurst, James W. *Law and Markets in United States History. Different Modes of Bargaining among Interests.* Madison, WI: University of Wisconsin Press, 1982. 207 p.
A sociological study of the market economy and its relationship to the legal system. The legal autonomy of the market, the money supply and public policy formation are several of the topics analyzed. Extensively footnoted.

367. Hyman, Herbert H. *Health Regulation.* Germantown, MD: Aspen Systems Corporation, 1977. 185 p.
An in-depth explanation of the National Health Planning and Resources Development Act of 1974. The regulation of health care expenditures and facilities as well as the 1974 act's intent and provisions are examined.

368. Jain, Avrind K. *Commodity Futures Markets and the Law of One Price.* Ann Arbor, MI: Division of Research, Graduate School of Business Administration, University of Michigan, 1980. 138 p.
A work which presents a model of price exchanges for commodities. The movement of prices is explained. Includes tabular charts and equations.

369. Jordan, William A. *Airline Regulation in America: Effects and Imperfections.* Baltimore, MD: Johns Hopkins University Press, 1970. 352 p.
This study of the airline industry analyzes the influence of the Civil Aeronautics Board and industry competition on consumer fares. Fares in major and minor markets are studied. Includes a bibliography as well as numerous tables and exhibits.

370. Joskow, Paul J. *Controlling Hospital Costs: The Role of Government Regulation.* Cambridge, MA: MIT Press, 1982. 211 p.
A study of the impact government health care policy has on hospital economics. The effects of government regulation on health care services and the economic structure of the American hospital system are assessed. Includes a brief bibliography and footnoted references.

371. Judson, Frederick N. *The Law of Interstate Commerce and Its Federal Regulation.* Chicago: Flood, 1916. 1066 p.
An in-depth text which cites statutory provisions establishing the ICC. The concurrent and exclusive powers of the commission are noted in detail.

372. Kagan, Robert A. *Regulatory Justice: Implementing a Wage-Price-Freeze.* New York: Russell Sage Foundation, 1978. 200 p.
This work evaluates the dynamics and inner workings of the administrative legal process. An examination of "freeze agencies and policy" is provided. A brief section explaining the research methods employed by the author is included.

373. Kalt, Joseph P. *The Economics and Politics of Oil Price Regulation: Federal Policy in the Post-Embargo Era.* Cambridge, MA: MIT Press, 1981. 327 p.
A study of the effect federal regulations have had on the price and supply of petroleum products. The impact of price regulation on distribution and efficiency are examined. Includes mathematical formulas, tabular charts and footnoted references.

374. Kelman, Steven J. *Regulation America, Regulation Sweden: A Comparative Study of Occupational Safety and Health Policy.* Cambridge, MA: MIT Press, 1981. 270 p.

This comparative analysis of administrative bureaucracy examines social systems, rule making processes and industry compliance levels in the United States and Sweden. Includes bibliographic references and statistical tables.

375. Kinter, Earl W. *An Antitrust Primer: A Guide to Antitrust and Trade Regulation Laws for Businessmen.* 2d ed. New York: Macmillan, 1973. 325 p.

An excellent work intended for corporate executives to help simplify the complexities of federal antitrust and trade law. Price fixing, mergers/acquisitions, justice department enforcement, antitrust exemptions and unfair methods of competition are several of the topics addressed. A selected bibliography and summaries of the principal antitrust statutes are provided.

376. Kneese, Allen V. *Economics and the Environment.* New York: Penguin Books, 1977. 120 p.

This study analyzes the environmental costs of production and consumption in modern economics. Research priorities in the environmental economics field are identified. Tables and footnoted references are provided.

377. Kneese, Allen V., and Bower, Blair T. *Managing Water Quality: Economics, Technology, Institutions.* Baltimore, MD: Johns Hopkins University Press, 1968. 328 p.

This study identifies the major issues and problems associated with water pollution control. Waste load management, effluent standards, water quality analysis and the future of water management control policy are examined. Includes tables and bibliographic references.

378. Kolko, Gabriel M. *Railroads and Regulation, 1877–1916.* Princeton, NJ: Princeton University Press, 1965. 273 p.

An exceptional history of government attempts to regulate railroad interests during their height of power. Includes a political analysis of Senate passage of the Elkins and Hepburn Acts. A bibliography of primary and secondary sources is provided.

379. Kottke, Frank J. *The Promotion of Price Competition Where Sellers Are Few.* Lexington, MA: Lexington Books, 1978. 227 p.

An essay which assesses the effect oligopolistic trade practices have on prices in a free market economy. Policies and proposals designed to promote greater price competition are presented. Includes footnoted references and appendices with supporting data.

380. Kraft, John, and Roberts, Blaine, eds. *Wage and Price Controls: The U.S. Experiment.* New York: Praeger, 1975. 151 p.

This edited collection of essays assesses the impact and effectiveness of controls. Alternatives to and an examination of industrial wage and price controls are presented. Blaine Roberts, Arthur Kraft, A. Bradley Askin and Sidney L. Jones are among the contributors to this work.

381. Lake, Laura. *Environmental Regulation.* New York: Praeger, 1982. 152 p.

An analysis of how the enforcement of environmental law is politicizing the U.S. court system and redefining the traditional concept of federalism. Includes a selected bibliography.

382. Lave, Lester B., and Omenn, Gilbert S. *Clearing the Air: Reforming the Clean Air Act: A Staff Paper.* Washington, DC: Brookings Institution, 1981. 51 p.

A critical assessment of the effectiveness of the 1970 Clean Air Act. As an alternative to the present means of enforcement, the authors recommend greater reliance be placed on economic incentives/deterrents instead of on administrative due process and procedure. Includes footnoted references, a glossary of terms and tables.

383. Leonard, H. Jeffrey. *Are Environmental Regulations Driving U.S. Industry Overseas?* Washington, DC: Conservation Foundation, 1984. 155 p.

An evaluation of the effects environmental and workplace regulations have on industrial location. The industrial sectors most likely to relocate, due to regulatory restrictions, are identified. Includes tabular charts and footnoted references.

384. Macaulay, Hugh H., and Yandel, Bruce. *Environmental Use and the Market.* Lexington, MA: Lexington Books, 1977. 145 p.
This excellent volume analyzes the relationship between environmental use and regulatory decisions via the marketplace. It is a concise study that is easy to follow and understand.

385. MacAvoy, Paul W., ed. *Federal Energy Administration Regulation: Report of the Presidential Task Force.* Washington, DC: American Enterprise Institute for Public Policy Research, 1977. 195 p.
This investigative report examines FEA regulation of the petroleum industry. The program's costs outweigh its benefits according to the findings of the task force. Recommendations designed to simplify and improve the regulation of the oil industry (during normal supply and shortage periods) are proposed.

386. MacAvoy, Paul W. *The Regulated Industries and the Economy.* New York: Norton, 1979. 160 p.
This work examines the growth of government regulation and recent attempts to deregulate the private sector. A brief analysis of health and safety regulation, regulatory reform and the benefits of environmental legislation are presented. Includes footnoted references and tables with supporting data.

387. McCaffrey, David P. *OSHA and the Politics of Health Regulation.* New York: Plenum Press, 1982. 192 p.
This work describes the development of Occupational Safety and Health Administration regulation during the 1970s. The political and economic factors of regulating the safety/health of the occupational workplace are examined. Includes footnoted references and tables with supporting data.

388. McCraw, Thomas K. *Prophets of Regulation: Charles Francis Adams, Louis D. Brandeis, James M. Landis, Alfred F. Kahn* Cambridge, MA: Harvard University Press, 1984. 387 p.
This biographical account describes the careers of several leading government officials and their influence on the course of regulation. The early years of industrialization (late nineteenth century), the progressive period, the New Deal and the 1970s are time periods of importance also examined. Includes bibliographic footnotes.

389. McFarland, Andrew S. *Public Interest Lobbies: Decision Making on Energy.* Washington, DC: American Enterprise Institute for Public Policy Research, 1976. 141 p.
A book which examines the organizational characteristics and positions of interest groups. Includes appendices of information on Common Cause, the Sierra Club and Consumer Federation of America. Footnoted references are provided.

390. McGee, John S. *In Defense of Industrial Concentration.* New York: Praeger, 1971. 167 p.
An analytical study of the positive impact monopolistic and oligopolistic concentration has on industry performance. Footnoted references and tables are provided.

391. McManis, Charles R. *The Law of Unfair Trade Practices in a Nutshell.* St. Paul, MN: West, 1983. 445 p.
An in-depth work which explains various aspects of business law. Trademarks, contractual relations, price discrimination and patent infringement are among the legal areas considered. A table of court cases is provided.

392. Maler, Karl-Goran. *Environmental Economics: A Theoretical Inquiry.* Baltimore, MD: Johns Hopkins University Press, 1974. 267 p.
A technical study of the effects of economic growth on environmental quality and services. An analysis of the economic problems associated with environmental policy is provided. Includes mathematical formulas, graphs and a brief bibliography.

393. Maney, Ardith L. *Representing the Consumer Interest.* Washington, DC: University Press of America, 1978. 378 p.
A book which examines the role elected officials, political parties and interest groups play in protecting the public from fraud and abuse. Includes a bibliography and tabular charts.

394. Meany, George; Blough, Roger M.; and Jacoby, Neil H. *Government Wage-Price Guideposts in the American Economy.* New York: School of Commerce, New York University, 1967. 82 p.
A discussion which explores the advisability of federal wage and price control policy. Includes explanatory and footnoted references.

395. Melnick, Rowell S. *Regulation and the Courts: The Case of the Clean Air Act.* Washington, DC: Brookings Institution, 1983. 404 p.
An excellent analysis of the impact judicial activism has had on federal regulation of air pollution. The congressional and bureaucratic politics of the Clean Air Act are among other topics examined. Includes footnoted references and an index of legal cases cited within the work.

396. Mendeloff, John. *Regulating Safety: An Economic and Political Analysis of Occupational Safety and Health Policy.* Cambridge, MA: MIT Press, 1979. 219 p.
An examination of OSHA's performance in setting workable job safety standards. Complaint and compliance procedures are discussed. Includes recommendations for improving the agency's effectiveness.

397. Meyer, John R., and Oster, Clinton V. *Deregulation and the New Airline Entrepreneurs.* Cambridge, MA: MIT Press, 1984. 240 p.
An analysis of government decontrol of the air transportation industry. The cost structure of short-haul air service, commuter airline safety and competitive financial strategies (for air carriers) are among the topics discussed. Includes tables with supporting data.

398. Minow, Newton N. *Equal Time: The Private Broadcaster and the Public Interest.* New York: Atheneum, 1964. 316 p.
A provocative work, by a former chairman of the FCC, which considers the relationship between the quality of programming, commercial sponsor demands and government regulation of broadcasting. Analyses of network news programming and educational television are presented. Lawrence Laurent has provided an editor's note to this interesting book.

399. Mintz, Morton. *By Prescription Only: A Report on the Role of the United States Food and Drug Administration.* Boston: Beacon Press, 1967. 446 p.
This study examines the ineffectual monitoring and regulation of pharmaceutical products by the FDA. Drug testing procedures, (doctor) conflicts of interest and the power of pharmaceutical firms are various aspects of the problem investigated. An index to drugs and explanatory references are provided.

400. Mitchell, Edward J., ed. *The Deregulation of Natural Gas.* Washington, DC: American Enterprise Institute for Public Policy Research, 1983. 163 p.
This edited collection of essays analyzes the controversial issue of government decontrol of the natural gas industry. The Natural Gas Policy Act's effect on intrastate and interstate pricing disparities is discussed. Benjamin Schlesinger (American Gas Association), Milton Russell, Robert Leone (Harvard Business School), and Robert Means (Federal Energy Regulation Commission) are among the contributors to this work.

401. Mitchell, Edward J., ed. *Perspectives on U.S. Energy Policy: A Critique of Regulation.* New York: Praeger, 1976. 256 p.
An edited work devoted to the study of how price controls have affected the natural gas industry. Includes tabular charts, footnoted references and economic equations.

402. Moore, W. S., ed. *Horizontal Divestiture: Highlights of a Conference on Whether Oil Companies Should Be Prohibited from Owning Nonpetroleum Energy Resources.* Washington, DC: American Enterprise Institute for Public Policy Research, 1977. 62 p.
A booklet which surveys the highlights of a conference concerned with the issue of oil industry ownership of coal, solar and other energy sources. The competitive, technological and organizational aspects of oil industry divestiture are discussed. Edward J. Mitchell, Gary Swenson, Morris Adelman and Thomas E. Kauper are among the conferees whose remarks are included within this work.

403. Nadel, Mark V. *The Politics of Consumer Protection.* Indianapolis, IN: Bobbs-Merrill, 1971. 257 p.

A concise history of the consumer protection movement. The role played by Congress, executive agencies and consumer advocates in formulating policy are discussed. Statistical tables and a brief bibliography are provided.

404. National Industrial Conference Board. *Basic Issues in Decontrol: An Economic Forum Discussion.* New York: The Board, 1952. 62 p.

Dialogue, from an economic forum, which addresses the efficacy of continuing wage and price controls in early post–World War II America. Donald Wallace, Edwin B. George, Jules Backman and A. D. H. Kaplan are among the economists contributing to this slim volume.

405. Neal, Harry E. *The Protectors: The Story of the Food and Drug Administration.* New York: J. Messner, 1968. 190 p.

This work briefly summarizes the need for FDA regulation of drugs and potentially hazardous substances. Quack remedies, poisons, label lures and the dangers of barbiturates are discussed. A readings list is provided.

406. Nicholas, James C. *State Regulation/Housing Prices.* New Brunswick, NJ: Rutgers, Center for Urban Policy Research, 1982. 130 p.

An analysis of real estate development costs in Florida. The effect of government regulation on construction costs is assessed. Includes a selected bibliography, footnoted references and charts.

407. Noll, Roger G., and Owen, Bruce M. *The Political Economy of Deregulation: Interest Groups in the Regulatory Process.* Washington, DC: American Enterprise Institute for Public Policy, 1983. 164 p.

This book assesses the impact of special interest groups. A series of case studies explore how commission decisions affect the private economy. Includes tabular charts and footnoted references.

408. Noll, Roger G.; Peck, M. J.; and McGowan, J. J. *Economic Aspects of Television Regulation.* Washington, DC: Brookings Institution, 1973. 342 p.

An examination of how government regulatory policies affect performance in the television industry. FCC policies which have an impact on television programming and licensing are evaluated. Includes explanatory references and appendices.

409. Nourse, Edwin G. *Price Making in a Democracy.* Washington, DC: Brookings Institution, 1944. 541 p.

An economic study which assesses the various forms of price fixing. Laissez-faire ideology, corporate growth, supply and demand considerations and management policy are among the related topics examined. Includes footnoted references and statistical tables.

410. Nutter, G. Warren, and Einhorn, Henry A. *Enterprise Monopoly in the United States: 1899–1958.* New York: Columbia University Press, 1969. 256 p.

The factors which determine the level of economic concentration in an industrial sector are examined in this study. The changing criteria for estimating the growth of monopolies are also discussed. Includes statistical tables, appendices and bibliographic references.

411. Park, R. E. *The Role of Analysis in Regulatory Decision-Making: The Case of Cable Television.* Santa Monica, CA: Rand, 1972. 114 p.

A collection of essays which explore the brief history of cable television regulation. Perspectives and opinions from members of the FCC, National Association of Broadcasters and the National Cable Television Association are presented. A chronology of cable television regulation and a bibliography are provided.

412. Parkyn, Brian. *Democracy, Accountability and Participation in Industry.* Bradford, West Yorkshire, England: MCB Publications, 1979. 152 p.

An examination of participatory management and policy making in the private sector. Community ownership, works councils, two-tier boards and glacier systems are among the topics discussed. Includes a glossary of terms.

413. Peltzman, Samuel. *Automobile Safety Regulation.* Washington, DC: American Enterprise Institute for Public Policy Research, 1975. 53 p.
This study summarizes the technical and economic aspects of mandated automobile safety devices. The effect of auto safety regulation on the highway death rate is ascertained. Bibliographic and explanatory footnotes are provided.

414. Pertschuk, Michael. *Revolt against Regulation: The Rise and Pause of the Consumer Movement.* Berkeley, CA: University of California Press, 1982. 165 p.
A FTC chairman's appraisal of the commission's role during the 1970s and 1980s. The influence of pressure groups, consumer movement strategies and the impact of congressional action are among the topics discussed. Includes footnoted references.

415. Peskin, Henry M., et al, eds. *Environmental Regulation and the U.S. Economy.* Baltimore, MD: Johns Hopkins University Press, 1981. 163 p.
This edited collection of papers examines the impact of environmental regulations on economic productivity and growth. The relationship between GNP and the quality of the environment is explored. Footnoted references and tabular charts with supporting data are provided.

416. Phillips, Almarin W. *Market Structure, Organization, and Performance: An Essay on Price Fixing and Combinations in Restraint of Trade.* Cambridge, MA: Harvard University Press, 1962. 257 p.
An examination of the abuses of monopolistic and oligopolistic trade practices. The steel, coal, hardwood and plate glass mirror industries are studied. Includes a table of legal cases.

417. Phillips, Charles F. *The Regulation of Public Utilities: Theory and Practice.* Arlington, VA: Public Utilities Reports, 1984. 812 p.
A textbook study of government regulation of the electrical power, natural gas, telecommunications and water industries. Rate structures, rate-of-return allowances and an appraisal of the regulatory process are among the areas covered. Includes the indexes of legal cases, names and subjects.

418. Pierce, Richard J., et al. *Economic Regulation: Energy, Transportation and Utilities.* Indianapolis, IN: Bobbs-Merrill, 1980. 1200 p.
An in-depth textbook study of regulatory policy and process in two major sectors of the economy. The regulation of natural gas, petroleum, public utilities and freight carriers is examined. The role of antitrust policy in the regulated sector is assessed.

419. *Proceedings of a Symposium on Rate Design Problems of Regulated Industries, Kansas City, MO., 1975.* Columbia, MO: University of Missouri, 1975. 232 p.
A collection of papers which analyze rate structures in the public utility and oil industries. Incremental cost pricing, marginal cost principles and two-tier pricing are among the topics discussed. Symposium participants include noted authorities Almarin Phillips, Donald A. Murry, James Tanner and Ernest Ellingson.

420. *Proceedings of the 1977 Symposium on Problems of Regulated Industries.* Sponsored by Foster Associates, Inc., et al. Columbia, MO: University of Missouri, 1977. 400 p.
This collection of papers examines rate regulation in the electric utility and natural gas industries. The measurement and application of price elasticity are discussed. Alfred E. Kahn, David Spann, Milton Russell and William E. Miller are among the contributors to the proceedings.

421. Quarles, John. *Cleaning Up America: An Insider's View of the Environmental Protection Agency.* Boston: Houghton Mifflin, 1976. 255 p.
A leading official's critical assessment of EPA's response to the public outcry against industry abuse of the environment. Includes photographs.

422. Quarles, John. *Federal Regulation of New Industrial Plants.* New York: Practising Law Institute, 1978. 272 p.
A series of essays which critically assess EPA powers to regulate industrial expansion and development. EPA regulatory decisions are depicted as powerful disincentives to investment. Legal challenges to specific EPA rules are cited.

423. Quirk, Paul J. *Industry Influence in Federal Regulatory Agencies.* Princeton, NJ: Princeton University Press, 1981. 260 p.

A provocative study which assesses the impact the private sector exerts over the appointment process. Data from the Federal Trade Commission and National Highway Traffic Safety Administration is assessed. Includes a bibliography and footnoted references.

424. Rhoads, Steven E. *Policy Analysis in the Federal Aviation Administration.* Lexington, MA: Lexington Books, 1974. 160 p.

An examination of FAA objectives and responsibilities by system analysts. A cost-benefit analysis of FAA facilities and regulations is discussed. Footnoted references are provided.

425. Rider, Barry, and French, Leigh. *The Regulation of Insider Trading.* London: Macmillan, 1979. 474 p.

This helpful compendium of securities trading examines regulations in the U.S., U.K., France, Australia and Hong Kong among other nations. Securities markets surveillance, timely disclosure requirements and self-regulating insider trader procedures are topics covered. International regulatory cooperation is also discussed.

426. Rodgers, William H. *Brown-Out: The Power Crisis in America.* New York: Stein and Day, 1972. 300 p.

An account of the political and economic problems associated with energy development in the United States. Federal and state regulation of public utilities is investigated. Explanatory footnotes are included.

427. Rosenbaum, Walter A. *The Politics of Environmental Concern.* 2d ed. New York: Praeger, 1977. 298 p.

A summary of the issues and events which have had an impact on the environmental protection movement of the 1970s. The controversies surrounding timber harvesting, surface mining practices, the disposal of solid waste and the enforcement of air pollution regulations are examined. Extensively footnoted.

428. Rothwell, Roy, and Zegveld, Walter. *Industrial Innovation and Public Policy: Preparing for the 1980's and the 1990's.* Westport, CT: Greenwood Press, 1981. 251 p.

This excellent study examines the effect of scientific and technological advances on industrial policy. The influence of government intervention on technological innovation is assessed. Includes footnoted references and tables with supporting data.

429. Sabatier, Paul A., and Mazmanian, Daniel A. *Can Regulation Work? The Implementation of the 1972 California Coastal Initiative.* New York: Plenum, 1983. 389 p.

This study describes the process and politics of the California Coastal Commission's implementation of the 1972 Coastal Zone Conservation Act. The evaluation and reformulation of the commission's (zoning) mandate is discussed. Extensive bibliographic references and a text of the 1972 act are provided.

430. Sanford, David, comp. *Hot War on the Consumer.* New York: Pitman, 1969. 280 p.

A provocative collection of essays which investigate the issue of product reliability and safety. Food and drug licensing, big business malpractice and insurance industry abuses are among the areas covered. Ralph Nader, James Ridgeway, David Sanford and Robert Coles are several of the consumer advocates contributing to this volume.

431. Scherer, Frederick M. *Industrial Market Structure and Economic Performance.* 2d ed. Chicago: Rand McNally, 1980. 632 p.

This economic study analyzes the relationship between the market and economic performance. It is particularly useful for understanding how regulation of industry affects the market and industrial performance.

432. Sichel, Werner, ed. *Salvaging Public Utility Regulation.* Lexington, MA: Lexington Books, 1976. 154 p.
> An edited collection of papers which address the issue of regulatory reform in the utility industry. The unanticipated consequences of direct utility regulation are assessed. James R. Nelson, David L. McNicol and Harry Trebing are among the economists contributing to this work. Includes footnoted references and tabular charts with supporting data.

433. Sichel, Werner, and Gies, Thomas G., eds. *Public Utility Regulation: Change and Scope.* Lexington, MA: Lexington Books, 1975. 103 p.
> An edited collection of essays which analyze the economics and structure of utility rates. Developments in the natural gas and electrical utility industries are discussed. Includes tabular charts with supporting data.

434. Smith, Peter F. *Protecting the Consumer: An Economic and Legal Analysis.* Oxford: M. Robertson, 1979. 286 p.
> Buyer redress, competition policy, deception prevention and market intervention are among the topics covered in this examination of consumer protection. Includes a bibliography, footnoted references and a table of consumer-related statutes.

435. Sullivan, Frank C. *Crisis of Confidence: Utilities, Public Relations and Credibility.* Canaan, NH: Phoenix Publishing, 1977. 129 p.
> An examination of the role public utilities play in the business sector of the economy. Industry attempts to improve public relations are explored. Includes a list of books cited in the text and a bibliography.

436. Susskind, Lawrence; Bacow, Lawrence; and Wheeler, Michael; eds. *Resolving Environmental Regulatory Disputes.* Cambridge, MA: Schenkman, 1983. 261 p.
> A collection of environmental case studies which cite examples of extra-judicial negotiation between the EPA, private firms and third parties. The judicial interpretation of new and existing EPA regulation is discussed.

437. Taneja, Nawal K. *Airlines in Transition.* Lexington, MA: Lexington Books, 1981. 247 p.
> An analysis of the air transportation industry following passage of the Airline Deregulation Act of 1978. The response of air carriers to rising fuel costs and inflationary pressures are examined. Includes tabular charts.

438. Tierney, John T. *Postal Reorganization: Managing the Public's Business.* Boston: Auburn House, 1981. 191 p.
> This book assesses the managerial changes within the U.S. Postal Service following its reorganization in 1971. Cost containment, labor relations, mechanization and managerial autonomy are among the topics discussed. Includes footnotes.

439. Trebing, Harry M., ed. *Performance under Regulation.* East Lansing, MI: Institute of Public Utilities, Michigan State University, 1968. 169 p.
> This edited collection of papers surveys the impact of regulatory policy on the efficiency of the private economy. The pricing practices, market structure and performance of regulated industries are examined. Includes footnoted references.

440. Twentieth Century Fund. *Electric Power and Government Policy.* New York: The Fund, 1948. 860 p.
> An in-depth examination of the relationship between government and the power industry. The regulation of rates, service and the financing of electric systems are discussed. Includes statistical tables and footnoted references.

441. Vietor, Richard H. *Environmental Politics and the Coal Coalition.* College Station, TX: Texas A & M University Press, 1980. 285 p.
> This book assesses the effects of strip mining regulation on the coal industry. The regulatory politics of enforcing coal mining and air pollution standards are among the topics addressed. Includes an appendix of tabular charts and a bibliography.

442. Viscusi, W. Kip. *Regulating Consumer Product Safety.* Washington, DC: American Enterprise Institute for Public Policy Research, 1984. 116 p.
A book which analyzes the need for voluntary consumer product safety standards. Product liability, insurance, the CPSC and accident trends are discussed. Includes a bibliography.

443. Viscusi, W. Kip. *Risk by Choice: Regulating Health and Safety in the Workplace.* Cambridge, MA: Harvard University Press, 1983. 200 p.
An analysis of the economic variables which influence health and safety regulation. The costs and benefits of establishing and enforcing health and safety standards are discussed. Includes footnoted references and a bibliography.

444. Wachter, Michael L., and Wachter, Susan M. *Toward a New U.S. Industrial Policy?* Philadelphia, PA: University of Pennsylvania Press, 1983. 514 p.
An edited work which examines the relationship between business and government. A supply-side approach as opposed to a conventional one is assessed. Extensively footnoted. John T. Dunlop, William W. Hogan, Irving B. Kravis and Donald T. Regan are among this volume's contributors.

445. Weber, Gustavus A. *The Food, Drug, and Insecticide Administration: Its History, Activities and Organization.* Baltimore, MD: Johns Hopkins University Press, 1928. 134 p.
An account of the origins and regulatory activities of the FDIA. The enforcement of the Tea, Naval Stores, Milk and Caustic Poison Acts are discussed. Includes a bibliography and appendices.

446. Weber, Nathan, ed. *Insurance Deregulation: Issues and Perspectives; Essays on the Regulation-Deregulation Controversy and Its Significance for Insurance Companies, Agents and Consumers.* New York: Conference Board, 1982. 46 p.
An edited collection of essays which assess the benefits and problems of the insurance industry. Market versus regulated rates, industry competition, regulatory politics and the future of insurance are discussed.

447. Weil, Gordon L. *Trade Policy in the 70's: A New Round.* New York: Twentieth Century Fund, 1969. 75 p.
A discussion of commodity regulation is presented. International, protectionist, free trade and agricultural policies are examined.

448. Weiss, Leonard W. *Case Studies in American Industry.* 3d ed. New York: Wiley, 1980. 381 p.
An economic study of U.S. market structure and performance. The effects of oligopolistic and monopolistic trade practices on the agricultural, electrical power, steel and retail sectors of the economy are examined. Includes footnoted references, graphs and tabular charts.

449. Weiss, Leonard W. *Trade Liberalization and the National Interest.* Washington, DC: U.S. Export Competitiveness Project, Center for Strategic and International Studies, Georgetown University, 1980. 52 p.
A paper which addresses the importance of American exports. An assessment of the Multilateral Trade Negotiations (MTN) is provided. Includes footnoted references and a bibliography.

REGULATORY AGENCIES

450. Abramson, Joan. *Old Boys, New Women.* New York: Praeger, 1979. 255 p.
This work surveys the legal and administrative problems associated with the enforcement of equal employment opportunity for women. Sex discrimination in the public and private sectors is analyzed. Includes an excellent bibliography.

451. Anderson, Kent. *Television Fraud: The History and Implications of the Quiz Show Scandals.* Westport, CT: Greenwood Press, 1978. 226 p.

A noteworthy assessment of TV game show deception in the late 1950s. Public reaction to the quiz show scandals is examined. Includes appendices and a bibliography.

452. Banning, William P. *Commercial Broadcasting Pioneer, the WEAF Experiment: 1922–1926.* Cambridge, MA: Harvard University Press, 1946. 308 p.

A study of AT&T's development of the first "pay" radio station. Programming formats, patent protection of technology and the introduction of government regulation are among the topics discussed. Includes copies of internal memoranda, footnoted references and photographs.

453. Barnouw, Erik. *The Golden Web.* New York: Oxford University Press, 1968. 391 p.

An excellent account of American radio and television broadcasting from the 1930s to 1953. The role of the media in reporting major events during this period is examined. Includes a bibliography and photographs.

454. Barnouw, Erik. *The Image Empire.* New York: Oxford University Press, 1970. 396 p.

A detailed study of television's impact on politics and popular culture from 1953 to 1970. The use of television by politicians in shaping public opinion and network news coverage are among the topics discussed. Includes appendices and photographs.

455. Barnouw, Erik. *A Tower in Babel.* New York: Oxford University Press, 1966. 344 p.

A historical account of radio from its origins at the turn of the century to 1933. The establishment of the FRC and the passage of the Radio Acts of 1917 and 1927 are among the topics featured. Includes a bibliography and photographs.

456. Barnouw, Erik. *Tube of Plenty: The Evolution of American Television.* New York: Oxford University Press, 1982. 552 p.

A brief history of commercial television in the United States. Topics discussed include FCC regulation and the medium's impact on national elections. Includes photographs.

457. Bernhardt, Joshua. *The Interstate Commerce Commission: Its History, Activities and Organization.* Baltimore, MD: Johns Hopkins University Press, 1923. 169 p.

An overview of ICC administrative machinery and regulatory activities. ICC regulation of railway commerce, in the public interest, is the central focus of this work. Includes appendices.

458. Bernstein, Irving. *The New Deal Collective Bargaining Policy.* Berkeley, CA: University of California Press, 1950. 178 p.

The consequences of federal recognition of the rights of unions to organize are examined. The effects of the Railway Labor Act, Wagner Act and National Relations Act on the size and regulation of labor unions are ascertained. A text of the National Labor Relations Act is included.

459. Bosland, Chelcie C. *Valuation Theories and Decisions of the Securities and Exchange Commission.* New York: Simmons-Boardman, 1964. 89 p.

An economic study of the valuation problem. Analyses of assessed, appraised, intrinsic, exchange and market values are presented.

460. Bromberg, Alan R. *Securities Law: Fraud, SEC Rule 10b-5.* New York: McGraw-Hill, 1977. 4 vols.

A compendium of SEC misrepresentation, deception and fraud (trading) provisions. A subject index and table of references are provided.

461. Cherington, Charles R. *The Regulation of Railroad Abandonments.* Cambridge, MA: Harvard University Press, 1948. 277 p.

This book examines ICC decisions allowing railroads to relinquish the operation of certain carrier routes. The ICC's control of railway commerce during the war is also discussed. Includes footnoted references.

462. Cherington, Paul W.; Hirsch, Leon V.; and Brandwein, Robert, eds. *Television Station Ownership: A Case Study of Federal Agency Regulation.* New York: Hastings House, 1971. 304 p.
A collection of case studies which examine FCC television station ownership requirements. Includes tables and appendices.

463. Clarkson, Kenneth W., and Muris, Timothy J., eds. *The Federal Trade Commission since 1970: Economic Regulation and Bureaucratic Behavior.* New York: Cambridge University Press, 1981. 379 p.
This edited volume concentrates on the activities of the FTC since 1970. It includes introductory chapters on the statutory power, and the legislative, judicial and executive constraints on the FTC. It includes several case studies of FTC actions, plus a summary of the FTC overall performance.

464. Cole, Barry G., and Oettinger, Mal. *Reluctant Regulators: The FCC and the Broadcasting Audience.* Reading, MA: Addison-Wesley, 1978. 310 p.
This book attacks the FCC for failure to regulate the communications industry in the public interest. The lack of public input during FCC deliberations is criticized.

465. Cox, Edward T., et al. *The Nader Report on the Federal Trade Commission.* New York: R. W. Barron, 1969. 241 p.
A task force report which examines FTC consumer-protection performance, enforcement techniques and data-gathering methods. Includes an appendix with tabular charts of supporting data.

466. de Bedts, Ralph F. *The New Deal's SEC: The Formative Years.* New York: Columbia University Press, 1964. 226 p.
A study which examines the historical origins of the Securities and Exchange Commission. The Commission's growth and function is analyzed. Includes an extensive bibliography.

467. Fellmeth, Robert C. *The Interstate Commerce Commission: The Public Interest and the ICC.* New York: Grossman, 1970. 423 p.
A Nader-sponsored report which investigates the ICC. The influence of corporate conglomerates, highway safety and the planned obsolescence of passenger trains are among the topics discussed. Includes a foreword by Ralph Nader, footnoted references and survey data.

468. Freeman, A. Myrick; Havemen, Robert H.; and Kneese, Allan V. *The Economics of Environmental Policy.* New York: Wiley, 1973. 184 p.
This work discusses the relationship between environmental quality, the market system and the enforcement of pollution control standards. The costs and benefits associated with environmental management are examined. Includes tabular charts.

469. *The FTC As an Antitrust Enforcement Agency: The Role of Section Five of the FTC Act in Antitrust.* Chicago: American Bar Association, Section of Antitrust Law, 1981. 2 vols.
An assessment of the FTC's performance in maintaining free market competition through its application of section five of the FTC Act. Internal FTC case procedures and related antitrust provisions are also discussed. Includes footnoted references.

470. Gaskill, Nelson B. *The Regulation of Competition.* New York: Harper and Row, 1936. 179 p.
A critical review of FTC performance by a former commission member. A series of case studies demonstrate FTC failure to restore free market conditions.

471. Green, Harold P., and Rosenthal, Alan. *Government of the Atom: The Integration of Powers.* New York: Atherton Press, 1963. 281 p.
A detailed study of nuclear regulation by the legislative and executive branches. Extensively footnoted.

472. Green, Mark J. *The Closed Enterprise System: Ralph Nader's Study Group Report on Antitrust Enforcement.* New York: Grossman, 1972. 588 p.
A two-volume report which examines the alleged failure of the federal government to effectively regulate market competition. The political difficulties associated with enforcing antitrust legislation are investigated. A foreword by Ralph Nader is provided.

473. Gross, Barry R. *Discrimination in Reverse: Is Turnabout Fair Play?* New York: New York University Press, 1978. 168 p.
This book assesses the policy implications of the Bakke decision. The competing claims of equity and hiring quotas are considered. Includes a foreword by Professor Sidney Hook.

474. Gross, James A. *The Making of the NLRB: A Study in Economics, Politics and the Law.* Albany, NY: State University of New York Press, 1974. 265 p.
A major study of the evolution of national labor policy under the NLRB. The role of the NLRB in resolving labor disputes on a case by case basis is discussed. Includes citations to the board's internal memoranda.

475. Gross, James A. *The Reshaping of the NLRB: National Labor Policy in Transition, 1937–1947.* Albany, NY: State University of New York Press, 1981. 379 p.
An analysis of the evolution of national labor policy under the NLRB. NLRB arbitration of labor disputes are discussed on a case by case basis. Includes citations to internal memoranda.

476. Grundfest, Joseph A. *Citizen Participation in Broadcast Licensing before the FCC.* Santa Barbara, CA: Rand, 1976. 195 p.
A survey of public input into the granting, renewal and revocation of broadcast licenses. The mechanisms for citizen involvement are examined. Includes legal and bibliographic citations.

477. Hammond, Matthew B. *Railway Rate Theories of the Interstate Commerce Commission.* Cambridge, MA: Harvard University Press, 1911. 200 p.
An assessment of the ICC's regulation of railway rate structure. The effect of specific ICC decisions on economic competition is assessed.

478. Harlan, John M. *The Federal Trade Commission.* Chicago: Callaghan and Co., 1916. 183 p.
A compendium of FTC rules and procedures for the regulation of commerce. Includes an analytical index.

479. Hawkins, Keith, and Thomas, John M. *Enforcing Regulation.* Boston: Kluwer-Nijhoff, 1984. 198 p.
A collection of essays which analyze administrative procedure and law. The enforcement of social, health and safety and surface mining regulations are investigated. Professors Donald Clelland, Robert A. Kagan and Susan S. Silbey are among the contributors to this work.

480. Hewlett, Richard G., and Anderson, Oscar E. *The New World.* University Park, PA: Pennsylvania State University Press, 1962. 766 p.
An AEC-sponsored account of the agency's origins and development. Problems of national security, legislative enactment and public education are among the topics examined. Includes appendices and footnoted references.

481. Hewlett, Richard G., and Duncan, Francis. *Atomic Shield, 1947/1952.* University Park, PA: Pennsylvania State University Press, 1969. 718 p.
A detailed history of the AEC's first six years. The regulatory problems encountered during the development of military, scientific and commercial applications are discussed. Includes footnoted references and appendices.

482. Hewlett, Richard G., and Duncan, Francis. *Nuclear Navy.* Chicago: University of Chicago Press, 1974. 477 p.
A historical survey of the bureaucratic and technological problems faced by the U.S. Navy in developing a nuclear-powered fleet. Includes appendices.

483. Hill, Herbert. *Black Labor and the American Legal System.* Washington, DC: Bureau of National Affairs, 1977. 455 p.
A study which examines the history of federal minority labor policy. Employment discrimination practices, the Fair Employment Practice Committee and the influence of labor unions are discussed.

484. Holt, William S. *The Federal Trade Commission: Its History, Activities and Organizations.* New York: Appleton, 1922. 80 p.
A brief account of the origins and role of the FTC from 1914 to 1921. The economic and quasi-judicial activities of the commission are discussed. Includes a classification chart of FTC activities and a bibliography.

485. Karmel, Roberta S. *Regulation by Prosecution: The Securities and Exchange Commission vs. Corporate America.* New York: Simon and Schuster, 1982. 400 p.
A political analysis of the administrative processes and jurisdictional powers of the SEC. Includes a list of SEC commissioners and former chairmen.

486. Katzmann, Robert A. *Regulatory Bureaucracy: The Federal Trade Commission and Antitrust Policy.* Cambridge, MA: MIT Press, 1980. 223 p.
A study of the decision-making process, goals, objectives and powers of the FTC. The commission's efforts to shape policy are examined. Includes footnoted references.

487. Kinsley, Michael E. *Outer Space and Inner Sanctums: Government, Business, and Satellite Communication.* New York: Wiley, 1976. 280 p.
A Nader-sponsored study of nonmilitary applications of telecommunication satellites. AT&T's most-favored status by federal agencies is criticized.

488. Knauss, Robert L. *Securities Regulation Sourcebook.* New York: Practising Law Institute, 1972. 1 vol.
This compendium of SEC rules and regulations cites disclosure and registration requirements as well as important commission releases. A text of the Securities and Exchange Act with amendments is provided.

489. Krasnow, Erwin G., et al. *The Politics of Broadcast Regulation.* New York: St. Martin's Press, 1982. 304 p.
An analysis of citizen, White House, industry and court participation in the formation of FCC regulatory policy. A series of case studies demonstrate the continuing need and importance of FCC regulation in the public interest. Recommendations for improving the regulation of the media are presented.

490. McCormick, Edward T. *Understanding the Securities Act and the SEC.* New York: American Book Co., 1948. 327 p.
This book discusses the Securities Act from its passage in 1933 to 1947. Extensively footnoted.

491. McFarland, Carl. *Judicial Control of the Federal Trade Commission and the Interstate Commerce Commission, 1920–1930.* Cambridge, MA: Harvard University Press, 1933. 214 p.
A comparative study of how court intervention has influenced FTC and ICC policy decisions and procedures. Free market trade implications are discussed. Extensive legal references.

492. Marshall, F. Ray, et al. *Employment Discrimination Law: The Impact of Legal and Administrative Remedies.* New York: Praeger, 1978. 153 p.
This study examines the effectiveness of antidiscrimination law. Combating employment discrimination in the shipbuilding and construction industries is studied. Includes tables, footnotes and a glossary of terms.

493. Mason, Lowell B. *The Language of Dissent.* Cleveland, OH: World Publishing Co., 1959. 314 p.
This study, by a former FTC commissioner, explores the problems associated with enforcing fair trade practices. Trade associations, states rights, enforcement ethics and price fixing are among the topics examined. An appendix of FTC minority opinions (from the late 1940s and early 50s) is provided.

494. Mitchell, Olivia S. *The Labor Market Impact of Federal Regulation: OSHA, ERISA, EEO and Minimum Wage.* Cambridge, MA: National Bureau of Research, 1982. 51 p.
A report which examines the effects of the federal minimum wage on employment. The consequences of minimum wage standards on worker health and safety, pension benefits and hiring practices are among the topics covered. Includes a bibliography.

495. Moore, Thomas G. *Freight Transportation Regulation: Surface Freight and the Interstate Commerce Commission.* Washington, DC: American Enterprise Institute for Public Policy Research, 1972. 98 p.
A brief history of the ICC which analyzes U.S. surface transportation industry rates and service. Congressional reform proposals are presented. Includes footnoted references.

496. Mosco, Vincent. *Reforming Regulation: The FCC and Innovations in the Broadcasting Market.* Cambridge, MA: Harvard University, Program on Information Technologies and Public Policy, 1976. 45 p.
A critical overview of FCC policy decisions. The inflexibility of FCC responses to technological and market changes is discussed. Includes tables, graphs and appendices.

497. Mosco, Vincent. *The Regulation of Broadcasting in the United States: A Comparative Analysis.* Cambridge, MA: Harvard University Program on Information Technologies and Public Policy, 1975. 294 p.
An analysis of four major FCC regulatory decisions. The effect on economic concentration is discussed.

498. Newcomb, Harry T. *The Work of the Interstate Commerce Commission.* Washington, DC: Press of Gibson Brothers, 1905. 102 p.
A booklet of editorials and articles which assess the activities of the ICC during its first year of existence. Railway rate regulation and the importance of railroad transportation to the economy are among the topics considered. Statistical tables are provided.

499. Okrent, David. *Nuclear Reactor Safety: On the History of the Regulatory Process.* Madison, WI: University of Wisconsin Press, 1981. 370 p.
A historical analysis of the nuclear power industry in the United States. The developments, controversy and politics of industry regulation are discussed. Reactor site criteria standards are also examined.

500. Phillips, Susan M., and Zecher, Richard J. *The SEC and the Public Interest.* Cambridge, MA: MIT Press, 1981. 177 p.
A historical and economic study of the Securities and Exhange Commission. Corporate disclosure requirements, the market structure for securities trading and the future of regional exchanges are among the topics covered. Includes tabular charts with supporting data, footnoted references and an extensive bibliography.

501. Posner, Richard A., and Scott, Kenneth E., eds. *Economics of Corporation Law and Securities Regulation.* Boston: Little, Brown, 1980. 384 p.
Capital structure, corporate acquisitions, insider trading and SEC regulation are among the topics covered in this edited collection of essays. Contributors to this work include William H. Beaver, Ralph K. Winter, Peter Holl and James H. Scott. Includes bibliographic notes and questions for each chapter.

502. Ray, Verne M., ed. *Interpreting FCC Broadcast Rules and Regulations.* Thurmont, MD: Tab Books, 1966–1972. 3 vols.
A practical guide, intended for broadcasters, which briefly clarifies Federal Communication Commission rules. The fairness doctrine, libel, FCC ownership philosophy and programming responsibility are among the areas covered.

503. Redford, Emmett S. *Public Administration and Policy Formation.* Austin, TX: University of Texas Press, 1956. 319 p.
A collection of federal and state regulatory studies. Banking, interstate commerce and natural gas regulation are among the topics covered. Includes explanatory and bibliographic references.

504. Rolph, Elizabeth S. *Nuclear Power and the Public Safety: A Study in Regulation.* Lexington, MA: Lexington Books, 1970. 213 p.
This study examines the growth and regulation of nuclear technology. The early commercialization of atomic energy is investigated. Includes an extensive bibliography and tabular charts.

505. Rolph, Elizabeth S. *Regulation of Nuclear Power: The Case of the Light Water Reactor.* Santa Monica, CA: Rand, 1977. 88 p.
A historical account of the AEC's administrative control of light water nuclear reactors from 1954 to 1974. The revision of AEC regulatory standards (in response to technological and safety considerations) is discussed. Includes tables and graphs.

506. Schattschneider, Elmer E. *Politics, Pressures and the Tariff.* New York: Prentice-Hall, 1935. 301 p.
This book examines the role special interest groups played in drafting and enacting the protective tariff revision of 1929–1930. Industry and agricultural protectionists are shown to have been successful in maintaining and extending trade restraints under the revision. Includes tables and appendices.

507. Schlei, Barbara L., and Grossman, Paul. *Employment Discrimination Law.* Washington, DC: Bureau of National Affairs, 1979. 1472 p.
A compendium of antidiscriminatory (hiring) statutory provisions. Affirmative action requirements, procedural due process and Executive Orders 11236 and 11375 are among the employment-related areas covered. Footnoted references and a table of cases are provided.

508. Siegel, Barry N. *Money in Crisis: The Federal Reserve, the Economy, and Monetary Reform.* San Francisco, CA: Pacific Institute for Public Policy Research, 1984. 361 p.
An edited work which assesses the need for monetary reform. The federal reserve system, the gold standard and a free market policy are among the topics discussed. Includes a selected bibliography, footnoted references, tabular charts and graphs.

509. Skolnick, Jerome H. *The Politics of Protest: A Report.* New York: Simon and Schuster, 1969. 276 p.
A task force report on demonstrations, protest and group violence. Antiwar, student and racial protests are analyzed. The judicial and social responses to civil disobedience are discussed. Includes a bibliography and footnoted references.

510. Skousen, K. Fred. *An Introduction to the SEC.* 2d ed. Cincinnati, OH: South-Western, 1980. 161 p.
A book which discusses the nature, origins and functions of the Securities and Exchange Commission. The impact of SEC disclosure requirements and regulations on financial markets are examined. An appendix of selected references and discussion points is provided.

511. Smith, Christopher. *FTC Trade Regulation: Advertising, Rulemaking, and the New Consumer Protection.* New York: Practising Law Institute, 1979. 632 p.
An explanation of Federal Trade Commission decisions. Legal and administrative precedents are cited.

512. Sovern, Michael I. *Legal Restraints on Racial Discrimination in Employment.* New York: Twentieth Century Fund, 1966. 270 p.
A book which examines the legal remedies for discrimination in hiring. Civil rights statutes, executive orders and state legislation are among the legal areas discussed. Includes a selected bibliography and footnoted references.

513. Stephens, Harold M. *Administrative Tribunals and the Rules of Evidence.* Cambridge, MA: Harvard University Press, 1933. 128 p.
A study of the legislation, rules and judicial decisions associated with regulatory commissions. The Interstate Commerce, Federal Trade and State Public Service Comissions are among the regulatory bodies studied. Footnoted references and appendices are provided.

514. Stone, Alan. *Economic Regulation and the Public Interest: The Federal Trade Commission in Theory and Practice.* Ithaca, NY: Cornell University Press, 1977. 314 p.

An excellent account of the origins, organization and role of the FTC. The regulatory activities and administrative domain of the commission are examined. Includes a bibliography and footnotes.

515. Tedrow, Joseph H. *Regulation of Transportation: Practice and Procedure before the Interstate Commerce Commission.* Dubuque, IA: W. C. Brown, 1947. 595 p.

A book which examines the regulatory activities of the ICC and other federal commissions. The operating rights, liabilities and entry route assignments of carriers are among the topics discussed. Includes an index of cases and a suggested readings list.

516. Thompson, Donald N. *The Economics of Environmental Protection.* Cambridge, MA: Winthrop, 1973. 278 p.

This book analyzes the economic considerations associated with pollution control. The legal and scientific approaches to pollution abatement are examined. Includes a glossary of terms and footnoted references.

517. Tybout, Richard A. *Government Contracting in Atomic Energy.* Ann Arbor, MI: University of Michigan Press, 1956. 226 p.

This work investigates the public ownership and private operation of the U.S. nuclear power industry. Cost plus fixed fee, variable price and fixed price contracts are assessed as government methods of procurement. Footnoted references and an appendix are provided.

518. Tyler, Poyntz, ed. *Securities, Exchanges and the SEC.* New York: H. W. Wilson, 1965. 201 p.

A concise introduction to security and commodity trading. The stock exchanges, bond ratings and role of the Securities and Exchange Commission in regulating the financial markets are topics explored. A bibliography is provided.

519. Wolkinson, Benjamin W. *Blacks, Unions and the EEOC: A Study of Administrative Futility.* Lexington, MA: Lexington Books, 1973. 175 p.

This work analyzes EEOC arbitration of seventy-five suits involving racial discrimination by organized labor. The study concludes that the agency was often unsuccessful in curbing unfair union practices and in compensating plaintiffs. Recommendations for improving the conciliation process are presented.

II. Economics of Regulation

GOVERNMENT INTERVENTION

520. Abernathy, W. J., and Chakravarthy, B. S. "Government Intervention and Innovation in Industry: A Policy Framework." *Sloan Management Review* 20 (Spring 1979): 3–18.

521. Andersen (Arthur) and Company. *Cost of Government Regulation: Study for the Business Roundtable: A Study of the Direct Incremental Costs Incurred by 48 Companies in Complying with the Regulations of Six Federal Agencies in 1977.* Chicago: A. Andersen, 1979. 355 p.

522. Ballard, Frederick; Mundheim, Robert; Weinstock, Lewis; and Wetzel, Carroll. "The Corporate Conscience and the Corporate Bar: A Panel." *Business Lawyer* 26 (January 1971): 959–69.

523. Barkdoll, G. L. "Perils and Promise of Economic Analysis for Regulatory Decision-Making." *Food Drug Cosmetic Law Journal* 34 (December 1979): 625–30.

524. Becker, William H. *The Dynamics of Business-Government Relations: Industry and Exports, 1893 to 1921.* Chicago: University of Chicago Press, 1982. 240 p.

525. Berg, Stanford V. "The Clean Clothes Act: A Fable." *Regulation* 5 (November–December 1981): 43–45.

526. Bernstein, Barton. "The Removal of War Production Board Controls on Business, 1944–1946." *Business Historical Review* 39 (Summer 1965): 243–60.

527. Berryman, Richard, and Schifter, Richard. "A Global Straitjacket: The New International Regulation." *Regulation* 5 (September–October 1981): 19–28.

528. Blumner, Sidney M., and Hefner, Dennis L., eds. *Readings in the Regulation of Business.* Scranton, PA: International Textbook, 1968. 407 p.

529. Boies, David, and Verkuil, Paul R. *Public Control of Business: Cases, Notes, and Questions.* Boston: Little, Brown, 1977. 1034 p.

530. Boisjoly, Russell P. "Optimal Financial Strategies under Threat of Bankruptcy: The Regulated and Unregulated Cases." D.B.A. dissertation, Indiana University, Graduate School of Business, 1978. 142 p.

531. Bork, Robert H. "Viewpoint: On Constitutional Economics." *Regulation* 7 (September–October 1983): 14–18.

532. Braithwaite, John. "The Limits of Economics in Controlling Harmful Corporate Conduct." *Law and Society Review* 16 (1981–82): 481–504.

533. Carroll, James D.; Flynn, Paul J.; and Dorsey, Thomas A. "Vertical Coalitions for Technology Transfer: Toward an Understanding of Intergovernmental Technology." *Publius* 9 (Summer 1979): 3–33.

534. Chilton, Kenneth W., and Weidenbaum, Murray L. "Government Regulation: The Small Business Burden." *Journal of Small Business Management* 20 (January 1982): 4–10.

535. Christiansen, Gregory B., and Havemen, Robert H. "Government Regulations and Their Impact on the Economy." *American Academy of Political and Social Science, Annals* 459 (January 1982): 112–22.

536. Coogan, Peter F. "The Effect of the Federal Tax Lien Act of 1966 upon Security Interests Created under the Uniform Commercial Code." *Harvard Law Review* 81 (May 1968): 1369–1418.

537. Coogan, Peter F. "Intangibles as Collateral under the Uniform Commercial Code." *Harvard Law Review* 77 (April 1964): 997–1036.

538. Coppock, Joseph D. "Government as Enterpriser-Competitor: The Case of the Electric Home and Farm Authority." *Explorations in Economic History* 1 (Winter 1964): 187–206.

539. Cornell, Nina W; Pelcovits, Michael D.; and Brenner, Steven R. "A Legacy of Regulatory Failure." *Regulation* 7 (July–August 1983): 37–42.

540. Cramton, Roger C. "Regulatory Structure and Regulatory Performance: A Critique of the Ash Council Report." *Public Administration Review* 32 (July–August 1972): 284–92.

541. Davidow, Joel, and Chiles, Lisa. "The United States and the Issue of the Binding or Voluntary Nature of International Codes of Conduct Regarding Restrictive Business Practices." *American Journal of International Law* 72 (April 1978): 247–71.

542. Davis, Lance, and Legler, John. "The Government in the American Economy, 1815–1902: A Quantitative Study." *Journal of Economic History* 26 (December 1966): 514–52.

543. DeFina, Robert. *Public and Private Expenditures for Federal Regulation of Business.* St. Louis, MO: Center for the Study of American Business, Washington University, November 1977. 56 p.

544. Diebold, John. "Business, Government and Science: The Need for a Fresh Look." *Foreign Affairs* 51 (April 1973): 555–72.

545. Dodge, Kristen, ed. *Government and Business, Prospects for Partnership.* Austin, TX: Lyndon B. Johnson School of Public Affairs, Lyndon Baines Johnson Library, 1980. 238 p.

546. Dubnick, Melvin J., and Walker, Lafayette. "Problems in U.S. Standard-Setting: The Implications of the Shift to Control Functions." *Midwest Review of Public Administration* 13 (March 1979): 25–49.

547. Dufault, Roland E. "The Businessman in Politics: The Role of the Regulatory Official in State Government." Ph.D. dissertation, Brown University, 1971. 298 p.

548. Dunlop, John T. "Viewpoint: New Approaches to Economic Policy." *Regulation* 3 (January–February 1979): 13–16.

549. Eads, George C. "Regulation and Technical Change: Some Largely Unexplored Influences." *American Economic Review; Papers and Proceedings* 70 (May 1980): 50–54.

550. Edwards, Corwin D. *Big Business and the Policy of Competition.* Cleveland, OH: Press of Western Reserve University, 1956. 180 p.

551. Engelbert, Arthur. "Short-Term Grants and Long-Range Goals: The Dilemma of Federal Policies." *Educational Record* 44 (April 1963): 161–64.

552. Fried, Charles. "Laissez Partir: The Borders of Freedom." *Regulation* 7 (September–October 1983): 43–45.

553. Friedmann, W. "Government Enterprise: A Comparative Analysis." In *Government Enterprise,* edited by J. F. Garner, pp. 303–36. London: Stevens, 1970.

554. Galbraith, J. K. "Government vs. Small Business." *Washington Monthly* 10 (September 1978): 42–44.

555. Glazer, Nathan. "Regulating Business and the Universities: One Problem or Two?" *Public Interest* 56 (Summer 1979): 43–65.

556. Grossfeld, Bernhard, and Ebke, Werner. "Controlling the Modern Corporation: A Comparative View of Corporate Power in the United States and Europe." *American Journal of Comparative Law* 26 (Summer 1978): 397–433.

557. Grunschlag, Dov M. "Administering Federal Programs of Production Adjustment." *Agricultural History* 49 (January 1975): 131–49.

558. Hanson, A. H. *Public Enterprise and Economic Development.* London: Routledge and Kegan Paul, 1959. 485 p.

559. Huszagh, S. M. "Exporter Perceptions of the US Regulatory Environment." *Columbia Journal of World Business* 16 (Fall 1981): 22–31.

560. Isaacs, Asher, and Slesinger, Reuben E. *Business, Government and Public Policy.* Princeton, NJ: Van Nostrand, 1964. 461 p.

561. Johnson, Arthur M. "Government-Business Relations: A Domestic View." *Business History Review* 38 (Summer 1964): 141–43.

562. Johnson, Arthur M. "Government-Business Relations: An International Approach." *Business History Review* 38 (Spring 1964): 1–3.

563. Johnson, G. E. "Theory of Labour Market Intervention." *Economica* 47 (August 1980): 309–29.

564. Jones, L. R. "Regulatory Review without Economists: Evaluating a Model for State Governments." *Public Administration Review* 42 (July–August 1982): 327–38.

565. Katz, Robert N. "Business Impact upon Regulatory Agencies." *California Management Review* 16 (Spring 1974): 102–08.

566. Kelman, Steven. "Regulation and Paternalism." *Public Policy* 29 (Spring 1981): 219–54.

567. Key, V. O. "Government Corporations." In *Elements of Public Administration,* edited by Fritz Morstein, pp. 219–45. Englewood Cliffs, NJ: Prentice-Hall, 1959.

568. Keyes, Lucile S. "The Protective Functions of Commission Regulation." *American Economic Review* 48 (May 1958): 544–52.

569. Kirkpatrick, Jeane J. "Global Paternalism—The UN and the New International Regulatory Order." *Regulation* 7 (January–February 1983): 17–22.

570. Kurezewski, Jacek, and Frieske, Kazimierz. "Some Problems in the Legal Regulation of the Activities of Economic Institutions." *Law and Society Review* 11 (Winter 1977): 489–506.

571. Lapinsky, M. "Role of the Economist in Regulatory Hearings." *Public Utilities Fortnightly* 90 (October 12, 1972): 37–41.

572. Larson, David A. "An Economic Analysis of the Webb-Pomerene Act." *Journal of Law and Economics* 13 (October 1970): 461–500.

573. Lascelles, David. "United States: Revolutionary Changes Ahead." *Banker* 132 (March 1982): 105–06.

574. Latimer, Hugh. "Premerger Notification." *Regulation* 3 (May–June 1979): 46–52.

575. Lee, L. W. "Theory of Just Regulation." *American Economic Review* 70 (December 1980): 848–62.

576. Littlefield, Durwood E. "Extra-Territorial Application of United States Regulatory Legislation: A Response by the Nation State to a Changing World." Ph.D. dissertation, Johns Hopkins University, 1977.

577. Litwak, Eugene. "Towards the Theory and Practice of Coordination between Formal Organizations." In *Organizations and Clients: Essays in the Sociology of Service,* edited by William R. Rosengren and Mark Lefton, pp. 137–86. Columbus, OH: Charles E. Merrill, 1970.

578. Loescher, Samuel M.; Stevens, Robert W.; and Grossack, Irvin M. "Limiting Corporate Power." *Journal of Economic Issues* 13 (June 1979): 557–82.

579. Lowi, Theodore. "American Business, Public Policy, Case Studies and Political Theory." *World Politics* 16 (July 1964): 677–715.

580. Martin, David D. "Our Changing Order." *Journal of Economic Issues* 13 (June 1979): 303–16.

581. McDermott, E. H. "Statutory and Regulatory Schemes for Dealing with Conflicts of Interest." *Illinois Bar Journal* 51 (September 1962): 36–43.

582. McKenzie, Richard B., and Macaulay, H. "A Bureaucratic Theory of Regulation." *Public Choice* 35 (1980): 297–314.

583. McKie, James W. "The Ends and Means of Regulation." In *Competition and Monopoly in the Domestic Telecommunications Industry,* pp. 86–95. Lexington, VA: Washington and Lee University Press, 1974.

584. Mescon, Timothy S., and Vozikis, George S. "Federal Regulation: What Are the Costs?" *Business* 34 (January–February 1982): 33–39.

585. Miller, James C. "Lessons of the Economic Impact Statement Program." *Regulation* 1 (July–August 1977): 14–21.

586. Miller, James C. "Regulators and Experts—A Modest Proposal." *Regulation* 1 (November–December 1977): 36–37.

587. Mund, Vernon A. *Government and Business.* 4th ed. New York: Harper and Row, 1965. 385 p.

588. Nager, Glen D. "Bureaucrats and the Cost-Benefit Chameleon." *Regulation* 6 (September–October 1982): 37–46.

589. Noam, E. "Choice of Governmental Level in Regulation." *Kyklos* 35 (1982): 278–91.

590. Noll, Roger G. "The Social Costs of Government Intervention." In *The Business-Government Relation: A Reassessment,* edited by N. H. Jacoby, pp. 56–64. Pacific Palisades, CA: Goodyear Publishing, 1975.

591. Pegrum, Dudley F. *Public Regulation of Business.* Rev. ed. Homewood, IL: Irwin, 1965. 766 p.

592. Pellerzi, Leo M. "Conceptual View of the Regulatory Process." *California Management Review* 16 (Spring 1974): 83–86.

593. Peltzman, Samuel. "Toward a More General Theory of Regulation." *Journal of Law and Economics* 19 (August 1976): 211–40.

594. Pillai, K. G. J. "Government Regulation in the Private Interest." *Journal of Air Law and Commerce* 40 (Winter 1974): 29–50.

595. Portney, Paul R. "How Not to Create a Job." *Regulation* 6 (November–December 1982): 35–38.

596. Posner, Richard A. "An Economic Theory of Privacy." *Regulation* 2 (May–June 1978): 19–26.

597. Reynolds, Lloyd G. "Foundations of an Institutional Theory of Regulation." *Journal of Economic Issues* 15 (September 1981): 641–56.

598. Rose, Michael D., ed. *Selected Federal Taxation Statutes and Regulations.* St. Paul, MN: West, 1985. 1402 p.

599. Ross, Stephen A. "On the Economic Theory of Agency and the Principle of Similarity." In *Essays of Economic Behavior under Uncertainty,* edited by M. Balch and D. McFadden, pp. 121–46. New York: North-Holland, 1974.

600. Ross, Stephen A. "The Economic Theory of Agency: The Principal's Problem." *American Economic Review* 63 (May 1973): 134–39.

601. Rowland, C. K., and Marz, Roger. "Gresham's Law: The Regulatory Analogy." *Policy Studies Review* 1 (1982): 572–80.

602. Sabatier, Paul A. "Regulatory Policy-Making: Toward a Framework of Analysis." *Natural Resources Journal* 17 (July 1977): 415–57.

603. Scalia, Antonin. "Regulatory Review and Management." *Regulation* 6 (January–February 1982): 19–21.

604. Schoeck, Helmut, and Wiggins, James W., eds. *The New Argument in Economics: The Public Versus the Private Sector; Papers.* Princeton, NJ: Van Nostrand, 1963. 264 p.

605. Schwartz, Bernard. *The Economic Regulation of Business and Industry: A Legislative History of U.S. Regulatory Agencies.* New York: Chelsea House, 1973. 5 vols.

606. Seidman, Harold. "Government-Sponsored Enterprise in the United States." In *The New Political Economy: The Public Use of the Private Sector,* edited by Bruce L. R. Smith, pp. 83–108. New York: Halsted, Wiley, 1975.

607. Shenefield, John H. "Viewpoint: Government Enterprise—A New Frontier for Regulatory Reformers." *Regulation* 3 (November–December 1979): 16–18.

608. Slesinger, Reuben E., and Isaacs, Asher. *Business, Government, and Public Policy.* 2d ed. Princeton, NJ: Van Nostrand, 1968. 459 p.

609. Spengler, Joseph H. "The Role of the State in Shaping Things Economic." *Journal of Economic History* 7 (1947): 123–43.

610. Stigler, George J. "Regulation: The Confusion of Means and Ends." In *Regulating New Drugs,* edited by Richard L. Landau, pp. 9–20. Chicago: University of Chicago Center for Policy Study, 1973.

611. Surrey, Stanley S. "Tax Incentives as a Device for Implementing Government Policy: A Comparison with Direct Government Expenditures." *Harvard Law Review* 83 (February 1970): 705–38.

612. Van Andel, Jay, and Devos, Richard M. "The Government Versus the Entrepreneur." *Policy Review* 10 (Fall 1979): 23–32.

613. Weidenbaum, Murray L. "Case for Economizing on Government Controls." *JEI (Journal of Economic Issues)* 9 (June 1975): 205–21.

614. Weidenbaum, Murray L. "The Effects of Government Contracting on Private Enterprise." *George Washington Law Review* 35 (December 1966): 378–84.

615. Weidenbaum, Murray L. "The High Cost of Government Regulation." *Challenge* 28 (November–December 1979): 32–39.

616. Weidenbaum, Murray L. "Overview of Government Regulations." *Journal of Commercial Bank Lending* 63 (January 1981): 27–36.

617. Wernette, John P. *Government and Business.* New York: Macmillan, 1964. 534 p.

INDUSTRY AND STATE

618. Abel, Albert S. "The Public Corporation in the United States." In *Government Enterprise,* edited by W. Friedmann and J. F. Garner, pp. 181–99. London: Stevens, 1970.

619. Agnelli, Giovanni. "The Strategic Role of the Western Business Community." *Washington Quarterly* 3 (Winter 1980): 126–32.

620. Alperovitz, G., and Faux, J. "Conservative Chic: Reindustrialization." *Social Policy* 11 (November 1980): 6–9.

621. Andrews, B. "Criticizing Economic Democracy." *Monthly Review* 32 (May 1980): 19–25.

622. Aronowitz, S. "Modernizing Capitalism." *Social Policy* 6 (May 1975): 19–27.

623. Averch, Harvey, and Johnson, Lee. "Behavior of the Firm under Regulatory Constraint." *American Economic Review* 52 (December 1962): 1052–69.

624. Baker, Donald I. "Holding Companies after the HUNT." *Antitrust Law Journal* 42 (1973): 707–48.

625. Bartlett, Roland W. *Modern Private Enterprise: Is It Successful?* Danville, IL: Interstate Printers and Publishers, 1973. 175 p.

626. Bauer, Raymond A.; Pool, Ithiel de Sola; and Dexter, Lewis A. *American Business & Public Policy; The Politics of Foreign Trade.* 2d ed. Chicago: Aldine Atherton, 1972. 499 p.

627. Bazelon, David L. "Big Business & The Democrats." *Commentary* 39 (May 1965): 39–46.

628. Bennett, James T., and DiLorenzo, Thomas J. "How the Government Evades Taxes." *Policy Reviews* 19 (Winter 1982): 71–89.

629. Black, L. S. "Shareholder Democracy and Corporate Governance." *Securities Regulation Law Journal* 5 (Winter 1978): 291–317.

630. Bleiberg, R. M. "Capitalism—A Year Later; Odds on Its Survival Have Lengthened." *Barrons* 59 (July 1979): 7–8.

631. Branson, William H. "The Myth of De-Industrialization." *Regulation* 7 (September–October 1983): 24–30.

632. Bruyn, Severyn T. H. *The Social Economy: People Transforming Modern Business.* New York: Wiley, 1977. 392 p.

633. Burdick, G. "Regulatory Recognition of Managerial Efficiency." *Public Utilities Fortnightly* 75 (March 4, 1965): 34–37.

634. Burness, H. S., et al. "Capital Contracting and the Regulated Firm." *American Economic Review* 70 (June 1980): 342–54.

635. "Business Climate Battle Moves to a New Arena." *Industrial Development* 147 (May 1978): 8–11.

636. Calkins, Francis J. "Feasibility in Plans of Corporate Reorganization under Chapter X." *Harvard Law Review* 61 (May 1948): 763–81.

637. Capitaman, William G. *Panic in the Boardrooms; New Social Realities Shake Old Corporate Structures.* Garden City, NY: Anchor Press, 1973. 300 p.

638. Carroll, T. M., and Ciscel, D. H. "Effects of Regulation on Executive Compensation." *Review of Economics and Statistics* 64 (August 1982): 505–09.

639. Cheleden, Algerdas N. "The Governmental Regulation of Business through the Doctrine of Public Interest in American Constitutional Law." Ph.D. dissertation, University of California, Los Angeles, 1947. 263 p.

640. Christiansen, Gregory B., and Haveman, Robert H. "Public Regulations and the Slowdown in Productivity Growth." *American Economic Review* 71 (May 1981): 320–25.

641. Cincotta, G. A. "Old Financial Rules No Longer Apply." *Duns Business Monthly* 119 (June 1982): 92–99.

642. Clarkson, Kenneth W., et al. "Regulating Chrysler Out of Business?" *Regulation* 3 (September–October 1979): 44–51.

643. Claybrook, Joan. "Viewpoint: Crying Wolf." *Regulation* 2 (November–December 1978): 14–16.

644. Coleman, W. T. "Government Regulation of Foreign Business Practices—A Reassessment." *Financial Executive* 48 (September 1980): 36–40.

645. Corson, John J. *Business in the Humane Society.* New York: McGraw-Hill, 1971. 314 p.

646. Cossman, E. Joseph. *How to Get $100,000 Worth of Services Free, Each Year, from the U.S. Government.* New York: F. Fell Publishers, 1975. 282 p.

647. Dean, J. "Effects of the Guidelines on Accounting for Regulatory Agencies." *Journal of Taxation* 18 (May 1963): 274–77.

648. "Discovery of Internal Corporate Investigations." *Stanford Law Review* 32 (July 1980): 1163–81.

649. Dixon, Paul R. "Guidance and Enforcement." *Business Lawyer* 22 (November 1966): 159–65.

650. Dundas, M. J., and George, B. C. "Responsibilities of Domestic Corporate Management under the Foreign Corrupt Practice Act." *Syracuse Law Review* 31 (Fall 1980): 865–905.

651. Epstein, Edwin A. *The Corporation in American Politics.* Englewood Cliffs, NJ: Prentice-Hall, 1969. 365 p.

652. Fedders, J. M. "Policing Internationalized U.S. Capital Markets: Methods to Obtain Evidence Abroad." *The International Lawyer* 18 (Winter 1984): 89–108.

653. Ferrara, R. C.; Starr, R. M; and Steinberg, M. I. "Disclosure of Information Bearing on Management Integrity and Competency." *Northwestern University Law Review* 76 (November 1981): 555–612.

654. Foglesong, R. E. "Business against the Welfare State." *Challenge* 26 (November–December 1983): 38–45.

655. Fox, Harrison W., and Schnitzer, Martin. *Doing Business in Washington, DC: How to Win Friends and Influence Government.* New York: Free Press, 1981. 240 p.

656. Freudenberger, Herman. "Fashion, Sumptuary Laws, and Business." *Business History Review* 37 (Spring–Summer 1963): 37–48.

657. Fried, Charles. "Viewpoint: Fast and Loose in the Welfare State." *Regulation* 3 (May–June 1979): 13–16.

658. Gay, Thomas E. "Creating the Virginia State Corporation Commission." *Virginia Magazine of History and Biography* 78 (October 1970): 464–80.

659. Gilbert, James B. *Designing the Industrial State: The Intellectual Pursuit of Collectivism in America, 1880–1940.* Chicago: Quadrangle Books, 1972. 335 p.

660. Graham, R. "Small Business: Beset, Bothered, and Beleaguered by Five Big Problems." *Nation's Business* 58 (February 1980): 22–31.

661. Greenough, W. C. "Keeping Corporate Governance in the Private Sector." *Business Horizons* 23 (February 1980): 71–74.

662. Hall, Ford P. *Government and Business.* 3d ed. New York: McGraw-Hill, 1949. 594 p.

663. Hancock, William A. *Executive's Guide to Business Law.* New York: McGraw-Hill, 1979. 1000 p.

664. Harron, Thomas J. *Law for Business Managers; The Regulatory Environment.* Boston: Holbrook Press, 1977. 428 p.

665. Hay, Robert D. *Introduction to Business.* New York: Holt, Rinehart and Winston, 1968. 528 p.

666. Hirschey, M., and Pappas, J. L. "Regulatory and Life Cycle Influences on Managerial Incentives." *Southern Economic Journal* 48 (October 1981): 327–34.

667. Holton, Richard. "Business and Government." *Daedalus* 98 (Winter 1969): 41–59.

668. Horowitz, David, ed. *Corporations and the Cold War.* New York: Monthly Review Press, 1969. 249 p.

669. Howard, Marshall C. *Legal Aspects of Marketing.* New York: McGraw-Hill, 1964. 173 p.

670. "Innovation, Technological Progress, and Research and Development." *American Economic Review* 70 (May 1980): 50–61.

671. Jacobe, Dennis. "The Business' Future Role Hangs on Structural Decisions." *Savings and Loan News* 104 (June 1983): 37–41.

672. Javits, Benjamin A. *Ownerism: A Better World for All through Democratic Ownership.* New York: Crown, 1969. 192 p.

673. Jennings, Marianne M., and Shipper, Frank. "Strategic Planning for Managerial-Political Interaction." *Business Horizons* 24 (July-August 1981): 44–51.

674. Johnson, Arthur T. "Public Sports Policy." *American Behavioral Scientist* 21 (January-February 1978): 319–44.

675. "Just Leave Us Alone: That's What Business Leaders Tell Washington." *Nation's Business* 68 (June 1980): 34–36.

676. Kanaga, W. S. "Corporate Governance—The New Battle Cry." *Financial Executive* 47 (September 1979): 12–19.

677. Kuhn, James W., and Berg, Ivar. *Values in a Business Society; Issues and Analyses.* New York: Harcourt, Brace and World, 1967. 309 p.

678. Laube, Richard Henry. "The Relationship between Some Characteristics of Corporate Boards and Operational Results." Ph.D. dissertation, University of Nebraska, 1966. 242 p.

679. Levin, Harvey J., ed. *Business Organization and Public Policy; A Book of Readings.* New York: Rinehart, 1958. 550 p.

680. Lincoln,' S. J. "Is There—And Should There Be—A Future for Industrial Revenue Bonds?" *Journal of Housing* 38 (November 1981): 535–39.

681. Linowitz, Sol M.; Malik, Charles H.; and Parker, Daniel. *International Business-Government Relations.* Washington, DC: American University, Center for the Study of Private Enterprise, 1970. 123 p.

682. Litke, A. L. "Tomorrow's Regulatory Accountants—Micros or Macros?" *Public Utilities Fortnightly* 81 (February 1968): 13–19.

683. Louden, J. Keith. *The Effective Director.* New York: AMACOM, 1975. 190 p.

684. Magill, R. F. "Prescription for Survival in a Regulated World." *Business Horizons* 23 (February 1980): 75–81.

685. Marcus, Alfred A. "Policy Uncertainty and Technological Innovation." *Academy of Management Review* 6 (July 1981): 443–48.

686. Marley, M. "Is Innovation Becoming a Thing of the Past?" *Iron Age* 222 (October 1979): 65–68.

687. Marsh, Sandra W., ed. *Current Business Views of Government Regulations.* Muncie, IN: Bureau of Business Research, College of Business, Ball State University, 1979. 61 p.

688. Martin, Albro. "Uneasy Partners: Government-Business Relations in Twentieth-Century American History." *Prologue* 11 (Summer 1979): 91–105.

689. Martin, David D. "Uses and Abuses of Economic Theory in the Social Control of Business." *Journal of Economic Issues* 8 (June 1974): 271–85, 301–07.

690. Mautz, Robert K., et al. *Internal Control in U.S. Corporations: The State of the Art: A Research Study and Report.* New York: The Foundation, 1980. 454 p.

691. May, Bruce E. "The Impact of Federal Social Regulation on the Research and Development Activities of the Industrial Innovative Process." D.B.A. dissertation, United States International University, 1981. 187 p.

692. McCaffrey, David P. "Corporate Resources and Regulatory Pressures: Toward Explaining a Discrepancy." *Administrative Science Quarterly* 27 (September 1982): 398–419.

693. McCraw, Thomas K. "Regulation in America: A Review Article." *Business History Review* 49 (Summer 1975): 159–83.

694. McCurdy, C. W. "American Law and the Marketing Structure of the Large Corporation, 1875–1890." *Journal of Economic History* 38 (September 1978): 631–49.

695. McKenzie, Richard B. "The Case for Plant Closures." *Policy Review* 15 (Winter 1981): 119–33.

696. McManus, G. J. "Regulatory Over-Kill Frustrates Industry." *Iron Age* 216 (December 1975): 18–22.

697. McQuaid, K. "Big Business and Public Policy in Contemporary United States." *Quarterly Review of Economics and Business* 20 (Summer 1980): 57–68.

698. Mechem, C. "Business and Government: Now Is the Time." *Public Management* 61 (January 1979): 4–6.

699. Metzger, H. P. "Coercive Utopians: Their Hidden Agenda." *Industrial Development* 148 (July 1979): 2–7.

700. Miller, Richard. *Plant Location Factors, United States, 1966.* Park Ridge, NJ: Noyes Development Corporation, 1966. 116 p.

701. Momboisse, R. M. "How to Survive in the Regulatory Jungle." *Management Review* 66 (September 1977): 43–47.

702. Montgomery, John D., and Katzman, Martin T. "Cui Bono? Measuring Income-Redistribution Effects of Capital Projects." *Administration and Society* 10 (August 1978): 235–55.

703. Mueller, Milton. "Spectrum Fees vs. Spectrum Liberation." *Regulation* 7 (May–June 1983): 21–25.

704. Nash, Gerald D. "Government and Business: A Case Study of State Regulation of Corporate Securities, 1850–1933." *Business History Review* 38 (Summer 1964): 144–62.

705. Orlebeke, J. "Administering Enterprise Zones: Some Initial Observations." *Urban Affairs Quarterly* 18 (September 1982): 31–38.

706. Paulszek, John L. *Will the Corporation Survive?* Reston, VA: Reston Publishing, 1977. 255 p.

707. Pertschuk, Michael. "Fable of Regulation: Dilemmas of the King." *Business and Society Review* 30 (Summer 1979): 52–54.

708. Phillips, Joseph. "The Relevance of Small Business Policy." *Centennial Review* 7 (Winter 1963): 95–112.

709. Popham, J. J. "1971 Consensus Agreement: The Perils of Unkept Promises." *Catholic University Law Review* 24 (Summer 1975): 813–32.

710. Powell, W. J. "Case for the Regulatory Accountant." *Public Utilities Fortnightly* 75 (January 7, 1965): 36–47.

711. "Pragmatism on Parade." *Fortune* 109 (February 20, 1984): 37–38.

712. Quinn, J. J., and Sommer, A. A. "Financial Reporting for Segments of a Business Enterprise." *Institute on Securities Regulation* 10 (1979): 1–37.

713. Quirk, Paul J. *Industry Influence in Federal Regulatory Agencies.* Princeton, NJ: Princeton University Press, 1981. 260 p.

714. Rabel, William H. "The Regulation of Separate Accounts." Ph.D. dissertation, University of Pennsylvania, 1974. 416 p.

715. Raffaele, Joseph A. *System and Unsystem; An Ethnic View of Organization and Society.* New York: Halsted Press, 1974. 458 p.

716. Rainey, Hal G. "Comparing Public and Private: Conceptual and Empirical Analysis of Incentives and Motivation among Government and Business Managers." Ph.D. dissertation, Ohio State University, 1977. 384 p.

717. Rainey, Hal G.; Backoff, Robert W.; and Levine, Charles H. "Comparing Public and Private Organizations." *Public Administration Review* 36 (March–April 1976): 233–44.

718. Reich, Robert B. "Making Industrial Policy." *Foreign Affairs* 60 (Spring 1982): 852–81.

719. Robinson, Richard D. "Interrelationship of Business Enterprise and Political Development." *Business History Review* 36 (Autumn 1962): 287–324.

720. Rosengren, William R. "The Careers of Clients and Organizations." In *Organizations and Clients: Essays in the Sociology of Service,* edited by William R. Rosengren and Mark Lefton, pp. 117–35. Columbus, OH: Charles E. Merrill, 1970.

721. Rothwell, Roy. "The Impact of Regulation on Innovation: Some U.S. Data." *Technological Forecasting and Social Change* 17 (May 1980): 7–34.

722. Roy, W. G. "Vesting of Interests and the Determinants of Political Power: Size, Network Structure, and Mobilization of American Industries, 1886–1905." *American Journal of Sociology* 86 (May 1981): 1287–310.

723. Ruder, William, and Nathan, Raymond. *The Businessman's Guide to Washington.* New York: Collier, 1975. 408 p.

724. Samuelson, A. T. "Accounting vs. Federal Regulation: Is There an Emerging Discipline?" *Management Accounting* 47 (October 1965): 14–21.

725. Scherer, Frederick M. "Sunlight and Antitrust: Discovering Each Industry's Inner Economic Logic." *Antitrust Law & Economics Review* 9 (1977): 41–53.

726. Schuyler, William E. "Small Business and the Proposed Patent Reform Act of 1967." *George Washington Law Review* 36 (October 1967): 122–35.

727. Seavoy, Ronald E. "The Public Service Origins of the American Business Corporation." *Business History Review* 52 (Spring 1978): 30–60.

728. Sethi, S. Prakash, ed. *The Unstable Ground: Corporate Social Policy in a Dynamic Society.* Los Angeles: Melville Publishing, 1976. 557 p.

729. Shaw, Gaylord. *How to Get Your Share of Government Treasure: A Guide to Valuable Benefits and Services.* New York: Simon and Schuster, 1975. 256 p.

730. Silberman, Laurence H. "Will Lawyering Strangle Democratic Capitalism." *Regulation* 2 (March–April 1978): 15–22.

731. Smith, Sammie L. "An Investigation of the Evolution of Last-In-First-Out Inventory Costing into a Generally Accepted Accounting Principle with Emphasis on the Influence of Federal Income Tax Regulations." Ph.D. dissertation, University of Arkansas, 1972. 254 p.

732. Sobel, Lester A., ed. *Corruption in Business.* New York: Facts on File, 1977. 230 p.

733. Sommers, Albert T., ed. *The Free Society and Planning: A Conversation on the Future of the Mixed Economy.* New York: Conference Board, 1975. 36 p.

734. Steiner, George A., and Steiner, John F., comps. *Issues in Business and Society.* 2d ed. New York: Random House, 1977. 560 p.

735. Stickells, Austin T. *Legal Control of Business Practice.* Mount Kisco, NY: Baker, Voorhis, 1965. 843 p.

736. Stockfisch, Jacob A., ed. *Planning and Forecasting in the Defense Industries.* Belmont, CA: Wadsworth, 1962. 292 p.

737. Symonds, E. "Economy Throttled by Red Tape." *Accountant* 181 (July 1979): 8–10.

738. Tarnowieski, Dale, ed. *Not of One Mind.* New York: AMACOM, 1976. 128 p.

739. Tassey, Gregory. "The Effectiveness of Venture Capital Markets in the US Economy." *Public Policy* 25 (Fall 1977): 479–97.

740. Trimm, John H. "A Socio-Structural Analysis of Selected Federal Regulatory Agencies Affecting Business Management." Ph.D. dissertation, Michigan State University, 1967. 240 p.

741. "United States: Nothing to Lose but Our Chains." *Economist* 269 (December 1978): 44–46.

742. Van Winden, F. "Interaction between State and Firms." *Oxford Economic Papers* 32 (November 1980): 428–52.

743. Vogel, David. "The Inadequacy of Contemporary Opposition to Business." *Daedalus* 109 (Summer 1980): 47–58.

744. Wakulla Conference, Wakulla, Fla., 1977. *A Seminar on Business Regulation: A Florida Perspective.* Lexington, KY: Council of State Governments, 1977. 42 p.

745. Walsh, Annmarie H. *The Public's Business: The Politics and Practices of Government Corporations.* Cambridge, MA: MIT Press, 1978. 436 p.

746. Webber, W. L., ed. "Regulation and Innovation." *Law and Contemporary Problems* 43 (Winter 1979): 1–149.

747. Weidenbaum, Murray L. *The Future of Business Regulation: Private Action and Public Demand.* New York: AMACOM, 1979. 183 p.

748. Weidenbaum, Murray L. "Way to Regulate the Regulatory Binge." *Business and Society Review* 20 (Winter 1976–77): 4–5.

749. Weidenbaum, Murray L. "Weidenbaum Analyzes Benefit-Cost Analysis." *Across the Board* 19 (February 1982): 66–70.

750. Weidenbaum, Murray L., and Munger, Michael C. "Viewpoint: Protection at Any Price?" *Regulation* 7 (July–August 1983): 14–18.

751. Weiss, E. J., and Schwartz, D. E. "Using Disclosure to Activate the Board of Directors." *Law and Contemporary Problems* 41 (Summer 1977): 63–114.

752. Wendel, Jeanne. "Firm-Regulator Interaction with Respect to Firm Cost Reduction Activities." *Bell Journal of Economics* 7 (Autumn 1976): 631–52.

753. Wiebe, Robert H. "Businessmen and Reform: A Study of the Progressive Movement." *Explorations in Economic History* 1 (Winter 1964): 276–78.

754. Wintner, Linda. *Business and the Cities: Programs and Practices.* New York: Conference Board, 1981. 17 p.

755. Wright, David M. *The Business Cycle and Political Freedom.* Bloomington, IN: Graduate School of Business, Indiana University, 1962. 11 p.

756. Yandle, Bruce. "Viewpoint: Bootleggers and Baptists—The Education of a Regulatory Economist." *Regulation* 7 (May–June 1983): 12–16.

757. Zimmerman, Rae T. "Formation of New Organizations to Manage Risk." *Policy Studies Review* 1 (May 1982): 736–47.

MARKET REGULATION

758. Adams, Walter. *Antitrust Issues, Are We Investing in the Future of Competition?* New York: Conference Board, 1981. 21 p.

759. "Aftermath of WHDH: Regulation by Competition or Protection of Mediocrity?" *University of Pennsylvania Law Review* 118 (January 1970): 368–409.

760. "Applicability of NEPA to Antitrust Law Enforcement Proceedings." *Connecticut Law Review* 10 (Fall 1977): 177–91.

761. Austern, H. Thomas. "Presumption and Percipience about Competitive Effect under Section 2 of the Clayton Act." *Harvard Law Review* 81 (February 1968): 773–819.

762. Bailey, E. E. "Contestability and the Design of Regulatory and Antitrust Policy." *American Economic Review; Papers and Proceedings* 71 (May 1981): 178–83.

763. Bailey, Martin J. "Government Operations and Inflation." *Proceedings of the Academy of Political Science* 33 (1979): 57–67.

764. Barber, William. "'Among the Most Techy Articles of Civil Police': Federal Taxation and the Adoption of the Whiskey Excise." *William and Mary Quarterly* 25 (January 1968): 58–84.

765. Bauer, Peter Tamas, comp. *Markets, Market Control and Marketing Reform; Selected Papers.* London: Weidenfeld and Nicolson, 1969. 421 p.

766. Benedict, M. K. "Attempts to Restrict Competition in Agriculture: The Government Programs." *American Economic Review* 44 (May 1954): 93–106.

767. Bergson, Herbert A. "Regulation v. Competition." *Insurance Law Journal* 406 (November 1956): 703–08.

768. Blecher, Maxwell M. "Attempt to Monopolize under Section 2 of the Sherman Act: 'Dangerous Probability' of Monopolization within the 'Relevant Market.'" *George Washington Law Review* 38 (December 1969): 215–22.

769. Bosworth, Barry P. "Cumulative Impacts of Regulation." *American Journal of Agricultural Economics* 61 (November 1979): 791–97.

770. Boulton, W. R. "Government Control: Business Strikes Back." *Business Horizons* 22 (August 1979): 61–66.

771. Bower, R. S. "Rising Capital Cost Versus Regulatory Restraint." *Public Utilities Fortnightly* 75 (March 4, 1965): 31–33.

772. Breit, William, and Elzinga, Kenneth C. "Antitrust Penalties and Attitudes toward Risk: An Economic Analysis." *Harvard Law Review* 86 (February 1973): 693–713.

773. Brennan, M. J., and Schwartz, E. S. "Consistent Regulatory Policy under Uncertainty." *Bell Journal of Economics* 13 (August 1982): 506–21.

774. Breslaw, J., and Smith, J. B. "Restrictiveness of Flexible Functional Forms and the Measurement of Regulatory Constraint." *Land Economics* 58 (November 1982): 553–58.

775. Brown, Kenneth M. "The Elusive Carrot: Tax Incentives for R and D." *Regulation* 8 (January–February 1984): 33–38.

776. Buland, George, and Fuhrman, Frederick. "Integrated Ownership: The Case for Removing Existing Restrictions on Common Ownership of the Several Forms of Transportation." *George Washington Law Review* 31 (October 1962): 156–85.

777. Burns, Malcolm R. "The Competitive Effects of Trust-Busting: A Portfolio Analysis." *Journal of Political Economy* 85 (August 1977): 717–40.

778. Cagan, Phillip. "Inflationary Effects of Government Interference in Markets." *Proceedings of the Academy of Political Science* 33 (1979): 26–41.

779. Campana, J. "Economics of Regulation: A Critique." *American Journal of Agricultural Economics* 61 (November 1979): 741–45.

780. Cargill, Thomas F., and Garcia, Gillian G. "The Impact of Deregulation on the Financial System." *Issues in Bank Regulation* 4 (Winter 1981): 1–11.

781. Coase, Ronald H. "George J. Stigler: An Appreciation." *Regulation* 6 (November–December 1982): 21–24.

782. "Controls on International Capital Movements: The Experience with Controls on International Financial Credits, Loans and Deposits." *Financial Market Trends* (November 1982): 1–13.

783. Crawford, Peter H. "Business Proposals for Government Regulation of Monopoly, 1887–1914." Ph.D. dissertation, Columbia University, 1963. 646 p.

784. Das, S. P. "On the Effect of Rate of Return Regulation under Uncertainty." *American Economic Review* 70 (June 1980): 456–60.

785. Dhiman, Om P. "An Inter-temporal Model of Firm Behavior under Uncertainty and Regulation." Ph.D. dissertation, University of New York, 1978. 212 p.

786. Doerfer, Gordon L. "The Limits on Trade Secret Law Imposed by Federal Patent and Antitrust Supremacy." *Harvard Law Review* 80 (May 1967): 1432–67.

787. Dominguez, George S. *Marketing in a Regulated Environment.* New York: Wiley, 1978. 341 p.

788. Dowd, Mary J. "The State in the Maryland Economy, 1776–1807." *Maryland Historical Magazine* 57 (June 1962): 90–92.

789. Dowd, Mary J. "The State in the Maryland Economy." *Maryland Historical Magazine* 57 (September 1962): 229–58.

790. Ekelund, R. B., and Higgins, R. S. "Capital Fixity, Innovations, and Long-Term Contracting: An Intertemporal Economic Theory of Regulation." *American Economic Review* 72 (March 1982): 32–46.

791. Elman, Philip. "Antitrust Enforcement: Retrospect and Prospect." *American Bar Association Journal* 53 (July 1967): 609–12.

792. Elzinga, Kenneth G. "The Antimerger Law: Pyrrhic Victories?" *Journal of Law and Economics* 12 (April 1969): 43–78.

793. Elzinga, Kenneth G. "Oligopoly: The Sherman Act and the New Industrial State." *Social Science Quarterly* 49 (June 1968): 49–57.

794. "Enforcing the Obligation to Present Controversial Issues: The Forgotten Half of the Fairness Doctrine." *Harvard Civil Rights Law Review* 10 (Winter 1975): 137–79.

795. Faith, R. L.; Leavens, D. R.; and Tollison, Robert D. "Antitrust Pork Barrel." *Journal of Law & Economics* 25 (October 1982): 329–42.

796. Fegenbaum, Susan K. "A Theory of Nonprofit Regulation and Firm Behavior." Ph.D. dissertation, University of Wisconsin at Madison, 1980. 298 p.

797. Feige, E. L., and Pearce, D. "Economically Rational Expectations: Are Innovations in the Rate of Inflation Independent of Innovations in Measures of Monetary and Fiscal Policy." *Journal of Political Economy* 84 (June 1976): 499–522.

798. Felton, John R. "Conglomerate Mergers, Concentration and Competition." *American Journal of Economics and Sociology* 30 (July 1971): 225–42.

799. Fiedler, Edgar R. "Inflation and Economic Policy." *Proceedings of the Academy of Political Science* 33 (1979): 113–31.

800. Financial Accounting Standards Board. *An Analysis of Issues Related to Effect of Rate Regulation on Accounting for Regulated Enterprises.* Stamford, CT: The Board, 1979. 137 p.

801. Fishbein, Richard. "Conglomerate Mergers and Economic Concentration." *Yale Review* 62 (Summer 1973): 507–19.

802. Froelich, Robert J. "The Benefits and Costs of Regulations—Perspectives from Both Government and Business." *American Review of Public Administration* 15 (Fall 1981): 259–65.

803. Gellhorn, Ernest. "Antitrust and Trade Regulation." *Regulation* 6 (January–February 1982): 22–23.

804. Gibbons, Gerald R. "Domestic Territorial Restrictions in Patent Transactions and the Antitrust Laws." *George Washington Law Review* 34 (June 1966): 893–926.

805. Goldberg, Victor P. "Institutional Change and the Quasi-Invisible Hand." *Journal of Law and Economics* 17 (October 1974): 461–96.

806. Goldberg, Victor P. "Regulation and Administered Contracts." *Bell Journal of Economics* 7 (Autumn 1976): 426–48.

807. Goldberg, Victor P. "Relational Exchange: Economics and Complex Contracts." *American Behavioral Scientist* 23 (January–February 1980): 337–52.

808. Gordon, R. J. "What Can Stabilization Policy Achieve?" *American Economic Review; Papers and Proceedings* 68 (May 1978): 335–41.

809. Green, Mark J., and Nader, Ralph. "Economic Regulation vs. Competition: Uncle Sam the Monopoly Man." *Yale Law Journal* 82 (April 1973): 871–89.

810. Gressley, Gene M. "Thurman Arnold, Antitrust, and the New Deal." *Business History Review* 38 (Summer 1964): 214–31.

811. Griffiths, David B. "Anti-Monopoly Movements in California, 1873–1898." *Southern California Quarterly* 52 (Summer 1970): 93–121.

812. Hale, G. E., and Hale, Rosemary D. "The Otter Tail Power Case: Regulation by Commission or Antitrust Laws." *Supreme Court Review* (1973): 99–122.

813. Hammond, A. S. "Now You See It, Now You Don't: Minority Ownership in an 'Unregulated' Marketplace." *Catholic University Law Review* 32 (Spring 1983): 633–63.

814. Handel, Sidney S. "Investment Behavior in the Regulated Industries." Ph.D. dissertation, University of California, Berkeley, 1965. 152 p.

815. Hemel, Eric I. "Rate Base Accounting and Allocative Efficiency for a Regulated Firm." Ph.D. dissertation, Stanford University, 1980. 96 p.

816. Henderson, D. W., and Sargent, T. "Monetary and Fiscal Policy in a Two-Sector Aggregative Model." *American Economic Review* 63 (June 1973): 345–65.

817. Hendon, William S., and Noakes, Wayne C. "Large Firms and Small Firms: Enforcement of the Clayton Act." *Antitrust Bulletin* 11 (September–December 1966): 949–62.

818. Herendeen, J. B. "Financial Model of the Regulated Firm and Implications of the Model for Determination of the Fair Rate of Return." *Southern Economic Journal* 42 (October 1975): 279–84.

819. Hofstadter, Richard. "Antitrust in America." *Commentary* 38 (August 1964): 47–53.

820. Holthausen, Duncan M. "The Firm under Regulation: An Analysis of Uncertainty, Incentives and Regulatory Lag." Ph.D. dissertation, Northwestern University, 1974. 321 p.

821. Howard, R. Hayden, ed. *Risk and Regulated Firms.* East Lansing, MI: Division of Research, Graduate School of Business Administration, Michigan State University, 1973. 5104 p.

822. Huber, Peter. "The Market for Risk." *Regulation* 8 (March–April 1984): 33–40.

823. Ismail, Hamzah B. "An Examination of the Application of Alternative Accounting Measurement Attributes to Rate Base Regulation—A Simulation Approach to Attribution." D.B.A. dissertation, Indiana University, 1978. 243 p.

824. Jacobs, Donald P., and Phillips, Almarin W. "The Commission on Financial Structure and Regulation: Its Organization and Recommendations." *Journal of Finance* 27 (May 1972): 319–28.

825. Johnson, Robert. "Government Regulation of Business Enterprise in Virginia, 1750–1820." Ph.D. dissertation, University of Minnesota, 1958. 441 p.

826. Jones, B. J. "The Brown Shoe Case and the New Antimerger Policy: Comment." *American Economic Review* 54 (June 1964): 407–12.

827. Jones, Frederick W. "Input Biases under Rate of Return Regulation: A Test of an Intertemporal Averch-Johnson Model." Ph.D. dissertation, University of Virginia, 1978. 166 p.

828. Jones, J. R. "Inflation and Regulation." *Public Utilities Fortnightly* 100 (August 1977): 17–20.

829. Jordan, William A. "Producer Protection, Prior Market Structure, and the Effects of Government Regulation." *Journal of Law and Economics* 15 (April 1972): 151–76.

830. Kahn, Alfred E. "Applications of Economics to an Imperfect World." *American Economic Review* 69 (May 1979): 1–13.

831. Kahn, Alfred E. "Applying Economics to an Imperfect World." *Regulation* 2 (November–December 1978): 17–27.

832. Kauper, Thomas E. "Antitrust—A Form of Regulation." *Regulation* 2 (September–October 1978): 54–57.

833. Kelman, Steven. "Competition among the States: The Ethics of Regulatory Competition." *Regulation* 6 (May–June 1982): 39–43.

834. Kelman, Steven. "Cost-Benefit Analysis—An Ethical Critique." *Regulation* 5 (January–February 1981): 33–40.

835. Kennedy, Joseph B. "Patent and Antitrust Policy: The Search for a Unitary Theory." *George Washington Law Review* 35 (March 1967): 512–61.

836. Khanna, S. K. "Economic Regulation and Technological Change: A Review of the Literature." *Public Utilities Fortnightly* 109 (January 1982): 35–44.

837. Kimball, James N. "The Economic Effect of Water Effluent Regulation and Enforcement upon Firm Behavior." Ph.D. dissertation, Virginia Polytechnic Institute and State University, 1979. 156 p.

838. Kintner, Earl W.; Romano, Salvatore A.; and Flipini, John C. "Cooperative Buying and Antitrust Policy: The Search for Competitive Equality." *George Washington Law Review* 41 (July 1973): 971–1005.

839. Kirzner, Israel M. *The Perils of Regulation: A Market-Process Approach.* Coral Gables, FL: Law and Economics Center, Miami School of Law, 1978. 25 p.

840. Klebaner, Benjamin J. "Potential Competition and the American Antitrust Legislation of 1914." *Business History Review* 38 (Summer 1964): 163–85.

841. Kleiner, Morris M.; Gay, Robert S.; and Greene, Karen. "Licensing, Migration, and Earnings: Some Empirical Insights." *Policy Studies Review* 1 (1982): 510–22.

842. Koehl, Dorothy S. "A Model of a Regulated Firm in a Capital Asset Pricing Model World." Ph.D. dissertation, Ohio State University, 1978. 103 p.

843. Koehn, Michael F. "Regulation and Risk in Financial Depository Intermediaries: A Comparative Analysis." Ph.D. dissertation, University of Pennsylvania, 1979. 255 p.

844. Kottke, Frank J. "Six Misconceptions of Pro-Competition Policy." *Journal of Economic Issues* 13 (June 1979): 543–55.

845. Kreps, Donald E. "A Study of the Impacts of Actions of Selected Parties upon Regulatory Program Effectiveness." D.B.A. dissertation, George Washington University, 1981. 279 p.

846. Krupnick, Alan; Magat, Wesley; and Harrington, Winston. "Understanding Regulatory Decision-Making: An Econometric Approach." *Policy Studies Journal* 11 (September 1982): 44–54.

847. Kuhlman, John M. "Incremental Decision-Making and Antitrust Policy." *Social Science Quarterly* 45 (December 1964): 239–48.

848. Liedquist, R. E. "Recent Developments in Regional Enforcement of the Antitrust Laws." *Antitrust Law Symposium* 1975 (1975): 38–48.

849. Lindblom, Charles E. "The Market as Prison." *Journal of Politics* 44 (May 1982): 324–36.

850. Litzenverger, R. H., and Sosin, H. B. "Comparison of Capital Structure Decisions of Regulated and Non-Regulated Firms." *Financial Management* 8 (Autumn 1979): 17–21.

851. Loevinger, Lee. "Regulation and Competition as Alternatives." *Antitrust Bulletin* 11 (January–April 1968): 101–40.

852. Loury, G. C. "Market Structure and Innovation." *Quarterly Journal of Economics* 93 (August 1979): 395–410.

853. Lovett, William A. "Teamwork, Markets, and Regulations: Distortions Arising from Legal Parochialism." *Journal of Economic Issues* 15 (June 1981): 409–22.

854. Machado, Ezequiel L. "Financial Planning in a Regulated Environment." Ph.D. dissertation, University of North Carolina, 1977. 191 p.

855. Madden, Carl H. "Government Controls Versus Market Discipline." *Proceedings of the Academy of Political Science* 33 (1979): 203–18.

856. Maule, C. J. "Antitrust and the Takeover Activity of American Firms in Canada." *Journal of Law and Economics* 11 (October 1968): 423–32.

857. McKie, James W. "Regulation and the Free Market: The Problem of Boundaries." *Bell Journal of Economics and Management Science* 1 (Spring 1970): 6–26.

858. McLeod, Philip W. "Regulation and the Capital Expansion Policy of a Monopoly." Ph.D. dissertation, Stanford University, 1980. 143 p.

859. Menzel, Donald C., and West, William. "Economic Regulatory Policy." *Policy Studies Journal* 9 (Summer 1981): 1085–86.

860. Moore, Thomas G. "The Purpose of Licensing." *Journal of Law and Economics* 4 (October 1961): 93–117.

861. Morgenfeld, I. R. "Antitrust and the Oligopoly Problem: 'Intellectual Pygmies' at the Enforcement Agencies?" *Antitrust Law and Economics Review* 9 (1977): 15–30.

862. Mueller, Charles, E. "Trustbusting and the Future of Capitalism: 'Small Could Be Beautiful.'" *Antitrust Law and Economics* Review 8 (1976): 47–80.

863. Musacchio, Robert A. "Optimal Capital Policies of a Regulated Firm." Ph.D. dissertation, University of Wisconsin—Milwaukee, 1980. 242 p.

864. Naim, Moise. "The Political Economy of Regulating Multinational Corporations." Ph.D. dissertation, Massachusetts Institute of Technology, 1979. 348 p.

865. Nathan, Jambu. "Concentration, Regulation, Sales, and Profitability: Their Influence on Top Level Executive Compensation for Large Corporations." Ph.D. dissertation, University of Cincinnati, 1980. 194 p.

866. Nicholson, James M. "A Revitalized Commission." *Antitrust Law Symposium* 437 (October 27, 1969): 29–37.

867. Niro, Raymond P., and Wigert, J. William. "Patents, Fraud and the Antitrust Laws." *George Washington Law Review* 37 (October 1968): 168–83.

868. Niss, James F., and Pledge, Michael T., eds. *Competition in Regulated Industries: Essays on Economic Issues.* Macomb, IL: Center for Business and Economic Research, Western Illinois University, 1975. 128 p.

869. Noll, Roger G. "The Economics and Politics of Regulation." *Virginia Law Review* 57 (1971): 1016–32.

870. Ordover, J., and Weiss, A., "Information and the Law: Evaluating Legal Restrictions on Competitive Contracts." *American Economic Review* 71 (May 1981): 399–404.

871. Orr, Lloyd. "Incentive for Innovation as the Basis for Effluent Charge Strategy." *American Economic Review* 66 (May 1976): 441–47.

872. Parr, Arnold F. "Theory of the Capital Decision in the Regulated Firm." Ph.D. dissertation, University of Oklahoma, 1968. 262 p.

873. Piott, Steven L. "From Dissolution to Regulation: The Popular Movement against Trusts and Monopoly in the Midwest, 1887–1913." Ph.D. dissertation, University of Missouri, 1978. 271 p.

874. "Political Surfing When Issues Break." *Harvard Business Review* 63 (January–February 1985): 72–81.

875. Posner, Richard A. "Statistical Study of Antitrust Enforcement." *Journal of Law and Economics* 13 (October 1970): 365–415.

876. Posner, Richard A. "Natural Monopoly and Its Regulation." *Stanford Law Review* 21 (February 1969): 548–643.

877. Posner, Richard A. "Taxation by Regulation." *Bell Journal of Economics and Management Science* 2 (Spring 1971): 22–50.

878. Posner, Richard A. "Theories of Economic Regulation." *Bell Journal of Economics and Management Science* 5 (Autumn 1974): 335–58.

879. Pulikonda, Nagabhushanam. "The Impact of Vertical Integration of Firms Subject to Regulatory Constraints." Ph.D. dissertation, University of Illinois at Urbana-Champaign, 1979. 174 p.

880. Quiggin, John. "A Theory of Anticipated Utility." *Journal of Economic Behavior and Organization* 3 (December 1982): 323–44.

881. Ratkowski, Alex J. "The Ingot Molds Decision: The Effects of Minimum Rate Regulation of Intermodal Competition." Ph.D. dissertation, University of Nebraska, 1975. 217 p.

882. Regnery, A. S. "Antitrust Reform: The Congressional Prognosis." *Trial* 15 (April 1979): 26–29.

883. Reinken, Paul E. "Let Us Now Praise Natural Monopoly." *Alternative* 8 (December 1974): 13–14.

884. Reuber, Grant L. "Antitrust and the Takeover Activity of American Firms in Canada: A Further Analysis." *Journal of Law and Economics* 12 (October 1969): 405–17.

885. Reuber, Grant L. "Antitrust and the Takeover Activity of American Firms in Canada: A Reply." *Journal of Law and Economics* 13 (April 1970): 257–59.

886. Reynolds, Robert J. "The Regulatory Process: An Analysis of Its Impact on Firm Behavior." Ph.D. dissertation, Northwestern University, 1970. 109 p.

887. Roberts, R. Blaine; Maddala, G. S.; and Enholm, Gregory. "Determinants of the Requested Rate of Return and Rate of Return Granted in a Formal Regulatory Process." *Bell Journal of Economics* 9 (Autumn 1978): 611–21.

888. Scheiber, Harry N. "Regulation, Property Rights, and Definition of the Market: Law and the American Economy." *Journal of Economic History* 41 (March 1981): 103–11.

889. Schelling, Thomas C. "Command and Control." In *Social Responsibility and the Business Predicament,* edited by James W. McKie, pp. 79–108. Washington, DC: Brookings Institution, 1974.

890. Schwert, George W. "Using Financial Data to Measure Effects of Regulation." *Journal of Law and Economics* 24 (April 1981): 121–58.

891. Scott, Austin W. "Spendthrift Trusts and the Conflict of Laws." *Harvard Law Review* 77 (March 1964): 845–72.

892. *Selected Structure and Allocation Problems in the Regulated Industries.* East Lansing, MI: Institute of Public Utilities, Michigan State University, 1969. 70 p.

893. Shaffer, Sherrill L. "Regulation, Risk and Information." Ph.D. dissertation, Stanford University, 1981. 132 p.

894. *Shifting Boundaries between Regulation and Competition: Criteria for an Enterprise System and the Experience Curve Model.* New York: Conference Board, 1980. 29 p.

895. Shrug, E. P. "On the Road with the Antitrusts' 'Phoenix': '84 Is Coming!" *Antitrust Law and Economics Review* 13 (1981): 101–17.

896. Sims, Joe. "Antitrust Comes to City Hall." *Regulation* 3 (July–August 1979): 35–43.

897. Sims, Joe, and Blumenthal, William. "The New Era in Antitrust." *Regulation* 6 (July–August 1982): 25–28.

898. Smartt, L. E. "Thinking about the Relative Merits of Regulation and Competition." *Public Utilities Fortnightly* 112 (December 8, 1983): 5–7.

899. Smith, F. Leslie. "Why Not Abolish Antitrust?" *Regulation* 7 (January–February 1983): 23–28.

900. Snowberger, V. "Sustainability Theory: Its Implications for Governmental Preservation of a Regulated Monopoly." *Quarterly Review of Economics and Business* 18 (Winter 1978): 81–89.

901. Spann, Robert M. "Rate of Return Regulation and Efficiency in Production: An Empirical Test of Averch-Johnson Thesis." *Bell Journal of Economics and Management Science* 5 (Spring 1974): 38–52.

902. Stempel, Guido H. "A New Analysis of Monopoly and Competition." *Columbia Journalism Review* 6 (Spring 1967): 11–12.

903. Stern, Louis W., and Grabner, John R. *Competition in the Marketplace.* Glenview, IL: Scott, Foresman, 1970. 160 p.

904. Stigler, George J. "Free Riders and Collective Action: An Appendix to Theories of Economic Regulation." *Bell Journal of Economics and Management Science* 5 (Autumn 1974): 359–65.

905. Stigler, George J. "The Process of Economic Regulation." *Antitrust Bulletin* 17 (Spring 1972): 207–36.

906. Stigler, George J. "The Theory of Economy Regulation." *Bell Journal of Economics and Management Science* 2 (Spring 1971): 3–21.

907. Stigler, George J. "Viewpoint: Economists and Public Policy." *Regulation* 6 (May–June 1982): 13–17.

908. Stiglitz, Joseph E. "Incentives, Risk, and Information: Notes towards a Theory of Hierarchy." *Bell Journal of Economics and Management Science* 6 (Autumn 1975): 552–79.

909. Straussman, J. D. "Spending More and Enjoying It Less: On the Political Economy of Advanced Capitalism: Review Article." *Comparative Politics* 13 (January 1981): 235–52.

910. Suk-Anarak, Weerasak. "Optimal Control Theory for Financing Models of Regulated Firms." Ph.D. dissertation, University of Wisconsin—Madison, 1980. 173 p.

911. Sweeney, George H. "Adoption of Cost-Saving Innovations by a Regulated Firm." *American Economic Review* 71 (June 1981): 437–47.

912. Sweeney, George H. "A Dynamic Theory of a Firm Subject to Regulation." Ph.D. dissertation , Northwestern University, 1978.

913. Tasch, Philip G. "Optimal Capital Policies for a Regulated Firm." Ph.D. dissertation, Johns Hopkins University, 1979. 171 p.

914. Thatcher, Janet S. "A Theoretical and Empirical Study of the Effect of Financial Leverage and Taxes on the Behavior of the Regulated and Unregulated Firm under Uncertainty." Ph.D. dissertation, University of Wisconsin—Madison, 1979. 252 p.

915. Thompson, M. J. "Monopoly, Competition, and Free Enterprise: Toward an Economic 'Point of No Return'?" *George Washington Law Review* 42 (August 1974): 901–20.

916. Tincher, William R. "Practical Aspects of Conducting Antitrust Proceedings: Post Hearing." *Antitrust Bulletin* 4 (September–October 1959): 683–91.

917. Toccillo, J. "Taxation by Regulation: The Case of Financial Intermediaries." *Bell Journal of Economics and Management Science* 8 (Autumn 1977): 577–87.

918. Trebing, Harry M., ed. *Performance under Regulation.* East Lansing, MI: Institute of Public Utilities, Michigan State University, 1968. 169 p.

919. Turner, Donald F. "Conglomerate Mergers and Section 7 of the Clayton Act." *Harvard Law Review* 78 (May 1965): 1313–95.

920. Ulrey, Ivon W. "The Economic Consequences of Regulated Monopoly Taxation." Ph.D. dissertation, Ohio State University, 1953. 217 p.

921. Walker, Myron, and Rothermel, Tim. "Political Activity and Tax Exempt Organizations Before and After the Tax Reform Act of 1969." *George Washington Law Review* 38 (July 1970): 1114–36.

922. Watson, Justin T. "A Regulatory View of Capital Adequacy." *Journal of Bank Research* 6 (Autumn 1975): 170–72.

923. Weaver, Suzanne. *Decision to Prosecute: Organization and Public Policy in the Antitrust Division.* Cambridge, MA: MIT Press, 1977. 196 p.

924. Weaver, Suzanne. "Viewpoint: Inhaber and the Limits of Cost-Benefit Analysis." *Regulation* 3 (July–August 1979): 14–16.

925. Weidenbaum, Murray L. *The Economics of Peacetime Defense.* New York: Praeger, 1974. 193 p.

926. Weidenbaum, Murray L. "Viewpoint: On Estimating Regulatory Costs." *Regulation* 2 (May–June 1978): 14–18.

927. Wending, W., and Werner, J. "Nonprofit Firms and the Economic Theory of Regulation." *Quarterly Review of Economics and Business* 20 (Autumn 1980): 6–18.

928. Williams, Walter, E. "Racial Reasoning in Unfree Markets—Preference, Prejudice, and Difference." *Regulation* 3 (March–April 1979): 39–48.

929. Wilson, R. A. "Barriers to Trustbusting: 'Efficiency' Myths and Timid Trustbusters." *Antitrust Law and Economics Review* 9 (1977): 19–39.

930. Wolf, C. "Theory of Nonmarket Failure: Framework for Implementation Analysis." *Journal of Law and Economics* 22 (April 1979): 107–39.

931. Yaakob, Izan H. "An Empirical Analysis of the Economic Effects of Mandatory Audit Regulation." Ph.D. dissertation, University of Chicago, 1978.

PUBLIC GOOD

932. Aiken, Michael, and Alford, Robert. "Community Structure and Innovation: The Case of Public Housing." *American Political Science Review* 64 (September 1970): 843–64.

933. American Public Works Association. *History of Public Works in the United States, 1776–1976,* edited by Ellis L. Armstrong, et al. Chicago: The Association, 1976. 736 p.

934. Aranson, Peter H., and Ordeshook, Peter. "Regulation, Redistribution, and Public Choice." *Public Choice* 37 (1981): 69–100.

935. Arrow, Kenneth J. "Political and Economic Evaluation of Social Effects and Externalities." In *The Analysis of Public Output,* edited by Julius Margolis, pp. 1–30. New York: Columbia University Press, 1970.

936. Benditt, Theodore M. "The Public Interest." *Philosophy and Public Affairs* 2 (Spring 1973): 291–311.

937. Browning, E. K. "Collective Choice and General Fund Financing." *Journal of Political Economy* 83 (April 1975): 377–90.

938. Buchanan, James M., and Tullock, Gordon. "Polluters' Profits and Political Response: Direct Controls Versus Taxes." *American Economic Review* 65 (March 1975): 135–47.

939. Burrows, P. "Pigovian Taxes, Polluter Subsidies, Regulation, and the Size of a Polluting Industry." *Canadian Journal of Economics* 12 (August 1979): 494–501.

940. Cervero, Robert. "Revitalizing Urban Transit—More Money or Less Regulation?" *Regulation* 8 (May–June 1984): 36–42.

941. Cohen, Harris S. "Professional Licensure, Organizational Behavior, and the Public Interest." *Milbank Memorial Fund Quarterly* 51 (Winter 1973): 73–88.

942. Chernick, Howard A. "Block Grants for the Needy: The Case of AFDC." *Journal of Policy Analysis and Management* 1 (1982): 209–22.

943. Davis, Saville R.; Kendall, Donald M.; and Stans, Maurice H. *Private Enterprise and the Urban Crisis.* Washington, DC: American University, Center for the Study of Private Enterprise, 1971. 68 p.

944. Dick, Everett. "Some Aspects of Private Use of Public Lands." *Journal of the West* 9 (January 1970): 24–32.

945. Downing, Paul B. "Policy Consequences of Indirect Regulatory Costs." *Public Policy* 29 (Fall 1981): 507–26.

946. Downs, Anthony. "The Public Interest: Its Meaning in a Democracy." *Social Research* 29 (Spring 1962): 1–36.

947. Eilbott, P., and Kempey, W. "New York City's Tax Abatement and Exemption Program for Encouraging Housing Rehabilitation." *Public Policy* 26 (Fall 1978): 571–97.

948. Farmer, Mary K., and Barrell, Ray. "Enterpreneurship and Government Policy: The Case of the Housing Market." *Policy Studies Review Annual* 6 (1982): 709–34.

949. Ferejohn, J. A. "Decisive Coalitions in the Theory of Social Choice." *Journal of Economic Theory* 15 (August 1977): 301–06.

950. Fischel, William A. "Equity and Efficiency Aspects of Zoning Reform." *Public Policy* 27 (Summer 1979): 301–31.

951. Fowler, E. P., and White, D. "Big City Downtowns: The Non-Impact of Zoning." *Policy Studies Journal* 7 (Summer 1979): 690–700.

952. Fowler, M. S. "Public's Interest." *Florida Bar Journal* 56 (March 1982): 213–17.

953. Frieden, Bernard J. "Housing Allowances: An Experiment That Worked." *Policy Studies Review Annual* 5 (1981): 476–97.

954. Frieden, Bernard J. "The New Regulation Comes to Suburbia." *Public Interest* 55 (Spring 1979): 15–27.

955. Gilb, Corinne L. "Self-Regulating Professions and the Public Welfare: A Case Study of the California State Bar." Ph.D. dissertation, Radcliffe College, 1957.

956. Goodall, Leonard E. "State Regulation of Local Indebtedness with Special Reference to Illinois and Michigan." Ph.D. dissertation, University of Illinois, 1962. 244 p.

957. Goodwin, Leonard, and Moen, Phyllis. "The Evolution and Implementation of Family Welfare Policy." *Policy Studies Journal* 8 (1980): 633–51.

958. Gottdiener, M., and Neiman, Max. "Characteristics of Support for Local Growth Control." *Urban Affairs Quarterly* 17 (September 1981): 55–73.

959. Graham, John D. "Some Explanations for Disparities in Life-Saving Investments." *Policy Studies Review* 1 (May 1982): 692–704.

960. Halteman, James. "Should Municipal Authority Water Firms Be Regulated? A Comparative Study between Private and Municipal Authority Firms." Ph.D. dissertation, Pennsylvania State University, 1974. 153 p.

961. Harford, J. D. "The Spatial Aspects of Local Public Goods: A Note." *Public Finance Quarterly* 7 (January 1979): 122–28.

962. Henrich, Frederick K. "A Role for Regulation: Early American Legislation to Protect the Public Interest." Ph.D. dissertation, University of New York, 1978. 476 p.

963. Hildreth, J. "Economists, Regulation, and Public Policy." *American Journal of Agricultural Economics* 61 (November 1979): 741–45.

964. Hoffman, John F. "An Analysis of the Theory, Application, and Current Experiences of the Participative Management Concept in Municipal Government Jurisdictions." Master's thesis, California State University, Long Beach, 1975.

965. Holtkamp, J. A. "Suburban Community Issue: Rebutting the Presumption That a Suburban Applicant Intends to Serve the Central City." *Federal Communications Bar Journal* 27 (1974): 81–106.

966. Hori, H. "Revealed Preference for Public Goods." *American Economic Review* 65 (December 1975): 978–91.

967. Humphrey, Craig R., and Buttel, Frederick H. "The Sociology of the Growth/No Growth Debate." *Policy Studies Journal* 9 (Winter 1980): 336–45.

968. Ippolito, R. A., and Masson, R. T. "Social Cost of Government Regulation of Milk." *Journal of Law and Economics* 21 (April 1978): 33–65.

969. Jackson, Jesse. "Reparations Are Justified for Blacks." *Regulation* 2 (September–October 1978): 24–29.

970. Janczyk, Joseph T., and Constance, William, C. "Impacts of Building Moratoria on Housing Markets within a Region." *Growth and Change* 11 (January 1980): 11–19.

971. Johnson, Knowlton W. "Police Interaction and Referral Activity with Personnel of Other Social Regulatory Agencies: A Multivariate Analysis." Ph.D. dissertation, Michigan State University, 1971. 183 p.

972. Kaish, Stanley. "What Is 'Just and Reasonable' in Rent Control? Why Historic Cost Is More Rational than Current Value." *American Journal of Economics and Sociology* 40 (April 1981): 129–37.

973. Kalleberg, A. L., et al. "Economic Segmentation, Worker Power, and Income Inequality." *American Journal of Sociology* 87 (November 1981): 651–83.

974. Khadduri, Jil, and Struyk, Raymond J. "Housing Vouchers for the Poor." *Journal of Policy Analysis and Management* 1 (1982): 196–208.

975. Kohlmeier, Louis M. "Effective Regulation in the Public Interest." *California Management Review* 16 (Spring 1974): 95–101.

976. Krooth, David, and Spragens, Jeffrey. "The Interest Assistance Programs—A Successful Approach to Housing Problems." *George Washington Law Review* 39 (May 1971): 789–817.

977. Lazin, F. A. "Federal Low-Income Housing Assistance Programs and Racial Segregation: Leased Public Housing." *Public Policy* 24 (Summer 1976): 337–60.

978. Lebowitz, Neil H. "Above Party, Class, or Creed: Rent Control in the United States, 1940–1947." *Journal of Urban History* 7 (August 1981): 439–70.

979. Leduc, Thomas. "Public Policy, Private Investment, and Land Use in American Agriculture, 1825–1875." *Agricultural History* 37 (January 1963): 3–9.

980. Leone, Robert. "The Real Costs of Regulation." *Harvard Business Review* 55 (November–December 1977): 57–66.

981. Lilley, William, and Miller, James C. "The New 'Social Regulation.'" *Public Interest* 47 (Spring 1977): 49–61.

982. Loeb, M. "Alternative Versions of the Demand-Revealing Process." *Public Choice* 29 (Spring 1977): 15–26.

983. Lowenthal, R. "Pluralism versus the Common Weal in the Industrial State." *Survey* 25 (Autumn 1980): 101–11.

984. MacFarlan, Sandra G. "A Property Rights Analysis of the Administration of the Food Stamp Program." Ph.D. dissertation, Duke University, 1981. 213 p.

985. Manvel, A. D. "Fiscal Impact of Revenue Sharing." *American Academy of Political and Social Science, Annals* 419 (May 1975): 36–49.

986. Marando, Vincent L. "A Metropolitan Lower Income Housing Allocation Policy." *American Behavioral Scientist* 19 (September–October 1975): 75–103.

987. Marx, T. G. "Egalitarian Regulation and the Pursuit of Self-Interest: Moral Conflicts for Private Enterprise." *Business Economics* 15 (September 1980): 36–40.

988. Maslove, Allan M. "Public Sector Decision Making and the Technology of Consumption." *Public Choice* 27 (Fall 1976): 59–70.

989. Merseth, Gale D. "Regulation and Income Redistribution: The Massachusetts Experience." D.B.A dissertation, Harvard University, 1979. 518 p.

990. Mills, Thomas A. "Municipal Agencies: An Empirical Study of Organizational Performance." Ph.D. dissertation, University of Pennsylvania, 1975. 349 p.

991. Mishan, E. J. "The Postwar Literature on Externalities: An Interpretative Essay." *Journal of Economic Literature* 9 (March 1971): 1–28.

992. Mitnick, Barry M. "A Typology of Conceptions of the Public Interest." *Administration and Society* 8 (May 1976): 5–28.

993. Mitnick, Barry M., and Weiss, Charles. "The Siting Impasse and a Rational Choice Model of Regulatory Behavior: An Agency for Power Plant Siting." *Journal of Environmental Economics and Management* 1 (1974): 150–71.

994. Moore, Mark H. "A 'Feasibility Estimate' of a Policy Decision to Expand Methadone Maintenance." *Public Policy* 26 (Spring 1978): 285–304.

995. Moore, Thomas G. "Comments on Aranson and Ordeshook's Regulation, Redistribution, and Public Choice." *Public Choice* 37 (1981): 101–06.

996. Morschauser, Joseph. *Public Issues, Private Interests.* New York: Conference Board, 1976. 11 p.

997. Mushkin, Selma J., and Vehorn, Charles L. "User Fees and Charges." *Governmental Finance* 6 (November 1977): 42–48.

998. Muskin, J. B., and Sorrentino, J. A. "Externalities in a Regulated Industry: The Aircraft Noise Problem." *American Economic Review* 67 (February 1977): 347–50.

999. Musolf, Lloyd D. "Public Enterprise and Economic Planning: A Comparative Perspective." *George Washington Law Review* 35 (December 1966): 362–77.

1000. Nagel, Stuart S., and Neef, M. "Finding an Optimum Choice, Level, or Mix in Public Policy Analysis." *Public Administration Review* 38 (September 1978): 404–12.

1001. Nivola, Pietro S. "Distributing a Municipal Service: A Case Study of Housing Inspection." *Journal of Politics* 40 (February 1978): 59–81.

1002. Palley, M. L. "Current Issues in Welfare Poverty Policy." *Policy Studies Journal* 6 (Spring 1978): 412–19.

1003. Piven, Francis F., and Cloward, Richard A. *Regulating the Poor: The Functions of Public Welfare.* New York: Pantheon, 1971. 389 p.

1004. Plott, Charles R. "Axiomatic Social Choice Theory: An Overview and Interpretation." *American Journal of Political Science* 20 (August 1976): 511–96.

1005. Plott, Charles R., and Meyer, Robert. "The Technology of Public Goods, Externalities, and the Exclusion Principle." "Comment" by Robert H. Haveman. In *Economic Analysis of Environmental Problems,* edited by Edwin S. Mills, pp. 65–94. New York: National Bureau of Economic Research, Columbia University Press, 1975.

1006. Posner, Richard A. "Social Costs of Monopoly and Regulation" *Journal of Political Economy* 83 (August 1975): 807–27.

1007. Raman, Krishnamurthy K. "Revenue Sharing and Local Government Modernization: The Case of Accounting, Auditing, and Financial Reporting." *Publius* 9 (Summer 1979): 75–88.

1008. Renshaw, Edward F., and Reer, D. "Government Budgets and Public Services: Some Criteria for Determining the Sources and Levels of Public Goods, Including Transport Services." *American Journal of Economics and Sociology* 38 (July 1979): 275–86.

1009. Roisman, Florence W. "The Right to Public Housing." *George Washington Law Review* 39 (May 1971): 691–733.

1010. Rothenberg, Jerome. "Comments on Preference Revelation for Public Policy Decision." *Policy and Politics* 4 (June 1976): 45–50.

1011. Salamon, Lester J., and Siegfried, John J. "Economic Power and Political Influence: The Impact of Industry Structure on Public Policy." *American Political Science Review* 71 (September 1977): 1026–43.

1012. Samuelson, Paul. "The Pure Theory of Public Expenditure." *Review of Economics and Statistics* 36 (November 1954): 387–89.

1013. Schelling, Thomas C. "On the Ecology of Micromotives." *Public Interest* 7 (Fall 1971): 61–98.

1014. Schubert, Glendon. "'The Public Interest' in Administrative Decision-Making: Theorem, Theosophy, or Theory?" *American Political Science Review* 51 (June 1957): 346–68.

1015. Schultze, Charles L. "Opinion: The Public Use of Private Interest." *Regulation* 1 (September–October 1977): 10–14.

1016. Schultze, Charles L. "The Role of Incentives, Penalties, and Rewards in Attaining Public Policy." In *Public Expenditures and Policy Analysis,* edited by R. H. Haveman and J. Margolis, pp. 145–72. Chicago: Markham, 1970.

1017. Shepherd, William G. "Regulation, Entry and Public Enterprise." In *Regulation in Further Perspective: The Little Engine That Might,* edited by William G. Shepherd and Thomas G. Gies, pp. 5–25. Cambridge, MA: Ballinger, 1974.

1018. Smeeding, Timothy M. "The Anti-Poverty Effect of In-Kind Transfers: A 'Good Idea' Gone Too Far?" *Policy Studies Journal* 10 (March 1982): 499–521.

1019. Smith, V. Kerry. "The Role of Innovation in the Provision of Local Public Goods." *Public Finance Quarterly* 4 (July 1976): 285–94.

1020. Smith, V. L. "Experiments with a Decentralized Mechanism for Public Good Decisions." *American Economic Review* 70 (September 1980): 584–99.

1021. Sorauf, Frank. "The Public Interest Reconsidered." *Journal of Politics* 19 (November 1957): 616–39.

1022. Sorg, James D. "A Theory of Individual Behavior in the Implementation of Policy Innovations." Ph.D. dissertation, Ohio State University, 1978. 441p,.

1023. Staaf, Robert J., and Tannian, Francis X., eds. *Externalities: Theoretical Dimensions of Political Economy.* New York: Dunellen, 1973. 354 p.

1024. Steiner, Peter O. "The Public Sector and the Public Interest." In *Public Expenditures and Policy Analysis,* edited by R. H. Haveman and J. Margolis, pp. 21–58. Chicago: Markham, 1970.

1025. Stockfisch, Jacob, A., and Edwards, D. J. "The Blending of Public and Private Enterprise: The SST as a Case in Point." *Public Interest* 14 (Winter 1969): 108–17.

1026. Stonecash, Jeff. "Local Policy Analysis and Autonomy: On Intergovernmental Relations in Theory Specification." *Comparative Urban Research* 5 (1978): 5–23.

1027. Stowe, Eric, and Rehfuss, John. "Federal Towns Policy: 'Muddling Through' at the Local Level." *Public Administration Review* 35 (May–June 1975): 222–28.

1028. Sufrin, S. C. "Regulation for Amenities." *Challenge* 26 (November–December 1983): 57–58.

1029. Suzumura, K. "Remarks on the Theory of Collective Choice." *Economica* 43 (November 1974): 381–90.

1030. Turvey, Ralph, ed. *Public Enterprise.* Harmondsworth, UK: Penguin Books, 1968.

1031. Viscusi, W Kip, and Zeckhauser, Richard J. "Optimal Standards with Incomplete Enforcement." *Public Policy* 27 (Fall 1979): 437–56.

1032. Weaver, Paul H. "Regulation, Social Policy, and Class Conflict." *Public Interest* 50 (Winter 1978): 45–63.

1033. Weber, Bruce A., and Bryson, John M. *Toward a Policy Impact Simulation Model: Identifying the Probable Effects of Alternative State Policy Tools.* Madison, WI: Lake Superior Project, Center for Geographic Analysis, Institute for Environmental Studies, University of Wisconsin—Madison, 1975. 68 p.

1034. Weingast, Barry R. *A Positive Model of Public Policy Formation: The Case of Regulatory Agency Behavior.* St. Louis, MO: Center for the Study of American Business, Washington University, 1978. 33 p.

1035. Weisbrod, B. A. "Distributional Effects of Collective Goods." *Policy Analysis* 5 (Winter 1979): 67–95.

1036. Weitzman, Martin L. "Optimal Rewards for Economic Regulation." *American Economic Review* 68 (September 1978): 683–91.

1037. Woodren, Robert L. "Helping the Poor Help Themselves." *Policy Review* 21 (Summer 1982): 73–86.

1038. Yandle, Bruce. "Conflicting Commons." *Public Choice* 38 (1982): 317–27.

1039. Zeckhauser, Richard, and Schaefer, Elmer. "Public Policy and Normative Economic Theory." In *The Study of Policy Formation,* edited by Raymond A. Bauer and Kenneth J. Gergen, pp. 27–102. New York: Free Press, 1968.

III. Politics of Regulation

ADMINISTRATION

1040. Adelman, Kenneth L. "Viewpoint: Biting the Hand That Loves Them." *Regulation* 6 (July-August 1982): 16–18.

1041. Anderson, Wayne F. "Intergovernmental Aid: Relief or Intrusion?" *National Civic Review* 69 (March 1980): 127–32.

1042. Arpaia, Anthony F. "The Independent Agency—A Necessary Instrument of Democratic Government." *Harvard Law Review* 69 (January 1956): 483–506.

1043. Attewell, Paul, and Gerstein, Dean R. "Government Policy and Local Practice." *American Sociological Review* 44 (April 1979): 311–27.

1044. Balzano, Michael P. "Putting the Skids to Meals on Wheels." *Regulation* 3 (September-October 1979): 52–54.

1045. Barfield, Claude E. "Unsnarling the Federal Grant System." *Regulation* 5 (September–October 1981): 37–46.

1046. Beckman, Norman, and Handerson, Harold, eds. *New Directions in Public Administration: The Federal View.* Reston, VA: The Bureaucrat, 1975. 209 p.

1047. Bosworth, Karl A. "Federal-State Administrative Regulations in the Regulation of Public Service Enterprises." Ph.D. dissertation, University of Chicago, 1943.

1048. Boynton, George Robert. *If Only We Had Known.* Bloomington, IN: Center for International Policy Studies, Indiana University, 1978. 17 p.

1049. Bozeman, Barry, and Dong, Kim. "Governing the 'Republic of Science': An Analysis of National Science Foundation Officials' Attitudes about Managed Science." *Polity* 14 (Winter 1981): 183–204.

1050. Brewer, W. D. "Regulation—The Balance Point." *Pepperdine Law Review* 1 (1974): 355–71.

1051. Brinkley, Alan. "Prelude." *Wilson Quarterly* 6 (Spring 1982): 51–61.

1052. Bulgaro, Patrick J., and Webb, Arthur Y. "Federal-State Conflicts in Cost Control." *Proceedings of the Academy of Political Science* 33 (1980): 92–110.

1053. Carlson, Allan C. "Regulators and Religion: Caesar's Revenge." *Regulation* 3 (May-June 1979): 27–34.

1054. Carty, J. P. "Politics of Regulation: Understanding the Regulatory Complex." *Personnel Administrator* 25 (June 1980): 25–30.

1055. Cochran, Clarke E. "Political Science and 'The Public Interest.'" *Journal of Politics* 36 (May 1974): 327–55.

1056. Colman, William. "The Role of the Federal Government in the Design and Administration of Intergovernmental Programs." *American Academy of Political and Social Science, Annals* 359 (May 1965): 23–34.

1057. *Conference on Regulatory Reform, Washington, DC, 1976. Proceedings, National Conference on Regulatory Reform.* Washington, DC: National Center for Productivity and Quality of Working Life, 1976. 274 p.

1058. Congressional Quarterly. *Regulation: Process and Politics.* Washington, DC: Congressional Quarterly, 1982. 184 p.

1059. Conklin, C. "PLLRC Revisited—A Potpourri of Memories." *Denver Law Journal* 54 (1977): 445–54.

1060. Connolly, William E. "On 'Interests' in Politics." *Politics and Society* 2 (Summer 1972): 459–77.

1061. *A Conversation with Michael Pertschuk: Held on January 11, 1979 at the American Enterprise Institute for Public Policy Research, Washington, DC.* Washington, DC: The Institute, 1979. 26 p.

1062. Cooper, Phillip J. "Public Law and Administration in the 80s." *Midwest Review of Public Administration* 14 (September 1980): 163–76.

1063. Crane, P. M. "Regulatory Agencies." *Journal of Social and Political Affairs* 1 (January 1976): 21–42.

1064. Cutler, Lloyd N., and Johnson, David R. "Regulation and the Political Process." *Yale Law Journal* 84 (June 1975): 1359–418.

1065. Davis, J. C. "Government Over-Regulation: It's Costing All of Us Money. " *Real Estate Today* 12 (June 1979): 26–31.

1066. Day, J. E. "Overregulation and Underachievement: An Analysis of the Regulatory Agencies." *Public Utilities Fortnightly* 80 (July 1967): 15–20.

1067. Debout, John E. "Form and Function: A Matter of Relationships." *National Civic Review* 68 (July 1979): 332–40.

1068. "Definition of a Branch under the McFadden Act." *Boston College Law Review* 19 (January 1978): 373–86.

1069. DeLong, James V. "How to Convince an Agency: A Handbook for Policy Advocates." *Regulation* 6 (September-October 1982): 27–36.

1070. Deutsch, Karl, and Rieselbach, Leroy. "Recent Trends in Political Theory and Political Philosophy." *American Academy of Political and Social Science, Annals* 86 (May 1973): 1250–81.

1071. Dubnick, Melvin J., and Gitelson, Alan R. "Regulatory Policy Analysis: Working in a Quagmire." *Policy Studies Review* 1 (1982): 423–35.

1072. Elazar, Daniel J. "The New Federalism: Can the States Be Trusted?" *Public Interest* 35 (Spring 1974): 89–102.

1073. Elliff, John. "Aspects of Federal Civil Rights Enforcement: The Justice Department and the FBI, 1939–1964." *Perspectives in American History* 5 (1971): 605–74.

1074. Englebert, Ernest. "Federal-State Relationships: Their Influence on Western Regional Growth." *Western Political Quarterly* 16 (September 1963): 686–707.

1075. Ethridge, Marcus E. "Legislative-Administrative Interaction as 'Intrusive Access': An Empirical Analysis." *Journal of Politics* 43 (May 1981): 473–92.

1076. Evans, Frank B., and Pinkett, Harold T., eds. *Research in the Administration of Public Policy; Papers and Proceedings.* Washington, DC: Howard University Press, 1975. 229 p.

1077. "Extraterritorial Service of Administrative Subpoenas." *Law and Policy in International Business* 13 (1981): 847–70.

1078. Fainsod, Merle. "Some Reflections on the Nature of Regulatory Process." *Public Policy* 1 (1940): 297–323.

1079. "Federal Administrative Agencies: A Panel." *Law Library Journal* 67 (November 1974): 466–81.

1080. Feldstein, Paul J. "The Political Environment of Regulation. " *Proceedings of the Academy of Political Science* 33 (1980): 6–20.

1081. Fesler, James W. "Independent Regulatory Establishments." In *Elements of Public Administration*, edited by Fritz M. Marx, pp. 207–35. New York: Prentice-Hall, 1946.

1082. Fox, J. R. "Breaking the Regulatory Deadlock." *Harvard Business Review* 59 (September-October 1981): 97–105.

1083. Froomkin, J. "Needed: A New Framework for the Analysis of Governmental Programs." *Policy Analysis* 2 (Spring 1976): 341–50.

1084. Goldbert, Victor P., and Peltzman, Sam. "Peltzman on Regulation and Politics." *Public Choice* 39 (1982): 291–300.

1085. Goldman, M.E. "'Something There Is That Doesn't Love a Wall': The Need for a Conceptual Approach to Professional Responsibility." *George Washington Law Review* 43 (March 1975): 713–28.

1086. Greer, Darryl G. "State-Level Coordination and Policy Implementation." *Policy Studies Journal* 10 (September 1981): 32–47.

1087. Grumet, Barbara R. "Who Is 'Due' Process?" *Public Administration Review* 42 (July-August 1982): 321–26.

1088. Hall, C. W. "Sensitive Payments or Services—Submitting Materials to the Government." *Tulane Tax Institute* 27 (1977): 26–31.

1089. Hayes, Richard E. "The Effect of Changes in Level of Civil Violence on Political Regulation Policy." Ph.D. dissertation, Indiana University, 1972. 341 p.

1090. Hein, Clarence, and Hady, Thomas. "Administrative Control of Municipal Incorporation: The Search for Criteria." *Western Political Quarterly* 19 (December 1966): 697–704.

1091. Holden, Matthew, ed. "Policy Content and the Regulatory Process." *American Behavioral Scientist* 19 (September 1975): 5–136.

1092. Homah, Richard. "The Regulated Libretto." *Regulation* 8 (March-April 1984): 45–46.

1093. Huber, Peter. "Exorcists vs. Gatekeepers in Risk Regulation." *Regulation* 7 (November-December 1983): 23–32.

1094. Huntington, Samuel P. "Clientalism: A Study in Administrative Politics." Ph.D. dissertation, Harvard University, 1951. 354 p.

1095. Jaffe, Louis L. "The Effective Limits of the Administrative Process: A Reevaluation." *Harvard Law Review* 67 (May 1954): 1105–35.

1096. Jaffe, Louis L. "The Illusion of the Ideal Administration." *Harvard Law Review* 86 (May 1973): 1183–99.

1097. Johanson, Robin B., and Rosen, Sanford J. "State and Local Regulation of Religious Solicitation of Funds: A Constitutional Perspective." *American Academy of Political and Social Science, Annals* 446 (November 1979): 116–35.

1098. Joskow, Paul J., and Noll, Roger. "Regulation in Theory and Practice: A Current Overview." In *Studies of Public Regulation*, edited by Gary Fromm, pp. 33–52. Cambridge, MA: MIT Press, 1981.

1099. Kahn, David. "Cryotology Goes Public." *Foreign Affairs* 58 (Fall 1979): 141–59.

1100. Karmel, Roberta S. "Ambivalent Reflections on Regulation." *UC Davis Law Review* 12 (March 1979): 95–103.

1101. Kay, Marvin L. "The Institutional Background to the Regulation in Colonial North Carolina." Ph.D. dissertation, University of Minnesota, 1962. 622 p.

1102. Kearny, Edward N. *Thurman Arnold, Social Critic; The Satirical Challenge to Orthodoxy.* Albuquerque, NM: University of New Mexico Press, 1970. 164 p.

1103. Kelman, Steven J. "Regulation for a Decent Society." *American Federationist* 86 (February 1979): 4–8.

1104. Kemp, K. "Symbolic and Strict Regulation in the American States." *Social Science Quarterly* 62 (September 1981): 516–26.

1105. Kemp, Kathleen A. "Instability in Budgeting for Federal Regulatory Agencies." *Social Science Quarterly* 63 (December 1982): 643–60.

1106. Kettl, Donald F. "Regulating the Cities." *Publius* 11 (Spring 1981): 111–25.

1107. Kimble, Cary. "In Pursuit of Well-Being." *Wilson Quarterly* 4 (Spring 1980): 61–74.

1108. Kintner, Earl W. "The Current Ordeal of the Administrative Process: In Reply to Mr. Hector." *Yale Law Journal* 69 (May 1960): 965–77.

1109. Kraft, Michael E. "The Use of Risk Analysis in Federal Regulatory Agencies: An Exploration." *Policy Studies Review* 1 (May 1982): 666–75.

1110. Laird, Michael J., and Thoms, William E. "End of the Line." *Loyola Law Review* 15 (1968–69): 263–80.

1111. Lambright, W. Henry. *Governing Science and Technology.* New York: Oxford University Press, 1976. 218 p.

1112. Leone, Richard C. "Public Interest Advocacy and the Regulatory Process." *American Academy of Political and Social Science, Annals* 400 (March 1972): 54–55.

1113. Levine, Charles H. "Organizational Design: A Post-Minnowbrook Perspective for the 'New' Public Administration." *Public Administration Review* 35 (July-August 1975): 425–35.

1114. Lewis, Earl M. "History of Public Regulation in New York State." Ph.D. dissertation, University of Chicago, 1952. 199 p.

1115. Lippitt, H. F. "State and Federal Regulatory Agencies—Conflict or Cooperation?" *Public Utilities Fortnightly* 85 (March 26, 1970): 33–38.

1116. Lovell, Catherine H. "Coordinating Federal Grants from Below." *Public Administration Review* 39 (September-October 1979): 432–39.

1117. Lukowski, Susan, and Grayson, Cary T., eds. *State Information and Federal Region Book.* Washington, DC: Potomac Books, 1973. 90 p.

1118. Machan, Tibor R. "Wronging Rights." *Policy Review* 17 (Summer 1981): 37–58.

1119. Malbin, Michael J. "Neither a Mountain nor a Molehill." *Regulation* 3 (May-June 1979): 41–45.

1120. Margolis, Michael, and Haque, Khondaker E. "Applied Tolerance or Fear of Government? An Alternative Interpretation of Jackman's Findings." *American Journal of Political Science* 25 (May 1981): 241–55.

1121. Medina, William A. "Factors Which Condition the Responses of Departments and Agencies to Centrally Mandated Management Improvement Approaches." Ph.D. dissertation, American University, 1978. 295 p.

1122. Meltzer, Bernard D. "The Weber Case: Double Talk and Double Standards." *Regulation* 3 (September-October 1979): 34–43.

1123. Mikulecky, Thomas J. "Intergovernmental Regulations Strategies for the Local Manager." *Public Administration Review* 40 (July-August 1980): 379–81.

1124. Miller, William E. "The Waterman Doctrine Revisited." *Georgetown Law Journal* 54 (Fall 1965): 5–29.

1125. Mitchell, W. L. "Federal Inroads into State Regulation." *Public Utilities Fortnightly* 76 (September 30, 1965): 92–98.

1126. Mitnick, Barry M. "Regulation and the Theory of Agency." *Policy Review* 1 (1982): 442–53.

1127. Moore, John E. "Recycling the Regulatory Agencies." *Public Administration Review* 32 (July-August 1972): 291–98.

1128. Morgan, Patrick M. "Academia and the Federal Government." *Policy Studies Journal* 10 (September 1981): 70–84.

1129. Mosher, Frederick C., ed. *Basic Documents of American Public Administration, 1776–1950.* New York: Holmes and Meier, 1976. 225 p.

1130. Norback, Craig T., and Norback, Peter. *Everything You Can Get from the Government for Free . . . or Almost for Free.* New York: Van Nostrand Reinhold, 1975. 233 p.

1131. Ostrom, Vincent. *The Intellectual Crisis in American Public Administration.* Rev. ed. Birmingham, AL: University of Alabama Press, 1974. 179 p.

1132. Payne, T. "Independent Regulatory Commission—A Search for the Public Interest: Statement of Problems and Implications." *Western Political Quarterly* 13 (September 1960): 73–75.

1133. Pertschuk, Michael. "Viewpoint: Needs and Licenses." *Regulation* 3 (March-April 1979): 14–16.

1134. Petersen, H. Craig. "An Empirical Test of Regulatory Effects." *Bell Journal of Economics and Management Science* 6 (Spring 1975): 111–26.

1135. Petkas, Peter J. "The U.S. Regulatory System: Partnership or Maze?" *National Civic Review* 69 (June 1981): 297–301.

1136. Pfiffner, James P. "Management and Central Controls Reconsidered." *Bureaucrat* 10 (Winter 1981–82): 13–16.

1137. Plumbee, John P., and Meier, Kenneth J. "Capture and Rigidity in Regulatory Administration." In *The Policy Cycle,* edited by Judith V. May and Aaron B. Wildavsky, pp. 215–34. Beverly Hills, CA: Sage Publications, 1979.

1138. Plumlee, John P. "Regulatory Administration and Organizational Rigidity: An Empirical Analysis." Ph.D. dissertation, Rice University, 1977. 198 p.

1139. Pogue, R. W. "Effects on Other Merger Transactions: Does the Government Abuse Its Newly Granted Power?" *American Bar Association Antitrust Law Journal* 48 (August 1979): 1471–86.

1140. Pool, Ithiel de Sola. "The New Censorship of Social Research." *National Civic Review* 69 (March 1980): 127–32.

1141. Presthus, Robert V. *Public Administration.* 6th ed. New York: Ronald Press, 1975. 432 p.

1142. Rabinovitz, Francine; Pressman, Jeffrey; and Rein, Martin. "Guidelines: A Plethora of Forms, Authors, and Functions." *Policy Sciences* 7 (December 1976): 399–416.

1143. Reagan, M. C., ed. "Regulatory Administration: Are We Getting Anywhere?" *Public Administration Review* 32 (July 1972): 283–310.

1144. Redford, Emmette S. "Perspectives for the Study of Government Regulation." *American Journal of Political Science* 6 (February 1962): 1–18.

1145. "Regulation—The First Year." *Regulation* 6 (January-February 1982): 19–40.

1146. "Regulatory Agencies: Boring Slowly, from Within." *Economist* 282 (March 1982): 45–46.

1147. Reich, Robert B. "Regulation by Confrontation or Negotiation?" *Harvard Business Review* 59 (May-June 1981): 82–93.

1148. Reid, J. D. "Government Regulatory Institutions: Origin and Evolution." *Journal of Economic History* 39 (March 1979): 321–22.

1149. Robinson, Glen O., and Gellhorn Ernest. *The Administrative Process.* St. Paul, MN: West, 1974. 928 p.

1150. Rudnick, Edward. "The Immigration and Naturalization Service and the Administration of the Naturalization and Citizenship Laws." *International Migration Review* 5 (Winter 1971): 420–35.

1151. Russell, H. L. "State Administrative Law—1978 Today and Tomorrow." *Public Utilities Fortnightly* 102 (November 1978): 82–87.

1152. Ryan, Edward J. "Management by Objectives in Perspective: A Comparative Study of Selected Federal Experience with the Fiscal Year 1975 Program." D.B.A. dissertation, George Washington University, 1976. 354 p.

1153. Sabatier, Paul A., and Mazmanian, Daniel. "The Conditions of Effective Implementation: A Guide to Accomplishing Policy Objectives." *Policy Analysis* 5 (Fall 1979): 481–504.

1154. Sabatier, Paul A., and Mazamanian, Daniel. "The Implementation of Public Policy: A Framework of Analysis." *Policy Studies Journal* 8 (1980): 538–60.

1155. Samprone, Joseph C., and Riddell-Dudra, Nancy. "State Regulatory Climate: Can It Be Predicted?" *Public Utilities Fortnightly* 108 (October 8, 1981): 41–43.

1156. Scalia, Antonin. "Guadalajara! A Case Study in Regulation by Munificence." *Regulation* 2 (March-April 1978): 23–29.

1157. Schenker, E. "Another Look at State Regulatory Agencies." *Public Utilities Fortnightly* 62 (1958): 1008–14.

1158. Schwarz, J. E. "The Hidden Truth about Regulation." *Challenge* 26 (November-December 1983): 54–56.

1159. Shaffer, J. D. "Observations on the Political Economics of Regulations." *American Journal of Agricultural Economics* 61 (November 1979): 721–31.

1160. Shannon, James A. "Thoughts on the Relationships between Science and Federal Programs." *Educational Record* 48 (Summer 1967): 214–23.

1161. Simon, Michael E. "What We Did." *Regulation* 3 (July-August 1979): 20–25.

1162. Solomon, Herbert. "Government-University Relationships and the Administration of Federal Research Funds." *Educational Record* 48 (Summer 1967): 236–41.

1163. Sommer, A. A. "Commission and the Bar: Forty Good Years." *Business Lawyer* 30 (November 1974): 5–14.

1164. Sommer, A. A. "New Day for Municipals." *Urban Law* 8 (Summer 1976): 461–73.

1165. Standish, T. K. "State Initiatives in State-Federal Relations." *American Economic Review* 70 (May 1980): 398–402.

1166. Staten, Michael E., and Umbeck, John R. "Close Encounters in the Skies: A Paradox of Regulatory Incentives." *Regulation* 7 (March-April 1983): 25–31.

1167. Stewart, Richard B. "Public Programs and Private Rights." *Harvard Law Review* 95 (April 1982): 1193–322.

1168. Tabb, W.K. "Government Regulations: Two Sides to the Story." *Challenge* 23 (November-December 1980): 40–48.

1169. Trebing, Harry M. "Critique of the Planning Function in Regulation." *Public Utilities Fortnightly* 79 (March 30, 1967): 15–24.

1170. Trull, Edna. "The Administration of Regulatory Inspectional Services in American Cities." Ph.D. dissertation, Columbia University, 1932. 184 p.

1171. Tyler, G. "Mythologies of a Simon-Pure Conservative."*Dissent* 26 (Spring 1979): 183–93.

1172. Uhl, A. "Regulatory Agencies." *American Federationist* 67 (October 1960): 16–20.

1173. United States. General Accounting Office. *Improving Management for More Effective Government: 50th Anniversary Lectures of the United States General Accounting Office, 1921–1971.* Washington, DC: U.S. Government Printing Office, 1972. 285 p.

1174. Welborn, David M., and Brown, Anthony E. "Power and Politics in Federal Regulatory Commissions." *Administration and Society* 12 (May 1980): 37–68.

1175. Whelan, Charles M. "Government Attempts to Define Church and Religion." *Ameriċan Academy of Political and Social Science, Annals* 446 (November 1979): 32–51.

1176. Wilson, James Q. "The Dead Hand of Regulation." *Public Interest* 25 (Fall 1971): 39–58.

1177. Wilson, James Q. "The Politics of Regulation." In *Social Responsibility and the Business Predicament*, edited by James W. McKie, pp. 135–68. Washington, DC: Brookings Institution, 1974.

1178. Wirt, John G.; Lieberman, Arnold J.; and Levien, Robert E. *R&D Management: Methods Used by Federal Agencies.* Lexington, MA: Lexington Books, 1975. 233 p.

1179. Worthing, Sharon L. "The State Takes Over a Church." *American Academy of Political and Social Science, Annals* 446 (November 1979): 136–48.

1180. Wozencraft, F. M. "Freedom of Information Act and the Agencies." *Public Utilities Fortnightly* 86 (September 1970): 69–70.

1181. Wright, Deil S. "New Federalism: Recent Varieties of an Older Species." *American Review of Public Administration* 16 (Spring 1982): 56–73.

BEHAVIOR OF REGULATORS

1182. Adams, George R. "The Carolina Regulators: A Note on Changing Interpretations." *North Carolina Historical Review* 49 (October 1972): 345–52.

1183. Archer, Stephen H. "Rating the Regulators." *State and Local Government Review* 14 (September 1982): 121–23.

1184. Bendix, Reinhard. *Higher Civil Servants in American Society: A Study of the Social Origins, the Careers, and the Power-Position of Higher Federal Administrators.* Boulder, CO: University of Colorado Press, 1949. 129 p.

1185. Berry, William D. "Theories of Regulatory Impact: The Rules of the Regulator, the Regulated and the Public." *Policy Studies Review* 1 (1982): 436–41.

1186. Beyer, William C. "Limited-Term and Excepted Appointments in the Civil Service—A Study of the Legal Provisions by Which They Are Regulated in Fifty-Nine Jurisdictions in the U.S." Ph.D. dissertation, University of Pennsylvania, 1952. 334 p.

1187. Bolster, Mel H. "The Strategic Deployment of Exceptional Talent: An Account of the Career Executive Roster's Short History." *Public Administrative Review* 27 (December 1967): 446–56.

1188. Boyd, A. S. "Scope and Philosophy of Regulatory Commissions." *Public Utilities Fortnightly* 65 (June 23, 1960): 909–14.

1189. Brigman, William E. "The Executive Branch and the Independent Regulatory Agencies." *Presidential Studies Quarterly* 11 (Spring 1981): 244–61.

1190. Brown, Richard M. *The South Carolina Regulators.* Cambridge, MA: Belknap Press, Harvard University Press, 1963. 230 p.

1191. Cohen, S. E. "Regulatory Agencies: Are They Independent?" *Industrial Marketing* 52 (February 1967): 138–39.

1192. Congressional Budget Office. *The Number of Federal Employees Engaged in Regulatory Activities.* Washington, DC: U.S. Government Printing Office, 1976. 16 p.

1193. Dinnerstein, Leonard. "The Senate's Rejection of Aubrey Williams as Rural Electrification Administrator." *Alabama Review* 21 (April 1968): 133–43.

1194. Dixon, Robert G. "Independent Commissions and Political Responsibility." *Public Utilities Fortnightly* 94 (October 1974): 88–91.

1195. Eckert, J. L. "Life Cycle of Regulatory Commissioners." *Journal of Law and Economics* 24 (April 1981): 113–20.

1196. Eckert, Ross D. "Regulatory Commission Behavior: Taxi Franchising in Los Angeles and Other Cities." Ph.D. dissertation, University of California, Los Angeles, 1968. 255 p.

1197. Edwards, Jack D. "Role Concepts of Federal Regulatory Officials." Ph.D. dissertation, Vanderbilt University, 1966. 151 p.

1198. Emmerich, Herbert. *Federal Organization and Administrative Management.* Birmingham, AL: University of Alabama Press, 1971. 304 p.

1199. Fenn, D. H. "Dilemmas for the Regulator." *California Management Review* 16 (Spring 1974): 87–94.

1200. Gerwig, Robert W. "Public Authorities in the United States." *Law and Contemporary Problems* 26 (Autumn 1961): 591–618.

1201. Grabosky, P. N., and Rosenbloom, David H. "Racial and Ethnic Integration in the Federal Service." *Social Science Quarterly* 56 (June 1975): 71–84.

1202. Heffron, Florence A. "The Independent Regulatory Commissioners." Ph.D. dissertation, University of Colorado, 1971. 493 p.

1203. Helco, Hugh. "Issue Networks and the Executive Establishment." In *The New American Political System,* edited by Anthony King, pp. 87–124. Washington, DC: American Enterprise Institute, 1978.

1204. Hilton, George W. "Basic Behavior of Regulatory Commissions." *American Economic Review; Papers and Proceedings* 62 (May 1972): 47–54.

1205. Holden, Matthew. "'Imperialism' in Bureaucracy." *American Political Science Review* 60 (December 1966): 943–51.

1206. Katz, Daniel, et al. *Bureaucratic Encounters; A Pilot Study in the Evaluation of Government Services.* Ann Arbor, MI: Survey Research Center, Institute for Social Research, University of Michigan, 1975. 264 p.

1207. Loevinger, Lee. "The Sociology of Bureaucracy." *The Business Lawyer* 24 (November 1968): 7–18.

1208. Mashaw, Jerry L. "Regulation, Logic, and Ideology." *Regulation* 3 (November-December 1979): 44–51.

1209. McFadden, Daniel. "The Revealed Preferences of a Government Bureaucracy: Empirical Evidence." *Bell Journal of Economics and Management Science* 7 (Spring 1976): 55–72.

1210. McFadden, Daniel. "The Revealed Preferences of a Government Bureaucracy: Theory." *Bell Journal of Economics and Management Science* 6 (Autumn 1975): 401–16.

1211. Meier, Kenneth J. "Representative Bureaucracy and Administrative Responsiveness: An Empirical and Theoretical Analysis." Ph.D. dissertation, Syracuse University, 1975. 291 p.

1212. Meier, Kenneth J., and Plumlee, John P. "Regulatory Administration and Organizational Rigidity." *Western Political Quarterly* 31 (March 1978): 80–95.

1213. Mekeel, C. L. "From the Ground Up: Bureaucratic Hurdles." *Hardware Age* 216 (November 1979): 83–86.

1214. Meyer, Marshall W., and Brown, M. Craig. "The Process of Bureaucratization." *American Journal of Sociology* 83 (September 1977): 364–85.

1215. Miller, John T. "The Civil Service Commission's New Hearing Examiner Recruitment Program." *Administrative Law Review* 17 (Fall 1964): 104–09.

1216. Mitnick, Barry M. "The Theory of Agency: The Policing 'Paradox' and Regulatory Behavior." *Public Choice* 24 (Winter 1975): 27–42.

1217. Nagel, Stuart S. "Regulatory Commissioners and Party Politics." In his *The Legal Process from a Behavioral Perspective*, pp. 237–44. Homewood, IL: Dorsey, 1969.

1218. Niskanen, William. "Bureaucrats and Politicians." *Journal of Law and Economics* 18 (December 1975): 617–43.

1219. Noll, Roger G. "The Behavior of Regulatory Agencies." *Review of Social Economy* 29 (March 1971): 15–19.

1220. Posner, Richard A. "The Behavior of Administrative Agencies." *Journal of Legal Studies* 1 (June 1972): 305–47.

1221. Reynolds, Harry W. "The Career Public Service and Statute Lawmaking in Los Angeles." *Western Political Quarterly* 18 (September 1965): 621–39.

1222. Roos, Noralow P., and Roos, Leslie L. "Reducing Potential Conflict between Evaluators and Administrators." *Policy Studies Journal* 6 (Summer 1978): 548–51.

1223. Rosenbloom, David H. "The Size of Public Bureaucracies: An Exploratory Analysis." *State and Local Government Review* 13 (September 1981): 115–23.

1224. Rothman, Stanley, and Lichter, S. R. "How Liberal Are Bureaucrats?" *Regulation* 7 (November-December 1983): 16–22.

1225. Rourke, Francis E. "Bureaucratic Autonomy and the Public Interest." *American Behavioral Scientist* 22 (May-June 1979): 537–46.

1226. Roy, William G. "The Politics of Bureaucratization and the US Bureau of Corporations." *Journal of Political and Military Sociology* 10 (Fall 1982): 183–99.

1227. Russell, Milton R., and Shelton, Robert B. "A Model of Regulatory Agency Behavior." *Public Choice* 20 (Winter 1974): 47–62.

1228. Saltzstein, Grace H. "Representative Bureaucracy and Bureaucratic Responsibility: Problems and Prospects." *Administration and Society* 10 (February 1979): 465–75.

1229. Seevers, G. L. "Regulator's Perspective on Regulatory Research." *American Journal of Agricultural Economics* 16 (November 1979): 787–90.

1230. Sibley, D. S., and Bailey, E. E. "Regulatory Commission Behavior: Myopic versus Forward Looking." *Economic Inquiry* 16 (April 1978): 249–56.

1231. Smith, Lincoln. "Academic Man as Regulatory Commissioner." *Public Utilities Fortnightly* 68 (August 1961): 145–54.

1232. Smith, Lincoln. "Accountants as Regulatory Commissioners." *Public Utilities Fortnightly* 59 (January 17, 1957): 93–104.

1233. Smith, Lincoln. "Businessmen as Regulatory Commissioners." *Journal of Business* 31 (April 1958): 132–44.

1234. Smith, Lincoln. "Engineers as Regulatory Commissioners." *Public Utilities Fortnightly* 60 (November 7, 1957): 718–27.

1235. Smith, Lincoln. "Lawyers as Regulatory Commissioners." *George Washington Law Review* 23 (March 1955): 375–428.

1236. Smith, Lincoln. "Laymen as Regulatory Commissioners." *Public Utilities Fortnightly* 63 (May 7, 1959): 673–82.

1237. Smith, Lincoln. "Professional Administrators as Regulatory Commissioners." *Public Utilities Fortnightly* 64 (August 13, 1959): 257–67.

1238. Smith, Lincoln. "Recent Trends in the Appointment of Commissioners." *Ohio State Law Journal* 13 (Autumn 1952): 479–502.

1239. Smith, Lincoln. "Should Regulatory Commissioners Come from Staff Personnel?" *Public Utilities Fortnightly* 66 (December 8, 1960): 871–88.

1240. Smith, Lincoln. "What a Regulatory Commissioner Needs to Know." *Public Utilities Fortnightly* 73 (March 26, 1964): 26–40.

1241. Smith, R. "Regulator's View on Rate Control." *Public Utilities Fortnightly* 84 (September 25, 1969): 26–34.

1242. Somers, Herman M. "The Federal Bureaucracy and the Change of Administration." *American Political Science Review* 48 (March 1954): 131–51.

1243. Sproull, Lee S. "Response to Regulation: An Organizational Process Framework." *Administration and Society* 12 (February 1981): 447–70.

1244. Stephens, Lester D. "The Appointment of the Commissioner of Agriculture in 1877: A Case Study in Political Ambition and Patronage." *Southern Quarterly* 15 (July 1977): 371–86.

1245. Swiss, James E. "Implementing Federal Programs: Administrative Systems and Organizational Effectiveness." Ph.D. dissertation, Yale University, 1976. 262 p.

1246. Thompson,. W. A., et al. "Performance of a Regulatory Agency as a Function of Its Structure and Client Environment: A Simulation Study." *Management Science* 28 (January 1982): 57–72.

1247. Trebing, Harry M. "What's Wrong with Commission Regulation?" *Public Utilities Fortnightly* 65 (May 12, 1960): 660–70.

1248. Tschudy, Ted N. "Advisory Committees as Boundary Linking Units: A Comparative Analysis of Notions from Public Policy and Organization Theory." Ph.D. dissertation, American University, 1976. 390 p.

1249. Tuohy, C. "Accounting Regulators Are Accountable Too." *CA Magazine* 114 (April 1981): 46–51.

1250. United States. General Accounting Office. *Better Evaluation Needed for Federal Civilian Employee Training, Civil Service Commission: Report to the Congress.* Washington, DC: U.S. General Accounting Office, 1974. 36 p.

1251. Untereiner, R. E. "Duties of a Commissioner." *Public Utilities Fortnightly* 62 (August 1958): 304–15.

1252. Vukasin, J. P. "Role of the State Commission." *Public Utilities Fortnightly* 90 (September 28, 1972): 71–73.

1253. Walton, Richard E. *Conflict and Integration in the Federal Bureaucracy.* Cambridge, MA: Present and Fellows of Harvard College, Advanced Research Projects Agency, 1971. 269 p.

1254. Welborn, David M., and Brown, Anthony E. *Regulatory Policy and Processes: The Public Service Commissions in Tennessee, Kentucky, and Georgia.* Knoxville, TN: Bureau of Public Administration, University of Tennessee, 1980. 151 p.

1255. West, W. F. "Institutionalizing Rationality in Regulatory Administration." *Public Administration Review* 43 (July-August 1983): 326–34.

1256. "What the State Commissioners Are Thinking about." *Public Utilities Fortnightly* 84 (November 20, 1969): 48–53.

1257. Wiley, Richard E. "Extent of Independence of Federal Regulatory Agencies. "*Public Utilities Fortnightly* 94 (October 1974): 33–36.

1258. Williamson, Oliver E. "Administrative Controls and Regulatory Behavior." In *Essays on Public Utility Pricing and Regulation,* edited by Harry M. Trebing, pp. 411–52. East Lansing, MI: Institute of Public Utilities, Graduate School of Business Administration, Michigan State University, 1971.

DEREGULATION

1259. Barks, J. V. "Newest Dirty Word: Deregulation." *Iron Age* 222 (May 1979): 23–26.

1260. Beck, Robert A. "Four Hard Deregulation Questions." *National Underwriters Life and Health* 87 (November 26, 1983): 11, 28–29.

1261. Caves, Douglas W. ; Christensen, Laurits R. ; and Tretheway, Michael W. "Airline Productivity under Deregulation." *Regulation* 6 (November-December 1982): 25–28.

1262. Clark, Robert C. "Deregulation Hearings Raise Conflict-of-Interest Issue." *Trusts and Estates* 121 (April 1982): 15–16.

1263. Cooke, Charles M. "Deregulation through Consolidation." *Education and Urban Society* 14 (August 1982): 457–83.

1264. Crickmer, B. "Regulation: How Much Is Enough?" *Nation's Business* 68 (March 1980): 26–30.

1265. "Deregulating America." *Business Week* (November 28, 1983): 80–96.

1266. Eason, H. "Deregulation: Dream Deferred." *Nation's Business* 72 (February 1984): 24–26.

1267. Easterbrook, Frank H. "Breaking Up Is Hard to Do." *Regulation* 5 (November-December 1981): 25–31.

1268. Edwards, A. L. "Regulate or Deregulate: A Bicentennial Question." *Crisis* 83 (January 1976): 27–31.

1269. Hale, David D. "What Financial Deregulation Is Doing to the US Economy." *Banker* 133 (October 1983): 27–33.

1270. Haley, Charles W. "Regulation, Deregulation, and Reregulation." *Business Forum* 8 (Summer 1983): 4–8.

1271. Herman, William R. "Deregulation: Now or Never! (Or Maybe Someday?)" *Public Administration Review* 36 (March-April 1976): 223–28.

1272. Hochman, Harold M. "The Over-Regulated City: A Perspective on Regulatory Procedures in the City of New York." *Public Finance Quarterly* 9 (April 1981): 197–219.

1273. Jacobe, Dennis. "Deregulation Brings the Threat of a Riskier Financial System." *Savings and Loan News* 103 (November 1982): 29–31.

1274. Kaufman, George G., et al. "Impact of Deregulation: Product Lines, Geographic Markets." *Bankers Monthly* 94 (May 1982): 19–23.

1275. Kaufman, George G., et al. "Implications of Deregulation for Product Lines and Geographical Markets of Financial Institutions/Discussant's Comments." *Journal of Bank Research* 14 (Spring 1983): 8–24.

1276. Kaus, R. M., and Frankel, G. "Decline and Fall of the American Way of Regulation." *Washington Monthly* 11 (July-August 1979): 34–45.

1277. Kristol, Irving. "Opinion: A Regulated Society?" *Regulation* 1 (July-August 1977): 12–13.

1278. Kurtz, H., and Chapman, S. "Federal Regulation: Too Much vs. Too Little." *Washington Monthly* 9 (December 1977): 28–39.

1279. Levine, Michael E. "Is Regulation Necessary?" *Yale Law Journal* 74 (July 1965): 1416–47.

1280. Mabley, Robert E., and Strack, Walter D. "Deregulation—A Green Light for Trucking Efficiency." *Regulation* 6 (July-August 1982): 36–42.

1281. Machan, Tibor R. "Some Normative Considerations of Deregulation." *Journal of Social and Political Studies* 3 (Winter 1978): 363–78.

1282. Miller, W. H. "Decade of Deregulation?" *Industry Week* 204 (January 1980): 17–19.

1283. Mitnick, Barry M. "Deregulation as a Process of Organizational Reduction." *Public Administration Review* 38 (July 1978): 350–57.

1284. Mitnick, Barry M. "Strategic Use of Regulation—And Deregulation." *Business Horizons* 24 (March-April 1981): 71–83.

1285. Nelson, Robert H. "Why the Sagebrush Revolt Burned Out." *Regulation* 8 (May-June 1984): 27–35.

1286. Prioleau, Gwendolyn D. "Decontrol vs. Deregulation: Heads, They Win; Tails, You Lose." *Harvard Law Journal* 23 (1981): 235–43.

1287. Puckett, Richard H. "Deregulation and the Principles of Regulation." *Bankers Magazine* 166 (March-April 1983): 86–88.

1288. Rabkin, Jeremy. "Viewpoint: The Stroke of a Pen." *Regulation* 5 (May-June 1981): 15–18.

1289. "Regulation and Deregulation: Does It Pay and How Much Does It Cost?" *Journal of Contemporary Business* 9 (1980): 1–171.

1290. Rose, J. C. "Economic Planning vs. Economic Deregulation." *Conference Board Record* 13 (April 1976): 18–21.

1291. Salkin, Michael S., and Van Dyke, Daniel T. "Toward Deregulation: Another Step." *Mortgage Banking* 43 (1983): 11–16.

1292. Samuels, Warren J., and Shaffer, James D. "Deregulation: The Principal Inconclusive Arguments." *Policy Studies Review* 1 (1982): 463–69.

1293. Smith, Frances B. "Deregulation: An Overview of What's Been Happening." *Credit* 9 (November-December 1983): 10–13.

1294. Smith, Paul F. "Deregulation in Perspective." *Business Forum* 8 (Summer 1983): 14–19.

1295. Thoryn, M. "Delights of Deregulation." *Nation's Business* 69 (November 1981): 46–48.

1296. Tullock, Gordon. "Achieving Deregulation—A Public Choice Perspective." *Regulation* 2 (November-December 1978): 50–54.

1297. Vander Weide, J. H., and Zalkind, J. H. "Deregulation and Oligopolistic Price-Quality Rivalry." *American Economic Review* 71 (March 1981): 144–54.

1298. Waters, L. L. "Deregulation for Better, or for Worse?" *Business Horizons* 17 (January-February 1981): 88–91.

1299. Weidenbaum, Murray L. "Regulation: How Washington Will Switch." *Nation's Business* 69 (February 1981): 26–30.

1300. Weiss, Julian. "De-Regulation: A Scorecard on Washington's Record." *May Trends* 16 (1983): 7–10.

1301. Wilson, George W. "Deregulation: How Far Should It Go?" *Indiana Law Journal* 51 (Spring 1976): 700–17.

1302. Wilson, George W. "Regulating and Deregulating Business." *Business Horizons* 25 (July-August 1982): 45–52.

LEGISLATION

1303. Aberbach, Joel D., and Rockman, Bert A. "Bureaucrats and Client Groups: A View from Capitol Hill." *American Journal of Political Science* 22 (November 1978): 818–32.

1304. Adams, Bruce, and Sherman, B. "Sunset Implementation: A Positive Partnership to Make Government Work." *Public Administration Review* 38 (January-February 1978): 78–82.

1305. Adams, Roger C. "The Land Use Policy and Planning Assistance Act of 1973: Legislating a National Land Use Policy." *George Washington Law Review* 41 (March 1973): 604–25.

1306. Alexander, Thomas G. "Teapot Dome Revisited: Reed Smoot and Conservation in the 1920s." *Utah Historical Quarterly* 45 (Fall 1977): 352–68.

1307. Austern, H. Thomas. "Congressional and Legal/Regulatory Developments under the Federal Food, Drug, and Cosmetic Act." *Food Drug Cosmetic Law Journal* 29 (December 1974): 588–95.

1308. Bardach, Eugene. "Policy Termination as a Political Process." *Policy Sciences* 7 (June 1976): 123–31.

1309. Barker, Joel. "The Arkansas Law on Obscenity and *Gent v. Arkansas*." *Arkansas Historical Quarterly* 29 (Spring 1970): 48–65.

1310. Benson, Lucy W. "Turning the Supertanker: Arms Transfer Restraint." *International Security* 3 (Spring 1979): 3–17.

1311. Berns, Walter. "On Pornography: Pornography vs. Democracy: The Case for Censorship." *Public Interest* 22 (Winter 1971): 3–24.

1312. Brown, D. Clayton. "Sam Rayburn and the Development of Public Power in the Southwest." *Southwestern Historical Quarterly* 78 (October 1974): 140–54.

1313. Bruff, Harold H., and Gellhorn, E. "Congressional Control of Administrative Regulation: A Study of Legislative Vetoes." *Harvard Law Review* 90 (May 1977): 1369–440.

1314. Burke, Albie. "Federal Regulation of Congressional Elections in Northern Cities, 1871–1894." Ph. D. dissertation, University of Chicago, 1968. 299 p.

1315. Calvert, Randall L., and Weingast, Barry R. "Runaway Bureaucracy and Congressional Oversight: Why Reforms Fail." *Policy Studies Review* 1 (1982): 557–64.

1316. Council of State Governments. *Occupational Licensing Legislation in the States.* Chicago: Council of State Governments, 1952. 106 p.

1317. Crafts, Edward, and Schrer, Susan. "Congressional Liaison in the Forest Service." *Forest History* 16 (October 1972): 12–17.

1318. Dempsey, P. S. "Congressional Intent and Agency Discretion—Never the Twain Shall Meet: The Motor Carrier Act of 1980." *Chicago-Kent Law Review* 58 (Winter 1981): 1–58.

1319. Edwards, Richard. "Economic Sophistication in Nineteenth-Century Congressional Tariff Debates." *Economic History* 30 (December 1970): 802–38.

1320. Ericson, J. E., and McCrocklin, James. "From Religion to Commerce: The Evolution and Enforcement of Blue Laws in Texas." *Social Science Quarterly* 45 (June 1964): 50–58.

1321. Fiorina, Morris P., and Noll, Roger G. "Voters, Bureaucrats and Legislators: A Rational Choice Perspective on the Growth of Bureaucracy." *Journal of Public Economics* 9 (1978): 239–54.

1322. Fishel, Leslie. "The Genesis of the First Wisconsin Civil Rights Act." *Wisconsin Magazine of History* 49 (Summer 1966): 324–33.

1323. Franklin, John H. "The Enforcement of the Civil Rights Act of 1875." *Prologue* 6 (Winter 1974): 225–35.

1324. Freedman, James O. "Legislative Delegation to Regulatory Agencies." *Proceedings of the Academy of Political Science* 34 (1981): 76–89.

1325. Greene, Barbara P. "The Politics of Regulation: Responsiveness and Control." Ph. D. dissertation, Indiana University, 1971. 236 p.

1326. Gregson, R. E. "Sunset in Colorado: The Second Round." *State Government* 53 (Spring 1980): 58–62.

1327. Heisler, Kenneth G. "A New Approach to Supervisory Legislation." *Business Lawyer* 22 (November 1966): 257–64.

1328. Hitt, M. A., et al. "Sunset Legislation and the Measurement of Effectiveness." *Personnel Management* 6 (May 1977): 188–93.

1329. Holbert, Robert L. "The Politics of Lobbying Regulation: The Roles of the Congress, Supreme Court, and Internal Revenue Service." Ph. D. dissertation, University of Arizona, 1970. 265 p.

1330. Jable, J. Thomas. "The Pennsylvania Sunday Blue Laws of 1779: A View of Pennsylvania Society and Politics during the American Revolution." *Pennsylvania History* 40 (October 1973): 413–26.

1331. Johnson, Arthur T. "Congress and Professional Sports: 1951–1978." *American Academy of Political and Social Science, Annals* 445 (September 1979): 102–15.

1332. Kerstein, Robert, and Judd, Dennis R. "Achieving Less Influence with More Democracy: The Permanent Legacy of the War on Poverty." *Social Science Quarterly* 61 (September 1980): 208–20.

1333. Kopel, G. H. "Sunset in the West." *State Government* 49 (Summer 1976): 135–38.

1334. Kramer, Susan W., and Canner, Glenn B. "The Current Status of Usury Legislation in the United States." *Issues in Bank Regulation* 6 (Summer 1982): 11–23.

1335. Lane, Edgar. "Statutory Regulation of Lobbying in the United States, with Special Reference to the Federal Regulation of Lobbying Act of 1946." Ph. D. dissertation, University of Michigan, 1949. 355 p.

1336. Levin, Arthur. "The Search for New Forms of Control." *Proceedings of the Academy of Political Science* 33 (1980): 1–5.

1337. March, Michael S. "Colorado's Sunset Review 1976–1981: An Experiment in State Regulatory Reform." *Policy Studies Review* 1 (1981): 491–502.

1338. McArdle, Richard E., and Maunder, Elwood R. "Wilderness Politics: Legislation and Forest Service Policy." *Journal of Forest History* 19 (October 1975): 166–79.

1339. Mindlin, Albert, and Duncan, John. "Municipal Fair Housing Legislation: Community Beliefs and Facts." *Phylon* 25 (Fall 1964): 217–37.

1340. Morgan, John A. "Regulation and Legislative Intent." *Proceedings of the Academy of Political Science* 33 (1980): 21–31.

1341. Moss, J. E. "Crisis of Corporate Accountability: A Legislator's View." *Journal of Corporate Law* 3 (Winter 1978): 251–65.

1342. Muskie, Edmund. "The Role of Congress in Promoting and Controlling Technological Advance." *George Washington Law Review* 36 (July 1968): 1138–49.

1343. Noll, Roger G. *The Political Economy of Deregulation: Interest Groups in the Regulatory Process.* Washington, DC: American Enterprise Institute for Public Policy Research, 1983. 164 p.

1344. Ogul, Morris S. *Congress Oversees the Bureaucracy: Studies in Legislative Supervision.* Pittsburgh, PA: University of Pittsburgh Press, 1976. 237 p.

1345. Place, J. B. M. "Special Interests: Democracy or Disaster?" *Journal of Commercial Bank Lending* 62 (July 1980): 17–24.

1346. Pursell, Carroll. "A Preface to Government Support of Research and Development: Research Legislation and the National Bureau of Standards, 1935–1941." *Technology and Culture* 9 (April 1968): 145–64.

1347. Ribicoff, A. A. "Ribicoff's Way with Regulations." *Across the Board* 17 (August 1980): 73–77.

1348. Richins, William D. "Economic Pressure Groups and Governmental Marketing Regulation in the Pacific Northwest." Ph. D. dissertation, University of Washington, 1950.

1349. Salomon, Kenneth D., and Wechsler, Lawrence H. "The Freedom of Information Act: A Critical Review." *George Washington Law Review* 38 (October 1969): 150–63.

1350. Scalia, Antonin. "The Freedom of Information Act Has No Clothes." *Regulation* 6 (March-April 1982): 14–19.

1351. Scalia, Antonin. "The Legislative Veto: A False Remedy for System Overload." *Regulation* 3 (November-December 1979): 19–26.

1352. Scher, Seymour. "Conditions for Legislative Control." *Journal of Politics* 25 (August 1963): 526–51.

1353. Scher, Seymour. "Congressional Committee Members as Independent Agency Overseers: A Case Study." *American Political Science Review* 54 (December 1960): 911–20.

1354. Schuck, Peter H. "The Graying of Civil Rights Law." *Public Interest* 60 (Summer 1980): 69–93.

1355. Scott, Andrew M., and Hall, M. *Congress and Lobbies: Image and Reality.* Chapel Hill, NC: University of North Carolina Press, 1960. 106 p.

1356. Sheridan, J. H. "Can Congress Control the Regulators?" *Industry Week* 188 (March 1976): 20–27.

1357. Shimberg, Benjamin. "Sunset Approach: The Key to Regulatory Reform?" *State Government* 49 (Summer 1976): 140–47.

1358. Simpson, Murray L. "1(b) or Not 1(b),. . . ?: Recognition of Legislative Intent in Judicial Interpretation of Investment Company Act of 1940." *George Washington Law Review* 40 (July 1972): 890–917.

1359. Slawson, W. David. "Standard Form Contracts and Democratic Control of Lawmaking Power." *Harvard Law Review* 84 (January 1971): 529–66.

1360. Steele, Henry. "Economic Reform Legislation: Drug Amendments Act of 1962." *American Journal of Economics and Sociology* 25 (January 1966): 39–52.

1361. Surrey, Stanley S. "The Congress and Tax Lobbyist—How Special Tax Provisions Get Enacted." *Harvard Law Review* 70 (May 1957): 1145–82.

1362. United States. General Accounting Office. *Evaluating a Performance Measurement System: A Guide for the Congress and Federal Agencies.* Washington, DC: U. S. General Accounting Office, 1980. 24 p.

1363. Vinyard, Dale. "The Congressional Committees on Small Business: Pattern of Legislative Committee-Executive Agency Relations." *Western Political Quarterly* 21 (September 1968): 391–99.

1364. Viscusi, W. Kip. "Presidential Oversight: Controlling the Regulators." *Journal of Policy Analysis and Management* 2 (Winter 1983): 157–73.

1365. Weaver, Valeria W. "The Failure of Civil Rights 1875–1883 and Its Repercussions." *Journal of Negro History* 54 (October 1969): 368–82.

1366. Weingast, Barry R. "A Representative Legislature and Regulatory Agency Capture." Ph. D. dissertation, California Institute of Technology, 1978. 191 p.

1367. Williams, Harold S. "The Effects on Competition of Federal Legislation Regulating Business." Ph. D. dissertation, University of Iowa, 1948.

1368. Woelfl, Paul A. "Federal Regulation of Political Activity." Ph. D. dissertation, St. Louis University, 1950. 227 p.

1369. Wyatt-Brown, Bertram. "The Civil Rights Act of 1875." *Western Political Quarterly* 18 (December 1965): 763–75.

REFORM

1370. Abrams, Richard, ed. *The Issue of Federal Regulation in the Progressive Era.* Chicago: Rand McNally, 1963. 58 p.

1371. American Enterprise Institute for Public Policy Research. *Government Regulation: Proposals for Procedural Reform, 1979, 96th Congress, 1st Session.* Washington, DC: American Enterprise Institute, 1979. 56 p.

1372. "An Implementation Problem in Institutional Reform Litigation." *Harvard Law Review* 91 (December 1977): 428–63.

1373. Aranson, Peter H. *The Uncertain Search for Regulatory Reform.* Coral Gables, FL: University of Miami Law and Economics Center, 1979. 23 p.

1374. Aron, Joan B. "Citizen Participation at Government Expense." *Public Administration Review* 39 (September 1979): 477–85.

1375. Aug, S. M. "How the Regulators Are Trying to Reform." *Nation's Business* 64 (August 1976): 16–20.

1376. Backoff, Robert W. "Operationalizing Administrative Reform for Improved Governmental Performance." *Administration and Society* 6 (May 1974): 73–106.

1377. Barton, S. E. "Property Rights and Human Rights: Efficiency and Democracy as Criteria for Regulatory Reform. "*Journal of Economic Issues* 17 (December 1983): 915–30.

1378. Battistoni, Gary R. "The Possibility of Recovery of Attorney's Fees by Successful Private Defendants in Federal Regulatory Actions." *Harvard Journal of Law and Public Policy* 3 (1980): 191–226.

1379. Bernstein, Marver H. "Independent Regulatory Agencies: A Perspective on Their Reform." *American Academy of Political and Social Science, Annals* 400 (March 1972): 14–26.

1380. Berry, Jeffrey M. "Citizen Groups and Alternative Approaches to Regulatory Reform." *Policy Studies Review* 1 (1982): 503–09.

1381. Brown, Clarence J. "A More Demanding Standard: The Brown-Bentsen Bills." *Regulation* 3 (May-June 1979): 20–23.

1382. Brown, David S. *The Public Advisory Board and the Tariff Study.* Indianapolis, IN: Bobbs-Merrill, 1956. 47 p.

1383. Buchholz, R. "Reducing the Cost of Paperwork." *Business Horizons* 23 (February 1980): 82–89.

1384. Butler, S., and Kane, R. P. "Improper Corporate Payments: The Second Half of Watergate." *Loyola University Law Journal* (Chicago) 8 (Fall 1976): 1–50.

1385. Caiden, Gerald E. "Administrative Reform: A View from the Field." *Policy Studies Journal* 8 (Winter 1979): 456–62.

1386. Campbell, T. C. "Should Regulatory Commissions Be Abolished, Modified, or Retained?" *Public Utilities Fortnightly* 92 (July 19, 1973): 17–23.

1387. Casbolt, G. "Reform of Regulation Still Being Proposed." *Public Utilities Fortnightly* 97 (February 1976): 14–16.

1388. Cassity, M. J. "Huey Long: Barometer of Reform in the New Deal." *Southern Atlantic Quarterly* 72 (Spring 1973): 255–69.

1389. Chandler, L. B., and Jaffee, D. M. "Regulating the Regulators: A Review of the FINE Regulatory Reforms." *Journal of Money, Credit and Banking* 9 (November 1977): 619–35.

1390. Clark, Timothy B. "It's Still No Bureaucratic Revolution, But Regulatory Reform Has a Foothold." *Naitonal Journal* 11 (1979): 1596–601.

1391. Dearstyne, Bruce W. "Regulation in the Progressive Era: The New York Public Service Commission." *New York History* 58 (July 1977): 331–47.

1392. DeMuth, Christopher C. "A Strategy for Regulatory Reform." *Regulation* 8 (March-April 1984): 25–29.

1393. Friedman, Milton, and Spector, Michael. "Tenement House Legislation in Wisconsin: Reform and Reaction." *American Journal of Legal History* 9 (January 1965): 41–63.

1394. Gellhorn, Ernest. "Reform as Totem—A Skeptical View." *Regulation* 3 (May-June 1979): 23–26.

1395. Goldberg, S. C. "Facilitating Discovery in Civil Securities Actions: The 1975 Amendments to the Freedom of Information Act of 1966." *New York Law Forum* 21 (Fall 1975): 277–89.

1396. Goldstein, B. "Screwing of the Average Man—Chapter XII: It's the Little Things That Count." *Washington Monthly* 11 (July-August 1979): 27–30.

1397. *Government Regulation: What Kind of Reform?: A Round Table Held on 11 September 1975 and Sponsored by the American Enterprise Institute for Public Policy Research and the Hoover Institution on War, Revolution and Peace.* Washington, DC: American Enterprise Institute for Public Policy Research, 1976. 60 p.

1398. Granat, Diane. "Government Operations: Scope of Regulatory Reform Bills Differ." *Congressional Quarterly Weekly Report* 40 (April 3, 1982): 740–42.

1399. Greenwald, C. S. "Who's Regulating the Regulators?" *Bankers Magazine* 164 (March-April 1981): 39–43.

1400. Halpern, Paul J. "The Corvair, the Pinto and Corporate Behavior: Implications for Regulatory Reform." *Policy Studies Review* 1 (1982): 540–45.

1401. Harris, O. "Improving the Regulatory Process." *Public Utilities Fortnightly* 64 (July 2, 1959): 19–26.

1402. Heim, G. F. "Regulatory Commissions of the Future: Fact or Fiction?" *Public Utilities Fortnightly* 78 (November 10, 1966): 32–36.

1403. Hershman, A. "Regulating the Regulators." *Dun's Review* 109 (January 1977): 34–36.

1404. "In the Public Interest: How to Regulate the Regulators." *Management Review* 66 (May 1977): 13–19.

1405. "Independence for Regulatory Agencies." *Public Utilities Fortnightly* 84 (August 14, 1969): 44–47.

1406. Jaffe, Louis L. "James Landis and the Administrative Process." *Harvard Law Review* 78 (1964): 319–28.

1407. Kangun, N., and Moyer, R. C. "Failings of Regulation." *Michigan State University Business Topics* 24 (Spring 1976): 5–14.

1408. Kaufman, Herbert. "All of Us Produce Red Tape." *Across the Board* 15 (September 1978): 29–34.

1409. Kirkpatrick, Jeane. "Viewpoint: Regulation, Liberty, and Equality." *Regulation* 1 (November-December 1977): 11–15.

1410. Klingaman, Murray O. "Administrative Reorganization in New York State Government: A Study of the Temporary State Commission on Coordination of State Activities." Ph. D. dissertation, New York University, 1967. 256 p.

1411. Lawrence, G. H., and Muchow, D. J. "Regulatory Reform: Maybe a Pill with Nothing But Side Effects." *Public Utilities Fortnightly* 105 (March 1980): 13–20.

1412. Litan, Robert E., and Nordhaus, William D. *Reforming Federal Regulation.* New Haven, CT: Yale University Press, 1983. 204 p.

1413. McKeage, Everett C. "Folklore of Regulation." *Public Utilities Fortnightly* 67 (March 1961): 361–68.

1414. Monaghan, J. R. "Regulatory Agencies under Fire." *Public Utilities Fortnightly* 84 (October 9, 1969): 36–38.

1415. Murphy, M. E. "Payoffs to Foreign Officials: Time for More National Responsibility." *American Bar Association Journal* 62 (April 1976): 480–82.

1416. "Music the Universal Healer: First Amendment Protection—Real or Illusory?" *North Carolina Central Law Journal* 7 (Spring 1976): 329–46.

1417. Neustadt, Richard M. "Taming the Paperwork Tiger." *Regulation* 5 (January-February 1981): 28–32.

1418. Noll, Roger G., and Owen, Bruce M. "What Makes Reform Happen?" *Regulation* 7 (March-April 1983): 19–24.

1419. Olson, Walter. "Where's the Reform?" *Regulation* 8 (March-April 1984): 30–32.

1420. Percy, C. H. "Prescription for Curing Our Regulatory Ills." *Nation's Business* 64 (December 1976): 25–28.

1421. Pertschuk, Michael. "Regulatory Reform through the Looking Glass." *American Bar Association Journal* 65 (April 1979): 556–60.

1422. "Regulatory Paperwork: A Company Assesses Its Costs in Time and Money." *Management Review* 68 (July 1979): 46–47.

1423. "Regulatory Reform." *Public Utilities Fortnightly* 65 (April 28, 1960): 609–12.

1424. Reich, Robert B. "Warring Critiques of Regulation." *Regulation* 3 (January-February 1979): 37–42.

1425. "Reorganizing the Regulatory Commissions." *Public Utilities Fortnightly* 67 (April 1961): 532–35.

1426. Ribicoff, Abe. "For Effectiveness and Efficiency S. 262." *Regulation* 3 (May-June 1979): 17–20.

1427. Richie, D. A. "Reforming the Regulatory Process: Why James Landis Changed His Mind." *Business History Review* 54 (Autumn 1980): 283–302.

1428. Ruckelshaus, W. D. "Government Regulation: Who Leads When the Law Can't Be Followed?" *Industrial Development* 149 (September-October 1980): 2–4.

1429. Scalia, Antonin. "Viewpoint: Regulatory Reform—The Game Has Changed." *Regulation* 5 (January-February 1981): 13–15.

1430. Schofield, W. M. "GAO Reports Limited Success Controlling Regulatory Agencies' Demands for Paperwork from the Public." *Financial Executive* 45 (January 1977): 32–35.

1431. Scholz, John T. "State Regulatory Reform and Federal Regulation." *Policy Studies Review* 1 (1982): 347–60.

1432. Schuck, Peter H. "Why Regulation Fails." *Harper's Magazine* 251 (September 1975): 16–30.

1433. Siedel, G. J. "Internal Accounting Controls under the Foreign Corrupt Practices Act: A Federal Law of Corporations." *American Business Law Journal* 18 (Winter 1981): 443–75.

1434. Swindler, Joseph C. "The Challenge to State Regulation Agencies: The Experience of New York State." *American Academy of Political and Social Science, Annals* 410 (November 1973): 106–19.

1435. Talbert, Roy. "Arthur E. Morgan's Ethical Code for the Tennessee Valley Authority." *East Tennessee Historical Society's Publications* 40 (1968): 119–27.

1436. Talbert, Roy. "Arthur E. Morgan's Social Philosophy and the Tennessee Valley Authority." *East Tennessee Historical Society's Publications* 41 (1969): 86–99.

1437. Thompson, Frederick, and Jones, L. R. "Fighting Regulation: The Regulatory Review." *California Management Life Underwriters* 23 (Winter 1980): 5–19.

1438. Tollison, Robert D. "An Historical Note on Regulatory Reform." *Regulation* 2 (November-December 1978): 46–49.

1439. United States. Office of Management and Budget. *Papers Relating to the President's Departmental Reorganization Program: A Reference Compilation.* Washington, DC: U. S. Government Printing Office, 1971. 288 p.

1440. U. S. President's Advisory Council on Executive Organization. *A New Regulatory Framework: Report on Selected Independent Regulatory Agencies.* Washington, DC: U. S. Government Printing Office, 1971. 198 p.

1441. Wardell, William. "Rx: More Regulation or Better Therapies?" *Regulation* 3 (September-October 1979): 25–33.

1442. Westin, A. F. "What's Wrong with Our Watchdog Agencies?" *Management Review* 49 (December 1960): 33–36.

1443. Willis, E. I. "Federal-State Regulatory Conflicts: There Ought to Be a Law." *Public Utilities Fortnightly* 86 (September 1970): 64–67.

1444. Wilson, James Q., and Rachal, Patricia. "Can the Government Regulate Itself?" *Public Interest* 46 (Winter 1977): 3–14.

1445. Winter, Ralph K. "Viewpoint: The Welfare State and the Decline of Electoral Politics." *Regulation* 2 (March-April 1978): 11–14.

1446. Wood, Lance D. "Restraining the Regulators: Legal Perspectives on a Regulatory Budget for Federal Agencies." *Harvard Journal on Legislation* 11 (Winter 1981): 1–33.

1447. Wynes, Charles E. "The Evolution of Jim Crow Laws in Twentieth Century Virginia." *Phylon* 28 (Winter 1967): 416–25.

RULE MAKING

1448. Alexander, George J. "A New Pragmatism in Robinson-Patman Interpretations?" *Syracuse Law Review* 15 (Spring 1964): 487–505.

1449. Auerbach, Carl A., et al. *The Legal Process: An Introduction to Decision-Making by Judicial, Legislative, Executive, and Administrative Agencies.* Edited by L. K. Garrison. San Francisco, CA: Chandler, 1961. 915 p.

1450. Barton, N. E., and Block, D. J. "Administrative Proceedings to Enforce the Foreign Corrupt Practices Act." *Securities Regulation Law Journal* 7 (Spring 1979): 40–53.

1451. Bell, R. G. "Administrative Law: Rule Making and a 'Hearing': A Tale of Two Cases (Three Rules) or What the Dickens!" *Georgia Law Review* 8 (Fall 1973): 19–75.

1452. Bullock, Charles S., and Regens, James L. "The Courts as a Source of Regulatory Revitalization: External Agenda Setting and Equal Education Programs." *Policy Studies Review* 1 (1982): 565–71.

1453. Byse, Clark. "Suing the 'Wrong' Defendant in Judicial Review of Federal Administrative Action: Proposals for Reform." *Harvard Law Review* 77 (November 1963): 40–60.

1454. Colon, Frank T. "Court and the Commissions: Ex Parte Contacts and the Sangamon Valley Case." *Federal Communication Bar Journal* 19 (1964–65): 67–87.

1455. Colon, Frank T. "Ex Parte Influences in Federal Regulatory Commissions." Ph. D. dissertation, University of Pittsburgh, 1963. 370 p.

1456. DeLong, James V. "Repealing Rules." *Regulation* 7 (May-June 1983): 26–30.

1457. Diplock, Kenneth. "Antitrust and Judicial Process." *Journal of Law and Economics* 7 (October 1964): 27–44.

1458. Dixon, Paul R. "Some Impediments to Policy Making." *Antitrust Law Symposium* 1969 (1969): 21–28.

1459. "The Downstairs Insider: The Specialist and Rule 10b-5." *New York University Law Review* 42 (October 1967): 695–715.

1460. Dunham, Allison. "Due Process and Commercial Law." *Supreme Court Review* (1972): 135–56.

1461. Dunkle, Margaret C. "Title IX: New Rules for an Old Game." *Teachers College Record* 76 (February 1975): 385–99.

1462. Dunlop, John T. "Limits of Legal Compulsion." *Labor Law Journal* 27 (February 1976): 67–74.

1463. Ehrlich, Isaac, and Posner, Richard A. "An Economic Analysis of Legal Rulemaking." *Journal of Legal Studies* 3 (January 1974): 257–86.

1464. Elman, Philip. "A Note on Administrative Adjudication." *Yale Law Journal* 74 (March 1965): 652–56.

1465. Epstein, H. S. "New Directions for Administrative Regulations." *Food Drug Cosmetic Law Journal* 30 (July 1975): 384–95.

1466. Ethridge, Marcus E. "Agency Responses to Citizen Participation Requirements: An Analysis of the Tennessee Experience." *Midwest Review of Public Administration* 14 (June 1980): 95–104.

1467. Ethridge, Marcus E. "Judicialized Procedures in Regulatory Policy Implementation: An Empirical Analysis of Policy Consequences." *Law and Policy Quarterly* 4 (January 1982): 119–38.

1468. "Federal Regulatory Agencies: A Need for Rules of Decision." *Virginia Law Review* 50 (May 1964): 652–743.

1469. Feld, Werner J. "The Court of Justice: The Invisible Arm." *American Academy of Political and Social Science, Annals* 440 (November 1978): 42–53.

1470. Ferrara, R. C. "Administrative Disciplinary Proceedings under Rule 2(e)." *Business Lawyer* 36 (July 1981): 1807–13.

1471. Fine, S. D. "Philosophy of Enforcement." *Food Drug Cosmetic Law Journal* 31 (June 1976): 324–32.

1472. Freyer, Tony A. "Negotiable Instruments and the Federal Courts in Antebellum American Business." *Business History Review* 50 (Winter 1965): 435–55.

1473. Fuchs, Ralph F. "Agency Development of Policy through Rulemaking." *Northwestern University Law Review* 59 (January-February 1965): 781–807.

1474. Funston, Richard. "Pornography and Politics: The Court, the Constitution, and the Commission." *Western Political Quarterly* 24 (December 1971): 635–52.

1475. Gamberoni, Narciso L. "An Analysis of Appellate Court Decisions Determining the Authority of Boards of Education and Their Agents to Establish Rules and Regulations Governing the Conduct of Pupils, 1900–1960." Ed. D. dissertation, University of Pittsburgh, 1961. 167 p.

1476. Gifford, Daniel J. "Decisions, Decisional Referents, and Administrative Justice." In *Administrative Discretion: Problems of Decision-Making by Governmental Agencies*, edited by Clark C. Havighurst, pp. 73–96. Dobbs Ferry, NY: Oceana Publications, 1974.

1477. Gruenbaum, S. H., and Oppenheimer, M. A. "Special Investigative Counsel: Conflicts and Roles." *Rutgers Law Review* 33 (Summer 1981): 865–904.

1478. Grumbly, T. P. "Pre-Regulation Research: The Triumph of Policy Analysis." *American Journal of Agricultural Economics* 61 (November 1979): 775–78.

1479. Hart, R. M., and Kapp, R. W. "Case against Administrative Restraint: Declaratory Status Orders under the Investment Company Act of 1940." *Cornell Law Review* 61 (January 1976): 231–55.

1480. Haynes, John E. "Democracy and the Due Process: The Case of Handicapped Education." *Regulation* 6 (November-December 1982): 29–34.

1481. Hearn, George H. "Administrative Due Process Hearing Requirements and the Federal Maritime Commission." *Duke Law Journal* 1970 (February 1970): 45–66.

1482. Hector, L. J. "Can Regulators Be Judges?" *Public Utilities Fortnightly* 66 (September 1, 1960): 289–96.

1483. Holden, Mathew. "Litigation and the Political Order." *Western Political Quarterly* 16 (December 1963): 771–81.

1484. Howard, A. E. Dick. "The Law: A Litigation Society?" *Wilson Quarterly* 5 (Summer 1981): 98–109.

1485. Jenks, Jeremiah W. "Economic Aspects of the Recent Decisions of the United States Supreme Court on Trusts." *Journal of Political Economy* 20 (April 1912): 346–57.

1486. Johnson, Charles A. "Judicial Decisions and Organizational Change: A Theory." *Administration and Society* 11 (May 1979): 27–51.

1487. Joskow, Paul L. "The Determination of the Allowed Rate of Return in a Formal Regulatory Hearing." *Bell Journal of Economics and Management Science* 3 (Autumn 1972): 632–44.

1488. "Judicial Review of Administrative 'Reason to Believe.' " *William and Mary Law Review* 23 (Fall 1981): 139–64.

1489. "The Jurisprudence of the Foreign Claims Settlement Commission of the United States: Creditor Claims." *Syracuse Law Review* 16 (Summer 1964): 809–44.

1490. Kaus, R. M. "Power to the People: Making the Constitution Work Again." *Washington Monthly* 11 (October 1979): 51–58.

1491. "LaSalle Revisited: The Use of Agency Subpoena Powers in Parallel Civil and Criminal Proceedings." *Seton Hall Law Review* 11 (1981): 716–48.

1492. Lee, L. S. "Coping with Regulatory Agency Records Requirements." *Public Utilities Fortnightly* 99 (April 1977): 55–59.

1493. *Legal Problems of Administrative Practice.* Davis, CA: University of California, School of Law, 1972. 649 p.

1494. Linder, Stephen H. "Policy Formulation in Executive Branch Agencies." Ph. D. dissertation, University of Iowa, 1976. 232 p.

1495. Majone, Giandomenico. "Process and Outcome in Regulatory Decision Making." *American Behavioral Scientist* 22 (May-June 1979): 561–84.

1496. Marchand, Donald A., and Tompkins, Mark E. "Information Management and Use in Public Organizations: Some Impacts on Citizen Participation." *State and Local Government Review* 13 (September 1981): 103–09.

1497. Marquardt, Ronald G., and Wheat, Edward M. "Hidden Allocators: Administrative Law Judges and Regulatory Reform." *Law and Policy Quarterly* 2 (October 1980): 472–94.

1498. Marsh, H. "Rule 2(e) Proceedings." *Business Law* 35 (April 1980): 987–1019.

1499. Martini, D. F. "Recent Agency Rulings and Court Decisions." *Georgetown Law Journal* 36 (May 1948): 612–13.

1500. McFarland, Carl. *Administrative Procedures and the Public Lands.* Charlottesville, VA: University of Virginia, 1969. 390 p.

1501. Minow, Newton N. "Suggestions for Improvement of the Administrative Process." *Administrative Law Review* 15 (Summer 1963): 146–66.

1502. "Modification of Procedural Formality in Agency Rule-Making Determinations: *Long Island v. United States* (318 F Supp 490)." *Indiana Law Journal* 46 (Summer 1971): 506–20.

1503. Moore, John E. "Informal Methods of Administrative Regulation: A Study of Three Federal Programs." Ph. D. dissertation, Princeton University, 1963.

1504. Mosburg, Lewis G. "The Permian Decision—A Study in Group Regulation." *Oklahoma Law Review* 19 (May 1966): 133–49.

1505. Murray, Stephen J. "Right to Hearing and Consideration: A Case Study of the Maritime Administration." *American University Law Review* 17 (June 1968): 466–99.

1506. Musolf, Lloyd D. "Independent Hearing Officers: The California Experiment." *Western Political Quarterly* 14 (March 1961): 195–213.

1507. Nathanson, Nathaniel L. "Report to the Select Committee on Ex Parte Communications in Informal Rule-Making Proceedings." *Administrative Law Review* 30 (Summer 1978): 377–408.

1508. Peck, Cornelius J. "Regulation and Control of Ex Parte Communications with Administrative Agencies." *Harvard Law Review* 76 (December 1962): 233–74.

1509. Pedersen, William F. "Formal Records and Informal Rulemaking." *Yale Law Journal* 85 (1975): 38–88.

1510. Pfeffer, Jeffrey. "Administrative Regulation and Licensing: Social Problem or Solution?" *Social Problems* 21 (April 1974): 468–79.

1511. Pickholz, M. G. "Expanding World of Parallel Proceedings." *Temple Law Quarterly* 53 (1980): 1100–13.

1512. Pickholz, M. G. "Parallel Enforcement Proceedings: Guidelines for the Corporate Lawyer." *Securities Regulation Law Journal* 7 (Summer 1979): 99–118.

1513. Pineda, Julian. "Policy Issues in Federal Contract Compliance: The Executive Order Program and Affirmative Action." Ph. D. dissertation, University of California, Santa Barbara, 1983. 343 p.

1514. Pines, W. L. "Regulatory Letters, Publicity and Recalls." *Food Drug Cosmetic Law Journal* 31 (June 1976): 352–65.

1515. Pollock, S. G. "Cure for Regulatory Lag: Efficient Case Load Management." *Public Utilities Fortnightly* 98 (July 1, 1976): 27–30.

1516. "Proxy Regulation and the Rule-Making Process: The 1954 Amendments (Bayne, Caplin, Emerson, Latcham)." *Virginia Law Review* 40 (May 1954): 387–431.

1517. Rabkin, Jeremy. "Captive of the Court: A Federal Agency in Receivership." *Regulation* 8 (May-June 1984): 16–26.

1518. Rabkin, Jeremy. "Forcing the Enforcers: Judicial Activism and the Politics of Regulatory Enforcement." Ph. D. dissertation, Harvard University, 1983. 442 p.

1519. Reed, O. L. "Must Quasi-Legislators, Like Caesar's Wife, Be above Suspicion? Recall of Rulemakers for Prejudice and Bias." *American Business Law Journal* 19 (Spring 1981): 1–29.

1520. Rees, Grover. "The Fall of the House of Usury: Federalism in the Supreme Court." *Regulation* 7 (May-June 1983): 31–37.

1521. "Right to a Jury Trial in FTCA Section 5(1) Civil Penalty Actions." *Iowa Law Review* 60 (December 1974): 378–94.

1522. Roche, John P. "Entrepreneurial Liberty and the Fourteenth Amendment." *Labor History* 4 (Winter 1963): 3–31.

1523. Rosener, J. B. "Making Bureaucracy Responsive: A Study of the Impact of Citizen Participation and Staff Recommendations on Regulatory Decision Making." *Public Administration Review* 42 (August 1982): 339–45.

1524. Rosener, J. B. "User-Oriented Evaluation: A New Way to View Citizen Participation." *Journal of Applied Behavioral Science* 17 (1981): 583–96.

1525. Rotkin, A. L. "Standard Forms: Legal Documents in Search of an Appropriate Body of Law." *Arizona State Law Journal* 1977 (1977): 599–624.

1526. Scalia, Antonin. "Two Wrongs Make a Right: The Judicialization of Standardless Rulemaking." *Regulation* 1 (July-August 1977): 38–41.

1527. Schmerer, Henry M. "Unreviewability of Emergency Orders of the Federal Aviation Agency—The Concept of Preventive Administrative Proceedings." *University of Miami Law Review* 17 (Spring 1963): 348–70.

1528. Schotland, R. A. "Institutional Disclosure: The Forgotten Stepchild of the Disclosure Family." *Georgetown Law Journal* 66 (June 1978): 1257–70.

1529. Schwartz, D. E., and Weiss, E. J. "Using Disclosure to Activate the Board of Directors." *Law and Contemporary Problems* 41 (Summer 1977): 63–114.

1530. Shapiro, David L., and Shelton, Robert B. "The Application of an Agency Decision-Making Model." *Public Choice* 32 (Winter 1972): 51–65.

1531. Shapiro, Martin. "On Predicting the Future of Administrative Law." *Regulation* 6 (May-June 1982): 18–25.

1532. Sindler, Allan P. "The Court's Three Decisions." *Regulation* 2 (September-October 1978): 15–23.

1533. Solomon, Richard A. "Why Uncle Sam Can't Lose a Case under Section 7 of the Clayton Act." *American Bar Association Journal* 53 (February 1967): 137–42.

1534. Stewart, Charles V. "Self-Conscious Interest and the Democratic Process: The Case of Citizens, Regulatory Agencies, and Federal Courts." *Law and Policy Quarterly* 1 (October 1979): 411–38.

1535. Stewart, Milton D. "The New Regulatory Flexibility Act." *American Bar Association Journal* 57 (January 1981): 66–68.

1536. "Stuffing the Rabbit Back into the Hat: Limited Waiver of the Attorney-Client Privilege in an Administrative Agency Investigation." *University of Pennsylvania Law Review* 130 (May 1982): 1198–228.

1537. Swinney, Everette. "Enforcing the Fifteenth Amendment, 1870–1877." *Journal of Southern History* 28 (May 1962): 202–18.

1538. Swinney, Everette. "*United States v. Powell Clayton*: Use of Federal Enforcement Acts in Arkansas." *Arkansas Historical Quarterly* 26 (Summer 1967): 143–54.

1539. Thomforde, F. H. "Controlling Administrative Sanctions." *Michigan Law Review* 74 (March 1976): 709–58.

1540. Thompson, Frederick, and Jones, L. R. "Reforming Regulatory Decision Making–The Regulatory Budget." *Sloan Management Review* 22 (Winter 1981): 53–61.

1541. Unruh, Jesse M. "The California Ombudsman." *Journal of the Constitutional and Parliamentary Studies* (India) 1 (April-June 1967): 13–20.

1542. Vig, Norman J., and Bruer, Patrick J. "The Courts and Risk Assessment." *Policy Studies Review* 1 (May 1982): 716–27.

1543. Whitehurst, G. William. "Suffocation by Regulation." *Journal of Social and Political Studies* 2 (Spring 1977): 17–24.

1544. Wilmoth, R. "Criminal Prosecutions, Inspections and Section 305 Hearings." *Food Drug Cosmetic Law Journal* 33 (July 1978): 360–68.

1545. Wright, Charles L. "A Note on the Decision Rules of Public Regulatory Agencies." *Public Choice* 31 (Fall 1977): 151–55.

1546. Wright, J. Skelly. "Commentary: Rulemaking and Judicial Review." *Administrative Law Review* 30 (Summer 1978): 461–66.

1547. Young, G. G. "Federal Corporate Law, Federalism, and the Federal Courts." *Law and Contemporary Problems* 41 (Summer 1977): 146–81.

IV. Regulatory Activities

BANKING

1548. Abramson, Victor. "Private Competition and Public Regulation." *National Banking Review* 1 (September 1963): 101–05.

1549. Adams, E. Sherman. "How Public Policies Affect Banking." *Revue Internationale de L'Histoire de la Banque* 8 (1974): 60–71.

1550. Adams, E. Sherman. "S&L's Continue Attack on Deregulation Act." *Professional Builder/Apartment Business* 46 (May 1981): 24–25.

1551. Adams, John A. "Money Market Mutual Funds: Has Glass-Steagall Been Cracked?" *Banking Law Journal* 99 (January 1982): 4–54.

1552. Alhadeff, David A. *Competition and Controls in Banking: A Study of the Regulation of Bank Competition in Italy, France and England.* Berkeley, CA: University of California Press, 1968. 384 p.

1553. Allen, J. Knight, and Smith, Robert H. *Economic Aspects of Federal Regulation of Bank Holding Companies.* Menlo Park, CA: Stanford Institute, 1955.

1554. Anderson, Richard B. "Survey of Executive Attitudes towards Federal Regulations in Banking, Trucking and Airlines." D.B.A. dissertation, United States International University, 1981. 80 p.

1555. "Are You Ready for the Hard Times Ahead?" *ABA Banking Journal* 74 (November 1982): 93–97.

1556. Aspinwall, Richard C. "Anticipating Banking Deregulation." *Journal of Business Strategy* 3 (Spring 1983): 84–86.

1557. Atkinson, Jay M. "A Study of Regulatory Goals and Controls: Firm Size in the Savings and Loan Industry." Ph.D. dissertation, Virginia Polytechnic Institute and State University, 1978. 149 p.

1558. Aug, S. M. "The Financial Revolution." *Nation's Business* 70 (April 1982): 47–50.

1559. Baker, Donald I. "An Antitrust Look at the One-Bank Holding Company Problem." *Economic and Business Bulletin* 22 (Winter 1970): 26–30.

1560. Baker, Donald I. "Competition's Role in the Regulation of Banking." *Bankers Magazine* 154 (Summer 1971): 75–82.

1561. "Bank Deregulation Impasse?" *Dun's Business Month* 123 (February 1984): 9–10.

1562. "Bankers as Brokers." *Business Week* (April 11, 1983): 70–74.

1563. "Banking Deregulation Will Not Be a Cure-All." *Business Week* (July 27, 1981): 28–29.

1564. "Banking Law—Bank Holding Company with Attributes of Traditional Branch Banking Does Not Violate State Branching Restrictions." *Catholic University Law Review* 27 (Winter 1978): 401–18.

1565. "Banking Legislation: What Administration Seeks." *Bankers Monthly* 100 (August 15, 1983): 18–19, 22.

1566. "Banking on Deregulation?" *Regulation* 3 (July–August 1979): 7–8.

1567. Barnard, Doug. "Deregulation 'Has Only Just Begun.'" *Bank Marketing* 15 (June 1983): 21–26.

1568. Barrett, F. "Comptroller's Shift to a Stronger Enforcement Posture: Self-Dealing and Unsound Banking Practices Are the Targets." *Banking Law Journal* 94 (Summer 1977): 725–42.

1569. Basch, Donald L. "Response to Regulatory Change: The Case of Now Accounts in Massachusetts, 1972–75." Ph.D. dissertation, Yale University, 1977. 343 p.

1570. Beebe, Jack H. "Banking Deregulation: How Far? How Fast?" *Commodity Journal* 16 (November–December 1981): 20–21.

1571. Beighley, H. Prescott; Boyd, John H.; and Jacobs, Donald P. "Bank Equities and Investor Risk Perceptions: Some Entailments for Capital Adequacy Regulation." *Journal of Bank Research* 6 (Autumn 1975): 190–201.

1572. Benson, Bruce L. "A Theoretical Analysis of Regulatory Policy: Bank Mergers and Holding Company Acquisitions." Ph.D. dissertation, Texas A&M University, 1978. 538 p.

1573. Berger, Frederick E. "The Emerging Transformation of the US Banking System." *Banker* 131 (September 1981): 25–26.

1574. Berger, Frederick E. "US Banking Regulations: On the Brink of Sweeping Reversals." *American Import/Export Management* 96 (January 1982): 80–82.

1575. Berle, Adolf A. "Banking under the Antitrust Laws." *Columbia Law Review* 49 (May 1949): 589–600.

1576. Betz, George Wesley. "Member Bank Borrowing from the Reserve Bank: A Micro-Analytic Analysis." Ph.D. dissertation, University of Wisconsin, 1967. 63 p.

1577. Billington, Wilbur T. "Bank Deregulation and Concentration—What Policy for Mergers?" *Economic Review* (Federal Reserve Bank of Kansas City) 68 (November 1983): 3–6.

1578. Bolton, P. "Trust Officers Divided over Deregulation." *Trusts and Estates* 123 (January 1984): 16–17.

1579. Booth, James R. "The Effect of Regulation Q on the Commercial Loan Market: Estimates of a Structural Model under Conditions of Disequilibrium." Ph.D. dissertation, University of Alabama, 1981. 251 p.

1580. Bradford, Frederick A. "Proposed National Banking Legislation." *American Economic Review* 20 (September 1930): 400–25.

1581. Brown, M. V. "Prospects for Banking Reform (FINE STUDY)." *Financial Analysts Journal* 32 (March 1976): 14–18.

1582. Browne, D. G. "Development and Practical Application of the Adjustable Rate Mortgage Loan: The Federal Home Loan Mortgage Corporation's Adjustable Rate Mortgage Loan Purchase Program and Mortgage Loan Instruments." *Missouri Law Review* 47 (Spring 1982): 179–224.

1583. Buckley, John M. "The Federal Home Loan Bank Board." *Federal Home Loan Bank Board Journal* 15 (June 1982): 4–15.

1584. Bursey, Barry. "It's Due Time: Federal Preemption of Due-on-Sale Controversies." *Arizona Law Review* 24 (Spring 1982): 371–89.

1585. Bush, V. "Richard Pratt: Overseeing the Restructuring of the Savings and Loan Business." *Savings and Loan News* 102 (June 1981): 60–62.

1586. Busher, S. A., et al. "Federal Deposit Insurance, Regulatory Policy, and Optimal Bank Capital." *Journal of Finance* 36 (March 1981): 51–60.

1587. Butcher, Willard C. "Unshackle the Banks!" *Chief Executive* (Spring 1982): 10–13.

1588. "Can Credit Unions Buck Competition from Deregulation." *New England Business* 4 (February 15, 1982): 34–36.

1589. Canner, G. "Community Reinvestment Act: A Second Progress Report." *Federal Reserve Bulletin* 67 (November 1981): 813–23.

1590. Carey, Roberta G. "Evaluation under the Bank Merger Act of the Competitive Factors Involved in Bank Mergers: The Regulatory Agencies Compared." *Journal of Monetary Economics* 1 (July 1975): 275–308.

1591. Carfang, Anthony J. "What Bank Deregulation Will Cost Treasures." *Cash Flow* 3 (June 1982): 28–31.

1592. Carosso, Vincent. "Washington and Wall Street: The New Deal and Investment Bankers, 1933–1940." *Business History Review* 44 (Winter 1970): 425–45.

1593. Carson, Deane C., and Motter, David. "Bank Entry and the Public Interest." *National Banking Review* 1 (June 1964): 469–512.

1594. Carter, William A. "Commercial Banking and the Antitrust Laws." *Antitrust Bulletin* 1 (January–April 1966): 144–80.

1595. Chase, Anthony G. "Emerging Financial Conglomerate: Liberalization of the Bank Holding Company Act." *Georgetown Law Journal* 60 (May 1972): 1225–51.

1596. Chase, Kristine L. "Interest Rate Deregulation, Branching, and Competition in the Savings and Loan Industry." *Federal Home Loan Bank Board Journal* 14 (November 1981): 2–6.

1597. Chase, Samuel B. "Financial Structure and Regulation: Some Knotty Problems." *Journal of Finance* 26 (May 1971): 585–97.

1598. Chase, Samuel B., and Mingo, John J. "The Regulation of Bank Holding Companies." *Journal of Finance* 30 (May 1975): 281–92.

1599. Clayton, Ronnie J., and Dubinsky, Alan J. "Executive Views of Deregulation: The Depository Institutions Deregulation and Monetary Control Act of 1980." *Journal of Retail Banking* 5 (Spring 1983): 52–59.

1600. Climo, Beth L., and Evans, Robert B. "Interest Rate Deregulation." *Business Lawyer* 37 (July 1982): 1381–89.

1601. Coats, Warren L. "Regulation D and the Vault Cash Game." *Journal of Finance* 28 (June 1973): 601–07.

1602. Coats, Warren L. "The September 1968 Changes in 'Regulation D' and Their Implications for Money Supply Control." Ph.D. dissertation, University of Chicago, 1972.

1603. Cobb, Joe. "Deregulation of Banking: How Far, How Fast?" *Journal of Retail Banking* 3 (September 1981): 39–45.

1604. Cocheo, Steve. "Complete Rate Freedom May Be Coming for Federal Credit Unions." *ABA Banking Journal* 74 (March 1982): 72–74.

1605. Cocheo, Steve. "For FDIC's Isaac, Thrifts Are Priority 1 But Deregulation Is Next." *ABA Banking Journal* 74 (July 1982): 41–45.

1606. Cocheo, Steve. "Home Loan Bank Board Chairman Pratt Tells What's on His Mind." *ABA Banking Journal* 74 (April 1982): 134–36.

1607. Cohan, Sandra B. "A Look at the Regulation of Interest Rate Ceilings on Time and Savings Deposits." *Magazine of Bank Administration* 49 (March 1973): 24–27.

1608. Cohen, Kalman J., and Reid, Samuel R. "Effects of Regulation, Branching, and Mergers on Banking Performance and Structure." *Southern Economic Journal* 34 (October 1967): 231–49.

1609. Coletta, Paolo E. "William Jennings Bryan and Currency and Banking Reform." *Nebraska History* 45 (March 1964): 31–58.

1610. Colton, Raymond R. "Regulation of New York Savings Bank and Trust Investments in Gas and Electric Corporation Securities, 1928–1950." Ph.D. dissertation, Columbia University, 1952. 373 p.

1611. "Commercial Bank Mergers: The Case for Procedural and Substantive Deregulation." *Harvard Law Review* 95 (June 1982): 1914–34.

1612. Congressional Quarterly. "Banking Deregulation." In *Regulation: Process and Politics,* pp. 99–103. Washington, DC: Congressional Quarterly, 1982.

1613. Cooke, W. P. "Banking Regulation, Profits and Capital Generation." *The Banker* 131 (August 1981): 21–33.

1614. Cox, Albert H. "Regulation of Interest on Deposits: An Historical Review." *Journal of Finance* 22 (May 1967): 274–99.

1615. Crew, A. C. "Supervision of Savings Institutions: A Review and Evaluation." *Federal Home Loan Bank Board Journal* 9 (September 1976): 19–21.

1616. Crooks, J. H. "Automated Investment Services: The Impact of Possible Glass-Steagall Revisions." *Trusts and Estates* 121 (June 1982): 23–25.

1617. Crowne, F. J. "Industry Reporting Requirements—Benefit or Burden?" *Federal Home Loan Bank Board Journal* 10 (March 1977): 7–12.

1618. Crum, Lawrence L. "Federal Regulation of Bank Holding Companies." Ph.D. dissertation, University of Texas, 1961. 376 p.

1619. "The CU System Is a Conglomerate Too." *Credit Union Magazine* 48 (September 1982): 13–14.

1620. Darnell, Jerome C. "Bank Holding Companies and Competition: The First National Bancorporation Case." *Banking Law Journal* 89 (April 1972): 291–317.

1621. Davis, Archie K. "Banking Regulation Today: A Banker's View." *Law and Contemporary Problems* 31 (Autumn 1966): 639–47.

1622. Davis, Blaine E. "The Impact of Regulation on Capital Budgeting in Public Utilities as a Problem in Optimal Control." Ed.D. dissertation, Johns Hopkins University, 1969. 109 p.

1623. "Decision/Removal of Institution from Membership: United States of America before the Federal Home Loan Bank Board." *Federal Home Loan Bank Board Journal* 15 (January 1982): 37–43.

1624. "Deregulation: Coping with the Unexpected." *Credit Union Magazine* 49 (February 1983): 46–50.

1625. "Deregulation: Implications for Agricultural Banking and the Economy." *Bank News* 81 (October 15, 1981): 15–16.

1626. Dezember, Rayburn S. "Bankers' Views on Regulatory Changes." *Issues in Bank Regulation* 7 (Autumn 1983): 3–6.

1627. Dhaliwal, D. S. "Disclosure Regulations and the Cost of Capital." *Southern Economic Journal* 45 (January 1949): 785–94.

1628. Dince, Robert R. "Deregulation and the Examiner: A Commentary and an Interview." *Issues in Bank Regulation* 7 (Summer 1983): 3–10.

1629. Dixon, George H. "The Right Approach to Regulating a Banking System." *Treasury Papers* 1 (April 1976): 6–7.

1630. Donoghue, William E. "Banking Deregulation and You." *Wealthbuilding* 5 (November 1983): 7–12, 14.

1631. Donoghue, William E. "The Deregulation Derby at Half-Time." *Trusts and Estates* 122 (September 1983): 45–48.

1632. Dorset, David C. "Bank Mergers and Holding Companies and the Public Interest." *Banking Law Journal* 80 (September 1963): 755–79.

1633. Downs, Anthony. "Financial Deregulation Has Impact on Real Estate." *National Real Estate Investor* 25 (December 1983): 30–34, 38.

1634. Draper, Malcolm. "Strategies for Assisting the Thrift Industry to Creatively Cope with the Rapidly Changing Financial Environment." *Federal Home Loan Bank Board Journal* 14 (December 1981): 8–10.

1635. Ebaugh, D. D. "Interpretation of the Bank Holding Company Leasing Regulation." *Banking Law Journal* 92 (November–December 1975): 1053–72.

1636. Edwards, Franklin R. "Bank Mergers and the Public Interest: A Legal and Economic Analysis of the 1966 Bank Merger Act." *Banking Law Journal* 85 (September 1968): 753–96.

1637. Edwards, Franklin R. "Economics of 'Tying' Arrangements: Some Proposed Guidelines for Bank Holding Company Regulation." *Antitrust Law and Economics Review* 6 (1973): 87–110.

1638. Edwards, J. "The 80/20 Rule under Deregulation." *Bank Marketing* 15 (February 1983): 22–25.

1639. Edwards, Linda N., and Edwards, Franklin R. "Measuring the Effectiveness of Regulation: The Case Study of Bank Entry Regulation." *Journal of Law and Economics* 17 (October 1974): 445–60.

1640. Edwards, Raoul D. "Banking and Commerce—Separate No Longer?" *United States Banker* 94 (June 1983): 40–46, 59.

1641. Edwards, Raoul D., and Fenimore, Watson. "Breaching Glass-Steagall: A Status Report." *United States Banker* 93 (September 1982): 18–23, 41.

1642. Eisenbeis, Robert A. "Differences in Federal Regulatory Agencies' Bank Merger Policies." *Journal of Money, Credit, and Banking* 7 (February 1975): 93–104.

1643. Eisenbeis, Robert A. "Regulation and Deregulation of Banking." *Bankers Magazine* 164 (March–April 1981): 25–33.

1644. Elston, Frank Arthur. "Nonmember Banks, Reserves, and Monetary Control." Ph.D. dissertation, University of Virginia, 1979.

1645. "Emerging Problems in the Bank Regulatory Structure." *Magazine of Bank Administration* 49 (May 1973): 46–48.

1646. England, Catherine, and Palffy, John. "An Optimistic Scenario for Small Banks." *Business Forum* 8 (Summer 1983): 25–27.

1647. Evans, Joel R. "Regulation of Bank Securities Activities." *Banking Law Journal* 91 (August 1974): 611–23.

1648. Falco, James F. "Section 7 of the Clayton Act and 'Control' in Bank Holding Company Regulation." *Antitrust Bulletin* 18 (Winter 1973): 715–41.

1649. Fand, David I. "Financial Regulation and the Allocative Efficiency of Our Capital Markets." *National Banking Review* 3 (September 1965): 55–63.

1650. "Federal Legislative and Regulatory Treatment of NOW Accounts." *Banking Law Journal* 91 (May 1974): 439–57.

1651. Fellows, J. A., and Beard, T. R. "Some Welfare Implications of Legal Restrictions on Commercial Bank Entry." *Journal of Bank Research* 11 (Autumn 1980): 159–68.

1652. Fishbaugh, C. W. "In Defense of Regulation Q." *Bankers Magazine* 154 (Autumn 1971): 22–26.

1653. Fisher, Clyde O. "Federal Control of Commercial Banking: A Proposal." *Journal of Political Economy* 35 (June 1927): 417–21.

1654. Flannery, Mark J. "Removing Deposit Rate Ceilings: How Will Bank Profits Fare?" *Business Review* (Federal Reserve Bank of Philadelphia) (March–April 1983): 13–20.

1655. "Flexible Fund Annuity: VALIC Revisited." *University of Pennsylvania Law Review* 115 (February 1967): 600–23.

1656. Fortune, P. "Effect of FHLB Bond Operations on Savings Inflows at Savings and Loan Associations: Comment." *Journal of Finance* 31 (June 1976): 963–72.

1657. Foust, James D. "U.S. Bankers vs. the Department of Justice: The 1966 Amendment to the Bank Merger Act, Banking Structure, and Regulation." *Revue Internationale de L'Histoire de la Banque* 9 (1974): 80–106.

1658. Fox, Guy H. "Regulation of Banking by the Comptroller of the Currency." Ph.D. dissertation, University of Texas, 1949. 200 p.

1659. Franz, Laurence W. "An Empirical Analysis of the Effectiveness of 'Operation Twist' and Changes in Regulation Q on the Yield Differential." Ph.D. dissertation, State University of New York, 1968. 132 p.

1660. Fraser, Donald R. "Deregulation and Depository Institutions." *Bankers Magazine* 166 (January–February 1983): 34–39.

1661. Fraser, Donald R. "The Future of Depository Institutions." *Texas Business Executive* 9 (Summer 1983): 16–20, 40.

1662. Fraser, Donald R., and Rose, Peter S. "Holding Company Expansion: When the Fed Says No." *Magazine of Bank Administration* 49 (December 1973): 36–40, 44.

1663. Friedman, Benjamin M. "Regulation Q and the Commercial Loan Market in the 1960s." *Journal of Money, Credit, and Banking* 7 (August 1975): 277–96.

1664. Frodin, Joanna H. "Electronics: The Key to Breaking the Interstate Banking Barrier." *Federal Reserve Philadelphia Business Review* (September–October 1982): 3–11.

1665. Furlong, Frederick T. "Banking Structure and the Theory of Economic Regulation." Ph.D. dissertation, University of California, Los Angeles, 1978. 134 p.

1666. Gardener, E. P. M. "Capital Adequacy and Banking Supervision—Towards a Practical System." *Journal of Bank Research* 13 (Summer 1982): 125–36.

1667. Gatell, Frank, "Secretary Taney and the Baltimore Pets: A Study in Banking and Politics." *Business History Review* 39 (Summer 1965): 205–27.

1668. Gaynor, R. L. "Trend in US Regulation of Foreign Banks." *The Banker* 131 (February 1981): 99–100.

1669. Geary, A. J. "Equal Credit Opportunity—An Analysis of Regulation B." *Business Lawyer* 31 (April 1976): 1641–58.

1670. Gebhardt, Lawrence. "Supremacy of the Bankruptcy Act: The New Standard of *Perez v. Campbell." George Washington Law Review* 40 (May 1972): 764–77.

1671. Gies, Thomas G. "Portfolio Regulations of Selected Financial Intermediaries: Some Proposals for Change." *Journal of Finance* 17 (May 1962): 302–10.

1672. Gilbert, Gary G. "An Analysis of Federal Regulatory Decisions on Market Extension Bank Mergers." *Journal of Money, Credit, and Banking* 7 (February 1975): 81–92.

1673. Gilbert, Gary G., and Peterson, Manfred. "Uniform Reserve Requirements on Demand Deposits: Some Policy Issues." *Journal of Bank Research* 5 (Spring 1974): 38–44.

1674. Godfrey. John M. "Deregulation: The Attack on Geographic Barriers." Federal Reserve Atlanta. *Economic Review* 66 (February 1981): 17–21.

1675. Golden, Joseph C. "Regulation Commercial Banking under the Bank Merger and Bank Holding Company Acts: As Amended." *Tennessee Law Review* 36 (Summer 1969): 706–27.

1676. Golembe, Carter H. "The Future Shape of Banking Regulation." *Journal of Finance* 26 (May 1971): 599–604.

1677. Goodman, Oscar R. "Antitrust and Competitive Issues in U.S. Banking Structure." *Journal of Finance* 26 (May 1971): 615–46, 650–51.

1678. Gorinson, Stanley M. "Depository Institution Regulatory Reform in the 1980's: The Issue of Geographic Restrictions." *Antitrust Bulletin* 28 (Spring 1983): 227–54.

1679. Grant, Philip. "The Bank Controversy and Connecticut Politics, 1834." *Connecticut Historical Society Bulletin* 33 (July 1968): 90–96.

1680. Grant, Philip. "The Bank Controversy and New Hampshire Politics, 1834–1835." *Historical New Hampshire* 23 (Autumn 1968): 19–33.

1681. Green, Andrew W. "Recommended Changes in Banking Regulation and Monetary Control Laws." *Bankers Magazine* 165 (November–December 1982): 42–46.

1682. Green, George D. "The Louisiana Bank Act of 1842: Policy Making during Financial Crisis." *Explorations in Economic History* 7 (Summer 1970): 399–412.

1683. Greenbaum, S. I., and Ali, M. M. "Entry, Control and the Market for Bank Charters." *Journal of Finance* 29 (May 1974): 525–35.

1684. Geguras, F., and Einhorn, T. "Regulatory Impact of Self-Service Banking." *Issues in Bank Regulation* 6 (Summer 1982): 3–10.

1685. Grunewald, A. E., and Wein, H. "Establishing a Branch Bank in Michigan." *Wayne Law Review* 19 (July 1973): 1137–50.

1686. Guenther, Harry P. "1970 Bank Holding Company Act Amendments and State Influence on Banking Structure." *Banking Law Journal* 89 (April 1972): 318–29.

1687. Haegele, M. "Financial Deregulation and the Commercial Account Officer." *Journal of Commercial Bank Lending* 65 (September 1982): 30–43.

1688. Hagerman, Robert L. "Government Regulation of Bank Financial Reporting: An Empirical Investigation." Ph.D. dissertation, University of Rochester, 1972. 158 p.

1689. Hagerman, Robert L. "The Value of Regulation F, an Empirical Test." *Journal of Banking Research* 3 (Autumn 1972): 178–85.

1690. Hall, George R. "Bank Holding Company Regulation." *Southern Economic Journal* 31 (April 1965): 342–55.

1691. Hall, William. "How the American System of Bank Regulation Developed." *The Banker* 124 (September 1974): 1101–08.

1692. Hawke, John D. "Deregulation and Self-Regulation: Illusion or Reality?" *Issues in Bank Regulation* 4 (Autumn 1980): 4–6.

1693. Hays, Fred H. "Interstate Banking: A Logical Step toward Financial Deregulation." *Texas Business Review* 57 (May–June 1983): 131–34.

1694. Haywood, Charles F. *Regulation Q and Monetary Policy.* Chicago: Association of Reserve City Bankers, 1971. 43 p.

1695. Hazleton, Jared. "Public Policy toward Bank Mergers: A Legal and Economic Evaluation." *Social Science Quarterly* 51 (September 1970): 295–308.

1696. Hector, Gary. "Tempting Thrifts to Become Spendthrifts." *Fortune* 108 (October 3, 1983): 193–94.

1697. Hogg, Russell. "Crystal-Ball Gazing." *Credit Union Executive* 23 (Summer 1983): 34–37.

1698. Holdsworth, John "Lessons of State Banking before the Civil War." *Proceedings of the Academy of Political Science* 30 (June 1971): 23–36.

1699. Horvitz, Paul M. "Can Commercial Banks Meet the Competition?" *NABW Journal* (National Association of Bank Women) 59 (January–February 1983): 5–7.

1700. Horvitz, Paul M. "The Committee on Interest and Dividends: An Assessment." *Policy Analysis* 3 (Winter 1977): 85–106.

1701. Horvitz, Paul M. "The Implications of the Deregulation Act for the Competitive Position of Depository Institutions." *Issues in Bank Regulation* 6 (Autumn 1982): 8–14.

1702. Horvitz, Paul M. "Stimulating Bank Competition through Regulatory Action." *Journal of Finance* 20 (March 1965): 1–13.

1703. Horvitz, Paul M., and Shull, Bernard. "The Bank Merger Act of 1960: A Decade After." *Antitrust Bulletin* 16 (Winter 1971): 859–89.

1704. Hugon, James H. "Federal Regulation of Bank Holding Companies." D.B.A. dissertation, University of Washington, 1964. 354 p.

1705. Hunt, Carle Manhart. "A Critical Analysis of the Credit Policies of the Federal Home Loan Bank Board: 1950–1966." D.B.A. dissertation, University of Southern California, 1968. 248 p.

1706. Hunter, Oakley. "The Federal National Mortgage Association: Its Response to Critical Financing Requirements of Housing." *George Washington Law Review* 39 (May 1971): 818–34.

1707. Isaac, William M. "Bank Regulation in a Changing Climate." *Bankers Monthly* 97 (November 1980): 18–22.

1708. Isaac, William M. "What's Needed Now: View of Bank Regulator." *Bankers Monthly* 100 (December 1983): 12–14.

1709. "Itchy Congress Moves on Bank Reform." *Business Week* (July 13, 1981): 24–25.

1710. Jackson, William. "Commercial Bank Regulation, Structure, and Performance." Ph.D. dissertation, Unviersity of North Carolina at Chapel Hill, 1974. 198 p.

1711. Jacobe, Dennis. "Deposit Insurance; Compatible with Deregulation?" *Savings and Loan News* 104 (April 1983): 36–42.

1712. Jacobe, Dennis. "In a Deregulated World, Bigger Banks Have an Advantage." *Savings and Loan News* 104 (February 1983): 31–33.

1713. Jacobe, Dennis. "The New Holding Company: An Old Idea in New Guise." *Savings Institutions* 104 (August 1983): 48–56.

1714. Jacobe, Dennis. "Regulators Net Worth Focus Deters Needed Restructuring." *Savings and Loan News* 103 (August 1982): 21–23.

1715. Jacobs, Donald P. "The Framework of Commercial Bank Regulations: An Appraisal." *National Banking Review* 1 (March 1964): 343–57.

1716. Jakubik, Jerome W. "Foreign Bank Reserve Requirements: Effects on Funding the International Loan." *Banking Law Journal* 100 (January 1983): 58–68.

1717. James, Christopher M. "A Theory of Bank Portfolio Allocations under Uncertainty and the Implications for Bank Regulation." Ph.D. dissertation, University of Michigan, 1978. 194 p.

1718. Johnson, Robert L. "Banking Changes." *South Dakota Business Review* 42 (August 1983): 4–6.

1719. Jones, Homer. "An Appraisal of the Rules and Procedures of Bank Supervision, 1929–39." *Journal of Political Economy* 48 (April 1940): 183–98.

1720. Juncker, George R. "A New Supervisory System for Rating Banks." In *Current Perspectives in Banking,* 2d ed., edited by Thomas M. Havrilesky and John T. Boorman, pp. 481–87. Arlington Heights, IL: AHM Publishing, 1980.

1721. Kalish, Lionel. "The 'Protest' in the Bank Entry Process." *Public Choice* 36 (1981): 287 99.

1722. Kalish, Lionel, and Alton, Gilbert R. "The Influence of Bank Regulation on the Operating Efficiency of Commercial Banks." *Journal of Finance* 28 (December 1973): 1287–1301.

1723. Kareken, John H. "The First Step in Bank Deregulation: What about the FDIC?" *American Economic Review* 73 (May 1983): 198–203.

1724. Kearl, J. R. "Piecemeal Deregulation: The Problems of Interest Rate Regulation and Mortgage Innovation." *Journal of Economics and Business* 33 (Fall 1980): 72–79.

1725. Keller, Bill. "Liberation of Bank Industry May Be Thwarted This Year by Fractured Finance Lobbies." *Congressional Quarterly Weekly Report* 40 (February 6, 1982): 187–91.

1726. Kent, R. J. "Evaluating the Bank Board's Liquidity and Special Advances Programs." *Federal Home Loan Bank Board Journal* 14 (August 1981): 13–16.

1727. King, D. R. "Feasibility in Chapter X Reorganizations." *American Bankruptcy Law Journal* 49 (Fall 1975): 323–99.

1728. King, John F., et al. "How Financial Institutions View Deregulation: Three Views—The Banking Industry/The Securities Industry/The Savings and Loan Industry." *Business Forum* 8 (Summer 1983): 20–24.

1729. Klebaner, Benjamin J. "Bank Holding Act of 1956." *Southern Economic Journal* 24 (January 1958): 313–26.

1730. Klima, Jerry V., and Fishkin, Martin E. "Massachusetts Omnibus Banking Act: Deregulation of a State's Banking Industry." *United States Banker* 93 (November 1982): 58–60.

1731. Koch, Donald L., and Steinhauser, Delores W. "Challenges for Retail Banking in the 80's." *Economic Review* (Federal Reserve Bank of Atlanta) 67 (May 1982): 13–19.

1732. Koehn, Michael F., and Santomer, A. M. "Regulation of Bank Capital and Portfolio Risk." *Journal of Finance* 35 (December 1980): 1235–44.

1733. Kreps, Clifton H. "Modernizing Banking Regulation." *Law and Contemporary Problems* 31 (Autumn 1966): 648–72.

1734. Kurtz, R. D., and Sinkey, J. R. "Bank Disclosure Policy and Procedures, and Adverse Publicity and Deposit Flows." *Journal of Bank Research* 4 (Autumn 1973): 177–84.

1735. Labreque, T. G. "How Current Rules Penalize Banking." *Bankers Monthly* 98 (December 1981): 18–20.

1736. Laird, R. H. "Looking Back: Board Has Long History of Enforcing Fair Home Lending Practices." *Federal Home Loan Bank Board Journal* 10 (May 1977): 2–6.

1737. Lawrence, Robert J. "Effects of Deregulation and Expanded Banking Activities on Bank Supervision." *Issues in Bank Regulation* 6 (Autumn 1982): 15–22.

1738. Leavitt, Brenton C. "Philosophy of Financial Regulation." *Banking Law Journal* 90 (August 1973): 632–48.

1739. Leavitt, Brenton C. "What the Fed Likes to See in a Bank Holding Company Application." *Banking Law Journal* 91 (April 1974): 320–21.

1740. Lee, Chris. "Chase Federal Savings: Coping with 'Dereg.'" *Training* 20 (October 1983): 171–73.

1741. Lifland, William T. "Banking and the Antitrust Laws." *Harvard Business Review* 45 (May 1967): 138–44.

1742. Linke, Charles M. "The Evolution of Interest Rate Regulation on Commercial Bank Deposits in the U.S." *National Banking Review* 3 (June 1966): 449–69.

1743. Linke, Charles M. "Interest Rate Regulation on Commercial Bank Deposits, Its Evolution and Impact in the State of Indiana." D.B.A. dissertation, Indiana University, 1966. 403 p.

1744. Linton, Robert E. "Through the Financial Looking Glass—1983: The Financial Services Industry." *Vital Speeches* 49 (September 1, 1983): 690–92.

1745. Long, Robert. "Regulation and Experimentation." *Magazine of Bank Administration* 50 (December 1974): 6–7.

1746. Lovett, William A., et al. "A Problem of Imagination: National Policy toward Multibank Integration." *Journal of Economic Issues* 13 (June 1979): 427–69.

1747. Lower, Robert C. "Savings and Loan Associations and the Futures Markets." *Emory Law Journal* 30 (Fall 1981): 1035–63.

1748. Luckett, William S. "Is Demand Deposit Regulation Necessary?" *Journal of Commercial Bank Lending* 7 (May 1971): 16–25.

1749. Marans, J. Eugene, and Murphy, John C. "Sorting Out the Banking Bills." *ABA Banking Journal* 75 (October 1983): 91–101.

1750. Market, Donald Raymond. "The Theory of 100 Per Cent Reserve Banking Historical Development and Critical Analysis." Ph.D. dissertation, Louisiana State University and Agricultural and Mechanical College, 1967. 242 p.

1751. Marlin, J. A. "Ideas on Bank Regulatory Reform." *Bankers Magazine* 153 (Winter 1970): 32–38.

1752. Martin, Preston. "A Case for Regulation Q." *Federal Home Loan Bank Board Journal* 25 (October 1970): 1–6.

1753. Martin, Preston. "Restructuring the Banking Industry: Is There a Need?" *Independent Banker* 32 (December 1982): 17–19.

1754. Masten, J. T., and Severiens, J. T. "Bank Holding Company Regulatory Experience since 1970." *Indiana Law Review* 8 (1975): 942–62.

1755. Mayne, Lucille S. "The Deposit Reserve Requirement Recommendations of the Commission on Financial Structure and Regulation: An Analysis and Critique." *Journal of Bank Research* 4 (Spring 1973): 41–51.

1756. Mayne, Lucille S. "Trends in Banking Structure and Regulation." *Journal of Finance* 26 (May 1971): 647–49.

1757. Mayor, Thomas H., and Fraser, John T. "An Analysis of Factors Used to Determine the Public Need for New Banks." *Southern Economic Journal* 43 (July 1976): 818–26.

1758. McAnaw, Richard. "Bankers and Politicians: The Not So Strange Bedfellows." *Michigan Academician* 5 (Spring 1973): 505–13.

1759. McCord, Thom. "A Regulatory Perspective: 'The Depository Institutions Act of 1982.'" *Issues in Bank Regulation* 6 (Autumn 1982): 3–7.

1760. McEvoy, George F. "Bank Loans and Regulation U." *Banking Law Journal* 84 (August 1967): 668–83.

1761. McNamar, T. "Treasury Encourages Support for Deregulation Bill." *Trusts and Estates* 121 (March 1982): 53–56.

1762. Meadows, E. "Small Banks Stand Up to the Goliaths." *Fortune* 103 (January 26, 1981): 28–31.

1763. Means L. "Office of the Federal Savings and Loan Insurance Corporation." *Federal Home Loan Bank Board Journal* 10 (April 1977): 26–32.

1764. Meer, J. M. "Reorganizations under the Bankruptcy and Holding Company Acts." *Texas Law Review* 27 (November 1948): 14–41.

1765. Meltzer, Allan H. "Major Issues in the Regulation of Financial Institutions." *Journal of Political Economy* 75 (August 1967): 482–511.

1766. Melvin, Donald J. "The Future Direction of Bank Regulation and Legislation." *Journal of Bank Research* 5 (Autumn 1974): 161–64.

1767. Merris, Randall C. "Monetary Policy, Bank Regulation and Banking Profits." Ph.D. dissertation, University of Kentucky, 1979. 258 p.

1768. Metzger, Robert O. "Banking Compensation: The Next Major Changed Forced by Deregulation." *Journal of Retail Banking* 5 (Spring 1983): 1–7.

1769. Metzger, Robert O. "Deregulation Calls for Changes in Organizational Structure." *Savings and Loan News* 103 (September 1982): 62–66.

1770. Miller, R. B. "What the Administration Is Doing to Banking." *Bankers Magazine* 165 (September–October 1982): 27–30.

1771. Miller, Roger L. "Distortion and Misuse of Rule 2(e)." *Securities Regulation Law Journal* 7 (Spring 1979): 54–75.

1772. Mingo, John J. "Regulatory Influence on Bank Capital Investments." *Journal of Finance* 30 (September 1975): 1111–21.

1773. Mintz, Steven. "Banking on Marketing." *Sales and Marketing Management* 130 (June 6, 1983): 43–48.

1774. Modesitt, L. E. "Mutual Fund—A Corporate Anomaly." *UCLA Law Review* 14 (August 1967): 1252–67.

1775. Mors, Wallace. "Recent Trends in State Regulation of Installment Credit." *Journal of Finance* 15 (May 1960): 191–205.

1776. Mors, Wallace. "State Regulation of Retail Installment Financing: Progress and Problems, Part I." *Journal of Business* 23 (October 1950): 199–218.

1777. Motter, David C. "Bank Formation and the Public Interest." *National Banking Review* 2 (March 1965): 299–350.

1778. Motter, David C. "Bank Mergers and Public Policy." *National Banking Review* 1 (September 1963): 89–100.

1779. Motter, David C., and Carson, Deane C. "Bank Entry and the Public Interest: A Case Study." *National Banking Review* 1 (June 1964): 469–512.

1780. Much, Marilyn. "More Reforms Await Banking Industry." *Industry Week* 210 (September 7, 1981): 131–32.

1781. Much, Marilyn. "Who Benefits from Interstate Banking?" *Industry Week* 218 (September 5, 1983): 52–56.

1782. Murane, William E. "The FDIC and Bank Regulations." *Banking Law Journal* 89 (June 1972): 483–98.

1783. Murphy, E. J. "Office of Industry Development." *Federal Home Loan Bank Board Journal* 10 (April 1977): 37–42.

1784. Murphy, Neil B., and Weiss, Steven T. "Restructuring Federal Regulation of Financial Institutions." *Bankers Magazine* 155 (Winter 1972): 71–77.

1785. Nadar, Ralph. "Regulators Who Kowtow to Bankers." *Business and Society Review* 36 (Winter 1980–1981): 37–42.

1786. Nadler, Paul S. "One-Bank Holding Companies: The Public Interest." *Harvard Business Review* 47 (May–June 1969): 107–13.

1787. Nalf, T., and Leaman, S. "Deregulation and the Mortgage Lender: A Mixed Blessing." *Mortgage Banker* 41 (June 1981): 36–37.

1788. Nash, James H., and Shapero, Benjamin P. "Control Relationships under the Bank Holding Company Act." *Banking Law Journal* 92 (June–July 1975): 618–30.

1789. "New Hampshire Focus Is on Interstate Banking, Deregulation, Market Niche." *Savings Bank Journal* 64 (October 1983): 41–43.

1790. "No. 2 Man in Treasury, Influential Administrator, on Bank Deregulation." *ABA Banking Journal* 74 (May 1982): 39–44.

1791. Norton, Joseph Jude. "The 1982 Banking Act and the Deregulation Scheme." *Business Lawyer* 38 (August 1983): 1627–51.

1792. Nowesnick, Mary. "Is the DIDC Doing Too Much, Too Soon—Or Still Not Enough?" *Savings and Loan News* 103 (March 1982): 50–54.

1793. O'Brien, Steven J. "The Development of Bank Regulation and Its Appropriate Competitive Standards—Grays Harbor, A Gathering Storm." *Business Lawyer* 31 (November 1976): 415–31.

1794. Oetking, Robert. "Fringe Banks Face New Regulation." *Bankers Monthly* 91 (February 1974): 30–34.

1795. Osborn, Neil, "What Happens after Glass-Steagall?" *Institutional Investor* 16 (February 1982): 67–78.

1796. Pakonen, Richard R. "The Differential Effect of Branch Law Regulation on Commercial Bank Entry." Ph.D. dissertation, Washington State University, 1969. 163 p.

1797. Parker, George G. "Now Management Will Make or Break the Bank: To Cope with the Deregulation Revolution, the Business of Banking Must Change Dramatically in the Next 20 Years." *Harvard Business Review* 59 (November–December): 140–48.

1798. Peltzman, Samuel. "Bank Entry Regulation: Its Impacts and Purpose." *National Banking Review* 3 (December 1965): 163–77.

1799. Peltzman, Samuel. "Capital Investment in Commercial Banking and Its Relationship to Portfolio Regulation." *Journal of Political Economy* 78 (January–February 1970): 1–26.

1800. Pettit, R. Richardson. "Structure and Performance in the Savings and Loan Industry: An Analysis of Operating Efficiency and Its Relation to Regulation." Ph.D. dissertation, University of California, 1969. 252 p.

1801. Phelps, Kenneth J., and Spedale, Iris R. "Reinterpreting Glass-Steagall: A Bank's Move into Brokerage." *Trusts and Estates* 122 (November 1983): 17–22.

1802. Phillips, Almarin W. "Regulatory Reform for the Deposit Financial Institutions—Retrospect and Prospects." *Journal of Financial and Quantitative Analysis* 9 (November 1974): 795–802.

1803. Phillips, Almarin W. "Structural and Regulatory Reform for Commercial Banking." In *Issues in Banking and Monetary Analyses,* edited by G. Pontecorvo, et al. pp. 103–24. New York: Holt, Rinehart and Winston, 1967.

1804. Phillips, Robert W. "Commercial Bank Mergers and the Antitrust Laws: An Analysis of the Application of Conventional Antitrust Criteria to a Quasi-Regulated Industry." D.B.A. dissertation, Indiana University, 1969. 472 p.

1805. Pierce, J. L. "FINE Study." *Journal of Money, Credit and Banking* 9 (November 1977): 605–18.

1806. Pistor, Charles. "The Economic Necessity of Bank Deregulation." *Financier* 6 (August 1982): 52–54.

1807. Pohn, G. W. "National Banks and the Future—One Regulator's Concerns." *Journal of Commercial Bank Lending* 57 (December 1974): 53–57.

1808. "Pratt Discusses the Bank Board's Proposed Thrift Institutions Restructuring Act." *Federal Home Loan Bank Board Journal* 14 (October 1981): 2–9.

1809. Pratt, Richard T. "A New Day Dawns for the Savings and Loan Industry." *Federal Home Loan Bank Board Journal* 14 (December 1981): 2–7.

1810. "Preparing for Competition without Regulation Q." *ABA Banking Journal* 74 (August 1982): 75–77.

1811. "Preston Martin Addresses Banking Deregulation." *ABA Banking Journal* 74 (October 1982): 70–73.

1812. Pyle, David H. "The Losses on Savings Deposits from Interest Rate Regulation." *Bell Journal of Economics and Management Science* 8 (Autumn 1974): 614–22.

1813. Raiford, Norman G. "South Carolina and the Second Bank of the United States: Conflict in Political Principle or Economic Interest?" *South Carolina Historical Magazine* 72 (January 1971): 30–43.

1814. Randall, K. A. "The Federal Deposit Insurance Corporation Regulatory Functions and Philosophy." *Law and Contemporary Problems* 31 (Autumn 1966): 696–712.

1815. "Reg Q—Quicksand for the Small Saver." *Citibank Monthly Economic Letter* 33 (May 1981): 5–7.

1816. Regan, D. "What's Wrong with Glass-Steagall." *Institutional Investor* 15 (October 1981): 21–22.

1817. "Regulation D." *Federal Reserve Bulletin* 66 (September 1980): 743–44.

1818. "Regulation K: Amendment and Interpretation." *Federal Reserve Bulletin* 66 (October 1980): 829–30.

1819. Reid, Samuel R. "The Bank Merger Act of 1960—A Decade After: Comment." *Antitrust Bulletin* 18 (Fall 1973): 449–62.

1820. Reid, Samuel R. "Legislation, Regulation, Antitrust, and Bank Mergers." *Banking Law Journal* 92 (May 1975): 427–36.

1821. "The Revolution in Financial Services." *Business Week* 28 (November 28, 1983): 88–89.

1822. Reynolds, Alan. "Dollars & Sense: It's Time We Invested in Rethinking the Regulation of Banking." *Reason* 14 (May 1982): 41–43.

1823. Rhoades, Stephen A. "The Implications of Financial Deregulation, Interstate Banking and Financial Supermarkets for Bank Merger Policy." *Magazine of Bank Administration* 59 (November 1983): 48–53.

1824. Richter, J. L. "Office of the Federal Home Loan Banks." *Federal Home Loan Bank Board Journal* 10 (April 1977): 23–25.

1825. Roberts, Neil E. "The Department of Justice and Regulation of the One-Bank Holding Company." *Bankers Magazine* 154 (Autumn 1971): 58–63.

1826. Roberts, Ray. "Evolution of Financial Audit Criteria with Emphasis on Selected Legal and Regulatory Influences 1917–1972." Ph.D. dissertation, University of Santa Clara, 1978. 373 p.

1827. Robertson, James L. "The Case for a Single Bank Regulatory Agency." In *Current Perspectives in Banking,* 2d ed., edited by Thomas M. Havrilesky and John T. Boorman, pp. 477–80. Arlington Heights, IL: AHM Publishing, 1980.

1828. Robertson, James L. "Federal Regulation of Banking: A Plan for Unification." *Law and Contemporary Problems* 31 (Autumn 1966): 673–95.

1829. Robinson, Stanley D. "Antitrust Developments Affecting Banks in General." *Banking Law Journal* 86 (November 1969): 980–1001.

1830. Roisman, Anthony Z. "Truth in Lending: Regulation Z—Its Limitations and Applicability." *George Washington Law Review* 37 (July 1969): 1154–70.

1831. Roos, Lawrence K. "Future Choices for Bankers." *Mississippi Business Review* 43 (June 1982): 3–6.

1832. Rose, Peter S. "Exodus: Why Banks Are Leaving the Fed." *Bankers Magazine* 159 (Winter 1976): 43–49.

1833. Rose, Peter S., and Fraser, Donald R. "State Regulation of Bank Holding Companies." *Bankers Magazine* 157 (Winter 1974): 42–48.

1834. Salley, Charles D. "Origins of the Regulatory Separation of Banking and Commerce." *Banking Law Journal* 93 (February 1976): 196–206.

1835. Santomero, A. M., and Siegel, J. J. "Bank Regulation and Macro-Economic Stability." *American Economic Review* 71 (March 1981): 39–53.

1836. Scheiber, Harry N. "Public Canal Finance and State Banking in Ohio, 1825–1837." *Indiana Magazine of History* 65 (June 1969): 119–32.

1837. Scott, Kenneth E. "Financial Institutions." *Regulation* 6 (January–February 1982): 32–34.

1838. Scott, Kenneth E. "The Uncertain Course of Bank Deregulation." *Regulation* 5 (May–June 1981): 40–45.

1839. Scott, Kenneth E., and Mayer, Thomas. "Risk and Regulation in Banking: Some Proposals for FDIC Reform." *Stanford Law Review* 23 (May 1971): 857–902.

1840. Seeley, Miles G. "Banks and Antitrust." *Business Lawyer* 21 (July 1966): 917–30.

1841. Selberfield, E. S. "Recent Litigation and Legislation in Lending." *Journal of Commercial Bank Lending* 50 (March 1968): 2–12.

1842. Senterfitt, D. T. "Glass-Steagall in Perspective." *Bankers Monthly* 99 (August 1982): 16–18.

1843. Shade, William G. "Banks and Politics in Michigan, 1835–1845: A Reconsideration." *Michigan History* 57 (Spring 1973): 28–52.

1844. Shapiro, Eli. "The Commission on Financial Structure and Regulation: Its Organization and Recommendations—Discussion." *Journal of Finance* 27 (May 1972): 336–39.

1845. Shay, Jerome W. "Capital Adequacy: The Regulator's Perspective." *Magazine of Bank Administration* 44 (October 1974): 22–25.

1846. Shay, Robert P. "An Evaluation of Regulation Was a Selective Device for the Control of Credit." Ph.D. dissertation, University of Virginia, 1951.

1847. Short, Eugenie D., and O'Driscoll, Gerald P. "Deposit Insurance and Financial Stability." *Business Forum* 8 (Summer 1983): 10–13.

1848. Short, Eugenie D., and O'Driscoll, Gerald P. "Deregulation and Deposit Insurance." *Economic Review* (Federal Reserve Bank of Dallas) (September 1983): 11–23.

1849. Silber, William L. "Open Market Rates and Regulation Q." *National Banking Review* 4 (March 1967): 299–303.

1850. Silber, William L. "Portfolio Substitutability, Regulations, and Monetary Policy." *Quarterly Journal of Economics* 83 (May 1969): 197–219.

1851. Silberfeld, E. S. "Long Arm of the Law Is Getting Longer." *Journal of Commercial Bank Lending* 54 (November 1971): 48–53.

1852. Skillern, F. L. "Federal Deposit Insurance Corporation and the Failed Bank: The Past Decade." *Banking Law Journal* 99 (March 1982): 233–58.

1853. Smith, Frances B., and Swope, Genilee. "A Restructured Financial Institutions World." *Credit* 8 (November–December 1982): 14–21.

1854. Smith, Paul F. "Structural Disequilibrium and the Banking Act of 1980." *Journal of Finance* 37 (May 1982): 385–93.

1855. Smith, Stanley D. "Regulatory Influence on Capital Investment in Large Bank Holding Companies." D.B.A. dissertation, Arizona State University, 1979. 113 p.

1856. Smith, W. F. "Interstate Banking Restrictions Outweigh Public Benefit." *Trusts and Estates* 121 (June 1982): 26–29.

1857. Solomon, A. M. "Fast-Changing Financial Landscape." *Bankers Monthly* 99 (February 1982): 16–17.

1858. Solomon, Elinor H. "Bank Merger Policy and Problems: A Linkage Theory of Oligopoly." *Journal of Money, Credit and Banking* 2 (August 1970): 323–36.

1859. Sprague, W. "Office of Examinations and Supervision." *Federal Home Loan Bank Board Journal* 10 (April 1977): 33–36.

1860. Stafford, John, and Eldine, Diana. "Reg-Q Critics Miss the Point." *Savings and Loan News* 97 (March 1976): 94–95.

1861. Stigler, George J. "The Commission on Financial Structure and Regulation: Its Organization and Recommendations—Discussion." *Journal of Finance* 27 (May 1972): 340–41.

1862. Storrs, T. I. "Freedom for Banks." *Journal of Finance* 30 (May 1975): 293–302.

1863. Struck, Peter L., and Mandell, Lewis. "The Effect of Bank Deregulation on Small Business: A Note." *Journal of Finance* 38 (June 1983): 1025–31.

1864. Stuhldreher, Thomas J. "The Federal Regulation of Foreign Banking in the United States: An Analysis of Attitudes and Implications." D.B.A. dissertation, Kent State University, 1979. 182 p.

1865. Swary, Itzhak. "Capital Adequacy Requirements and the Regulation of Bank Holding Companies." Ph.D. dissertation, University of Rochester, 1979. 230 p.

1866. Sweet, William. "Banking Deregulation." *Editorial Research Reports* (August 7, 1981): 575–92.

1867. Sylla, Richard. "Federal Policy, Banking Market Structure, and Capital Mobilization in the United States, 1863–1913." *Journal of Economic History* 29 (December 1969): 657–86.

1868. Teater, David D. "The Future of Premiums in a Deregulated Environment." *Bank Marketing* 14 (August 1982): 18–19.

1869. Thompson, T. W. "Banking Commentary." *United States Banker* 93 (August 1982): 6–10.

1870. Tomaskovic-Devey, D., and McKinlay, J. "Bailing Out the Banks: The United States and Private International Debt." *Social Policy* 11 (January–February 1981): 8–17.

1871. Torgovnik, Efraim. "Policy Development through the Study Commission Device: The Case of the Rhode Island Special Commission to Appraise the Financial Operation of the State-Government and the Matter of State-Local Financial Relations." Ph.D. dissertation, New York University, 1966. 265 p.

1872. "US Deregulation: A Cleaner Structure." *The Banker* 133 (October 1983): 69–70.

1873. Van Lenten, W. L. "Freedom of Information Act: What It Is and How It Affects the Bank Board." *Federal Home Loan Bank Board Journal* 15 (January 1982): 10–12.

1874. Vanlandingham, M. H. "Regulation Q and Commercial Bank Liquidity: 1966 and 1969." Ph.D. dissertation, University of Florida, 1972. 225 p.

1875. Verbrugge, James A. "The Effects of Pledging Regulations on Bank Asset Composition." *Journal of Bank Research* 4 (Autumn 1973): 168–76.

1876. Verkuil, Paul R. "Perspectives on Reform of Financial Institutions." *Yale Law Journal* 83 (June 1974): 1349–81.

1877. Vernon, Jack P. "Regulatory Barriers to Branching and Merger and Concentration in Banking Markets." *Southern Economic Journal* 37 (January 1971): 349–55.

1878. Vestner, Eliot N. "Trends and Developments in State Regulation of Banks." *Banking Law Journal* 90 (June 1973): 464–78.

1879. Via, J. William. "Some Thoughts on Evaluating the Tripartite Federal Bank Regulatory System." *Banking Law Journal* 93 (May 1973): 509–24.

1880. Volcker, Paul A. "Toward a National Review of Banking Change." *United States Banker* 94 (June 1983): 56–59.

1881. "Voluntary Disclosure Code for the Banking Industry." *Banking Law Journal* 95 (January 1978): 4–27.

1882. Waddell, Harry. "Competition Crowding in on Small-Town Banks." *ABA Banking Journal* 75 (March 1983): 118–23.

1883. Waite, Donald C. "Deregulation and the Banking Industry: When Deregulation Comes to Banking Who Will the Winners—and Losers—Be?" *Bankers Magazine* 165 (January–February): 26–35.

1884. Walker, David A. "Effects of Deregulation on the Savings and Loan Industry." *Financial Review* 18 (February 1983): 94–110.

1885. Wallich, Henry C. "One Chance in a Generation: Guideposts for the Commission on Financial Structure and Regulation." *Journal of Money, Credit and Banking* 3 (February 1971): 21–30.

1886. Walsh, C. E. "Taxation of Interest Income, Deregulation and the Banking Industry." *Journal of Finance* 38 (December 1983): 1529–42.

1887. Waxberg, Stanley D., and Robinson, Stanley D. "Chaos in Federal Regulation of Bank Mergers: A Need for Legislative Revision." *Banking Law Journal* 82 (May 1965): 377–94.

1888. "We Want Government off Your Backs." *Credit Union Magazine* 48 (March 1982): 16–18.

1889. Wemple, William J., and Cutler, Kenneth. "Federal Bank Merger Law and the Antitrust Laws." *Banking Law Journal* 79 (June 1962): 461–73.

1890. Weston, J. Fred. "Regulatory Reform for the Deposit Financial Institutions— Retrospect and Prospects: Comment." *Journal of Financial and Quantitative Analysis* 9 (November 1974): 831–33.

1891. "What Tomorrow's Banking System Will Look Like." *U.S. News and World Report* 94 (May 16, 1983): 71–72.

1892. White, B. B. "Foreign Banking in the United States: A Regulatory and Supervisory Perspective." *Federal Reserve Bank of New York Quarterly Review* 7 (Summer 1982): 48–58.

1893. White, Eugene N. "The Regulation and Reform of the Dual Banking System, 1900–1928." Ph.D. dissertation, University of Illinois at Urbana-Champaign, 1980. 292 p.

1894. White, Michael. "Barriers to Interstate Banking Begin to Crumble." *Savings and Loan News* 103 (January 1982): 44–49.

1895. White, Roger S. "State Regulation of Commercial Banks, 1781–1843." Ph.D. dissertation, University of Illinois, 1971. 137 p.

1896. Willacy, A. B., and Willacy, H. M. "Conglomerate Bank Mergers and Clayton 7: Is Potential Competition the Answer?" *Banking Law Journal* 93 (February 1976): 148–95.

1897. Willie, Frank. "State Banking: A Study in Dual Regulation." *Law and Contemporary Problems* 31 (Autumn 1966): 733–48.

1898. Williams, Larry L. "Banking and the Antitrust Laws." *Banking Law Journal* 81 (May 1964): 377–92.

1899. Wooley, John T. "Monetary Policy, Instrumentation, and the Relationship of Central Banks and Government." *American Academy of Political and Social Science, Annals* 434 (November 1977): 151–73.

1900. Wu, H., and Cornell, L. "Merger Myopia: An Economic View of Supreme Court Decisions on Bank Mergers." *Virginia Law Review* 59 (May 1973): 860–84.

1901. Yaari, Uzi. "The Regulation of Interest Paid by Banks on Demand Deposits." Ph.D. dissertation, Unviersity of Chicago, 1972. 114 p.

1902. Yesley, J. "Federal Laws Regulating Bank Mergers and the Acquisitions of Banks by Registered Bank Holding Companies." *Economic Review* (Federal Reserve Bank of Cleveland) (January 1971): 18–27.

COMMUNICATION

1903. "Administrative Law—Communications—Developing Standards for Diversification of Broadcasting Formats." *Texas Law Review* 52 (March 1974): 558–69.

1904. "Administrative Law: Current Progress of Native American Broadcasting—Status of Indian Ownership." *American Indian Law Review* 4 (Summer 1976): 91–98.

1905. Albert, J. A. "Constitutional Regulation of Televised Violence." *Virginia Law Review* 64 (December 1978): 1299–345.

1906. Albert, J. A. "Federal and Local Regulation of Cable Television." *University of Colorado Law Review* 48 (Summer 1977): 501–23.

1907. Allen, G. "Television Game." *American Opinion* 19 (December 1976): 1–6.

1908. Anthony, Robert A. "Towards Simplicity and Rationality in Comparative Broadcast Licensing Proceedings." *Stanford Law Review* 24 (November 1971): 1–115.

1909. Baird, Frank L. "Congress' Role is Regulation: Radio and Television Programming." Ph.D. dissertation, University of Texas, 1964. 439 p.

1910. Bennett, Sandra W. "Ascertainment of Community Needs by Public Television Stations: A Study of KPBS, WOSU, WVIZ, WETA, and the Alabama Educational Television Commission." Ph.D. dissertation, Ohio State University, 1971. 421 p.

1911. Besen, Stanley M. "Deregulating Telecommunications—Sorting Out Mixed Signals." *Regulation* 2 (March–April 1978): 30–36.

1912. Besen, Stanley M. "Economics of the Cable Television 'Consensus.'" *Journal of Law and Economics* 17 (April 1974): 39–51.

1913. Besen, Stanley M., and Krattenmaker, Thomas G. "Regulating Network Television: Dubious Premises and Doubtful Solutions." *Regulation* 5 (May–June 1981): 27–34.

1914. Besen, Stanley M., and Soligo, R. "Economics of the Network-Affiliate Relationship in the Television Broadcasting Industry." *American Economic Review* 63 (June 1973): 259–68.

1915. Bilik, Eugene W. "The Image Candidates: An Appraisal of Political Broadcast Regulation Based on Television Coverage of the 1961 Mayoral Campaigns in New York City." Ph.D. dissertation, New York University, 1966. 342 p.

1916. Botein, M. "Citizen Participation in the Regulation of Cable Television." *Catholic University Law Review* 24 (Summer 1975): 777–94.

1917 Botein, M. "New Copyright Act and Cable Television—A Signal of Change." *Bulletin of the Copyright Society of the U.S.A.* 24 (October 1974): 1–17.

1918. Brenner, D. L. "Government Regulation of Radio Program Format Changes." *University of Pennsylvania Law Review* 127 (November 1978): 56–110.

1919. Brice, J. O. "Regulatory Commission and the Press." *Public Utilities Fortnightly* 66 (September 15, 1960): 379–85.

1920. Chazen, Leonard, and Ross, Leonard. "Federal Regulation of Cable Television: The Visible Hand." *Harvard Law Review* 83 (June 1970): 1820–841.

1921. Church, Thomas W. "Conspiracy Law and Seditious Speech Offenses: Constitutional Ramifications of the Use of Criminal Conspiracy as a Device for the Regulation of Political Speech." Ph.D. dissertation, Cornell University, 1973. 186 p.

1922. Coase, Ronald H. "Payola in Radio and Television Broadcasting." *Journal of Law and Economics* 22 (October 1979): 269–328.

1923. "Communications Law—Cable Television." *Annual Survey of American Law* 1977 (1977): 577–94.

1924. "Communications Law—Growing Deference to the Broadcaster's First Amendment Rights." *Annual Survey of American Law* 1976 (1976): 399–425.

1925. "Community Antenna Television: The New Federal Exercise of Jurisdiction." *Iowa Law Review* 51 (Winter 1966): 366–84.

1926. "Computer Services and the Federal Regulation of Communications." *University of Pennsylvania Law Review* 116 (December 1967): 328–46.

1927. Cosson, D. "Development of Regulation of Common Carrier Communications: Its Basis, Objectives, Methods and the Social and Political Underpinnings with Emphasis on the Dichotomy of Joint Federal/State Regulation." *Federal Communications Law Journal* 28 (1975): 132–46.

1928. Crandall, Robert W. "Regulation of Television Broadcasting: How Costly Is the 'Public Interest'?" *Regulation* 2 (January–February 1978): 31–39.

1929. Davidson, W. M., and Kraus, C. R. "New Approaches to Telephone Regulation by State Commissions." *Public Utilities Fortnightly* 93 (January 17, 1974): 36–39.

1930. "Delays Seen in Integration of GTE—United Telecom Packet Net." *Data Communications* 15 (February 1986): 62–64.

1931. "Developments in the Law—Deceptive Advertising." *Harvard Law Review* 80 (March 1967): 1005–1163.

1932. Digianni, John. "An Examination of Government Regulation of U.S. Broadcasting as Manifested in the Communications Act of 1934." *Historian* 73 (Spring 1975): 31–39.

1933. Dinneen, Patricia M. "Departures from Efficiency in Regulated Industries: The Case of International Telecommunications." Ph.D. dissertation, Massachusetts Institute of Technology, 1980. 271 p.

1934. "Diversity Ownership in Broadcasting Affirmative Policy in Search of an Author." *University of Florida Law Review* 27 (Winter 1975): 502–30.

1935. Doron, Gideon. "How Smoking Increased When TV Advertising of Cigarettes Was Banned." *Regulation* 3 (March–April 1979): 49–52.

1936. "Federal Regulation of Radio Broadcasting—Standards and Procedures for Regulating Format Changes in the Public Interest." *Rutgers Law Review* 28 (Spring 1975): 966–85.

1937. Fleming, Horace W. "Administrative Regulation of Obscenity: A Comparison of Four State Literature Commissions." Ph.D. dissertation, Vanderbilt University, 1973. 504 p.

1938. Freidman, Jane. "Erotica, Censorship, and the United States Post Office Department." *Michigan Academician* 4 (Summer 1971): 7–16.

1939. Friedenn, R. M. "Computer Inquiries: Mapping the Communications/Information Processing Terrain." *Federal Communications Law Journal* 33 (Winter 1981): 55–115.

1940. Garwood, Griffith L. "New Look at Credit Advertising under Regulation Z." *Banking Law Journal* 91 (January 1974): 48–59.

1941. Geller, Henry. "Making Cable TV Pay? The Copyright Controversy." *Regulation* 5 (May–June 1981): 35–39.

1942. Geller, Henry. "Telecommunications." *Regulation* 6 (January–February 1982): 24–26.

1943. Geller, Max A. "The Federal Regulation of Advertising." Ph.D. dissertation, New York University, 1951. 354 p.

1944. Givens, Richard A. "Refusal of Radio and Television Licenses on Economic Grounds." *Virginia Law Review* 46 (November 1960): 1391–406.

1945. Goldstein, J. "Communications, Property Rights, and Broadcasting Vouchers." *Canadian Public Policy* 8 (Winter 1982): 45–56.

1946. Hamburg, M. I. "Use of Broadcasting Facilities: A Matter of Fairness." *New York Law Forum* 21 (Fall 1975): 209–30.

1947. Haring, John R. "Competition, Regulation, and Performance in the Commercial Radio Broadcasting Industry." Ph.D. dissertation, Yale University, 1975. 216 p.

1948. Hennock, F. B. "Free Air Waves—An Administrative Dilemma: Address." *Women Lawyers Journal* 36 (Fall 1950): 5–8, 26–29.

1949. "High Potential in Law Power: A Model for an Efficient Low Power Television Service" *Federal Communications Law Journal* 33 (Summer 1981): 419–69.

1950. Immerwahr, John, et al. "Public Attitudes toward Freedom of the Press." *Public Opinion Quarterly* 46 (Summer 1982): 177–94.

1951. Inocentio, Eusebio S. "Differences in Perspective of Public Policy Issues in Broadband Cable Communications—A Comparison of Federal, State and Local Regulatory Views." Ph.D. dissertation, University of Pennsylvania, 1975.

1952. "Interdependence of Communications and Data Processing: An Alternative Proposal for the Second Computer Inquiry." *Northwestern University Law Review* 73 (May–June 1978): 307–58.

1953. Irwin, Manley R., and McKee, Robert E. "Vertical Integration and the Communication Equipment Industry: Alternatives for Public Policy." *Cornell Law Review* 53 (February 1968): 446–72.

1954. Jameson, Kay C. "The Influence of the United States Court of Appeals for the District of Columbia on Federal Policy in Broadcast Regulation, 1929–1971." Ph.D. dissertation, University of Southern California, 1972. 566 p.

1955. Jorgensen, Norman E.; Schwartz, Louis; and Woods, Robert A. "Programming Diversity in Proposals for New Broadcast Licenses." *George Washington Law Review* 32 (April 1964): 769–807.

1956. Joskow, Paul L., and Nelson, P. "Effects of FTS Advertising Regulation." *Journal of Law and Economics* 24 (December 1981): 403–59.

1957. Kahn, Frank J. "Cable, Competition, and the Commission." *Catholic University Law Review* 24 (Summer 1975): 854–71.

1958. Katz, Michael L., and Willig, Robert D. "The Case for Freeing AT&T." *Regulation* 7 (July–August 1983): 43–52.

1959. Kuklin, S. B. "Continuing Confusion: The Renewal of Broadcast Licenses." *St. Louis University Law Journal* 27 (February 1983): 95–144.

1960. "Letting the Marketplace Select Radio Entertainment Formats." *Loyola Law Review* 27 (Fall 1981): 1250–65.

1961. Levin, Harvey J. "Federal Control of Entry in the Broadcast Industry." *Journal of Law and Economics* 5 (October 1962): 49–68.

1962. "Liberating Radio: Judicial Review of Administrative Agencies' Rulemaking Authority." *Denver Law Journal* 59 (1982): 537–61.

1963. Lichty, Lawrence W. "Television in America: Success Story." *Wilson Quarterly* 5 (Winter 1981): 52–65.

1964. "Listeners' Rights: Public Intervention in Radio Format Changes." *St. John's Law Review* 49 (Summer 1975): 714–47.

1965. Loevinger, Lee. "Religious Liberty and Broadcasting." *George Washington Law Review* 33 (March 1965): 631–59.

1966. Ludlam, C. E. "Abatement of Corporate Image Environmental Advertising." *Ecology Law Quarterly* 4 (1974): 247–78.

1967. Maddalena, Samuel A. "The Management of International Telecommunications: A Study of the Role of U.S. Government Regulation." D.P.S. dissertation, Pace University, 1980. 336 p.

1968. Marks, H. E., and Bell, S. R. "Computer Communications: Government Regulation." *Washington University Law Quarterly* 1977 (Summer 1977): 479–92.

1969. Mayer, J. W., and Botein, M. "Ashbacker Rites in Administrative Practice: A Case Study of Broadcast Regulation." *New York Law School Law Review* 24 (1978): 461–80.

1970. McCormick, Charlie A. "Intrastate Telephone Regulation: A Public Choice Approach." Ph.D. dissertation, Virginia Polytechnic Institute and State University, 1978. 89 p.

1971. McDougald, William W. "Federal Regulation of Political Broadcasting: A History and Analysis." Ph.D. dissertation, Ohio State University, 1964. 327 p.

1972. McKerns, Joseph P. "Industry Skeptics and the Radio Act of 1927." *Journalism History* 4 (Winter 1976–1977): 128–31.

1973. McKinney, Jerome B. "The Regulation of Telephonic Communication in Missouri." Ph.D. dissertation, University of Missouri, 1969. 276 p.

1974. Metzger, Stanley D., and Burrus, Bernie R. "Radio Frequency Allocation in the Public Interest: Federal Government and Civilian Use." *Duquesne University Law Review* 4 (Fall 1965): 1–96.

1975. Mitchell, Bridger M., and Smiley, R. H. "Cable, Cities, and Copyrights." *Bell Journal of Economic and Management Science* 5 (Spring 1974): 235–63.

1976. Murphy, T. P. "Federal Regulatory Policy and Communications Satellites." *American Journal of Economics and Sociology* 31 (October 1982): 337–52.

1977. "National Policy in the 'Public Interest'—A Marriage of Necessity in the Communications Act of 1934." *University of Pennsylvania Law Review* 114 (January 1966): 386–94.

1978. Nelson, Richard W. "Regulating Technical Change: The Case of Communication Satellites." Ph.D. dissertation, Yale University, 1971. 266 p.

1979. "New Approach to the Regulation of Broadcast Programming: The Public Nuisance Doctrine." *American University Law Review* 28 (Winter 1979): 239–77.

1980. "New Copyright Law and Cable Television, Interpretation and Implications." *Performing Arts Review* 7 (1977): 176–95.

1981. "Newspaper-Broadcast Combinations in the Same Community: How Much Divestiture for the Sake of Diversity?" *Brigham Young University Law Review* 1978 (1978): 675–705.

1982. O'Riordan, K. L. "Examination of the Application of Common Carrier Regulation to Entities Providing New Telecommunications Services." *Case Western Reserve Law Review* 29 (Spring 1979): 577–602.

1983. Oruk, Peter B. "South African Broadcasting Corporation: An Instrument of Afrikaner Political Power." *Journal of Southern African Affairs* 3 (January 1978): 55–64.

1984. "OTP Cable Proposals: An End to Regulatory Myopia." *Catholic University Law Review* 24 (Fall 1974): 91–117.

1985. "Pay Television: The Pendulum Swings toward Deregulation." *Washburn Law Journal* 18 (Fall 1978): 86–104.

1986. Pearson, D. B. "Cable: The Thread by Which Television Competition Hangs." *Rutgers Law Review* 27 (Summer 1974): 800–35.

1987. Petrick, Michael J. "'Equal Opportunities' and 'Fairness' in Broadcast Coverage of Politics." *American Academy of Political and Social Science, Annals* 427 (September 1976): 73–83.

1988. "Private Diplomacy and Public Business: Public Supervision of the Communications Satellite Corporation." *University of Chicago Law Review* 45 (Winter 1978): 419–49.

1989. "Regulation of Competing First Amendment Rights: A New Fairness Doctrine Balance after CBS? (*Columbia Broadcasting System, Inc. v. Democratic Nat. Comm.* 93 Sup Ct 2080)." *University of Pennsylvania Law Review* 122 (May 1974): 1283–329.

1990. "Regulation of Corporate Image Advertising." *Minnesota Law Review* 59 (November 1974): 189–222.

1991. "Regulatory Approach to Diversifying Commercial Television Entertainment." *Yale Law Journal* 89 (March 1980): 694–718.

1992. "Regulatory Approaches to Television Network Control of the Program Procurement Process: An Historical Perspective." *Fordham Urban Law Journal* 8 (1979–1980): 563–95.

1993. Reich, Leonard S. "Research, Patents, and the Struggle to Control Radio: A Study of Big Business and the Uses of Industrial Research." *Business History Review* 51 (Summer 1977): 208–35.

1994. Rice, D. M. "Regulation of Direct Broadcast Satellites: International Constraints and Domestic Options." *New York Law School Law Review* 25 (1980): 813–62.

1995. Robinson, Kenneth. "Some Thoughts on Broadcasting Reform." *Regulation* 7 (May–June 1983): 17–20.

1996. Roche, Francis H. "Economic Regulation of Educational Television, 1952–1968." Ph.D. dissertation, Unversity of Notre Dame, 1968. 222 p.

1997. Rose, Louis A. "Monopoly Rents of VHF Television Stations: A Study in Industry and Regulatory Commission Behavior." Ph.D. dissertation, University of California at Los Angeles, 1970. 264 p.

1998. Ruch, Richard H. "The Regulation of Network Broadcasting." Ph.D. dissertation, Harvard University, 1950.

1999. Schmidt, Orville H. "Space Age Regulation: An Examination of Certain Regulatory Problems Arising out of the Communications Satellite Act of 1962." Ph.D. dissertation, West Virginia University, 1967. 270 p.

2000. Schneyer, T. J. "Overview of Public Interest Law Activity in the Communications Field." *Wisconsin Law Review* 1977 (1977): 619–83.

2001. Schwartz, Herman. "Governmentally Appointed Directors in a Private Corporation—The Communications Satellite Act of 1962." *Harvard Law Review* 79 (December 1965): 350–65.

2002. "Scrambling Battle of Distributorship." *Broadcasting* 110 (March 24, 1986): 66–68.

2003. Sethi, S. Prakash, "Case (for and against) the Imposition of Proof of Accuracy or Substantiation Requirements on Advocacy—or Issue-Oriented Corporate Image-Advertising." *Wayne Law Review* 23 (July 1977): 1229–59.

2004. Shafer, Edward. "An Assessment of the Role of Federal Regulation in the Development of the Cable Television Industry." D.B.A. dissertation, George Washington University, 1980. 401 p.

2005. Simmons, S. J. "Problem of 'Issue' in the Administration of the Fairness Doctrine." *California Law Review* 65 (May 1977): 546–96.

2006. Skitol, R. A. "Defense of a False Advertising Case." *Food and Drug Cosmetic Law Journal* 33 (February 1978): 48–58.

2007. Smith, J. C. "Primer on the Regulatory Development of CATV (1950–72)." *Howard Law Journal* 18 (1975): 729–60.

2008. Somerville, Don S. "A Study of Local Regulations and Group Actions on the Circulation of Newsstand Publications." Ph.D. dissertation, University of Illinois at Urbana-Champaign, 1956. 252 p.

2009. Sommer, Michael H. "A Criticism of News Broadcasting and Regulatory Issues in the Richards Case." Ph.D. dissertation, University of Southern California, 1969. 161 p.

2010. Sparkes, Vernone M. "Municipal Agencies for the Regulation of Cable Television: A Study of Current Developments and Issues." Ph.D. dissertation, Indiana University, 1974. 189 p.

2011. Sterk, S. E. "Law of Comparative Advertising; How Much Worse Is 'Better' than 'Great.'" *Trademark Reporter* 67 (July–August 1977): 368–406.

2012. Sterling, Christopher H. "Newspaper Ownership of Broadcast Stations, 1920–68." *Journalism Quarterly* 46 (Summer 1969): 227–36, 254.

2013. Stewart, I. "Telecommunications Management: The Strategy of Organizational Location." *Public Administration Review* 23 (September 1963): 149–54.

2014. "Still Deregulating after All These Years." *Broadcasting* 106 (April 23, 1984): 37–38.

2015. "Study of the Significant Departures from the Administrative Procedure Act as Found in the 1952 Amendments to the Communications Act of 1934." *University of Cincinnati Law Review* 37 (Fall 1954): 469–80.

2016. Sullivan, John P. "Editorials and Controversy: The Broadcaster's Dilemma." *George Washington Law Review* 32 (April 1964): 719–68.

2017. Synchef, R. M. "Municipal Ownership of Cable Television Systems." *University of San Francisco Law Review* 12 (Winter 1978): 205–55.

2018. "Telecommunications-Broadcast Licensing-Divestiture Required in Cases of Local Cross-Ownership of Newspapers and Broadcast Media." *Dickenson Law Review* 82 (Fall 1977): 193–204.

2019. Thompson, Willard L. "Self-Regulation in Advertising." Ph.D. dissertation, University of Illinois at Urbana-Champaign, 1958. 430 p.

2020. "The Use and Reliability of Survey Evidence in Deceptive Advertising Cases." *Oregon Law Review* 62 (1983): 561–602.

2021. Volner, I.D. "Broadcast Regulation: Is There Too Much 'Public Interest'?" *University of Cincinnati Law Review* 43 (1974): 267–89.

2022. Wall, T. H., and Jacob, J. B. "Communications Act Amendments, 1952—Clarity or Ambiguity." *Georgetown Law Journal* 41 (January 1953): 135–81.

2023. Wall, T. W. "Section 309 of the Communications Act—The Renewal Provision—A Need for Change." *Administrative Law Review* 25 (Fall 1973): 407–13.

2024. Ware, Harold. "The Impact of Technological Change on Regulation: The Emerging Land Mobile Communications Industry." Ph.D. dissertation, Cornell University, 1978. 216 p.

2025. White, Melvin R. "History of Radio Regulation Affecting Program Policy." Ph.D. dissertation, University of Wisconsin, 1949. 279 p.

2026. Wiley, Richard E. "Procedural Accommodation of Federal and State Regulatory Interests in Cable Television." *Administrative Law Review* 25 (Spring 1973): 213–23.

2027. Williams, Robert J. "The Politics of American Broadcasting: Public Purposes and Private Interests." *Journal of American Studies* 10 (December 1976): 329–40.

2028. Williamson, Oliver E. "Franchise Bidding for Natural Monopoly—In General and with Respect to CATV." *Bell Journal of Economics and Management Science* 7 (Spring 1976): 73–104.

2029. Wills, James R., and Ryans, John R. "Attitudes toward Advertising: A Multinational Study." *Journal of International Business Studies* 13 (Winter 1982): 121–30.

2030. Wilson, Hall T. "The Regulation of Standard Radio Broadcasting, 1934–1952: Defining the Public Interest through Licensing Policies." Ph.D. dissertation, Rutgers University, 1968. 404 p.

2031. Winokur, Dena. "The Influence of Legal and Voluntary Restraints upon the Gatekeeping Function in the Regulation of Retail Advertising Copy: A Case Study of the *New York Times.*" Ph.D. dissertation, Ohio University, 1975. 370 p.

CONSUMERISM

2032. Adams, Walter. "Consumer Needs and Consumer Sovereignty in the American Economy." *Journal of Business* 35 (July 1962): 264–77.

2033. "Advertising: The Deception Standard." *Washburn Law Journal* 18 (Spring 1979): 600–05.

2034. Anderson, Sigurd. "Struggle for the Consumer's Dollar." *Antitrust Bulletin* 8 (May–June 1963): 517–30.

2035. Berlin, Philip D. "The Performance Effects of Government Regulation on the Ethical Drug Industries of France, England and the United States." Ph.D. dissertation, Harvard University, 1965.

2036. Berman, David R. "Consumerism and the Regulatory System: Paradigms of Reform." *Policy Studies Review* 1 (1982): 454–62.

2037. Black, E. "Great Contact Lens Con." *Washington Monthly* 12 (September 1980): 23–29.

2038. Breen, Denis A. "Regulation and Household Moving Costs." *Regulation* 2 (September–October 1978): 51–54.

2039. Byington, S. J. "Public Regulation of Consumer Products and Product Liability—The Interface." *Forum* 14 (Fall 1978): 327–38.

2040. Climo, Beth L. "The New Truth-in-Lending." *Issues in Bank Regulation* 5 (Autumn 1981): 15–19.

2041. Colantoni, Claude S.; Davis, O. A.; and Swaminuthan, M. "Imperfect Consumers and Welfare Comparisons of Policies Concerning Information and Regulation." *Bell Journal of Economics and Management Science* 7 (Autumn 1976): 602–15.

2042. "Consumer Protection—The Magnuson-Moss Act." *Annual Survey of American Law* 1976 (1976): 257–83.

2043. "Corrective Advertising: An Advertiser's Atonement." *University of Florida Law Review* 30 (Winter 1978): 490–500.

2044. "Corrective Advertising and the Limits of Virginia Pharmacy." *Stanford Law Review* 32 (November 1979): 121–42.

2045. "Corrective Advertising: Panacea or Punishment." *Duquesne Law Review* 17 (1978–1979): 169–87.

2046. "Corrective Advertising—The New Response to Consumer Deception." *Columbia Law Review* 72 (February 1972): 415–31.

2047. Davis, Frederick G., et al. "Regulation of Consumer Credit Insurance." *Law and Contemporary Problems* 33 (Autumn 1968): 718–36.

2048. Diederich, B. F. "Protection of Consumer Interests under the Federal Aviation Act." *Journal of Air Law and Commerce* 40 (Winter 1974): 1–28.

2049. Doherty, Neville. "Competition in the Provision of Dental Services—Impacts on Providers and Consumers: An Introduction." *Journal of Health Politics, Policy and Law* 5 (Winter 1981): 588–92.

2050. Donoghue, William E. "Deregulation of Consumer Checking Accounts Damages Banks." *Trusts and Estates* 122 (March 1983): 26–28.

2051. Epstein, Richard A. "Manville: The Bankruptcy of Product Liability Law." *Regulation* 6 (September–October 1982): 14–19.

2052. Federal Credit Legislation Subcommittee of the Corporation, Banking, and Business Law Committee. American Bar Association, Young Lawyers Division. *Federal Regulation of Consumer Credit.* Boston: Warren, Gorham and Lamont, 1981. 497 p.

2053. Foreman, Carol T. "The Consumer and Food." *Current History* 78 (May 1980): 218–21, 228.

2054. Freidman, Robert S. "Representation in Regulatory Decision Making: Scientific, Industrial, and Consumer Inputs to the FDA." *Public Administration Review* 38 (May–June 1978): 205–14.

2055. Gambitta, Richard A. L.; May, Marlynn L.; and Foster, James C. "Governing through Courts: Consumer Perspectives." *Law and Policy Quarterly* 3 (April 1981): 123–24.

2056. "GAO Blasts Agency Enforcement of Consumer Credit Laws." *Savings and Loan News* 102 (March 1981): 12–15.

2057. Gertz, Elmer. "The Black Laws of Illinois." *Journal of the Illinois State Historical Society* 56 (Autumn 1963): 454–73.

2058. Gilhooley, M. "Federal Regulation of Cosmetics: An Overview." *Food Drug Cosmetic Law Journal* 33 (May 1978): 231–38.

2059. Grabowski, Henry G., and Vernon, J. M. "Consumer Protection Regulation in Ethical Drugs." *American Economic Review, Papers and Proceedings* 67 (February 1977): 359–64.

2060. Greenberger, M. D. "Consumer Advocate's View of the FDA's Procedures and Practices." *Food Drug Cosmetic Law Journal* 32 (June 1977): 293–99.

2061. Grimes, Warren. "Control of Advertising in the United States and Germany: Volkswagen Has a Better Idea." *Harvard Law Review* 84 (June 1971): 1769–800.

2062. Gurol, M., and Mann, Richard A. "Objective Approach to Detecting and Correcting Deceptive Advertising." *Notre Dame Lawyer* 54 (October 1978): 73–101.

2063. Harris, James R. "A Model Statute to Regulate Unfair Advertising and Sales Practices in Alabama." Ph.D. dissertation, University of Florida, 1973. 296 p.

2064. Heggie, Ian G. "Consumer Response to Public Transport Improvements and Care Restraint: Some Practical Findings." *Policy and Politics* 5 (June 1977): 47–70.

2065. Herbst, Anthony F. "Truth in Lending, Regulation Z: Comments on Closed-End Contract Interest Rate Disclosure Requirements." *Journal of Bank Research* 3 (Summer 1972): 95–101.

2066. Herrmann, Robert O. "Consumer Protection: Yesterday, Today and Tomorrow." *Current History* 78 (May 1980): 193–96, 226–27.

2067. Hessler, R. M., and Walters, M. J. "Consumer Evaluation Research: Implications for Methodology, Social Policy, and the Role of the Sociologist." *Sociological Quarterly* 17 (Winter 1976): 74–89.

2068. Hohner, Robert. "Prohibition and Virginia Politics: *William Hodges Mann versus Henry St. George Tucker,* 1909." *Virginia Magazine of History and Biography* 74 (January 1966): 88–107.

2069. Hohner, Robert. "Prohibition Comes to Virginia: The Referendum of 1914." *Virginia Magazine of History and Biography* 75 (October 1967): 473–88.

2070. Howington, Arthur. "John Barley Corn Subdued: The Enforcement of Prohibition in Alabama." *Alabama Review* 23 (July 1970): 212–25.

2071. Jackson, Charles O. "Muckraking and Consumer Protection: The Case of the 1938 Food, Drug and Cosmetic Act." *Pharmacy in History* 13 (1971): 103–10.

2072. Jensen, Raymond A. "Effect of Federal Truth in Lending Act and Regulation Z on Real Estate." *Real Property, Probate, and Trust Journal* 4 (Spring 1969): 11–28.

2073. Jones, Mary G., and Boyer, Barry B. "Improving the Quality of Justice in the Marketplace: The Need for Better Consumer Remedies." *George Washington Law Review* 40 (March 1972): 357–415.

2074. Kass, Benny. "S.2589 and the Uniform Consumer Credit Code: A Comparison of Consumer Protections." *George Washington Law Review* 37 (July 1969): 1131–53.

2075. Kawaja, Michael N. "Regulation of the New York State Consumer Finance Industry." Ph.D. dissertation, Columbia University, 1964. 210 p.

2076. Kripke, Homer. "Consumer Credit Regulation: A Creditor Oriented Viewpoint." *Columbia Law Review* 68 (March 1969): 445–87.

2077. Lancaster, K. J. "A New Approach to Consumer Theory." *Journal of Political Economy* 74 (April 1966): 132–57.

2078. Leland, Hayne E. "Quacks, Lemons, and Licensing: A Theory of Minimum Quality Standards." *Journal of Political Economy* 87 (December 1979): 1328–46.

2079. Madel, Mark V. "Consumerism: A Coalition in Flux." *Policy Studies Journal* 4 (Autumn 1975): 31–35.

2080. Maney, Ardith L. "Regulating Business in New York City: The Departments of Markets, Licenses and Consumer Affairs, 1933–1973." Ph.D. dissertation, Columbia University, 1975. 381 p.

2081. Mangione, Thomas W., and Fowler, Floyd J. "Enforcing the Gambling Laws." *Journals of Social Issues* 35 (Summer 1979): 115–28.

2082. McClure, J. A. "Toward a Neo-Consumerism." *Trial* 14 (February 1978): 33–35.

2083. McNeil, Kenneth, et al. "Market Discrimination against the Poor and the Impact of Consumer Disclosure Laws: The Used Car Industry." *Law and Society Review* 13 (Spring 1979): 695–720.

2084. McNulty, Paul J. "Consumer and the Producer." *Yale Review* 58 (June 1969): 537–48.

2085. Morey, R. S. "FDA Publicity against Consumer Products—Time for Statutory Revitalization?" *Business Lawyer* 30 (November 1974): 165–78.

2086. Nader, Ralph. "Consumerism and Legal Services: The Merging of Movements." *Law and Society Review* 11 (1976): 247–56.

2087. Percy, C. H. "Need for an Agency for Consumer Advocacy." *Trial* 14 (February 1978): 30–32.

2088. Perkins, J. H. "Inflation by Regulation: The Consumer Is the Victim." *Across the Board* 16 (July 1979): 78–80.

2089. Pitofsky, Robert. "Beyond Nader: Consumer Protection and the Regulation of Advertising." *Harvard Law Review* 90 (February 1977): 661–701.

2090. Preston, Homer J. "Distributor, Producer, and Consumer Knowledge and Opinion of the Pennsylvania Milk Control Commission and Its Regulatory Functions." Ph.D. dissertation, Pennsylvania State University, 1950. 303 p.

2091. "Regulation of Investment Advisers." *Stanford Law Review* 14 (July 1962): 827–47.

2092. Richardson, Barrie. "State Regulations of Retail Installment Credit—Revolving Credit Sales." Ph.D. dissertation, Indiana University, 1963.

2093. Riska, Elainne, and Taylor, James A. "Consumer Attitudes toward Health Policy and Knowledge." *Journal of Health Politics, Policy and Law* 3 (Spring 1978): 112–23.

2094. Schweig, Barry B. "The Consumer as Plaintiff." *Current History* 78 (May 1980): 197–200.

2095. Scotton, Donald W. "A Study of the Regulation of Consumer Installment Credit." Ph.D. dissertation, University of Illinois, 1952. 283 p.

2096. Shay, Robert P. "Justification for Direct Regulation of Consumer Credit Reappraised." *Journal of Finance* 8 (May 1953): 272–77.

2097. Shick, Blair C. "Need for Increased Regulation of Consumer Credit." *Credit World* 62 (December 1973): 11–15.

2098. Skolnick, Jerome H. "The Dilemmas of Regulating Casino Gambling." *Journal of Social Issues* 35 (Summer 1979): 129–43.

2099. Stonebraker, Michael. "Evaluating Consumer Product Hazards." *Policy Sciences* 7 (September 1976): 337–50.

2100. Tedlow, Richard S. "From Competitor to Consumer: The Changing Focus of Federal Regulation of Advertising, 1914–1938." *Business History Review* 55 (Spring 1981): 35–58.

2101. Thaler, Richard, and Gould, William. "Public Policy toward Life Saving: Should Consumer Preferences Rule?" *Journal of Policy Analysis and Management* 1 (1982): 223–42.

2102. Twinem, Lynn K. "New York Leads the Way in Consumer Legislation." *New York State Bar Journal* 42 (October 1970): 540–47.

2103. Wade, John W., and Kamenshine, Robert D. "Restitution for Defrauded Consumers: Making the Remedy Effective through Suit by Governmental Agency." *George Washington Law Review* 37 (July 1969): 1031–66.

2104. Williams, Carla S. "FDA's Consumer Consultant Program." *Food Drug Cosmetic Law Journal* 16 (September 1961): 569–75.

2105. Wines, Michael. "Administration, Critics Play Legal Cat and Mouse Game on Agency Rules: Consumer and Environmental Critics Have Been Filing Lawsuits to Block Weakening of Regulations." *National Journal* 14 (December 18, 1982): 2,157–60.

2106. Winter, Ralph K. *The Consumer Advocate vs. the Consumer.* Washington, DC: American Enterprise Institute, 1972. 16 p.

2107. Winter, Ralph K. "Regulation of the Consumer Finance Industry: A Reappraisal of Its Economic Impact." Ph.D. dissertation, Ohio State University, 1967. 187 p.

EDUCATION

2108. Allen, Russ, and Clark, Jill. "State Policy Adoption and Innovation: Lobbying and Education." *State and Local Government Review* 13 (January 1981): 18–25.

2109. Atkin, J. Myron. "The Government in the Classroom." *Daedalus* 109 (Summer 1980): 85–97.

2110. Battle, Haron. "State Involvement in the Urban Education Crisis." *Journal of Negro Education* 42 (Summer 1973): 315–21.

2111. Bok, Derek C. "The Federal Government and the University." *Public Interest* 15 (Winter 1980): 80–101.

2112. Bradshaw, James A. "Survey of Laws, Regulations, and Administrative Procedures Relating to Learning Disability and Other Related Programs in the Various States." Ed.D. dissertation, University of Idaho, 1971. 209 p.

2113. Brown, Paul R. "A Study of Rules and Regulations of Boards of Education in New Jersey." Ph.D. dissertation, Rutgers University, 1951. 134 p.

2114. Bullock, Charles S. "The Office for Civil Rights and Implementation of Desegregation Programs in the Public Schools." *Policy Studies Journal* 8 (1980): 597–616.

2115. Butler, Edward R. "Legal Issues Pertaining to the Regulation of Pupil Control Interpreted in Light of Certain Social Changes, 1828–1900." Ph.D. dissertation, University of Pittsburgh, 1956. 145 p.

2116. Cleary, Robert E. "Federal Higher Education Policy: A View from the Campus." *Policy Studies Journal* 10 (September 1981): 85–95.

2117. Cone, William H. "Development of School Committee Policy and Administrative Regulations in Longmeadow, Massachusetts." Ph.D. dissertation, Harvard University, 1962.

2118. Cooke, Robert P. "An Analysis of the Opinions of Undergraduate Students and Their Parents Regarding Rules, Regulations, and Disciplinary Procedures." Ed.D. dissertation, Indiana University, 1971. 231.

2119. Crowell, Robert A. "Regulations Pertaining to Missouri's Teachers, Principals and Superintendents as Defined by Written Rules and Regulations of the Local Boards of Education." Ed.D. dissertation, University of Missouri—Columbia, 1950. 323 p.

2120. DeBruin, Hendrik C. "State Regulation of Local School District Financial Administration." Ph.D. dissertation, University of Arizona, 1962. 221 p.

2121. Determan, Dean, and Ware, Gilbert. "New Dimensions in Education: Title VI of the Civil Rights Act of 1964." *Journal of Negro Education* 35 (Winter 1966): 5–10.

2122. Douglas, Stephen. "Policy Issues in Sport and Athletics." *Policy Studies Journal* 7 (Autumn 1978): 137–51.

2123. Emerson, William J. "Financing Public Schools in Michigan, An Analysis and Criticism of the Effect of State Regulations on the Operation of Public Schools." Ed.D. dissertation, Wayne State University, 1955. 236 p.

2124. Erbe, Wesley A. "A Proposed Program of Policies, Regulations, and Criteria for the Approval of Iowa Public Secondary Schools." Ph.D. dissertation, University of Iowa, 1956. 159 p.

2125. Farrar, Donald L. "A Written Codification of the Policies, Rules and Regulation for the Public Schools of White Plains, New York." Ph.D. dissertation, Columbia University, 1960.

2126. Fike, George J. "The Evolution of the Regulatory Functions of the Department of Public Instruction in Pennsylvania (1834–1952)." Ph.D. dissertation, University of Pittsburgh, 1954. 241 p.

2127. Guthrie, James W. "The Future of Federal Education Policy." *Education and Urban Society* 14 (August 1982): 511–30.

2128. Hamilton, Bette Everett, and Yohalem, Daniel. "The Effects of Federal Deregulation: The Case of Handicapped Children." *Education and Urban Society* 14 (August 1982): 399–423.

2129. Hamilton, William J. "The Regulation of Proprietary Schools in the United States." Ph.D. dissertation, University of Pennsylvania, 1958. 356 p.

2130. Harmon, James J. "A Case Study: The Identification, Clarification, Development, and Codification of the Policies, Rules, and Regulations of the Board of Education of Lawrence, Kansas." Ed. D. dissertation, University of Kansas, 1962. 592 p.

2131. Hartstein, Jacob I. "State Regulatory and Supervisory Control of Higher Education in New York from Its Beginning through the Civil War." Ph.D. dissertation, New York University, 1945. 224 p.

2132. Hendrick, Irving. "Academic Revolution in California: A History of Events Leading to the Passage and Implementation of the 1961 Fisher Bill on Teacher Certification. Part I." *Southern California Quarterly* 49 (Summer 1967): 127–66.

2133. Hendrick, Irving. "Academic Revolution in California: A History of Events Leading to the Passage and Implementation of the 1961 Fisher Bill on Teacher Certification. Part II." *Southern California Quarterly* 49 (Fall 1967): 253–95.

2134. Hendrick, Irving. "Academic Revolution in California: A History of Events Leading to the Passage and Implementation of the 1961 Fisher Bill on Teacher Certification. Part III." *Southern California Quarterly* 49 (Winter 1967): 359–406.

2135. Hilton, Harry H. "Regulatory and Supervisory Services for Privately Owned Correspondence, Business, Trade, and Technical Schools and Their Representatives as Provided by the State Education Agencies in the Fifty States." Ed.D. dissertation, University of Nebraska—Lincoln, 1964. 202 p.

2136. Himmelheber, John W. "An Analysis of Recent Higher Court Decisions on the Regulation of Public School Pupil Conduct." Ph.D. dissertation, Indiana State University, 1971. 247 p.

2137. Hoachlander, E. Gareth. "Considering Deregulation in Education: Experience with the Vocational Education Act." *Education and Urban Society* 14 (August 1982): 425–41.

2138. Jackman, Mary R. "Education and Policy Commitment to Racial Integration." *American Journal of Political Science* 25 (May 1981): 256–69.

2139. Jackson, Russell A. "Rules, Regulations, Standards and Legal Aspects of State Provisions for Programs for Early Childhood Education." Ed.D. dissertation, Temple University, 1970. 420 p.

2140. Joyner, Thomas. "Legalization and Regulation of Professions and Occupations in New York State." Ph.D. dissertation, Syracuse University, 1951. 354 p.

2141. Kavanaugh, Allen H. "An Analysis of State Laws and Selected Handbooks to Determine the Pattern of Rules and Regulations Exercised by School Boards in the Control of Local Schools." Ed.D. dissertation, University of Northern Colorado, 1953. 166 p.

2142. Kelley, Dean. "State Regulations of the Participation of Pupils of Private Schools in Title I of the Federal Aid to Education Act of 1965." *Church and State* 8 (Autumn 1966): 415–29.

2143. Kirkland, Billy R. "The Perceptions of Selected Groups of Practitioners, Regulators, and Educators in Real Estate and Related Fields Regarding the Effects of the Revised Real Estate License Act on Educational Institutions and Various Segments of the Real Estate Industry in Texas." Ph.D. dissertation, East Texas State University, 1978. 367 p.

2144. Landes, William, and Solomon, Lewis. "Compulsory Schooling Legislation: An Economic Analysis of Law and Social Change in the Nineteenth Century." *Journal of Economic History* 32 (March 1972): 54–91.

2145. LaNoue, George R. "Is the Federal Government Controlling Education? The Federal Tailors." *Education and Urban Society* 9 (February 1977): 197–214.

2146. Leslie, John M. "The Organization and Administration of the Program of Vocational Education in Private Trade Schools for New York State: An Analysis of the Laws and Regulations of the Several States Concerning Private Trade Schools Resulting in an Administrative Handbook." Ed.D. dissertation, New York University, 1960. 308 p.

2147. Long, Robert P. "State Laws, Regulations, and Recommendations Related to the Grade Organization of Junior High Schools in the Fifty States, with Particular Reference to Connecticut." Ph.D. dissertation, University of Connecticut, 1970. 283 p.

2148. Marcus, Lawrence R., and Hollander, Edward T. "The Capital and the Campus—Each in Its Proper Place." *Policy Studies Journal* 10 (September 1981): 19–32.

2149. Martin, Donald L. "Will the Sun Set on Occupational Licensing?" *State Government* 53 (Summer 1980): 157–60.

2150. McClure, Phyllis. "Deregulation of Title I: A Lesson to Be Learned from the Past." *Education and Urban Society* 14 (August 1982): 443–55.

2151. Medhurst, Richard Russell. "Legal Regulation of the Social Work Profession: With Special Reference to the California Registered Social Worker Program." D.S.W. dissertation, University of Southern California, 1959. 267 p.

2152. Merrow, John. "The Politics of Federal Educational Policy: The Case of Educational Renewal." *Teachers College Record* 76 (September 1974): 19–38.

2153. Morford, John A. "The Teacher as Lawmaker: A Study of the Extent of and Limits to Teachers' Power to Make Rules and Regulations as Shown by an Analysis of the Decisions of American Courts." Ed.D. dissertation, University of Idaho, 1963. 239 p.

2154. Murray, Jeanne M. "Development and Application of a Methodology for Policy Design: New Directions for the Role of Governmental Regulation in University Affairs." Ph.D. dissertation, American University, 1980. 320 p.

2155. Nelson, Arvid E. "A History of the Policies, Rules, and Regulations of the Public Schools of Omaha, Nebraska from 1870 to 1964." Ed.D. dissertation University of Nebraska—Lincoln, 1969. 491 p.

2156. Nihan, James F. "A Study of State Laws and State Education Department Regulations for Safety Education in the Public Schools of the United States." Ed.D. dissertation, New York University, 1961. 352 p.

2157. Orlich, Donald C. "A Case Study of the Development and Codification of School Board Policies and Administrative Regulations." Ed.D. dissertation, Montana State University, 1963. 255 p.

2158. Rabkin, Jeremy. "Behind the Tax-Exempt Schools Debate." *Public Interest* 68 (Summer 1982): 21–36.

2159. Rand, Maritt J. "Rules and Regulations for Noncity School Districts in California." Ph.D. dissertation, University of Southern California, 1952.

2160. Rowen, Robert B. "The Impact of Federal Legislation on School Social Work." *Social Work* 12 (April 1967): 109–15.

2161. Sellers, Robert. "A Methodology for Evaluating University Public Service Outreach to State and Local Government." *State and Local Government Review* 11 (May 1979): 64–69.

2162. Shannon, Wilburn A. "Planning, Developing, and Implementing of School Committee Policies and Administrative Regulations in Scituate, Massachusetts." Ph.D. dissertation, Harvard University, 1966.

2163. Stern, David, and Timar, Thomas. "Conflict and Choice in Public Education." *Education and Urban Society* 14 (August 1982): 485–510.

2164. Stern, Robert N. "Competitive Influences on the Interorganizational Regulation of College Athletics." *Administrative Science Quarterly* 26 (March 1981): 15–32.

2165. Strong, Donald V. "Teacher Perception of School Board Regulations and Administrative Policies: Springfield, Illinois." Ph.D. dissertation, Southern Illinois University, 1963. 92 p.

2166. Templeton, Wayne K. "Legislative Regulation of Teachers' Salaries." Ed.D. dissertation, University of Southern California, 1963. 169 p.

2167. Vaughn, William P. "Separate and Unequal: The Civil Rights Act of 1875 and Defeat of the School Integration Clause." *Social Science Quarterly* 48 (September 1967): 146–54.

2168. Whitten, Milton R. "The Status of Illinois School Programs for Children with Learning Disabilities with Implications for Changes in Rules and Regulations." Ph.D. dissertation, Southern Illinois University, 1970. 207 p.

2169. Vitullo-Martin, Thomas. "Federal Policies and Private Schools." *Proceedings of the Academy of Political Science* 33 (1978): 124–35.

ENERGY

2170. Al-Bassam, Sadik M. "An Evaluation of OPEC Conservation Regulation Systems of the Hydrocarbon Resources: The Case of Kuwait." Ph.D. dissertation, University of Texas at Austin, 1980. 629 p.

2171. Alesi, Louis De. "An Economic Analysis of Government Ownership and Regulation: Theory and the Evidence from the Electric Power Industry." *Public Choice* 19 (Fall 1974): 1–42.

2172. Anderson, Mark W. "Regulatory Policy toward Domestic Crude Oil Production." *Policy Sciences* 12 (October 1980): 245–64.

2173. Aron, Joan B. "Intergovernmental Politics of Energy." *Policy Analysis* 5 (Fall 1979): 451–71.

2174. Atkinson, Edward L. "Federal Regulation of Natural Gas—The Independent Producers' Status." *Southwestern Law Journal* 13 (Fall 1959): 425–505.

2175. Attwell, J. E. "Acquiring, Developing, and Transporting Natural Gas for the Industrial or Other End User." *Rocky Mountain Mineral Law Institute* 23 (1977): 825–40.

2176. Attwell, J. E. "Project Financing for Offshore and Onshore Gas Facilities: Regulatory Problems Involved." *Oil and Gas Law and Taxation Institute* 28 (1977): 292–307.

2177. Bergman, Elihu. "American Energy Dependence: A Failure of Political Authority." *Middle East Review* 12 (Fall 1979): 5–10.

2178. Berner, Arthur, and Scoggins, Sue. "Oil and Gas Drilling Programs—Structure and Regulation." *George Washington Law Review* 41 (March 1973): 471–504.

2179. Bissell, Richard E. "The Role of the International Oil Companies." *Current History* 74 (May–June 1978): 202–05, 227.

2180. Bond, John R. "Oiling the Tax Committee in Congress, 1900–1974: Subgovernment Theory, the Over-Representation Hypothesis, and the Oil Depletion Allowance." *American Journal of Political Science* 23 (November 1979): 651–64.

2181. Breyer, Stephen, and MacAvoy, Paul W. "The Natural Gas Shortage and the Regulation of Natural Gas Producers." *Harvard Law Review* 86 (April 1973): 941–87.

2182. Carver, John A. "Governmental and Regulatory Aspects of the Energy Crisis." *Institute on Mineral Law* 20 (1973): 105–21.

2183. Carver, John A. "Significant Regulatory Developments under the Natural Gas Act in 1968." *Oil and Gas Law and Taxation Institute* 20 (1969): 1–25.

2184. "Case for a White Market in the Allocation of Natural Gas during Shortages." *Texas Law Review* 57 (March 1979): 615–39.

2185. Castle, Emery; Kelso, Maurice; and Gardner, Delworth. "Water Resources Development: A Review of the New Federal Evaluation Procedures." *American Journal of Agricultural Economics* 45 (November 1963): 693–704.

2186. Cockrell, W. F. "Exceptions to Federal Regulations for Management of the Energy Crisis: The Emerging Agency Case Law." *Oklahoma Law Review* 28 (Summer 1975): 530–44.

2187. Cockrell, W. F. "Federal Regulation of Energy: Evolution of the Exceptions Process." *Administrative Law Review* 27 (Summer 1975): 233–53.

2188. Cohen, Robert L., and Lichter, S. R. "Nuclear Power—The Decision Makers Speak." *Regulation* 7 (March–April 1982): 32–37.

2189. "Colloquy on the Trial of a Case before the FERC: The Administrative Law Judge's Perspective." *Energy Law Journal* 3 (1982): 317–30.

2190. Colwell, Leonard F. "The Federal Regulation of Distribution of Industrial Fuels and Its Effect on Their Competitive Position in the Market." Ph.D. dissertation, American University, 1969. 335 p.

2191. Conine, G. B., and Niebrugge, T. W. "Dedication under the Natural Gas Act: Extent and Escape." *Oklahoma Law Review* 30 (Fall 1977): 735–833.

2192. Cook, Earl. "The Role of History in the Acceptance of Nuclear Power." *Social Science Quarterly* 63 (March 1982): 3–15.

2193. Copp, Emmanuel A. "Governmental Regulation and Industry Structure in Petroleum Refining: An Anatomy of Policy Failure, 1948–1973." Ph.D. dissertation, Texas A&M University, 1974. 346 p.

2194. Copp, Emmanuel A. *Regulating Competition in Oil: Government Intervention in the U.S. Refining Industry, 1948–1975.* College Station, TX: Texas A&M University Press, 1976. 280 p.

2195. Cormie, C. "Incremental Pricing under the Natural Gas Policy Act of 1978." *Denver Law Journal* 57 (1979): 1–20.

2196. Dacy, Douglas C., and Kuenne, Robert E. "Simple Theories in Complex Contexts: The Gasoline Misfueling Problem." *Journal of Policy Analysis and Management* 1 (1982): 269–72.

2197. Dam, Kenneth. "Implementation of Import Quotas: The Case of Oil." *Journal of Law and Economics* 14 (April 1971): 1–60.

2198. Davidson, Paul. "Public Policy Problems of the Domestic Crude Oil Industry." *American Economic Review* 53 (March 1963): 85–108.

2199. DeAlessi, Louis. "An Economic Analysis of Government Ownership and Regulation: Theory and the Evidence from the Electric Power Industry." *Public Choice* 19 (Fall 1974): 1–42.

2200. DeAlessi, Louis. "Managerial Tenure under Private and Government Ownership in the Electric Power Industry." *Journal of Political Economy* 82 (May 1974): 645–53.

2201. DeAlessi, Louis. "Some Effects of Ownership on the Wholesale Prices of Electric Power." *Economic Inquiry* 13 (December 1975): 526–38.

2202. DeSeyn, R. J., and Mandelbaum, P. "Electric Power Politics and the Uses of Science." *Public Utilities Fortnightly* 112 (September 29, 1983): 28–34.

2203. DiLeon, A. M. "Introduction to the Mandatory Petroleum Allocation Regulations." *Louisiana Bar Journal* 22 (September 1974): 107–21.

2204. Dimopoulos, Dionissios A. "Pricing Schemes for Regulated Enterprises and Their Implications in the Case of Electricity." Ph.D. dissertation, Columbia University, 1979. 83 p.

2205. Dunn, Lewis A. "Nuclear Gray Marketeering." *International Security* 1 (Winter 1977): 107–18.

2206. Easterbrook, Gregg. "Synthetic Progress: The Fifth Annual Report of the Energy Security Corporation, July 15, 1984." *Regulation* 3 (November–December 1979): 40–43.

2207. Eichner, Donald O. "The Inter-American Nuclear Energy Commission: Its Goals and Achievements." Ph.D. dissertation, American University, 1968. 206 p.

2208. Ely, Northcutt. "One OPEC Is Enough!" *Regulation* 5 (November–December 1981): 19–24.

2209. Emery, Edward D. "An Investigation of the Potential Welfare Effects Associated with Rate of Return Regulation of the Steam-Electric Industry in the United States." Ph.D. dissertation, University of Minnesota, 1969. 123 p.

2210. "Energy Reorganization Act of 1974: More Power to the People?" *Loyola University Law Journal* (Chicago) 7 (Spring 1976): 410–30.

2211. Fajaee, Ahmad A. "The Organization of Petroleum Exporting Countries (An Inquiry Pertaining to the Trends Leading to the Creation of This Regulatory Mechanism)." Ph.D. dissertation, American University, 1964. 235 p.

2212. Fiorino, Daniel J. "The Federal Courts and the Regulatory Process: The Cases of Natural Gas and Broadcasting." Ph.D. dissertation, Johns Hopkins University, 1977. 425 p.

2213. Flittie, William J., and Armour, James L. "The Natural Gas Act Experience—A Study in Regulatory Aggression and Congressional Failure to Control the Legislative Process." *Southwestern Law Journal* 19 (September 1965): 448–522.

2214. Formby, J. P., and Harrison, J. L. "Regional Distortions in Natural Gas Allocations: A Legal and Economic Analysis." *North Carolina Law Review* 57 (October 1978): 57–89.

2215. Garbarino, Robert P. "How a Lawyer 'Builds' a Nuclear Power Plant." *Villanova Law Review* 7 (Summer 1962): 587–610.

2216. Gerwig, Robert W. "Natural Gas Production: A Study of Costs of Regulation." *Journal of Law and Economics* 5 (October 1962): 69–92.

2217. Gilinsky, Victor. "Plutonium Proliferation and the Price of Reprocessing." *Foreign Affairs* 57 (Winter 1978–1979): 374–86.

2218. Gold, Fern R., and Ebinger, Charles K. "The Government's Role in the Energy Crisis." *Current History* 74 (July–August 1978): 27–30, 35–37.

2219. Goldmuntz, Lawrence. "American Energy Policies." *Middle East Review* 14 (Spring–Summer 1982): 13–23.

2220. Gordon, Richard L. "Hobbling Coal—Or How to Serve Two Masters Poorly." *Regulation* 2 (July–August 1978): 36–45.

2221. Green, Harold P. "Nuclear Power Licensing and Regulation." *American Academy of Political and Social Science Annals* 400 (March 1972): 116–26.

2222. Greene, Julian M. "An Empirical Analysis of Rate-of-Return Regulation and Its Effect on Investment in Steam-Electric Generation." Ph.D. dissertation, University of Minnesota, 1971. 129 p.

2223. Greer, Thomas V. "Marketing of Natural Gas from the Permian Basin: Producer Practices and Federal Regulation, 1954–1963." Ph.D. dissertation, University of Texas, 1964. 167 p.

2224. Grossman, Henry. "The Problem of Reasonable Market Prices in the Regulation of Independent Producers of Natural Gas." Ph.D. dissertation, Georgetown University, 1961.

2225. Gruening, Ernest H. *The Public Pays: A Study of Power Propaganda.* New and enl. ed. New York: Vanguard Press, 1964. 273 p.

2226. Haase, B. L. "Federal Role in Implementing the Natural Gas Policy Act of 1978." *Houston Law Review* 16 (July 1979): 1067–80.

2227. Habicht, E. R. "America's Hidden Energy Policy: Federal Regulation and Taxation." *Current History* 74 (May–June 1978): 219–21.

2228. Hall, Clyde L. "Federal Regulation of the Natural Gas Industry with Special Reference to the Problems of Interstate Transmission." Ph.D. dissertation, Ohio State University, 1950.

2229. Hall, R. E., and Pindyck, R. S. "The Conflicting Goals of National Energy Policy." *Public Interest* 47 (Spring 1977): 3–15.

2230. Haney, R. L., et al. "Hidden Cost of Federal Energy Legislation." *California Management Life Underwriters* 22 (Fall 1979): 13–22.

2231. Hansen, John A. "Competitive Aspects of the United States Petroleum Pipeline Industry: Implications for Regulatory Policy." Ph.D. dissertation, Yale University, 1980. 195 p.

2232. Hausman, J. A. "Project Independence Report: An Appraisal of U.S. Energy Needs up to 1985." *Bell Journal of Economics and Management Science* 6 (Autumn 1975): 517–51.

2233. Hawkins, Clark A. "The Cost Problem in the Field Price Regulation of Natural Gas." Ph.D. dissertation, Purdue University, 1964. 289 p.

2234. Helfrich, Ralph W. "Administrative Regulation of Natural Gas Rates, 1898–1938." Ph.D. dissertation, Indiana University, 1962. 359 p.

2235. Henderson, Carter. "More Regulation Needed: America's Energy Policy Tomorrow." *Current History* 74 (July–August 1978): 23–26, 33–34.

2236. Herman, S. A. "Introductions to Natural Gas Curtailments." *Law Notes* 11 (Spring 1975): 33–38.

2237. Horwich, George, and Weimer, David L. "The Next Oil Shock—Giving the Market a Chance." *Regulation* 8 (March–April 1984): 16–24.

2238. Huie, William O. "Apportionment of Oil and Gas Royalties." *Harvard Law Review* 78 (June 1965): 1534–67.

2239. Huitt, Ralph K. "National Regulation of the Natural Gas Industry." Ph.D. dissertation, University of Texas, 1950.

2240. Ingles, Joseph L. "The Missouri Public Service Commission: A Preliminary Survey." Ph.D. dissertation, University of Missouri, 1968. 274 p.

2241. Johnson, James P. "Drafting the NRA Code of Fair Competition for the Bituminous Coal Industry." *Journal of American History* 53 (December 1966): 521–41.

2242. Joskow, Paul L. "Approving Nuclear Power Plants: Scientific Decisionmaking or Administrative Charade?" *Bell Journal of Economics and Mangement Science* 5 (Spring 1974): 320–32.

2243. Joskow, Paul L., and MacAvoy, Paul W. "Regulation and the Financial Condition of the Electric Power Companies in the 1970s." *American Economic Review* 65 (May 1975): 295–301.

2244. Joskow, Paul L., and Pindyck, Robert S. "Synthetic Fuels—Should the Government Subsidize Non-Conventional Energy Supplies?" *Regulation* 3 (September–October 1979): 18–24.

2245. Kaufman, Burton I. "Oil and Antitrust: The Oil Cartel Case and the Cold War." *Business History Review* 51 (Spring 1977): 35–56.

2246. Keating, William T. "Politics, Energy, and the Environment: The Role of Technology Assessment." *American Behavioral Scientist* 19 (September–October 1975): 37–74.

2247. Kennedy, W. McNeil, and Wander, Herbert S. "Texas Gulf Sulphur, A Most Unusual Case." *Business Lawyer* 20 (July 1965): 1057–74.

2248. Kerrigan, Mark L. "Decision Making in the Management of Energy Regulation." *Public Administration Review* 39 (November–December 1979): 553–55.

2249. Kindt, John W. "Offshore Siting of Nuclear Power Plants." *Ocean Development and International Law* 8 (1980): 57–103.

2250. Klausner, Samuel Z. "The Energy Social System." *American Academy of Political and Social Science, Annals* 444 (July 1979): 1–22.

2251. Langdon, J. C. "FEA Price Controls for Crude Oil and Refined Petroleum Products." *Oil and Gas Law and Taxation Institute* 26 (1975): 55–100.

2252. "Legal Considerations in Nuclear Power Plant Siting in Light of the Energy Reorganization Act of 1974." *New England Law Review* 10 (Spring 1975): 305–23.

2253. Lemann, N. "Why the Sun Will Never Set on the Federal Empire." *Washington Monthly* 88 (September 1976): 32–41.

2254. Lewis, Ben W. "Public Policy and the Growth of the Power Industry." *Journal of Economic History* 7 (1947): 47–55.

2255. Longin, Thomas C. "Coal, Congress and the Courts: The Bituminous Coal Industry and the New Deal." *West Virginia History* 35 (January 1974): 101–30.

2256. Lovejoy, Wallace F. "The Regulation of Natural Gas and Its Economic Background." Ph.D. dissertation, University of Wisconsin, 1956. 535 p.

2257. Matthew, Dieter. "Regulating the Coal Industry: Federal Coal Mine Health and Safety and Surface Mining Policy Development." Ph.D. dissertation, University of Pittsburgh, 1977. 296 p.

2258. Mead, Walter J. *Energy and the Environment: Conflict in Public Policy.* Washington, DC: American Enterprise Institute for Public Policy Research, 1978. 36 p.

2259. Mead, Walter J. "The National Energy Program Evaluated." *Current History* 74 (July–August 1978): 9–12, 31–33.

2260. Milligan, C. E. "Anatomy of a Gas Purchase Contract." *Rocky Mountain Mineral Law Institute* 23 (1977): 771–802.

2261. Mitchell, Edward J. "Viewpoint: New Ideas about Oil Mergers." *Regulation* 8 (March–April 1984): 13–15.

2262. Mitchell, Edward J. "Viewpoint: Oil, Film, and Folklore." *Regulation* 2 (July–August 1978): 17–20.

2263. Mitchell, Edward J., and Chaffetz, Peter R. *Toward Economy in Electric Power.* Washington, DC: American Enterprise Institute for Public Policy Research, 1975. 32 p.

2264. Moe, Ronald C. "Government Corporations and the Erosion of Accountability: The Case of the Proposed Energy Security Corporation." *Public Administration Review* 39 (November–December 1979): 566–71.

2265. Moody, R. "Uncertainty in Natural Gas Regulation and Legislation—A Dilemma for the Gas Producer and His Attorney." *Rocky Mountain Mineral Law Institute* 22 (1976): 695–730.

2266. Morgan, Richard G. "Application and Enforcement of the Natural Gas Policy Act of 1978: Administrative and Legal Problems." *Rocky Mountain Mineral Law Institute* 25 (1979): 13.1–13.37.

2267. "National Energy Goals and FEA's Mandatory Crude Oil Allocation Program." *Virginia Law Review* 61 (May 1975): 903–37.

2268. "Natural Gas Rate Regulation: The Conflict in the Application of the Just and Reasonable Standard." *Tulsa Law Journal* 12 (1976): 293–322.

2269. Navarro, Peter. "Electric Utility Regulation and National Energy Policy." *Regulation* 5 (January–February 1981): 20–27.

2270. Navarro, Peter. "Save Now, Freeze Later—The Real Price of Cheap Electricity." *Regulation* 7 (September–October 1983): 31–36.

2271. Nelkin, Dorothy, and Sills, David L. "Some Social and Political Dimensions of Nuclear Power: Examples from Three Mile Island." *American Political Science Review* 75 (March 1981): 132–45.

2272. Nelson, Robert M. "Undue Diligence—The Mine-It-or-Lose-It Rule for Federal Coal." *Regulation* 7 (January–February 1983): 34–38.

2273. Nordhauser, Norman. "Origins of Federal Oil Regulation in the 1920's." *Business History Review* 47 (Spring 1973): 53–71.

2274. Nowak, G. P., and Watts-Fitzgerald, A. C. "Regulatory Incentives for Development of Congeneration Facilities." *Natural Resources Law* 13 (1981): 613–31.

2275. Olson, Charles E. "Regulatory Needs under Changing Technology in the Electric Power Industry." Ph.D. dissertation, University of Wisconsin, 1968. 139 p.

2276. Oppedahl, Richard A. "An Analysis of the Use of Cost of Capital Concepts in Natural Gas Pipeline Rate Regulation." D.B.A. dissertation, University of Washington, 1967. 170 p.

2277. Orren, Lowell Harris. "A General Equilibrium Model of Optimal Rate of Return Regulation with an Application to Electricity." Ph.D. dissertation, University of Minnesota, 1979. 67 p.

2278. Pelsoci, Thomas M. "The Energy Crisis and the New Breed of Regulators: A Study of State Public Utility Commissions." *Midwest Review of Public Administration* 13 (March 1979): 51–61.

2279. Phelps, Charles E., and Smith, Rodney. "Petroleum Regulation: The False Dilemma of Decontrol." *Policy Studies* 3 (1979): 237–40.

2280. Pindyck, Robert S. "The Natural Gas Industry." *Current History* 74 (May–June 1978): 215–17, 229.

2281. Rankin, Bob. "New Department Given Wide Energy Powers." *Congressional Quarterly* 35 (July 30, 1977): 1581–84.

2282. "Refund Beneficiaries and Refund Credits under the Natural Gas Act." *University of Chicago Law Review* 41 (Summer 1974): 792–813.

2283. Regens, James L., and Rycroft, Robert W. "Administrative Discretion in Energy Policy-Making: The Exceptions and Appeals Program of the Federal Energy Administration." *Journal of Politics* 43 (August 1981): 875–88.

2284. "Regulating Independent Gas Producers: The First Area Attempt." *University of Pennsylvania Law Review* 115 (November 1966): 84–87.

2285. Renshaw, Edward F. "The Decontrol of U.S. Oil Production." *Energy Policy* 8 (March 1980): 38–49.

2286. Rosenberg, Laurence C. "Natural-Gas-Pipeline Rate Regulation: Marginal Cost Pricing and the Zone-Allocation Problem." *Journal of Political Economy* 75 (March–April 1967): 159–68.

2287. Rowen, Henry R., and Rowen, Beverly C. "Nuclear Power: A Boon or a Menace?" *Current History* 74 (July–August 1978): 19–22, 38–48.

2288. Rycroft, Robert W. "The United States Oil Industry." *Current History* 74 (May–June 1978): 193–97, 225–26.

2289. Scott, Michael J. "Some Implications of Petroleum Conservation Regulation." Ph.D. dissertation, University of Washington, 1975. 297 p.

2290. Scott, N. Kenneth. "The Federal Certificate Regulation of Producer Gas Sales: Initial Rates and Related Problems." *Southwestern Law Journal* 18 (December 1964): 570–700.

2291. "Securities Act of 1933—Resale of Assignments of Oil and Gas Leases as Security—Investment Contract." *George Washington Law Review* 12 (June 1944): 494–96.

2292. Shoup, Carl S. "Envoi—The National Energy Act of 1978." *Growth and Change* 10 (January 1979): 90–92.

2293. Smith, V. Kerry. "Regulating Energy: Indicative Planning or Creeping Nationalization." *Policy Studies* 3 (1979): 203–26.

2294. Stahr, Walter. "The Priority Energy Project Act: A New Remedy for the Law's Delay." *Publius* 10 (Winter 1980): 93–99.

2295. "State and Local Regulation Affecting Performance of Commercial Plowshare Projects." *Atomic Energy Law Journal* 12 (Summer 1970): 184–206.

2296. "Supreme Court Denies Extension of Federal Regulation of Natural Gas Producers." *Natural Resources Journal* 20 (January 1980): 187–98.

2297. Symington, Stuart. "The Washington Nuclear Mess." *International Security* 1 (Winter 1977): 71–78.

2298. Temples, J. R. "Politics of Nuclear Power: A Sub-Government in Transition." *Political Science Quarterly* 95 (Summer 1980): 239–60.

2299. Tiano, J. Richard. "Limits of Federal Regulation of Natural Gas Curtailments." *Georgetown Law Journal* 64 (October 1975): 27–41.

2300. Tiano, J. Richard, and Zimmer, M. J. "Wheeling for Cogeneration and Small Power Production Facilities." *Energy Law Journal* 3 (1982): 95–109.

2301. United States. Library of Congress. Congressional Research Service. *Federal Energy Reorganization: Historical Perspective.* Washington, DC: U.S. Government Printing Office, 1976. 1359 p.

2302. Van Tine, K. K. "Enforcement Issues under the Natural Gas Act of 1938 and the Natural Gas Policy Act of 1978." *Houston Law Review* 16 (July 1979): 1025–65.

2303. Von Hippel, Frank. "Looking Back on the Rasmussen Report." *Bulletin of the Atomic Scientists* 33 (February 1977): 42–47.

2304. Watson, James W. "The Effects of Federal Energy Administration Regulations and State Dealer-Day-in-Court Laws on Service at Gasoline Stations." Ph.D. dissertation, University of California, Los Angeles, 1978. 177 p.

2305. Webb, Michael, and Pearce, David. "The Economics of Energy Analysis." *Energy Policy* 3 (December 1975): 318–31.

2306. Werner, Roy A. "The Economic Impact of American Oil Dependency." *Current History* 74 (July–August 1978): 1–4, 35.

2307. Wilms, Wellford W. "Soft Policies for Hard Problems: Implementing Energy Conserving Building Regulations in California." *Public Administration Review* 42 (November–December 1982): 553–61.

2308. Wolf, C. P. "The Accident at Three Mile Island: Social Science Perspectives." *Policy Studies Review Annual* 4 (1980): 371–76.

2309. Wright, Arthur W. "Energy Policy and Deregulation: Two Hot Topics, or Does Smoke Necessarily Mean There's Fire?" *Growth and Change* 10 (January 1979): 4–13.

2310. Zerbe, Richard O. "Monopoly, the Emergence of Oligopoly and the Case of Sugar Refining." *Journal of Law and Economics* 13 (October 1970): 501–15.

ENVIRONMENT

2311. Altree, Lillian R., and Baxter, William F. "Legal Aspects of Airport Noise." *Journal of Law and Economics* 15 (April 1972): 1–113.

2312. Alviani, J. D. "Federal Regulation: The New Regimen." *Boston College Environmental Affairs Review* 9 (1980): 285–309.

2313. Andrews, Richard N. L. "Values Analysis in Environmental Policy." *Policy Studies Journal* 9 (Winter 1980): 369–78.

2314. Bailey, Kenneth R. "Development of Surface Mine Legislation 1939–1967." *West Virginia History* 30 (April 1969): 525–29.

2315. Barde, Robert. "Arthur E. Morgan, First Chairman of TVA." *Tennessee Historical Quarterly* 30 (Fall 1971): 299–314.

2316. Beard, Daniel P. "United States Environmental Legislation and Energy Resources: A Review." *Geographical Review* 65 (April 1975): 229–44.

2317. Benveniste, Guy. *Regulation and Planning: The Case of Environmental Politics.* San Francisco, CA: Boyd and Fraser Publishing, 1981. 207 p.

2318. Berns, Walter. "Viewpoint: Mining the Seas for a Brave New World." *Regulation* 5 (November–December 1981): 15–18.

2319. Berry, M. P. "Water Management in Crisis." *Public Administration Review* 37 (September–October 1977): 472–77.

2320. Bird, Richard M., and Waverman, Leonard."Some Fiscal Aspects of Controlling Industrial Water Pollution." In *Economic Thinking and Pollution Problems,* edited by D. A. L. Auld, pp. 75–102. Toronto, Ontario: University of Toronto Press, 1972.

2321. Bleser, Carol R. "The South Carolina Land Commission: A Study of a Reconstruction Institution." Ph.D. dissertation, Columbia University, 1966. 258 p.

2322. Brady, Gordon L., and Bower, Blair T. "Effectiveness of the U.S. Regulatory Approach to Air Quality Management: Stationary Sources." *Policy Studies Journal* 11 (September 1982): 66–76.

2323. Brenner, Michael J. *The Political Economy of America's Environmental Dilemma.* Lexington, MA: Lexington Books, 1973. 177 p.

2324. Brickman, Ronald, and Jaranoff, Sheria. "Concepts of Risk and Safety in Toxic Substances Regulation: A Comparison of France and the United States." *Policy Studies Journal* 9 (Winter 1980): 394–403.

2325. Broadus, James M. "Corruption and Regulation: New York Policy and Kentucky Surface Mining." Ph.D. dissertation, Yale University, 1976. 230 p.

2326. Burke, S. H. "Small Scale Hydroelectric Development and Federal Environmental Law: A Guide for the Private Developer." *Boston College Environmental Affairs Review* 9 (1981–1982): 815–61.

2327. Calvert, Jerry W. "The Social and Ideological Bases of Support for Environmental Legislation: An Examination of Public Attitudes and Legislative Action." *Western Political Quarterly* 32 (September 1979): 327–37.

2328. Carleton, William G. "Government's Historic Role in Conservation." *Current History* 58 (June 1970): 321–27.

2329. Cart, Theodore W. "The Lacey Act: America's First Nationwide Wildlife Statute." *Forest History* 17 (October 1973): 4–13.

2330. Cart, Theodore W. "'New Deal' for Wildlife: A Perspective on Federal Conservation Policy, 1933–1940." *Pacific Northwest Quarterly* 63 (July 1972): 113–20.

2331. Carter, Roberta C. "The Responses of the American Automobile Industry to Environmental Protection: A Study of Regulatory Experience." D.B.A. dissertation, University of Colorado at Boulder, 1979. 297 p.

2332. Chan, Arthur H. "The Nature of Water Resources Policy and Policymaking." *American Journal of Economics and Sociology* 41 (January 1982): 85–93.

2333. Clarke, James W. "Environment, Process and Policy." *American Political Science Review* 68 (December 1969): 1172–82.

2334. Coletta, Paolo E. "'The Most Thankless Task': Bryan and the California Alien Land Legislation." *Pacific Historical Review* 36 (May 1967): 163–88.

2335. Cowdrey, Albert E. "Pioneering Environmental Law: The Army Corps of Engineers and the Refuse Act." *Pacific Historical Review* 44 (August 1975): 331–49.

2336. Crandall, Robert W. "The Environment." *Regulation* 6 (January–February 1982): 29–31.

2337. Cuzan, Alfred G. "A Critique of Collectivist Water Resources Planning." *Western Political Quarterly* 32 (September 1979): 320–26.

2338. David, Martin H.; Joeres, Erhard; and Peirce, Jeffrey. "Phosphorus Pollution Control in the Lake Michigan Watershed." *Policy Analysis* 6 (Winter 1980): 47–60.

2339. "Denial of Hearing at Three Mile Island Held to Be Error." *Natural Resources Journal* 21 (October 1981): 911–18.

2340. Doria, J. J. "Radiation Regulation." *Environment* 21 (December 1979): 25–31.

2341. Downing, Paul B., and Brady, Gordon L. "Implementing the Clean Air Act: A Case Study of Oxident Control in Los Angeles." *Natural Resources Journal* 18 (April 1978): 237–83.

2342. Downing, Paul B., and Kimball, James N. "Enforcing Pollution Control Laws in the U.S." *Policy Studies Journal* 11 (September 1982): 55–65.

2343. Downing, Paul B., and Watson, William D. "The Economics of Enforcing Air Pollution Controls." *Journal of Environmental Economics and Management* 1 (1974): 219–36.

2344. Downs, Anthony. "Up and Down with Ecology: The Issue Attention Cycle." *Public Interest* 28 (Summer 1972): 38–50.

2345. EcoSystems, Incorporated. *An Impact Assessment of Three Federal Regulations.* McLean, VA: EcoSystems, 1974. 155 p.

2346. Edelman, Sidney. "Federal Air and Water Control: The Application of the Commerce Power to Abate Interstate and Intrastate Pollution." *George Washington Law Review* 33 (June 1965): 1067–87.

2347. Ethridge, Marcus E. "The Effect of Administrative Procedure on Environmental Policy Implementation: A Comparative State Study." Ph.D. dissertation, Vanderbilt University, 1979. 211 p.

2348. Fanara, Philip. "Pollution Control in Regulation Industries: A Theoretical and Empirical Analysis." Ph.D. dissertation, Indiana University, 1980. 220 p.

2349. Farley, Mary. "Colorado and the Arkansas Valley Authority." *Colorado Magazine* 48 (Summer 1971): 221–34.

2350. Farrell, John H. "A Survey of Professional Attitudes toward Public Forest Regulation in the United States." Ph.D. dissertation, State University of New York, 1955. 105 p.

2351. Ferrar, Terry A., and Horst, Robert L. "Effluent Charges—A Price on Pollution." *Atmospheric Environment* 8 (1974): 657–67.

2352. Foreman, Christopher H. "Against the Tide: Federal Regulators and the Fishermen of New England." Ph.D. dissertation, Harvard University, 1980. 282 p.

2353. Foreman, Christopher H. "Sea of Troubles: Managing New England's Fisheries." *Regulation* 6 (July–August 1982): 43–48.

2354. Freeman, A. Myrick. "Residuals Charges for Pollution Control: A Policy Evaluation." *Science* 177 (July 28, 1982): 322–29.

2355. Gates, Paul. "The California Land Act of 1851." *California Historical Quarterly* 50 (December 1971): 395–430.

2356. Gates, Paul. "Charts of Public Land Sales and Entries." *Journal of Economic History* 24 (March 1964): 22–28.

2357. Gates, Paul. "Public Land Issues in the United States." *Western Historical Quarterly* 2 (October 1971): 363–76.

2358. Gatewood, Willard. "Conservation and Politics in the South, 1899–1906." *Georgia Review* 16 (Spring 1962): 30–42.

2359. Gerhardt, Paul H. "Air Pollution Control: Benefits, Costs, and Inducements." In *Public Prices for Public Products,* edited by Selma Mushkin, pp. 153–71. Washington, DC: Urban Institute, 1972.

2360. Gibson, Frank K. "The Regulation and Control of Water Pollution in West Virginia." Ph.D. dissertation, University of North Carolina, 1955. 930 p.

2361. Gilmour, Robert S., and McCauley, John A. "Environmental Preservation and Politics: The Significance of 'Everglades Jetport.'" *Political Science Quarterly* 90 (Winter 1975–1976): 719–38.

2362. Glass, Mary Ellen. "The First Nationally Sponsored Arid Land Reclamation Project: The Newlands Act in Churchill County, Nevada." *Nevada Historical Society Quarterly* 14 (Spring 1971): 5–12.

2363. Gopalakrishnan, C. "Water Resource Development: A Case History of Montana." *American Journal of Economics and Sociology* 30 (October 1971): 421–28.

2364. Gosdin, John Mark. "The Environmental Impact Statement Process: The Texas Experience." Ph.D. dissertation, University of Texas at Austin, 1982. 318 p.

2365. Gretz, Malcolm, and Walter, Benjamin. "Environmental Policy and Competitive Structure: Implications of the Hazardous Waste Management Program." *Policy Studies Journal* 9 (Winter 1980): 404–13.

2366. Gricar, Barbara G. "The Environmental Imperative Created by Government Regulation: Predicting Organizational Response." Ph.D. dissertation, Case Western Reserve, 1979. 191 p.

2367. Gulley, D. A. "State Response to Mineral Development." *State Government* 53 (Winter 1980): 7–10.

2368. Hagenstein, P. R. "Commissions and Public Land Policies: Setting the Stage for Change." *Denver Law Journal* 54 (1977): 619–61.

2369. Hahn, Robert W., and McRae, Gregory J. "Application of Market Mechanisms to Pollution." *Policy Studies Review* 1 (February 1982): 470–76.

2370. Hall, George. "Conservation as a Public Policy Goal." *Yale Review* 51 (March 1962): 400–13.

2371. Hall, R. M. "Evolution and Implementation of EPA's Regulatory Program to Control the Discharge of Toxic Pollutants to the Nation's Waters." *Natural Resources Law* 10 (1977): 507–29.

2372. Haller, P. H. "U.S. Environmental Protection Agency: Procedures of Administrative Resolution of Bid Protests under Construction Grants." *Wisconsin Bar Bulletin* 50 (November 1977): 10–15.

2373. Halteman, James. "Private Water Supply Firms and Municipal Authorities: A Comparative Analysis in Pennslyvania." *State and Local Government Review* 11 (January 1979): 29–34.

2374. Hamilton, Herbert H. "Regulation of Land Use by Local Governments for Aesthetic Purposes." Ph.D. dissertation, Indiana University, 1961. 255 p.

2375. Hamilton, Lawrence. "The Federal Forest Regulation Issue." *Forest History* 9 (April 1965): 2–11.

2376. Hardy, Michael. "The Implications of Alternative Solutions for Regulating the Exploitation of Seabed Minerals." *International Organization* 31 (Spring 1977): 313–42.

2377. Harman, Bryan D. "The National Capital Planning Commission and the Land-Use Planning Process in the District of Columbia." Ph.D. dissertation, American University, 1967. 323 p.

2378. Harrison, David, and Portney, Paul R. "Making Ready for the Clean Air Act." *Regulation* 5 (March–April 1981): 24–31.

2379. Haskell, Elizabeth H., and Price, Victoria S. *State Environmental Management; Case Studies of Nine States.* New York: Praeger, 1973. 283 p.

2380. Heckert, R. E. "Environmental Alternatives and Social Goals." *American Academy of Political and Social Science, Annals* 444 (July 1979): 102–11.

2381. Hickel, Walter. "The U.S. Department of the Interior and the Economic Geology of the West." *Journal of the West* 10 (January 1971): 129–32.

2382. Hoffman, Abraham. "Origins of a Controversy: The U.S. Reclamation Service and the Owens Valley-Los Angeles Water Dispute." *Arizona and the West* 19 (Winter 1977): 333–46.

2383. Hoover, Roy O. "Public Law 273 Comes to Shelton: Implementing the Sustained-Yield Forest Management Act of 1944." *Journal of Forest History* 22 (April 1978): 86–101.

2384. Hundley, Norris. "The Politics of Reclamation: California, the Federal Government, and the Origins of the Boulder Canyon Act—A Second Look." *California Historical Quarterly* 52 (Winter 1973): 292–325.

2385. Ingram, Helen; Laney, Nancy; and McCain, John R. "Water Scarcity and the Politics of Plenty in the Four Corners States." *Western Political Quarterly* 32 (September 1979): 298–306.

2386. Johnson, Ralph W. "Regulation of Commercial Salmon Fishermen: A Case of Confused Objectives." *Pacific Northwest Quarterly* 55 (October 1964): 141–45.

2387. Jones, Charles O. *Clean Air: The Policies and Politics of Pollution Control.* Pittsburgh, PA: University of Pittsburgh Press, 1975. 372 p.

2388. Jones, Charles O. "Speculative Augmentation in Federal Air Pollution Policy-Making." *Journal of Politics* 36 (May 1974): 438–64.

2389. Joskow, Paul L. "Inflation and Environmental Concern: Structural Change in the Process of Public Utility Price Regulation." *Journal of Law and Economics* 17 (October 1974): 291–327.

2390. Jurewitz, John L. "The Internalization of Environmental Costs in the Private Electric Utility Industry: A Theoretical Analysis of Alternative Environmental Policies under Rate-of-Return Regulation." Ph.D. dissertation, University of Wisconsin—Madison, 1978. 691 p.

2391. Kane, H. Scott. "The Nature of Conflict in the Regulatory Process: A Study of the Clean Air Act Amendments of 1982." Ph.D. dissertation, George Washington University, 1983. 286 p.

2392. Keisar, Sharon A. "Regulating Demands in Four Local Development Districts of Western North Carolina." Ph.D. dissertation, University of North Carolina, 1974. 275 p.

2393. King, Andrew J. "Law and Land Use in Chicago: A Prehistory of Modern Zoning." Ph.D. dissertation, University of Wisconsin, 1976. 454 p.

2394. Kmiec, Douglas W. "Manufactured Home Siting: Regulatory Challenges and a Proposal for Federal Deregulation." *Zoning and Planning Law Report* 6 (April 1983): 113–17.

2395. Kneese, Allen V. "Discharge Capacity of Waterways and Effluent Charges." In *Public Prices for Public Products,* edited by Selma Mushkin, pp. 133–51. Washington, DC: Urban Institute, 1972.

2396. Kneese, Allen V. "Strategies for Environmenal Management." *Public Policy* 19 (Winter 1971): 37–52.

2397. Kneese, Allen V., and Schultze, Charles L. *Pollution, Prices, and Public Policy.* Washington, DC: Brookings Institution, 1975. 125 p.

2398. Kneisel, Robert P. "The Impact of the California Coastal Zone Conservation Commission on the Local Housing Market: A Study of Two Regional Coastal Commissions." Ph.D. dissertation, University of California, 1979. 278 p.

2399. Koch, Walton B. "The Alaska Native Land Claims Bill: Pay Off or Rip Off?" *Michigan Academician* 6 (Winter 1974): 299–305.

2400. Korr, Charles. "William Hammond Hall: The Failure of Attempts at State Water Planning in California, 1878–1888." *Southern California Quarterly* 45 (December 1963): 305–22.

2401. Krier, James E., and Ursin, Edmund. *Pollution and Policy: A Case Essay on California and Federal Experience with Motor Vehicle Air Pollution 1940–1975.* Berkeley, CA: University of California Press, 1977. 401 p.

2402. Kusler, Jon A. *Strengthening State Wetland Regulations.* Washington, DC: Environmental Law Institute, 1978. 147 p.

2403. Lee, Linda. "Factors Affecting Land Use Change at the Urban-Rural Fringe." *Growth and Change* 10 (October 1979): 25–31.

2404. Lewis, Leonard J., and Rooker, C. Keith. "Domestic Uranium Procurement History and Problems." *Land and Water Law Review* 1 (1966): 449–71.

2405. Liebman, Ernst. "The National Water Commission—Problems and Issues." *Natural Resources Lawyer* 5 (Fall 1972): 640–67.

2406. Lundquist, Lennart J. "Do Political Structures Matter in Environmental Politics? The Case for Air Pollution Control in Canada, Sweden, and the United States." *American Behavioral Scientist* 17 (May–June 1974): 731–50.

2407. Lynch, Myra C. "State Control of Low Level Nuclear Waste Disposal." *Natural Resources Journal* 17 (October 1977): 683–90.

2408. Majone, Giandomenico. "Choice among Policy Instruments for Pollution Control." *Policy Analysis* 2 (Fall 1976): 589–613.

2409. Majone, Giandomenico. "Standard Setting and the Theory of Institutional Choice: The Case of Pollution Control." *Policy and Politics* 4 (December 1975): 35–51.

2410. Mandelker, Daniel R. *Environment and Equity: A Regulatory Challenge.* New York: McGraw-Hill, 1981. 162. p.

2411. Marcus, Alfred A., et al. "Alternative Arrangements for Cost Effective Pollution Abatement: The Need for Implementation Analysis." *Policy Studies Review* 1 (February 1982): 477–83.

2412. Massay, Glenn F. "Legislators, Lobbyists and Loopholes: Coal Mining Legislation in West Virginia, 1875–1901." *West Virginia History* 32 (April 1971): 135–70.

2313. Mayer, Harold. "Politics and Land Use: The Indiana Shoreline of Lake Michigan." *Annals of the Association of American Geographers* 54 (December 1964): 508–23.

2414. McCraw, Thomas K. "Triumph and Irony—The TVA." *Proceedings IEEE* 64 (September 1976): 1372–80.

2415. McEntyre, John G. "A Suggested Revision of the Laws of Kansas Regulating Land Surveying and Land Registration." Ph.D. dissertation, Cornell University, 1954. 206 p.

2416. McEvoy, A. F. "Economy, Law, and Ecology in the California Fisheries to 1925." *Journal of Economic History* 41 (March 1981): 195–97, 199–201.

2417. McHugh, J. L. "Rise and Fall and World Whaling: The Tragedy of the Commons Illustrated." *Journal of International Affairs* 31 (Spring–Summer 1977): 23–33.

2418. McKean, Roland N. "Enforcement Costs in Environmental and Safety Regulation." *Policy Analysis* 6 (Summer 1980): 269–90.

2419. McKinnon, J. E. "Federal Water Pollution Control Act—Industrial Challenges to Effluent Limitations." *Boston College Environmental Affairs Law Review* 7 (1979): 545–66.

2420. Melnick, Rowell S. "Into the Regulatory Thicket: The Impact of Court Decisions on Federal Regulation of Air Pollution." Ph.D. dissertation, Harvard University, 1980. 499 p.

2421. Mendelsohn, Robert O. "Towards Efficient Regulation of Air Pollution from Coal-Fired Power Plants." Ph.D. dissertation, Yale University, 1978. 383 p.

2422. Menzel, Donald C., and Edgmon, Terry D. "The Struggle to Implement a National Surface Mining Policy." *Publius* 10 (Winter 1980): 81–91.

2423. Michlitsch, Joseph F. "Organizational Responses to Perceived Environmental Uncertainty: A Test of the Dominance of Uncertainty in the Regulatory Segment." Ph.D. dissertation, University of Minnesota, 1980. 236 p.

2424. Milbrath, Lester W., and Inscho, Frederick R. "The Environmental Problem as a Political Problem: An Agenda of Environmental Concerns for Political Scientists." *American Behavioral Scientist* 17 (May–June 1974): 623–50.

2425. Miles, Mike, and Mann, Richard A. "State Land Use Planning: The Current Status and Demographic Rational." *American Planning Association Journal* 45 (January 1979): 48–61.

2426. Mitrick, Jerry M. "Incentive Systems in Environmental Regulation." *Policy Studies Journal* 9 (Winter 1980): 379–93.

2427. Moore, Richard. "The Arizona Bureau of Mines." *Journal of the West* 10 (January 1971): 136–40.

2428. Munn, Robert F. "The First Fifty Years of Strip Mining in West Virginia, 1916–1965." *West Virginia History* 35 (October 1973): 66–74.

2429. Murphy, Arthur W. "National Environmental Policy Act and the Licensing Process: Environmentalist Magna Carta or Agency Coup de Grace?" *Columbia Law Review* 72 (October 1972): 963–1007.

2430. Nagel, Stuart S. "Incentives for Compliance with Environmental Law." *American Behavioral Scientist* 17 (May–June 1974): 690–710.

2431. Nash, Gerald D. "The California State Board of Forestry, 1883–1960." *Southern California Quarterly* 47 (September 1965): 291–302.

2432. Nash, Gerald D. "The California State Land Office 1858–1898." *Huntington Library Quarterly* 27 (August 1964): 347–56.

2433. Navarro, Peter. "The 1977 Clean Air Act Amendments: Energy, Environmental, Economic, and Distributional Impacts." *Public Policy* 29 (Spring 1981): 121–46.

2434. Nieman, Max, and Lovell, Catherine. "Federal and State Mandating—A First Look at the Mandate Terrain." *Administration and Society* 14 (November 1982): 343–72.

2435. Nokolai, L. A.; Elam, R.; and Boseman, Barry. "Financial Statement Modeling: Analyzing the Pollution-Control Tax Incentive." *Policy Analysis* 5 (Spring 1979): 243–54.

2436. Null, James A. "The Politics of Water Resource Management through Arizona Water-Related Regulatory Agencies." Ph.D. dissertation, University of Arizona, 1970. 331 p.

2437. Oakeshott, Gordon. "Notes on the Nevada Bureau of Mines." *Journal of the West* 10 (January 1971): 152–53.

2438. Orr, Lloyd D. "Social Costs, Incentive Structures, and Environmental Policies." *Western Political Quarterly* 32 (September 1979): 286–97.

2439. Pashigian, B. P. "How Large and Small Plants Fare under Environmental Regulation." *Regulation* 7 (September–October 1983): 19–23.

2440. Paterson, D. G. "The North Pacific Seal Hunt, 1886–1910: Rights and Regulations." *Explorations in Economic History* 14 (April 1977): 97–119.

2441. Pisani, Donald J. "Federal Reclamation and Water Rights in Nevada." *Agricultural History* 51 (July 1977): 540–58.

2442. Polenberg, Richard. "Conservation and Reorganization: The Forest Service Lobby, 1937–1938." *Agricultural History* 39 (October 1965): 230–39.

2443. Pool, John. "Statement on the Controlled Dangerous Substances Act of 1969 (S. 3246) by the New York Academy of Medicine." *Bulletin of the New York Academy of Medicine* 46 (July 1970): 509–10.

2444. Portney, Paul R. "Efficient Use of Standards and Enforcement: The Case of Pollution Control." *Policy Analysis* 5 (Fall 1979): 521–24.

2445. Pratt, Joseph A. "Growth or a Clean Environment? Responses to Petroleum-Related Pollution in the Gulf Coast Refining Region." *Business History Review* 52 (Spring 1978): 1–29.

2446. Rabin, Robert L. "Ozone Depletion Revisited—EPA Regulation of Chlorofluorocarbons." *Regulation* 5 (March–April 1981): 32–38.

2447. Raucher, Robert L. "Regulating the Quality of Drinking Water: An Economic Analysis of the Safe Drinking Water Act of 1974." Ph.D. dissertation, University of Wisconsin—Madison, 1980. 340 p.

2448. Regnell, John B. "Conflicting Intergovernmental Relations in Environmental Regulatory Policy Development: The National and Arizona's Air Pollution Control Administration, 1971–1974." Ph.D. dissertation, Arizona State University, 1974. 282 p.

2449. Richardson, Elmo R. "Federal Park Policy in Utah: The Escalante National Monument Controversy of 1935–1940." *Utah Historical Quarterly* 33 (Spring 1965): 109–33.

2450. Richardson, Genevra. "Policing Pollution: The Enforcement Process." *Policy Studies Journal* 11 (September 1982): 153–64.

2451. Rickson, R. E. "Dimensions of Environmental Management: Legitimation of Government Regulation by Industrial Managers." *Environment and Behavior* 9 (March 1977): 15–40.

2452. Roberts, Frances C. "Politics and Public Land Disposal in Alabama's Formative Period." *Alabama Review* 22 (July 1969): 163–74.

2453. Roberts, Marc J. "Organizing Water Pollution Control: The Scope and Structure of River Basin Authorities." *Public Policy* 19 (Winter 1971): 75–141.

2454. Roberts, Marc J. "River Basin Authorities: A National Solution to Water Pollution." *Harvard Law Review* 83 (May 1970): 1527–56.

2455. Roberts, Marc J., and Stewart, Richard B. "Energy and the Environment." In *Setting National Priorities: The Next Ten Years,* edited by Henry Owen and Charles L. Schultze, pp. 411–56. Washington, DC: Brookings Institution, 1976.

2456. Roos, Leslie L., and Roos, Noralou P. "Pollution, Regulation, and Evaluation." *Law and Society Review* 6 (May 1972): 509–29.

2457. Rose-Ackerman, Susan. "Effluent Charges: A Critique." *Canadian Journal of Economics* 6 (1973): 512–28.

2458. Rose-Ackerman, Susan. "Market Models for Water Pollution Control: Their Strengths and Weaknesses." *Public Policy* 25 (Summer 1977): 383–406.

2459. Rosenbaum, Nelson. "Statutory Structure and Policy Implementation: The Case of Wetlands Regulation." *Policy Studies Journal* 8 (1980): 575–96.

2460. Rothenberg, Jerome. "The Physical Environment." In *Social Responsibility and the Business Predicament,* edited by James W. McKie, pp. 191–215. Washington, DC: Brookings Institution, 1974.

2461. Ruff, Larry E. "The Economic Common Sense of Pollution." *Public Interest* 19 (Spring 1970): 69–85.

2462. Ryan, Michael J. "A Goal Programming Approach to Land Use Economics, Planning and Regulation." Ph.D. dissertation, University of Texas at Austin, 1974. 162 p.

2463. Sabatier, Paul A., and Mazmanian, Daniel. "Regulating Coastal Land Use in California, 1973–1975." *Policy Studies Journal* 11 (September 1982): 88–102.

2464. Saddler, Gordon T. "The Appalachian Regional Commission: Selected Aspects of Institutions and Processes and Their Relationship to Natural and Human Resources Development." Ph.D. dissertation, West Virginia University, 1969. 669 p.

2465. Salamon, L. M. "The Time Dimension in Policy Evaluation: The Case of the New Deal Land-Reform Experiments." *Public Policy* 27 (Spring 1979): 129–83.

2466. Saloutos, Theodore. "Land Policy and Its Relation to Agricultrual Production and Distribution, 1862 to 1933." *Journal of Economic History* 22 (December 1962): 445–60.

2467. Samuels, Warren J., and Schmid, A. Allan. "Polluters' Profit and Political Response: The Dynamics of Rights Creation." *Public Choice* 28 (Winter 1976): 99–105.

2468. Scheiber, Harry N. "Land Reform, Speculation, and Governmental Failure: The Administration of Ohio's State Canal Lands, 1836–60." *Prologue* 7 (Summer 1975): 85–98.

2469. Scheiber, Harry N. "The Road to Munn: Eminent Domain and the Concept of Public Purpose in the State Courts." In *Perspectives in American History,* edited by Donald Fleming and Bernard Bailyn, vol. 5, pp. 329–402. Cambridge, MA: Harvard University, 1971.

2470. Scheiber, Harry N. "State Policy and the Public Domain: The Ohio Canal Lands." *Journal of Economic History* 25 (March 1965): 86–113.

2471. Schlottmann, Alan M. "Environmental Regulation and the Allocation of Coal: A Regional Analysis." Ph.D. dissertation, Washington University, 1975. 285 p.

2472. Searle, Newell. "Minnesota National Forest: The Politics of Compromise, 1898–1908." *Minnesota History* 42 (Fall 1971): 242–67.

2473. Selznick, Philip. *TVA and the Grass Roots: A Study in the Sociology of Formal Organization.* Berkeley, CA: University of California Press, 1949. 274 p.

2474. Shapiro, Edward. "The Southern Agrarians and the Tennessee Valley Authority." *American Quarterly* 22 (Winter 1970): 791–806.

2475. Smathers, Webb M. "A Mixed Integer Method for Analyzing the Impact of Surface Mining Regulations on Economies with Public and Private Goods." Ph.D. dissertation, University of Kentucky, 1980. 208 p.

2476. Starbuck, William H. "Organizations and Their Environments." In *Handbook of Industrial and Organizational Psychology,* edited by Marvin D. Dunnettee, pp. 1069–123. Chicago: Rand McNally, 1976.

2477. Steen, Harold K. "Grazing and the Environment: A History of Forest Service Stock-Reduction Policy." *Agricultural History* 49 (January 1975): 238–42.

2478. Stout, Joe A. "Cattlemen, Conservationists and the Taylor Grazing Act." *New Mexico Historical Review* 45 (October 1970): 311–32.

2479. Strausberg, Stephen F. "Indiana and the Swamp Lands Act: A Study in State Administration." *Indiana Magazine of History* 73 (September 1977): 191–203.

2480. Street, Donald R. "An Economic Analysis of Regulated Fee Fishing Lakes in Pennsylvania." Ph.D. dissertation, Pennsylvania State University, 1965. 150 p.

2481. Swain, Donald C. "The Bureau of Reclamation and the New Deal, 1933–1940." *Pacific Northwest Quarterly* 61 (July 1970): 137–46.

2482. Swain, Donald C. "The Founding of the National Park Service." *American West* 6 (September 1969): 6–9.

2483. Swain, Donald C. "The National Park Service and the New Deal, 1933–1940." *Pacific Historical Review* 41 (August 1972): 312–32.

2484. Swain, Donald C. "The Passage of the National Park Service Act of 1916." *Wisconsin Magazine of History* 50 (Autumn 1966): 4–17.

2485. Taggart, William Arend. "The Innovation and Diffusion of Environmental Policies in the American States." Ph.D. dissertation, Florida State University, 1982. 314 p.

2486. Taylor, S. A., and Wayland, S. "The Federal Water Pollution Control Act Amendments of 1972." *Natural Resources Journal* 17 (July 1977): 513–19.

2487. Teitenberg, T. H. "Derived Decision Rules for Pollution Control in a General Equilibrium Space Economy." *Journal of Environmental Economics and Management* 1 (May 1974): 3–16.

2488. Teitenberg, T. H. "Spatially Differentiated Air Pollutant Emission Charges: An Economic and Legal Analysis." *Policy Studies Review Annual* 3 (1979): 277–90.

2489. Thompson, John T. "Governmental Responses to the Challenges of Water Resources in Texas." *Southwestern Historical Quarterly* 70 (July 1966): 44–64.

2490. Thompson, Roger C. "Politics in the Wilderness: New York's Adirondack Forest Preserve." *Forest History* 6 (Winter 1963): 14–23.

2491. Vietor, Richard H. "Environmental Politics in Pennsylvania: The Regulation of Surface Mining, 1961–1973." *Pennsylvania History* 45 (January 1978): 19–46.

2492. Walton, Scott D. *American Business and Its Environment.* New York: Macmillan, 1966. 654 p.

2493. Warner, Kenneth E. "Clearing the Airwaves: The Cigarette Ad Ban Revisited." *Policy Analysis* 5 (Fall 1979): 435–50.

2494. Weaver, Glen D. "Nevada's Federal Lands." *Annals of the Association of American Geographers* 59 (March 1969): 27–49.

2495. Weinstein, Milton C. "Decision Making for Toxic Substances Control: Cost-Effective Information Development for the Control of Environmental Carcinogen." *Public Policy* 27 (Summer 1979): 333–83.

2496. Wengert, Norman. "The Ideological Basis of Conservation and Natural Resources Policies and Programs." *American Academy of Political and Social Science, Annals* 344 (November 1962): 65–75.

2497. Wenner, Lettie M. "Enforcement of Water Pollution Control Law." *Law and Society Review* 6 (May 1972): 481–507.

2498. Wenner, Lettie M. "Pollution Control: Implementation Alternatives." *Policy Analysis* 4 (Winter 1978): 47–65.

2499. Whatley, George C., and Cook, Sylvia. "East Florida Land Commission: A Study in Frustration." *Florida Historical Quarterly* 50 (July 1971): 39–52.

2500. Whitaker, Adelynne H. "A History of Federal Pesticide Regulation in the United States to 1947." Ph.D. dissertation, Emory University, 1974. 473 p.

2501. White, Arthur O. "The Niagara Grab and the Precedent of Federal Regulation of Niagara Falls." *Niagara Frontier* 22 (Winter 1975): 78–87.

2502. White, Henry G. "Forest Regulation—A Study of Public Control of Cutting Practices on Private Forest Land in the United States." Ph.D. dissertation, University of Minnesota, 1949. 243 p.

2503. White, Lawrence J. "Effluent Charges as a Faster Means of Achieving Pollution Abatement." *Public Policy* 24 (Winter 1976): 111–25.

2504. White, Ron D. "The Anatomy of Nonmarket Failure: An Examination of Environmental Policies." *American Economic Review* 66 (May 1976): 454–58.

2505. White, Ron D. "Growth versus Conservation: A Veblenian Perspective." *Journal of Economic Issues* 12 (June 1978): 427–33.

2506. Wilson, `H. "California CZM Plan to Delay OCS Action." (California Coastal Commission) *Oil and Gas Journal* 76 (October 1978): 55–58.

2507. Witt, William E. "A Communications Approach to the Study of a Natural Resources Issue: Shoreland Zoning in Wisconsin Counties. Survey of State, Regional, and County Interests, and Multivariate Analysis of County Shoreland Development, and Regional Planning Commission Membership, and Circulation of News on Shoreland Zoning." Ph.D. dissertation, University of Wisconsin, 1970. 220 p.

2508. Yandle, Bruce. "The Emerging Market in Air Pollution Rights." *Regulation* 2 (July–August 1978): 21–29.

2509. Yearwood, Richard M. "The Law and Administration of Subdivision Regulation: A Study in Land Use Control." Ph.D. dissertation, University of Florida, 1966. 344 p.

HEALTH

2510. Albritton, Robert B. "Cost-Benefits of Measles Eradication: Effects of a Federal Intervention." *Policy Analysis* 4 (Winter 1978): 1–21.

2511. Altman, Drew. "The Politics of Health Care Regulation: The Case of the National Health Planning and Resources Development Act." *Journal of Health Politics, Policy and Law* 2 (Winter 1978): 560–80.

2512. Altman, Drew, and Sapolsky, H. "Writing the Regulations for Health." *Policy Sciences* 7 (December 1976): 417–38.

2513. Annis, Edward R. "Government Health Care: First the Aged, then Everyone." *Current History* 45 (August 1963): 104–09, 119.

2514. Auster, R. D. "Incentives in a Government Controlled Health Sector?" *Policy Studies Journal* 5 (Spring 1977): 295–300.

2515. Barkdoll, G. L. "Type III Evaluations: Consultation and Consensus." *Public Administration Review* 40 (March 1980): 174–79.

2516. Battistella, Roger M., and Eastaugh, Steven R. "Hospital Cost Containment." *Proceedings of the Academy of Political Science* 3 (1980): 192–205.

2517. Bellush, Jewel. "The Politics of Liquor." *New York History* 45 (April 1964): 114–34.

2518. Berkowitz, Monroe. "Occupational Safety and Health." *American Academy of Political and Social Science, Annals* 443 (May 1979): 41–53.

2519. Bjorkman, James W., and Altenstetter, Christa. "Accountability in Health Care: An Essay on Mechanisms, Muddles, and Mires." *Journal of Health Politics, Policy and Law* 4 (Fall 1979): 360–81.

2520. Bolotin, Fredric N. "The Impact of Government Regulatory Policy: The Case of Alcohol Beverage Control Laws." Ph.D. dissertation, State University of New York at Binghamton, 1983. 207 p.

2521. Brandt-Rauf, Sherry I., and Brandt-Rauf, Paul W. "Occupational Health Ethics: OSHA and the Courts." *Journal of Health Politics, Policy and Law* 5 (Fall 1980): 523–35.

2522. Brieger, Gert. "Sanitary Reform in New York City: Stephen Smith and the Passage of the Metropolitan Health Bill." *Bulletin of the History of Medicine* 40 (September-October 1966): 407–29.

2523. Brisson, E.L. "A Look at the Bioresearch Monitoring Program: The Agency Perspective." *Food Drug Cosmetic Law Journal* 38 (April 1983): 184–89.

2524. Brooks, Carol. "The Early History of the Anti-Contraceptive Laws in Massachusetts and Connecticut." *American Quarterly* 17 (Spring 1966): 3–23.

2525. Buntz, C. Gregory; Macaluso, Theodore F.; and Azarow, Jay Allen. "Federal Influence on State Health Policy." *Journal of Health Politics, Policy and Law* 3 (Spring 1978): 71–86.

2526. Burt, R.A. "The Limits of Law in Regulating Health Care Decisions." *Hastings Center Report* 7 (December 1977): 29–32.

2527. Cannizzaro, John F., and Rosenfeld, Madelon M. "Laetrile and the FDA: A Case of Reverse Regulation." *Journal of Health Politics, Policy and Law* 3 (Summer 1978): 181–95.

2528. Caplan, Arthur L. "Kidneys, Ethics, and Politics: Policy Lessons of the ESRD Experience." *Journal of Health Politics, Policy and Law* 6 (Fall 1981): 488–503.

2529. Carleton, William G. "Government and Health before the New Deal." *Current History* 72 (May-June 1977): 196–97, 223–24.

2530. Checkoway, Barry, and Doyle, Michael. "Community Organizing Lessons for Health Care Consumers." *Journal of Health Politics, Policy and Law* 5 (Summer 1980): 213–26.

2531. Chopra, J. G. "Current Regulatory Status of Foods for Special Dietary Uses." *American Journal of Public Health* 66 (April 1976): 351–53.

2532. Cirn, John T. "The New York Cost-of-Regulation Study: A Severe Case of Myopia." *Journal of Health Politics, Policy and Law* 6 (Summer 1981): 321–27.

2533. Cleary, T. F. "Pleading and Practice before the Occupational Safety and Health Review Commission." *Labor Law Journal* 24 (December 1973): 779–87.

2534. Cohen, Harris S. "Regulatory Politics and American Medicine." *American Behavioral Scientist* 19 (September-October 1975): 122–36.

2535. Comanor, William S. "The Drug Industry and Medical Research: The Economics of the Kefauver Committee Investigations." *Journal of Business* 39 (January 1966): 12–18.

2536. Comanor, William S. "Health Manpower and Government Planning: A Review of the GMENAC Report." *Regulation* 5 (May-June 1981): 47–49.

2537. Connerton, Marguerite M. "Accident Control through Regulation: The 1969 Coal Mine Health and Safety Act Experience." Ph.D. dissertation, Harvard University, 1978.

2538. Conrad, Douglas A., and Emerson, Marie L. "State Dental Practice Acts: Implications for Competition." *Journal of Health Politics, Policy and Law* 5 (Winter 1981): 610–30.

2539. Copper, Theodore, and Olimpio, Nicholas. "Medical Education." *Proceedings of the Academy of Political Science* 33 (1980): 32–44.

2540. Covell, Ruth M. "The Impact of Regulation on Health Care Quality." *Proceedings of the Academy of Political Science* 33 (1980): 111–25.

2541. Crane, Stephen C. "The Legislative Marketplace: A Model of Political Exchange to Explain State Health Regulatory Policy." Ph.D. dissertation, University of Michigan, 1981. 428 p.

2542. Curran, W. J. "Administrative Warrants for Health and Safety Inspections." *American Journal of Public Health* 68 (October 1978): 1029–30.

2543. Curran, W. J. "Occupational Safety and Health: Unconstitutional Searches." *American Journal of Public Health* 67 (July 1977): 684–85.

2544. Dana, B. "Consumer Health Education." *Proceedings of the Academy of Political Science* 32 (1977): 182–92.

2545. Deshaw, Charles G. "An Evaluation of the Established Regulations Employed by the States to Ensure the Health and Safety of Varsity Competitors in Secondary Schools." Ed. D. dissertation, New York University, 1948. 133 p.

2546. Dismukes, K. "Recombinant DNA: A Proposal for Regulation." *Hastings Center Report* 7 (April 1977): 25–30.

2547. Dixon, Paul R. "Guidance and Enforcement." *Food Drug Cosmetic Law Journal* 22 (March 1967): 177–84.

2548. Dolan, Andrew K. "Antitrust Law and Physician Dominance of Other Health Practitioners." *Journal of Health Politics, Policy and Law* 4 (Winter 1980): 675–90.

2549. Dorsey, R. "American Psychiatric Association and the Food and Drug Administration: An Analysis and Proposal for Action." *American Journal of Psychiatry* 135 (September 1978): 1049–58.

2550. Drake, David F. "The Cost of Hospital Regulation." *Proceedings of the Academy of Political Science* 33 (1980): 45–59.

2551. Drake, David F., and Kozak, David M. "A Primer on Antitrust and Hospital Regulation." *Journal of Health Politics, Policy and Law* 3 (Fall 1978): 328–44.

2552. DuVal, Merlin K., and Den Boer, James. "Consumer Health Education." *Proceedings of the Academy of Political Science* 33 (1980): 168–81.

2553. Eickhoff, Harold W. "The Organization and Regulation of Medicine in Missouri, 1883–1901." Ph. D. dissertation, University of Missouri—Columbia, 1964. 309 p.

2554. Eilers, Robert D. "Regulation of Blue Cross and Blue Shield Plans." Ph. D. dissertation, University of Pennsylvania, 1961. 352 p.

2555. Ettling, Albert J. *The Germ of Laziness: Rockefeller Philanthropy and Public Health in the New South.* Cambridge, MA: Harvard University Press, 1981. 263 p.

2556. Faden, Ruth R., et al. "Disclosure Standards and Informed Consent." *Journal of Health Politics, Policy and Law* 6 (Summer 1981): 255–84.

2557. Fairbanks, James D. "Politics, Economics and the Public Morality: State Regulation of Gambling, Liquor, Divorce and Birth Control." Ph. D. dissertation, Ohio State University, 1975. 366 p.

2558. Falkson, Joseph L. "Market Reform, Health Interest and HMOs." *Policy Studies Journal* 9 (1980–1981): 213–20.

2559. Farrow, Michael, and Juberg, Richard. "Genetics and Laws Prohibiting Marriage in the United States." *Journal of the American Medical Association* 93 (July 28, 1969): 534–38.

2560. Fausold, Martin L. "James W. Wadsworth Sr. and the Meat Inspection Act of 1906 " *New York History* 51 (January 1971): 43–62.

2561. Field, Robert I. "Patterns in the Laws on Health Risks." *Journal of Policy Analysis and Management* 1 (1982): 257–60.

2562. Fisk, M. "Drug Regulation Reform: To Disclose or Not to Disclose." *Trial* 15 (March 1979): 53–55.

2563. Frech, Harry E. "The Regulation of Health Insurance." Ph. D. dissertation, University of California, Los Angeles, 1974. 150 p.

2564. Galblum, Trudi W. "Health Care Cost Containment Experiments: Policy, Individual Rights, and the Law." *Journal of Health Politics, Policy and Law* 3 (Fall 1978): 375–87.

2565. Ginzberg, E. "Health Services Industry: Realism in Social Control." *Journal of Economic Issues* 8 (June 1974): 381–94.

2566. Glick, Lee E. "An Analysis of the Effect of Federal Regulatory Policies on Major Chains in Retail Food Distribution." Ph. D. dissertation, University of Pittsburgh, 1965. 192 p.

2567. Goldberg, Lawrence F., and Greenberg, Warren. "The Effect of Physician-Controlled Health Insurance: *U. S. v. Oregon State Medical Society.*" *Journal of Health Politics, Policy and Law* 2 (Spring 1977): 48–78.

2568. Goldstein, E. M. "Medical Devices: Soon Federal Control." *Trial* 12 (February 1975): 68–69.

2569. Gordon, Richard S., ed. *Issues in Health Care Regulation.* New York: McGraw-Hill, 1980. 375 p.

2570. Grabowski, Henry G., et al. "Estimating the Effects of Regulation on Innovation: An International Comparative Analysis of the Pharmaceutical Industry." *Journal of Law and Economics* 21 (April 1978): 133–63.

2571. Hall, John W. "The Regulation of Commercial Health Insurance for the Individual." Ph. D. dissertation, University of Pennsylvania, 1960. 808 p.

2572. Halperin, J. A. "From Investigation to Marketplace: Moving Drugs through the System." *Food Drug Cosmetic Law Journal* 36 (April 1981): 166–74.

2573. Hamilton, J. S. "Administrative Practice in Aviation Medical Proceedings." *Emory Law Journal* 26 (Summer 1977): 565–88.

2574. Hamilton, Kenneth L. "An Application of Socioeconomic Accounting to Analysis of Nursing Home Regulatory Policy." Ph. D. dissertation, Georgia Institute of Technology, 1979. 162 p.

2575. Hanft, Ruth S., and Eichenholz, Joseph. "The Regulation of Health Technology." *Proceedings of the Academy of Political Science* 33 (1980): 148–57.

2576. Harney, Malachi. "The U. S. Bureau of Narcotics." *Current History* 53 (July 1967): 23–30, 50.

2577. Hastings, Anne H. "The Strategies of Government Inrtervention: An Analysis of Federal Education and Health Care Policy." Ph. D. dissertation, University of Virginia, 1982. 369 p.

2578. Havender, William R. "Ruminations on a Rat-Saccharin and Human Risk." *Regulation* 3 (March-April 1979): 17–24.

2579. Havighurst, Clark C. *Deregulating the Health Care Industry: Planning for Competition.* Cambridge, MA: Ballinger, 1982. 500 p.

2580. Headen, Alvin E. "Measuring the Effect of Economic Regulation: Certificate of Need Regulation of Hospitals in Massachusetts 1972–1978." Ph. D. dissertation, Massachusetts Institute of Technology, 1981. 179 p.

2581. Hess, Fritz. "An Analysis of the Codes Regulating Selected School Sanitary Facilities." Ph. D. dissertation, Columbia University, 1961.

2582. Hickman, D. H. "Advisory Committees at FDA—A Legal Perspective." *Food Drug Cosmetic Law Journal* 29 (July 1974): 395–408.

2583. Hodgson, Godfrey. "The Politics of American Health Care." *Atlantic* 232 (October 1973): 45–61.

2584. Hughes, Charles F. "Commissioner Colburn and Blue Cross: A Study of Decision-Making within the Regulatory Process in Michigan." Ph. D. dissertation, University of Michigan, 1966. 346 p.

2585. Hyman, P. M. "What Is Happening to OTC Drugs?" *Food Drug Cosmetic Law Journal* 33 (April 1978): 203–15.

2586. Hynes, Charles J. "The Regulation of Nursing Homes: A Case Study." *Proceedings of the Academy of Political Science* 33 (1980): 126–36.

2587. Judd, Leda R. "Federal Involvement in Health Care after 1945." *Current History* 72 (May-June 1977): 201–06, 227.

2588. Kaiser, Donald L., et al. "The Effects of Departmental Resources on Compliance with Mandated Standards: Assessment of Local Health Agencies." *State and Local Government Review* 10 (September 1978): 82–87.

2589. Kane, Nancy M. "Hospital Strategy: The Implications of the Managerial View for Public Policy and Regulation." D. B. A. dissertation, Harvard University, 1981. 394 p.

2590. Kay, Bonnie J., and Neal, James R. "Regulatory Policy and Abortion Clinics: Implications for Planning." *Journal of Health Politics, Policy and Law* 3 (Spring 1978): 43–53.

2591. Keiser, Robert K. "The New Regulation of Health and Safety." *Political Science Quarterly* 95 (Fall 1980): 479–91.

2592. Kelman, Steven J. *Regulating America, Regulating Sweden: A Comparative Study of Occupational Safety and Health Policy* Cambridge, MA: MIT Press, 1981. 270 p.

2593. Kett, Joseph F. *The Formation of the American Medical Profession; The Role of Institutions,* 1780–1860. New Haven, CT: Yale University Press, 1968. 217 p.

2594. Kingsdale, Jon M. "Marrying Regulatory and Competitive Approaches to Health Care Cost Containment." *Journal of Health Politics, Policy and Law* 3 (Spring 1978): 20–42.

2595. Kushman, John E. "Pricing Dental Services: A Market Testing Approach." *Journal of Health Politics, Policy and Law* 5 (Winter 1981): 634–49.

2596. Laubach, Gerald D. "Federal Regulation and Pharmaceutical Innovation." *Proceedings of the Academy of Political Science* 33 (1980): 60–90.

2597. Lave, Lester B. "Lessons from Benzene." *American Statistician* 36 (August 1982): 260–61.

2598. Lien-fu Huang. "Controlling Inflation of Medicare Physicians' Fees." *Policy Analysis* 3 (Summer 1977): 325–39.

2599. Linderman, T. G. "Freedom of Information—Animal Drug Regulations." *Food Drug Cosmetic Law Journal* 33 (June 1978): 274–80.

2600. Lipscomb, Joseph. "Deregulation of Paraprofessionals and Health Care Cost Containment: The Case of Dentistry." *Policy Studies Review* 1 (1982): 523–31.

2601. Lipsky, Michael, and Lounds, Morris. "Citizen Participation and Health Care: Problems of Government Induced Participation." *Journal of Health Politics, Policy and Law* 1 (Spring 1976): 85–111.

2602. Mahler, Julianne A. "Barriers to Coordinating Health Services Regulatory Programs." *Journal of Health Politics, Policy and Law* 6 (Fall 1981): 528–41.

2603. Matzen, Clement W. "California State Regulation of Family Care Homes for the Mentally Ill: An Historical Inquiry." D. S. W. dissertation, University of Southern California, 1968. 395 p.

2604. McCaffrey, David P. "Assessment of OSHA's Recent Effects on Injury Rates." *Journal of Human Resources* 18 (Winter 1983): 130–46.

2605. McCarthy, Carol M. "Regulation and Compliance Activity in New York State Acute Care Hospitals." Ph. D. dissertation, New York University, 1978. 497 p.

2606. McClure, Walter. "On Broadening the Definition of and Removing Regulatory Barriers to a Competitive Health Care System." *Journal of Health Politics, Policy and Law* 3 (Fall 1978): 303–27.

2607. Meyer, Jack A. "Viewpoint: Health Care Reform and Market Discipline—Federalism Strikes Back." *Regulation* 6 (November-December 1982): 16–20.

2608. Miller, P. S. "IND/NDA Rewrite: Rewritten." *Food Drug Cosmetic Law Journal* 36 (July 1981): 354–62.

2609. Moran, R. D. "Discretionary Review by the Occupational Safety and Health Review Commission: Is It Necessary?" *University of Colorado Law Review* 46 (Winter 1974): 139–56.

2610. Moran, R. D. "Oversight of Penalty Increases and Adjudicatory Function under the Occupational Safety and Health Act of 1970." *Federal Bar Journal* 33 (Spring 1974): 138–48.

2611. Morey, R. S. "GMPs and GLPs—Where Are We Going?" *Food Drug Cosmetic Law Journal* 32 (October 1977): 459–68.

2612. Morgareidge, Kenneth. "Getting FDA Clearance for Food Additives." *Food Drug Cosmetic Law Journal* 19 (July 1964): 364–73.

2613. Mowitz, Robert. "The Nuisance Doctrine and Public Health Regulation in New York State." Ph. D. dissertation, Syracuse University, 1948.

2614. Mueller, John. "The Politics of Fluoridation in Seven California Cities." *Western Political Quarterly* 19 (March 1966): 54–67.

2615. Mugleston, William F. "Cornpone and Potlikker: A Moment of Relief in the Great Depression." *Louisiana History* 16 (Summer 1975): 279–88.

2616. O'Keefe, Harold F. "Food and Drug Administration Industry Information Programs." *Food Drug Cosmetic Law Journal* 21 (January 1966): 52–56.

2617. O'Reilly, J. T. "Role of Corporate Counsel in Defense of FDA Court Actions." *Food Drug Cosmetic Law Journal* 35 (June 1980): 370–75.

2618. "OSHA at the Threshold: Setting Permissible Exposure Levels for Known Carcinogens after American Petroleum Institute (*Industrial Union Dept., AFL-CIO v. American Petroleum Institute*, 100 S Ct 2844)." *San Diego Law Review* 18 (July 1981): 633–61.

2619. Page, J. A., and Munsing, P. N. "Occupational Health and the Federal Government: The Wages Are Still Bitter." *Law and Contemporary Problems* 38 (Summer 1974): 650–68.

2620. Palley, Howard A. "Policy Formulation in Health: Some Considerations of Governmental Constraints on Pricing in the Health Delivery System." *American Behavioral Scientist* 17 (March-April 1974): 572–84.

2621. Pape, S. M. "Meetings and Correspondence, Including FOI Consideration." *Food Drug Cosmetic Law Journal* 32 (May 1977): 226–35.

2622. Parle, William M. "State Regulation of the Economic Performance of Hospitals: A Comparative Study." Ph. D. dissertation, University of South Carolina, 1978. 231 p.

2623. Peltzman, Samuel. "The Benefits and Costs of New Drug Regulation." In *Regulating New Drugs*, edited by Richard L. Landau, pp. 113–211. Chicago: University of Chicago Center for Policy Study, 1973.

2624. Peskoe, M. P. "Submissions and Petitions under the FDA's Procedural Regulations." *Food Drug Cosmetic Law Journal* 32 (May 1977): 216–25.

2625. Pilot, L. R. "FDA Update." *Food Drug Cosmetic Law Journal* 32 (March 1977): 113–20.

2626. Pollard, Michael R. "Fostering Competition in Health Care." *Proceedings of the Academy of Political Science* 33 (1980): 158–67.

2627. Prindle, Richard. "The Antismoking Program of the Public Health Service." *Bulletin of the New York Academy of Medicine* 44 (December 1968): 1514–20.

2628. "Publicity and the FDA." *Food Drug Cosmetic Law Journal* 28 (July 1973): 436–46.

2629. Pursell, Carroll. "The Administration of Science in the Department of Agriculture, 1933–1940." *Agricultural History* 42 (July 1968): 231–40.

2630. Rankin, Winton B. "FDA's Organization: The Reasons for Change." *Food Drug Cosmetic Law Journal* 22 (December 1967): 660–66.

2631. Rice, Dorothy P. "Health Facilities in the United States." *Current History* 72 (May-June 1977): 211–14, 230.

2632. Richards, E. P. "OSHA Regulations: Access to Employer-Held Medical Information." *Trial* 16 (November 1980): 8–9.

2633. Robinson, Nelson M. "Regulatory Systems and Hospital Standards." Ph. D. dissertation, Syracuse University, 1954. 594 p.

2634. Roemer, Milton I. "The Foreign Experience in Health Service Policy." *Proceedings of the Academy of Political Science* 33 (1980): 206–23.

2635. Rorrie, Colin C., and Shannon, Terry E. "Health Planning: Experience and Expectations." *State and Local Government Review* 12 (May 1980): 45–50.

2636. Rosner, George. "Criminal Liability for Deceiving the Food and Drug Administration." *Food Drug Cosmetic Law Journal* 20 (August 1965): 446–68.

2637. Rothschild, L. "Newest Regulatory Agency in Washington." *Food Drug Cosmetic Law Journal* 33 (February 1978): 86–93.

2638. Rothstein, M. A. "Judicial Review of Decisions of the Occupational Safety and Health Review Commission—1973–1978: An Empirical Study." *Chicago-Kent Law Review* 56 (Spring 1980): 607–33.

2639. Rubinstein, Eli A. "Warning: The Surgeon General's Research Program May Be Dangerous to Preconceived Notions." *Journal of Science Issues* 32 (Fall 1976): 18–34.

2640. Rucklin, Hirsch S. "A New Strategy for Regulating Long-Term Care Facilities." *Journal of Health Politics, Policy and Law* 2 (Summer 1977): 190–211.

2641. Rulis, A. M., and Ronk, R. J. "Cyclic Review—Looking Forward?" *Food Drug Cosmetic Law Journal* 36 (April 1981): 156–65.

2642. Rushefsky, Mark E. "A Critique of Market Reform in Health Care: The 'Consumer-Choice' Health Plan." *Journal of Health Politics, Policy and Law* 5 (Winter 1981): 720–41.

2643. Saber, F. A. "Laetrile: Is It Really a Matter of Free Choice?" *American Journal of Public Health* 67 (September 1977): 871–72.

2644. Saltman, Richard B., and Young, David W. "The Hospital Power Equilibrium: An Alternative View of the Cost Containment Dilemma." *Journal of Health Politics, Policy and Law* 6 (Fall 1981): 391–418.

2645. Sapolsky, Harvey M. "The Political Obstacles to the Control of Cigarette Smoking in the United States." *Journal of Health Politics, Policy and Law* 5 (Summer 1980): 277–90.

2646. Scarlett, T. "FDA's Regulatory Proposals for the Management of Advisory Committees." *Food Drug Cosmetic Law Journal* 30 (August 1975): 503–08.

2647. Schmidt, A. M. "FDA—Social Trend and Regulatory Reform." *Food Drug Cosmetic Law Journal* 31 (November 1976): 605–15.

2648. Schmidt, A. M. "FDA Today: Critics, Congress and Consumerism." *Food Drug Cosmetic Law Journal* 29 (November 1974): 575–84.

2649. Schmidt, A. M. "Some Homework Is Needed." *Food Drug Cosmetic Law Journal* 32 (February 1977): 67–75.

2650. Schmidt, Robert Milton. "Law, Medicine and Public Policy: The Sickle Cell Anemia Control Act of 1972: A Case Study." Ph. D. dissertation, Emory University, 1982. 269 p.

2651. Schweitzer, Mary M. "Economic Regulation and the Colonial Economy: The Maryland Tobacco Inspection Act of 1747." *Journal of Economic History* 40 (September 1980): 551–69.

2652. Seidman, David. "The Politics of Policy Analysis: Protection or Overprotection in Drug Regulation." *Regulation* 1 (July-August 1977): 22–37.

2653. Shupack, R. A. "Inspectional Process: A Statutory Overview." *Food Drug Cosmetic Law Journal* 33 (December 1978): 697–709.

2654. Smith, Roland B. "An Evaluation of the Connecticut Food and Drug Commission with Special Reference to the Supervision of Drug and Cosmetic Advertising Labeling." Ph. D. dissertation, Columbia University, 1959. 374 p.

2655. Solo, Robert. "Regional Building Codes Formulated and Enforced by the Federal Bureau of Standards." *Journal of Economic Issues* 15 (March 1981): 173–75.

2656. Somers, Anne R. "Social, Economic, and Health Aspects of Mandatory Retirement." *Journal of Health Politics, Policy and Law* 6 (Fall 1981): 542–57.

2657. Spellman, William E., and Jorgenson, Mark R. "The Social and Revenue Effects of State Alcoholic Beverage Control." *American Journal of Economics and Sociology* 41 (January 1982): 77–83.

2658. Spence, G. K. "FDA Trade Secret Procedures and Standards." *Food Drug Cosmetic Law Journal* 35 (June 1980): 362–69.

2659. Spiller, R. M. "How to Handle an FDA Inspection." *Food Drug Cosmetic Law Journal* 33 (March 1978): 101–08.

2660. Sponholtz, Lloyd. "The Politics of Temperance in Ohio, 1880–1912." *Ohio History* 85 (Winter 1976): 4–27.

2661. Stribling, J. H. "Regulation of Food Labeling and Advertising by the Food and Drug Administration." *Food Drug Cosmetic Law Journal* 33 (January 1978): 4–11.

2662. Summerson, William H. "The Role of Scientific Research in the Food and Drug Administration." *Food Drug Cosmetic Law Journal* 20 (July 1963): 427–32.

2663. Swanson, J. W. "How to Handle an FDA Inspection—The Inspector's View." *Food Drug Cosmetic Law Journal* 33 (March 1978): 109–15.

2664. Taylor, M. R. "Seizures and Injunctions: Their Role in FDA's Enforcement Program." *Food Drug Cosmetic Law Journal* 33 (November 1978): 596–606.

2665. Temin, P. "Origin of Compulsory Drug Prescriptions." *Journal of Law and Economics* 22 (April 1979): 91–105.

2666. Tesh, Sylvia. "Disease Casuality and Politics." *Journal of Health Politics, Policy and Law* 6 (Fall 1981): 369–90.

2667. Thompson, Frank J., and Campbell, Richard W. "Implementation and Service Error: Veterans Administration Health Care and the Commercial Market Option." *Journal of Health Politics, Policy and Law* 6 (Fall 1981): 419–43.

2668. Ullmann, Steven G. "Regulation and Reimbursement in the Long Term Health Case Industry: The Case of New York State." Ph. D. dissertation, University of Michigan, 1980. 215 p.

2669. United States. General Accounting Office. *FDA Drug Approval: A Lengthy Process That Delays the Availability of Important New Drugs: Report to the Subcommittee on Science, Research and Technology, House Committee on Science and Technology.* Washington, DC: U. S. Government Printing Office, 1980. 83 p.

2670. Urban, Raymond, and Mancke, Richard. "Federal Regulation of Whiskey Labelling: From the Repeal of Prohibition to the Present." *Journal of Law and Economics* 15 (October 1972): 411–26.

2671. Viscusi, W. Kip. "Health and Safety." *Regulation* 6 (January-February 1982): 34–36.

2672. Vocci, F. J. "Drug Enforcement Administration: Scheduling Policy and Classification." *Food Drug Cosmetic Law Journal* 35 (December 1980): 691–97.

2673. Walden, J. R. "FDA with a Capital 'L'" *Food Drug Cosmetic Law Journal* 31 (December 1976): 649–55.

2674. Walker, Forrest A. "Compulsory Health Insurance: 'The Next Great Step in Social Legislation.'" *Journal of American History* 56 (September 1969): 290–304.

2675. Waterlow, J. C. "Uses of Recommended Intakes—The Purpose of Dietary Recommendations." *Food Policy* 4 (May 1979): 107–14.

2676. Weeda, D. F. "FDA Seizure and Injunction Actions: Judicial Means of Protecting the Public Health." *Food Drug Cosmetic Law Journal* 35 (February 1980): 112–21.

2677. Wellford, Harrison. *Sowing the Wind: A Report from Ralph Nader's Center for Study of Responsive Law on Food Safety and the Chemical Harvest.* New York: Grossman, 1972. 384 p.

2678. Whelan, Elizabeth. "The Politics of Cancer." *Policy Review* 10 (Fall 1979): 33–46.

2679. White, William D. "Why is Regulation Introduced in the Health Sector? A Look at Occupational Licensure." *Journal of Health Politics, Policy and Law* 4 (Fall 1979): 536–52.

2680. Willeman, Thomas R. "Regulatory Response to Variations in the Supply of Nursing Home Beds." *Public Policy* 27 (Fall 1979): 257–67.

2681. Wunsch, James L. "Prostitution and Public Policy: From Regulation to Suppression, 1858–1920." Ph.D. dissertation, University of Chicago, 1976. 175 p.

2682. Zervox, C., and Rodricks, J. V. "FDA's Ban of DES in Meat Production." *American Statistician* 36 (August 1982): 278–83.

INDUSTRY

2683. Allen, John E., and Roberts, Miriam. "The Oregon Department of Geology and Mineral Industries." *Journal of the West* 10 (January 1971): 154–57.

2684. American Management Association. General Management Division. *Technical Planning in the Defense Industry.* New York: The Association, 1963. 23 p.

2685. Anderson, R. C. "Public Policies toward the Use of Scrap Materials." *American Economic Review; Papers and Proceedings* 67 (February 1977): 355–58.

2686. Arden, J. Lea. "Cotton Textiles and the Federal Child Labor Act of 1916." *Labor History* 16 (Fall 1975): 485–94.

2687. Baack, Bennett D., and Ray, Edward J. "Tariff Policy and Comparative Advantage in the Iron and Steel Industry: 1870–1929." *Explorations in Economic History* 11 (Fall 1973): 3–23.

2688. Benson, Edward A. "Common Stock Underwriting Commissions and Their Correlates from 1960 to 1970." Ph.D. dissertation, University of Texas, 1971. 201 p.

2689. Berninger, Louis M. "An Economic Analysis of the Wisconsin Floriculture Industry with Special Reference to the Wholesale Commission Firms." Ph. D. dissertation, University of Wisconsin, 1959. 218 p.

2690. Block, F. "Beyond Corporate Liberalism." *Social Problems* 24 (February 1977): 352–61.

2691. Braeutigam, Ronald R. "Analysis of Fully Distributed Cost Pricing in Regulated Industries." *Bell Journal of Economics and Management Science* 11 (Spring 1980): 182–96.

2692. Bromley, D. W. "Economics and Public Decisions: Roles of the State and Issues in Economic Evaluation." *Journal of Economic Issues* 10 (December 1976): 811–38.

2693. Brunner, K., and Meckling, W. H. "Perception of Man and the Conception of Government." *Journal of Money, Credit and Banking* 9 (February 1977): 70–85.

2694. Calleo, D. P. "Business Corporations and the National State." *Social Research* 41 (Winter 1974): 702–18.

2695. Caves, Douglas W. "Measuring Productivity Growth in the U. S. Railroad Industry with an Estimate of Losses Resulting from Economic Regulation." Ph. D. dissertation, University of Wisconsin—Madison, 1980. 302 p.

2696. Chee, Choung. "National Regulation of Fisheries in International Law." Ph. D. dissertation, New York University, 1964. 329 p.

2697. Chelius, James R. "An Analysis of Industrial Safety Regulation." Ph. D. dissertation, University of Chicago, 1974. 339 p.

2698. David, Paul A. "Learning by Doing and Tariff Protection: A Reconsideration of the Case of the Antebellum United States Cotton Textile Industry." *Journal of Economic History* 30 (September 1970): 521–601.

2699. Davis, Allen. "The Campaign for the Industrial Relations Commission, 1911–1913." *Mid-America* 45 (October 1963): 211–28.

2700. Doron, Gideon. "Administrative Regulation of an Industry: The Cigarette Case." *Public Administration Review* 39 (March-April 1979): 163–70.

2701. Doron, Gideon. "Public Regulation of the Cigarette Industry: Theory, Measurement, Fact." Ph. D. dissertation, University of Rochester, 1978. 205 p.

2702. Eads, George C. *Chemicals as a Regulated Industry: Implications for Research and Product Development.* Santa Monica, CA: Rand, 1979. 36 p.

2703. Early, Allen. "Regulation of Life Insurance in Texas: A Study of the Impact of Regulatory Policies on Industry Structure, Behavior and Performance." Ph. D. dissertation, University of Oklahoma, 1974. 288 p.

2704. Francois, Michele B. "Federal Regulations, Processing Costs and Scale of Plant in the Louisiana Sugar Cane Industry." Ph. D. dissertation, Tulane University, 1971. 199 p.

2705. Frese, Joseph R., and Judd, Jacob, eds. *American Industrialization, Economic Expansion, and the Law.* Tarrytown, NY: Sleepy Hollow Press, 1981. 251 p.

2706. Galbraith, John K. *The New Industrial State.* 3d ed., rev. Boston: Houghton Mifflin, 1978. 438 p.

2707. Gardner, Ella P. "Implementing the Social Legislation of the 60s and 70s: A Descriptive Study of Industry Participation in Selected Rulemaking Proceedings." D. B. A. dissertation, George Washington University, 1982. 308 p.

2708. Gruchy, A. G. "Government Intervention and the Social Control Business: The Neoinstitutionalist Position." *Journal of Economic Issues* 8 (June 1974): 235–53.

2709. Harper, Donald V. "Economic Regulation of the Motor Trucking Industry by the States." Ph. D. dissertation, University of Illinois, 1957. 437 p.

2710. Hartley, K., and Watt, P. A. "Profits, Regulation and the UK Aerospace Industry." *Journal of Industrial Economics* 29 (June 1981): 413–28.

2711. Hillman, A. L. "Declining Industry and Political Support Protectionist Motives." *American Economic Review* 72 (December 1982): 1180–87.

2712. Himmelberg, Robert F. "Business, Antitrust Policy, and the Industrial Board of the Department of Commerce, 1919." *Business History Review* 42 (Spring 1968): 1–23.

2713. Himmelberg, Robert F. "The War Industries Board and the Antitrust Question in November 1918." *Journal of American History* 52 (June 1965): 59–74.

2714. Irwin, Manley R., and Stanley, Kenneth B. "Regulatory Circumvention and Holding Company." *Journal of Economic Issues* 8 (June 1974): 375–411.

2715. Johnson, Leland L. "Behavior of the Firm under Regulatory Constraint: A Reassessment." *American Economic Review; Papers and Proceedings* 63 (May 1973): 90–97.

2716. Kennedy, T. E. "Regulated Firm with a Fixed Proportion Production Function." *American Economic Review* 67 (December 1977): 968–71.

2717. Koch, C. James, and Leone, Robert A. "The Clean Water Act: Unexpected Impacts on Industry." *Harvard Environmental Law Review* 3 (1979): 84–111.

2718. Kosonen, P. "Contemporary Capitalism and the Critique of Political Economy: Methodological Aspects." *Acta Sociologica* 20 (1977): 369–84.

2719. Krueger, A. O., and Tuncer, B. "Empirical Test of the Infant Industry Argument." *American Economic Review* 72 (December 1982): 1142–52.

2720. Lauterbach, A. "Convergence Controversy Revisited." *Kyklos* 29 (1976): 733–54.

2721. Leamer, E. E., et al. "Empirical Analysis of the Composition of Manufacturing Employment in the Industrialized Countries." *European Economic Review* 9 (April 1977): 1–19.

2722. Lee, Harold O. "A Critical Study of Exceptional Accounting Practices in Selected Regulated Industries." Ph.D. dissertation, University of Texas, 1969. 290 p.

2723. Leonard, William N. "Industry, Trade and Tariffs." *Current History* 43 (August 1962): 103–10.

2724. Magat, W. A., ed. "Managing the Transition to Deregulation." *Law and Contemporary Problems* 44 (Winter 1981): 1–195.

2725. Melody, William H. "Marginal Utility of Marginal Analysis in Public Policy Formulation." *Journal of Economic Issues* 8 (June 1974): 287–300.

2726. Metzgar, J. "Public Policy and Steel." *Dissent* 29 (Summer 1982): 325–29.

2727. Mirakhor, A. "Efficient Allocation of Resources in a Regulated and Unionized Monopoly." *Southern Economic Journal* 42 (April 1976): 725–29.

2728. Nadel, Mark V. "Hidden Dimension of Public Policy: Private Governments and the Policy Making Process." *Journal of Politics* 37 (February 1975): 2–34.

2729. Nash, Gerald D. "Industry and the Federal Government: 1850–1933." *Current History* 48 (June 1965): 321–37, 364.

2730. National Industrial Conference Board. *The Conference Board Presents the Crisis of the Free Market.* by F. A. Harper, et al. New York: The Board, 1945. 83 p.

2731. National Industrial Conference Board. Division of Public Affairs. *Government in Business.* New York: The Board, 1964. 32 p.

2732. National Industrial Conference Board. *Government-Industry Conference.* New York: The Board, 1965. 78 p.

2733. Nickell, S. J. "Influence of Uncertainty on Investment." *Economic Journal* 87 (March 1977): 47–70.

2734. Ohl, John R. "The Navy, the War Industries Board, and the Industrial Mobilization for War, 1917–1918." *Military Affairs* 40 (February 1976): 17–22.

2735. Oster, S. "Strategic Use of Regulatory Investment by Industry Subgroups." *Economic Industry* 20 (October 1982): 604–18.

2736. Petersen, William M. "Economic Determinants of Legislation, Regulatory Behavior and Market Performance in the Automobile Insurance Industry." Ph. D. dissertation, Harvard University, 1981.

2737. Petras, J. F. "State Capitalism and the Third World." *Journal of Contemporary Asia* 6 (1976): 432–43.

2738. Pfunder, M. R. "Report to the Section 7 (Clayton Act) Committee of the Antitrust Section of the American Bar Assocation on the Implications of Judicial Review of a Denial of Early Termination under the Hart-Scott-Rodino Premerger Notification Plan." *Antitrust Law Journal* 51 (1982): 739–63.

2739. Phillips, Almarin W., and Stevenson, Rodney E. "Historical Development of Industrial Organization." *History of Political Economy* 6 (Fall 1974): 324–42.

2740. Piette, Michael J., and Desvousges, William H. "Behavior of the Firm: The US Petroleum Pipeline Industry under Regulatory Constraint." *Growth and Change* 12 (April 1981): 17–22.

2741. Pittman, Russell. "The Effects of Industry Concentration and Regulation on Contributions in Three 1972 U. S. Senate Campaigns." *Public Choice* 27 (Fall 1976): 71–80.

2742. Pratt, Joseph A. "The Petroleum Industry in Transition: Antitrust and the Decline of Monopoly Control in Oil." *Journal of Economic History* 40 (December 1980): 815–37.

2743. Price, Glenn. "Robert F. Stockton and the American Character in the Middle of the 19th Century Part II: Stockton as Promoter and Entrepreneur: Ships, Guns, Canals, Railroads and the Public Interest." *Pacific Historian* 9 (February 1965): 33–44.

2744. Proxmire, William. "Economic Regulations in Five Major Industries: Bank Regulations at the Federal Level. " *Challenge* 19 (November-December 1976): 51–52.

2745. Purcell, Susan Kaufman. "Business-Government Relations in Mexico: The Case of the Sugar Industry." *Comparative Politics* 13 (January 1981): 211–33.

2746. Richards, Bronwyn K. "The Economics and Law of a Semi-Regulated Industry: The Philadelphia National Bank Case." Ph. D. dissertation, Columbia University, 1981. 581 p.

2747. Roberts, Keith. "Antitrust Problems in the Newspaper Industry." *Harvard Law Review* 82 (December 1968): 319–66.

2748. Rogers, C. P. "Mergers in Regulated Industries: The Role of the Regulatory Agency." *St. Mary's Law Journal* 7 (1975): 297–318.

2749. Rutherford, Malcolm. "Veblen on Owners, Managers, and the Control of Industry." *History of Political Economy* 12 (Fall 1980): 434–48.

2750. Saloutos, Theodore. "Protection and Industry, 1866–1919." *Current History* 42 (June 1962): 339–43, 364.

2751. Samprone, Joseph C. "State Rate Regulation of the Property-Liability Insurance Industry." Ph. D. dissertation, University of California, Santa Barbara, 1975. 138 p.

2752. Savage, William W. "The Cherokee Strip Live Stock Association: The Impact of Federal Regulation on the Cattleman's Last Frontier." Ph. D. dissertation, University of Oklahoma, 1972. 145 p.

2753. Schmalensee, Richard. "Antitrust and the New Industrial Economics." *American Economic Review; Papers and Proceedings* 72 (May 1982): 24–28.

2754. Schmalensee, Richard. "Valuing Changes in Regulated Firms' Input Prices." *Southern Economic Journal* 43 (January 1977): 1346–51.

2755. Sheahan, John B. "Competition versus Regulation as a Policy Aim for the Telephone Equipment Industry." Ph. D. dissertation, Harvard University, 1954. 385 p.

2756. Shepherd, William G. "Entry as a Substitute for Regulation." *American Economic Review; Papers and Proceedings* 63 (May 1973): 98–105.

2757. "Shipping Industry Seeks a Safe Haven: Merger Jurisdiction for the FMC?" *Law and Policy in International Business* 5 (1973): 274–91.

2758. Smith, R. L. "Franchise Regulation: An Economic Analysis of State Restrictions on Automobile Distribution." *Journal of Law and Economics* 25 (April 1982): 125–57.

2759. Smith, V. Kerry. "Implications of Regulation for Induced Technical Change." *Bell Journal of Economics and Management Science* 5 (Autumn 1974): 623–32.

2760. Steedman, I. "State and the Outcome of the Pasinetti Process." *Economic Journal* 82 (December 1972): 1387–95.

2761. Stein, J. L., and Borts, G. H. "Behavior of the Firm under Regulatory Constraint." *American Economic Review* 62 (December 1972): 964–70.

2762. Strumpel, B. "Changing Face of Advanced Industrial Economies: A Post-Keynesian View." *Political Studies* 10 (October 1977): 299–322.

2763. Takayama, A. "Behavior of the Firm under Regulatory Constraint." *American Economic Review* 59 (June 1969): 255–60.

2764. Temin, P. "Technology, Regulation, and Market Structure in the Modern Pharmaceutical Industry." *Bell Journal of Economics and Management Science* 10 (Autumn 1979): 429–46.

2765. Turkel, G. "Rational Law and Boundary Maintenance: Legitimating the 1971 Lockheed Loan Guarantee." *Law and Society Review* 15 (1980–1981): 41–77.

2766. Turner, Max W. "State Regulation of the Motion Picture Industry." Ph. D. dissertation, University of Iowa, 1947. 293 p.

2767. Urofsky, Melvin I. "Josephus Daniels and the Armor Trust." *North Carolina Historical Review* 45 (July 1968): 237–63.

2768. U. S. Congress. Office of Technology Assessment. *U. S. Industrial Competitiveness: A Comparison of Steel, Electronics, and Automobiles.* Washington, DC: Congress of the U. S., Office of Technology Assessment, 1981. 27 p.

2769. Vanderzell, John H. "State Legislation Relating to Standards Development in Building Regulation." Ph. D. dissertation, Syracuse University, 1955. 286 p.

2770. Varela, Oscar A. "General Equilibrium versus Partial Equilibrium Economic and Financial Analysis with Respect to the Impact of a Rate of Return on Investment Regulatory Constraint in the Motor Carrier Industry." Ph. D. dissertation, University of Alabama, 1980. 289 p.

2771. Vogel, David. "Business Distrust of Government." *Center Magazine* 10 (November 1977): 69–78.

2772. Ward, Charles S. "Collective Bargaining in Industry: Its Evolution under National Government Regulation, 1933–1935." Ph. D. dissertation, University of Minnesota, 1972. 329 p.

2773. Wend, Jared S. "Public Regulation of the Fluid-Milk Industry in Detroit, Michigan." Ph. D. dissertation, University of Michigan, 1952. 250 p.

2774. Whitten, David O. "Tariff and Profit in the Antebellum Louisiana Sugar Industry." *Business History Review* 44 (Summer 1970): 226–33.

2775. Wiens, E. G. "Government Enterprise: An Instrument for the Internal Regulation of Industry." *Canadian Journal of Economics* 13 (February 1980): 124–32.

2776. Williams, H. R. "U. S. Trade Adjustment Assistance to Mitigate Injury from Import Competition." *American Journal of Economics and Sociology* 36 (October 1977): 381–92.

2777. Wise, Kenneth T. "The Effects of OSHA Regulations on the U. S. Lead Industry: An Economic Impact and Econometric Modeling Analysis." Ph. D. dissertation, Massachusetts Institute of Technology, 1979. 517 p.

2778. Yelton, Emery J. "Regulation of the Pari-Mutual Industry." Ph. D. dissertation, University of Florida, 1974. 177 p.

2779. Zaid, Mayer N. "On the Social Control of Industries." *Social Forces* 57 (September 1978): 79–102.

2780. Zerbe, Richard O. "Seattle Taxis: Deregulation Hits a Pothole." *Regulation* 7 (November-December 1983): 43–48.

2781. Zweier, Paul. "Performance of a Vertically Integrated Manufacturer under Indirect Regulation." Ph. D. dissertation, Ohio State University, 1968. 275 p.

LABOR

2782. Albritton, Robert B. "Measuring Public Policy: Impacts of the Supplemental Security Income Program." *American Journal of Political Science* 23 (August 1979): 559–78.

2783. Asher, Robert. "Business and Workers' Welfare in the Progressive Era: Workmen's Compensation Reform in Massachusetts, 1880–1911." *Business History Review* 43 (Winter 1969): 452–75.

2784. Asher, Robert. "The 1911 Wisconsin Workmen's Compensation Law: A Study in Conservative Labor Reform." *Wisconsin Magazine of History* 57 (Winter 1973–1974): 123–40.

2785. Asher, Robert. "The Origins of Workmen's Compensation in Minnesota." *Minnesota History* 44 (Winter 1974): 142–53.

2786. Asher, Robert. "Radicalism and Reform: State Insurance of Workmen's Compensation in Minnesota, 1910–1933." *Labor History* 14 (Winter 1973): 19–41.

2787. Baird, V. C. "Industrial Union Department, *AFL-CIO v. American Petroleum Institute*: Limiting OSHA's Authority to Regulate Workplace Carcinogens under the Occupational Safety and Health Act." *Boston College Environmental Affairs Law Review* 9 (1981–1982): 623–85.

2788. Balmer, Donald. "The Role of Political Leadership in the Passage of Oregon's Migratory Labor Legislation." *Western Political Quarterly* 15 (March 1962): 146–56.

2789. Barber, Bernard. "Control and Responsibility in the Powerful Professions." *Political Science Quarterly* 93 (Winter 1978–79): 599–615.

2790. Begun, James W. ; Crowe, Edward; and Feldman, Roger. "Occupational Regulation in the States: A Casual Model." *Journal of Health Politics, Policy and Law* 6 (Summer 1981): 229–54.

2791. Beiser, Edward, and Silberman, Jonathan. "The Political Party Variable: Workmen's Compensation Cases in the New York Court of Appeals." *Polity* 3 (Summer 1971): 521–30.

2792. Benham, Lee, and Benham, Alexandra. "Regulating through the Professions: A Perspective on Information Control." *Journal of Law and Economics* 18 (October 1975): 421–47.

2793. Brewer, Thomas L. "State Anti-Labor Legislation: Texas—A Case Study." *Labor History* 11 (Winter 1970): 58–76.

2794. Brozen, Yale. "Minimum Wage Rates and Household Workers." *Journal of Law and Economics* 5 (October 1962): 103–10.

2795. Burkhauser, Richard V., and Smeeding, Timothy M. "The Net Impact of the Social Security System on the Poor." *Policy Studies Review Annual* 6 (1982): 137–56.

2796. Burns, Arthur. "Some Reflections of the Employment Act." *Political Science Quarterly* 77 (December 1962): 481–504.

2797. Campbell, Colin D. "Social Insurance in the United States: A Program in Search of an Explanation." *Journal of Law and Economics* 12 (October 1969): 249–65.

2798. Cassell, Frank. "Immigration and the Department of Labor." *American Academy of Political and Social Science, Annals* 367 (September 1966): 105–14.

2799. Chambers, Donald E. "Workmen's Compensation in the United States: The Effects of Fifty Years of Local Control and Private Enterprise on the Administration of a Social Welfare Programme." *Journal of Social Policy* 4 (October 1975): 337–48.

2800. Collins, Adrian A. "Pension Regulation: A Study of Need and Feasibility." D. B. A. dissertation, George Washington University, 1967. 300 p.

2801. Collins, Morris W. "State Regulation of Discrimination in Employment." Ph. D. dissertation, Harvard University, 1953. 251 p.

2802. Conner, Valerie Jean. "The National War Labor Board: 1918–1919." Ph. D. dissertation, University of Virginia, 1974. 277 p.

2803. Cooper, George, and Sobol, Richard. "Seniority and Testing under Fair Employment Laws: A General Approach to Objective Criteria of Hiring and Promotion." *Harvard Law Review* 82 (June 1969): 1598–1679.

2804. Cowan, Edward. "Apples and Aliens—Growers Challenge Feds over Who Does the Picking." *Regulation* 2 (November-December 1978): 40–45.

2805. Cuff, Robert, and Urofsky, Melvin. "The Steel Industry and Price-Fixing during World War I." *Business History Review* 44 (Autumn 1970): 291–306.

2806. Davidson, Emmett. "A Survey of Public Regulation of Labor Union Practices." Ph. D. dissertation, University of Missouri, 1950. 252 p.

2807. "Employment Law—Sex Discrimination—Fourth Circuit Holds Private Employer's Denial of Pregnancy-Related Disability Benefits Sex Discrimination and Violative of Title VII." *South Carolina Law Review* 28 (June 1976): 219–33.

2808. Evans, Robert. "'Render unto Caesar': Federal District Courts and Unfair Labor-Practice Jurisdiction." *Journal of Business* 39 (July 1966): 400–12.

2809. Feldstein, M. "Facing the Social Security Crisis." *Public Interest* 47 (Spring 1977): 88–100.

2810. Feldstein, M. "Social Insurance." *Public Policy* 25 (Winter 1977): 81–115.

2811. Felt, Jeremy P. "The Child Labor Provisions of the Fair Labor Standards Act." *Labor History* 11 (Fall 1970): 467–81.

2812. Felt, Jeremy P. "The Regulation of Child Labor in New York State, 1886–1942, with Emphasis upon the Work of the New York Child Labor Committee." Ph. D. dissertation, Syracuse University, 1959., 315 p.

2813. Ferguson, William C. "An Analysis of the Wage Stabilization Board's Criteria in Wage Determination." Ph. D. dissertation, University of Iowa, 1955. 197 p.

2814. Goldberg, Joseph. "Labor-Management since World War II." *Current History* 48 (June 1965): 346–52.

2815. Gomberg, William. "The Problem of Arbitration—The Resolution of Public Sector Disputes." *Proceedings of the American Philosophical Society* 118 (October 1974): 409–14.

2816. Halaby, N. E. "Dispute between the FAA and PATCO: Conflicting Views." *Journal of Air Law and Commerce* 47 (Winter 1982): 275–80.

2817. Halter, Gary. "The Effects of the Hatch Act on the Political Participation of Federal Employees." *American Journal of Political Science* 16 (November 1972): 723–29.

2818. Hancock, K. J. "The Reduction of Unemployment as a Problem of Public Policy, 1920–1929." *Economic History Review* 15 (December 1962): 328–43.

2819. Harris, Milton, and Raviv, Artur. "Some Results on Incentive Contracts with Applications to Education and Employment, Health Insurance, and Law Enforcement." *American Economic Review* 68 (March 1978): 20–30.

2820. Harrison, B., and Kanter, S. "Political Economy of States' Job-Creation Business Incentives." *American Institute of Planners Journal* 44 (October 1978): 424–35.

2821. Hayashi, Paul M., and Trapani, John M. "Rate of Return Regulation and the Regulated Firm's Choice of Capital-Labor Ratio: Further Empirical Evidence on the Averch-Johnson Model." *Southern Economic Journal* 42 (January 1976): 384–98.

2822. "Hearing on Protest Challenging Grant of Construction Permit Cannot Be Limited to Oral Argument on Allegations of Protest If Facts Raise Other Relevant Issues (*Clarksburg Publ. Co. v. FCC*, 225 F 2d 511)." *Harvard Law Review* 69 (April 1956): 1137–40.

2823. Hearn, George H. "Recent Law of the Federal Maritime Commission and Collective Bargaining." *Journal of Maritime Law* 6 (October 1974): 31–46.

2824. Hermann, D. H. J. "Clerical Employees, Religious Enterprises, and Collective Bargaining." *Labor Law Journal* 35 (April 1984): 205–15.

2825. Hoar, W. P. "How Government Creates Unemployment." *American Opinion* 20 (December 1971): 11–18.

2826. Hoffmann, Carl, and Reed, John. "Sex Discrimination?—The XYZ Affair." *Policy Studies* 5 (1981): 549–67.

2827. Horton, Raymond D. "Public Employee Labor Relations under the Taylor Law." *Proceedings of the Academy of Political Science* 31 (May 1974): 161–74.

2828. Horwich, George. "Regulating Retirement—The Indirect Costs." *Regulation* 2 (May-June 1978): 27–36.

2829. Jackson, R. "Job-Discrimination and the Use of Bonuses." *American Journal of Economics and Sociology* 32 (October 1973): 351–66.

2830. "Jurisdiction—Federal Maritime Commission Has Jurisdiction under Section 15 of the Shipping Act to Review Assessment Formulas in Collective Bargaining Agreements." *Vanderbilt Journal of Transnational Law* 8 (Spring 1975): 493–504.

2831. Kamer, G. J. "Employee Participation in Settlement Negotiations and Proceedings before the OSHRC." *Labor Law Journal* 31 (April 1980): 208–22.

2832. Katz, L. A. "Investigation and Conciliation of Employment Discrimination Charges under Title VII: Employers' Rights in an Adversary Process." *Hastings Law Journal* 28 (March 1977): 877–929.

2833. Kelly, Matthew A. "Regulation of Hours of Labor of Federal Employees Including Employees of Public Contractors." Ph. D. dissertation, Princeton University, 1946. 351 p.

2834. Kerr, Thomas. "The New York Factory Investigating Commission and the Minimum-Wage Movement." *Labor History* 12 (Summer 1971): 373–91.

2835. Kleinsorge, Paul L., and Smith, Robert E. "Compulsory Arbitration: A Broad View." *Current History* 49 (August 1965): 97–105, 118.

2836. Koch, J. V., and Chizmar, J. F. "Sex Discrimination and Affirmative Action in Faculty Salaries." *Economic Inquiry* 14 (March 1976): 16–24.

2837. Kosugi, Takeo. "Regulation of Practice by Foreign Lawyers." *American Journal of Comparative Law* 27 (Fall 1979): 678–703.

2838. Kroger, W. "Out of Work, but in the Money." *Nation's Business* 67 (September 1979): 88–90.

2839. Kutler, Stanley I. "Labor, the Clayton Act, and the Supreme Court." *Labor History* 3 (Winter 1962): 19–38.

2840. Lauderbaugh, Richard A. "Business, Labor, and Foreign Policy: U. S. Steel, the International Steel Cartel, and Recognition of the Steel Workers Organizing Committee." *Politics and Society* 6 (1976): 433–57.

2841. Ledvinka, James. *Federal Regulation of Personnel and Human Resource Management.* Boston: Kent Publishing, 1982. 274 p.

2842. Leman, Christopher. "Patterns of Policy Development: Social Security in the United States and Canada." *Public Policy* 25 (Spring 1977): 261–91.

2843. Lubove, Roy. "Workmen's Compensation and the Prerogatives of Voluntarism." *Labor History* 8 (Fall 1967): 254–79.

2844. Lucas, John. "The Unholy Experiment—Professional Baseball's Struggle against Pennsylvania Sunday Blue Laws 1926-1934." *Pennsylvania History* 38 (April 1971): 163–75.

2845. Mabry, Bevars D. "An Analysis of State Labor Laws Regulating Trade Union Activities." Ph. D. dissertation, Tulane University, 1959. 567 p.

2846. Malik, Mukhtar A. "Some Economic Effects of Minimum Wage Regulation in the United States and Postwar Period." Ph. D. dissertation, University of Michigan, 1963. 238 p.

2847. "Mandatory Retirement of Airline Pilots: An Analysis of the FAA's Age 60 Retirement Rule." *Hastings Law Journal* 33 (September 1981): 241–61.

2848. Marlow, Arthur C. "State Regulation of Private Employment Agencies." Ph. D. dissertation, St. Louis University, 1958. 209 p.

2849. Marlow, Michael L. "The Impact of Different Government Units in the Regulation of the Workplace Environment." *Public Choice* 37 (1981): 349–56.

2850. McAhren, Robert W. "Making the Nation Safe for Childhood: A History of the Movement for Federal Regulation of Child Labor, 1900–1938." Ph. D. dissertation, University of Texas, 1967. 280 p.

2851. McConnell, Michael W. "Affirmative Action after Teal: A New Twist or a Turn of the Screw?" *Regulation* 7 (March-April 1983): 38–44.

2852. Mitchell, Daniel J., and Azevedo, Ross E. *Wage-Price Controls and Labor Market Distortions.* Los Angeles: Institute of Industrial Relations, University of California, 1976. 17 p.

2853. Nash, Gerald D. "The Influence of Labor on State Policy 1860–1920: The Experience of California." *California Historical Quarterly* 42 (September 1963): 241–57.

2854. Nelson, Dalmas H. "Regulation of the Political Activity of Federal Employees." Ph. D. dissertation, Harvard University, 1957.

2855. Nelson, Daniel. "The Origins of Unemployment Insurance in Wisconsin." *Wisconsin Magazine of History* 51 (Winter 1967–1968): 109–21.

2856. Newland, Chseter. "Trends in Public Employee Unionization." *Journal of Politics* 26 (August 1964): 586–611.

2857. Northrup, Herbert R., and Bloom, Gordon F. *Government and Labor; The Role of Government in Union-Management Relations.* Homewood, IL: R. D. Irwin, 1963. 507 p.

2858. Nourse, Edwin. "The Employment Act and the 'New Economics.'" *Virginia Quarterly Review* 45 (Autumn 1969): 595–612.

2859. Nudd, Howard C. "A Survey of Current Provisions in the Seniority Regulation of Selected Industries in Ohio." Ph. D. dissertation, Ohio State University, 1955. 206 p.

2860. Papier, William. "Does Father Know Best? The Case of State Employment Agencies." *Regulation* 6 (March-April 1982): 43–46.

2861. Paster, Irving I. "National Minimum Wage Regulation in the United States." Ph. D. dissertation, University of Michigan, 1948. 377 p.

2862. Pati, G. C., and Reilly, C. W. "Reversing Discrimination: A Perspective." *Labor Law Journal* 29 (January 1978): 9–25.

2863. "Permissible Scope of Title VII Actions." *Seton Hall Law Review* 8 (1977): 493–538.

2864. Pickup, Robert. "Michigan Public-Employee Relations." *Proceedings of the Academy of Political Science* 30 (April 1971): 94–106.

2865. Pomper, Gerald. "Labor Legislation: The Revision of Taft-Hartley in 1953–1954." *Labor History* 6 (Spring 1965): 143–58.

2866. Porter, David. "Senator Carl Hatch and the Hatch Act of 1939." *New Mexico Historical Review* 48 (April 1973): 151–64.

2867. Rapp, Michael T., and Wible, Roger L. "Freedom of Political Activity for Civil Servants: An Alternative to Section 9(a) of the Hatch Act." *George Washington Law Review* 41 (March 1973): 626–40.

2868. Reilly, Sheila A. "Disputes between Federal Agencies and Their Employees." *Chicago Bar Record* 63 (May-June 1982): 320–27.

2869. Reynolds, Harry W. "Merit Controls, the Hatch Acts, and Personnel Standards in Intergovernmental Relations." *American Academy of Political and Social Science, Annals* 359 (May 1965): 81–93.

2870. Reynolds, Lloyd G. "Policies Concerning Labor-Management Relations." *Proceedings of the Academy of Political Science* 30 (June 1971): 74–81.

2871. Rist, Ray C. "Beyond the Quantitative Cul-de-Sac: A Qualitative Perspective on Youth Employment Programs." *Policy Studies Journal* 10 (March 1982): 522–38.

2872. Ritland, Raymond W. "A Study of State and Federal Regulation of the Closed Shop." Ph. D. dissertation, University of Iowa, 1952.

2873. Romanofsky, Peter. "'The Public Is Aroused': The Missouri Children's Code Commission 1915–1919." *Missouri Historical Review* 68 (January 1974): 204–22.

2874. Rubin, Harold. "Labor Relations in State and Local Governments." *Proceedings of the Academy of Political Science* 30 (April 1971): 14–28.

2875. Sandon, Leo. "When Kansas Said Yes to 'Right-to-Work. '" *Midwest Quarterly* 4 (April 1963): 269–81.

2876. Satorius, John A. "Congress and the Judiciary: Congressional Oversight and Judicial Policy-Making in Securities and Labor Regulation." Ph. D. dissertation, Harvard University, 1977. 261 p.

2877. Saway, Charles P. "The Employment Effect of Minimum Wage Regulation in the Southern Pine Lumber Industry." Ph. D. dissertation, Indiana University, 1959. 400 p.

2878. Schneider, S. M. "Unprotected Minority: Employers and Civil Rights Compliance." *Labor Law Journal* 29 (January 1978): 3–8.

2879. Schramm, Carl J. "Regulating Hospital Labor Costs: A Case Study in the Politics of State Rate Commissions." *Journal of Health Politics, Policy and Law* 3 (Fall 1978): 364–74.

2880. Schuck, Peter H. "Litigation, Bargaining, and Regulation." *Regulation* 3 (July-August 1979): 26–34.

2881. Sedgwick, Robert C. "Federal Regulation of Union Unfair Practices against Employees." Ph. D. dissertation, Syracuse University, 1953.

2882. Sgontz, Larry G. "The Experience with the Provisions of the Labor Management Reporting and Disclosure Act Regulating the Internal Affairs of Labor Unions." Ph. D. dissertation, University of Illinois, 1964. 189 p.

2883. Sher, Stanley O. "The Federal Maritime Commission and Labor Related Matters: The Aftermath of the Volkswagenwerk Decision." *Journal of Maritime Law and Commerce* 3 (July 1972): 647–81.

2884. Sherman, Frederick E., and Black, Dennis B. "The Labor Board and the Private Nonprofit Employer: A Critical Examination of the Board's Worthy Cause Exemption." *Harvard Law Review* 83 (April 1970): 1323–51.

2885. Sherman, Richard B. "The Rejection of the Child Labor Amendment." *Mid-America* 45 (January 1963): 3–17.

2886. Shimberg, Benjamin; Esser, Barbara F. ; and Kruger, Daniel H. *Occupational Licensing: Practices and Policies.* Washington, DC: Public Affairs Press, 1973. 258 p.

2887. Shostak, Arthur. "Appeals from Discrimination in Federal Employment: A Case Study." *Social Forces* 47 (December 1963): 174–78.

2888. Siegel, Nathan, and Lawton, Mary. "Stalemate in 'Major' Disputes under the Railway Labor Act—The President and Congress." *George Washington Law Review* 32 (October 1963): 8–22.

2889. Silard, John. "Labor Board Regulation of Union Discipline after Allis-Chalmers, Marine Workers and Scofield." *George Washington Law Review* 38 (December 1969): 187–98.

2890. Smith, Lowell C. "An Evaluation of Public Policy Proposals for the Regulation of Private Pension Plan Eligibility Requirements and Vesting Provisions." Ph. D. dissertation, University of Alabama, 1969. 380 p.

2891. Stambler, Moses. "The Effect of Compulsory Education and Child Labor Laws on High School Attendance in New York City, 1898–1917." *History of Education Quarterly* 8 (Summer 1968): 189–214.

2892. Stein, Bruno. "Wage Stabilization in the Korean War Period: The Role of the Subsidiary Wage Boards." *Labor History* 4 (Spring 1963): 161–77.

2893. Vidich, Arthur J. "The Moral, Economic, and Political Status of Labor in American Society." *Social Research* 49 (Autumn 1982): 752–90.

2894. Wagaman, David G. "The Evolution of Some Legal-Economic Aspects of Collective Bargaining by Public Employees in Nebraska since 1919." *Nebraska History* 58 (Winter 1977): 475–89.

2895. Walker, Roger W. "The AFL and Child-Labor Legislation: An Exercise in Frustration." *Labor History* 11 (Summer 1970): 323–40.

2896. Weber, Arnold R. "The Role of the U. S. Department of Labor in Immigration." *International Migration Review* 4 (Summer 1970): 31–46.

2897. Weinstein, James. "Big Business and the Origins of Workmen's Compensation." *Labor History* 8 (Spring 1967): 156–74.

2898. Welch, Finis. "The Rising Impact of Minimum Wages." *Regulation* 2 (November-December 1978): 28–39.

2899. White, William D., and Marmor, Theodore R. "New Occupations, Old Demands: The Public Regulation of Paraprofessionals." *Journal of Policy Analysis and Management* 1 (1982): 243–56.

2900. Wiley, Norbert. "America's Unique Class Politics: The Interplay of the Labor, Credit and Commodity Markets." *American Sociological Review* 32 (August 1967): 529–40.

2901. Wines, Michael. "Regulation Writing in Washington, DC: Making Days Stretch into Years; A 1978 Law to Help Displaced Airline Workers, Which the Labor Department Has Still Not Implemented, Illustrates How Congress Does Not Always Have the Last Word." *National Journal* 14 (November 13, 1982): 1937–40.

PRICES

2902. Abe, M. A., and Brush, B. C. "On the Regulation of Price and Service Quality: The Taxicab Problem." *Quarterly Review of Economics and Business* 16 (Autumn 1976): 105–11.

2903. Abrahams, Paul. "Agricultural Adjustment during the New Deal Period: The New York Milk Industry: A Case Study." *Agricultural History* 39 (April 1965): 92–101.

2904. Almon, Clopper; Belzer, David; and Taylor, Peter. "Prices in Input-Output: The INFORUM Experience in Modeling the U. S. Deregulation of Domestic Oil." *Journal of Policy Modeling* 1 (September 1979): 399–412.

2905. Anderson, James E. "Who Benefits from Farm Programs?" *Proceedings of the Academy of Political Science* 34 (1982): 144–56.

2906. Arnow, Kathryn Smul. *The Attack on the Cost of Living Index.* Washington, DC: Committee on Public Administration Cases, 1951. 166 p.

2907. Arrow, Kenneth J., and Kalt, Joseph P. "Viewpoint: Why Oil Prices Should Be Decontrolled." *Regulation* 3 (September-October 1979): 13–17.

2908. Backman, Jules, ed. *Price Practices and Price Policies: Selected Writings.* New York: Ronald Press, 1953. 660 p.

2909. Barron, John, and Umbeck, John. "A Dubious Bill of Divorcement: The Case of Oil Refiners and Gas Stations." *Regulation* 7 (January-February 1983): 29–33.

2910. Bernstein, Barton. "The Clash of Interests: The Postwar Battle between the Office of Price Administration and the Department of Agriculture." *Agricultural History* 41 (January 1967): 45–58.

2911. Bernstein, Marver H. "Enforcing Government Regulations: The Experience of the Office of Price Administration." Ph. D. dissertation, Princeton University, 1948. 457 p.

2912. Blackwell, Roger D. "Price Levels of Funerals: An Analysis of the Effects of Entry Regulation in a Differentiated Oligopoly." Ph. D. dissertation, Northwestern University, 1966. 344 p.

2913. Blinder, A. S. and Goldfeld, S. "New Measures of Fiscal and Monetary Policy, 1958–73." *American Economic Review* 66 (December 1976): 780–96.

2914. Boddewyn, Jean J. "The Protection of Washington Wines: A Case Study in the State Regulation of Business." D. B. A. dissertation, University of Washington, 1964. 291 p.

2915. Breimyer, Harold. "Fifty Years of Federal Marketing Programs." *American Journal of Agricultural Economics* 45 (November 1963): 749–58.

2916. Breyer, Stephen. "Taxes as a Substitute for Regulation." *Growth and Change* 10 (January 1979): 39–52.

2917. Brimmer, A. F. "Alternative Monetary-Fiscal Policies and Sectoral Credit Flows." *American Economic Review; Papers and Proceedings* 64 (May 1974): 112–20.

2918. Campbell, Colin, ed. *Wage-Price Controls in World War II, United States and Germany: Reports by Persons Who Observed and Participated in the Programs.* Washington, DC: American Enterprise Institute for Public Policy Research, 1971. 73 p.

2919. Carney, Michael T. "Real Estate Brokerage Commission Rates: Price Fixing in Home Brokerage." Ph. D. dissertation, University of California, Los Angeles, 1981. 251 p.

2920. Cochrane, James L., and Griepentrog, Gary L. "Sulphur and the U. S. Government: Price Fighting in the 1960's." *Economic Inquiry* 16 (July 1978): 360–84.

2921. Cowee, John W. *Federal Regulation of Insurance.* Madison, WI: University of Wisconsin, School of Commerce, Bureau of Business Research and Service, 1949. 89 p.

2922. Crandal, Robert W. "Paying for Government Policy through the Price Level." *Proceedings of the Academy of Political Science* 33 (1979): 42–56.

2923. Dethloff, Henry. "Missouri Farmers and the New Deal: A Case Study of Farm Policy Formulation on the Local Level." *Agricultural History* 39 (July 1965): 141–46.

2924. Eckel, Leonard G. "The Regulation of Treasury Stock Transactions." Ph. D. dissertation, University of Michigan, 1969. 325 p.

2925. Eisenach, Jeffrey A., and Miller, James C. "Price Competition on the NYSE." *Regulation* 5 (January-February 1981): 16–19.

2926. Elzinga, Kenneth G. "Predatory Pricing: The Case of the Gunpowder Trust." *Journal of Law and Economics* 13 (April 1970): 223–40.

2927. Epstein, Richard A. "Products Liability: The Gathering Storm." *Regulation* 1 (September-October 1977): 15–20.

2928. Erickson, W. Bruce. "Price-Fixing Conspiracies: Their Long-Term Impact." *Journal of Industrial Economics* 24 (March 1976): 189–202.

2929. Ferreira, Joseph. *Some Analytical Aspects of Driver Licensing and Insurance Regulation.* Cambridge, MA: Massachusetts Institute of Technology Operations Research Center, 1971. 243 p.

2930. Fite, Gilbert. "Farmer Opinion and the Agriculture Adjustment Act, 1933." *Journal of American History* 48 (March 1962): 656–73.

2931. Ford, Robert A. "The Regulation of Life Insurance in Alabama." Ph. D. dissertation, University of Alabama, 1957.

2932. Frieberg, Albert M. "The Milk Business in Boston: A Case Study of Government Economic Regulation." Ph. D. dissertation, Harvard University, 1950.

2933. Gordon, Robert M., and Hanke, Steve H. "Federal Milk Marketing Orders: A Policy in Need of Analysis." *Policy Analysis* 4 (Winter 1978): 23–31.

2934. Grant, R. M. "Recent Developments in the Control of Price Discrimination in Countries outside North America." *Antitrust Bulletin* 26 (Fall 1981): 593–632.

2935. Gray, Robert C. "The Development, Structure, and Regulation of the Fertilizer Industry in Virginia." Ph. D. dissertation, Virginia Polytechnic Institute and State University, 1963. 256 p.

2936. Greco, Anthony J. "State Regulation of Fluid Milk and the Processor-Retailer Margin." Ph. D. dissertation, University of Tennessee, 1978. 125 p.

2937. Hall, Tom G. "The Aiken Bill, Price Supports and the Wheat Farmer in 1948." *North Dakota History* 39 (Winter 1972): 13–22, 47.

2938. Hamilton, James L. "Regulation and Congestion in the Markets for Flue-Cured Leaf Tobacco." Ph. D. dissertation, Duke University, 1969. 300 p.

2939. Harrington, Diana R. "The Capital Asset Pricing Model and Regulated Utility Cost of Equity Determination." D. B. A. dissertation, University of Virginia, 1979. 438 p.

2940. Herbert, B. G. "Delivered Pricing as Conspiracy and as Discrimination: The Legal Status." *Law and Contemporary Problems* 15 (1950): 181–226.

2941. Hersh, Mona S. "Milk Distribution: A Study in Market Structure and Regulation." Ph. D. dissertation, Southern Methodist University, 1966.

2942. Higgins, T. "Road Pricing: Managing the Risks." *Policy Analysis* 3 (Fall 1977): 579–82.

2943. Hill, Raymond D. "Capital Market Equilibrium and the Regulation of Property-Liability Insurance." Ph. D. dissertation, Massachusetts Institute of Technology, 1978. 156 p.

2944. Hjort, H. W. "Regulation and Economic Analysis in the U.S. Department of Agriculture." *American Journal of Agricultural Economics* 61 (November 1979): 746–50.

2945. Hollas, Daniel R. "Regulation, Pricing and Performance of Municipally Owned Electric Utilities." Ph. D. dissertation, University of Illinois, 1977. 193 p.

2946. Holtz, Milton E. "Agricultural Administration under the Patent Office, 1836–1862." *South Dakota History* 5 (Spring 1975): 123–49.

2947. Hsia, Ke T. "Depreciation under Changing Price Levels in Public Utility Regulation." Ph. D. dissertation, University of Wisconsin, 1966. 202 p.

2948. Hughes, Charles E. "An Investigation of the Regulation of Holding Company Operations in the Insurance Business." D.B.A. dissertation, Georgia State University, 1970. 226 p.

2949. Johnson, Herbert E. "Regulation and Price Policies in the Production of Natural Gas." Ph. D. dissertation, University of Illinois, 1951. 325 p.

2950. Johnson, Kenneth R. "The Troy Case: A Fight against Discriminatory Freight Rates." *Alabama Review* 22 (July 1969): 175–87.

2951. Johnson, Leland L. "Why Local Rates Are Rising." *Regulation* 7 (July-August 1983): 31–36.

2952. Joskow, Paul L. "Pricing Decisions of Regulated Firms: A Behavioral Approach." *Bell Journal of Economics and Management Science* 4 (Spring 1973): 118–40.

2953. Just, Richard. "A Methodology for Investigating the Importance of Government Intervention in Farmers' Decisions." *American Journal of Agricultural Economics* 55 (August 1973): 441–52.

2954. Kaufman, Henry M., and Marcis, R. G. "Hunt Commission Recommendations and the Determination and Control of the Money Supply." *Journal of Money, Credit and Banking* 7 (August 1975): 343–58.

2955. Kempel, P. M. "New Guides for the Law Book Industry." *Michigan State Bar Journal* 54 (December 1975): 938–55.

2956. Kensicki, Peter R. "History of Insurance Regulation in Ohio, 1803–1879." D. B. A. dissertation, Georgia State University, 1972. 303 p.

2957. Kirkpatrick, M. W. "Federal Regulation of Life and Disability Insurance Advertising." *Forum* 11 (Summer 1976): 1029–39.

2958. Knight, Bruce. "Ballad of the 'Right Price.'" *Regulation* 2 (November–December 1978): 12–13.

2959. Knutson, Ronald D. "Price and Trade Practice Regulation in the Minnesota Dairy Industry." Ph.D. dissertation, University of Minnesota, 1967. 352 p.

2960. Kosters, Marvin H. "Counting the Costs." *Regulation* 3 (July-August 1979): 17–19.

2961. Kwoka, John E. "Federal Milk Market Regulation Objectives and Impact." Ph. D. dissertation, University of Pennsylvania, 1972. 212 p.

2962. Latto, L. J. "Variable Life Insurance—Round Three." *Insurance Law Journal* 1975 (April 1975): 216–20.

2963. Lee, James. "The Ohio Agricultural Commission, 1913–1915." *Ohio History* 79 (Summer-Autumn 1970): 219–30.

2964. Lie, Kye Uck. "Price Discrimination and Monopoly Regulation." Ph. D. dissertation, New York University, 1974. 190 p.

2965. Lindsay, David S. "Pricing Tactics, Regulation and Successive Monopoly." Ph. D. dissertation, University of California, Los Angeles, 1978. 132 p.

2966. MacAvoy, Paul W., and Pindyck, Robert S. *Price Controls and the Natural Gas Shortage.* Washington, DC: American Enterprise Institute for Public Policy Research, 1975. 81 p.

2967. MacAvoy, Paul W., and Snow, John W., eds. *Regulation of Entry and Pricing in Truck Transportation.* Washington, DC: American Enterprise Institute for Public Policy Research, 1977. 301 p.

2968. McCallum, B. T. "Price-Level Stickiness and the Feasibility of Monetary Stabilization Policy with Rational Expectations." *Journal of Political Economy* 85 (June 1977): 627–34.

2969. McConnell, F. Britton. "State Regulation v. State Regulation plus Regulation by Multiple, Decentralized, Independent Federal Agencies." *Insurance Law Journal* 1956 (November 1956): 697–703.

2970. Mackay, Malcolm. "The Regulation of Health Insurance." *Proceedings of the Academy of Political Science* 33 (1980): 81–91.

2971. McMillan, Samuel S. *Individual Firm Adjustments under OPA: A Study in the Dynamics of Flexible Pricing.* Bloomington, IN: Principia Press, 1949. 256 p.

2972. McNamee, Bernard J. "Territorial Price Discrimination under the Robinson-Patman Act." *George Washington Law Review* 37 (December 1968): 293–323.

2973. McPherson, Roy L. "The Regulation of Life Insurance in Texas." Ph. D. dissertation, University of Texas, 1950.

2974. Manley, Robert. "A Note on Government and Agriculture: A Nineteenth Century Nebraska View." *Nebraska History* 45 (September 1964): 237–52.

2975. Marshall, Robert A. "Life Insurance Company Mergers and Consolidations—Rationale, Ramifications, and Regulation." Ph. D. dissertation, University of Pennsylvania, 1968. 396 p.

2976. Martin, Michael V. "An Economic Analysis of the Social Cost of Regulated Value-of-Service Wheat and Barley Rail Rates in the Upper Midwest." Ph. D. dissertation, University of Minnesota, 1978. 201 p.

2977. Mead, Walter J. "The Use of Taxes, Regulation and Price Controls in the Energy Sector." *Policy Studies* 3 (1979): 227–36.

2978. Miller, David Bruce. "Origins and Functions of the Federal Farm Board." Ph. D. dissertation, University of Kansas, 1973. 411 p.

2979. Miller, Edythe S. "Rate Structure Reform: A Review of the Current Debate." *Journal of Economic Issues* 12 (September 1978): 609–26.

2980. Minasian, Jora R. "Television Pricing and the Theory of Public Goods." *Journal of Law and Economics* 7 (October 1964): 71–86.

2981. Mitchell, Daniel J. B. "Wage-Price Controls and Inflation." *Proceedings of the Academy of Political Science* 31 (1975): 114–26.

2982. Munch, P., and Smallwood, D. E. "Solvency Regulation in the Property-Liability Insurance Industry: Empirical Evidence." *Bell Journal of Economics and Management Science* 11 (Spring 1980): 261–79.

2983. Nadel, Mark. "Auto Insurance—The Irrelevance of Regulation." *Regulation* 6 (March-April 1982): 37–42.

2984. Nadler, Paul S. "Pricing under Deregulation." *Bankers Magazine* 166 (September-October 1982): 33–38.

2985. National Industrial Conference Board. *The Conference Board Economic Forum Presents: Price Control in a Defense Economy.* New York: The Board, 1950. 64 p.

2986. Nichols, Ellsworth. *Rate of Return.* Washington, DC: Public Utilities Reports, 1955. 502 p.

2987. O'Donnell, John L., ed. *Adapting Regulation to Shortages, Curtailment, and Inflation.* East Lansing, MI: Division of Research, Graduate School of Business Administration, Michigan State University, 1977. 237 p.

2988. Otto, Ingolf H. "Regulation of Insurance in the United States by the Federal Government." Ph. D. dissertation, Washington University, 1959.

2989. Paul, Chris W. "Competition in the Medical Profession: A Test of the Economic Theory of Regulation." Ph. D. dissertation, Texas A&M University, 1979. 131 p.

2990. Peltzman, Samuel. "Pricing in Public and Private Enterprises: Electric Utilities in the United States." *Journal of Law and Economics* 14 (April 1971): 109–47.

2991. Poole, Robert W. "Monetary Policies in the United States, 1965–74." *Proceedings of the Academy of Political Science* 31 (1975): 91–104.

2992. "Price Control." *Annals of Public and Co-operative Economy* 52 (October-December 1981): 421–502.

2993. Quirin, George D. "The Regulation of Field Prices for Natural Gas under the Natural Gas Act." Ph. D. dissertation, Princeton University, 1961. 380 p.

2994. Ramsett, David E., and Heck, Tom R. "Wage and Price Controls: A Historical Survey." *North Dakota Quarterly* 45 (Autumn 1977): 5–22.

2995. Rawson, William S. *Public Regulation of Milk Prices: The South Carolina Experience.* Columbia, SC: Bureau of Business and Economic Research, University of South Carolina, 1974. 83 p.

2996. Roberts, Tanya. "Federal Price Regulation of Close Substitutes for Fresh Drinking Milk: History, Economic Analysis, and Welfare Implications." Ph. D. dissertation, University of Washington, 1979. 221 p.

2997. Rockoff, Hugh. "The Response of the Giant Corporations to Wage and Price Controls in World War II." *Journal of Economic History* 41 (March 1981): 123–28.

2998. Rodriguez, C. A. "Short-and-Long-Run Effects of Monetary and Fiscal Policies under Flexible Exchange Rates and Perfect Capital Mobility." *American Economic Review* 69 (March 1979): 176–82.

2999. Roulac, Stephen E. "Real Property Investment: Public Policy, Valuation, Regulatory and Management Considerations of Real Estate Investment Programs." Ph. D. dissertation, Stanford University, 1978.

3000. Saulnier, Raymond J. "An Appraisal of Federal Fiscal Policies: 1961–1967." *American Academy of Political and Social Science, Annals* 379 (September 1968): 63–71.

3001. Scherr, Bruce A., and Babb, Emerson. "Pricing Public Goods: An Experiment with Two Proposed Pricing Systems." *Public Choice* 23 (Fall 1975): 35–48.

3002. Schlesinger, James R. "Emerging Attitudes toward Fiscal Policy." *Political Science Quarterly* 77 (March 1962): 1–18.

3003. Schulz, Norbert. "On Fixed Price Equilibria as a Microfoundation of Price Regulation." Ph. D. dissertation, University of California, Berkeley, 1980. 131 p.

3004. Seelye, Alfred L. "Fluid Milk Price Control in World War II: OPA—Region 5." D. C. S. dissertation, Indiana University, 1950. 244 p.

3005. Siddayao, Corazon M. "The Role of Field Price Regulation of Natural Gas in Its Use for Electricity Generation." Ph. D. dissertation, George Washington University, 1975. 246 p.

3006. Sivesind, C., and Hurley, K. "Choosing an Operating Target for Monetary Policy." *Quarterly Journal of Economics* 94 (February 1980): 199–203.

3007. Sjoblom, Kriss A. "Essays on Information and Regulation by Price and on Induced Innovation and the Rate of Return to Investment." Ph. D. dissertation, Yale University, 1980. 303 p.

3008. Solberg, Harry J. "The Regulation of Fire Insurance Rates." Ph. D. dissertation, University of Wisconsin, 1957. 205 p.

3009. Spencer, Clarence A. "The Regulation of Fire Insurance in Alabama with Special Emphasis upon Rate Regulation." Ph. D. dissertation, University of Alabama, 1967. 359 p.

3010. Stark, John. "Coordination of Monetary Policy: Unfinished Business." *George Washington Law Review* 35 (December 1966): 318–28.

3011. Stich, R. S. "Price of Efficiency. " *Public Utilities Fortnightly* 81 (February 1968): 19–23.

3012. Surrey, Stanley S. "Treasury Department Regulatory Material under the Tax Code." *Policy Sciences* 7 (December 1976): 505–18.

3013. Thompson, Victor A. "The Regulatory Process in OPA Rationing." Ph. D. dissertation, Columbia University, 1951. 466 p.

3014. Trebing, Harry M., and Howard, R. Hayden, eds. *Rate of Return under Regulation, New Directions and Perspectives.* East Lansing, MI: Institute of Public Utilities, Michigan State University, 1969. 217 p.

3015. Wade, Charles E. "The Regulation of Securities in Oklahoma." Ph. D. dissertation, University of Oklahoma, 1966. 240 p.

3016. Wakefield, S. A. "Allocation, Price Control and the FEA: Regulatory Policy and Practice in the Political Arena." *Rocky Mountain Mineral Law Institute* 21 (1976): 257–84.

3017. Weitzman, Martin L. "Prices vs. Quantities." *Review of Economic Studies* 61 (October 1974): 477–91.

3018. West, D. A. "Adjusting Rates to Cost of Capital." *Public Utilities Fortnightly* 100 (September 1977): 19–23.

3019. White, Lawrence J. "Quality Variation When Prices Are Regulated." *Bell Journal of Economics and Management Science* 3 (Autumn 1972): 425–36.

3020. Wolfinger, Raymond E., and Greenstein, Fred I. "The Repeal of Fair Housing in California: An Analysis of Referendum Voting." *American Political Science Review* 62 (September 1968): 753–69.

3021. Woodward, Lynn N. "Residential Real Estate Brokerage Commission Structure and a Survey of Home Sellers' Perceptions of Alternative Fee Schedules or Compensation Plans." Ph. D. dissertation, University of Wisconsin—Madison, 1980. 371 p.

3022. Worsinger, L. "'New and More Drastic Remedies for Vertical Restraints and Resale Price Fixing. '" *Antitrust Law Symposium* 1976 (1976): 38–51.

3023. Yohe, Gary W. "A Comparison of Price Controls and Quantity Controls under Uncertainty." Ph. D. dissertation, Yale University, 1975. 243 p.

PRODUCTS

3024. Anderson, James E. "Agricultural Marketing Orders and the Process and Politics of Self-Regulation." *Policy Studies Review* 2 (August 1982): 97–111.

3025. Arrington, Leonard J. "Science, Government, and Enterprise in Economic Development: The Western Beet Sugar Industry." *Agricultural History* 41 (January 1967): 1–18.

3026. Baumer, David L. "Federal Regulation of the Dairy Industry: Costs, Benefits, and Legal Constraints." Ph. D. dissertation, University of Virginia, 1980. 234 p.

3027. Bergstrom, T. C., and Goodman, R. P. "Private Demands for Public Goods." *American Economic Review* 63 (June 1973): 280–96.

3028. Breen, John J. "An Economic Analysis of the Regulation of Milk by the State of Rhode Island." Ph. D. dissertation, Clark University, 1957. 331 p.

3029. Croll, Robert F. "Government Regulation of Automobile Distribution, 1933–1963: An Economic Analysis of Its Causes and Consequenses." D. B. A. dissertation, Indiana University, 1969. 591 p.

3030. Dahl, D. C. "Regulation Analysis as a Research Focus in Agricultural Economics." *American Journal of Agricultural Economics* 61 (November 1979): 776–94.

3031. Dahlgran, Roger A. "Welfare Losses and Interregional Income Transfers Due to Regulation of U. S. Dairy Markets." Ph. D. dissertation, North Carolina State University at Raleigh, 1980. 271 p.

3032. Dew, Lee A. "The Blytheville Case and Regulation of Arkansas Cotton Shipments." *Arkansas Historical Quarterly* 38 (Summer 1979): 116–30.

3033. Dykstra, David L. "Patent and Proprietary Medicines: Regulations Control Prior to 1906." Ph. D. dissertation, University of Wisconsin, 1951.

3034. Gardner, B. L. "Economic Analysis of the Regulation of Agriculture." *American Journal of Agricultural Economics* 61 (November 1979): 732–40.

3035. Guerin, Charles L. "The Federal Regulation of Pesticides." Ph. D. dissertation, University of Massachusetts, 1983. 489 p.

3036. Head, John G. "Public Goods and Public Policy." *Public Finance* 17 (1962): 197–219.

3037. Koenker, R. W., and Perry, M. K. "Product Differentiation, Monopolistic Competition, and Public Policy." *Bell Journal of Economics and Management Science* 12 (Spring 1981): 217–31.

3038. Lower, R. C. "Regulation of Commodity Options." *Duke Law Journal* 1978 (December 1978): 1095–145.

3039. Lurie, Jonathan. "Commodities Exchanges, Agrarian 'Political Power,' and the Antioption Battle, 1890–1894." *Agricultural History* 48 (January 1974): 115–25.

3040. Lurie, Jonathan. "The Commodities Exchanges and Federal Regulation, 1922–1974: The Decline of Self-Government?" *Policy Studies Journal* 6 (Summer 1978): 488–93.

3041. Parry, Stanton P. "Some Problems in Extending Federal Milk Order Regulation in Michigan." Ph. D. dissertation, Michigan State University, 1958. 245 p.

3042. Pellish, Harold. "Regulation of Insurance by the State of New York." Ph. D. dissertation, New York University, 1962. 412 p.

3043. Price, David E. "The Politics of Sugar." *Review of Politics* 33 (April 1971): 212–32.

3044. Prybutok, Benn. "Federalism without Washington: The Insurance Regulatory Environment in the United States." *Publius* 12 (Spring 1982): 79–97.

3045. Rayward, W. Boyd. "Manufacture and Copyright: Past History Remaking." *Journal of Library History* 3 (January 1968): 7–31.

3046. Reinmuth, Dennis F. "The Regulation of Reciprocal Insurance Exchanges." Ph. D. dissertation, University of Pennsylvania, 1964. 243 p.

3047. Roberts, N. Keith, and Gardner, Delworth. "Livestock and the Public Lands." *Utah Historical Quarterly* 32 (Summer 1964): 285–300.

3048. Roos, Nestor R. "Government Regulations of Fire Insurance." D. B. A. dissertation, Indiana University, 1960. 226 p.

3049. Rudd, Benjamin W. "Notable Dates in American Copyright." *Quarterly Journal of the Library of Congress* 28 (April 1971): 137–43.

3050. Schiffrin, M. J. "Individual Product Licensure." *Food Drug Cosmetic Law Journal* 32 (January 1977): 21–26.

3051. Scruggs, Otey M. "The Bracero Program under the Farm Security Administration, 1942–1943." *Labor History* 3 (Spring 1962): 149–68.

3052. Shiffler, Neil F. "Analysis of Regulations Affecting the Marketing of Fluid Milk under Pennsylvania Milk Control." Ph. D. dissertation, University of Pittsburgh, 1961. 145 p.

3053. Sichel, Werner. "Fire Insurance: Imperfectly Regulated Collusion." Ph. D. dissertation, Northwestern University, 1964. 216 p.

3054. Stanley, Richard E. "A Marketing Appraisal of the Promotional Activities of the Florida Citrus Commission from 1935 to 1960." Ph. D. dissertation, University of Florida, 1962. 279 p.

3055. Swantz, Alexander. "Economic Effects of Federal Regulations of Fluid Milk Markets with Special Reference to the Minneapolis, St. Paul Market." Ph. D. dissertation, University of Minnesota, 1951.

3056. Tiano, J. Richard. "Federal Jurisdiction over Producer Sales in the State of Production." *Natural Resources Journal* 17 (January 1977): 97–111.

3057. Weisbrod, Steven R. "The Regulation of the Securities Portfolios of Life Insurance Companies." Ph. D. dissertation, University of Chicago, 1978.

3058. Whitaker, Arthur R. "The Regulation of Ex Post Insurance Rates." Ph. D. dissertation, University of Pennsylvania, 1965. 263 p.

3059. Wiggins, Steven N. "Product Quality Regulation and Innovation in the Pharmaceutical Industry. " Ph. D. dissertation, Massachusetts Institute of Technology, 1979. 179 p.

3060. Winter, Ralph K. "Information on Regulation in Life Insurance: An Economic Analysis." Ph. D. dissertation, University of California, Berkeley, 1979. 179 p.

3061. Wood, Glenn L. "Life Insurance Policy Loans: Nature, Uses, Practices, and Regulation." Ph. D. dissertation, University of Pennsylvania, 1963. 294 p.

SAFETY

3062. Adams, L. J. "Cosmetic or Drug? FDA's OTC Drug Review Program Provides Some Answers and Raises New Questions." *Food Drug Cosmetic Law Journal* 35 (February 1980): 98–111.

3063. "Alcohol and Highway Safety: The National Highway Traffic Safety Administration's Approach to the Drunk Driving Problem." *Police Chief* 49 (December 1982): 24–27.

3064. Allen, G. "Growing Resistance by Small Business." *American Opinion* 20 (May 1977): 31–33.

3065. Allera, E. J. "FDA's Combination Animal Drug Policy—Is It Feasible? Or, Should Elsie Be the Only One Getting Milked?" *Food Drug Cosmetic Law Journal* 33 (June 1978): 267–73.

3066. Allera, E. J. "FDA's Use of Guidelines, Notices of Proposed Rulemaking, and Compliance Policies as De Facto Rules: An Abuse of Discretion." *Food Drug Cosmetic Law Journal* 36 (May 1981): 270–80.

3067. Ames, C. C., and McCracken, S. C. "Framing Regulatory Standards to Avoid Formal Adjudication: The FDA as a Case Study." *California Law Review* 64 (January 1976): 14–73.

3068. Auchter, T. G. "OSHA: A Year Later." *Labor Law Journal* 33 (April 1982): 195–201.

3069. Bachrach, E. E. "The Food and Drug Administration Cosmetic Inspection: An Industry Approach." *Food Drug Cosmetic Law Journal* 38 (October 1983): 373–82.

3070. Banta, H. D., and Thacker, S. B. "Policies toward Medical Technology: The Case of Electronic Fetal Monitoring." *American Journal of Public Health* 69 (September 1979): 931–35.

3071. Barnes, Joseph W. "The Arson Years: Fire Protection, Fire Insurance, and Fire Politics 1908–1910." *Rochester History* 38 (1976): 1–47.

3072. Bauman, John F. "Safe and Sanitary without the Costly Frills: The Evolution of Public Housing in Philadelphia, 1929–1941." *Pennsylvania Magazine of History and Biography* 101 (January 1977): 114–28.

3073. Bayer, R. "Women, Work and Reproductive Hazards." *Hastings Center Report* 12 (October 1982): 14–19.

3074. Becker, R. H. "Is the Over-the-Counter Drug Review Program Still Viable?" *Food Drug Cosmetic Law Journal* 38 (October 1983): 349–54.

3075. Bennett, A. R. "Committee or Commissioner." *Food Drug Cosmetic Law Journal* 32 (July 1977): 323–29.

3076. Bisogni, C. "Food Safety Laws Eyed in Washington." *Human Ecology Forum* 13 (Summer 1982): 18–20.

3077. Bisogni, C. "Widening Debate over Food Additives." *Human Ecology Forum* 10 (Fall 1979): 15–18.

3078. Blank, R. H., and Ostheimer, J. M. "An Overview of Biomedical Policy: Life and Death Issues." *Policy Studies Journal* 8 (Winter 1979): 470–79.

3079. Boden, Leslie I. "Underground Coal Mining Accidents and Government Enforcement of Safety Regulation." Ph. D. dissertation, Massachusetts Institute of Technology, 1977. 163 p.

3080. Boggan, E. C. "FDA's Combination Drug Policy." *Food Drug Cosmetic Law Journal* 30 (May 1975): 276–87.

3081. Bollier, D. "The Deregulation of Carcinogens." *Business and Society Review* 48 (Winter 1984): 13–18.

3082. Brunt, W. Van. "Advisory Opinions." *Food Drug Cosmetic Law Journal* 32 (July 1977): 304–11.

3083. Burditt, G. M. "Quo Vadit FDA?" *Food Drug Cosmetic Law Journal* 38 (April 1983): 87–92.

3084. Cabana, B. E. "Bioavailabilty/Bioequivalence." *Food Drug Cosmetic Law Journal* 32 (November 1977): 513–26.

3085. Celeste, A. C. "Inevitable FDA Inspection." *Food Drug Cosmetic Law Journal* 34 (January 1979): 32–39.

3086. Clark, Franklin D. "The Regulatory Functions of the Food and Drug Administration." *Food Drug Cosmetic Law Journal* 16 (August 1961): 500–07.

3087. Cleary, T. F. "Some Aspects of Agency Review of Initial Decisions of Administrative Law Judges." *Labor Law Journal* 31 (September 1980): 531–38.

3088. Cody, William F. "Authoritative Effect of FDA Regulations." *Business Lawyer* 24 (January 1969): 479–91.

3089. Cook, Philip J. "The Effect of Gun Availability on Violent Crime Patterns." *American Academy of Political and Social Science, Annals* 455 (May 1981): 63–79.

3090. Cooper, I. P. "FDA, the BATF, and Liquor Labeling: A Case Study of Interagency Jurisdictional Conflict." *Food Drug Cosmetic Law Journal* 34 (July 1979): 370–90.

3091. Cornell, Nina W., and Noll, Roger G. "Safety Regulation." In *Setting National Priorities: The Next Ten Years*, edited by Henry Owen and Charles L. Schultze, pp. 457–504. Washington, DC: Brookings Institution, 1976. 618 p.

3092. Cribbett, James R. "Report from the Division of Pharmacology." *Food Drug Cosmetic Law Journal* 16 (December 1961): 738–43.

3093. Davidson, D. J. "View from the Bench." *Food Drug Cosmetic Law Journal* 32 (May 1977): 236–44.

3094. Davis, A. D. "Food and Drug Administration Plans and Programs." *Food Drug Cosmetic Law Journal* 21 (January 1966): 57–64.

3095. "Defining Contours of OSHA Inspection Warrants." *Brooklyn Law Review* 48 (Fall 1981): 105–36.

3096. Diprima, F. P. "Some Partisan Musings on the OTC Review and the Advertising RTTs." *Food Drug Cosmetic Law Journal* 32 (1977): 405–13.

3097. Donadio, R. E. "OSHA Criteria for Laboratory Proficiency in Blood Lead Analysis." *American Journal of Public Health* 72 (April 1982): 404–05.

3098. Eads, George C. "The Benefits of Better Benefits Estimation." In *The Benefits of Health and Safety Regulation*, edited by Allen R. Ferguson and E. Phillip LeVeen, pp. 43–52. Cambridge, MA: Ballinger, 1981.

3099. Edwards, Charles C. "Meeting New Challenges." *Food Drug Cosmetic Law Journal* 28 (January 1973): 4–12.

3100. Eiermann, H. J. "The Food and Drug Administration's Cosmetics Inspection Program." *Food Drug Cosmetic Law Journal* 38 (January 1983): 53–57.

3101. Elengold, M. "Freedom of Information Policy at the FDA." *Food Drug Cosmetic Law Journal* 35 (November 1980): 627–32.

3102. "FDA Disclosure of Safety and Effectiveness Data: A Legal and Policy Analysis." *Duke Law Journal* 1979 (February 1979): 286–326.

3103. "FDA's Over-the-Counter Drug Review: Expeditious Enforcement by Rulemaking." *University of Michigan Journal of Law Reform* 11 (Fall 1977): 142–61.

3104. "The FDA's Public Board of Inquiry and the Aspartame Decision." *Indiana Law Journal* 58 (1982–1983): 627–49.

3105. "The Food and Drug Administration: Law, Science, and Politics in the Evaluation and Control of New Drug Technology." *Northwestern University Law Review* 67 (January-February 1973): 858–914.

3106. "Food and Drug Administration—Medical Devices Amendments to the Food, Drug, and Cosmetic Act Gives the FDA the Power to Regulate the Manufacture and Use of Medical Devices through Recommendations by Expert Panels—21 U. S. C. A. : 360c-360j (West Supp. 1977)." *Temple Law Quarterly* 50 (1977): 1105–18.

3107. Forte, Wesley E. "Food and Drug Administration and the Economic Adulteration of Foods." *Food Drug Cosmetic Law Journal* 21 (October-November 1966): 533–48.

3108. "Generic Drugs: Breaking the Definitional Barriers to FDA Regulations." *Northwestern University Law Review* 76 (November 1981): 613–39.

3109. Giemza, R. A. "Credibility Factor: North Carolina's Approach to Radar Training and Certification." *Police Chief* 50 (January 1983): 38–41.

3110. Goddard, James L. "The Year in Review." *Food Drug Cosmetic Law Journal* 22 (February 1967): 92–99.

3111. Goldsmith, Frank. "Controlling Occupational Hazards." *Proceedings of the Academy of Political Science* 32 (1977): 106–20.

3112. "The Good-Faith Exception to the Exclusionary Rule: Should It Apply to OSHA Enforcement Proceedings?" *University of Dayton Law Review* 9 (Fall 1983): 95–112.

3113. Goyan, J. E. "Future of the FDA under a New Administration." *Food Drug Cosmetic Law Journal* 36 (February 1981): 60–65.

3114. Graebner, William. "The Coal-Mine Operator and Safety: A Study of Business Reform in the Progressive Period." *Labor History* 14 (Fall 1973): 483–505.

3115. Greene, R. J. "Informal FDA Hearings." *Food Drug Cosmetic Law Journal* 32 (August 1977): 354–60.

3116. Guttenberger, A. E. "Use of Summary Judgment by the FDA to Avoid Formal Adjudication: In the Public Interest?" *Food Drug Cosmetic Law Journal* 36 (August 1981): 396–419.

3117. Hadley, J. E., and Richman, G. L. "Impact of Benzene (*Industrial Union Dept. AFL-CIO v. American Petroleum Institute*, 100 S Ct 2844) and Cotton Dust (*American Textile Mfrs. Institute, Inc. v. Donovan*, 100 S Ct 2478): Restraints on the Regulations of Toxic Substances." *Administrative Law Review* 34 (Winter 1982): 59–77.

3118. Hadwiger, D. F. "Nutrition, Food Safety and Farm Policy." *Proceedings of the Academy of Political Science* 34 (1982): 79–88.

3119. Hamilton, Robert W. "Rulemaking on a Record by the Food and Drug Administration." *Texas Law Review* 50 (August 1972): 1132–94.

3120. Hansen, A. W. "FDA Inspection: Preparing for the Inevitable." *Food Drug Cosmetic Law Journal* 36 (December 1981): 641–46.

3121. Harlow, D. R. "FDA's OTC Drug Review: The Development and an Analysis of Some Aspects of the Procedure." *Food Drug Cosmetic Law Journal* 32 (June 1977): 248–74.

3122. Harter, Philip J. "In Search of OSHA." *Regulation* 1 (September-October 1977): 33–39.

3123. Hartmann, E. "L-Tryptophan: A Rational Hypnotic with Clinical Potential." *American Journal of Psychiatry* 134 (April 1977): 366–70.

3124. Harvey, George Y. "Citizens Advisory Committee." *Food Drug Cosmetic Law Journal* 16 (December 1961): 749–55.

3125. Harvey, John L. "Current Developments in Food and Drug Administration." *Business Lawyer* 17 (November 1961): 130–36.

3126. Harvey, John L. "Report on the Growth, Organization, Operations and Plans of the Food and Drug Administration." *Business Lawyer* 20 (November 1964): 151–57.

3127. Hayes, A. H. "Accomplishments at FDA and a Look Toward the Future." *Food Drug Cosmetic Law Journal* 38 (January 1983): 64–76.

3128. Hayes, A. H. "Major Regulatory Challenges Confronting the FDA." *Food Drug Cosmetic Law Journal* 36 (November 1981): 565–72.

3129. Hoffman, J. E. "FDA's New Forms of Public Hearing—Choosing among the Alternatives." *Food Drug Cosmetic Law Journal* 32 (July 1977): 330–39.

3130. Hogan, R. B. "FTCA: Recovering for Injuries Caused by Negligent OSHA Inspections." *Trial* 18 (October 1982): 82–85.

3131. Hornbrook, Mark C. "Medicinal Drugs: Risks and Regulation." *Current History* 78 (May 1980): 201–05, 223–26.

3132. Hornbrook, Mark C. "Prescription Drugs: Problems for Public Policy." *Current History* 72 (May-June 1977): 215–22, 228–29.

3133. Hutt, Peter B. "Food and Drug Regulation in Transition." *Food Drug Cosmetic Law Journal* 35 (May 1980): 283–99.

3134. Hutt, Peter B. "Future of the Food and Drug Administration." *Food Drug Cosmetic Law Journal* 30 (December 1975): 694–705.

3135. Hutt, Peter B. "Regulatory History of DES." *American Statistician* 36 (August 1982): 267.

3136. Hyman, P. M. "Participating in a TRR." *Food Drug Cosmetic Law Journal* 32 (August 1977): 369–79.

3137. Janssen, W. F. "Food and Drug Administration Celebrates 75 Years of Consumer Protection—An Album from the Archives." *Public Health Reports* 96 (November-December 1981): 487–94.

3138. Jenkins, Roland E. "A Comparative Study of State Food and Drug Regulatory Programs." Ph. D. dissertation, Ohio State University, 1976. 233 p.

3139. Kahan, J. S. "Criminal Liability under the Federal Food, Drug, and Cosmetic Act—The Large Corporation Perspective." *Food Drug Cosmetic Law Journal* 36 (June 1981): 314–31.

3140. Kanig, J. L. "Advisory Committees: An Expanding Concept in the Field of Drug Regulation: The Perspective of a Liaison Representative." *Food Drug Cosmetic Law Journal* 29 (July 1974): 353–59.

3141. Kelleher, W. A. "FDA Inspection and Restricted Devices." *Food Drug Cosmetic Law Journal* 33 (July 1978): 331–41.

3142. Kennedy, D. "FDA and the Future." *Food Drug Cosmetic Law Journal* 34 (January 1979): 13–19.

3143. Kennedy, D. "Remarks of the Commissioner of Food and Drugs." *Food Drug Cosmetic Law Journal* 32 (September 1977): 384–91.

3144. King, R. A. "Economic Research Conference on US Food System Regulation." *American Journal of Agricultural Economics* 61 (November 1979): 836–38.

3145. Kingham, R. F. "Comments on the Proposed Revisions of FDA's New Drug Regulations." *Food Drug Cosmetic Law Journal* 38 (January 1983): 58–63.

3146. Kirk, J. Kenneth. "Standard-Setting FDA." *Food Drug Cosmetic Law Journal* 24 (August 1969): 408–12.

3147. Kurtz, H. "Real Problem with the FDA." *Washington Monthly* 9 (July-August 1977): 59–62.

3148. Kushen, Allan S. "FDA: A Case Study in Administrative 'Legislation.'" *Business Lawyer* 24 (November 1968): 261–66.

3149. Land, S. J. "Current Issues Relating to FDA Regulation of New Drugs." *Food Drug Cosmetic Law Journal* 38 (January 1983): 29–34.

3150. Larrick, George P. "Decision Making in the Food and Drug Administration." *Food Drug Cosmetic Law Journal* 20 (April 1965): 197–207.

3151. Lasagna, Louis. "Who Will Adopt the Orphan Drugs?" *Regulation* 3 (November-December 1979): 27–32.

3152. Laughlin, Stanley. "LSD-25 and the Other Hallucinogens: A Pre-Reform Proposal." *George Washington Law Review* 36 (October 1967): 23–59.

3153. Leff, Carol S., and Leff, Mark H. "The Politics of Ineffectiveness: Federal Firearms Legislation, 191–38." *American Academy of Political and Social Science, Annals* 455 (May 1981): 48–62.

3154. Lepkowski, Wil. "The Saccharin Debate: Regulation and the Public Taste." *Hastings Center Report* 7 (December 1977): 5–7.

3155. Levin, Michael. "Politics and Polarity—The Limits of OSHA Reform." *Regulation* 3 (November-December 1979): 33–39.

3156. Levine, Selma M. "Separation of Functions in FDA Administrative Proceedings." *Food Drug Cosmetic Law Journal* 23 (March 1968): 132–41.

3157. Lewis-Beck, Michael S., and Alford, John R. "Can Government Regulate Safety? The Coal Mine Example." *American Political Science Review* 74 (September 1980): 745–56.

3158. Link, Mary. "Proposed Saccharin Ban Causes Controversy." *Congressional Quarterly* 35 (March 26, 1977): 539–41.

3159. Long, J. M. "Cosmetic Industry Concerns Arising from Recent FDA Activities." *Food Drug Cosmetic Law Journal* 35 (June 1980): 392–400.

3160. MacCarthy, M. "Review of Some Normative and Conceptual Issues in Occupational Safety and Health." *Boston College Environmental Affairs Law Review* 9 (1981–1982): 773–814.

3161. Macklin, Ruth. "On the Ethics of Not Doing Scientific Research." *Hastings Center Report* 7 (December 1977): 11–13.

3162. Mallino, David L. "The Politics of Occupational Cancer: Federal Regulation of Industrial Carcinogens." Ph. D. dissertation, University of Maryland, 1980. 417 p.

3163. Mamana, Joseph M. "FDA's Obligations under the 1966 Public Information Act." *Food Drug Cosmetic Law Journal* 22 (October 1967): 563–68.

3164. "Mandatory Food and Drug Recalls: An Analysis of a Developing FDA Enforcement Tool." *Food Drug Cosmetic Law Journal* 36 (December 1981): 669–87.

3165. "Mandatory Food and Drug Recalls—An Analysis of a Developing FDA Enforcement Tool." *Utah Law Review* 1980 (1980): 809–28.

3166. Marvel, Mary K. "Implementation and Safety Regulation: Variations in Federal and State Administration under OSHA." *Administration and Society* 14 (May 1982): 15–33.

3167. McGrew, J. L. "How to Let in the Sunshine without Getting Burned: Protecting Your Rights before Advisory Committees." *Food Drug Cosmetic Law Journal* 30 (September 1975): 536–44.

3168. McKay, F. E. "Lawyers of the FDA—Yesterday and Today." *Food Drug Cosmetic Law Journal* 30 (October 1975): 621–28.

3169. McLean, Robert A., and Schneck, Ronald G. "Client Group Attitudes toward Alternative Forms of Industrial Safety Regulation." *Policy Studies Journal* 8 (Winter 1979): 392–400.

3170. McNamara, S. H. "FDA Inspection: What You Need to Know to Protect Your Company." *Food Drug Cosmetic Law Journal* 36 (May 1981): 245–57.

3171. McNamara, S. H. "The Food and Drug Administration Over-the-Counter Drug Review—Concerns of the Cosmetic Industry." *Food Drug Cosmetic Law Journal* 38 (October 1983): 289–98.

3172. McNamara, S. H. "New Age of FDA Rule-Making." *Food Drug Cosmetic Law Journal* 31 (July 1976): 393–403.

3173. Mendeloff, John. "Does Overregulation Cause Underregulation? The Case of Toxic Substances." *Regulation* 5 (September-October 1981): 47–52.

3174. Merrill, R. A. "FDA and Effects of Substantive Rules." *Food Drug Cosmetic Law Journal* 35 (May 1980): 270–82.

3175. Merrill, R. A. "Risk-Benefit Decisionmaking by the Food and Drug Administration." *George Washington Law Review* 45 (August 1977): 994–1012.

3176. Meyers, Earl L. "FDA Role in the Labeling of Blood Bank Products." *Food Drug Cosmetic Law Journal* 17 (February 1962): 169–74.

3177. Mills, N. "Brown-Lung Cotton-Mill Blues." *Dissent* 26 (Winter 1978): 8–11.

3178. Moore, Mark H. "Keeping Handguns from Criminal Offenders." *American Academy of Political and Social Science, Annals* 455 (May 1981): 92–109.

3179. Mugridge, Donald. "The United States Sanitary Commission in Washington, 1861–1865." *Records of the Columbia Historical Society of Washington, DC* 1960–1962 (1960–1962): 134–49.

3180. Myers, Lee. "An Experiment in Prohibition." *New Mexico Historical Review* 40 (October 1965): 293–307.

3181. Nanes, Allan. "Federal Control of Firearms: Is It Necessary?" *Current History* 53 (July 1967): 38–42.

3182. Neely, A. S. "FDA Inspection Authority—Is There an Outer Limit?" *Food Drug Cosmeitc Law Journal* 33 (December 1978): 710–25.

3183. Nichols, A. L., and Zeckhauser, Richard. "Government Comes to the Workplace: An Assessment of OSHA." *Public Interest* 49 (Fall 1977): 39–69.

3184. Norcross, M. A. "Animal Drug Control: The Challenge of Coordination—An FDA Intraagency Perspective." *Food Drug Cosmetic Law Journal* 38 (April 1983): 141–46.

3185. Norton, D. B. "Constitutionality of Warrantless Inspections by the Food and Drug Administration." *Food Drug Cosmetic Law Journal* 35 (January 1980): 25–43.

3186. Oi, Walter. "Safety at Any Price." *Regulation* 1 (November-December 1977): 16–23.

3187. O'Keefe, D. F. "Legal Issues in Food Establishment Inspections." *Food Drug Cosmetic Law Journal* 33 (March 1978): 121–33.

3188. Orlofsky, J. "Fourth Amendment—Administration Searches and Seizures." *Journal of Criminal Law and Criminology* 69 (Winter 1978): 552–62.

3189. "OSHA and the Exclusionary Rule: The Cost of Constitutional Protection." *Wake Forest Law Review* 19 (October 1983): 819–44.

3190. Pearson, Jessica S. "Organizational Response to Occupational Injury and Disease: The Case of the Uranium Industry." *Social Forces* 57 (September 1978): 23–41.

3191. "Permissible Scope of OSHA Complaint Inspections." *University of Chicago Law Review* 49 (Winter 1982): 203–34.

3192. "Permissible Scope of OSHA Inspection Warrants." *Cornell Law Review* 66 (August 1981): 1254–69.

3193. Perry, Charles S. "Government Regulation of Coal Mine Safety: Effects of Spending under Strong and Weak Laws." *American Politics Quarterly* 10 (July 1982): 303–14.

3194. Pettus, Beryl E. "OSHA Inspection Costs, Compliance Costs and Other Outcomes: The First Decade." *Policy Studies Review* 1 (1982): 596–614.

3195. Plott, Charles R. "Occupational Self-Regulation: A Case Study of the Oklahoma Dry Cleaners." *Journal of Law and Economics* 8 (October 1965): 195–222.

3196. Powledge, Tabitha M. "Recombinant DNA: Backing Off on Legislation." *Hastings Center Report* 7 (December 1977): 8–10.

3197. Rothschild, D. P. FDA's Regulations—A Model for the Future?" *Food Drug Cosmetic Law Journal* 32 (August 1977): 344–53.

3198. Schmidt, A. M. "Food and Drug Administration's Enforcement Policy." *Food Drug Cosmetic Law Journal* 30 (December 1975): 687–93.

3199. Smith, D. J. "Detention and Seizure of Imports by the Food and Drug Administration." *Food Drug Cosmetic Law Journal* 33 (December 1978): 726–33.

3200. Spiker, Earl G., and Stafford, P. Gordon. "A Look at FDA's New Rules of Practice—And Problems Still Unsolved." *Food and Drug Cosmetic Law Journal* 21 (September 1966): 448–57.

3201. Steele, Henry. "Monopoly and Competition in the Ethical Drugs Market." *Journal of Law and Economics* 5 (October 1962): 131–64.

3202. Stimson, R. A. "FDA's Standards Policy." *Food Drug Cosmetic Law Journal* 35 (May 1980): 300–05.

3203. Sturniolo, E. J. "FDA's Sterilization Compliance Program." *Food Drug Cosmetic Law Journal* 36 (September 1981): 460–68.

3204. Swanson, S. M. "Quantitative Risk Assessment in Light of the Benzene Decision." *American Statistician* 36 (August 1982): 262–63.

3205. Thomas, W. A. "Supreme Court Review of the OSHA Benzene Standard." *American Statistician* 36 (August 1982): 264–65.

3206. Thompson, Frank J. "Deregulation by the Bureaucracy: OSHA and the Aegean Quest for Error Correction." *Public Administration Review* 42 (May-June 1982): 202–12.

3207. Vernon, D. H. "Labyrinthine Ways: The Handling of Food, Drug, Device and Cosmetic Cases by the Federal Trade Commission since 1938." *Food Drug Cosmetic Law Journal* 8 (June 1953): 367–93.

3208. Viscusi, W. Kip. "Impact of Occupational Safety and Health Regulation." *Bell Journal of Economics and Management Science* 10 (Spring 1979): 117–40.

3209. Weiss, Roger W. "The Case for Federal Meat Inspection Examined." *Journal of Law and Economics* 7 (October 1964): 107–20.

3210. White, Larry. "The Return of the Thief: The Repeal of Prohibition and the Adventist Response." *Adventist Heritage* 5 (Winter 1978): 34–46.

3211. Williams, Albert P., et al. *Policy Analysis for Federal Biomedical Research.* Santa Monica, CA: Rand, 1976. 50 p.

3212. Wolfe, Margaret R. "The Agricultural Experiment Station and Food and Drug Control: Another Look at Kentucky Progressivism, 1898–1916." *Filson Club Historical Quarterly* 49 (October 1975): 323–38.

3213. Wollan, Michael. "Controlling the Potential Hazards of Government-Sponsored Technology." *George Washington Law Review* 36 (July 1968): 1105–37.

3214. Woodby, Kathleen R., and Smith, F. Leslie. "The Cigarette Commercial Ban: A Pattern for Change." *Quarterly Journal of Speech* 60 (December 1974): 431–41.

3215. Yandle, Bruce. "Social Regulation Controversy: The Cotton Dust Standard." *Social Science Quarterly* 63 (March 1982): 58–69.

3216. Yingling, G. L. "Effect of the FDA's OTC Drug Review Program on the Cosmetic Industry." *Food Drug Cosmetic Law Journal* 33 (February 1978): 78–85.

3217. Young, A. L. "Recent Developments under FOIA and FACA Directly Affecting the Pharmaceutical Industry." *Food Drug Cosmetic Law Journal* 31 (September 1976): 507–20.

TRADE

3218. Abbott, Alden. "Missing the Boat on Export Trading Companies." *Regulation* 6 (November-December 1982): 39–44.

3219. Albjerg, Victor L. "High Tariff and World Trade: 1920–1932." *Current History* 42 (June 1962): 344–49.

3220. "American Cyanamid Co. 3 Trade Reg Rep—16527—(Aug. 8, 1963)." *New York University Law Review* 38 (December 1963): 1191–200.

3221. Ashmen, Roy. "Price Determination in the Butter Market: The Elgin Board of Trade, 1872–1917." *Agricultural History* 36 (July 1962): 156–62.

3222. Barfield, Claude. "'Our Share of the Booty': The Democratic Party Cannonism, and the Payne-Aldrich Tariff." *Journal of American History* 57 (September 1970): 308–23.

3223. Basevi, Giorgio. "The Restrictive Effect of the U. S. Tariff and Its Welfare Value." *American Economic Review* 58 (September 1968): 840–52.

3224. Bayard, Thomas O. "Regulation of International Trade in Primary Products: Cartels and Other Commodity Accords." Ph. D. dissertation, Cornell University, 1979. 334 p.

3225. Berry, Thomas S. "The Effect of Business Conditions on Early Judicial Decisions Concerning Restraint of Trade." *Journal of Economic History* 10 (May 1950): 30–44.

3226. Bronz, George. "Tariff Commission as a Regulatory Agency." *Columbia Law Review* 61 (March 1961): 463–89.

3227. Cady, John F. "Structural and Competitive Effects of Retail Trade Regulation: A Study of the Impact of Public Policy in the Retail Market for Prescription Drugs." Ph. D. dissertation, State University of New York at Buffalo, 1975. 245 p.

3228. Carleton, William G. "Tariffs and the Rise of Sectionalism." *Current History* 53 (June 1962): 333–38.

3229. Chatfield, Robert E. "An Economic Analysis of the Holder in Due Course Trade Regulation Rule." Ph. D. dissertation, Purdue University, 1979. 161 p.

3230. Coats, A. W. "Political Economy and the Tariff Reform Campaign of 1903." *Journal of Law and Economics* 11 (April 1968): 181–229.

3231. Cox, Charles C. "The Regulation of Futures Trading." Ph. D. dissertation, University of Chicago, 1975.

3232. Crane, M., and Walker, J. C. "Who Can Sue and Be Sued under Section 36(a) of the Investment Company Act of 1940." *Business Law* 32 (January 1977): 417–25.

3233. Davies, Warnock. "International Business and U. S. Foreign Policy: Precedents in the Political Use of the Power to Regulate Commerce with Foreign Nations." Ph. D. dissertation, Fletcher School of Law and Diplomacy, 1979.

3234. De La Torre, Jose. "Corporate Adjustments and Import Competiton in the U. S. Apparel Industry." *Journal of International Business Studies* 8 (Spring-Summer 1977): 5–21.

3235. Detzer, David. "Businessmen, Reformers, and Tariff Revision: The Payne-Aldrich Tariff of 1909." *Historian* 35 (February 1973): 196–204.

3236. Dew, Lee A. "The Arkansas Tap Line Cases: A Study in Commerce Regulation." *Arkansas Historical Quarterly* 29 (Winter 1970): 327–44.

3237. Dew, Lee A. "The Owensboro Cattle Cases: A Study in Commerce Regulation." *Filson Club Historical Quarterly* 49 (April 1975): 195–203.

3238. Dix, George. "The Death of the Commerce Court: A Study in Institutional Weakness." *American Journal of Legal History* 8 (July 1964): 238–60.

3239. Dobson, John M. "Six Decades of Stalemate: The Changing Mandate of the US Tariff Commission." *Midwest Review of Public Administration* 14 (December 1980): 269–79.

3240. Evans, John W. "The General Agreement on Tariffs and Trade." *International Organizations* 22 (Winter 1968): 72–98.

3241. "Financial Deregulation Ripples into Futures." *Commodities: The Magazine of Futures Trading* 11 (August 1982): 40–42.

3242. Flint, Richard E. "An Analysis and Evaluation of Policies Concerning Regulation of the Activities of Specialists Trading on the New York Stock Exchange." Ph. D. dissertation, University of Texas, 1971. 455 p.

3243. Franklin, W. Neil, ed. "Act for the Better Regulation of the Indian Trade, Virginia, 1714." *Virginia Magazine of History and Biography* 72 (April 1964): 141–51.

3244. Frederick, Kenneth D. "Production Controls under the International Coffee Agreements." *Journal of Interamerican Studies and World Affairs* 12 (April 1970): 255–69.

3245. Friend, Irwin, and Herman, Edward S. "Professor Stigler on Securities Regulation: A Further Comment." *Journal of Business* 38 (January 1965): 106–10.

3246. Friend, Irwin, and Westerfield, Randolph. "Required Disclosure and the Stock Market: Comment." *American Economic Review* 65 (June 1975): 467–72.

3247. Fray, Earl H., and Radebaugh, Lee H., eds. *Regulation of Foreign Direct Investment in Canada and the United States.* Provo, UT: Brigham Young University International Center, 1983. 198 p.

3248. Gonzalez, Mario. "Regulation of Indian Traders: A Historical Perspective." *American Indian Law Review* 5 (Winter 1977): 312–42.

3249. Gottlieb, Amy Z. "The Influence of British Trade Unionists on the Regulation of the Mining Industry in Illinois, 1872." *Labor History* 19 (Summer 1978): 397–415.

3250. Gottschalk, Doris D. "The Remote Computing Services Industry in the U. S. : A Profile of Its Technology, Structure, Regulation, Competition, and Economic Outlook." Ph. D. dissertation, Golden Gate University, 1980. 306 p.

3251. Gould, Lewis L. "Diplomats in the Lobby: Franco-American Relations and the Dingley Tariff of 1897." *Historian* 39 (August 1977): 659–80.

3252. Guither, Harold. "Commodities Exchanges, Agrarian 'Political Power,' and the Antioption Battle: Comment." *Agricultural History* 48 (January 1974): 126–29.

3253. Handler, Milton, ed. *Cases and Materials on Trade Regulation.* 4th ed. Brooklyn, NY: Foundation Press, 1967. 1347 p.

3254. Hawke, G. R. "The United States Tariff and Industrial Protection in the Late Nineteenth Century." *Economic History Review* 28 (February 1975): 84–99.

3255. Hunt, Michael S. "Trade Associations and Self-Regulation: Major Home Appliances." In *Regulating the Product: Quality and Variety*, edited by R. Caves and M. Roberts, pp. 35–39. Cambridge, MA: Ballinger, 1975.

3256. "Insider Trading without Disclosure—Theory of Liability." *Ohio State Law Journal* 28 (Summer 1967): 472–82.

3257. Kant, Chander. "Theory of Multinational Firms under Regulatory Constraints." Ph. D. dissertation, Southern Methodist University, 1980. 142 p.

3258. Kenkel, Joseph F. "The Tariff Commission Movement: The Search for a Nonpartisan Solution of the Tariff Question." Ph. D. dissertation, University of Maryland, 1962. 137 p.

3259. Keohane, Robert O., and Ooms, Van Doorn. "The Multinational Firm and International Regulations." *International Organization* 29 (Winter 1975): 169–209.

3260. Khan, Kabir-ur-Rahman. "The International Tin Agreement, 1976: An Assessment of Its Regulatory Machine as an Instrument of International Policy." *Resources Policy* 5 (June 1979): 83–94.

3261. Kintner, Earl W. "The Trade Court Proposal: An Examination of Some Possible Defects." *American Bar Association Journal* 44 (May 1958): 441–44.

3262. Kottman, Richard N. "The Canadian-American Trade Agreement of 1935." *Journal of American History* 52 (September 1965): 275–96.

3263. Krasner, Stephen D. "Business Government Regulations: The Case of the International Coffee Agreement." *International Organizations* 27 (Autumn 1973): 495–516.

3264. Kripke, Homer. "Where Are We on Securities Disclosure after the Advisory Committee Report?" *Securities Regulation Law Journal* 6 (Summer 1978): 99–132.

3265. Lefkowitz, Louis J. "New York: Criminal Infiltration of the Securities Industry." *American Academy of Political and Social Science, Annals* 347 (May 1963): 51–57.

3266. Leith, J. Clark. "The Effect of Tariffs on Production, Consumption, and Trade: A Revised Analysis." *American Economic Review* 61 (March 1971): 74–81.

3267. Lesh, W. T. "Federal Regulation of Over-the-Counter Brokers and Dealers in Securities." *Harvard Law Review* 59 (October 1946): 1237–75.

3268. Levin, David S. "Regulating the Securities Industry: The Evolution of a Government Policy." Ph. D. dissertation, Columbia University, 1969. 430 p.

3269. Levine, T. A. "Developments in Securities Law: An Address." *Law Library Journal* 70 (November 1977): 501–08.

3270. Lipton, D. A. "Special Study of the Options Market: Its Findings and Recommendations." *Securities Regulation Law Journal* 7 (Winter 1980): 299–346.

3271. Lowenfels, Lewis D. "Section 16(b): A New Trend in Regulating Insider Trading." *Cornell Law Review* 54 (November 1968): 45–64.

3272. Lurie, Jonathan. "The Chicago Board of Trade, 1874–1905, and the Development of Certain Rules and Regulations Governing Its Operation: A Study in the Effectiveness of Internal Regulation." Ph. D. dissertation, University of Wisconsin, 1970. 363 p.

3273. Lurie, Jonathan. "Private Associations, Internal Regulation and Progressivism: The Chicago Board of Trade as a Case Study." *American Journal of Legal History* 16 (July 1972): 215–38.

3274. Mann, B. A., and Schneider, C. W. "Disclosure of 'Soft Information. '" *Institute on Securities Regulation* 10 (1979): 169–95.

3275. McKay, Thomas A. "Federal Regulation of Trading on the New York Stock Exchange." Ph. D. dissertation, New York University, 1949. 245 p.

3276. Miller, Debra L. "Panacea or Problem? The Proposed International Code of Conduct for Technology Transfer." *Journal of International Affairs* 33 (Spring-Summer 1979): 43–62.

3277. Miller, Richard G. "The Tariff of 1832: The Issue that Failed." *Filson Club Historical Quarterly* 49 (July 1975): 221–30.

3278. Mitchell, Broadus. "The Abominable Tariff-Making, 1789–1828." *Current History* 42 (June 1962): 327–32.

3279. Morrison, Rodney J. "The Canadian-American Reciprocal Trade Agreement of 1874: A Pennsylvanian's View." *Pennsylvania Magazine of History and Biography* 102 (October 1978): 457–68.

3280. Perlow, Gary H. "The Multilateral Supervision of International Trade: Has the Textiles Experiment Worked?" *American Journal of International Law* 75 (January 1981): 93–133.

3281. Polopulus, Leo, and Fuller, Varden. "Policies and Politics in Determining Sugar Quotas." *Social Science Quarterly* 43 (March 1963): 331–40.

3282. Pope, Clayne. "The Impact of the Ante-Bellum Tariff on Income Distribution." *Explorations in Economic History* 9 (Summer 1972): 375–422.

3283. Porter, David. "Senator Pat Harrison of Mississippi and the Reciprocal Trade Act of 1940." *Journal of Mississippi History* 36 (November 1974): 363–76.

3284. Poulshock, S. Walter. "Pennsylvania and the Politics of the Tariff, 1880–1888." *Pennsylvania History* 29 (July 1962): 291–305.

3285. Pozen, R. "Competition and Regulation in the Stock Markets." *Michigan Law Review* 73 (December 1974): 317–96.

3286. Prentice, E. Parmalee, and Egan, John G. *The Commerce Clause of the Federal Constitution.* Littleton, CO: F. B. Rothman, 1981. 386 p.

3287. Pursell, Carroll. "Tariff and Technology: The Foundation and Development of the American Tin-Plate Industry, 1872–1900." *Technology and Culture* 3 (Summer 1962): 267–84.

3288. Re, E. D. "Foreign Claims Settlement Commission and the Adjudication of International Claims." *American Journal of International Law* 56 (July 1962): 728–34.

3289. "Reflections 10b–5 in the 'Pool' of Commodity Futures Antifraud." *Houston Law Review* 14 (May 1977): 899–924.

3290. Robertson, James L. "Adjustment Assistance under the Trade Expansion Act of 1962: A Will-o'-the-Wisp." *George Washington Law Review* 33 (June 1965): 1088–125.

3291. Rothenberg, Stuart. "The Impact of Affluence: Restrictions on Foreign Investment in Canada." *American Review of Canadian Studies* 9 (Autumn 1979): 72–84.

3292. Rubin, Alfred P. "United States Export Controls: An Immodest Proposal." *George Washington Law Review* 36 (March 1968): 633–47.

3293. Salehizadeh, Mehdi. "Developing Countries' Regulations of Foreign Direct Investment: A Theoretical and Empirical Analysis." Ph. D. dissertation, University of Wisconsin—Madison, 1980. 220 p.

3294. Sanders, Pieter. "Implementing International Codes of Conduct for Multinational Enterprises." *American Journal of Comparative Law* 30 (Spring 1982): 241–54.

3295. Schatz, Arthur W. "The Reciprocal Trade Agreements Program and the 'Farm Vote,' 1934–1940." *Agricultural History* 46 (October 1972): 498–514.

3296. Scheick, Donald B. "The Regulation of Commodity Currency in Colonial Virginia." Ph. D. dissertation, Indiana University, 1954. 337 p.

3297. Scheinberg, Stephen. "Invitation to Empire: Tariffs and American Economic Expansion in Canada." *Business History Review* 47 (Summer 1973): 218–38.

3298. Scher, Irving. *Manual of Federal Trade Regulations Affecting Retailers.* new ed. New York: National Retail Merchants Association, 1969. 2 vol.

3299. Schlup, Leonard. "Henry C. Hansbrough and the Fight against the Tariff in 1894." *North Dakota History* 45 (Winter 1978): 4–9.

3300. Schmutz, A. W. "Payments to Foreign Consultants: Procedures and Remedies." *Institute on Securities Regulation* 7 (1976): 49–69.

3301. Schwartz, Warren F. "Antidumping Duties for Japanese TVs." *Regulations* 3 (May-June 1979): 53–56.

3302. Short, Joe N. "American Business and Foreign Policy: Cases in Coffee and Cocoa Trade Regulation." Ph. D. dissertation, Columbia University, 1974. 350 p.

3303. Shue, Henry. "Exporting Hazards." *Ethics* 91 (July 1981): 579–606.

3304. Smith, Edward C. "Trademarks and Antitrust: The Misuse Defense under Section 33(b) (7) of the Lanham Act." *Harvard Journal of Law and Public Policy* 4 (Summer 1981): 161–98.

3305. Smith, Malcolm D. H. "Administrative Discretion in Foreign Trade Regulation: A Comparative Analysis of Regulation in the United States, Australia, and Japan." S. J. D. dissertation, Harvard University, 1976.

3306. Snyder, John R. "Edward P. Costigan and the United States Tariff Commission." Ph. D. dissertation, University of Colorado, 1966. 243 p.

3307. Stone, Alan. "The Politics of Trade Regulation: Towards a Theory of Regulatory Behavior." Ph. D. dissertation, University of Chicago, 1972. 345 p.

3308. "Tariff Commission Upheld on Exclusion Order Based on Contested Patent." *Columbia Law Review* 56 (November 1956): 1119–21.

3309. Terrill, Tom E. "David A. Well, the Democracy, and Tariff Reduction, 1877–1894." *Journal of American History* 56 (December 1969): 540–55.

3310. Tharp, Paul A. "Transnational Enterprises and International Regulation: A Survey of Various Approaches in International Organizations." *International Organization* 30 (Winter 1976): 47–73.

3311. Tontz, Robert L., and Angelidis, Alex D. "The Farm Surplus and Tariff Reform." *Current History* 43 (August 1962): 95–102.

3312. Tool, Kent. "Farm Surpluses, Exports, and the Common Market." *Midwest Quarterly* 5 (October 1963): 47–57.

3313. Torodash, Martin. "Underwood and the Tariff." *Alabama Review* 20 (April 1967): 115–30.

3314. United States Congress. House of Representatives. Committee on Interstate and Foreign Commerce. Subcommittee on Oversight and Investigations. *Federal Regulation and Regulatory Reform: Report.* 94th Congress, 2d session. Washington, DC: U. S. Government Printing Office, 1976. 749 p.

3315. U. S. Congress. House of Representatives. Subcommittee on Oversight and Investigations, Committee on Interstate and Foreign Commerce. *Regulatory Reform—Volume I: Quality of Regulators.* 94th Congress, 1st session. Washington, DC: U.S. Government Printing Office, 1975. 95 p.

3316. Unrau, William E. "Joseph G. McCoy and Federal Regulation of the Cattle Trade." *Colorado Magazine* 43 (Winter 1966): 32–43.

3317. Vance, Roger P. "The First Federal Customs." *U. S. Naval Institute Proceedings* 102 (March 1976): 47–53.

3318. Vernon, Raymond. "Multinationals: No Strings Attached." *Foreign Policy* 33 (Winter 1978–1979): 121–34.

3319. Vernon, Raymond. "Storm over the Multinationals: Problems and Prospects." *Foreign Affairs* 55 (January 1977): 243–62.

3320. Williams, John A. "The Bituminous Coal Lobby and the Wilson-Gorman Tariff of 1894. " *Maryland Historical Magazine* 68 (Fall 1973): 273–87.

3321. Winiecki, Jan. "Japan's Imports and Exports of Technology Policy." *Studies in Comparative International Development* 14 (Fall-Winter 1979): 45–62.

TRANSPORTATION

3322. Adams, Henry C. "A Decade of Federal Railway Regulation." *Atlantic Monthly* 81 (April 1898): 433–43.

3323. "'Agreements' and Mergers: The Scope of Federal Maritime Commission Jurisdiction." *Washington University Law Quarterly* 1975 (1975): 182–90.

3324. Avery, George A. "Breaking the Cycle: Regulation and Transportation Policy." *Urban Affairs Quarterly* 8 (June 1973): 423–38.

3325. Axelrod, Donald. "Government Covers the Waterfront: An Administrative Study of the Background, Origin, Development, and Effectiveness of the Bistate Waterfront Commission of New York Harbor, 1953–1966." D. P. A. dissertation, Syracuse University, 1967. 542 p.

3326. Baldwin, John R. *The Regulatory Agency and the Public Corporation: The Canadian Air Transport Industry.* Cambridge, MA: Ballinger, 1975. 252 p.

3327. Barke, Richard P., et al. "A Political Theory of Regulation with Some Observations on Railway Abandonment." *Public Choice* 39 (1982): 73–111.

3328. Barnum, John W. "Midwest Railroads and Northeast Lessons." *Regulation* 2 (July-August 1978): 30–35.

3329. Barr, Alwyn. "Federal Aid for Texas Rivers and Harbors, 1867–1900." *Social Studies* 16 (Summer 1977): 233–44.

3330. Barton, Frank, and Nupp, Byron. "Regulation and Economic Performance in Transportation." *George Washington Law Review* 31 (October 1962): 186–97.

3331. Benson, Lee. *Merchants, Farmers, and Railroads: Railroad Regulation and New York Politics, 1850–1887.* New York: Russell and Russell, 1969, 1955. 310 p.

3332. Bloch, T. S., and Stein, R. J. "Public Counsel Concept in Practice: The Regional Rail Reorganization Act of 1973." *William and Mary Law Review* 16 (Winter 1974): 215–36.

3333. Boger, Dan C. "Economic Aspects of the Regulated Inland Waterway Freight Transportation Industry." Ph. D. dissertation, University of California, Berkeley, 1979. 163 p.

3334. Boyer, K. D. "Minimum Rate Regulation, Modal Split Sensitivities, and the Railroad Problem." *Journal of Political Economy* 85 (June 1977): 493–512.

3335. Breen, Denis A. "The Economic Effects of Regulation: The Case of Motor Carriers of Household Goods." Ph. D. dissertation, Ohio State University, 1975. 236 p.

3336. Broeze, Frank. "The New Economic History, the Navigation Acts, and the Continental Tobacco Market, 1770–1790." *Economic History Review* 26 (November 1973): 668–78.

3337. Burton, William. "Wisconsin's First Railroad Commission: A Case Study in Apostasy." *Wisconsin Magazine of History* 45 (Spring 1962): 190–98.

3338. Bushnell, Eleanore, and Driggs, Don. "Business, Government, and Technological Progress in the Aircraft Industry, 1923." *Business Historical Review* 38 (Summer 1964): 258–64.

3339. Caine, Stanley P. "Railroad Regulation in Wisconsin, 1903–1910: An Assessment of a Progressive Reform." Ph. D. dissertation, University of Wisconsin, 1967. 363 p.

3340. Caine, Stanley P. "Why Railroads Supported Regulation: The Case of Wisconsin, 1905–1910." *Business History Review* 44 (Summer 1970): 175–89.

3341. Campbell, Randolph. "The Case of the 'Three Friends': An Incident in Maritime Regulation during the Revolutionary War." *Virginia Magazine of History and Biography* 74 (April 1966): 190–224.

3342. Carnell, Richard S. "Francis G. Newlands and the National Incorporation of the Railroads." *Nevada Historical Society Quarterly* 19 (Spring 1976): 3–25.

3343. Carson, Robert B. "Railroads and Regulation Revisited—A Note on Problems of Historiography and Ideology." *Historian* 34 (May 1972): 437–46.

3344. Caudill, Edwin G. "Regulatory Policy, Railroad Consolidation and Transportation Efficiency." Ph. D. dissertation, American University, 1968. 305 p.

3345. Caves, Douglas W. ; Christensen, Laurits R. ; and Swanson, Joseph A. "The High Cost of Regulating U. S. Railroads." *Regulation* 5 (January-February 1981): 41–46.

3346. Cochran, Thomas C. *Railroad Leaders, 1845–1890: The Business Mind in Action.* Cambridge, MA: Harvard University Press, 1953. 564 p.

3347. Cohen, Richard E. "Will Carter Be Able to Apply the Brakes to Trucking Regulation?" *National Journal* 9 (May 14, 1977): 748–53.

3348. "Comparative Hearings for Air Route Authorizations: Transplanting the Ashbacker Doctrine." *New York University Law Review* 40 (November 1965): 928–47.

3349. "Competitive Policy in Airline Deregulation." *American University Law Review* 28 (Summer 1979): 537–76.

3350. "Consent Order Arbitration by the AAA: The Ryder System Experience." *Arbitration Journal* 35 (June 1980): 13–17.

3351. Constantin, Jim A. "The Development of Regulation of International Aviation: United States Participation and Policy." Ph. D. dissertation, University of Texas, 1950.

3352. Cowen, Janna L. "The Operating Ratio and Alternative Earnings Control Standards for Regulated Highway Freight Carriers." Ph. D. dissertation, University of Nebraska—Lincoln, 1979. 253 p.

3353. "A Critical Analysis of the Department of Transportation." *Journal of Air Law and Commerce* 33 (Spring 1967): 314–33.

3354. Cummings, Donald G. "The Economics of Conference Rate-Making and Regulation in Ocean Freight Liner Shipping." Ph. D. dissertation, Tulane University, 1975. 475 p.

3355. Cunningham, J. C. "Administrative History of the Federal Maritime Commission's Self-Policing Rules." *Journal of Maritime Law and Commerce* 11 (October 1979): 43–66.

3356. Darby, Larry F. "An Evaluation of Federal Regulation of Common Motor Carriage." Ph. D. dissertation, Indiana University, 1969. 228 p.

3357. Daughety, A. F., and Inaba, F. S. "Analysis of Regulatory Change in the Transportation Industry." *Review of Economics and Statistics* 63 (May 1981): 246–55.

3358. Davison, Charles M. "Transportation Regulation: How Much? How Long?" *Virginia Law Review* 50 (January 1964): 5–22.

3359. Dearstyne, Bruce W. "Railroads and Railroad Regulation in New York State, 1900–1913." Ph. D. dissertation, Syracuse University, 1974. 406 p.

3360. De Vany, Arthur. "Time in the Budget of the Consumer: The Theory of Consumer Demand and Labor Supply under a Time Constraint." Ph. D. dissertation, University of California, Los Angeles, 1970. 145 p.

3361. "Diminishing Power of the FMC in the Aftermath of Seatrain." *Texas International Law Journal* 9 (Fall 1974): 359–76.

3362. Doezema, William R. "Maneuvering within the System: Railroad Responses to State and Federal Regulation, 1870–1916." Ph. D. dissertation, Kent State University, 1978. 330 p.

3363. Doezema, William R. "Railroad Management and the Interplay of Federal and State Regulation, 1885–1916." *Business History Review* 50 (Summer 1976): 153–78.

3364. Douglas, George W., and Miller, James C. "Quality Competition, Industry Equilibrium, and Efficiency in the Price-Constrained Airline Market." *American Economic Review* 64 (September 1974): 657–69.

3365. Due, John F. "Revolution in Transportation Analysis and Policy. " *American Behavioral Scientist* 23 (January-February 1980): 353–82.

3366. Dunn, James A. "The Debate on Public Ownership of U. S. Railroads: A Comparative Perspective." In *Economic Regulatory Policies*, edited by James E. Anderson, pp. 149–58. Carbondale, IL: Southern Illinois University Press, 1976.

3367. Eads, George C. "Airline Capacity Limitation Controls: Public Vice or Public Virtue?" *American Economic Review* 64 (May 1974): 365–71.

3368. Eckert, Ross D. "On the Incentives of Regulators: The Case of Taxicabs." *Public Choice* 14 (Spring 1973): 83–100.

3369. Elazar, Daniel J. "The Inauguration of Minnesota's Railroad System: A Study in Federal-State Collaboration." *Journal of the West* 5 (April 1966): 225–50.

3370. Elliott, Frank N. "The Causes and Growth of Railroad Regulation in Wisconsin: 1848–1876." Ph. D. dissertation, University of Wisconsin, 1956. 338 p.

3371. Emery, S. W. "The Merchant Marine Act of 1970." *U. S. Naval Institute Proceedings* 97 (March 1971): 38–43.

3372. Farnham, Wallace. "The Pacific Railroad Act of 1862." *Nebraska History* 43 (September 1962): 141–68.

3373. "Federal Maritime Commission Determination that Conference Rates Were Unjustly Discriminatory or Unfair to Competing Carrier Is Binding on Maritime Administrator in Determining Whether to Recover Subsidies Paid in Past." *Journal of Maritime Law and Commerce* 2 (October 1970): 179–90.

3374. "Federal Maritime Commission Jurisdiction over Terminal Operators." *Journal of Maritime Law and Commerce* 12 (January 1981): 209–32.

3375. "*Federal Maritime Commission v. Anglo-Canadian Shipping Company* 335 F 2d 255." *California Law Review* 53 (May 1965): 681–91.

3376. "Federal Regulation of Air Transportation and the Environmental Impact Problem." *University of Chicago Law Review* 35 (Winter 1968): 317–41.

3377. "Federal Regulation of Trucking: The Emerging Critique." *Columbia Law Review* 63 (March 1963): 460–514.

3378. Felton, John R. "The Costs and Benefits of Motor Truck Regulation." *Policy Studies* 3 (1979): 143–56.

3379. Flynn, Paul P. "Aviation Congestion: Law, Technology and Regulation." S. J. D. dissertation, Southern Methodist University, 1973.

3380. "*FMC v. DeSmedt,* 336 F 2d 464." *Louisiana Law Review* 52 (April 1967): 1032–34.

3381. Freeman, J. W., and Gerson, R. W. "Motor Carrier Operating Rights Proceedings—How Do I Lose Thee?" *Transportation Law Journal* 11 (1979): 13–64.

3382. Fremlin, Robert. "Primary Jurisdiction and the Federal Maritime Commission." *Hastings Law Journal* 18 (May 1967): 733–93.

3383. Fritzsche, David J. "The Relevance of Consumer Response Data for Regulatory Decision-Making: The Commuter Airlines, A Case Study." D. B. A. dissertation, Indiana University, 1972. 136 p.

3384. Fruhan, William E. *The Fight for Competitive Advantage: A Study of the United States Domestic Trunk Air Carriers.* Boston: Division of Research, Graduate School of Business Administration, Harvard University, 1972. 200 p.

3385. Fuller, John W. "Current Issues in the Regulation of Motor Vehicle Sizes and Weights." Ph. D. dissertation, Washington State University, 1968. 404 p.

3386. Fuller, John W. "Inflationary Effects on Transportation." *American Academy of Political and Social Science, Annals* 456 (July 1981): 112–22.

3387. Gellman, Aaron J. "Effect of Regulation on Aircraft Choice." Ph. D. dissertation, Massachusetts Institute of Technology, 1968.

3388. Ginsburg, Douglas H. "Making Automobile Regulation Work: Policy Options and a Proposal." *Harvard Journal of Law and Public Policy* 2 (Summer 1979): 73–102.

3389. Glasner, David. "The Effect of Rate Regulation on Automobile Insurance Premiums." Ph. D. dissertation, University of California, Los Angeles, 1977. 132 p.

3390. Gliddon, Reverdy T. "Administrative Regulation of Commercial Air Transport." Ph. D. dissertation, University of Texas, 1958. 408 p.

3391. Goodman, Gilbert. "Government Policy toward Commercial Aviation, Competition and the Regulation of Rates." Ph. D. dissertation, Columbia University, 1945. 122 p.

3392. Gordon, James S. "Shipping Regulation and the Federal Maritime Commission." *University of Chicago Law Review* 37 (Fall 1969–Winter 1970): 90–158, 256–94.

3393. Goss, R. O. "U. S. A. Legislation and the Foreign Shipowner, A Critique." *Industrial Economist* 12 (November 1963): 1–19.

3394. Graham, David R., and Kaplan, Daniel P. "Airline Deregulation Is Working." *Regulation* 6 (May-June 1982): 26–32.

3395. Hallin, Richard R. "The Tri-State Transportation Commission: A Capability Analysis of a Metropolitan Policy Subsystem." Ph. D. dissertation, Columbia University, 1969. 554 p.

3396. Hamilton, J. S. "Appellate Practice in Air Safety Proceedings." *Southwestern University Law Review* 10 (1978): 247–66.

3397. Harbeson, Robert W. "Railroads and Regulation, 1877–1916: Conspiracy or Public Interest?" *Journal of Economic History* 27 (1967): 230–42.

3398. Harrison, David. "Controlling Automotive Emissions: How to Save More Than $1 Billion per Year and Help the Poor Too." *Public Policy* 25 (Fall 1977): 527–53.

3399. Herbst, Anthony F., and Wu, Joseph S. K. "Some Evidence of Subsidization: The U. S. Trucking Industry, 1900–1920." *Journal of Economic History* 33 (June 1973): 417–33.

3400. Herrin, Glen W. "The Applicability of Generally Accepted Accounting Principles to a Regulated Industry: Air Transportation." Ph. D. dissertation, University of Alabama, 1965. 295 p.

3401. Hill, C. E., and Borenstein, M. A. "Airline Passenger Safety: Two Studies in FAA Dalliance." *Trail* 14 (August 1978): 36–39.

3402. Howe, J. "Airworthiness: The Government's Role." *Forum* 17 (Winter 1982): 645–55.

3403. Huttsel, Ray C. "The Impact of Entry Regulation by the Nebraska Public Service Commission upon the Motor Carrier Industry in Nebraska." Ph. D. dissertation, University of Nebraska, 1979. 387 p.

3404. "In General—Noncarrier Holding Company May Attain Carrier Status by Acquiring Integrated Railroad System (*Breswick & Co. v. U. S.* 138 F Supp 123). " *Harvard Law Review* 69 (May 1956): 1335–37.

3405. Jacobs, B. A. "Commuter Aircraft Rules up in the Air." *Industry Week* 207 (April 1979): 79–82.

3406. Johnson, James C. "An Economic and Regulatory Analysis of the Merger and Consolidation Movement in the Motor Trucking Industry." Ph. D. dissertation, University of Minnesota, 1970. 616 p.

3407. Johnson, Tobe. "The Waterfront Commission of New York Harbor: A Case Study of a Bi-State Regulatory Agency." Ph. D. dissertation, Columbia University, 1963. 381 p.

3408. Jones, William K. "Licensing of Domestic Air Transportation." *Journal of Air Law and Commerce* 30 (Spring 1964): 113–72.

3409. Jordan, William A. "Economic Effects of Airline Regulation." Ph. D. dissertation, University of California, Los Angeles, 1968. 739 p.

3410. Kafoglis, Milton. "A Paradox of Regulated Trucking: Valuable Operating Rights in a 'Competitive' Industry." *Regulation* 1 (September-October 1977): 27–32.

3411. Kahn, Alfred E. "Deregulation of Air Transportation—Getting from Here to There." *Policy Studies* 3 (1979): 174–202.

3412. Kahn, Mark L. "Industrial Regulations in the Airlines: The Interaction of Unions, Managements and Government in a Regulated and Subsidized Industry." Ph. D. dissertation, Harvard University, 1950.

3413. Kamp, Jaap. "Air Charter Regulation: A Legal, Economic, and Consumer Study." D. B. A. dissertation, Indiana University, Graduate School of Business, 1975. 189 p.

3414. Kasun, J. R., and Ruprecht, T. K. "Your Highway Taxes at Work: Caltrans and the Arcata Freeway." *Policy Analysis* 3 (Spring 1977): 219–38.

3415. Katz, Stanley M. "A Three-Dimensional Demand Model of the Competition between Regulated Rail and Motor Transportation in the United States." Ph. D. dissertation, University of Pennsylvania, 1970. 223 p.

3416. Keeler, Theodore E. "Airline Regulation and Market Performance." *Bell Journal of Economics and Management Science* 3 (Autumn 1972): 399–424.

3417. Kennedy, Edward M. "Competition in the Airlines." *Regulation* 1 (November-December 1977): 24–35.

3418. Kerr, K. Austin. "A New View of Government Regulation: The Case of the Railroads." *Kansas Quarterly* 2 (Summer 1970): 102–10.

3419. Keyes, Lucile S. "The Transpacific Route Investigation: Historical Background and Some Major Issues." *Journal of Air Law and Commerce* 34 (Winter 1968): 3–26.

3420. Kitch, Edmund W. "The Yellow Cab Antitrust Case." *Journal of Law and Economics* 15 (October 1972): 327–35.

3421. Kittrie, Nicholas N. "United States Regulation of Foreign Airlines Competition." *Journal of Air Law and Commerce* 29 (Winter 1963): 1–11.

3422. Kolczynski, P. J., and Harrison, J. R. "Government Liability for Certification of Aircraft?" *Journal of Air Law and Commerce* 44 (1978): 23–45.

3423. Kolko, Gabriel M. *Railroads and Regulation, 1877–1916.* New York: Norton, 1965. 284 p.

3424. Kovarik, J. A. "Procedures before the Federal Aviation Administration." *Journal of Air Law and Commerce* 42 (Winter 1976): 11–37.

3425. Kutish, L. John. "Truck Regulations Forming Barriers to the Marketing of Wisconsin Fluid Dairy Products." Ph. D. dissertation, University of Wisconsin, 1952.

3426. Leduc, Thomas. "Carriers, Courts, and the Commodities Clause." *Business History Review* 39 (Spring 1965): 57–73.

3427. Levin, Mark M., and Stram, Bruce N. "Nursing the Railroads Back to Health." *Regulation* 5 (September-October 1981): 29–36.

3428. Lewis, W. David, and Newton, Wesley P. "The Delta-C&S Merger: A Case Study in Airline Consolidation and Federal Regulation." *Business History Review* 53 (Summer 1979): 161–79.

3429. Lidinsky, R. A., and Colson, D. A. "Federal Regulation of American Port Activities." *International Trade Law Journal* 6 (Fall-Winter 1981–1982): 38–57.

3430. Liipfert, Eugene T. "Consolidation and Competition in Transportation: The Need for an Effective and Consistent Policy." *George Washington Law Review* 31 (October 1962): 106–35.

3431. Lissitzyn, Oliver J. "International Aspects of Air Transport in American Law." *Journal of Air Law and Commerce* 33 (Winter 1967): 86–101.

3432. Llorca, M. R. "Anti-Trust Exemption of Shipping Conferences." *Journal of Maritime Law* 6 (January 1975): 287–98.

3433. Long, Durward. "Florida's First Railroad Commission, 1887–1891: Part I." *Florida Historical Quarterly* 42 (October 1963): 103–24.

3434. Long, Durward. "Florida's First Railroad Commission 1887–1891: Part II." *Florida Historical Quarterly* 42 (January 1964): 248–57.

3435. Loschky, David. "Studies of the Navigation Acts: New Economic Non-History?" *Economic History Review* 26 (November 1973): 689–701.

3436. Lowe, Margaret. "Pro-Con: Deregulation of the Airline Industry." *Congressional Quarterly* 33 (May 10, 1975): 977–80.

3437. Madole, D. W. "Improving Aircraft Type Certification." *Forum* 17 (Winter 1982): 627–44.

3438. Mallach, Stanley. "The Origins of the Decline of Urban Mass Transportation in the United States, 1890–1930." *Urbanism Past and Present* 8 (Summer 1979): 1–17.

3439. Margolin, Edward. "The Gray Area Problem in Transportation." *George Washington Law Review* 31 (October 1962): 136–55.

3440. Margolis, Howard. "The Politics of Auto Emissions." *Public Interest* 49 (Fall 1977): 3–21.

3441. "Maritime Law—Merger Jurisdiction—Federal Maritime Commission Jurisdiction under Section 15 of the Shipping Act Does Not Extend to Transactions Which Are 'In Substance' Mergers, Notwithstanding Possible Commission Jurisdiction over Specific Conditions Affixed to a Merger Agreement." *George Washington Law Review* 43 (January 1975): 635–47.

3442. "Maritime Law—Mergers—The Federal Maritime Commission Is without Authority to Approve Mergers of Shipping Lines under Section 15 of the Shipping Act." *George Washington Law Review* 40 (December 1971): 322–30.

3443. Martin, Albro. "The Troubled Subject of Railroad Regulation in the Gilded Age—A Reappraisal." *Journal of American History* 61 (September 1974): 339–71.

3444. Mathews, Craig. "Certificated Air Service at Smaller Communities: The Need for Service as a Determinant of Regulatory Policy." *Journal of Air Law and Commerce* 34 (Winter 1968): 27–61.

3445. May, Timothy J. "The Status of Federal Maritime Commission Shipping Regulation under Principles of International Law." *Georgetown Law Journal* 54 (Spring 1966): 794–856.

3446. McAfee, Ward. "Local Interests and Railroad Regulation in California during the Granger Decade." *Pacific Historical Review* 37 (February 1968): 51–66.

3447. McClelland, Peter. "The New Economic History and the Burdens of the Navigation Acts: A Comment." *Economic History Review* 26 (November 1973): 679–86.

3448. McClintock, William R. "Early Railroad Regulation in Michigan: 1850–1863." Ph. D. dissertation, University of Wyoming, 1976. 231 p.

3449. Melton, Lee J. "A Re-examination of Contract Carrier Regulation and Exempt Provisions of the Motor Carrier Act of 1935 and Their Impact on Common Carriers." Ph. D. dissertation, Louisiana State University and Agricultural and Mechanical College, 1953.

3450. Mercer, Lloyd. "Land Grants to American Railroads: Social Cost or Social Benefit?" *Business History Review* 43 (Summer 1969): 134–51.

3451. Mercer, Lloyd. "Taxpayers or Investors: Who Paid for the Land-Grant Railroads?" *Business History Review* 46 (Autumn 1972): 279–94.

3452. Meyer, J. S. "Section 419 of the Airline Deregulation Act: What Has Been the Effect on Air Service to Small Communities?" *Journal of Air Law and Commerce* 47 (Fall 1981): 151–85.

3453. Miller, George H. *Railroads and the Granger Laws.* Madison, WI: University of Wisconsin Press, 1971. 296 p.

3454. Monkkonen, Eric. "Can Nebraska or Any State Regulate Railroads? *Smyth v. Ames,* 1898." *Nebraska History* 54 (Fall 1973): 365–82.

3455. Moore, Thomas G. "Deregulating Transportation—Tracking the Progress." *Regulation* 2 (March-April 1978): 37–44.

3456. Moore, Thomas G. "Rail and Truck Reform: The Record So Far." *Regulation* 7 (November-December 1983): 33–42.

3457. Moore, Thomas G. "Transportation." *Regulation* 6 (January-February 1982): 27–28.

3458. Morton, Alexander L. "Emerging Structural Changes in Transport and Public Utilities: Northeast Railroads: Restructured or Nationalized?" *American Economic Review* 65 (May 1975): 284–88.

3459. Narodick, Kit G. "Competition and Regulation in the Domestic Air Freight Industry." Ph. D. dissertation, Columbia University, 1967. 207 p.

3460. Nash, Gerald D. "The California Railroad Commission, 1876–1911." *Southern California Quarterly* 44 (December 1962): 287–306.

3461. National Academy of Sciences. *Regulatory Reform in the U. S. Trucking Industry.* Washington, DC: Transportation Research Board, 1978. 93 p.

3462. "National Transportation Policy and the Regulation of Motor Carriers." *Yale Law Journal* 71 (December 1961): 307–29.

3463. Norvell, James. "The Railroad Commission of Texas: Its Origin and History." *Southwestern Historical Quarterly* 68 (April 1965): 465–80.

3464. "Ocean Shipping Conferences and the Federal Maritime Commission." *Cornell Law Review* 53 (July 1968): 1070–93.

3465. Olson, Josephine E. "Discrimination in Motor Carrier Class Rates: The Effects of Regulation." Ph. D. dissertation, Brown University, 1970. 160 p.

3466. Orion, Henry. "Domestic Air Cargo, 1945–1965: A Study of Competition in a Regulated Industry." Ph. D. dissertation, Columbia University, 1967. 466 p.

3467. Osborn, P. F. "Procedure for Obtaining Interstate Motor Carrier Franchise." *Alabama Law* 11 (October 1950): 409–19.

3468. Panzar, John C. "Regulation, Service Quality, and Market Performance: A Model of Airline Rivalry." Ph. D. dissertation, Stanford University, 1975. 118 p.

3469. Parker, Francis H., and Gorman, Gilbert. "Rail Planning—Crisis and Opportunity." *Journal of the American Institute of Planners* 43 (January 1977): 13–23.

3470. Peterson, Robert L. "State Regulation of Railroads in Texas, 1836–1920." Ph. D. dissertation, University of Texas, 1960. 513 p.

3471. Phillips, Charles F. *The Economics of Regulation; Theory and Practice in the Transportation and Public Utility Industries.* Rev. ed. Homewood, IL: R. D. Irwin, 1969. 774 p.

3472. Pierce, Burton. "The Nature and Extent of Long Range Planning in the Transportation Regulatory Agencies." Ph. D. dissertation, Stanford University, 1971. 289 p.

3473. Porter, Michael E., and Sagansky, Jeffrey F. "Information, Politics, and Economic Analysis: The Regulatory Decision Process in the Air Freight Cases." *Public Policy* 24 (Spring 1976): 263–307.

3474. Powell, H. Benjamin. "Coal and Pennsylvania's Transportation Policy, 1825–1828." *Pennsylvania History* 38 (April 1971): 134–51.

3475. "Pre-Implementation Review under Section 15 of the Shipping Act of 1916." *Loyola University Law Journal* (Chicago) 9 (Fall 1977): 248–65.

3476. "Private Carriage on Trial: Competition in the Motor-Transportation Industry." *Stanford Law Review* 21 (May 1969): 1204–26.

3477. Pruitt, Charles. "People Doing What They Do Best: The Professional Engineers and NHTSA." *Public Administration Review* 39 (July-August 1979): 363–70.

3478. Pustay, Michael W., and Frew, James R. "Motor Carrier Regulation and Service to Small Communities." *Growth and Change* 13 (July 1982): 2–10.

3479. "Railroad Modification Act of 1948." *Stanford Law Review* 1 (June 1949): 676–99.

3480. "Railroads—Voluntary Merger—Dissenting Shareholders' Rights to Be Determined Solely by Federal Law: *Schwabacher v. United States*, 68 Supreme Court 958." *University of Pennsylvania Law Review* 97 (November 1948): 130–31.

3481. Redford, Emmette S. *The Regulatory Process, with Illustrations from Commercial Aviation.* Austin, TX: University of Texas Press, 1969. 336 p.

3482. Reed, Alan. "The Omaha-Council Bluffs Metro Area Transit and the 13-C Controversy." *Midwest Review of Public Administration* 14 (March 1980): 41–50.

3483. Reed, Merl E. "Government Investment and Economic Growth: Louisiana's Ante Bellum Railroads." *Journal of Southern History* 28 (May 1962): 183–201.

3484. Roberts, Derrell C. "Governor Joseph E. Brown of Georgia and the Texas and Pacific Railroad." *West Texas Historical Association Yearbook* 46 (1970): 184–86.

3485. Roberts, Edward C. "Criteria for the Award of a Foreign Air Route to a Domestic Air Carrier." *South Carolina Law Review* 15 (1963): 867–927.

3486. Rogoff, Edward G. "Theories of Economic Regulation Tested on the Case of the New York City Taxicab Industry." Ph. D. dissertation, Columbia University, 1980. 241 p.

3487. Rothwell, Jack C. "The Conservation Program of the Railroad Commission and the Structure of Crude Oil Prices in Texas." Ph. D. dissertation, University of Texas, 1958. 267 p.

3488. Samuelson, Robert J. "The Truckers and the Feds—A Tangled Relationship." *National Journal* 11 (January 6, 1979): 4–8.

3489. "Section 801 of the Federal Aviation Act—The President and the Award of International Ari Routes to Domestic Carriers: A Proposal for Change." *New York University Law Review* 45 (May 1970): 517–38.

3490. Seldon, Zena A. "The Economic Implications of Alternative Air Transport Regulatory Practices: A Canada-United States Comparison." Ph. D. dissertation, University of Manitoba, 1979. 571 p.

3491. Sequin, Chanel J. "The Transportation of New Motor Vehicles: An Analysis of Commission and Industry Performance." Ph. D. dissertation, Michigan State University, 1962. 308 p.

3492. Skowronek, Stephen. "National Railroad Regulation and the Problem of State-Building: Interests and Institutions in Late Nineteenth-Century America." *Politics and Society* 10 (1981): 225–50.

3493. Smykay, Edward W. "The National Association of Railroad and Utility Commissioners as the Originators and Promoters of Public Policy for Public Utilities." Ph. D. dissertation, University of Wisconsin, 1956. 443 p.

3494. Southard, William R. "An Analysis of the Transportation Regulation Legislative Process." Ph. D. dissertation, University of Texas, 1968. 231 p.

3495. Spady, Richard H. "Econometric Estimation of Cost Functions for the Regulated Transportation Industries." Ph. D. dissertation, Massachusetts Institute of Technology, 1978. 222 p.

3496. Spann, Robert M., and Erickson, Edward W. "The Economics of Railroading: The Beginning of Cartelization and Regulation." *Bell Journal of Economics and Management Science* 1 (Autumn 1970): 227–44.

3497. Sparling, Lee I. "Regulatory Distortions in Transportation and Telecommunications." Ph. D. dissertation, California Institute of Technology, 1980. 137 p.

3498. Spiller, Pablo T. "Quality, Capacity and Regulation: An Analysis of the Airline Industry." Ph. D. dissertation, University of Chicago, 1980. 169 p.

3499. Sprague, Stuart S. "Kentucky and the Navigation of the Mississippi: The Climactic Years 1793–1795." *Register of the Kentucky Historical Society* 71 (October 1973): 364–92.

3500. "State Power to Order Railroad Trackage Agreements." *Stanford Law Review* 12 (May 1960): 674–81.

3501. Stover, John F. *American Railroads.* Chicago: University of Chicago Press, 1961. 302 p.

3502. Sutton, Robert M. "The Origins of American Land-Grant Railroad Rates." *Business History Review* 40 (Spring 1966): 66–76.

3503. Swing, John T. "The Law of the Sea." *Proceedings of the Academy of Political Science* 32 (1977): 128–41.

3504. Szerszen, Carol A. "The Impact of Regulation on Collective Bargaining in the Commercial Airline Industry." Ph. D. dissertation, University of Illinois at Urbana-Champaign, 1979. 305 p.

3505. Thornton, Robert L. "Governments and Airlines." *International Organizations* 25 (Summer 1971): 541–53.

3506. Thurston, William N. "Management-Leadership in the United States Shipping Board 1917–1918." *American Neptune* 32 (July 1972): 155–70.

3507. Tobin, Richard J. "Safety-Related Defects in Motor Vehicles and the Evaluation of Self-Regulation." *Policy Studies Review* 1 (February 1982): 532–39.

3508. Treleven, Dale E. "Railroads, Elevators, and Grain Dealers: The Genesis of Antimonopolism in Wisconsin." *Wisconsin Magazine of History* 52 (Spring 1969): 205–22.

3509. Vaden, Tec. "Truckers Fear Continued Deregulation Drive." *Congressional Quarterly* 34 (November 27, 1976): 3249–54.

3510. Vietor, Richard H. "Businessmen and the Political Economy: The Railroad Rate Controversy of 1905." *Journal of American History* 64 (June 1977): 47–66.

3511. Walton, Gary M. "The New Economic History and the Burdens of the Navigation Acts." *Economic History Review* 24 (November 1971): 533–42.

3512. Weckstein, Herman B., and Weckstein, Donald T. "The Oklahoma Furniture Case: New Shadings in the Gray Area of Motor Carrier Regulation." *George Washington Law Review* 32 (March 1964): 533–53.

3513. Weinberg, Lee S. "*Askew vs. American Waterways Operators, Inc.* : The Emerging New Federalism." *Publius* 8 (Fall 1978): 37–53.

3514. Welborn, David M. "The Certification of Motor Common Carriers of Property: A Study in National Regulatory Administration." Ph. D. dissertation, University of Texas, 1962. 513 p.

3515. Whipple, Glen D. "An Economic Motor Carrier Industry in Washington." Ph. D. dissertation, Washington State University, 1980. 216 p.

3516. White, Lawrence J. "U. S. Mobile Source Emissions Regulation: The Problems of Implementation." *Policy Studies Journal* 11 (September 1982): 77–88.

3517. Whitney, Scott C. "Integrity of Agency Judicial Process under the Federal Aviation Act: The Special Problem Posed by International Airline Route Awards." *William and Mary Law Review* 14 (Summer 1973): 787–815.

3518. Whitton, Rex M. "Bureau of Public Roads." *Historic Preservation* 18 (November-December 1966): 250–55.

3519. "Who Governs the Ports? A Lacuna in the Law of Shipping Regulation." *Loyola Law Review* 26 (Summer 1980): 627–80.

3520. Williams, Ernest W. "Transportation Prices: Their Initiation and Regulation." *Virginia Law Review* 50 (April 1964): 377–412.

3521. Williams, Stephen F. "Getting Downtown—Relief of Highway Congestion through Pricing." *Regulation* 5 (March-April 1981): 45–50.

3522. Wilson, James A. "Southwestern Cattlemen and Railroad Regulation: A Matter of Dollars and Sense." *Rocky Mountain Social Science Journal* 7 (April 1970): 89–98.

3523. Winham, Gilbert R. "We Are Driven: The Auto Crisis." *Foreign Policy* 43 (Summer 1981): 155–65.

3524. "*Yellow Transit Freight Lines, Inc. v. U. S.* 221 F Supp 465." *Harvard Law Review* 77 (June 1964): 1520–23.

UTILITIES

3525. "Administrative Agencies—Separating the Jurisdictional Authorities of State and Federal Administrators in the Regulation of the Physical Equipment within the Nation's Telephone Network." *University of Toledo Law Review* 8 (Spring 1977): 733–64.

3526. Alyea, Paul E. *Assessment of Public Utilities in Alabama.* Birmingham, AL: Bureau of Public Administration, University of Alabama, 1952. 142 p.

3527. Anaza, John A. "Telephone Regulation in Nebraska: A Study in the Commission Control of Rates." Ph. D. dissertation, University of Nebraska, 1971. 290 p.

3528. Anderson, Alma J. "The Coping Behavior of a State Regulatory Commission: Decision-Making at the California Public Utilities Commission." Ph. D. dissertation, University of California, Davis, 1977. 221 p.

3529. Anderson, James E. "The Public Utility Commission of Texas: A Case of Capture or Rapture?" *Policy Studies Review* 1 (1982): 484–90.

3530. Andrews, Francis J. "Diversification and the Public Utility Holding Company Act." *Public Utilities Fortnightly* 110 (December 23, 1982): 24–28.

3531. Armstrong, D. H. "Focusing on Regulatory Issues." *Public Utilities Fortnightly* 86 (August 1970): 17–21.

3532. Bailey, Harry A. "Independence, Regulation, and the Kansas Corporation Commission." *Public Utilities Fortnightly* 77 (May 12, 1966): 15–24.

3533. Bailey, Harry A. "The State Corporation Commission: A Study of the Law and Practice of Public Utility Regulation in Kansas." Ph. D. dissertation, University of Kansas, 1964. 255 p.

3534. Baughman, Martin L. "Energy and the Electric Utilities." *Current History* 74 (May-June 1978): 210–14, 228.

3535. Bell, James P. "Pricing by User Class: A Study of Electric Utility Costs and Price Discrimination under Regulation." Ph. D. dissertation, University of California, Berkeley, 1978. 204 p.

3536. Berry, William D. "Economic Regulation by State Commissions: The Case of the Electric Utility Industry." Ph. D. dissertation, University of Minnesota, 1980. 297 p.

3537. Berry, William D. "Utility Regulation in the States: The Policy Effects Professionalism and Salience to the Consumer." *American Journal of Political Science* 23 (May 1979): 263–77.

3538. Blackford, Mansel G. "Businessmen and the Regulation of Railroads and Public Utilities in California during the Progressive Era." *Business History Review* 44 (Autumn 1970): 307–19.

3539. Blank, Blanche D. "Municipal Regulatory Licensing: A Study of Sixteen American Cities." Ph. D. dissertation, Columbia University, 1951. 293 p.

3540. Brock, Barbara H. "A Study of the Development and Change of the Uniform System of Accounts for Electric Utilities in New York State from 1900 to 1977 and the Reconciliation to Theories of Regulation." Ph. D. dissertation, University of New York, 1978.

3541. Brown, Robert W., ed. *New Directions in Utility Marketing; Selected Papers from the Fifteenth Annual Public Utilities Marketing Seminar.* Ann Arbor, MI: Bureau of Business Research, University of Michigan, 1970. 79 p.

3542. Buchanan, Norman S. "The Capital Account and the Rate of Return in Public Utility Operating Companies." *Journal of Political Economy* 43 (February 1935): 50–68.

3543. "Carroll Subcommittee Hearings." *Public Utilities Fortnightly* 66 (December 22, 1960): 963–65.

3544. Chandrasekaran, Perinkolam R. "The Impact of Regulatory Lag on Holding Period Returns of Common Stockholders of Electric Utilities." D. B. A. dissertation, Texas Tech University, 1980. 104 p.

3545. "Changes in Regulatory Agencies Expected." *Public Utilities Fortnightly* 75 (February 4, 1965): 43–44.

3546. Chessler, David S. "Price Discrimination by Electric Utilities and the Effect of State Regulation on the Rate Structure." Ph. D. dissertation, Columbia University, 1974. 292 p.

3547. Clare, Kenneth G. "An Analysis of Dual Regulation of Electric Utility and Natural Gas Industries." Ph. D. dissertation, University of Southern California, 1950.

3548. Clayton, John E. "Public Utility Regulation in Georgia." Ph. D. dissertation, University of Pennsylvania, 1957. 212 p.

3549. Clemens, Eli W. *Economics and Public Utilities.* New York: Appleton-Century-Crofts, 1950. 765 p.

3550. Climer, James H.; Face, Howard K.; and Hetu, Stuart C., eds. *Public Utilities in a Changing Society: Responsibilities and Prospects for Marketing; Papers.* Ann Arbor, MI; Bureau of Business Research, Graduate School of Business Administration, University of Michigan, 1969. 93 p.

3551. Courville, Leon. "Regulation and Efficiency in the Electric Utility Industry." *Bell Journal of Economics and Management Science* 5 (Spring 1974): 53–74.

3552. Coyle, Eugene P. "The Theory of Investment of the Regulated Firm—In the Special Context of Electric Power." Ph. D. dissertation, Boston College, 1969. 138 p.

3553. Crew, Michael A., ed. *Analyzing the Impact of Regulatory Change in Public Utilities.* Lexington, MA: Lexington Books, 1985. 192 p.

3554. Crew, Michael A., and Kleindorfer, Paul R. "Reliability and Public Utility Pricing." *American Economic Review* 68 (March 1978): 31–40.

3555. Cudahy, R. D. "Role of the Regulator in Utility Financing." *Public Utility Fortnightly* 98 (November 18, 1976): 29–31.

3556. Culpepper, Robert C. "A Study of the Effect of Certain Alternative Accounting Methods of Regulatory Decisions in the Gas Utility Industry." Ph. D. dissertation, University of Arkansas, 1969. 168 p.

3557. Demsetz, Harold. "Why Regulate Utilities?" *Journal of Law and Economics* 11 (April 1968): 55–65.

3558. Dilorenzo, Thomas J. "Utility Profits, Fiscal Illusion, and Local Public Expenditures." *Public Choice* 38 (1982): 243–52.

3559. Dirlam, Joel B. "The Regulation of Security Issues under the Public Utility Holding Company Act." Ph. D. dissertation, Yale University, 1947. 271 p.

3560. Donohue, E. J., and Hille, S. J. "National Transportation Policy and the Regulatory Agencies." *Michigan State University Business Topics* 19 (Spring 1971): 67–75.

3561. Doran, John J., et al. *Electric Utility Cost Allocation Manual.* Washington, DC: National Association of Regulatory Utility Commissioners, 1973. 124 p.

3562. *Economic Data on the Regulation of Utility and Transportation Companies.* Washington, DC: The National Association of Regulatory Utility Commissioners, 1974. 270 p.

3563. *Educational Contributions by Public Utilities and Other Regulated Industries as an Allowable Operating Expense for Rate-Making Purposes.* New York: Council for Financial Aid to Education, 1972. 44 p.

3564. Eiteman, David K. "Effect of Regulation under Alternate Rate Base Types upon Telephone and Electric Utility Earnings." Ph. D. dissertation, Northwestern University, 1959. 375 p.

3565. Elstein, Steve. *State Initiatives for Electric Utility Rate Reform.* Lexington, KY: Council of State Governments, 1978. 14 p.

3566. Erickson, Maurice J. "Impact of the Courts on the Practices of the Public Utility Commissions." Ph. D. dissertation, University of Texas, 1954.

3567. Fairclough, Adam. "The Public Utilities Industry in New Orleans: A Study in Capital, Labor and Government, 1894–1929." *Louisiana History* 22 (Winter 1981): 45–65.

3568. Feinn, Barbara A. "Public Utility Regulation in Connecticut." Ph. D. dissertation, Yale University, 1952.

3569. Finlayson, Ronald A. *The Public Utility Holding Company under Federal Regulation.* Chicago: University of Chicago Press, 1946. 41 p.

3570. Flax, L. "Will the Utility Service Obligation Become a Victim of Economic Theory?" *Public Utilities Fortnightly* 105 (March 1980): 21–25.

3571. Garfield, Paul J. "Recent Developments in Wisconsin Public Utility Regulation." Ph. D. dissertation, University of Wisconsin, 1955. 105 p.

3572. Garfield, Paul J., and Lovejoy, Wallace F. *Public Utility Economics.* Englewood Cliffs, NJ: Prentice-Hall, 1964. 505 p.

3573. Gault, John C. *Public Utility Regulation of an Exhaustible Resource: The Case of Natural Gas.* New York: Garland Publishers, 1979. 317 p.

3574. Glaeser, Martin G. *Public Utilities in American Capitalism.* New York: Macmillan, 1957. 624 p.

3575. Gormley, William T. "Alternative Models of the Regulatory Process: Public Utility Regulation in the States." *Western Political Quarterly* 35 (September 1982): 297–317.

3576. Gormley, William T. "Public Advocacy in Public Utility Commission Proceedings." *Journal of Applied Behavioral Science* 17 (1981): 446–62.

3577. Gross, Paul T. "True Yields Earned in Electric Public Utilities Operating under Alternative Regulatory Formulae and Managerial Investment Practices." Ph. D. dissertation, Columbia University, 1967. 162 p.

3578. Hall, C. "Corporate Background of the Texas Utilities Company." *Southwestern Social Science Quarterly* 28 (December 1947): 225–34.

3579. Haring, Joseph E., and Humphrey, Joseph F., eds. *Utility Regulation during Inflation.* Los Angeles: Economics Research Center, Occidental College, 1972. 217 p.

3580. Hass, Jerome E. *Public Utility Investment Analysis.* Ithaca, NY: Center for Environmental Quality Management, Cornell Energy Project, Cornell University, 1971. 10 p.

3581. Hendricks, W. "Effect of Regulation on Collective Bargaining in Electric Utilities." *Bell Journal of Economics and Management Science* 6 (Autumn 1975): 451–65.

3582. Hoeber, Ralph C. "The Development of Public Utility Regulation in Oregon." Ph. D. dissertation, University of Wisconsin, 1949. 200 p.

3583. Holmberg, Steven R. *Public Utility Research: A Synthesis of Current and Classic Energy and Communications Utility Research.* Potomac, MD: PMR Publishing, 1979. 303 p.

3584. Holmberg, Stevan R. "Public Utility Strategic Planning." D. B. A. dissertation, Indiana University, 1971. 612 p.

3585. "How Much New Law Does Landis Want?" *Public Utilities Fortnightly* 67 (January 1961): 98–100.

3586. Jackson, Raymond. "An Empirical Evaluation of Electric Utility Regulation." Ph. D. dissertation, Boston University, 1967. 157 p.

3587. Jaffee, Bruce L. "Aspects of the Regulated Public Utility: Misallocation, Marginal Cost Pricing, and Depreciation." Ph. D. dissertation, Johns Hopkins University, 1971. 168 p.

3588. Jarrell, Gregg A. "Demand for State Regulation of the Electric Utility Industry." *Journal of Law and Economics* 21 (October 1978): 269–95.

3589. Jarett, Jeffrey E. "The Profit Performance of Electric and Gas Utilities as Opposed to Non-Regulated Industries: An Analysis." Ph. D. dissertation, New York University, 1968. 210 p.

3590. Johnson, Harold L. "Public Utility Regulation and the Bell System: A Case Study in the Effectiveness of Social Control." Ph. D. dissertation, University of Texas, 1952.

3591. Joskow, Paul L. "A Behavioral Theory of Public Utility Regulation." Ph. D. dissertation, Yale University, 1972. 237 p.

3592. "Judicial Review for the FAA: An Additional Safeguard for Aviation Safety." *American University Law Review* 29 (Summer 1980): 713–39.

3593. Kahn, Alfred E. "Between Theory and Practice: Reflections of a Neophyte Public Utility Regulator." *Public Utilities Fortnightly* 95 (January 1975): 29–33.

3594. Kamerschen, David R., et al. "Political Determinants of Rates in Electric Utilities." *Policy Studies Review* 1 (February 1982): 546–56.

3595. Keig, N. G., et al. "State Regulation of Water Utilities." *Public Utilities Fortnightly* 86 (August 1970): 19–25.

3596. Kirch, Robert V. "Administrative Regulation of a Public Utility: A Case Study." Ph. D. dissertation, Indiana University, 1955. 393 p.

3597. Kreider, Lawrence E., et al. *The Public Utility Industry and Indiana Economic Growth: Predictive Model Study.* Bloomington, IN: Indiana University, Graduate School of Business, 1971. 300 p.

3598. Lamb, Terrence J. "Indian-Government Relations on Water Utilization in the Salt and Gila River Valleys of Southern Arizona." *Indian Historian* 10 (Summer 1977): 38–48.

3599. "Landis Report." *Public Utilities Fortnightly* 67 (January 1961): 114–17.

3600. Lawler, William C. "Efficiency Measurement in the Regulated Sector: An Empirical Study of the Massachusetts Electric Utility Industry Employing the Williamson Expense Preference Theory in a Pooled Regression Model." Ph. D. dissertation, University of Massachusetts, 1981. 176 p.

3601. Leary, L. W. "Voting Rights in Preferred Stock Issues under the Public Utility Holding Company Act of 1935." *Texas Law Review* 27 (June 1949): 749–74.

3602. Lerner, Abba P. "Conflicting Principles of Public Utility Price Regulation." *Journal of Law and Economics* 7 (October 1964): 61–70.

3603. Lindsay, William W. "Investment Risk as Affected by the Regulation of Public Utility Prices." Ph. D. dissertation, Ohio State University, 1962. 260 p.

3604. Livingstone, John L. "The Effects of Alternative Accounting Methods on Regulatory Rate of Return Decisions in the Electric Utility Industry." Ph. D. dissertation, Stanford University, 1966. 244 p.

3605. Manus, Peter C. "Regulated Public Utilities." *Proceedings of the Academy of Political Science* 31 (1975): 62–77.

3606. McCracken, Paul W. *Economic Progress and the Utility Industry.* Ann Arbor, MI: Bureau of Business Research, University of Michigan, 1964. 44 p.

3607. McDonald, F. "Samuel Insull and the Movement for State Utility Regulatory Commissions." *Business History Review* 32 (Autumn 1958): 241–54.

3608. McKenna, W. J. "CWA Policy toward Regulatory Commissions." *Public Utilities Fortnightly* 62 (August 1958): 236–41.

3609. Moore, Charles G. "An Econometric Evaluation of State Electric Utility Regulation Using a Measure of Manhours of Regulatory Input." Ph. D. dissertation, Northwestern University, 1969. 143 p.

3610. "More Regulatory Probing in 1961?" *Public Utilities Fortnightly* 65 (June 23, 1960): 915–17.

3611. Morgan, Richard E. *The Rate Watcher's Guide: How to Shape Up Your Utility's Rate Structure.* Washington, DC: Environmental Action Foundation, 1980. 108 p.

3612. Moszer, Irene E. "The Effect of Rate of Return Regulation on the Investment Criteria of the Firm: Its Impact on Growth, A Study of the Electric Utility Industry." Ph. D. dissertation, Bryn Mawr College, 1970. 183 p.

3613. Nelson, Randy A. "Regulation and Technical Change in the Electric Utility Industry: 1948–1975." Ph. D. dissertation, University of Illinois at Urbana-Champaign, 1979. 175 p.

3614. *New Challenges to Public Utility Management: Proceedings of the Sixth Annual Conference, 24–25 April 1973.* East Lansing, MI: Institute of Public Utilities, Division of Research, Graduate School of Business Administration, Michigan State University, 1974. 263 p.

3615. Nord, David. "The Experts versus the Experts: Conflicting Philosophies of Municipal Utility Regulation in the Progressive Era." *Wisconsin Magazine of History* 58 (Spring 1975): 219–36.

3616. Oezol, Cengiz. "Monopoly Regulation and a Description of the Behavior of Electric Utility Firms: Some Theoretical and Statistical Analyses." Ph. D. dissertation, Vanderbilt University, 1971. 195 p.

3617. Penland, Gael P. "Investment Behavior of Regulated Electric Utilities in the United States, 1964–1977." Ph. D. dissertation, University of Florida, 1979. 132 p.

3618. Peterson, Edward D. "Selected Issues Arising from Government Regulation of the Public Utility Industries." Ph. D. dissertation, Indiana University, 1960. 355 p.

3619. Peterson, William A. "An Application of a Method of Depreciation Accounting to Problems of Accounting for Federal Income Taxes with Particular Attention to Regulated Gas and Electric Utilities." Ph. D. dissertation, University of Michigan, 1963. 219 p.

3620. Phillips, Charles F. "Landis Report: Boon or Bane?" *Public Utilities Fortnightly* 67 (February 1961): 217–24.

3621. Priest, A. J. *Principles of Public Utility Regulation: Theory and Application.* Charlottesville, VA: Michie, 1969. 2 vols. 936 p.

3622. Ram-Mohan, Sita Raman. "Public Utility Regulation in a Changing Environment." Ph. D. dissertation, Purdue University, 1978. 101 p.

3623. Richardson, L. K. "Should Integrated Regional Power Systems Be Promoted?" *Public Utilities Fortnightly* 98 (August 12, 1976): 21–25.

3624. Robinson, H. Leslie. "The Hickenlooper Amendment and the IPC." *Pacific Historian* 14 (Spring 1970): 22–52.

3625. Robinson, Nelson M., and Petty, John R. *Public Utility Services in Tennessee: A Study for Subcommittee I, Tennessee Legislative Council Committee.* Knoxville, TN: Bureau of Public Administration, University of Tennessee, 1966. 141 p.

3626. Rodgers, P. "NARUC's Quest for Regulatory Excellence." *Public Utilities Fortnightly* 92 (September 13, 1973): 23–26.

3627. Roehm, Harper A. "An Examination of Rules and Procedures of the Florida Public Service Commission and an Evaluation of Their Applicability in Regulating the Municipally Owned Electric Utilities in Florida." D. B. A. dissertation, Florida State University, 1972. 225 p.

3628. Roosevelt, Franklin D. "Government Regulation of Public Utilities." *Proceedings of the Academy of Political Science* 30 (June 1941): 44–51.

3629. Rucker, T. Donald. "The Problem of State Regulation of Strikes in Privately Owned Public Utilities with Particular Emphasis on Illinois, Minnesota, and New York." Ph. D. dissertation, Syracuse University, 1952.

3630. Russell, Milton R. "An Economic Analysis of the Public-Utility and Area-Price Methods of Federal Regulation of the Independent Producers of Natural Gas." Ph. D. dissertation, University of Oklahoma, 1963. 370 p.

3631. Salmond, John A. "Postscript to the New Deal: The Defeat of the Nomination of Aubrey W. Williams as Rural Electrification Administrator in 1945." *Journal of American History* 61 (September 1974): 417-36.

3632. Salmonson, Roland F., ed. *Public Utility Accounting: Models, Mergers, and Information Systems.* East Lansing, MI: Institute of Public Utilities, Michigan State University, 1971. 237 p.

3633. Samuels, Warren J. "Public Utilities and the Theory of Power." In *Perspectives in Public Regulation: Essays on Political Economy,* edited by Milton Russell, pp. 1-27. Carbondale, IL: Southern Illinois University Press, 1973.

3634. Samuels, Warren J., and Trebing, Harry M., eds. *A Critique of Administrative Regulation of Public Utilities.* East Lansing, MI: Institute of Public Utilities, Division of Research, Michigan State University, 1972. 344 p.

3635. Sanders, Albert N. "State Regulation of Public Utilities by South Carolina, 1879-1935." Ph. D. dissertation, University of North Carolina, 1956.

3636. Savas, E. S. "An Empirical Study of Competition in Municipal Service Delivery." *Public Administration Review* 37 (November-December 1977): 717-24.

3637. Scheiber, Harry N. "The Rate-Making Power of the State in the Canal Era: A Case Study." *Political Science Quarterly* 77 (September 1962): 397-413.

3638. Sharaf, Hussein, A. "An Evaluation of the Regulative Aspects of Accounting Requirements for Public Utilities in the United States." Ph. D. dissertation, University of Illionis, 1959. 408 p.

3639. Shepherd, William G., and Geis, Thomas G., eds. *Utility Regulation; New Directions in Theory and Policy.* New York: Random House, 1966. 284 p.

3640. Sichel, Werner, and Gies, Thomas G., eds. *Applications of Economic Principles in Public Utility Industries.* Ann Arbor, MI: Division of Research, Graduate School of Business Administration, University of Michigan, 1981. 155 p.

3641. Smith, Clifford E. "State Regulation and the Incentive for Exceptional Managerial Performance in Investor-Owned Public Utilities." Ph. D. dissertation, Iowa State University, 1964. 171 p.

3642. Smith, Gerald W. "Regulatory Policies on Liberalized Depreciation and Their Effects upon Public Utilities." Ph. D. dissertation, Iowa State University, 1961. 168 p.

3643. Smith, Howard R. "The Changing Pattern of Utility Regulations." Ph. D. dissertation, Louisiana State University and Agricultural and Mechanical College, 1945. 288 p.

3644. Smith, Lincoln. "State Utility Commissioners—1978." *Public Utilities Fortnightly* 101 (February 16, 1978): 9-15.

3645. Smith, Nelson L. "Administrative Process." *Public Utilities Fortnightly* 64 (September 24, 1959): 549-59.

3646. Stelzer, Irwin M. "Electric Utilities—Next Stop for Deregulators?" *Regulation* 6 (July-August 1982): 29-35.

3647. Stigler, George J., and Friedland, Claire. "What Can Regulators Regulate?: The Case of Electricity." *Journal of Law and Economics* 5 (October 1962): 1-16.

3648. Suelflow, James E. *Public Utility Accounting: Theory and Application.* East Lansing, MI: Institute of Public Utilities, Michigan State University, 1973. 325 p.

3649. Tapon, F. "Electric Public Utilities in the United States: A Simulation Model of the Process of Rate of Return Setting by State Regulatory Commissions." *Simulation and Games* 9 (September 1978): 289–300.

3650. Thomas, Norman C. "The Judicial Impact on Administrative Regulation: A Study of Public Utility Regulation in New Jersey." Ph. D. dissertation, Princeton University, 1959. 362 p.

3651. Trachsel, Herman H. *Public Utility Regulation.* Chicago: R. D. Irwin, 1947. 538 p.

3652. Trebing, Harry M. "Broadening the Objectives of Public Utility Regulation." *Land Economics* 53 (February 1977): 106–22.

3653. Trebing, Harry M. "The Chicago School versus Public Utility Regulation." *Journal of Economic Issues* 10 (March 1976): 97–126.

3654. Trebing, Harry M., ed. *Essays on Public Utility Pricing and Regulation.* East Lansing, MI: Institute of Public Utilities, Division of Research, Michigan State University, 1971. 469 p.

3655. Trebing, Harry M., ed. *New Dimensions in Public Utility Pricing.* East Lansing, MI: Division of Research, Graduate School of Business Administration, Michigan State University, 1976. 619 p.

3656. Trebing, Harry M. "Realism and Relevance in Public Utility Regulation." *Journal of Economic Issues* 8 (June 1974): 209–33.

3657. Trout, Robert R. "Utility Regulation under Inflation." Ph. D. dissertation, University of California, Los Angeles, 1978. 215 p.

3658. Troxel, Charles E. *Economics of Public Utilities.* New York: Rinehart, 1947. 892 p.

3659. Turner, George E., ed. *Trends and Topics in Utility Regulation.* Washington, DC: Public Utilities Reports, 1969. 859 p.

3660. Turvaville, Lester J. "A Dynamic Model for Measuring Managerial Performance in Regulated Electric Utilities." Ph. D. dissertation, Georgia Institute of Technology, 1967. 182 p.

3661. Vaughan, C. M., and Sharpe, J. K. "Public Utility Regulatory Policies Act: Implications for Regulatory Commission Reform." *Public Administration Review* 41 (May-June 1981): 387–91.

3662. Voeltz, Herman C. "Genesis and Development of a Regional Power Agency in the Pacific Northwest, 1933–1943." *Pacific Northwest Quarterly* 53 (April 1962): 65–76.

3663. Wallace, C. G., and Johnson, Harold O. "Municipally Owned Power Plants in Nebraska." *Nebraska History* 43 (September 1962): 197–202.

3664. Weigel, John R. "Executive Bonus Programs and Efficiency in Electric Utility Regulation." Ph. D. dissertation, Washington State University, 1981. 152 p.

3665. Welch, Francis X. *Cases and Text on Public Utility Regulation.* Rev. ed. Washington, DC: Public Utilities Reports, 1968. 755 p.

3666. Werth, Alix E. "The Effects of Regulatory Policy on the Cost of Equity Capital and the Value of Equity in the Electric Utility Industry." Ph. D. dissertation, Massachusetts Institute of Technology, 1980. 186 p.

3667. Wich, Henry S. "A Construct for Incentive Regulation of Public Utility Firms." Ph. D. dissertation, St. Louis University, 1966. 138 p.

3668. York, Stanley, and Malko, Robert J. "Utility Diversification: A Regulatory Perspective." *Public Utilities Fortnightly* 111 (January 6, 1983): 15–20.

3669. Young, Harold H. *Forty Years of Public Utility Finance.* Charlottesville, VA: University Press of Virginia, 1965. 205 p.

V. Major Regulatory Agencies

CIVIL AERONAUTICS BOARD

3670. "Administrative Law—Civil Aeronautics Act—Supersession Pro Tanto of the Antitrust Laws." *Boston College Industrial and Commercial Law Review* 4 (Spring 1963): 734–38.

3671. "Administrative Law—Domestic Airline Service to Communities—CAB 'Inadequacy of Service' Rulings." *Notre Dame Lawyer* 36 (August 1961): 539–52.

3672. "Administrative Law—Inspection Powers—CAB Agents May, without Formal Process, Inspect Only Those Records in the Possession of a Regulated Air Carrier Which Are Reasonably Relevant to an Investigation within the CAB's Jurisdiction." *Journal of Air Law and Commerce* 43 (1977): 602–12.

3673. "Administrative Law—Primary Jurisdiction—Civil Aeronautics Board Regulations Held No Bar to Ticketholder in Pursuance of Civil Remedy in Federal Court." *New York University Law Review* 45 (May 1970): 560–70.

3674. "Airline Route Abandonment and Temporary Discontinuance—State Opposition to CAB Pre-emption." *Notre Dame Lawyer* 38 (April 1963): 343–49.

3675. "The American-Eastern Application: Crucial Test of CAB Merger Policy." *University of Pennsylvania Law Review* 111 (December 1962): 195–219.

3676. "Antitrust—Primary Jurisdiction of the CAB—The District Court Had Jurisdiction to Issue a Preliminary Injunction upon Foremost's Prima Facie Showing of Antitrust Violations." *Journal of Air Law and Commerce* 43 (1977): 184–97.

3677. Ballard, F. A. "Federal Regulation of Aviation." *Harvard Law Review* 60 (October 1947): 1235–81.

3678. Berman, Bradley. "The Civil Aeronautics Board." In *The Politics of Regulation,* edited by James Q. Wilson, pp. 107–38. New York: Basic Books, 1980.

3679. Boros, Howard S. "Intervention in Civil Aeronautics Board Proceedings." *Administrative Law Review* 17 (Fall 1964): 5–38.

3680. Boyd, Alan S. "The Promotion of Civil Aeronautics and the CAB." *Journal of Air Law and Commerce* 31 (Spring 1965): 126–32.

3681. Brown, Anthony E. "The Politics of Deregulating the Civil Aviation Industry." Ph.D. dissertation, University of Tennessee, 1982. 303 p.

3682. "CAB and Labor Jurisdiction." *Journal of Air Law and Commerce* 33 (Spring 1967): 334–48.

3683. "CAB—Exemption Policy and Procedure—Hawaiian Inter-Island Carriers." *Journal of Air Law and Commerce* 33 (Winter 1967): 192–99.

3684. "CAB Regulation of International Aviation." *Harvard Law Review* 75 (January 1962): 575–89.

3685. "CAB Regulation of Supplemental Air Carriers." *Harvard Law Review* 76 (May 1963): 1450–71.

3686. Calkins, G. Nathan. "The Role of the Civil Aeronautics Board in the Grant of Operating Rights in Foreign Air Carriage." *Journal of Air Law and Commerce* 22 (Summer 1955): 253–70.

3687. Callison, J. W. "Airline Deregulation—Only Partially a Hoax: The Current Status of the Airline Deregulation Movement." *Journal of Air Law and Commerce* 45 (Summer 1980): 961–1000.

3688. Caves, Richard E. "The Kennedy Subcommittee's 'Civil Aeronautics Board Practices and Procedures.'" *Bell Journal of Economics and Management Science* 7 (Autumn 1976): 733–36.

3689. "The Civil Aeronautics Board as Promoter." *Virginia Law Review* 54 (May 1968): 741–71.

3690. "The Civil Aeronautics Board as Trustees of the Public Interest." *University of San Francisco Law Review* 5 (April 1971): 392–403.

3691. "Civil Aeronautics Board Held to Have Exclusive Jurisdiction to Grant Injunctive Relief against Acts Allegedly in Violation of Antitrust Laws." *Columbia Law Review* 63 (May 1963): 923–34.

3692. Comisky, H. A. "International Airlines and Their Tour Operations—Competition on the Fringe of Regulation." *Journal of Air Law and Commerce* 43 (1977): 71–118.

3693. Corber, Robert J. "Administrative Law Practice Manual: Civil Aeronautics Board." *Administrative Law Review* 16 (Winter–Spring 1964): 199–204.

3694. Costantino, James. "An Evaluation of the Civil Aeronautics Board's Regulatory Policy with Respect to the Promotional Fares of the Domestic Trunk Air Carriers." Ph.D. dissertation, American University, 1971. 238 p.

3695. Crump, Irving. *Our Airliners.* New York: Dodd, Mead, 1941. 249 p.

3696. David, P. T. "Local Financing of Federal-Aid Airports." *Public Management* 28 (September 1946): 258–62.

3697. Dempsey, P. S. "Rise and Fall of the Civil Aeronautics Board—Opening Wide the Floodgates of Entry." *Transportation Law Journal* 11 (1979): 91–185.

3698. de Seife, Rodolphe J. A. "Practice by Laymen before the Civil Aeronautics Board." *Federal Bar Journal* 15 (April–June 1955): 168–76.

3699. Douglas, George W., and Miller, James C. "CAB's Domestic Passenger Fare Investigation." *Bell Journal of Economics and Management Science* 5 (Spring 1974): 205–22.

3700. Dupre, S. C. "Thinking Person's Guide to Entry/Exit Deregulation in the Airline Industry." *Transportation Law Journal* 9 (1977): 273–307.

3701. "Economic Regulation of Foreign Air Carriers by the CAB: Its Legality and Reviewability." *Georgetown Law Journal* 51 (Spring 1963): 593–604.

3702. Einzig, Robert S. "Civil Aeronautics Board Control over Domestic Routes and Competition 1938–1952." Ph.D. dissertation, University of Michigan, 1953. 574 p.

3703. "Federal Preemption of State Law: The Example of Overbooking in the Airline Industry." *Michigan Law Review* 74 (May 1976): 1200–21.

3704. Fisk, Winston M. *Administrative Procedure in a Regulatory Commission: The Civil Aeronautics Board and the New York-Chicago Case.* Indianapolis, IN: Bobbs-Merrill, 1965. 96 p.

3705. Galardi, Lawrence J. "Use of Civil Aeronautics Board Investigation Materials in Civil Litigation." *Brooklyn Law Review* 32 (December 1965): 58–88.

3706. Gillick, J. E. "Recent Developments in Airline Tariff Regulation: Procedural Due Process and Regulatory Reform." *Transportation Law Journal* 9 (1977): 67–96.

3707. Gilliland, Whitney. "The Role of the Civil Aeronautics Board in Licensing Foreign Air Carriers." *Journal of Air Law and Commerce* 32 (Spring 1966): 236–41.

3708. Gilliland, Whitney. "The Role of the Civil Aeronautics Board in the Development of the Domestic Air Carrier Route System." *Notre Dame Lawyer* 47 (October 1971): 32–56.

3709. Heath, Marvin W. "Domestic Route Regulation by the Civil Aeronautics Board." Ph.D. dissertation, University of Chicago, 1951. 114 p.

3710. Hector, L. J. "CAB Member Calls for Major Reforms in Regulatory Agencies." *Public Utilities Fortnightly* 64 (September 24, 1959): 513–14.

3711. Hopkins, G. "Maybe We Should Help Pan Am." *Washington Monthly* 8 (September 1976): 53–61.

3712. Hopkins, G. "Texas Airline War." *Washington Monthly* 8 (March 1976): 12–19.

3713. "Impact of the Aeronautics Board's Regulations on Price Structure in the Airline Industry." *Georgia Law Review* 11 (Winter 1976): 619–40.

3714. Jordan, William A. "Airline Performance under Regulation: Canada vs. the United States." *Research in Law and Economics* 1 (1979): 35–79.

3715. Kahn, Alfred E., and Roach, M. "Paean to Legal Creativity." *Administrative Law Review* 31 (Winter 1979): 97–114.

3716. Kelleher, H. D. "Deregulation and the Practicing Attorney." *Journal of Air Law and Commerce* 44 (1978): 261–96.

3717. Keplinger, B. "Examination of Traditional Arguments on Regulation of Domestic Air Transport." *Journal of Air Law and Commerce* 42 (Winter 1976): 187–212.

3718. Landy, Burton A. "Cooperative Agreements Involving Foreign Airlines: A Review of the Policy of the United States Civil Aeronautics Board." *Journal of Air Law and Commerce* 35 (Autumn 1969): 575–90.

3719. Larson, Dean M. "An Evaluation of Regulation by the Civil Aeronautics Board of Airlines Operating within the Conglomerate Form." Ph.D. dissertation, American University 1972. 302 p.

3720. Levine, Michael E. "Regulating Airmail Transportation." *Journal of Law and Economics* 18 (October 1975): 317–59.

3721. Mauer, R. S. "Use of Discovery Procedures before the CAB." *Administrative Law Review* 18 (Winter–Spring 1966): 157–76.

3722. Olson, Clifton V. "Policy Objectives in Airline Regulation: An Analysis of the Performance of the CAB." Ph.D. dissertation, Tulane University, 1979. 104 p.

3723. Olson, Clifton V., and Trapani, John M. "Who Has Benefited from Regulation of the Airline Industry?" *Journal of Law and Economics* 24 (April 1981): 75–93.

3724. Panzar, John C. "Regulation, Deregulation, and Economic Efficiency: The Case of the CAB." *American Economic Review* 70 (May 1980): 311–15.

3725. Peck, E., and Stephan, G. "Overview of Domestic Aviation Route Awards." *Journal of the Beverly Hills Bar Association* 10 (September–October 1976): 9–53.

3726. Pfeiffer, Paul N. "Shortening the Record in CAB Proceedings through Elimination of Unnecessary and Hazardous Cross-Examination." *Journal of Air Law and Commerce* 22 (Summer 1955): 286–97.

3727. *"Pillai v. Civil Aeronautics Board* (485 F 2d 1018)—CAB Regulation of International Airfares." *Temple Law Quarterly* 47 (Spring 1974): 620–39.

3728. Pilson, Neal. "The Exemption Provision of the Civil Aeronautics Act: The Problems Inherent in the Exercise of 'Pure' Administrative Power." *Journal of Air Law and Commerce* 29 (Autumn 1963): 255–98.

3729. Pomeroy, Leslie K. "An Evaluation in Terms of the Public Interest of the Civil Aeronautics Board's Route Strengthening Policy for Local Service Air Carriers." Ph.D. dissertation, American University, 1970. 248 p.

3730. "Regulation by Civil Aeronautics Board Promoting the Air Freight Forwarding Industry." *Journal of International Law and Economics* 6 (January 1972): 287–95.

3731. "The Rulemaking Procedure of the Civil Aeronautics Board: The Blocked Space Service Problem." *Boston College Industrial and Commercial Law Review* 8 (Fall 1966): 133–46.

3732. Russell, H. L. "CAB and the Consumer." *Journal of Air Law and Commerce* 40 (Winter 1974): 51–60.

3733. Seddig, Robert G. "Regulatory Policy Making in the Civil Aeronautics Board." Ph.D. dissertation, Princeton University, 1971. 426 p.

3734. Stodola, Edward T. "Problems in Expedition and Disposition of Large Administrative Proceedings at the Civil Aeronautics Board." *Journal of Air Law and Commerce* 28 (Summer 1961–1962): 238–59.

3735. *"Transcontinental Bus System, Inc. v. CAB*, 383 F 2d 466." *Texas Law Review* 46 (December 1967): 254–60.

3736. Travers, Arthur H. "An Examination of the CAB's Merger Policy." *University of Kansas Law Review* 15 (March 1967): 227–63.

COMMODITY FUTURES TRADING COMMISSION

3737. "Federal Regulation of Commodity Option Trading—Is the Customer Protected?" *St. Mary's Law Journal* 9 (1977): 53–71.

3738. Gaine, J. G. "1978 Sunset Review of the CFTC: Analysis and Comment." *Record of the Association of the Bar of the City of New York* 34 (April 1979): 290–99.

3739. Greenstone, W. D. "CFTC and Government Reorganization: Preserving Regulatory Independence." *Business Lawyer* 33 (November 1977): 163–219.

3740. Greenstone, W. D. "What Every Trial Lawyer Should Know about Commodities Law." *Trial* 17 (April 1981): 24–27.

3741. Guttman, E. "Futures Trading Act of 1978: The Reaffirmation of CFTC-SEC Coordinated Jurisdiction over Security/Commodities." *American University Law Review* 28 (Fall 1978): 1–35.

3742. Hewitt, J. O. "Commodities and Securities." *Institute on Securities Regulation* 7 (1976): 339–53.

3743. Horwitz, D. L., and Markham, Jesse W. "Sunset on the Commodity Futures Trading Commission: Scene II." *Business Lawyer* 39 (November 1983): 67–100.

3744. Hudson, R. A. "Customer Protection in the Commodity Futures Market." *Boston University Law Review* 58 (January 1978): 1–43.

3745. Johnson, P. F. "Commodity Futures Trading Commission Reauthorization Process: A View from the Trenches." *Detroit College of Law Review* (Spring 1979): 1–50.

3746. Johnson, P. F. "Perimeters of Regulatory Jurisdiction under the Commodity Futures Trading Commission Act." *Drake Law Review* 25 (Fall 1975): 61–74.

3747. Markham, Jesse W. "Investigations under the Commodity Exchange Act." *Administrative Law Review* 31 (Summer 1979): 285–327.

3748. Markham, Jesse W. "Regulation of International Transactions under the Commodity Exchange Act." *Fordham Law Review* 48 (November 1979): 129–58.

3749. Markham, Jesse W. "Seventh Amendment and CFTC Reparations Proceedings." *Iowa Law Review* 68 (October 1982): 87–122.

3750. Sackheim, M. S. "Judicial Equitable Enforcement of Federal Commodities Laws." *American University Law Review* 32 (Summer 1983): 945–83.

3751. Schief, W. R., and Markham, Jesse W. "Nation's 'Commodity Cops'—Efforts by the Commodity Futures Trading Commission to Enforce the Commodity Exchange Act." *Business Lawyer* 34 (November 1978): 19–61.

3752. Shipe, A. L. "Private Litigation before the Commodity Futures Trading Commission." *Administrative Law Review* 33 (Winter 1981): 153–71.

3753. Smith, M. Van. "Commodity Futures Trading Commission and the Return of the Bucketeers; A Lesson in Regulatory Failure." *North Dakota Law Review* 57 (1981): 7–41.

3754. Tendick, D. L., and Gaine, J. G. "Introducing the Regulator: The Commodity Futures Trading Commission." *Business Lawyer* 35 (March 1980): 751–63.

CONSUMER PRODUCT SAFETY COMMISSION

3755. Barr, C. J. "Requiem for Pactra: The Scope of Agency Discretion to Deny an Opportunity for a Hearing under Section 701(e)." *Food Drug Cosmetic Law Journal* 38 (October 1983): 334–48.

3756. Boehme, Lillian R. "Safetycrats: They're Protecting You from Doors." *American Opinion* 17 (January 1974): 21–25, 38.

3757. Byington, S. J. "Chairman Details Changes in Hazard Policy." *Trial* 13 (September 1977): 9–13.

3758. Grabowski, Henry G., and Vernon, J. M. "Consumer Product Safety Regulation." *American Economic Review; Papers and Proceedings* 68 (May 1978): 284–89, 299–300.

3759. Hermanson, Judith A. "Avenue of Access: The Consumer Product Safety Commission Advisory Council." *Public Administration Review* 35 (September 1975): 541–46.

3760. Hermanson, Judith A. "Regulatory Reform by Statute: The Implications of the Consumer Product Safety Commission's Offeror System." *Public Administration Review* 38 (March 1978): 151–55.

3761. Hoffman, Mathew E. "The Consumer Product Safety Commission: In Search of a Regulatory Pattern." *Columbia Journal of Law and Social Problems* 12 (1976): 393–450.

3762. Kahan, J. S. "Reporting of Substantial Product Hazards under Section 15 of the Consumer Product Safety Act." *Administrative Law Review* 30 (Spring 1978): 289–315.

3763. Kelman, Steven J. "Regulation by the Numbers—A Report on the Consumer Product Safety Commission." *The Public Interest* 36 (Summer 1974): 83–102.

3764. Linneman, P. "Effects of Consumer Safety Standards: The 1973 Mattress Flammability Standard." *Journal of Law and Economics* 23 (October 1980): 461–79.

3765. Merrill, R. A. "CPSC Regulation of Cancer Risks in Consumer Products: 1972–1981." *Virginia Law Review* 67 (October 1981): 1261–375.

3766. Russell, T. M. "Consumer Product Safety Act—A Brief Overview." *Food Drug Cosmetic Law Journal* 30 (September 1975): 555–66.

3767. Statler, S. M. "CPSC: Only a Beginning." *Trial* 16 (November 1980): 77–81.

3768. Statler, S. M. "Let the Sunshine in?" *American Bar Association Journal* 67 (May 1981): 573–75.

3769. Thomas, Lacy G. "Essays of the Regulation of Consumer Product Safety." Ph.D. dissertation, Duke University, 1979. 130 p.

3770. Weingast, Barry R. "Consumer Product Safety." *Current History* 78 (May 1980): 206–08, 228.

ENVIRONMENTAL PROTECTION AGENCY

3771. "Achieving Better Management: An Interview with Dr. John P. Horton." *EPA Journal* 8 (January–February 1982): 12–15.

3772. Adamkus, V. V. "Progressive Environmental Control." *EPA Journal* 8 (September–October 1982): 6–9.

3773. Alm, A. L., and Barnes, A. J. "Dealing with Toxic Substances; Present and Future." *EPA Journal* 9 (December 1983): 13–17.

3774. Blumm, M. C. "Clean Water Act's Section 404 Permit Program Enters Its Adolescence: An Institutional and Programmatic Perspective." *Ecology Law Quarterly* 8 (1980): 409–72.

3775. Bronstein, Daniel A., and Wennerberg, L. S. "Section 8(b) of the Toxic Substances Control Act: A Case Study of Government Regulation of the Chemical Industry." *Natural Resources Lawyer* 13 (1981): 704–27.

3776. Brumm, Harold J., and Dick, Daniel T. "Federal Environmental Policy and R&D on Water Pollution Abatement." *American Economic Review* 66 (May 1976): 448–53.

3777. *The Clean Air Act, Proposals for Revisions: 1981, 97th Congress, 1st Session.* Washington, DC: American Enterprise Institute for Public Policy Research, 1981.

3778. Cluster, R. C., and Gilbertson, W. E. "Training and Education of Environmental Health Manpower." *American Journal of Public Health* 69 (February 1979): 118–22.

3779. Cohen, N. H. "Settling Litigation: A New Role for Regulatory Lawyers." *American Bar Association Journal* 67 (July 1981): 878–81.

3780. Cohen, S. E. "Superfund Community Relations Policy." *EPA Journal* 7 (June 1981): 29–34.

3781. "Consumer Product Safety Commission: In Search of a Regulatory Pattern." *Columbia Journal of Law and Social Problems* 12 (1976): 393–450.

3782. Dabelko, D. D. "Political Aspects of Environmental Quality." *EPA Journal* 7 (July–August 1981): 7–8.

3783. Daneke, Gregory A. "Future of Environmental Protection: Reflections on the Difference between Planning and Regulating." *Public Administration Review* 42 (May–June 1982): 227–33.

3784. De Benedictis, N. "You Have a Friend in Pennsylvania." *EPA Journal* 7 (September–October 1981): 24–25.

3785. Debevoise, Thomas M., and Madden, William J. "The Impact of the National Environmental Policy Act upon Administration of the Federal Power Act." *Land and Water Law Review* 8 (1973): 93–124.

3786. Deland, M. R., and Gaines, S. E. "New PSD Regulations: EPA Seeks to Resolve the Continuing Controversy." *Natural Resources Lawyer* 13 (1981): 523–51.

3787. Docksai, M. F. "EPA Issues Toxic Wastes Regulations." *Trial* 16 (May 1980): 13–14.

3788. Dorfman, Nancy. "Who Will Pay for Pollution Control? The Distribution by Income of the Burden of the National Environmental Protection Programs, 1972–1980." *National Tax Journal* 28 (March 1975): 101–15.

3789. Dorrler, S. "EPA's Environmental Response Team—On Call around the Clock." *EPA Journal* 7 (June 1981): 32–33.

3790. Doty, Robert A. "Life Cycle Theories of Regulatory Agency Behavior: The Los Angeles Air Pollution Control District." Ph.D. dissertation, University of California, Riverside, 1977. 266 p.

3791. Durant, Robert F. "EPA, TVA, and Pollution Control: A Comparative Analysis of Intragovernmental Policy Implementation." Ph.D. dissertation, University of Tennessee, 1981. 213 p.

3792. "EPA and the Marine Environment." *EPA Journal* 7 (March 1981): 24–25.

3793. "EPA Management Strategies and Goals." *EPA Journal* 9 (October 1983): 16–17.

3794. "EPA Ordered to Revise Clean Air Stack Height Regulations." *Public Utilities Fortnightly* 112 (November 10, 1983): 42–43.

3795. "EPA Paves Way for PCB Burning." *EPA Journal* 8 (January–February 1982): 20–23.

3796. "EPA Reorganized." *EPA Journal* 7 (July–August 1981): 5–7.

3797. "EPA Sets Standards for Radiation from Active Uranium Mills." *Trial* 19 (December 1983): 13–14.

3798. "EPA Use of Private Contractors in Overview Inspections under the Clean Air Act." *Wayne Law Review* 29 (Summer 1983): 1415–32.

3799. "*EPA v. National Crushed Stone Association.*" *Columbia Journal of Environmental Law* 7 (Spring 1982): 165–78.

3800. "EPA Water Pollution Control Center Internationally Recognized." *EPA Journal* 8 (September–October 1982): 26–27.

3801. "EPA's Responsibilities under RCRA: Administrative Law Issues." *Ecology Law Quarterly* 9 (1981): 555–78.

3802. "FBI to Aid in Hazardous Waste Investigation." *EPA Journal* 7 (July–August 1981): 20–22.

3803. "Federal Water Pollution Control Act—Industrial Challenges to Effluent Limitations." *Boston College Environmental Affairs Law Review* 7 (1979): 545–66.

3804. "Federal Water Pollution Laws: A Critical Lack of Enforcement by the Environmental Protection Agency." *San Diego Law Review* 20 (August 1983): 945–62.

3805. Findley, M. E., et al. "Assessment of the Environmental Protection Agency's Asbestos Hazard Evaluation Algorithm." *American Journal of Public Health* 73 (October 1983): 1179–81.

3806. Floy, K. R. "Prevention of Significant Deterioration of Air Quality—The Regulations after Alabama Power." *Boston College Environmental Affairs Law Review* 9 (1980–1981): 13–61.

3807. Frankel, G. "Tragedy of TOSCA: Chemical Poisoning the EPA Can't Control." *Washington Monthly* 11 (July–August 1979): 42–45.

3808. Freeman, A. Myrick, and Haveman, Robert H. "Water Pollution Control, River Basin Authorities, and Economic Incentives: Some Current Policy Issues." *Public Policy* 19 (Winter 1971): 53–74.

3809. Gaines, Sanford. "Decision Making Procedures at the Environmental Protection Agency." *Iowa Law Review* 62 (February 1977): 839–908.

3810. Garland, George A., and Weddle, Bruce R. "Shaving Solid Waste Collection Costs." *Nation's Cities* 12 (February 1974): 13–17.

3811. Goetze, D. "Shaping of Environmental Attitudes in Air Pollution Control Agencies." *Public Administration Review* 41 (July–August 1981): 423–30.

3812. Gorsuch, A. M. "1980's—A Decade of Challenge. *EPA Journal* 8 (January–February 1982): 4–9.

3813. "Hazardous Substances—Environmental Protection Agency's Final Notification Rule under the Toxic Substances Control Act, Section 12(b)." *Texas International Law Journal* 16 (Summer 1981): 546–53.

3814. Jameson, R. "EPA Goes on Switch Hunt." *Trial* 15 (August 1979): 14–15.

3815. Johnson, E. L. "Risk Assessment in an Administrative Agency." *American Statistician* 36 (August 1982): 232–39.

3816. Kellogg, J., and Kellogg, D. "EPA, Guam, and Environmental Education." *EPA Journal* 7 (January 1981): 30–31.

3817. "Key Appointments Move Forward." *EPA Journal* 8 (January–February 1982): 26–28.

3818. Kramer, B. M. "Air Quality Modeling: Judicial, Legislative and Administrative Reactions." *Columbia Journal of Environmental Law* 6 (Spring 1979): 236–64.

3819. Kroger, W. "EPA's Formula May Be Hazardous to the Chemical Industry." *Nation's Business* 67 (August 1979): 70–72.

3820. "Markets in Air: Problems and Prospects of Controlled Trading." *Harvard Environmental Law Review* 5 (1981): 377–430.

3821. Martin, R. W. "EPA and Administrative Inspections." *Florida State University Law Review* 7 (Winter 1979): 123–37.

3822. Montgomery, M. "EPA's Role in Educating Youth." *EPA Journal* 7 (January 1981): 26–28.

3823. National Academy of Engineering. Coordinating Committee on Air Quality Studies. *Air Quality and Automobile Emission Control: A Report.* Washington, DC: U.S. Government Printing Office, 1974. 4 vols.

3824. Naturale, C. P. "EPA Limits Industrial Growth in Clean Air Areas." *Trial* 14 (September 1978): 14–15.

3825. Naturale, C. P. "Regulating Marlboro Country." *Trial* 14 (April 1978): 60–61.

3826. "New Criminal Enforcement Unit Established at EPA." *EPA Journal* 8 (January–February 1982): 24–25.

3827. "New Hazardous Waste Management System: Regulation of Wastes or Wasted Regulation?" *Harvard Environmental Law Review* 5 (1981): 89–129.

3828. "On a Two-Way Street: The Superfund Community Relations Program." *EPA Journal* 8 (July–August 1982): 8–9.

3829. "Regulating Hazardous Wastes: An Interview with Rita Lavalle." *EPA Journal* 8 (July–August 1982): 2–5.

3830. "Regulation of Pesticides by the Environmental Protection Agency." *Ecology Law Quarterly* 5 (1976): 233–63.

3831. Reitze, A. W., and Reitze, G. L. "Visit to the Castle." *Environment* 16 (September 1974): 3–4.

3832. Rosenthal, Albert J. "The Federal Power to Protect the Environment: Available Devices to Compel or Induce Desired Conduct." *Southern California Law Review* 45 (Spring 1972): 397–449.

3833. Ruckelshaus, W. D. "Science, Risk, and Public Policy: Ruckelshaus Outlines Major Issues." *EPA Journal* 9 (July 1983): 3–8.

3834. Sabatier, Paul A. "Social Movements and Regulatory Agencies: The NAPCA-EPA Citizen Participation Program." Ph.D. dissertation, University of Chicago, 1974.

3835. Schneider, M. W. "Criminal Enforcement of Federal Water Pollution Laws in an Era of Deregulation." *Journal of Criminal Law and Criminology* 73 (Summer 1982): 642–74.

3836. "Science and EPA." *EPA Journal* 7 (July–August 1981): 10–11.

3837. "Science for the Future." *EPA Journal* 8 (March–April 1982): 15–17.

3838. "Searching for Environmental Safety." *EPA Journal* 9 (November 1983): 2–19.

3839. Sielen, A. "Initiatives to Protect the Seas." *EPA Journal* 7 (March 1981): 8–10.

3840. Squiteri, Raymond L. "The Theory and Practice of Environmental Regulation with a Case Study of EPA's 1979 New Source Performance Standards." Ph.D. dissertation, Stanford University, 1981. 179 p.

3841. Thornton, L. "EPA Policy on Delayed Compliance Orders: A Need for Clarification." *Natural Resources Law* 11 (1979): 755–59.

3842. "Tighter EPA Management Planned." *EPA Journal* 7 (November–December 1981): 2–4.

3843. Trump, C. G. "Public Eye on Pollution; Read the Small Print." *Environment* 16 (December 1974): 13–16.

3844. Viscusi, W. Kip. "The Informational Requirements for Effective Regulatory Review: An Analysis of the EPA Lead Standard." *Policy Studies Review* 1 (May 1982): 686–91.

3845. Whitney, V. "EPA and Federal Information Centers." *EPA Journal* 7 (June 1981): 24–25.

EQUAL EMPLOYMENT OPPORTUNITY COMMISSION

3846. "Access to EEOC Files Concerning Private Employers." *University of Chicago Law Review* 46 (Winter 1979): 477–98.

3847. "Administrative Law—Title VII—A Consent Order Is Not a 'Written Interpretation or Opinion' of the EEOC." *Notre Dame Lawyer* 56 (February 1981): 520–28.

3848. "Administrative Law—Weight of EEOC Guidelines in Evaluation of Employment Selection Procedures." *Tulane Law Review* 50 (January 1976): 397–403.

3849. Beller, A. H. "Economics of Enforcement of an Antidiscrimination Law: Title VII of the Civil Rights Act of 1964." *Journal of Law and Economics* 21 (October 1978): 359–80.

3850. Beller, A. H. "Occupational Segregation by Sex: Determinants and Changes." *Journal of Human Resources* 17 (Summer 1982): 371–92.

3851. Belton, Robert. "Title VII of the Civil Rights Act of 1964: A Decade of Private Enforcement and Judicial Developments." *St. Louis University Law Journal* 20 (1976): 225–307.

3852. "Beyond *Equal Employment Opportunity Commission v. Associated Dry Goods Corp.* (101 S Ct 817): A New Defense of the EEOC's Role in the Title VII Enforcement Process." *California Law Review* 70 (May 1982): 816–49.

3853. "Binding Effect of EEOC-Initiated Actions." *Columbia Law Review* 80 (March 1980): 395–419.

3854. Blumrosen, Alfred. "Administrative Creativity: The First Year of the Equal Employment Opportunity Commission." *George Washington Law Review* 38 (May 1970): 695–752.

3855. Bompey, S. H., and Witten, R. E. "Settlement of the Title VII Disputes: Shifting Patterns in a Changing World." *Journal of College and University Law* 6 (1979–1980): 317–43.

3856. Bronfman, Lois A. M. "The Impact of Rules and Regulations Prohibiting Sex Discrimination in Employment: A Study of Response Patterns in Oregon." Ph.D. dissertation, University of Oregon, 1973. 250 p.

3857. Bumpass, T. M. "Application of Rule 23 of the Federal Rules of Civil Procedure to Actions Brought by the Equal Employment Opportunity Commission." *Case Western Reserve Law Review* 29 (Winter 1979): 343–95.

3858. Carmichael, Stokely, and Hamilton, Charles V. *Black Power: The Politics of Liberation in America.* Harmondsworth, England: Penguin, 1969. 199 p.

3859. Cayer, N. J., and Schaefer, R. C. "Affirmative Action and Municipal Employees." *Social Science Quarterly* 62 (September 1981): 487–94.

3860. "Certification of EEOC Class Suits under Rule 23." *University of Chicago Law Review* 46 (Spring 1979): 690–735.

3861. "Civil Rights—Employment Discrimination—An Unintentional Omission of a Procedural Prerequisite for Filing Suit under Title VII of the Civil Rights Act of 1964 Does Not Bar Suit by the EEOC against Employer Unless Prejudice Results." *University of Cincinnati Law Review* 46 (1977): 289–97.

3862. "Civil Rights—Title VII—Equal Employment Opportunity Commission—Right of Charging Parties to Pre-Litigation Access to EEOC Files." *Wayne Law Review* 25 (July 1979): 1105–18.

3863. Clark, Kenneth B. "The Civil Rights Movement: Momentum and Organization." *Journal of the American Academy of Arts and Sciences* 95 (Winter 1966): 239–67.

3864. "Class Actions—EEOC May Seek Classwide Relief without Being Certified as a Class Representative under Rule 23." *Tulane Law Review* 55 (December 1980): 237–50.

3865. Connolly, M. J., and Connolly, W. B. "Equal Employment Opportunities: Case Law Overview." *Mercer Law Review* 29 (Spring 1978): 677–744.

3866. Cornelius, S. F., and Oneglia, S. B. "Sexual Harassment in the Workplace: The Equal Employment Opportunity Commission's New Guidelines." *St. Louis University Law Journal* 26 (December 1981): 39–61.

3867. "Current Trends in Pregnancy Benefits—1972 EEOC Guidelines Interpreted." *DePaul Law Review* 24 (Fall 1974): 127–42.

3868. "Disclosure of EEOC Files to Title VII Litigants." *New York University Law Review* 54 (November 1979): 1013–34.

3869. "Early Access to Investigations of Employment Discrimination: *H. Kessler & Co. v. Equal Employment Opportunity Commission.*" *Southwestern Law Journal* 27 (December 1973): 872–81.

3870. "EEOC Regulatory Intervention: An Undeveloped Means of Enforcing Title VII." *Georgetown Law Journal* 62 (July 1974): 1753–70.

3871. "*EEOC v. University of New Mexico* (504 F 2d 1296)—Tenth Circuit Reduces Standards for Production of Employee Personnel Files in EEOC Investigations." *Utah Law Review* 1975 (Spring 1975): 264–78.

3872. Elisbury, D. "Equal Employment Opportunity Commission Procedural Regulations: An Evaluation by the Practicing Bar." *William and Mary Law Review* 16 (Spring 1975): 555–66.

3873. "Employment Testing and the Federal Executive Agency Guidelines on Employee Selection Procedures: One Step Forward and Two Steps Backward for Equal Employment Opportunity." *Catholic University Law Review* 26 (Summer 1977): 852–74.

3874. "Factually or Statistically Based Commissioner's Charge: A New Approach to EEOC Enforcement of Title VII." *Boston University Law Review* 63 (May 1983): 645–71.

3875. Feagin, Joe R., and Feagin, Clairece B. *Discrimination American Style: Institutional Racism and Sexism.* Englewood Cliffs, NJ: Prentice-Hall, 1978. 190 p.

3876. Fee, Teresa M. "Enforcement of Title VII by the EEOC: A Critical Assessment of the Federal Government's Efforts at Eliminating Sex Discrimination in Employment." Ph.D. dissertation, University of California, Riverside, 1982. 445 p.

3877. Fleming, Harold C. "The Federal Executive and Civil Rights: 1961–65. *Journal of the American Academy of Arts and Sciences* 94 (Fall 1965): 921–48.

3878. "Georgia Power Case: Another Federal Agency Comes of Age: Or, 'My God! Our Employer-Client's Testing Practices Are Being Challenged by the EEOC?'" *Marquette Law Review* 57 (1974): 515–57.

3879. Glazer, Nathan. *Affirmative Discrimination: Ethnic Inequality and Public Policy.* New York: Basic Books, 1978. 248 p.

3880. Glazer, Nathan. "Affirmative Discrimination: Where Is It Going?" *International Journal of Comparative Sociology* 20 (March–June 1979): 14–30.

3881. Golden, H. B. "Sex Discrimination and Hair-Length Requirements under Title VII of the Civil Rights Act of 1964—The Long and Short of It." *Labor Law Journal* 25 (June 1974): 336–51.

3882. Hunter, M. J., and Branch, M. C. "Equal Employment Opportunities: Administrative Procedures and Judicial Developments under Title VII of the Civil Rights Act of 1964 and the Equal Employment Opportunity Act of 1972." *Howard Law Journal* 18 (1975): 543–82.

3883. Jenkins, L. L. "Developments at the Equal Employment Opportunity Commission." *New York University Conference on Labor* 29 (1976): 93–114.

3884. Jones, James E. "The Development of the Law under Title VII since 1965: Implications of the New Law." *Rutgers Law Review* 30 (Fall 1976): 1–61.

3885. "Jurisidictional Conflicts in Minority Employment Relations: NLRB and EEOC." *University of San Francisco Law Review* 2 (October 1967): 149–63.

3886. Katzell, R. A. "EEO in Relation to Personnel Testing and Selection." *New York University Conference on Labor* 30 (1977): 101–07.

3887. Krzystofiak, F., and Newman, J. "Empirical Evaluation of a Fair Employment Standard." *Psychological Reports* 50 (June 1982): 1079–84.

3888. "Labor Law—The Equal Employment Opportunity Commission Is Not Limited to 180 Days from the Filing of a Charge in Which to Bring Suit against an Employer." *Texas Tech Law Review* 6 (Spring 1975): 1163–69.

3889. Landy, F. J. "Adventures in Implied Psychology: On the Value of True Negatives." *American Psychologist* 33 (August 1978): 756–60.

3890. Leach, D. E. "Title VII of the Civil Rights Act and the EEOC: An Agency in the Midst of Change." *Mercer Law Review* 29 (Spring 1978): 661–76.

3891. Leventer, J. C. "Sexual Harassment and Title VII: EEOC Guidelines, Condition Litigation, and the United States Supreme Court." *Capital University Law Review* 10 (Spring 1981): 481–97.

3892. Lomax, Louis E. *The Negro Revolt.* Rev. ed. New York: Harper and Row, 1971. 377 p.

3893. Martin, R. W. "EEOC's New Sexual Harassment Guidelines: Civility in the Workplace." *Nova Law Journal* 5 (Spring 1981): 405–19.

3894. McLain, L. "EEOC Sexual Harassment Guidelines: Welcome Advances under Title VII?" *University of Baltimore Law Review* 10 (Winter 1981): 275–337.

3895. "Meaning of 'Public' in Section 709(e) of the 1964 Civil Rights Act and Access to Information Gathered by the EEOC." *Kentucky Law Journal* 67 (1978–1979): 430–40.

3896. Modjeska, L. "Regressive Reorganization of Federal Employment Discrimination Laws." *Missouri Law Review* 44 (Fall 1979): 680–90.

3897. "New EEOC Guidelines on Discrimination Because of Sex: Employer Liability for Sexual Harassment under Title VII." *Boston University Law Review* 61 (March 1981): 535–62.

3898. "No Class at All: An Examination of Federal Rule 23 and the EEOC." *Cardozo Law Review* 2 (Fall 1980): 97–125.

3899. Northrup, Herbert R., and Larson, John A. *The Impact of the AT&T—EEO Consent Decree.* Philadelphia, PA: Industrial Research Unit, Wharton School, University of Pennsylvania, 1979. 239 p.

3900. Norton, E. H. "Overhauling the EEOC." *Labor Law Journal* 28 (November 1977): 683–95.

3901. Novick, M. R. "Federal Guidelines and Professional Standards." *American Psychologist* 36 (October 1981): 1035–46.

3902. Oneglia, S. B., and Cornelius, S. F. "Sexual Harassment in the Workplace: The Equal Employment Opportunity Commission's New Guidelines." *St. Louis University Law Journal* 26 (December 1981): 39–61.

3903. Peck, Cornelius J. "Equal Employment Opportunity Commission: Developments in the Administrative Process 1965–1975." *Washington Law Review* 51 (October 1976): 831–65.

3904. Perry, L. W. "Mandate and Impact of Title VII." *Labor Law Journal* 26 (December 1975): 743–49.

3905. Plitt, E. A. "Sexual Harassment." *Police Chief* 50 (December 1983): 18–19.

3906. "Potential of Expanded Arbitration in Resolving Title VII Claims in Light of *Alexander v. Gardner-Denver* (94 Sup Ct 1011) and New Equal Employment Opportunity Commission Policy." *Loyola University Law Journal* (Chicago) 7 (Spring 1976): 334–50.

3907. "Pregnancy and Sex-Based Discrimination in Employment: A Post-Aiello Analysis." *University of Cincinnati Law Review* 44 (1975): 57–80.

3908. "Regulatory Agencies and Equal Employment Opportunities—Implications of the AT&T Settlement." *Connecticut Law Review* 6 (Fall 1973): 86–124.

3909. Reiter, M. A. "Applicability of Rule 23 to EEOC Suits: An Examination of *EEOC v. D. H. Holmes Co.* (556 F 2d 787)." *Syracuse Law Review* 28 (1977): 741–61.

3910. Reiter, M. A. "Equal Employment Opportunity Commission and 'Duplicitous Suits': An Examination of *EEOC v. Missouri Pacific Railroad Co.* (493 F 2d 71)." *New York University Law Review* 49 (December 1974): 1130–59.

3911. Rodriguez, A., and Gallegos, T. E. "Improving EEOC Services to the Hispanic Community." *Los Angeles Bar Journal* 34 (December 1983): 739–46.

3912. Sape, George P., and Hart, Thomas J. "Title VII Reconsidered: The Equal Employment Opportunity Act of 1972." *George Washington Law Review* 40 (July 1972): 824–89.

3913. Schweitzer, G. E. "Rights of Federal Employees Named as Alleged Discriminatory Officials." *Public Administration Review* 37 (January 1977): 58–63.

3914. "Sexual Harassment in the Workplace: New Guidelines from the EEOC." *Loyola Law Review* 27 (Spring 1981): 512–31.

3915. Shattuck, C. A. "Current Issues in EEOC Litigation." *New York University Conference on Labor* 36 (1983): 1–19.

3916. Shawe, S. D. "Employment Discrimination—The Equal Employment Opportunity Commission and the Deferral Quagmire." *University of Baltimore Law Review* 5 (Spring 1976): 221–46.

3917. Slate, D. L. "Strengthening EEOC Litigation." *Labor Law Journal* 35 (February 1984): 67–70.

3918. Spurlock, D. L. "EEOC's Compliance Process: The Problems of Selective Enforcement." *Los Angeles Bar Journal* 26 (July 1975): 296–408.

3919. Stewart, Debra W. "Organizational Variables and Policy Impact: EEO." *Policy Studies Journal* 8 (Summer 1980): 870–78.

3920. "Time Limitations on the Filing of Title VII Suits by the Equal Employment Opportunity Commission." *Washington and Lee Law Review* 35 (Winter 1978): 215–38.

3921. "Use of EEOC Investigative Files in Title VII Actions." *Boston University Law Review* 61 (November 1981): 1245–69.

FEDERAL COMMUNICATIONS COMMISSION

3922. "A Strange Animal: The FCC and Broadcast EEO." *Communications and the Law* 6 (April 1984): 25–46.

3923. "Access to Broadcasters' Financial Statements Filed with the FCC: The Freedom of Information Act Alternative." *George Washington Law Review* 42 (November 1973): 145–61.

3924. "Achieving Diversity in Media Ownership: Bakke and the FCC." *California Law Review* 67 (January 1979): 231–55.

3925. "Administrative Agencies—Federal Communications Commission—FCC Lacks Jurisdiction over Two-Way Non-Video Intrastate Communications on Cable Television Leased Access Channels." *Harvard Law Review* 89 (April 1976): 1257–70.

3926. "Administration Law—Communications Law—FCC Authority over Cable Television." *Wisconsin Law Review* (1979): 962–86.

3927. "Administrative Law—Communications Law—FCC Diversity of Ownership Rules Challenged." *Wisconsin Law Review* 1978 (1978): 269–97.

3928. "Administrative Law—Communications—The FCC Lacks the Power to Force Cable Television Systems into a Common Carrier Capacity." *Southern Illinois University Law Journal* 5 (March 1980): 125–36.

3929. "Administrative Law—Federal Communications Commission—FCC Jurisdiction over Extraterritorial Radio Broadcasting." *Law and Policy in International Business* 6 (1974): 608–13.

3930. Albert, J. A. "FCC Assumes a New Role as Regulator of Broadcast Advertising and Candidates' Access." *St. John's Law Review* 54 (Winter 1980): 289–328.

3931. Albert, J. A. "Federal Investigation of Video Evangelism: The FCC Probes the PTL Club." *Oklahoma Law Review* 33 (Fall 1980): 782–823.

3932. "*Allegany County Broadcasting Corporation v. FCC* (348 F 2d 778)." *Federal Communications Bar Journal* 20 (1966): 58–67.

3933. "*American Security Council Education Foundation v. Federal Communications Commission* (607 F 2d 438): An Increased Burden of Proof in Fairness Doctrine Complaints." *American University Law Review* 29 (Fall 1979): 181–204.

3934. "Appeals Court Backs FCC in KSN Case." *Broadcasting* 105 (October 31, 1983): 59–60.

3935. "*Banzhaf v. FCC*: FCC's Fairness Doctrine Applies to Cigarette Ads." *George Washington Law Review* 37 (July 1969): 1293–98.

3936. "Bar Association Files Comments on Proposed Change in Rules on Consolidations and Dismissals." *Federal Communications Bar Journal* 16 (1958): 124–28.

3937. "Bar Association Files Comments on Proposed Change in Rules on Interlocutory Appeals." *Federal Communications Bar Journal* 16 (1958): 129–31.

3938. Barnett, Stephen. "The FCC's Nonbattle against Media Monopoly." *Columbia Journalism Review* 11 (January–February 1973): 43–50.

3939. Barron, Jerome A. "The Federal Communications Commission's Fairness Doctrine: An Evaluation." *George Washington Law Review* 30 (October 1961): 1–41.

3940. Barton, M. F. "Conditional Logit Analysis of FCC Decisionmaking." *Bell Journal of Economics and Management Science* 10 (Autumn 1979): 399–411.

3941. Baughman, James L. "Warriors in the Wasteland: The Federal Communications Commission and American Television, 1958–1967." Ph.D. dissertation, Columbia University, 1981. 560 p.

3942. Baxter, William F. "Regulation and Diversity in Communications Media." *American Economic Review; Papers and Proceedings* 64 (May 1974): 392–99.

3943. Bazelon, David L. "FCC Regulation of the Telecommunications Press." *Duke Law Journal* 1974 (May 1974): 213–51.

3944. Bazelon, David L. "The First Amendment and the 'New Media'—New Directions in Regulating Telecommunications." *Federal Communications Law Journal* 31 (1979): 37–52.

3945. Bazelon, David L. "On the Fortieth Anniversary of the Federal Communications Commission." *Federal Communications Bar Journal* 27 (1974): 1–6.

3946. Beizer, Robert A., and Quale, John C. "Judicial Review of FCC Decisions: 1972." *Federal Communications Bar Journal* 25 (1973): 251–72.

3947. Bennet, Robert W. "Media Concentration and the FCC: Focusing with a Section Seven Lens." *Northwestern University Law Review* 66 (May–June 1971): 159–98.

3948. Bennett, W. J. "Censorship for the Common Good." *Public Interest* 52 (Summer 1978): 98–102.

3949. Berkman, Dave. "A Modest Proposal: Abolishing the FCC." *Columbia Journalism Review* 4 (Fall 1965): 34–37.

3950. Berman, P. J. "CATV Leased-Access Channels and the FCC: The Intractable Jurisdiction Question." *Notre Dame Lawyer* 51 (December 1975): 145–86.

3951. Besen, Stanley M. "Copyright Liability for Cable Television: Compulsory Licensing and the Coase Theorem." *Journal of Law and Economics* 21 (April 1978): 67–95.

3952. Botein, M. "FCC's Restrictions on Employees' Publications: A Failure of Communication?" *Federal Communications Bar Journal* 27 (1974): 231–50.

3953. Botein, M. "Jurisdictional and Antitrust Considerations in the Regulation of the New Communications Technologies." *New York Law School Law Review* 25 (1980): 863–903.

3954. Bowie, N. A., and Whitehead, J. W. "Federal Communications Commission's Equal Employment Opportunity Regulation—An Agency in Search of a Standard." *Black Law Journal* 5 (1977): 313–52.

3955. Boyd, M. "Getting a Handle on AT&T." *Washington Monthly* 10 (January 1979): 37–47.

3956. Boyd, William M. "Ineffective Federal Regulation: The FCC and Television Editorializing." Ph.D. dissertation, University of California, Berkeley, 1972.

3957. Boyer, K. C., and Wirth, M. O. "Economics of Regulation by Policy Directive: FCC Public-Interest Requirements." *Quarterly Review of Economics and Business* 21 (Spring 1981): 77–96.

3958. Brenner, D. L. "Communications Regulation in the Eighties: The Vanishing Drawbridge." *Administrative Law Review* 33 (Spring 1981): 255–68.

3959. Brinton, Avard W. "A Case Study in Regulation by Independent Commission." Ph.D. dissertation, Harvard University, 1964.

3960. Byrne, C. A. "RKO General." *St. Louis University Law Journal* 27 (February 1983): 145–70.

3961. "Cable Television and Content Regulation: The FCC, the First Amendment and the Electronic Newspaper." *New York University Law Review* 51 (April 1976): 133–47.

3962. "Cablecasting: A Myth or Reality—Authority of the Federal Communications Commission to Regulate Local Program Origination on Cable Television—An Evaluation of the Commission's Cable-Casting Rules after *United States v. Midwest Video Corporation* (92 Sup Ct 1860)." *Rutgers Law Review* 26 (Summer 1973): 804–37.

3963. Cahill, Robert V. "'Fairness' and the FCC." *Federal Communications Bar Journal* 21 (1967): 17–25.

3964. "CATV Franchise Fee: Incentive for Regulation, Disincentive for Innovation." *Syracuse Law Review* 30 (Spring 1979): 741–65.

3965. Chamberlin, B. F "Lessons in Regulating Information Flow: The FCC's Weak Track Record in Interpreting the Public's Interest Standard." *North Carolina Law Review* 60 (June 1982): 1057–113.

3966. Chamberlin, William F. "A History of Public Issues Programming Regulation by the Federal Communications Commission: More Rhetoric than Action." Ph.D. dissertation, University of Washington, 1977. 413 p.

3967. "Children's Television Programming and the FCC: Background for Affirmative Regulation." *New England Law Review* 14 (1979–1980): 627–59.

3968. Chisman, Forrest P. "Public Interest and FCC Policy Making." *Journal of Communication* 27 (Winter 1977): 77–84.

3969. Coase, Ronald H. "Federal Communications Commission." *Journal of Law and Economics* 2 (October 1959): 1–40.

3970. "Collapse of Consensus: Effects of the Deregulation of Cable Television." *Columbia Law Review* 81 (April 1981): 612–38.

3971. Collins, Daniel F. "Judicial Review of FCC Decisions, 1968–1969." *Federal Communications Bar Journal* 23 (1969): 57–68.

3972. Collins, T. A. "Local Service Concept in Broadcasting: An Evaluation and Recommendation for Change." *Iowa Law Review* 65 (March 1980): 553–635.

3973. Comanor, William S., and Mitchell, Bridger M. "The Costs of Planning: The FCC and Cable Television." *Journal of Law and Economics* 15 (April 1972): 177–206.

3974. "Common Carriers under the Communications Act." *University of Chicago Law Review* 48 (Spring 1981): 409–38.

3975. "Communication–Administrative Law–The FCC Has the Rulemaking Authority to Ban the Creation of Commonly Owned, Co-Located Daily Newspaper-Broadcast-Station Combinations, While Declining to Require Broad Divestiture of Existing Combinations." *University of Cincinnati Law Review* 47 (1978): 503–13.

3976. "Communications—Cross-Ownership Divestiture—Judicial Power to Extend FCC Divestiture Orders." *Wayne Law Review* 24 (July 1978): 1421–38.

3977. "Communications—The FCC, as an Alternative to Divestment of Western Electric, Ordered Greater Autonomy for the Bell Operating Companies in Purchasing Decisions." *Catholic University Law Review* 27 (Fall 1977): 152–65.

3978. "Communications Law—Broadcasting Indecent but Not Obscene Language—When the FCC Finds That a Pig Has Entered the Parlor . . . ." *University of Detroit Journal of Urban Law* 57 (Fall 1979): 95–121.

3979. "Communications Law—*CBS v. FCC* (101 S Ct 2813): The Supreme Court Upholds FCC Regulations Restricting Broadcaster Discretion in Accepting Political Advertising." *North Carolina Law Review* 60 (June 1982): 1141–57.

3980. "Communications Law—District of Columbia Circuit Vacates FCC Decision Not to Promulgate Rules Which Would Require a Hearing When Assignee of Broadcast License Proposes Change in Entertainment Programming Format of Station." *Temple Law Quarterly* 53 (1980): 362–86.

3981. "Communications Law—FCC Lacks Authority to Promulgate Rules Controlling Content of Cablecast Programing Unless Such Regulations Promote Objectives Previously Held Valid in the Regulation of Broadcast Programing." *Catholic University Law Review* 27 (Winter 1978): 432–48.

3982. "Communications Law: Newspaper/Broadcast Cross-Ownership v. FCC's Policy of Diversity." *Washburn Law Journal* 17 (Spring 1978): 638–47.

3983. "Communications Law–Television–Antisiphoning Rules Governing Movie and Sports Content of Pay Cable Television Exceeded Jurisdiction of FCC under Federal Communications Act." *Villanova Law Review* 23 (March 1978): 507–613.

3984. "Comparing the Incomparable: Towards a Structural Model for FCC Comparative Broadcast License Renewal Hearings." *University of Chicago Law Review* 43 (Spring 1976): 573–612.

3985. "Computer or Communications? Allocation of Functions and the Role of the Federal Communications Commission." *Federal Communications Bar Journal* 27 (1974): 161–230.

3986. "Concentration of Ownership of the Media of Mass Communication: An Examination of New FCC Rules on Cross Ownership of Colocated Newspapers and Broadcast Stations." *Emory Law Journal* 24 (Fall 1975): 1121–63.

3987. "Constitutional Considerations of Multiple Media Ownership Regulated by the Federal Communications Commission." *American University Law Review* 24 (Summer 1975): 1217–50.

3988. "Constitutional Law—Administrative Law—Evidentiary Hearings Required When a Significant Sector of the Listening Public Protests the Loss of an Economically Viable and Unique Program Format." *Notre Dame Lawyer* 55 (June 1980): 848–59.

3989. "Constitutional Law—Freedom of Speech—Federal Communications Commission's Fairness Doctrine Is Constitutional." *Villanova Law Review* 13 (Winter 1968): 393–99.

3990. "Constitutionality of the FCC's Television-Cable Cross-Ownership Restrictions." *Federal Communications Law Journal* 34 (Winter 1982): 1–48.

3991. Cox, Kenneth A. "The FCC, the Constitution, and Religious Broadcast Programming." *George Washington Law Review* 34 (December 1965): 196–218.

3992. Cox, Kenneth A. "The Federal Communications Commission." *Boston College Industrial and Commercial Law Review* 11 (May 1970): 595–688.

3993. "The Criteria Employed by the Federal Communications Commission in Granting Mutually Exclusive Applications for Television Facilities." *Georgetown Law Journal* 45 (Winter 1956–1957): 265–81.

3994. Crotts, Glenna G. "The Public Information Function of the Federal Communications Commission." Ph.D. dissertation, University of Illinois at Urbana-Champaign, 1974. 328 p.

3995. "The Darkened Channels: UHF Television and the FCC." *Harvard Law Review* 75 (June 1962): 1578–607.

3996. "DBS, the FCC, and the Prospects for Diversity and Consumer Sovereignty in Broadcasting." *Computer Law Journal* 4 (Winter 1984): 551–72.

3997. "Development of New Public Interest Standards in the Format Change Cases." *Catholic University Law Review* 25 (Winter 1976): 364–79.

3998. "Discrimination or Discriminating Licensing?: FCC Policy and Newspaper Ownership of TV Stations, 1945–1970." *Administrative Law Review* 30 (Summer 1978): 423–46.

3999. "Diversification and the Public Interest: Administrative Responsibility of the FCC." *Yale Law Journal* 66 (January 1957): 365–96.

4000. "Diversification in Communication: The FCC and Its Failing Standards." *Utah Law Review* 1969 (June 1969): 494–519.

4001. Doerfer, John C. "Federal Communications Commission and the Antitrust Law." *Antitrust Law Symposium* 1960 (1960): 57–62.

4002. Douglas, Cathleen H. "Broadcast Media: Whose Message?" *Trial* 14 (May 1978): 26–30, 61.

4003. Dystel, J. J., and Johnson, N. "Day in the Life: The Federal Communications Commission." *Yale Law Journal* 82 (July 1973): 1575–634.

4004. "Ex Parte Contacts in Informal Rulemaking: *Home Box Office, Inc. v. FCC* and *Action for Children's Television v. FCC.*" *California Law Review* 65 (December 1977): 1315–31.

4005. "Ex Parte Contacts with the Federal Communications Commission." *Harvard Law Review* 73 (April 1960): 1178–98.

4006. "Ex Parte Contacts within the FCC: Problem in Accountability." *Ohio State Law Journal* 42 (1981): 751–69.

4007. Fagan, K. H. "Direct Broadcast Satellites and the FCC: A Case Study in the Regulation of New Technology." *Federal Bar News and Journal* (November 1982): 378–83.

4008. "Fairness, Freedom and Cigarette Advertising: A Defense of the Federal Communications Commission." *Columbia Law Review* 67 (December 1967): 1470–89.

4009. "FCC and Equal Employment Regulation: How the 'Zone of Reasonableness' Promotes 'Neutrality-in-Favor-of-the Licensee.'" *University of San Francisco Law Review* 13 (Spring 1979): 691–720.

4010. "FCC and Minorities: An Evaluation of FCC Policies Designed to Encourage Programming Responsive to Minority Needs." *Columbia Journal of Law and Social Problems* 16 (1981): 561–89.

4011. "FCC Applies Fairness Doctrine to Cigarette Commercials." *Fordham Law Review* 36 (December 1967): 341–45.

4012. "FCC Comparative Hearings." *Harvard Law Review* 64 (April 1951): 947–58.

4013. "FCC Comparative Renewal Hearings: The Role of the Commission and the Role of the Court." *Boston College Law Review* 21 (January 1980): 421–54.

4014. "FCC Computer Inquiry: Interfaces of Competitive and Regulated Markets." *Michigan Law Review* 71 (November 1972): 172–202.

4015. "FCC Content Regulation of Cable Pay-Television: The Threat of Pacifica." *Cumberland Law Review* 9 (Winter 1979): 811–29.

4016. "FCC's Deregulation of Cable Television: The Problem of Unfair Competition and the 1976 Copyright Act." *Hofstra Law Review* 10 (Winter 1982): 591–607.

4017. "FCC Disclaims Power to Limit Competition in Broadcasting." *Columbia Law Review* 57 (November 1957): 1036–38.

4018. "FCC Failure to Eradicate Employment Discrimination by Broadcast Licensees." *St. Louis University Law Journal* 21 (1977): 1560–69.

4019. "FFC—First Amendment—Constitutionality of Proscribing Drug Related Songs." *New York Law Forum* 19 (Spring 1974): 902–15.

4020. "FCC Investigation and Regulation of College Carrier-Current Radio Stations." *Columbia Journal of Law and Social Problems* 8 (Winter 1972): 196–221.

4021. "FCC Minority Distress Sale Policy: Public Interest v. the Public's Interest." *Wisconsin Law Review* 1981 (1981): 365–97.

4022. "FCC's New Equation for Radio Programming: Consumer Wants—Public Interest." *Duquesne Law Review* 19 (Spring 1981): 507–38.

4023. "FCC: Protector or Censor?" *Southern California Law Review* 38 (1965): 634–43.

4024. "FCC Regulation of Broadcast News: First Amendment Perils of Conflicting Standards of Review." *Fordham Law Review* 48 (May 1980): 1226–50.

4025. "FCC Regulation of Cable Television." *New York University Law Review* 54 (April 1979): 204–36.

4026. "The FCC's Role in Providing Equal Employment Opportunity for Minority Groups." *Boston University Law Review* 53 (May 1973): 657–710.

4027. "FCC Syndicated Exclusivity Rule and Alternatives to Nonduplication Protection." *UC Davis Law Review* 15 (Fall 1981): 189–226.

4028. "*FCC v. Midwest Video Corp.* (99 Sup Ct 1435): Public Access Teetering on the Tightrope of FCC Jurisdiction over Cable Television." *Idaho Law Review* 16 (Fall 1979): 123–41.

4029. "*FCC v. National Citizens Committee for Broadcasting* (98 Sup Ct 2096): A Closer Step to Complete Media Regulation." *Cumberland Law Review* 9 (Winter 1979): 851–68.

4030. "FCC's Cable Television Jurisdiction: Deregulation by Judicial Fiat." *University of Florida Law Review* 30 (Summer 1978): 718–51.

4031. "FCC's Deregulation of Cable Television: The Problem of Unfair Competition and the 1976 Copyright Act." *Hofstra Law Review* 10 (Winter 1982): 591–631.

4032. "FCC's Proposal to Deregulate Radio: Is It Permissible under the Communications Act of 1934?" *Federal Communications Law Journal* 32 (Spring 1980): 223–68.

4033. "FCC's Proposed CATV Regulations." *Stanford Law Review* 21 (June 1969): 1685–1713.

4034. "The FCC's Proposed CATV Regulations: Riding Herd on the Bonanza." *Columbia Journal of Law and Social Problems* 5 (April 1969): 169–91.

4035. "FCC's Recession of the 1970 Television-Cable Cross-Ownership Rule." *American University Law Review* 26 (Spring 1977): 688–725.

4036. "Federal Communications Commission and the Bell System: Abdication of Regulatory Responsibility." *Indiana Law Journal* 44 (Spring 1969): 459–77.

4037. "The Federal Communications Commission and Comparative Broadcast Hearings: WHDH as a Case Study in Changing Standards." *Boston College Industrial and Commercial Law Review* 10 (Summer 1969): 943–71.

4038. "The Federal Communications Commission and Program Regulation—Violation of the First Amendment?" *Nebraska Law Review* 41 (June 1962): 826–46.

4039. "The Federal Communications Commission and Regulation of CATV." *New York University Law Review* 43 (March 1968): 117–39.

4040. "Federal Communications Commission: Control of 'Deceptive Programming.'" *University of Pennsylvania Law Review* 108 (April 1960): 868–92.

4041. "Federal Communications Commission—Fairness Doctrine—Requirement That a Fairness Doctrine Complaint Establish a Prima Facie Case Defining a Specific Issue." *Villanova Law Review* 25 (January 1980): 386–402.

4042. "Federal Communications Commission—Power of Commission to Deny Application for Use of Frequencies without Hearing (*Bendix Aviation Corp. v. FCC* 272 F 2d 533)." *New York Law Forum* 6 (July 1960): 337–42.

4043. "Federal Communications Commission Regulation of Domestic Computer Communications: A Competitive Reformation." *Buffalo Law Review* 22 (Spring 1973): 947–84.

4044. "Federal Communications Commission—Review of Regulations Relating to Provision of Data Processing Services by Communications Common Carriers." *Boston College Industrial and Commercial Law Review* 15 (November 1973): 162–85.

4045. "*Federal Communications Commission v. National Citizens Committee for Broadcasting* (98 Sup Ct 2096): FCC Cross-Ownership Ban Upheld." *New England Law Review* 14 (Fall 1978): 337–69.

4046. "The Federal Communications Commission's Fairness Regulations: A First Step towards Creation of a Right of Access to the Mass Media." *Cornell Law Review* 54 (January 1969): 294–305.

4047. Fenton, Bruce S. "Federal Communications Commission and the License Renewal Process." *Suffolk University Law Review* 5 (Winter 1971): 389–425.

4048. Ferris, C. D. "Common Carrier Regulation for the Future." *Harvard Journal on Legislation* 17 (Spring 1980): 241–52.

4049. Ford, Fredrick W. "The Impact of Judicial Review on the Federal Communications Commission." *West Virginia Law Review* 63 (December 1960): 25–39.

4050. "Fortieth Anniversary of the Federal Communications Commission." *Federal Communications Bar Journal* 27 (1974): 109–60.

4051. Frawley, A. C. "Revised Expectations: A Look at the FCC's Equal Employment Opportunity Policies." *Federal Communications Law Journal* 32 (Summer 1980): 291–313.

4052. "Future of the Radio Format Change Controversy: The Case for the Competitive Marketplace." *William and Mary Law Review* 22 (Winter 1980): 281–319.

4053. Gard, S. W. "Impact of Pacifica Foundation on Two Traditions of Freedom of Expression." *Cleveland State Law Review* 27 (1978): 465–503.

4054. Geller, Henry. "Courts Can Open up the Media." *Center Magazine* 11 (January 1978): 21–23.

4055. Geller, Henry. "Modest Proposal for Modest Reform of the Federal Communications Commission." *Georgetown Law Journal* 63 (February 1975): 705–24.

4056. Geller, Henry. "Viewpoint: Talk vs. Action at the FCC." *Regulation* 7 (March-April 1983): 15–18.

4057. Goldberg, Henry. "FCC Broadcast License Renewal Reform: Two Comments on Recent Legislative Proposals—Introduction." *George Washington Law Review* 42 (November 1973): 67–114.

4058. Goldberg, Henry, and Couzens, Michael. "'Peculiar Characteristics': An Analysis of the First Amendment Implications of Broadcast Regulation." *Federal Communications Law Journal* 31 (1979): 113–29.

4059. Goldoff, A. C. "TV Advertising Is Injurious to You . . . ." *Social Policy* 7 (May 1976): 26–31.

4060. Gormley, William T. "An Evaluation of the FCC's Cross-Ownership Policy." *Policy Analysis* 6 (Winter 1980): 61–84.

4061. Gormley, William T. "A Test of the Revolving Door Hypothesis at the FCC." *American Journal of Political Science* 23 (November 1979): 665–83.

4062. Grams, John A. "An Analysis of Federal Communications Commission Actions in the Licensing of Newspaper-Affiliated Broadcasting Stations to 1970." Ph.D. dissertation, University of Wisconsin—Madison, 1973. 332 p.

4063. Grundfest, J. "Participation in FCC Licensing." *Journal of Communication* 27 (Winter 1977): 85–88.

4064. Grundfest, Joseph A. *Citizen Participation in Broadcast Licensing before the FCC.* Santa Monica, CA: Rand, 1976. 195 p.

4065. Grunewald, Donald. "The Entrepreneur and the Federal Communications Commission: A Study of Comparative Television Licensing." Ph.D. dissertation, Harvard University, 1962.

4066. Hammond, A. S. "Federal Communications Commission's Cable Accent Rule and the Fiction of Public Anticipation." *Black Law Journal* 5 (1977): 369–83.

4067. Hardy, A. R., and Secrest, L. W. "Religious Freedom and the Federal Communications Commission." *Valparaiso University Law Review* 16 (Fall 1981): 57–101.

4068. "Henry Rivera: Much More Than Minority Commissioner." *Broadcasting* 104 (January 1983): 103.

4069. Hoffer, M. D. "Power of the FCC to Regulate Cable Pay-TV: Jurisdictional and Constitutional Limitations." *Denver Law Journal* 53 (1976): 477–500.

4070. "Home Box Office and the FCC's Reasonably Ancillary Jurisdiction." *Washington and Lee Law Review* 35 (Winter 1978): 197–214.

4071. "Hughes Aircraft Co., Applications of, No. 19,812 (F.C.C., Sept. 12, 1973)." *Law and Policy in International Business* 6 (1974): 605–07.

4072. Hyde, R. H. "FCC Policy and Procedures Relating to Hearings on Broadcast Applications in Which a New Applicant Seeks to Displace a Licensee Seeking Renewal." *Duke Law Journal* 1975 (May 1975): 253–78.

4073. "Impact of Quality Programming on FCC Licensing." *Louisiana Law Review* 23 (December 1962): 85–106.

4074. "*Implications of Citizens Communications Center v. FCC.*" *Columbia Law Review* 71 (December 1971): 1500–20.

4075. "Invalidation of Mandatory Cable Access Regulations: *FCC v. Midwest Video Corp.* (99 Sup Ct 1435)." *Pepperdine Law Review* 7 (Winter 1980): 469–89.

4076. Jennings, John K. "The Regulators and the Regulated: A Study of Broadcasters' Perceptions of Federal Communications Commission Members and FCC Voting Behavior." Ph.D. dissertation, Stanford University, 1975. 311 p.

4077. "Judicial Review of FCC Program Diversity Regulation." *Columbia Law Review* 75 (March 1975): 401–40.

4078. "Judicial Role of the FCC Decisionmaking Process: A Perspective on the Court-Agency Partnership in the Entertainment Format Cases." *Boston College Law Review* 21 (July 1980): 1067–109.

4079. Kahn, Frank J. "Radio: Regulating Format Diversity." *Journal of Communication* 32 (Winter 1982): 181–91.

4080. Kahn, F. J. "The FCC's Regulation of Economic Injury in Broadcasting, 1934–1966." Ph.D. dissertation, New York University, 1967. 252 p.

4081. Kehoe, Thomas J. "Federal Communications Commission Regulation of the American Telephone & Telegraph Company 1965–74." Ph.D. dissertation, New York University, 1978. 282 p.

4082. Kelso, R., and Pinchuk, D. F. "Personal Attack Rule and Professional Occupations: Consistency in FCC Decision-Making." *California Western Law Review* 16 (1980): 399–421.

4083. Klos, Thornton A. "FCC Programming Regulations since 1960." Ph.D. dissertation, University of Texas at Austin, 1973. 283 p.

4084. Kolson, K. L. "Broadcasting in the Public Interest: The Legacy of Federal Communications Commissioner Nicholas Johnson." *Administrative Law Review* 30 (Winter 1978): 133–65.

4085. Krasnow, Erwin G. "The Ninety-First Congress and the Federal Communications Commission." *Federal Communications Bar Journal* 24 (1970–1971): 97–176.

4086. Krasnow, Erwin G., and Shooshan, Harry M. "Congressional Oversight: The Ninety-Second Congress and the Federal Communications Commission." *Harvard Journal on Legislation* 10 (February 1973): 297–329.

4087. Krasnow, Erwin G., and Shooshan, Harry M. "Congressional Oversight: The Ninety-Second Congress and the Federal Communications Commission." *Federal Communications Bar Journal* 26 (1973): 81–117.

4088. Krattenmaker, Thomas G., and Metzger, A. R. "FCC Regulatory Authority over Commercial Television Networks: The Role of Ancillary Jurisdiction." *Northwestern University Law Review* 77 (November 1982): 403–91.

4089. Lacey, L. J. "Electric Church: An FCC-'Established' Institution?" *Federal Communications Law Journal* 31 (Spring 1979): 235–75.

4090. Lee, R. E. "FCC and Regulatory Duplication: A Case of Overkill?" *Notre Dame Lawyer* 51 (December 1975): 235–50.

4091. Lee, R. E. "Federal Communications Commission's Impact on Product Advertising." *Brooklyn Law Review* 46 (Spring 1980): 463–86.

4092. Levin, Harvey J. "Regulatory Efficiency, Reform and the FCC." *Georgetown Law Journal* 50 (Fall 1961): 1–45.

4093. Lewit, E. M., et al. "Effects of Government Regulation on Teenage Smoking." *Journal of Law and Economics* 24 (December 1981): 545–73.

4094. Lichty, Lawrence W. "The Impact of FRC and FCC Commissioners' Backgrounds on the Regulation of Broadcasting." *Journal of Broadcasting* 6 (Spring 1962): 97–110.

4095. Lichty, Lawrence W. "Members of the Federal Radio Commission and Federal Communications Commission 1927–1961." *Journal of Broadcasting* 6 (Winter 1961–1962): 23–34.

4096. Linker, Jan H. "Public Intervenors and the Public Airwaves: The Effect of Interest Groups on Federal Communications Commission Decisions Decisions." Ph.D. dissertation, Emory University, 1981. 184 p.

4097. Locke, K. W. "FCC: Newest Labor Law Agency?" *Labor Law Journal* 29 (November 1978): 732–38.

4098. Loeb, G. H. "Communications Act Policy toward Competition: A Failure to Communicate." *Federal Communications Law Journal* 30 (March 1978): 1–56.

4099. Loevinger, Lee. "The Issues in Program Regulation." *Federal Communications Bar Journal* 20 (1966): 3–15.

4100. "Lot Is Cast into the Lap: Federal Communications Commission Mistreatment of State Lottery Broadcasts." *Loyola University Law Journal* (Chicago) 6 (Spring 1975): 407–29.

4101. Maher, D. W. "Purity versus Plugola: A Study of the Federal Communications Commission's Sponsorship Identification Rules." *DePaul Law Review* 23 (Spring 1974): 903–36.

4102. McCain, T. A., and Hofstetter, C. R. "Leaders of Opinion for Ascertainment in the Black Community: The Method Is the Message." *Social Science Journal* 19 (January 1982): 27–44.

4103. McDonald, D. "Media's Conflict of Interests." *Center Magazine* 9 (November 1976): 15–35.

4104. McKerns, Charles J., and Robbertson, Charles J. "Disciplinary Powers under the Communications Act Amendments of 1960: A Review." *Federal Communications Bar Journal* 19 (1964–1965): 3–26.

4105. McLauchlan, William P. "Agency-Clientele Relations: A Study of the Federal Communications Commission." *Washington University Law Quarterly* 1977 (Spring 1977): 257–306.

4106. "Media Cross-Ownership—The FCC's Inadequate Response." *Texas Law Review* 54 (January 1976): 336–71.

4107. Meek, Edwin E. "Eugene Octave Sykes, Member and Chairman of Federal Communications Commission and Federal Radio Commission, 1927–1939." *Journal of Mississippi History* 36 (November 1974): 377–86.

4108. Movshin, L. J., and Wheatley, R. B. "FCC's Computing Devices Rules—A Case Study on the Regulation of the Computer." *Emory Law Journal* 30 (Spring 1981): 513–81.

4109. "National Public Radio Satellite System: FCC Jurisdiction over a New Communications Technology." *Rutgers Journal of Computers, Technology and the Law* 8 (1980): 135–46.

4110. "1958 Report of the Committee on Communications of the Administrative Law Section, American Bar Association." *Federal Communications Bar Journal* 16 (1958): 108–23.

4111. "Of Common Carriage and Cable Access: Deregulation of Cable Television by the Supreme Court." *Federal Communications Law Journal* 34 (Winter 1982): 167–92.

4112. "Offensive Speech and the FCC." *Yale Law Journal* 79 (June 1970): 1343–68.

4113. Paper, Lewis J. "Judicial Scrutiny of the FCC: The Illusion of Usurpation." *Boston University Law Review* 52 (Fall 1972): 659–89.

4114. Park, R. E. "How Analysis Affects Decision-Makers' Views: A Bayesian Model." *Journal of Political Economy* 82 (September 1974): 1041–48.

4115. Parker, E. C. "Telecommunications Policy and the Public Interest." *Freedomways* 22 (1982): 163–68.

4116. Parkman, A. "Economic Analysis of the FCC's Multiple Ownership Rules." *Administrative Law Review* 31 (Spring 1979): 205–21.

4117. Parkman, A. "FCC's Allocation of Television Licenses: Regulation with Inadequate Information." *Albany Law Review* 46 (Fall 1981): 22–58.

4118. Peltier, Linda. "The Public Interest in Balanced Programming Content: The Case for FCC Regulation of Broadcasters' Format Changes." *George Washington Law Review* 40 (July 1972): 933–63.

4119. Pennybacker, John H., and Braden, Waldo. *Broadcasting and the Public Interest.* 2d ed. Belmont, CA: Wadsworth, 1978. 467 p.

4120. "Policy Paralysis in WESH: A Conflict between Structure and Operations in the FCC Comparative Renewal Process." *Federal Communications Law Journal* 32 (Winter 1980): 55–104.

4121. Possner, Karen B. "An Historical Analysis of the ABC-ITT Merger Proceeding before the Federal Communications Commission: 1966–1967." Ph.D. dissertation, University of Iowa, 1975. 173 p.

4122. Powe, L. A. "American Voodoo: If Television Doesn't Show It, Maybe It Won't Exist." *Texas Law Review* 59 (May 1981): 879–918.

4123. Powell, Robert S. "The Politics of Regulation: The FCC and Cable Television." Ph.D. dissertation, Princeton University, 1976. 291 p.

4124. "Power of the FCC to Regulate Newspaper-Broadcast Cross-Ownership: The Need for Congressional Clarification." *Michigan Law Review* 75 (August 1977): 1708–31.

4125. Pridgen, D. "Advertising and Marketing on Cable Television: Whither the Public Interest?" *Catholic University Law Review* 31 (Winter 1982): 227–71.

4126. "Primer on Docket Number 18110: The New FCC Cross-Ownership Rules." *Marquette Law Review* 59 (1976): 584–604.

4127. "Program Diversity in the Broadcast Media and the FCC: The Section 310(b) Labyrinth—A Delicate Balance." *Boston College International and Comparative Law Review* 17 (November 1975): 25–52.

4128. "Radio and Television." *Law and Contemporary Problems* 22 (Fall 1957): 541–696.

4129. "Radio and Television Station Transfers: Adequacy of Supervision under the Federal Communications Act." *Indiana Law Journal* 20 (Spring 1955): 351–65.

4130. "Radio: Broadcasting 'Obviously Offensive and Patently Vulgar' Material Warrants FCC Denial of License Renewal." *Minnesota Law Review* 47 (January 1963): 465–73.

4131. "Radio Station Lease Providing for Flexible Rental Based on Gross Income Disapproved." *Harvard Law Review* 63 (December 1949): 354–56.

4132. Ramey, Carl R. "The Federal Communications Commission and Broadcast Advertising: An Analytical Review." *Federal Communications Bar Journal* 20 (1966): 71–116.

4133. Rappaport, R. W. "Emergence of Subscription Cable Television and Its Role in Communications." *Federal Communications Bar Journal* 29 (1976): 301–34.

4134. "Recognition of Legitimate Renewal Expectancies in Broadcast Licensing." *Washington University Law Quarterly* 58 (1980): 409–38.

4135. Redburn, T. "Wedding Presents, Cigars, and Deference." *Washington Monthly* 7 (June 1975): 4–10.

4136. "Regulated Industries—Federal Communications Commission—Supreme Court Invalidates Regulations Requiring Cable Broadcasters to Provide Public Access." *Creighton Law Review* 13 (Spring 1980): 1023–43.

4137. "Regulation of Program Content by the FCC." *Harvard Law Review* 77 (February 1964): 701–16.

4138. "Right of Third Party to Hearing on Petition for Intervention in FCC Proceedings." *Columbia Law Review* 49 (April 1949): 579–82.

4139. Robinson, Glen O. "Federal Communications Commission: An Essay on Regulatory Watchdogs." *Virginia Law Review* 64 (March 1978): 169–262.

4140. Rosenblum, Victor G. "How to Get into TV: The FCC and Miami's Channel 10." In *The Uses of Power*, edited by Alan Westin, pp. 173–228. New York: Harcourt, Brace and World, 1962.

4141. Samet, H. "Computers and Communications: The FCC Dilemma in Determing What to Regulate." *DePaul Law Review* 28 (Fall 1978): 71–103.

4142. Scharfeld, Arthur W. "1955 Report of the Committee on Communications of the Administrative Law Section, American Bar Association." *Federal Communications Bar Journal* 14 (1955): 165–82.

4143. Schement, J. R., and Singleton, L. A. "Onus of Minority Ownership: FCC Policy and Spanish-Language Radio." *Journal of Communication* 31 (Spring 1981): 78–83.

4144. Schilz, Harold L. "New Techniques for Expediting Hearings in FCC Proceedings." *Columbia Law Review* 55 (June 1955): 830–46.

4145. Schuessler, T. L. "FCC Regulation of the Network Television Program Procurement Process: An Attempt to Regulate the Laws of Economics." *Northwestern University Law Review* 73 (May-June 1978): 227–306.

4146. Schuessler, T. L. "Structural Barriers to the Entry of Additional Television Networks: The Federal Communication Commission's Spectrum Management Policies." *Southern California Law Review* 54 (July 1981): 875–1000.

4147. Schwartz, Louis, and Woods, Robert A. "One Year in Life of the Three-Year Rule." *Federal Communications Bar Journal* 19 (1964–1965): 3–12.

4148. "Separation of Functions in the Federal Communications Commission." *South Dakota Law Review* 14 (Spring 1969): 358–75.

4149. Sewell, S. F. "Guide to Public Inspection of Broadcast Station Files and Program Logs." *Federal Communications Law Journal* 32 (Winter 1980): 1–18.

4150. Shapiro, W. "Liberal Plot to Kill God." *Washington Monthly* 7 (October 1975): 21–30.

4151. "Shareholder Control and FCC Regulation of Corporate Broadcast Licensees." *Wisconsin Law Review* 1967 (Summer 1967): 774–80.

4152. Sharp, S. A., and Lively, D. "Can the Broadcaster in the Black Hat Ride Again? 'Good Character' Requirement for Broadcast Licensees." *Federal Communications Law Journal* 32 (Spring 1980): 173–203.

4153. Shoenberger, A. E. "FCC, Cable TV, and Visions of Valhalla: Judicial Scrutiny of Complex Rulemaking and Institutional Competence." *University of Richmond Law Review* 14 (Fall 1979): 113–54.

4154. "Simmon vs. Fowler at FCC Meeting." *Broadcasting* 106 (March 26, 1984): 28–29.

4155. Simmons, S. J. "FCC's Personal Attack and Political Editorial Rules Reconsidered." *University of Pennsylvania Law Review* 125 (May 1977): 990–1022.

4156. Smith, Edward C. "Practice and Procedure before the Federal Communications Commission as Viewed by a Hearing Examiner." *Oklahoma Law Review* 7 (August 1954): 276–84.

4157. Spitzer, M. L. "Multicriteria Choice Processes: An Application of Public Choice Theory to Bakke, the FCC, and the Courts." *Yale Law Journal* 88 (March 1979): 717–79.

4158. Spitzer, M. L. "Radio Formats by Administrative Choice." *University of Chicago Law Review* 47 (Summer 1980): 647–87.

4159. Stambler, Arthur. "The Declaratory Order at the Federal Communications Commission." *Federal Communications Bar Journal* 21 (1967): 123–33.

4160. "Standing to Protest before the FCC." *Columbia Law Review* 55 (February 1955): 209–25.

4161. Stern, L. R. "Evolution of Cable Television Regulation: A Proposal for the Future." *Urban Law Annual* 21 (1981): 179–215.

4162. Stern, R. H. "The Federal Communications Commission and Television: The Regulatory Process in an Environment of Rapid Technical Innovation." Ph.D. dissertation, Harvard University, 1951. 354 p.

4163. Stern, R. H. "Television in the Thirties: Emerging Patterns of Technical Development, Industrial Control and Governmental Concern." *American Journal of Economics and Sociology* 23 (July 1964): 285–301.

4164. Stokes, John M. "The Lack of Discovery in Federal Communications Commission Proceedings—An Exercise in the Denial of Basic Fairness." *George Washington Law Review* 32 (December 1963): 328–64.

4165. Stoodley, B. H. "Bias in Reporting the FCC Investigation." *Public Opinion Quarterly* 24 (Spring 1960): 92–98.

4166. "Storming the AT&T Fortress: Can the FCC Deregulate Competitive Common Carrier Services?" *Federal Communications Law Journal* 32 (Spring 1980): 205–32.

4167. "Struggle to Define Character in FCC License Renewal Decisions: RKO General, Inc. (78 FCC 2d 1)." *Boston College Law Review* 22 (January 1981): 409–37.

4168. "Summary Disposal of Protests to Federal Communications Commission." *Fordham Law Review* 25 (Winter 1956–1957): 777–92.

4169. Swift, Richard F. "Judicial Review of FCC Decisions: 1970–1971." *Federal Communications Bar Journal* 25 (1972): 66–81.

4170. "Telecommunication—Right of Access—Section 312(a) (7) of Federal Communications Act Provides Affirmative Right of Individual Access to Broadcast Time for Federal Political Candidates." *St. Mary's Law Journal* 13 (1982): 692–704.

4171. "Television Programming, Communication Research, and the FCC." *University of Pittsburgh Law Review* 23 (June 1962): 993–1009.

4172. "Television Service and the FCC." *Texas Law Review* 46 (November 1968): 1100–217.

4173. "Testing FCC Fairness Doctrine Inquiry." *Marketing and Media Decisions* 19 (September 1984): 24.

4174. "The Texarkana Agreement as a Model Strategy for Citizen Participation in FCC License Renewals." *Harvard Journal on Legislation* 7 (May 1970): 627–43.

4175. "UHF and the FCC: The Search for a Television Allocations Policy." *University of Florida Law Review* 28 (Winter 1976): 399–438.

4176. "Unleashing Cable TV, Leashing the FCC: Constitutional Limitations on Government Regulation of Pay Television." *Fordham Urban Law Journal* 6 (Spring 1978): 647–65.

4177. "Use of Section 214 of the Communications Act of 1934 to Control Shifts in Corporate Control over Common Carriers." *Catholic University Law Review* 29 (Summer 1980): 891–913.

4178. Wall, T. H. "Program Evaluation by Federal Communications Commission: An Unconstitutional Abridgment of Free Speech?" *Georgetown Law Journal* 40 (November 1951): 1–40.

4179. Warner, H. P. "Administrative Process of the Federal Communications Commission." *Southern California Law Review* 19 (March 1946): 191–243.

4180. Warner, H. P. "Administrative Process of the Federal Communications Commission." *Southern California Law Review* 19 (July 1946): 312–48.

4181. Webbink, Douglas W. "The Budget Priorities of the Federal Communications Commission: A Note." *Federal Communications Bar Journal* 25 (1972): 53–65.

4182. Wheatley, R. B., and Movshin, L. J. "FCC's Computing Devices Rules—A Case Study on the Regulation of the Computer." *Emory Law Journal* 30 (Spring 1981): 513–81.

4183. Wilkinson, G. "Colonialism through the Media." *Indian History* 7 (Summer 1974): 29–32.

4184. Williams, Wenmouth. "Impact of Commissioner Background on FCC Decisions: 1962–1975." *Journal of Broadcasting* 20 (Spring 1976): 239–60.

4185. Willis, John W. "Judicial Review of FCC Decisions, 1965–1966." *Federal Communications Bar Journal* 20 (1966): 169–74.

4186. Willis, John W. "Judicial Review of FCC Decisions, 1966–1967." *Federal Communications Bar Journal* 21 (1967): 111–16.

4187. "The Wire Mire: The FCC and CATV." *Harvard Law Review* 79 (December 1965): 366–90.

4188. Wollert, James A. "Regulatory Decision-Making: The Federal Communications Commission (1966–1975)." Ph.D. dissertation, Michigan State University, 1976. 218 p.

4189. "*WORZ, Inc. v. FCC* (345 F 2d 85)—A New Rule of Procedure in Television Licensing." *University of Pennsylvania Law Review* 114 (April 1966): 939–48.

4190. "*Writers Guild v. FCC* (423 F Supp 1064): Duty of the Networks to Resist Governmental Regulation." *Syracuse Law Review* 28 (Spring 1977): 583–607.

FEDERAL ELECTION COMMISSION

4191. Anderson, J. B. "Campaign Financial Law Balances Money's Influence." *Trial* 13 (April 1977): 35–37.

4192. Baker, Riley. "Negro Voter Registration in Louisiana, 1879–1964." *Louisiana Studies* 4 (Winter 1965): 332–50.

4193. Baran, J. W. "Federal Election Commission: A Guide for Corporate Counsel." *Arizona Law Review* 22 (1980): 519–38.

4194. Bolton, John R. "Government Astride the Political Process—The Federal Election Commission." *Regulation* 2 (July-August 1978): 46–55.

4195. Buchanan, William, and Rowe, Leonard. "Campaign Funds in California: What the Records Reveal." *California Historical Quarterly* 41 (September 1962): 195–210.

4196. Curtis, T. B. "Reflections on Voluntary Compliance under the Federal Election Campaign Act." *Case Western Reserve Law Review* 29 (Summer 1979): 830–55.

4197. Epstein, Edwin M. "An Irony of Electoral Reform." *Regulation* 3 (May-June 1979): 35–41.

4198. "Federal Election Commission, the First Amendment, and Due Process." *Yale Law Journal* 89 (May 1980): 1199–224.

4199. "Federal Election Reform: An Examination of the Constitutionality of the Federal Election Commission." *Notre Dame Lawyer* 51 (February 1976): 451–66.

4200. Lindsay, David S. "The Doctrine of Agency and Publicity in the Regulation of Campaign Finance." Ph.D. dissertation, Florida State University, 1969. 334 p.

4201. Malbin, Michael J. "What Should Be Done About Independent Campaign Expenditures?" *Regulation* 6 (January-February 1982): 41–46.

4202. McDevitt, Roland D. "Congressional Campaign Finance and the Consequences of Its Regulation." Ph.D. dissertation, University of California, Santa Barbara, 1978. 212 p.

4203. Murphy, John G. "Federal Election Commission: A Rebuttal." *Regulation* 2 (September-October 1978): 42–50.

4204. Nelson, Dalmas H., and Hoffman, Paul. "Federal Employees and Voting in Federal Elections." *Western Political Quarterly* 22 (September 1969): 581–93.

4205. Pittman, Russell. "Market Structures and Campaign Contributions." *Public Choice* 31 (Fall 1977): 37–52.

4206. "Reflections on the Election Commission—An Interview with Neil O. Staebler." *Regulation* 3 (March-April 1979): 33–38.

4207. Richards, E. L. "In Search of a Consensus on the Future of Campaign Finance Laws: *California Medical Association v. Federal Election Commission.*" *American Business Law Journal* 20 (Summer 1982): 243–67.

4208. Rosenthal, Albert J. "The Constitution and Campaign Finance Regulation after *Buckley v. Valeo.*" *American Academy of Political and Social Science, Annals* 425 (May 1976): 124–33.

4209. Sarasohn, Stephen B. "The Regulation of Parties and Nominations in Michigan: The Politics of Election Reform." Ph.D. dissertation, Columbia University, 1953. 443 p.

4210. Staats, Elmer B. "Impact of the Federal Election Campaign Act of 1971." *American Academy of Political and Social Science, Annals* 425 (May 1976): 98–113.

FEDERAL ENERGY REGULATORY COMMISSION

4211. Adams, J. R. "Curtailment of Natural Gas Service by the Federal Power Commission: Possible Remedies for Industry." *Louisiana Bar Journal* 24 (March 1977): 267–78.

4212. "Administrative Law—Contract Law—FPC Summary Action in Natural Gas Pipeline Interim Curtailment Practice." *Boston College International and Comparative Law Review* 17 (January 1976): 260–86.

4213. "Administrative Law—The Federal Power Commission Is Not Compelled to Recommend Federal Construction of a Water Power Development Merely because Power from Such a Project Could Be Marketed More Cheaply Due to the Superior Credit Position and Freedom from Taxation of the United States." *Georgetown Law Journal* 45 (Summer 1957): 688–91.

4214. "Administrative Law—Natural Gas Act—Federal Power Commission Held to Have Jurisdiction over Direct Sales of Interstate Gas." *Indiana Law Review* 6 (March 1973): 589–603.

4215. Aitken, H. G. J. "Midwestern Case: Canadian Gas and the Federal Power Commission." *Canadian Journal of Economics* 25 (May 1959): 129–43.

4216. Attwell, J. E. "Federal Energy Regulatory Commission Developments." *Oil and Gas Law and Taxation Institute* (Southwestern Legal Foundation) 32 (1981): 49–82.

4217. Attwell, J. E. "Natural Gas and the Federal Energy Regulatory Commission: Drawbacks of Federal Natural Gas Regulation." *Tulsa Law Journal* 13 (1978): 751–70.

4218. Attwell, J. Evans. "Present Status of FPC Regulation of Natural Gas Producers." *Oil and Gas Law and Taxation Institute* (Southwestern Legal Foundation) 17 (1966): 1–22.

4219. Bagge, Carl E. "Federal Power Commission." *Boston College Industrial and Commercial Law Review* 11 (May 1970): 689–721.

4220. Benton, J. E. "Jurisdiction of the Federal Power Commission and of State Agencies in the Regulation of the Electric Power and Natural Gas Industries." *George Washington Law Review* 14 (December 1945): 53–80.

4221. Bonbright, James C. "Contributions of the Federal Power Commission to the Establishment of the Prudent Investment Doctrine of Ratemaking." *George Washington Law Review* 14 (December 1945): 136–51.

4222. Bragdon, Earl D. "The Federal Power Commission and the Regulation of Natural Gas: A Study in Administrative and Judicial History." Ph.D. dissertation, Indiana University, 1962. 323 p.

4223. Brewer, William A. "The Federal Power Commission and 'The Folklore of Capitalism.'" *American Bar Association Journal* 48 (May 1962): 438–41.

4224. Breyer, Stephen A., and MacAvoy, Paul W. "The Federal Power Commission and the Coordination Problem in the Electrical Power Industry." *Southern California Law Review* 46 (June 1973): 661–712.

4225. "Conservation and the Commission: The Growth of Regulation of the End Use of Natural Gas by the Federal Power Commission." *Environmental Affairs* 3 (1974): 527–62.

4226. "*Consolidated Gas Supply Corp. v. Federal Power Commission*, 520F 2d 1176." *Washburn Law Journal* 15 (1976): 480–84.

4227. "Constitutional Law: Interstate Commerce: Authority of FPC to Control the Use of Natural Gas." *Oklahoma Law Review* 14 (May 1961): 199–202.

4228. Cox, W. E., and Walker, W. R. "Jurisdiction of the Federal Power Commission over Non-Power Water Uses." *Land and Water Law Review* 5 (1970): 65–68.

4229. Davidson, Sidney. "The Plant Accounting Regulations of the Federal Power Commission—A Critical Analysis." Ph.D. dissertation, University of Michigan, 1950. 213 p.

4230. Debevoise, T. M. "Role of the Federal Energy Regulatory Commission in Licensing Small Hydroelectric Projects." *Vermont Law Review* 5 (Fall 1980): 279–93.

4231. Diener, William P. "Producer Rate Regulation—Rulemaking at the Federal Power Commission." *Natural Resources Lawyer* 5 (Summer 1972): 378–88.

4232. "Effect of the Natural Gas Policy Act of 1978 on Administrative Interpretation of Natural Gas Sales Contracts." *Georgetown Law Journal* 69 (October 1980): 133–49.

4233. "Electric Utility Jurisdiction of the Federal Power Commission." *New York University Law Review* 40 (December 1965): 1129–58.

4234. "Expanding Jurisdiction of the Federal Power Commission and the Problem of Federal-State Conflict." *Vanderbilt Law Review* 18 (October 1965): 1847–68.

4235. "Federal Power Commission—Approval of Securities Issue by Public Utility—Duty to Investigate Allegations of Anticompetitive Conduct Raised by Intervenors in a Section 204 Proceeding." *Boston College International and Comparative Law Review* 15 (February 1974): 578–95.

4236. "Federal Power Commission Control over River Basin Development." *Virginia Law Review* 51 (May 1965): 663–85.

4237. "Federal Power Commission—Extention of Jurisdiction over Wholesale Sales—Sales held to Be Jurisdictional If Made by a Member of an Integrated Interstate Power Pool." *Boston University Law Review* 46 (Fall 1966): 552–67.

4238. "Federal Power Commission, Job Bias, and *NAACP v FPC* (96 Sup Ct 1806)." *Akron Law Review* 10 (Winter 1977): 531–56.

4239. "Federal Power Commission: Recent Developments in Regulation of Independent Producers." *Oklahoma Law Review* 27 (Winter 1974): 78–86.

4240. "Federal Power Commission Resolves Conflict between Priority and Preference in Favor of Private Power Producers." *Montana Law Review* 26 (Spring 1965): 246–54.

4241. "Federal Power Commission Silver Anniversary, 1920–1945: A Symposium." *George Washington Law Review* 14 (December 1945): 1–272.

4242. "Federal Power Commission's Noncompliance with the National Environmental Policy Act: Statutory Impossibility and Delegation." *Boston University Law Review* 55 (July 1975): 575–97.

4243. "Federally Enforceable Delivery Obligation—More Uncertainty for Natural Gas Producers." *Houston Law Review* 16 (July 1979): 1171–203.

4244. Fiorino, Daniel J. "Judicial-Administrative Interaction in Regulatory Policy Making: The Case of the Federal Power Commission." *Adminstrative Law Review* 28 (Winter 1976): 41–88.

4245. FitzGerald, John L. "Adoption of Federal Power Commission Pricechanging Rules without Evidentiary Hearing: Statutory Collision." *Southwestern Law Review* 18 (June 1964): 236–71.

4246. Foster, J. Rhoads; Garfield, Paul J.; and Herz, Henry. "FPC Regulation of Sales of Electric Energy at Wholesale." *Virginia Law Review* 51 (January 1965): 76–104.

4247. "FPC and Indefinite Price Escalation Clauses: Remedy for Administrative Breakdown." *Yale Law Journal* 73 (June 1964): 1283.

4248. "FPC Held to Lack Power to Deny Transportation Certificate on Ground That Intended Use of Gas Is Inferior." *Columbia Law Review* 60 (November 1960): 1043–47.

4249. "FPC Must Consider Allegations of a Retail Price Squeeze in Setting Wholesale Rates." *Washington University Law Quarterly* 1977 (Spring 1977): 317–25.

4250. "FPC Order 533 and Natural Gas Shortages—Too Little, Too Late." *University of Toledo Law Review* 7 (Winter 1976): 653–82.

4251. "FPC Regulation of Independent Producers of Natural Gas." *Harvard Law Review* 75 (January 1962): 549–68.

4252. "*FPC v. Louisiana Power and Light Co.* (92 Sup Ct 1827)." *Louisiana Law Review* 33 (Winter 1973): 335–39.

4253. Francis, Charles I. "Area Price Regulation of Gas Producer Rates by the Federal Power Commission." *Dickinson Law Review* 68 (Spring 1964): 237–56.

4254. French, T., and Poland, S. S. "Federal Power Commission Practice." *Practical Lawyer* 2 (October 1956): 77–81.

4255. Gatchell, W. W. "Role of the Federal Power Commission in Regional Development." *Iowa Law Review* 32 (January 1947): 283–95.

4256. Gilbert, W. P. "Decision for Illinois: Natural Gas and the FPC." *Illinois Bar Journal* 43 (April 1955): 666–69.

4257. Gilliam, C. L. "Natural Gas: Congress, the FPC, and the Flickering Flame." *Oil and Gas Law and Taxation Institute* (Southwestern Legal Foundation) 27 (1976): 1–27.

4258. Gooch, G. "FPC Update." *Oil and Gas Law and Taxation Institute* (Southwestern Legal Foundation) 28 (1977): 65–76.

4259. Helms, Robert B. *Natural Gas Regulation; An Evaluation of FPC Price Controls.* Washington, DC: American Enterprise Institute for Public Policy Research, 1974. 83 p.

4260. Hendry, James B. "A Critique of Federal Power Commission Policy with Respect to Cost Allocations for Natural Gas Pipe Lines." Ph.D. dissertation, Columbia University, 1956. 250 p.

4261. Hetherwick, G. L. "FPC Procedure—Handling the 'Normal Case.'" *Institute on Mineral Law* 15 (1968): 152–55.

4262. "Independent Natural Gas Producers, the FPC and the Courts: A Case of Judicial Intermeddling." *Texas Law Review* 53 (May 1975): 784–830.

4263. "Jurisdiction of the Federal Power Commission over Importation of Liquefied Natural Gas." *Natural Resources Lawyer* 4 (April 1971): 276–90.

4264. "Jurisdiction of the Federal Power Commission under the Natural Gas Act—Commingled Gas." *Louisiana Law Review* 24 (April 1964): 600–18.

4265. "Jurisdiction of the FPC over Thermal Electric Power Plants." *William and Mary Law Review* 18 (Summer 1977): 761–86.

4266. Kelly, Thomas C. "The Federal Power Commission and the Regulation of the Natural Gas Industry: A Study in Environmental Inputs." Ph.D. dissertation, University of Maryland, 1964. 300 p.

4267. Kitch, Edmund W. "Regulation of the Field Market for Natural Gas by the Federal Power Commission." *Journal of Law and Economics* 11 (October 1968): 243–80.

4268. Kohler, E. L. "Development of Accounting for Regulatory Purposes by the Federal Power Commission." *George Washington Law Review* 14 (December 1945): 152–73.

4269. Koplin, H. T. "Conservation and Regulation: The Natural Gas Allocation Policy of the Federal Power Commission." *Yale Law Journal* 64 (May 1955): 840–62.

4270. Lea, C. F. "The Federal Power Commission as an Agency of Congress." *George Washington Law Review* 14 (December 1945): 5–8.

4271. "The Legality of FPC Regulation of Independent Gas Producers by Area Price Fixing." *Georgetown Law Journal* 50 (Winter 1961): 250–84.

4272. Lewis, Ben W. "Role of the Federal Power Commission Regarding the Power Features of Federal Projects." *George Washington Law Review* 14 (December 1945): 96–113.

4273. "Liberalized Depreciation: About-Face by the FPC." *Virginia Law Review* 50 (March 1964): 298–336.

4274. Lorne, Simon M. "Natural Gas Pipelines, Peak Load Pricing and the Federal Power Commission." *Duke Law Journal* 1972 (April 1972): 85–113.

4275. MacAvoy, Paul W. "The Formal Work-Product of the Federal Power Commissioners." *Bell Journal of Economics and Management Science* 2 (Spring 1971): 379–95.

4276. Marston, P. M., and Hollis, S. S. "Review and Assessment of the FERC Natural Gas Enforcement Program." *Houston Law Review* 16 (July 1979): 1105–27.

4277. McLauchlan, William P. "Federal Hearing Examiners and the Federal Power Commission." Ph.D. dissertation, University of Wisconsin, 1968. 389 p.

4278. Melody, William H. "Public Utility Regulation: Economic Analysis, Accounting Control, and Federal Power Commission Rate Policy." Ph.D. dissertation, University of Nebraska, 1966. 413 p.

4279. Miller, John C. "Jurisdiction of the Federal Power Commission over the Price of Gas in the Field." Ph.D. dissertation, University of Iowa, 1960. 297 p.

4280. Mogel, W. A. "Federal Power Commission's Authority to Set Area Rates by Rulemaking." *Seton Hall Law Review* 5 (Fall 1973): 31–63.

4281. Moody, R. "FERC Inheritance—Unresolved Problems in Producer Regulation." *Oil and Gas Law and Taxation Institute* 29 (1978): 417–53.

4282. Moore, C. A. "New Trial Program at the Federal Energy Regulatory Commission." *Energy Law Journal* 3 (1982): 337–42.

4283. Morgan, Richard G., and Garrison, C. W. "Enforcement Policies and Procedures of the Federal Energy Regulatory Commission." *Tulsa Law Journal* 15 (Spring 1980): 501–31.

4284. Morris, Everett L. "Earnings of the Electric Utility Industry 1966–1968 Based on Regulatory Accounting Principles Prescribed by the Federal Power Commission Compared with What Would Have Been Reported If Utilities Had Utilized Generally Accepted Accounting Principles Prescribed by the Accounting Principles Board of the American Institute of Certified Public Accountants." D.B.A. dissertation, George Washington University, 1971. 779 p.

4285. Mosburg, Lewis G. "Regulation of the Independent Producer by the Federal Power Commission." *Oklahoma Law Review* 16 (August 1963): 249–88.

4286. Muys, J. C. "Federal Power Commission Allocation of Natural Gas Supply Shortages: Prorationing, Priorities and Perplexity." *Rocky Mountain Mineral Law Institute* 20 (1975): 301–58.

4287. "New Approaches by the FPC to the Regulation of Natural Gas Producers: An Evaluation." *Vanderbilt Law Review* 17 (June 1964): 1200–34.

4288. "Of Birds, Bees, and the FPC." *Yale Law Journal* 77 (November 1967): 117–38.

4289. "*Office of Consumers' Counsel v. FERC*: The Great Plains Gasification Decision." *University of Pittsburgh Law Review* 43 (Fall 1981): 141–67.

4290. Pierce, Richard J. "Producer Regulation under the Natural Gas Policy Act." *Oil and Gas Law and Taxation Institute* (Southwestern Legal Foundation) 31 (1980): 99–129.

4291. "Power versus the Environment: Who Wins and Why? *Hudson River Fishermens Association v. Federal Power Commission* (498 F 2d 827), Latest Chapter in the Storm King Controversy." *New England Law Review* 10 (Spring 1975): 279–303.

4292. "Prudent Operator Standard and FERC Authority." *Texas Law Review* 57 (March 1979): 661–74.

4293. "Public or Private Power—Responsibilities of the FPC." *Indiana Law Journal* 29 (Summer 1954): 560–78.

4294. Rahbany, K. Phillip. "Licensing of Water Power Projects by the Federal Power Commission." Ph.D. dissertation, University of Wisconsin, 1958. 364 p.

4295. "Regulated Industries: Antitrust: Federal Power Commission Required to Give Presumptive Weight to Antitrust Policy." *Law and the Social Order* 1969 (1969): 92–104.

4296. "Regulated Industries—Natural Gas Regulation—The FPC Has Jurisdiction under the Natural Gas Act to Regulate the Curtailment of Natural Gas Deliveries to Direct Sale Consumers." *Georgetown Law Journal* 61 (February 1973): 833–43.

4297. Rhyne, C. S. "Municipal Interest in the Work of the Federal Power Commission." *George Washington Law Review* 14 (December 1945): 247–60.

4298. Riggs, S. H., and Yost, J. S. "Practice and Procedure before the Federal Power Commission." *George Washington Law Review* 14 (December 1945): 114–35.

4299. Ross, C. R. "Landis Report and the Federal Power Commission 1962." *Public Utilities Fortnightly* 70 (September 1962): 449–53.

4300. Ross, William W. "Discovery and Federal Power Commission." *Administrative Law Review* 18 (Winter–Spring 1966): 177–82.

4301. Rotstan, John A. "An Inquiry into the Political Order Underlying the Independent Federal Regulatory Commissions: A Case Study of the Federal Power Commission." Ph.D. dissertation, Claremont Graduate School, 1966. 358 p.

4302. Schapiro, D. "Effects of Federal Power Commission Accounting Orders on Dividend Legality." *Yale Law Journal* 59 (March 1950): 597–621.

4303. Schwartz, C. P. "Federalism and Anadromous Fish: *FPC v. Oregon.*" *George Washington Law Review* 23 (April 1955): 535–47.

4304. Smith, D. S. "Jurisdictional Transfers under the Department of Energy Act." *Oil and Gas Law and Taxation Institute* (Southwestern Legal Foundation) 29 (1978): 375–415.

4305. Smith, Nelson L. "The Federal Power Commission and Pipeline Markets: How Much Competition?" *Columbia Law Review* 68 (April 1968): 664–89.

4306. Steves, Sterling W. "FPC Gas Tariff—Solution to the Rate Change Dilemma of the Independent Producer?" *Southwestern Law Journal* 15 (1961): 46–83.

4307. Stone, O. L. "Federal Power Commission and the Producer of Natural Gas." *Institute on Mineral Law* 8 (1961): 22–25.

4308. Sullivan, John P. "Federal Power Commission Jurisdiction over Commingled Sales of Natural Gas: A Problem in Judicial and Administrative Legislation." *George Washington Law Review* 30 (April 1962): 638–81.

4309. Swidler, Joseph C. "The Federal Power Commission—A Program for the Future." *Antitrust Bulletin* 7 (July–August 1962): 567–81.

4310. Tiano, J. Richard. "Natural Gas Distribution Companies as Explorers: The NOMECO Doctrine." *Detroit College of Law Review* 1977 (Summer 1977): 259–77.

4311. Varner, H. H. "Standards of Due Process in Federal Power Commission Litigation." *Institute on Mineral Law* 10 (1963): 66–68.

4312. Wheat, Carl E. "Administration by the Federal Power Commission of the Certificate Provisions of the Natural Gas Act." *George Washington Law Review* 14 (December 1945): 194–216.

4313. Wheeler, B. K. "The Federal Power Commission as an Agency of Congress." *George Washington Law Review* 14 (December 1945): 1–4.

4314. Wolf, Justin R. "Federal Power Commission Regulation of Independent Natural Gas Producers." *Rocky Mountain Mineral Law Institute* 9 (1964): 191–204.

FEDERAL RESERVE SYSTEM

4315. Abrams, R. K., et al. "Monetary Policy Reaction Functions, Consistent Expectations, and the Burns Era." *Journal of Money, Credit and Banking* 12 (February 1980): 30–42.

4316. Ahearn, Daniel S. "Aspects of Federal Reserve Policy, 1951–1959: Facts and Controversies." Ph.D. dissertation, Columbia University, 1961. 584 p.

4317. Allen, G. "Bankruptcy; The Conspiracy Against the Economy." *American Opinion* 17 (October 1974): 1–8.

4318. Alperstein, Leslie M. "A Reevaluation of the Determinants of Member Bank Borrowing from the Federal Reserve." Ph.D. dissertation, University of Pittsburgh, 1967. 133 p.

4319. Apostolidis, Panayotis, A. "An Investigation of Selected Operating Ratios with Emphasis on Size of Member Banks of the Eleventh Federal Reserve District for the Years 1960–1969." Ph.D. dissertation, University of Arkansas, 1973. 257 p.

4320. Axilrod, S. H., and Lindsey, D. E. "Federal Reserve System Implementation of Monetary Policy: Analytical Foundations of the New Approach." *American Economic Review; Papers and Proceedings* 71 (May 1981): 246–52.

4321. Bach, Christopher L. "Federal Reserve Policy 1955–1958." Ph.D. dissertation, Case Western Reserve University, 1968. 296 p.

4322. Balles, John J. "Federal Reserve Monetary Policy in Transition, 1940–1950." Ph.D. dissertation, Ohio State University, 1952.

4323. Barnett, W. A., ed. "Econometric Modeling and Policy Design at the Federal Reserve." *Journal of Econometrics* 15 (January 1981): 3–173.

4324. Belkora, Abdelhak. "Federal Reserve Policy in the Two Post-Accord Recessions, 1953–54, 1957–58." Ph.D. dissertation, University of Colorado, 1960. 224 p.

4325. Bell, Joe A. "Costs of Regulation in Commercial Banking: The Tenth Federal Reserve District." Ph.D. dissertation, Oklahoma State University, 1980. 93 p.

4326. Benston, George J. "Federal Reserve Membership." In *Current Perspectives in Banking,* 2d ed., edited by Thomas M. Havrilesky and John T. Boorman, pp. 526–45. Arlington Heights, IL: AHM Publishing, 1980.

4327. Bergland, Allan E. "The Response to Monetary Policy in the Eleventh Federal Reserve District 1954–1963." Ph.D. dissertation, University of Arizona, 1967. 168 p.

4328. Billington, Wilbur T. "Income in the Tenth Federal Reserve District: A Study in Economic Development." Ph.D. dissertation, University of Minnesota, 1952. 133 p.

4329. Black, Robert P. "An Analysis of the Impacts of the 1953 and 1954 Reductions in Federal Reserve Member Bank Reserve Requirements." Ph.D. dissertation, University of Virginia, 1955. 360 p.

4330. Bowers, Patricia F. "An Analysis of the Influence of the Federal Reserve Bank of New York upon the Policy Decisions of the Federal Reserve System, 1946–1956." Ph.D. dissertation, New York University, 1965. 314 p.

4331. Brenner, Patricia E. "The Impact of Federal Reserve Regulations on the Eurodollar Market." Ph.D. dissertation, Stanford University, 1974. 164 p.

4332. Brimmer, F., and Sinai, A. "Rational Expectation and the Conduct of Monetary Policy." *American Economic Review; Papers and Proceedings* 71 (May 1981): 259–67.

4333. Broesamle, John J. "The Struggle for Control of the Federal Reserve System, 1914–1917." *Mid-America* 52 (October 1970): 280–97.

4334. Buehler, John E., and Fand, David I. "The Federal Reserve and Monetary Policy." *Michigan Academician* 1 (Spring 1969): 21–36.

4335. Bunting, R. L. "Debt Management Proposal." *Southern Economic Journal* 25 (January 1959): 338–42.

4336. Carson, Deane C. "Federal Reserve Support of Treasury Refunding Operations." Ph.D. dissertation, Clark University, 1956. 196 p.

4337. Clifford, Albert J. "The Independence of the Federal Reserve System." Ph.D. dissertation, University of Pennsylvania, 1961. 371 p.

4338. Cooper, Jack L. "Member Bank Borrowing from the Federal Reserve Bank of Chicago, 1951–1966." Ph.D. dissertation, University of North Carolina at Chapel Hill, 1968. 258 p.

4339. Cooper, Jerome P. *Development of the Monetary Sector. Prediction and Policy Analysis in the FRB-MIT-Penn Model.* Lexington, MA: Lexington Books, 1973. 225 p.

4340. Danne, James D. "The Fifth Federal Reserve District: A Study in Regional Economics." Ph.D. dissertation, Harvard University, 1949. 168 p.

4341. Davidson, Philip H. "The Credit Availability Doctrine—Its Theroretical and Practical Role in Federal Reserve Policy." Ph.D. dissertation, University of Illinois at Urbana-Champaign, 1971. 108 p.

4342. D'Antonio, Louis J. "An Empirical Investigation of the Risk-Return Characteristics of Commercial Banks which Have Left the Federal Reserve System." D. B A. dissertation, University of Colorado at Boulder, 1978. 163 p.

4343. "Deregulation: The Attack on Geographic Barriers." *Economic Review* (Federal Reserve Bank of Atlanta) 66 (February 1981): 17–21.

4344. Diggins, James R. "A Short Term Model of Federal Reserve Behavior in the 1970's." Ph.D. dissertation, Harvard University, 1978.

4345. Dreese, George R. "A Study of the Borrowing Patterns of Eighteen Cleveland Territory, Fourth Federal Reserve District Member Banks over the Period 1961–1965." Ph.D. dissertation, Ohio State University, 1965. 151 p.

4346. Dugger, William M. "Federal Reserve Open-Market Strategy in Transition." Ph.D. dissertation, University of Texas at Austin, 1974. 225 p.

4347. Edgar, Danford M. "A Critique of Federal Reserve-Federal Open Market Committee Activities in the Post-Accord Period 1953–1969." Ph.D. dissertation, University of Oklahoma, 1971.

4348. Eltohamy, Abdel-Moneim Ahmed. "The Burdens/The Benefits of Federal Reserve Membership and the Pricing of Bank Services." Ph.D. dissertation, University of Nebraska, 1981. 185 p.

4349. "Equal Credit Opportunity." *Federal Reserve Bulletin* 63 (February 1977): 101–07.

4350. Fair, R. C. "Sensitivity of Fiscal Policy Efforts to Assumptions about the Behavior of the Federal Reserve." *Econometrica* 46 (September 1978): 1165–79.

4351. Feige, E. L., and McGee, R. "Has the Federal Reserve Shifted from a Policy of Interest Rate Targets to a Policy of Monetary Aggregate Targets?" *Journal of Money, Credit and Banking* 11 (November 1979): 381–404.

4352. Fergusson, Donald A. "A Reconsideration of the Functions and Structures of the Federal Reserve System." Ph.D. dissertation, University of Chicago, 1951.

4353. Ford, W. F., and Tuccillo, J. A. "Monetary Policy Implications of the Hunt Commission Report." *Quarterly Review of Economics and Business* 13 (Autumn 1973): 93–103.

4354. Fulmer, John G. "An Investigation into the Effects of Federal Reserve System Membership on Individual Commercial Banks." Ph.D. dissertation, University of Alabama, 1970. 537 p.

4355. Gagnon, Joseph, and Yokas, Steve. "Recent Developments in Federal and New England Banking Laws." *New England Economic Review* (Federal Reserve Bank of Boston) (January/February 1983): 18–27.

4356. Garcia, Gillian, et al. "The Garn-St. Germain Depository Institutions Act of 1982." *Economic Perspectives* (Federal Reserve Bank of Chicago) 7 (March/April 1983): 3–31.

4357. Gibson, Jo-Anne T. "The Response to Monetary Policy in the Sixth Federal Reserve District, 1960–1969." Ph.D. dissertation, University of Mississippi, 1972. 331 p.

4358. Gilbert, Alton R. "Will the Removal of Regulation Q Raise Mortgage Interest Rates?" *Federal Reserve Bank of St. Louis Review* 63 (December 1981): 3–12.

4359. Glass, Carter. "The Opposition to the Federal Reserve Bank Bill." *Proceedings of the Academy of Political Science* 30 (June 1971): 37–43.

4360. Goldfeld, S. M. "New Monetary Control Procedures." *Journal of Money, Credit and Banking* 14 (February 1982): 148–155.

4361. Gray, H. Peter. "Bank Regulation, Bank Profitability, and Federal Reserve Membership." *National Banking Review* 2 (December 1964): 143–88.

4362. Guenther, Harry P. "Commercial Bank Lending and Investing Behavior during a Period of Restrictive Federal Reserve Monetary Policy." D.B.A. dissertation, Indiana University, 1959. 256 p.

4363. Guffey, Roger, "After Deregulation: The Regulatory Role of the Federal Reserve." *Economic Review* (Federal Reserve Bank of Kansas City) 68 (June 1983): 3–7.

4364. *A Guide to Federal Reserve Regulations.* Dallas, TX: Federal Reserve Bank of Dallas, 1982.

4365. Jaroudi, Jamil A. "Federal Reserve Behavior Revisited." Ph.D. dissertation, Northwestern University, 1981. 391 p.

4366. Havrilesky, T. M., et al. "Tests of the Federal Reserve's Reaction to the State of the Economy: 1964–1974." *Social Science Quarterly* 55 (March 1975): 835–52.

4367. Herman, Edward S. "The Transamerica Case: A Study of the Federal Reserve Board Antitrust Proceedings." Ph.D. dissertation, University of California, Berkeley, 1953.

4368. Hester, D. D. "On the Adequacy of Policy Instruments and Information when the Meaning of Money is Changing." *American Economic Review; Papers and Proceedings* 72 (May 1982): 40–42.

4369. Hubbard, Carl M. "Federal Reserve Membership, Bank Size, and Bank Location: Their Effects on Selected Operating Ratios and Profitability of Texas Commercial Banks." Ph.D. dissertation, Texas Tech University, 1975. 118 p.

4370. Humphrey, Joseph F. "The Role of the Manager of the Federal Reserve System Open Market Account 1951–1961." Ph.D. dissertation, University of Southern California, 1970. 338 p.

4371. "Is the Federal Reserve's Monetary Control Policy Misdirected?" *Journal of Money, Credit and Banking* 14 (February 1982): 119–47.

4372. Johannes, J. M., and Rasche, R. H. "Can the Reserve's Approach to Monetary Control Really Work?" *Journal of Money, Credit and Banking* 13 (August 1981): 298–313.

4373. Johnson, Eldon C. "The Impact of Federal Reserve Membership, Commercial Banking Structures and Bank Size on the Transmission of Monetary Policy." D. B. A. dissertation, University of Colorado at Boulder, 1978. 136 p.

4374. Johnston, Robert D. "An Analysis of the Responsiveness of Classes of Commercial Banks within the Sixth District to Federal Reserve System Monetary Policy Actions: 1962–1971." Ph.D. dissertation, University of Alabama, 1974. 380 p.

4375. Jones, David M. "Member Bank Borrowings from the Federal Reserve: An Analysis." Ph.D. dissertation, University of Pennsylvania, 1969. 179 p.

4376. Kane, E. J. "All for the Best: The Federal Reserve Board's 60th Annual Report." *American Economic Review* 64 (December 1974): 835–50.

4377. Kareken, John H. "Deposit Insurance Reform or Deregulation Is the Cart, Not the Horse." *Federal Reserve Bank of Minneapolis Quarterly Review* 7 (Spring 1983): 1–9.

4378. Kareken, John H. "Deregulating Commercial Banks: The Watchword Should Be Caution." *Federal Reserve Bank of Minneapolis Quarterly Review* 5 (Spring/Summer 1981): 1–5.

4379. Kaufman, George G. "Responses of Selected Commercial Banks to Federal Reserve Policy, 1 January 1957 to 1 April 1959." Ph.D. dissertation, University of Iowa, 1962. 324 p.

4380. Kaufman, George G., et al. "Deregulation of the Financial Sector." *Economic Perspectives* (Federal Reserve Bank of Chicago) 6 (Fall 1982): 26–36.

4381. King, Frank B. "Future Holding Company Lead Banks. Federal Reserve Standards and Record." *Journal of Bank Research* 13 (Summer 1982): 72–79.

4382. King, Frank B., et al. "IRAs in the Southeast: A Laboratory for Deregulation." *Economic Review* (Federal Reserve Bank of Atlanta) 67 (May 1982): 4–12.

4383. Knight, Robert E. "Federal Reserve System Policies and Their Effects on the Banking System." Ph.D. dissertation, Harvard University, 1968.

4384. Konstas, Panos. "From Bills Only to Operation Twist: A Study of Federal Reserve Open Market Operations for the Period 1953–1964." Ph.D. dissertation, Oklahoma State University, 1956. 170 p.

4385. Landes, William J. "Federal Reserve Membership Transition and the Impact upon Bank Systematic Risk." Ph.D. dissertation, University of Cincinnati, 1981. 145 p.

4386. Lawler, T. A. "Federal Reserve Policy Strategy and Interest Rate Seasonality." *Journal of Money, Credit and Banking* 11 (November 1979): 494–99.

4387. Lengyel, Thomas J. "Federal Reserve Even Keel Policy: An Historical and Empirical Analysis. Ph.D. dissertation, Louisiana State University and Agricultural and Mechanical College, 1971. 194 p.

4388. Leroy, S. F. "Monetary Control Lagged under Reserve Accounting." *Southern Economic Journal* 46 (October 1979): 460–70.

4389. Leroy, S. F., and Waud, R. N. "Applications of the Kalman Filter in Short-Run Monetary Control." *International Economic Review* 18 (February 1977): 195–207.

4390. Levine, Jules M. "Federal Reserve Monetary Management and the Linkage Framework for Implementing Monetary Policy." Ph.D. dissertation, Indiana University, 1969.

4391. Lieberman, C. "Note on the Impact of Electronic Funds Transfers on the Effectiveness of Monetary Policy." *Economic Inquiry* 17 (October 1979): 613–17.

4392. Linger, Irving O. "The Role of Clearing under the Federal Reserve System." Ph.D. dissertation, University of Texas at Austin, 1958. 293 p.

4393. Lombra, Raymond E. "Federal Reserve Behavior: Identification, Rationale and Implications." Ph.D. dissertation, Pennsylvania State University, 1971. 120 p.

4394. Mach, Anthony. "The Institutional, Statistical, and Analytical Importance of Federal Reserve Check Collections." Ph.D. dissertation, Boston College, 1967. 215 p.

4395. Markese, John D. "The Even Keel Policy of the Federal Reserve System—Origin, Definition, Implementation, and Import." Ph.D. dissertation, University of Illinois at Urbana-Champaign, 1971. 142 p.

4396. Mayne, Lucille S. "The Effect of Federal Reserve System Membership on the Profitability of Illinois Banks, 1961–1963." Ph.D. dissertation, Northwestern University, 1966. 331 p.

4397. McCalmont, David B. "Redistribution of Gold Reserves among Federal Reserve Banks." Ph.D. dissertation, Johns Hopkins University, 1960.

4398. Mceboy, Raymond H. "The Effects of Federal Reserve Operation, 1929–1936." Ph.D. dissertation, University of Chicago, 1950.

4399. Mckinley, Gordon W. "The Federal Reserve System in the Period of Crisis, 1930–1935." Ph.D. dissertation, Ohio State University, 1949. 214 p.

4400. Mcmahon, Marshall E. "Federal Reserve Behavior 1923–1931." Ph.D. dissertation, Vanderbilt University, 1972.

4401. McMillin, W. D., and Beard, T. R. "Short Run Impact of Fiscal Policy on the Money Supply." *Southern Economic Journal* 47 (July 1980): 122–35.

4402. McNeill, C. R. "Depository Institutions Deregulation and Monetary Control Act of 1980." *Federal Reserve Bulletin* 66 (June 1980): 444–53.

4403. Miller, Lewis C. "The Distribution of Member Bank Reserve among the Twelve Federal Reserve Districts, 1948–1964." Ph.D. dissertation, Yale University, 1967. 122 p.

4404. Morris, Russel D. "An Analysis of Certain Aspects of the Federal Reserve System Payments Mechanism Program." Ph.D. dissertation, Ohio State University, 1973. 188 p.

4405. Nadler, Paul S. "Federal Policy Since the March 1951 Accord." Ph.D. dissertation, New York University, 1958.

4406. Pihera, James A. "A Reaction Function for the Federal Reserve System, 1974–1977." Ph.D. dissertation, Georgia State University, 1979. 235 p.

4407. Poole, Robert W. "Federal Reserve Operating Procedures; A Survey and Evaluation of the Historical Record Since October 1979." *Journal of Money, Credit and Banking* 14 (November 1982): 626–32.

4408. Poole, Robert W. "Making of Monetary Policy: Description and Analysis." *Economic Inquiry* 13 (June 1975): 253–65.

4409. Prinzinger, Joseph M. "The Effect of Membership Status in the Federal Reserve System on Bank Profit: A National Study." Ph.D. dissertation, Georgia State University—College of Business Administration, 1974. 198 p.

4410. Rasking, Leo J. "The Federal Reserve System: An Administrative Agency for Contemporary Monetary Policy?" *George Washington Law Review* 35 (December 1966): 299–317.

4411. Rogalski, R. J., and Vinso, J. D. "Analysis of Monetary Aggregates." *Journal of Money, Credit and Banking* 10 (May 1978): 252–66.

4412. Salley, Charles D. "Concentration in Banking Markets: Regulatory Numerology of Useful Merger Guidelines?" *Federal Reserve Bank of Atlanta, Monthly Review* (November 1972): 186–93.

4413. Salley, Charles D. "A Decade of Holding Company Regulations in Florida." *Federal Reserve Bank of Atlanta, Monthly Review* (July 1970): 90–97.

4414. Sapp, Robert H. "An Examination of the Evidence from Federal Reserve Reaction Functions." Ph.D. dissertation, Duke University, 1980. 164 p.

4415. Schecter, Henry B. "Call for Economic Stability in the Interest of Housing." *Journal of Housing* 37 (January 1980): 20.

4416. Scott, William A. "Banking Reserves under the Federal Reserve Act." *Journal of Political Economy* 22 (April 1914): 332–44.

4417. Shapiro, R. J. "Politics and the Federal Reserve." *Public Interest* 66 (Winter 1982): 119–39.

4418. Sing, Francis P. "Open Market Operations of the Federal Reserve System in the Postwar Period, 1946 through 1959." Ph.D. dissertation, New York University, 1962.

4419. Skaggs, Neil T. "An Analysis of Federal Reserve Behavior: A Public Choice Approach." Ph.D. Dissertation, Duke University, 1980. 174 p.

4420. Sullivan, James J. "Alternative Models of Federal Reserve Behavior." Ph.D. dissertation, Johns Hopkins University, 1968. 161 p.

4421. Taylor, Phillip H. "An Inquiry into the Quantity and Quality of Officer Manpower in the Member Banks of the Eleventh District of the Federal Reserve System Relative to the Needs of These Banks." Ph.D. dissertation, University of Arkansas, 1966. 209 p.

4422. Torto, Raymond G. "An Endogenous Treatment of the Federal Reserve System in a Macro-Econometric Model." Ph.D. dissertation, Boston College, 1969. 166 p.

4423. Towey, Richard E. "Commercial Bank Time Deposits and Some of Their Implications for Federal Reserve Policy." Ph.D. dissertation, University of California at Berkeley, 1967. 318 p.

4424. Treichel, Edward A. "An Explanation of Federal Reserve Behavior: Objectives, Lags and Flexibility." Ph.D. dissertation, University of Iowa, 1976. 272 p.

4425. Trescott, P. B. "Federal Reserve Policy in the Great Contraction: A Counterfactual Assessment." *Explorations in Economic History* 19 (July 1982): 211–20.

4426. United States. Federal Reserve Bank of Boston. *The Regulation of Financial Institutions: Proceedings of a Conference Held at Melvin Village, New Hampshire, October 1979.* Boston: Federal Reserve Bank of Boston, 1980. 263 p.

4427. Upshaw, William F. "Bank Affiliates and Their Regulation." *Monthly Review* (March 1973): 14–19.

4428. Voss, Wellington J. "History of the Department Store Indexes of the Federal Reserve System." Ph.D. dissertation, Catholic University of America, 1952. 40 p.

4429. Walker, Charles E. "Federal Reserve Policy and the Government Security Market." Ph.D. dissertation, University of Pennsylvania, 1955. 306 p.

4430. Wells, John D. "A Measurement of the Relationships of Federal Reserve System Open Market Policies to the Yield Structure of United States Government Securities." Ph.D. dissertation, University of Texas at Austin, 1961. 429 p.

4431. West, Robert C. "The Depository Institutions Deregulation Act of 1980: A Historical Perspective." *Federal Reserve Kansas City Economic Review* 67 (February 1982): 3–13.

4432. Whitbread, Joseph E. "A Test of a Total Reserves Based Open-Market Operations Strategy for the Federal Reserve, 1953–1969." Ph.D. dissertation, Syracuse University, 1973. 186 p.

4433. Whitesell, William E. "The Federal Reserve System's Bills Only Policy." Ph.D. dissertation, University of Texas at Austin, 1963. 396 p.

4434. Wicker, Elmus R. "A Reconsideration of Federal Reserve Policy during the 1920–1921 Depression." *Journal of Economic History* 26 (June 1966): 223–38.

4435. Wood, Oliver G. "The Federal Reserve System's Operation Nudge." Ph.D. dissertation, University of Florida, 1965. 334 p.

4436. Woolley, John T. "Monetarists and the Politics of Monetary Policy." *American Academy of Political and Social Science, Annals* 459 (January 1982): 148–60.

4437. Wouldenberg, Henry W. "The Seasonal Effects of Federal Reserve Policy." Ph.D. dissertation, Michigan State University, 1968. 96 p.

4438. Yang, Jai-Hoon. "The Determinants of Membership in the Federal Reserve System." Ph.D. dissertation, University of California at Los Angeles, 1973. 159 p.

4439. Yantek, Thomas A. "The Federal Reserve System: A Study in Postwar Political Economy." Ph.D. dissertation, State University of New York at Stony Brook, 1982. 213 p.

4440. Yohe, W. P. "Mysterious Career of Walter W. Stewart, Especially 1922-1930." *History of Political Economy* 14 (Winter 1982): 583-607.

4441. Yun, Peter S. "An Investigation of the Attitudes of the Federal Reserve Open Market Committee to Wages and Employment, 1951-1967." Ph.D. dissertation, University of Georgia, 1975. 234 p.

FEDERAL TRADE COMMISSION

4442. Acheson, Eleanor D., and Tauber, Mark. "The Limits of FTC Power to Issue Consumer Protection Orders." *George Washington Law Review* 40 (March 1972): 496-526.

4443. "Ad Substantiation Program: You Can Fool All of the People Some of the Time and Some of the People All of the Time, but Can You Fool the FTC?" *American University Law Review* 30 (Winter 1981): 429-76.

4444. "Administrative Agencies—Federal Trade Commission—Unfair Competition—Advertising—The Federal Trade Commission Has the Power to Order Corrective Advertising in Cases Where the Lingering Effect of Prior Advertising Influences Future Consumer Decision." *University of Cincinnati Law Review* 47 (1978): 129-39.

4445. "Adminstrative Law—Federal Trade Commission—Authority to FTC to Issue Substantive Rules is Upheld." *Tulsa Law Review* 48 (April 1974): 697-703.

4446. "Administrative Law—FTC Denied Substantive Rulemaking Power." *Kansas Law Review* 21 (Winter 1973): 198-211.

4447. "Administrative Law—Judicial Control—Appellate Review of Federal Trade Commission Proceedings." *Michigan Law Review* 57 (June 1959): 1190-214.

4448. "Administrative Law—Magnuson-Moss Warranty—Federal Trade Commission Improvement Act—The FTC Can Obtain Equitable Relief for Deceptive Trade Practices." *Texas Law Review* 53 (May 1975): 831-40.

4449. "Administrative Law—Powers of Agencies—An Order of the Federal Trade Commission Must Have the Concurrence of a Majority of the Full Commission." *Harvard Law Review* 80 (May 1967): 1589-93.

4450. "Administrative Law—Trade Regulation—Federal Trade Commission Authority to Order Corrective Advertising." *Wisconsin Law Review* 1978 (1978): 605-25.

4451. "Advertising, Product Safety, and a Private Right of Action under the Federal Trade Commission Act." *Hofstra Law Review* 2 (Summer 1974): 669-91.

4452. "*American Home Products Corp. v. FTC,* 695 F. 2d 681." *Duquesne Law Review* 22 (Fall 1983): 273-98.

4453. "Analysis of the FTC Line of Business and Corporate Patterns Reports Litigation." *Cleveland State Law Review* 28 (1979): 83-114.

4454. Anderson, Sigurd. "Federal Trade Commission—What Is It and What Does It Do?" *South Dakota Law Review* 4 (Spring 1959): 117-48.

4455. Angel, A. R. "How a FTC Staff Attorney Makes a Record in a FTC Rulemaking Proceeding." *Antitrust Bulletin* 22 (Summer 1977): 327-339.

4456. "Antitrust Law—Investigatory Powers—Federal Trade Commission Has the Right to Obtain Private Copies of Privileged Census Information." *Vanderbilt Law Review* 15 (June 1962): 1009-16.

4457. "Applicability of NEPA's Environmental Impact Statement Requirement of Federal Trade Commission Adjudications." *Albany Law Review* 42 (Spring 1978): 506–21.

4458. Auerbach, Carl A. "Federal Trade Commision: Internal Organization and Procedure." *Minnesota Law Review* 48 (January 1964): 383–522.

4459. "Authority of the Federal Trade Commission to Order Corrective Advertising." *Boston College Law Review* 19 (July 1978): 899–938.

4460. Badal, R. G. "Restrictive State Laws and the Federal Trade Commission." *Administrative Law Review* 29 (Spring 1977): 239–64.

4461. Baker, Eugene R., and Baum, David J. "Section 5 of the Federal Trade Commission Act: A Continuing Process of Redefinition." *Villanova Law Review* 7 (Summer 1962): 517–62.

4462. Banta, Henry M., and Field, H. Robert. "FTC Orders Issued under the Price Discrimination Law: An Evaluation." *Antitrust Law and Economics Review* 3 (Winter 1969–1970): 89–118.

4463. Barton, Edgar E. "Scope of Federal Trade Commission Orders in Price Discrimination Cases." *Business Lawyer* 14 (July 1959): 1053–61.

4464. Baum, Daniel J. "The Consumer and the Federal Trade Commission." *Journal of Urban Law* 44 (Fall 1966): 71–88.

4465. Baum, Daniel J. "The Federal Trade Commission and the War on Poverty." *U.C.L.A. Law Review* 14 (May 1967): 1071–88.

4466. Baum, Daniel J. "Federal Trade Commission Orders under the Robinson-Patman Act." *Administrative Law Review* 16 (Winter–Spring 1964). 89–98.

4467. Baum, Daniel J. "FTC Citizens' Advisory Committee." *Administrative Law Review* 17 (Winter–Spring 1965): 201–05.

4468. Baum, Daniel J. "Program of Enforcement: Comment and Correspondence between Congressman Roush and the Federal Trade Commission." *Administrative Law Review* 16 (Fall 1963): 42–49.

4469. Baum, Daniel J. "Reorganization, Dealy and the Federal Trade Commission." *Administrative Law Review* 15 (Winter–Spring 1963): 92–110.

4470. Bennett, J. P. "Post-Complaint Discovery in Administrative Proceedings: the FTC as a Case Study." *Duke Law Journal* 1975 (May 1975): 329–46.

4471. "*Benrus Watch Co. v. FTC,* 352 F 2d 313." *Syracuse Law Review* 17 (Summer 1966): 792–96.

4472. Berger, Raoul. "Removal of Judicial Functions from Federal Trade Commission to a Trade Court: A Reply to Mr. Kintner." *Michigan Law Review* 59 (December 1960): 199–229.

4473. Berman, J. "New Policy of Federal Trade Commission and Recent Decisions on Trade Regulation." *Commercial Law Journal* 59 (September 1954): 240–44.

4474. Bernacchi, M. D. "Advertising and Its Discretionary Control by the FTC: A Need for Empirically Based Criteria." *Journal of Urban Law* 52 (November 1974): 223–66.

4475. Bernard, K. S. "Handling the 'News': A Proposed Approach for the Federal Trade Commission." *Arizona Law Review* 21 (1979): 1031–48.

4476. Bethell, Tom. "Breakfastgate: The FTC vs. the Cereal Companies." *Policy Review* 16 (Spring 1981): 13–32.

4477. Bickart, D. O. "Civil Penalties under Section 5(m) of the Federal Trade Commission Act." *University of Chicago Law Review* 44 (Summer 1977): 761–803.

4478. "Big Brother's War on Television Advertising: How Extensive is the Regulatory Authority of the Federal Trade Commission?" *Southwestern Law Journal* 33 (June 1979): 683–701.

4479. Bowers, E. W. "Legislative Reform is on the Agenda for FTC, Sec." *Iron Age* 223 (March 1980): 55–57.

4480. Boyer, Barry B. "Funding Public Participation in Agency Proceedings: The Federal Trade Commission Experience." *Georgetown Law Journal* 70 (October 1981): 51–172.

4481. Brandel, Ronald E., and DeLong, J. "FTC Role in Consumer Credit." *Business Law* 33 (February 1978): 965–80.

4482. Brandel, Roland E., and Sodergren, John A. "FTC and Banking: Power without Limit." *ABA Banking Journal* 74 (June 1982): 203–11.

4483. Brennan, Bruce J. "Affirmative Disclosure in Advertising and Control of Packaging Design under the Federal Trade Commission Act." *Business Lawyer* 20 (November 1964): 133–44.

4484. Brin, Royal H. "Jurisdiction of the Federal Trade Commission in the Field of Insurance." *Texas Law Review* 37 (December 1958): 198–206.

4485. Burrus, Bernie R., and Savarese, Ralph J. "Institutional Decision-Making and the Problem of Fairness in FTC Antitrust Enforcement." *Georgetown Law Journal* 53 (Spring 1965): 656–74.

4486. Burrus, Bernie R., and Teter, Harry. "Antitrust: Rulemaking v. Adjudication in the FTC." *Georgetown Law Journal* 54 (Summer 1966): 1106–30.

4487. Campbell, Michael E., and Phears, Harold W. "Federal Trade Commission: Restitution as an FTC Remedy." *George Washington Law Review* 41 (May 1973): 940–50.

4488. Campbell, T. J. "Antitrust Enforcement at the FTC: An Interview." *Antitrust Law and Economics Review* 14 (1982): 91–110.

4489. Carlson, M. B. "Fierce Fight over Deregulation at the Federal Trade Commission." *California Lawyer* 3 (January 1983): 40–43.

4490. Casey, Sharon C. "Franchisors and the FTC: State Regulation and Federal Preemption." *Harvard Journal of Law and Public Policy* 3 (1980): 155–90.

4491. "Civil Penalties and the Federal Trade Commission Improvements Act." *Southwestern Law Journal* 30 (Spring 1976): 454–80.

4492. Clanton, David A. "Antitrust Realities and Directions." *Chicago Bar Record* 62 (March/April 1981): 230–38.

4493. Clanton, D. A. "Trade Associations and the FTC." *Antitrust Bulletin* 22 (Summer 1977): 307–15.

4494. Clarkson, Kenneth W., and Muris, Timothy J. "Constraining the Federal Trade Commission: The Case of Occupational Regulation." *University of Miami Law Review* 35 (November 1980): 77–130.

4495. "Clayton Act—FTC Actions and the Requirements of Section 5." *University of Colorado Law Review* 42 (August 1970): 189–95.

4496. Cohen, Dorothy. "The Federal Trade Commission and the Regulation of Advertising in the Consumer Interest." Ph.D. dissertation, Columbia University, 1967. 239 p.

4497. Cohn, Fletcher G. "Some Practical Aspects of Conducting an Antitrust Hearing before the Federal Trade Commission." *Antitrust Bulletin* 4 (September–October 1959): 665–74.

4498. Collier, C. J. "Report from the Federal Trade Commission." *American Bar Association Antitrust Law Journal* 45 (Spring 1976): 163–68.

4499. "Commercial Speech and the FTC: A Point of Departure from the Traditional First Amendment Analysis Regarding Prior Restraint." *New England Law Review* 16 (1980–1981): 793–829.

4500. Connor, Martin F. "The Defense of Abandonment in Proceedings before the Federal Trade Commission." *Georgetown Law Journal* 49 (Summer 1961): 722–36.

4501. Connor, Martin F. "FTC Procedure Revisions: A Critique." *Villanova Law Review* 7 (Spring 1963): 359–88.

4502. "Constitutional Law—Federal Trade Commission Asserts Jurisdiction over Insurance Advertising in Interstate Commerce." *Notre Dame Lawyer* 32 (March 1957): 319–24.

4503. "Consumer Protection—the Federal Trade Commission's Remedial Power: Commission Efforts. Legislative Developments." *Annual Survey of American Law* 1973/74 (Summer 1974): 701–16.

4504. "Consumer Protection—Remedies of the Federal Trade Commission—Expansion to Include Limitations of Contracts." *Tulane Law Review* 47 (February 1973): 436–46.

4505. Cornfeld, R. S. "New Approach to an Old Remedy: Corrective Advertising and the Federal Trade Commission." *Iowa Law Review* 61 (February 1976): 693–721.

4506. "Corrective Advertising—the Federal Trade Commission's Response to Residual Deception." *Connecticut Law Review* 10 (Summer 1978): 1035–55.

4507. "Corrective Advertising and the FTC: No, Virginia, Wonder Bread Doesn't Help Build Strong Bodies Twelve Ways." *Michigan Law Review* 70 (December 1971): 374–99.

4508. "'Corrective Advertising' Orders of the Federal Trade Commission." *Harvard Law Review* 85 (December 1971): 477–506.

4509. "Court Upholds FTC Order Requiring Advertiser of Baldness Cure to Indicate Product is Ineffective in Most Cases." *Columbia Law Review* 60 (December 1960): 1184–87.

4510. Craswell, R. "Identification of Unfair Acts and Practices by the Federal Trade Commission." *Wisconsin Law Review* 1981 (1981): 107–53.

4511. Crespin, Jack. "A History of the Development of the Consumer Protection Activities of the Federal Trade Commission." Ph.D. dissertation, New York University, 1975. 704 p.

4512. "Critique of the Administrative Conference Report on Federal Trade Commission Rulemaking. Panel Discussion." *American Bar Association Antitrust Law Journal* 48 (1979): 1755–94.

4513. Davidson, K. M., and Doutherty, A. F. "Limitation without Regulation: The FTC's Bureau of Competition Approach to Conglomerage Mergers." *Utah Law Review* 1980 (1980): 95–154.

4514. Davis, Cullom. "The Transformation of the Federal Trade Commission. 1914–1929." *Journal of American History* 49 (December 1962): 437–55.

4515. Davis, George C. "The Federal Trade Commission: Promise and Practice in Regulating Business, 1900–1929." Ph.D. dissertation, University of Illinois, 1969. 295 p.

4516. Davis, George C. "Transformation of the Federal Trade Commission, 1914–1929." *Mississippi Valley Historical Review* 49 (December 1962): 437–55.

4517. "Debate: The Federal Trade Commission under Attack: Should the Commission's Role be Changed?" *American Bar Association Antitrust Law Journal* 49 (August 1980): 1481–97.

4518. "Deceptive Advertising and the Federal Trade Commission: A Perspective." *Pepperdine Law Review* 6 (Spring 1979): 439–83.

4519. "Deceptive Advertising, FTC Fact Finding and the Seventh Amendment." *Fordham Law Review* 43 (March 1975): 606–23.

4520. Decker, R. K. "New Directions for the Federal Trade Commission. Introductory Remarks." *American Bar Association Antitrust Law Journal* 42 (1972–1973): 55–77.

4521. Denger, M. L. "Unfairness Standard and FTC Rulemaking: The Controversy over the Scope of the Commission's Authority." *American Bar Association Antitrust Law Journal* 49 (Summer 1980): 53–108.

4522. Dietrich, Ronald. "The FTC and Regulations Affecting Banks." *Banking Law Journal* 89 (June 1972): 514–23.

4523. Dilks, Russell C. "A Stepchild Gains Small Favor: The FTC and the Meeting Competition Defense under the Robinson-Patman Act." *Business Lawyer* 21 (January 1966): 481–97.

4524. Dixon, Paul R. "FTC in 1966: Some Hopes and Resolutions." *Antitrust Law Symposium* 1966 (1966): 19–33.

4525. Dixon, Paul R. "The Federal Trade Commission in 1961." *Antitrust Law Symposium* 1962 (1962): 16–28.

4526. Dixon, Paul R. "Federal Trade Commission in 1962." *Antitrust Law Symposium* 1963 (1963): 28–39.

4527. Dixon, Paul R. "Federal Trade Commission in 1963." *Antitrust Law Symposium* 1964 (1964): 18–26.

4528. Dixon, Paul R. "The Federal Trade Commission: Its Fact-Finding Responsibilities and Powers." *Marquette Law Review* 46 (Summer 1962): 17–28.

4529. Dixon, Paul R. "Practice and Procedure before the Federal Trade Commission." *New York Law Forum* 9 (March 1963): 31–63.

4530. Dixon, Paul R. "Program Planning at the Federal Trade Commission." *Administrative Law Review* 19 (July 1967): 408–15.

4531. Dixon, Paul R. "Trademarks, the Federal Trade Commission, and the Lanham Act." *Trademark Reporter* 68 (July–August 1978): 463–70.

4532. Dixon, William D. "Federal Trade Commission Advisory Opinions." *Administrative Law Review* 18 (Fall 1965): 65–79.

4533. Dolan, R. J. "How an Association is Investigated and What is the Government Looking for—A Federal Trade Commission Perspective." *Antitrust Bulletin* 22 (Summer 1977): 273–86.

4534. Dole, E. H. "Cost-Benefit Analysis Versus Protecting the Vulnerable: The FTC's Special Interest Groups." *Antitrust Law and Economics Review* 9 (1977): 15–30.

4535. Douglas, George W. "Minority View Claims FTC Deception Policy Statement is a Radical Departure." *Television/Radio Age* 31 (February 20, 1984): 97–98.

4536. "Due Process in FTC Rulemaking." *Arizona State Law Journal* 1979 (1979): 543–62.

4537. Dyer, Thomas M., and Ellis, James B. "The FTC's Claim of Substantive Rule-Making Power: A Study in Opposition." *George Washington Law Review* 41 (December 1972): 330–47.

4538. Easterbrook, Gregg. "Stuck on Baltic Place: Why the Government Loses at Monopoly." *Washington Monthly* 11 (December 1979): 40–48.

4539. Elman, Philip. "Agency Decision-Making: Adjudication by the Federal Trade Commission." *Food Drug Cosmetic Law Journal* 19 (October 1964): 508–12.

4540. Elman, Philip. "The Federal Trade Commission and the Administrative Process." *Antitrust Bulletin* 8 (July–August 1963): 607–16.

4541. Elman, Philip. "Rulemaking Procedures in the FTC's Enforcement of the Merger Law." *Harvard Law Review* 78 (December 1964): 395–92.

4542. Elrod, L. D. "Federal Trade Commission: Deceptive Advertising and the Colgate-Palmolive Company." *Washburn Law Journal* 12 (Winter 1973): 133–50.

4543. "Emerging Issues under the Magnuson-Moss Warranty—Federal Trade Commission Improvement Act. Pt2. FTC Improvement Act." *American Bar Association Antitrust Law Journal* 45 (Spring 1976): 96–129.

4544. Emerling, Carol G. "The FTC Goes to the People." *American Bar Association Journal* 58 (February 1972): 171–74.

4545. "*Encyclopedia Britannica, Inc. v. FTC* (605 F 2d 964)—Beyond a 'Reasonable Remedy'?" *DePaul Law Review* 29 (Spring 1980): 951–71.

4546. England, W. H. "Federal Trade Commission's Corporation Reports." *American Statistical Association Journal* 42 (March 1947): 22–24.

4547. Engman, L. A. "Report from the Federal Trade Commission." *American Bar Association Law Journal* 44 (Spring 1975): 161–68.

4548. Erickson, A. R. "Federal Trade Commission Today: The New Improved Improvements Act." *Hastings Constitutional Law Quarterly* 3 (Summer 1976): 849–78.

4549. Erickson, W. Bruce. "Unfair Trade Practices under Section 5 of the Federal Trade Commission Act—A Statistical Evaluation." *Antitrust Bulletin* 22 (Fall 1977): 643–71.

4550. Everette, Donnie L. "The Federal Trade Commission and Consumer Representation." D.B.A. dissertation, Harvard University, 1978. 159 p.

4551. "Evidence, Federal Trade Commission Hearings: Proponent Must Show Good Cause for Evidence to be Received in Camera." *Minnesota Law Review* 46 (March 1962): 778–85.

4552. "'Extrinsic Misrepresentations' in Advertising under Section 5(a) of the Federal Trade Commission Act." *University of Pennsylvania Law Review* 114 (March 1966): 725–33.

4553. "Federal Trade Commission—Adjudicatory Proceedings—Receipt of Evidence in Camera." *Michigan Law Review* 60 (March 1962): 647–50.

4554. "The Federal Trade Commission and Reform of the Administrative Process." *Columbia Law Review* 62 (April 1962): 671–707.

4555. "The Federal Trade Commission and the Corrective Advertising Order." *University of San Francisco Law Review* 6 (April 1972): 367–85.

4556. "Federal Trade Commission—False Advertising—Corrective Advertising Remedy." *Duquesne Law Review* 16 (1977–1978): 797–812.

4557. "Federal Trade Commission Franchise Disclosure Rule." *John Marshall Law Review* 13 (Spring 1980): 637–77.

4558. "Federal Trade Commission Guides against Deceptive Pricing, 2 Trade Reg. Rep.–7897 (FTC Jan. 8, 1964)." *New York University Law Review* 39 (November 1964): 884–89.

4559. "Federal Trade Commission Improvement Act Section 5(m)(1)(B): Minimum Alterations to Preserve Constitutionality." *Arizona State Law Journal* 1981 (1981): 1020–48.

4560. "Federal Trade Commission Proceedings and Section 5 of the Clayton Act: Application and Implications." *Michigan Law Review* 64 (April 1966): 1156–64.

4561. "The Federal Trade Commission: The New Administration after One Year." *Antitrust Law Journal* 51 (1982): 533–688.

4562. "Federal Trade Commission—Trade Rule on Games of Chance in the Food Retailing and Gasoline Industries—16 C. F. R.—419.1 (1969)." *Ohio State Law Journal* 31 (Summer 1970): 610–17.

4563. "*Federal Trade Commission v. Compagnie De Saint-Gobain-Pont-A-Mousson* (636 F 2d 1300): International Service of Administrative Process." *George Washington Journal of International Law and Economics* 16 (1981): 119–41.

4564. "Federal Trade Commission's Power to Protect Consumers Sued in Inconvenient Forums." *Texas Law Review* 55 (November 1977): 1416–26.

4565. Ferguson, John R., et al. "Consumer Ignorance as a Source of Monopoly Power: FTC Staff Report on Self-Regulation, Standardization, and Product Differentiation." *Antitrust Law and Economics Review* 5 (Winter 1971–1972): 79–102.

4566. "First Amendment Limitations on FTC Corrective Advertising Orders." *Georgetown Law Journal* 66 (August 1978): 1473–513.

4567. "First Amendment Restrictions on the FTC's Regulation of Advertising." *Vanderbilt Law Review* 31 (March 1978): 349–73.

4568. Fischbach, J. T. "Need to Improve Consistency in the Application and Interpretation of Section 337 of the Tariff Act of 1930 and Section 5 of the Federal Trade Commission Act." *Georgia Journal of International and Comparative Law* 8 (Winter 1978): 65–79.

4569. Forman, William H. "The Consumer Advisory Board of New Orleans: A Federal Trade Commission Experiment." *Urban Lawyer* 4 (Fall 1972): 757–64.

4570. Forte, Wesley E. "Food and Drug Administration, Federal Trade Commission and the Deceptive Packaging of Foods." *Food Drug Cosmetic Law Journal* 21 (April-May 1966): 205–25, 248–74.

4571. Fortney, A. P. "Consumer Credit Compliance and the Federal Trade Commission: Sketching the New Directions." *Business Lawyer* 39 (May 1984): 1305–14.

4572. Fox, Edward J. "The Contribution of the Federal Trade Commission to the Public Regulation of Advertising." Ph.D. dissertation, University of California, Berkeley, 1950. 376 p.

4573. Fraizer, C. C. "Federal Trade Commission Jurisdiction?" *Insurance Counsel Journal* 22 (October 1955): 467–71.

4574. "Franchisors and the FTC: State Regulation and Federal Preemption." *Harvard Journal of Law and Public Policy* 3 (1980): 155–90.

4575. "The Freedom of Information Act and the Federal Trade Commission: A Study in Malfeasance." *Harvard Civil Rights Law Review* 4 (Spring 1969): 345–77.

4576. Freer, Robert E. "The Federal Trade Commission—A Study in Survival." *Business Lawyer* 26 (July 1971): 1505–26.

4577. French, John D. "The Federal Trade Commission and the Public Interest." *Minnesota Law Review* 49 (January 1965): 539–52.

4578. "FTC Ad Substantiation Program." *Georgetown Law Journal* 61 (July 1973): 1427–51.

4579. "FTC and Corrective Advertising: Act One." *American Business Law Journal* 17 (Summer 1979): 246–56.

4580. "FTC and 'No-Fault' Monopolies: It's against the Single-firm Variety." *Antitrust Law and Economics Review* 10 (1978): 21–36.

4581. "FTC and the Generic Doctrine: A New RX for Pharmaceutical Trademarks." *Tulsa Law Journal* 15 (1979): 327–47.

4582. "FTC Attempts to Abolish Vicarious Liability Defenses for Deceptive Sales Practices: Strict Liability for Manufacturers?" *Hastings Law Journal* 25 (April 1974): 1142–64.

4583. "FTC Deceptive Advertising Regulation: A Proposal for the Use of Consumer Behavior Research." *Northwestern University Law Review* 76 (February 1982): 946–79.

4584. "FCC Decides against Must-Carry Appeal." *Broadcasting* 109 (August 1985): 28.

4585. "FTC 5 and Robinson-Patman: Unfair Method of Legislation or Fair Method of Administration." *Villanova Law Review* 11 (Fall 1965): 113–24.

4586. "FTC Has Power to Issue Subpoenas in Proceedings to Enforce Section 2 of the Clayton Act (*FTC v. Menzies* 145 F Supp 164)." *Harvard Law Review* 70 (June 1957): 1476–79.

4587. "FTC Holder in Due Course Rule: Neither Creditor Ruination nor Consumer Salvation." *Southwestern Law Journal* 31 (Winter 1977): 1097–123.

4588. "FTC Regulation of Endorsements in Advertising: In the Consumer's Behalf?" *Pepperdine Law Review* 8 (March 1981): 697–745.

4589. "FTC Regulation of Interstate Land Sales." *Houston Law Review* 12 (March 1975): 708–31.

4590. "FTC Regulation of TV Advertising to Children—They Deserve a Break Today." *University of Florida Law Review* 30 (Fall 1978): 946–78.

4591. "FTC Rulemaking: The Standard for Disqualification of a Biased Commissioner." *St. Mary's Law Journal* 12 (1981): 734–53.

4592. "FTC Substantive Rulemaking: An Evaluation of Past Practice and Proposed Legislation." *New York University Law Review* 48 (April 1973): 135–70.

4593. "FTC v. Funeral Industry: Round One." *Lincoln Law Review* 11 (1980): 193–203.

4594. "The FTC's Claim of Substantive Rule-Making Power: A Study in Opposition." *George Washington Law Review* 41 (December 1972): 330–47.

4595. "FTC's Holder-In-Due-Course Rule: An Ineffective Means of Achieving Optimality in the Consumer Credit Market." *UCLA Law Review* 25 (April 1978): 821–61.

4596. "FTC's Newly Recognized Power to Issue Substantive Intra-Agency Rules or Why the Sleeping Beauty of Section 6(g) was Awakened by Court Order." *Loyola University Law Journal* (Chicago) 5 (Winter 1974): 107–39.

4597. Gage, R. J. "Discriminating Use of Information Disclosure Rules by the Federal Trade Commission." *U.C.L.A. Law Review* 26 (June 1979): 1037–83.

4598. Gard, S. W. "Purpose and Promise Unfulfilled: A Different View of Private Enforcement under the Federal Trade Commission Act." *Northwestern University Law Review* 70 (May–June 1975): 274–91.

4599. Gautschi, Frederick H. "Adjudicative Decisions in the Federal Trade Commission." Ph.D. dissertation, University of California, 1978. 256 p.

4600. Gellhorn, Ernest. "Distinguished Alumni Lecture—Regulatory Reform and the Federal Trade Commissions's Antitrust Jurisdiction." *Tennessee Law Review* 49 (Spring 1982): 471–510.

4601. Gellhorn, Ernest. "The New Gibberish at the FTC." *Regulation* 2 (May/June 1978): 37–42.

4602. Gellhorn, Ernest. "Trading Stamps S&H and the FTC's Unfairness Doctrine." *Duke Law Journal* 1983 (November 1983): 903–58.

4603. Gellhorn, Ernest. "The Treatment of Confidential Information by the Federal Trade Commission: Pretrial Practices." *University of Chicago Law Review* 36 (Fall 1968): 113–84.

4604. Gellhorn, Ernest. "The Treatment of Confidential Information by the Federal Trade Commission: The Hearing." *University of Pennsylvania Law Review* 116 (January 1968): 401–34.

4605. Gellhorn, Ernest. "Two's a Crowd: The FTC's Redundant Antitrust Powers." *Regulation* 5 (November–December 1981): 32–42.

4606. Gettleman, Arthur. "Advertising and the Federal Trade Commission." *Antitrust Bulletin* 7 (March–April 1962): 259–71.

4607. *"Gifford-Hill & Co. v. FTC* (Trade Reg Rep—1974 Trade Cas—75,348—D.D.C., Nov. 14, 1974): Does NEPA Apply to Law Enforcement Adjudicatory Functions of an Agency?" *Duke Law Journal* 1975 (August 1975): 743–52.

4608. Glennon, Anthony J. "The Trade Practice Conference Procedure of the Federal Trade Commission, 1935–1956." Ph.D. dissertation, Fordham University, 1959.

4609. Goldberg, Victor P. "Enforcing Resale Price Maintenance: The FTC Investigation of Lenox." *American Business Law Journal* 18 (Summer 1980): 225–58.

4610. Goldberg, Victor P. "Resale Price Maintenance and the FTC: The Magnavox Investigation." *William and Mary Law Review* 23 (Spring 1982): 439–500.

4611. Graves, K., and Hall, B. "Crisis at the FTC." *Human Ecology Forum* 11 (Summer 1980): 28–31.

4612. Gwynne, John W. "The Better Business Bureaus and the Federal Trade Commission." *Antitrust Bulletin* 2 (September-December 1957): 702–10.

4613. Hagen, Willis W. "Ethics, Marketing and the Federal Trade Commision." *American Business Law Journal* 5 (Fall 1967): 171–84.

4614. Hagen, Willis W. "The State of the Collective Liver of the Federal Trade Commissioners." *Marquette Law Review* 47 (Winter 1963–1964): 342–58.

4615. Halverson, James T. "Consumer Credit Regulation by the Federal Trade Commission." *Banking Law Journal* 90 (June 1973): 479–96.

4616. Halverson, James T. "FTC Antitrust Enforcement Policies with Respect to Business Practices in an Inflation and Shortage Economy." *Antitrust Law Symposium* 1975 (1975): 89–109.

4617. Halverson, James T. "Federal Trade Commission's Injunctive Powers under the Alaskan Pipeline Amendments: An Analysis." *Northwestern University Law Review* 69 (January–February 1975): 872–85.

4618. Hammer, S. N. "FTC Knights and Consumer Daze: The Regulation of Deceptive or Unfair Advertising." *Arkansas Law Review* 32 (Fall 1978): 446–69.

4619. Handler, Milton. "The Fiftieth Anniversay of the Federal Trade Commission." *Columbia Law Review* 64 (March 1964): 385–89.

4620. Harkrader, Carleton A. "Fictitious Pricing and the FTC: A New Look at an Old Dodge." *St. John's Law Review* 37 (December 1962): 1–28.

4621. Harris, Brian F. "Shared Monopoly and Antitrust Policy: An Empirical Investigation of the Effects of the Federal Trade Commission's Restructuring Proposals for the Cereal Industry." Ph.D. dissertation, Michigan State University, 1978. 265 p.

4622. Hay, G. A. "The FTC and Pricing: Of Predation and Signaling." *Antitrust Law Journal* 52 (August 1983): 409–17.

4623. Healey, John S. "The Federal Trade Commission Advertising Substantiation Program and Changes in the Content of Advertising in Selected Industries." Ph.D. dissertation, University of California, 1978. 182 p.

4624. Henke, Michael J. "Federal Trade Commission Hearings: Rights of a Non-Party to Protect Its Witnesses and Documents." *American University Law Review* 21 (September 1971): 130–55.

4625. "The History of Section 6 of the Federal Trade Commission Act." *Record* 27 (April 1972): 221–29.

4626. Hobbs, C. O. "Legal Issues in FTC Trade Regulation Rules." *Food Drug Cosmetic Law Journal* 32 (September 1977): 414–22.

4627. Hoffman, J. E. "Participating Effectively in Proceedings at the FTC." *Food Drug Cosmetic Law Journal* 32 (May 1977): 200–15.

4628. Hoge, J. F. "Federal Trade Commission at the Gates." *Michigan State Bar Journal* 29 (December 1950): 13–18, 34.

4629. Howrey, E. F. "Federal Trade Commission: A Revaluation of Its Responsibilities." *American Bar Association Journal* 40 (February 1954): 113–17.

4630. "Insurance—Federal Trade Commission—Regulation by State Where Unfair Trade Practice Originates Does not Oust FTC Jurisdiction under McCarran Act." *Vanderbilt Law Review* 14 (March 1961): 656–62.

4631. "Insurance—Regulation under the McCarran-Ferguson Act—FTC Jurisdiction Not Ousted by a State Statute Purporting to Control Deceptive Advertising Mailed to Other States." *Michigan Law Review* 59 (March 1961): 794–98.

4632. "International Trade: FTC Service of Subpoenae Abroad—FTC Improvements Act of 1980, Pub. L. No. 96-252, 13, 94 Stat. 374, 380 (1980)." *Harvard International Law Journal* 22 (Spring 1981): 458–64.

4633. "Interview with James C. Miller, III, Chairman, Federal Trade Commission." *American Bar Association Antitrust Law Journal* 51 (March/April 1982): 3–21.

4634. "Interview with James C. Miller III, Chairman, Federal Trade Commission." *Antitrust Law Journal* 53 (1984): 5–26.

4635. "Investigatory Powers of the Federal Trade Commission." *Northwestern University Law Review* 53 (March/April 1958): 109–16.

4636. Jaenicke, D. W. "Herbert Croly, Progressive Ideology, and the FTC Act." *Political Science Quarterly* 93 (Fall 1978): 471–493.

4637. Jenkins, John A. "How to End the Endless Delay at the FTC." *Washington Monthly* 8 (June 1976): 42–50.

4638. Johnson, S. Z. "Treatment of Confidential Documents by the Federal Trade Commission." *American Bar Association Antitrust Law Journal* 46 (Winter 1978): 1017–61.

4639. Jones, Mary G. "The Importance of Credit in our Competitive Economy and the Role of the Federal Trade Commission." *New England Law Review* 4 (Spring 1969): 111–19.

4640. "Jurisdiction of the Federal Trade Commission over the Accident and Health Insurance Industry." *Georgetown Law Journal* 45 (Fall 1956): 85–99.

4641. "Jurisdictional Fetter on the FTC." *Yale Law Journal* 76 (July 1967): 1688–700.

4642. "Jurisdictional Overlap between the Federal Trade Commission and the Consumer Product Safety Commission: Toward a Rational Delineation of Regulatory Duties." *George Washington Law Review* 42 (August 1974): 1114–40.

4643. Kamp, A. R. "In Re Borden: The FTC Goes Sour on Trademarks." *Business Lawyer* 35 (January 1980): 501–16.

4644. Kanwit, S. W. "FTC Enforcement Efforts Involving Trade and Professional Associations." *American Bar Association Antitrust Law Journal* 46 (Summer 1977): 640–52.

4645. Kanwit, S. W. "Federal Trade Commission and Insurance Mergers." *Insurance Law Journal* 1980 (Fall 1980): 73–78.

4646. Kaplan, E. "Federal Trade Commission and Equitable Remedies." *American Universities Law Review* 25 (Fall 1975): 173–99.

4647. "*Katharine Gibbs School v. FTC* (612 F 2d 658): Restricting the Federal Trade Commission's Trade Regulation Rulemaking Authority under the Magnuson-Moss Act." *New York University Law Review* 56 (April 1981): 183–205.

4648. Katzman, Robert A. "Federal Trade Commission." In *The Politics of Regulation.* Edited by James Q. Wilson, pp. 152–87. New York: Basic Books, 1980.

4649. Katzman, Robert A. *Regulatory Bureacracy: The Federal Trade Commission and Antitrust Policy.* Cambridge, MA: MIT Press, 1980. 223 p.

4650. Kauper, Thomas E. "Cease and Desist: The History, Effect, and Scope of Clayton Act Orders of the Federal Trade Commission." *Michigan Law Review* 66 (April 1968): 1095–210.

4651. Kauper, Thomas E. "*FTC v. Jantzen* (356 F 2d 253): Blessing, Disaster, or Tempest in a Teapot?" *Michigan Law Review* 64 (June 1966): 1523–50.

4652. Keating, W. J. "FTC Authority to Order Compulsory Trademark Licensing: Is 'Realemon' Really Real Lemon?" *Dickinson Law Review* 85 (Winter 1981): 191–99.

4653. Keating, William T. "Politics, Technology and the Environment." Ph.D. dissertation, 1974. 396 p.

4654. Kestenbaum, L. "Rulemaking beyond APA: Criteria for Trial-Type Procedures and the FTC Improvement Act." *George Washington Law Review* 44 (August 1976): 679–709.

4655. Kintner, Earl W. "Federal Trade Commission in 1960—Apologia Pro Vita Nostra." *Antitrust Law Symposium* 1961 (1961): 21–44.

4656. Kintner, Earl W. "Federal Trade Commission Regulation of Food, Drug and Cosmetic Advertising." *Business Lawyer* 16 (November 1960): 81–97.

4657. Kintner, Earl W. "The Revitalized Federal Trade Commission: A Two-Year Evaluation." *New York University Law Review* 30 (June 1955): 1143–93.

4658. Kintner, Earl W., and Smith, C. "Emergence of the Federal Trade Commission as a Formidable Consumer Protection Agency." *Mercer Law Review* 26 (Spring 1975): 651–88.

4659. Kintner, Earl W.; Smith, C.; and Goldston, D. B. "Effect of the Federal Trade Commission Improvements Act of 1980 on the FTC's Rulemaking and Enforcement Authority." *Washington University Law Quarterly* 58 (1980): 847–59.

4660. Kirkpatrick, M. W. "FTC Rulemaking in Historical Perspective." *American Bar Association Antitrust Law Journal* 48 (August 1979): 1561–69.

4661. Kitch, Edmund W. "Viewpoint: Taxi Reform—The FTC Can Hack It." *Regulation* 8 (May/June 1984): 13–15.

4662. Knapp, S. J. "Commercial Speech, the Federal Trade Commission and the First Amendment." *Memphis State University Law Review* 9 (Fall 1978): 1–56.

4663. Knowlton, Donald. "Jurisdiction of the Federal Trade Commission over Trade Practices in Insurers." *Insurance Law Journal* 1955 (October 1955): 673–78.

4664. Koch, C. H., and Martin, B. "FTC Rulemaking through Negotiation." *North Carolina Law Review* 61 (January 1983): 275–311.

4665. Kruse, L. E. "Deconcentration and Section 5 of the Federal Trade Commission Act." *George Washington Law Review* 46 (January 1978): 200–32.

4666. Lane, E. W. "Schechter and the FTC: A Roving Commission." *Business Lawyer* 39 (November 1983): 153–70.

4667. Lang, J. C. "Legislative History of the Federal Trade Commission Act." *Washburn Law Journal* 13 (Winter 1974): 6–25.

4668. Larsen, Paul. "The Federal Trade Commission, Clayton 7, and Bigness in the Dairy Industry." *Oregon Law Review* 45 (February 1966): 85–113.

4669. LaRue, Paul H. "FTC Expertise: A Legend Examined." *Antitrust Bulletin* 16 (Spring 1971): 1–31.

4670. Lemke, William F. "The Federal Trade Commission's Use of Investigational Subpoenas." *Loyola University Law Journal* (Chicago) 1 (Winter 1970): 15–32.

4671. Lemke, William F. "Souped up Affirmative Disclosure Orders of the Federal Trade Commission." *University of Michigan Journal of Law Reform* 4 (Winter 1970): 180–83.

4672. "The Limits of FTC Power to Issue Consumer Protection Orders." *George Washington Law Review* 40 (March 1972): 496–526.

4673. Long, Thad G. "The Adminstrative Process: Agonizing Reappraisal in the FTC." *George Washington Law Review* 33 (March 1965): 671–91.

4674. Lyons, Erin K. "The Role of Government Regualtion: A Case Study of the Federal Trade Commission." M.A. thesis, University of Louisville, 1982. 85 p.

4675. MacIntyre, A. Everette. "Federal Trade Commission after 50 Years." *Antitrust Law Symposium* 1964 (1964): 61–108.

4676. MacIntyre, A. Everette. "The Federal Trade Commission's Antitrust Function." *U.C.L.A. Law Review* 14 (May 1967): 997–1027.

4677. MacIntyre, A. Everette, and Volhard, Joachim J. "Federal Trade Commission." *Boston College Industrial and Commercial Law Review* 11 (May 1970): 723–83.

4678. MacIntryre, A. Everette, and Volhard, Joachim J. "The Federal Trade Commission and Incipient Unfairness." *George Washington Law Review* 41 (March 1973): 407–45.

4679. MacNee, James M. "The FTC and Trade Association Statistics." *Antitrust Bulletin* 7 (September–October 1962): 753–766.

4680. "Magnuson-Moss Amendments to the Federal Trade Commission Act: Improvements or Broken Promises?" *Iowa Law Review* 61 (October 1975): 222–59.

4681. "Magnuson-Moss Warranty—Federal Trade Commission Improvement Act: Protecting Consumers through Product Warranties." *Washington and Lee Law Review* 33 (Winter 1976): 163–79.

4682. Mahaney, M. C., and Tschoegl, A. E. "Determinants of FTC Antitrust Activity." *Adminstrative Law Review* 35 (Winter 1983): 1–32.

4683. Maher, J. A. "Rule of Law and FTC: Thesis and Antithesis? Some Proposals." *Dickinson Law Review* 86 (Spring 1982): 403–46.

4684. Maher, J. A. "Two Little Words and FTC Goes Local." *Dickinson Law Review* 80 (Winter 1976): 193–217.

4685. "Mail-Order Insurance: The FTC Rides Again." *Maryland Law Review* 24 (Fall 1964): 417–31.

4686. Mancke, R. B. "Petroleum Conspiracy: A Costly Myth." *Public Policy* 22 (Winter 1974): 1–13.

4687. Marble, R. D. "Federal Regulation of Life Insurance by the Federal Trade Commission." *Federation of Insurance Counsel Quarterly* 30 (Summer 1980): 319–34.

4688. Marinelli. A. J. "Federal Trade Commission's Authority to Determine Unfair Practices and Engage in Substantive Rulemaking." *Ohio Northern University Law Review* 2 (1974): 289–98.

4689. Mason, Lowell B. "'A Funny Thing Happened on the Way to the Federal Trade Commission.'" *Antitrust Law Symposium* 1964 (1964): 1–10.

4690. Matteoni, Norman E. "An Antitrust Argument: Whether a Federal Trade Commission Order Is within the Ambit of the Clayton Act's Section 5." *Notre Dame Law* 40 (February 1965): 158–70.

4691. May, John W. "The Federal Trade Commission's Standards of Economic Control." Ph.D. dissertation, University of Pittsburgh, 1948.

4692. McCarthy, J. T. "Trademarks, Antitrust and the Federal Trade Commission." *John Marshall Law Review* 13 (Fall 1979): 151–62.

4693. McKewn, J. "FTC v. Xerox Litigation: Implications for the United States Patent System." *Catholic University Law Review* 24 (Fall 1974): 1–28.

4694. Mead, J. M. "How the FTC Fights Evil Business Practices." *American Federationist* 58 (November 1951): 26–28.

4695. Meyer, L. G. "Some Brief Reflections on Shadows, Mirrors and Revolving Doors: Case Selection at the Federal Trade Commission." *American Bar Association Antitrust Law Journal* 46 (Spring 1977): 575–85.

4696. Mezines, Basil J., and Parker, Lewis F. "Discovery before the Federal Trade Commission." *Administrative Law Review* 18 (Winter–Spring 1966): 55–74.

4697. Millstein, Ira M. "Federal Trade Commission and the Excision of Trademarks." *Trademark Reporter* 55 (October 1965): 805–11.

4698. Minotti, A. M. "Federal Trade Commission Takes Another Look at Dual Distribution under the Robinson-Patman Act." *Texas Bar Journal* 44 (May 1981): 473–74.

4699. "Moog-Niehoff Decision—The FTC and Enforcement for Enforcement's Sake." *Northwestern University Law Review* 53 (September–October 1958): 510–20.

4700. Moore, Charles R. "Regulation of Deceptive Practices by the Federal Trade Commission." *Food Drug Cosmetic Law Journal* 16 (February 1961): 102–15.

4701. Mueller, Charles E. "Access to Corporate Papers under the FTC Act." *University of Kansas Law Review* 11 (October 1962): 77–105.

4702. Mueller, Charles E. "FTC and the Monopoly Problem: Trustbusing a 'Revolutionary' Concept in America?" *Antitrust Law and Economics Review* 7 (1975): 9–24.

4703. Mueller, Charles E. "See No Monopolies, Hear No Critics: The Sad Case of the Federal Trade Commission." *Antitrust Law and Economics Review* 12 (1980): 56–72.

4704. Muris, Timothy J. "Rules without Reason—The Case of the FTC." *Regulation* 6 (September/October 1982): 20–26.

4705. "*National Petroleum Refiners Association v. Federal Trade Commission* (340 F Supp 1343): Authority of FTC to Promulgate Trade Regulation Rules." *South Dakota Law Review* 18 (Winter 1973): 243–50.

4706. Nelson, T. H. "Politicization of FTC Rulemaking." *Connecticut Law Review* 8 (Spring 1976): 413–48.

4707. "The 'New' Federal Trade Commission and the Enforcement of the Antitrust Laws." *Yale Law Journal* 65 (November 1955): 34–85.

4708. Offen, N. H. "How FTC Proposed Rules Affect Trade Associations and Their Members." *Antitrust Bulletin* 22 (Summer 1977): 317–26.

4709. Oleson, R. C. "Consumer Protection: New Hope Following Failure of Civil and Criminal Remedies." *Journal of Criminal Law and Criminology* 66 (September 1975): 271–85.

4710. Oppenheim, S. Chesterfield. "Guides to Harmonizing Section 5 of the Federal Trade Commission Act with the Sherman and Clayton Acts." *Michigan Law Review* 59 (April 1961): 821–54.

4711. Orlans, M. H. "FTC Regulation of FTC Drug and Cosmetics Advertising." *Food Drug Cosmetic Law Journal* 36 (March 1981): 100–05.

4712. Orlans, M. H. "Phase I of the FTC's Food Advertising Rule: Its Scope and Impact." *Food Drug Cosmetic Law Journal* 36 (May 1981): 220–28.

4713. Palmer, Roy C. "Federal Trade Commission Jurisdiction." *Insurance Law Journal* 1964 (February 1964): 69–76.

4714. Parkany, John. "Federal Trade Commission Enforcement of the Robinson-Patman Act, 1946–1952." Ph.D. dissertation, Columbia University, 1955. 312 p.

4715. Pauker, M. "Case for FTC Regulation of Television Advertising Directed toward Children." *Brooklyn Law Review* 46 (Spring 1980): 513–46.

4716. Pearson, Richard N. "Section 5 of the Federal Trade Commission Act as Antitrust: A Comment." *Boston University Law Review* 47 (Winter 1967): 1–19.

4717. Peltzman, Samuel. "Effects of FTC Advertising Regulation." *Journal of Law and Economics* 24 (December 1981): 403–59.

4718. "Permissible Scope of Cease and Desist Orders: Legislation and Adjudication by the FTC." *University of Chicago Law Review* 29 (Summer 1962): 706–27.

4719. Pertschuk, Michael. "Consumer Priorities, Macro-Concentration, and the Scope of the FTC's Deconcentration Authority." *Antitrust Law and Economics Review* 9 (1977): 31–42. 4720.

4720. Pertschuk, Michael. "Report from the Federal Trade Commission." *American Bar Association Antitrust Law Journal* 47 (April 1978): 765–73.

4721. Peterman, J. L. "*Federal Trade Commission v. Brown Shoe Company*." *Journal of Law and Economics* 18 (October 1975): 361–419.

4722. Pfunder, M. R. "Premerger Notification after One Year: An FTC Staff Perspective." *Antitrust Law Journal* 48 (August 1979): 1487–1501.

4723. *"Pillsbury Co. v. FTC,* 354 F 2d 952." *Virginia Law Review* 52 (June 1966): 946–54.

4724. Pitofsky, Robert. "On the Record—New Perceptions at the Federal Trade Commission." *ALI-ABA Course Materials Journal* 3 (February 1979): 6–8.

4725. Pollick, Earl E. "Pre-Complaint Investigations by the Federal Trade Commission." *Antitrust Bulletin* 9 (January–February 1964): 1–26.

4726. Popper, L. M. "New FTC Rulemaking Proceeding: A Guide to Effective Participation." *Law Notes* 12 (Fall 1976): 81–87.

4727. Posner, Richard A. "The Federal Trade Commission." *University of Chicago Law Review* 37 (Fall 1969): 47–89.

4728. "Preservation of Consumer Claims and Defenses: Miller's Tale Tolled by FTC (or is it?)." *Mississippi Law Journal* 47 (September 1976): 768–88.

4729. Pridgen, D., and Preston, I. L. "Enhancing the Flow of Information in the Marketplace: From Caveat Emptor to Virginia Pharmacy and beyond at the Federal Trade Commission." *Georgia Law Review* 15 (Summer 1980): 635–80.

4730. "The Prima Facie Effect of Federal Trade Commission Orders in Clayton Act Treble Damage Actions." *Duke Law Journal* 1970 (April 1970): 351–73.

4731. "Private Enforcement and Rulemaking under the Federal Trade Commission Act: Expansion of FTC Responsibility." *Northwestern University Law Review* 69 (July–August 1974): 462–88.

4732. "A Private Right of Action under Section Five of the Federal Trade Commission Act." *Hastings Law Journal* 22 (May 1971): 1268–88.

4733. "Proposed FTC Regulation of Consumer Financing." *Georgetown Law Journal* 60 (June 1972): 1563–79.

4734. "Proprietary Vocational School Abuses: Can the FTC Cure Them?" *Catholic University Law Review* 24 (Spring 1975): 603–22.

4735. Quinn, James P. "The Responsibilities of the FTC under Public Law 15." *Insurance Law Journal* 1956 (December 1956): 778–800.

4736. Rabkin, Jeremy. "Rulemaking, Bias, and the Dues of Due Process at the FTC." *Regulation* 3 (January/February 1979): 43–47.

4737. Reich, Robert B. "Consumer Protection and the First Amendment: A Dilemma for the FTC?" *Minnesota Law Review* 61 (May 1977): 705–41.

4738. Reilly, John R. "The Role of the Federal Trade Commission." *Food Drug Cosmetic Law Journal* 22 (June 1967): 338–43.

4739. "Restitution for Consumer Fraud under Section Five of the Federal Trade Commission Act." *Valparaiso University Law Review* 10 (Fall 1975): 69–125.

4740. Richards, J. I., and Zakia, R. D. "Pictures: An Advertiser's Expressway through FTC Regulation." *Georgia Law Review* 16 (Fall 1981): 77–134.

4741. Riegel, Q. "FTC in the 1980's: An Analysis of the FTC Improvements Act of 1980." *Antitrust Bulletin* 26 (Fall 1981): 449–86.

4742. Rockefeller, Edwin S., and Wald, Robert L. "Antitrust Enforcement by the Federal Trade Commission and the Department of Justice: A Primer for Small Business." *Dickinson Law Review* 66 (Spring 1962): 251–67.

4743. "Rodale Press, Inc. "Trade Reg Rep (Transfer Binder 1963–65) 16864 (FTC 1964)." *Michigan Law Review* 63 (June 1965): 1499–503.

4744. Roll, D. L. "Dual Enforcement of the Antitrust Laws by the Department of Justice and the FTC: The Liaison Procedure." *Business Law* 31 (July 1976): 2075–85.

4745. Rushefsky, Norman, and Cantor, Herbert I. "FTC Section 5 Powers and the Pfizer-Cyanamid Imbroglio: Where do We Go from Here, or 'You Ain't Seen Nothing Yet.'" *Journal of the Patent Office Society* 51 (July 1969): 414–45.

4746. Ryan, William D. "The Development of the Federal Trade Commission's Authority to Regulate Advertising." Ph.D. dissertation, University of Illinois at Urbana-Champaign, 1968. 304 p.

4747. Scanlon, P. D. "Brand Advertising and the FTC: 'Catching the Seed, Ignoring the Weed.'" *Antitrust Law and Economics Review* 7 (1974–1975): 21–28.

4748. Scanlon, P. D. "Confirmation Hearings on the New FTC Chairman: Some Questions from the 'Review.'" *Antitrust Law and Economics Review* 6 (Winter 1972–1973): 15–42.

4749. Scanlon, P. D. "Measuring the 'Performance' of the FTC: The Wrong Kind of Numbers Game Again." *Antitrust Law and Economics Review* 7 (1974): 15–26.

4750. Scanlon, P. D. "Policy Planning at the FTC: A Commissioner Who Really Believes in It?" *Antitrust Law and Economics Review* 6 (1973): 35–58.

4751. Scher, Irving. "Recent Federal Trade Commission Developments." *Antitrust Law Journal* 46 (Summer 1977): 950–64.

4752. Schoenberg, W. "Basing Point Decision." *American Federationist* 56 (January 1949): 30–32.

4753. Schwartz, T. M. "Regulating Unfair Practices under the FTC Act: The Need for a Legal Standard of Unfairness." *Akron Law Review* 11 (Summer 1977): 1–28.

4754. "Scope of Current Questionnaire Investigations by the Federal Trade Commission." *Notre Dame Lawyer* 37 (March 1962): 379–89.

4755. "Scope of Federal Trade Commission Rulemaking: *Katherine Gibbs School v. FTC* (612 F 2d 658)." *New England Law Review* 16 (1980–1981): 917–77.

4756. Sebert, John A. "Obtaining Monetary Redress for Consumers through Action by the Federal Trade Commission." *Minnesota Law Review* 57 (December 1972): 225–87.

4757. "Section 14 of the Lanham Act—FTC Authority to Challenge Generic Trademarks." *Fordham Law Review* 48 (March 1980): 437–70.

4758. Seidman, Albert G. "What's New—What's on Top at the Federal Trade Commission?" *Food Drug Cosmetic Law Journal* 17 (March 1962): 181–87.

4759. Shipley, D. E. "Generic Trademarks, the FTC and the Lanham Act: Covering the Market with Formica." *William and Mary Law Review* 20 (Fall 1978): 1–32.

4760. Shrug, E. P. "Case against Antitrust 'Planning' at the FTC." *Antitrust Law and Economics Review* 6 (1973): 43–50.

4761. Simon, W. "Case against the Federal Trade Commission." *University of Chicago Law Review* 19 (Winter 1952): 297–338.

4762. Sloan, J. B. "Antitrust: Shared Information between the FTC and the Department of Justice." *Brigham Young University Law Review* 1979 (1979): 883–910.

4763. "Small Business before the Federal Trade Commission." *Yale Law Journal* 75 (January 1966): 487–503.

4764. Smith, J. C. "Practicing Communications Law—The Tangents: The Federal Communications Commission and the Federal Trade Commission." *Adminstrative Law Review* 32 (Summer 1980): 457–76.

4765. Smith, Leonidas C. "Thirty Years of Federal Trade Commission Concern with Broadcast Advertising, 1938–1968." Ph.D. dissertation, Ohio University, 1970. 378 p.

4766. "Some Antitrust Advice for FTC: Go out of Business." *Antitrust Law and Economics Review* 15 (1983): 15–58.

4767. "Standard Setting in Agency Adjudications under the Federal Trade Commission Improvement Act." *George Washington Law Review* 46 (January 1978): 233–50.

4768. "Standards of Disqualification for Federal Trade Commissioners in 'Hybrid' Proceedings." *Washington and Lee Law Review* 37 (Fall 1980): 1359–70.

4769. "State Action Exemption and Antitrust Enforcement under the Federal Trade Commission Act." *Harvard Law Review* 89 (February 1976): 715–51.

4770. Stewart, Joseph, and Cromartie, Jane S. "Partisan Presidential Change and Regulatory Policy: The Case of the FTC and Deceptive Practices Enforcement, 1938–1974." *Presidential Studies Quarterly* 12 (Fall 1982): 568–73.

4771. Stockell, M. L. "Federal Trade Commission and Trademarks." *Trademark Reporter* 54 (July 1964): 500–06.

4772. Stone, Alan. "The FTC and Advertising Regulation." *Public Policy* 21 (Spring 1973): 203–34.

4773. Stouffer, William H. "The Federal Trade Commission and Unfair Competitive Methods." Ph.D. dissertation, University of Virginia, 1926.

4774. "Subpoena Power of FTC in Clayton Act Proceedings Upheld." *Columbia Law Review* 57 (June 1957): 890–93.

4775. "Substantive Rulemaking and the FTC." *Fordham Law Review* 42 (October 1973): 178–96.

4776. "Substantive Rule-Making in the Federal Trade Commission: The Validity of Trade Regulation Rules." *Iowa Law Review* 59 (February 1974): 629–39.

4777. Surrency, Erwin C. "Federal Trade Commission." *Law Library Journal* 51 (February 1958): 28–33.

4778. Swanson, Carl L. "Revolution at the Federal Trade Commission." *American Bar Association Journal* 57 (February 1971): 132–34.

4779. Sweeny, Charles A. "Federal Trade Commission Control of False Advertising of Foods, Drugs and Cosmetics." *Food Drug Cosmetic Law Journal* 12 (October 1957): 606–16.

4780. Tackacs, W. E. "Pressures for Protectionism: An Empirical Analysis." *Economic Inquiry* 19 (October 1981): 687–93.

4781. Thompson, M. J. "Advertising and the FTC: The Role of Information in a Free-Enterprise Economy." *Antitrust Law and Economics Review* 6 (1973): 73–82.

4782. Thompson, M. J. "FTC Strikes Again: Rooting Out 'Low' Prices in the Bread Industry." *Antitrust Law and Economics Review* 7 (1975): 85–96.

4783. Thompson, M. J. "Mergers, Monopolization, and Marketing: The Problem of Priorities at the FTC." *Antitrust Law and Economics Review* 7 (1974): 27–36.

4784. Tifford, J. M. "Federal Trade Commission Trade Regulation Rule on Franchises and Business Opportunity Ventures." *Business Lawyer* 36 (April 1981): 101051–59.

4785. Tollison, Robert D. "Economic Analysis at the FTC: An Interview." *Antitrust Law and Economics Review* 14 (1982): 45–90.

4786. "Trade Regulation—Deceptive Trade Practices—The Federal Trade Commission Act and Recent Oregon Legislation," *Oregon Law Review* 45 (February 1966): 132–39.

4787. "Trade Regulation: The Federal Trade Commission Has the Authority to Order Corrective Advertising to Dispel the Effects of Past Deception." *Catholic University Law Review* 27 (Summer 1978): 803–17.

4788. "Trade Regulation—Use of Registered Mail by Federal Trade Commission to Subpoena Foreign Citizens Abroad Violates International Law." *Vanderbilt Journal of Transnational Law* 14 (Summer 1981): 663–76.

4789. "Trade Rules and Trade Conferences—The FTC and Business Attack Deceptive Practices, Unfair Competition, and Antitrust Violation." *Yale Law Journal* 62 (May 1953): 912–53.

4790. Turk, Peter B. "The Federal Trade Commission Hearings on Modern Advertising Practices: A Continuing Inquiry into Television Advertising." Ph.D. dissertation, University of Wisconsin, 1977. 276 p.

4791. "Unfair Trade Practices—Packers and Stockyards Act—Federal Trade Commission Lacks Jurisdiction over Grocery Chain Owning Meat Packing Plant." *Notre Dame Lawyer* 33 (December 1957): 121–23.

4792. "Unfairness without Deception: Recent Positions of the Federal Trade Commission." *Loyola University Law Journal* (Chicago) 5 (Summer 1974): 537–61.

4793. "*Universal-Rundle Corporation v. FTC,* 352 F 2d 831." *New York University Law Review* 41 (November 1966): 964–69.

4794. "The Use of Section 5 of the Federal Trade Commission Act in Robinson-Patman Enforcement: A Desirable End through Questionable Means." *Duke Law Journal* 1963 (Winter 1963): 145–53.

4795. Vaill, E. E. "Federal Trade Commission: Should It Continue as Both Prosecutor and Judge in Antitrust Proceedings?" *Southwestern University Law Review* 10 (1978): 763–94.

4796. Vanravenswaay, Eileen O. "Professionals in the Regulatory Process: A Study of Staff Attorney Decision Making at the Federal Trade Commission." Ph.D. dissertation, Carnegie-Mellon University, 1980. 489 p.

4797. Verkuil, Paul R. "Preemption of State Law by the Federal Trade Commission." *Duke Law Journal* 1976 (May 1976): 225–47.

4798. Wald, Robert L. "FTC Settlement Procedures." *Litigation* 5 (Spring 1979): 8–11.

4799. Wallace, R. A., and Douglas, P. H. "Antitrust Policies and the New Attack on the Federal Trade Commission." *University of Chicago Law Review* 19 (Summer 1952): 684–723.

4800. Walters, J. "The Federal Trade Commission Warns Associations: We're Not Going to Play Footsie." *Association Management* 36 (January 1984): 53–56.

4801. "*Warner-Lambert Co. v. FTC*: Corrective Advertising Gives Listerine a Taste of Its Own Medicine." *Northwestern University Law Review* 73 (December 1978): 957–79.

4802. "*Warner-Lambert Co. v. FTC*: The Possibilities and Limitations of Corrective Advertising." *New England Law Review* 13 (Fall 1977): 348–68.

4803. Waters, T. J. "How Legal Counsel for a Trade Association Participates in an FTC Rulemaking Preceeding and Protects His Members." *Antitrust Bulletin* 22 (Summer 1977): 341–54.

4804. Weinberger, Caspar W. "Arbitration and the Federal Trade Commission." *Arbitration Journal* 25 (1970): 65–72.

4805. Weinberger, Caspar W. "Federal Trade Commission of the 1970's" *Antitrust Law Journal* 39 (1969–1970): 411–26.

4806. Weinberger, Caspar W. "Federal Trade Commission: Progress and a New Profile." *Case Western Reserve Law Review* 22 (November 1970): 5–10.

4807. Weingast, Barry R. and Moran, Mark J. "Bureaucratic Discretion or Congressional Control? Regulatory Policymaking by the Federal Trade Commission." *Journal of Political Economy* 91 (October 1983): 765–800.

4808. Weingast, Barry R., and Moran, Mark J. "The Myth of Runaway Bureaucracy—The Case of the FTC." *Regulation* 6 (May/June 1982): 33–38.

4809. West, William F. "Judicial Rulemaking Procedures in the FTC: A Case of Their Causes and Effects." *Public Policy* 29 (Spring 1981): 197–218.

4810. West, William F. "Politics of Administrative Rulemaking." *Public Adminstration Review* 42 (September/October 1982): 420–26.

4811. Westen, T. "First Amendment: Barrier or Impetus to FTC Advertising Remedies?" *Brooklyn Law Review* 46 (Spring 1980): 487–512.

4812. White, P. A. "FTC: Wrong Agency for the Job of Adjudication." *American Bar Association Journal* 61 (October 1975): 1242–45.

4813. Whiting, R. A., et al. "Title II of the Magnuson-Moss Warranty—Federal Trade Commission Improvement Act." *American Bar Association Antitrust Law Journal* 44 (1975): 508–33.

4814. Williams, R. L. "Authority of Federal Agencies to Impose Discovery Sanctions: The FTC—A Case in Point." *Georgetown Law Journal* 65 (February 1977): 739–71.

4815. Wilson, Robert D. "Federal Trade Commission Orders and the Clayton Act Section 5: A Reexamination." *Antitrust Bulletin* 12 (Spring 1967): 27–47.

4816. Wilson, Robert D. "Judicial Review of Federal Trade Commission Action: An Analysis of Factors Influencing the Courts." *Antitrust Bulletin* 13 (Winter 1968): 1271–305.

4817. "Yes. FTC, There is a Virginia: The Impact of *Virginia State Board of Pharmacy v. Virginia Citizens Consumer Council, Inc* (96 Sup Ct 1817) on the Federal Trade Commission's Regulation of Misleading Advertising." *Boston University Law Review* 57 (November 1977): 833–63.

4818. Young, J. H. "Federal Trade Commission and the States: The Search for Regulatory Authority." *Federal Bar News and Journal* 38 (Winter 1979): 1–20.

INTERNATIONAL TRADE COMMISSION

4819. "Administering the Revised Antidumping Law: Allocating Power between the ITC and the Court of International Trade." *Virginia Journal of International Law* 22 (Summer 1982): 883–910.

4820. Bergsten, C. F. "U.S. Trade Policy and the World Economy." *Atlantic Community Quarterly* 15 (Winter 1977–1978): 442–49.

4821. Brown, P. "Unfair Methods of Competition in Importation: The Expanded Role of the U.S. International Trade Commission under 337 of the Tariff Act of 1930, as Amended by the Trade Act of 1974." *Business Lawyer* 31 (April 1976): 1627–39.

4822. Brunda, B. B. "Patent Preliminary Injunctions in the International Trade Commission." *Journal of Patent Office Society* 65 (November 1983): 632–47.

4823. Brunsvold, B. G. "Analysis of the United States International Trade Commission as a Forum for Intellectual Property Disputes." *Journal of the Patent Office Society* 60 (August 1978): 505–26.

4824. Dobson, John M. *Two Centuries of Tariffs: The Background and Emergence of the United States International Trade Commission.* Washington, DC: International Trade Commision, 1976. 144 p.

4825. Duval, D. K. "Adjudication under Statutory Time Limits: The ITC Experience." *Adminstrative Law Review* 32 (Fall 1980): 733–47.

4826. Easton, E. R. "Administration of Import Trade Statutes: Possibilities for Harmonizing the Investigative Techniques and Standards of the International Trade Commission." *Georgia Journal of International and Comparative Law* 10 (Winter 1980): 65–84.

4827. "Examination of ITC Determinations on Imports: The Basis for 'Substantial Injury.'" *International Trade Law Journal* 6 (Spring/Summer 1980/81): 242–60.

4828. Foster, F. D. and McDermid, J. F. "U.S. International Trade Commission's 30-day Inquiry under the Anti-dumping Act: Section 201 (c) (2)." *Mercer Law Review* 27 (Spring 1976): 657–80.

4829. Glick, L. A. "Settling Unfair Trade Practice Cases under Section 337 of the Tariff Act of 1930." *Harvard International Law Journal* 21 (Winter 1980): 129–60.

4830. Hemmendinger, N.; Barringer, W. H.; and Kossl, T. L. "Section 337: A Case for Repeal or Change." *Georgia Journal of International and Comparative Law* 8 (Winter 1978): 81–114.

4831. Herrington, W. W. "Unfair Practices in the Import Trade: Proceedings by the United States International Trade Commission under Section 337 of the Tariff Act of 1930." *Journal of Business Law* 1982 (March 1982): 162–68.

4832. "Interpretive History of the Escape Clause under the Trade Act of 1974." *Journal of International Law and Economics* 12 (1978): 531–90.

4833. "ITC Injury Determination in Countervailing Duty Investigations." *Law and Policy in International Business* 15 (1983): 987–1008.

4834. Kaye, H., and Plaia, P. "Developments in Unfair Trade Practices in International Trade: A Review of the Third and Fourth Years under Section 337 as Amended by the Trade Act of 1974." *Journal of the Patent Office Society* 61 (March 1979): 115–82.

4835. Klayman, L. E. "United States International Trade Commission: Co-Equal of the FTC in Regulating Unfair Methods of Competition." *Lawyer of the Americas* 10 (Spring 1978): 1–40.

4836. Leonard, W. E., and Foster, F. D. "Metamorphosis of the U.S. International Trade Commission under the Trade Act of 1974." *Virginia Journal of Internaitonal Law* 16 (Summer 1976): 719–77.

4837. McDermid, J. F. "Trade Act of 1974: Section 337 of the Tariff Act and the Public Interest." *Vanderbilt Journal of Transnational Law* 11 (Summer 1978): 421–80.

4838. Minchew, D. "Expanding Role of the United States International Trade Commission." *Mercer Law Review* 27 (Winter 1976): 429–40.

4839. Minchew, D., and Webster, R. D. "Regulating Unfair Practices in International Trade: The Role of the United States International Trade Commission." *Georgia Journal of International and Comparative Law* 8 (Winter 1978): 27–45.

4840. "Remedying Unfair Trade Practices in Imports: A Study of the International Trade Commission." *Boston University International Law Journal* 2 (Spring 1983): 133–54.

4841. "Revitalization of Section 337 of the Tariff Act of 1930 under the Trade Act of 1974." *Journal of International Law and Economics* 11 (1976): 167–200.

4842. "Section 337: An Activist ITC." *Law and Policy in International Business* 14 (1982): 905–26.

4843. "Trade Law—Notice and Opportunity to Be Heard in a 'Good Cause' Determination Proceeding under Section 201 (e) of the Trade Act of 1974 Are Not Required by the Provisions of the Act Itself or by Constitutional Due Process." *Georgia Journal of International and Comparative Law* 9 (Fall 1979): 654–66.

4844. "Trends in Antidumpting Decisions: The ITC's Use of Certain Economic Indicators." *International Trade Law Journal* 4 (Summer 1979): 230–42.

INTERSTATE COMMERCE COMMISSION

4845. "Administrative Law—Carriers—The Interstate Commerce Commission's Authority to Approve Tolerance Regulations—Their Effectiveness." *North Carolina Law Review* 34 (June 1956): 482–92.

4846. "Administrative Law—Interstate Commerce Commission Failed to Show Rational Basis for General Finding that Carriers of Recyclable Waste Products Serve the Public Convenience and Necessity." *Texas Law Review* 53 (March 1975): 539–51.

4847. "Administrative Law—Powers of Agencies—The Interstate Commerce Commission and Discontinuance of Railroads under the Transportation Act of 1958." *Michigan Law Review* 57 (June 1959): 1258–60.

4848. Aitchison, C. B. "Call for Cooperation in Simplifying and Winnowing Evidence." *I.C.C. Practitioners' Journal* 16 (April 1949): 625–30.

4849. Aldredge, J. H. "Interstate Commerce Commission and Its Work." *Alabama Law* 12 (July 1951): 264–70.

4850. Alexis, Marcus, and Moore, Thomas G. "The Applied Theory of Regulation, Political Economy at the Interstate Commerce Commission." *Public Choice* 39 (1982): 5–32.

4851. Allen, B. J. "Nature, Effectiveness, and Importance of Motor Common Carrier Service Obligations." *American Economic Review; Papers and Proceedings* 71 (May 1981): 110–15.

4852. Allen, Gary. "Railroads: from Regulation to Takeover." *American Opinion* 17 (April 1974): 49–51.

4853. Allen, W. B. "ICC Behavior on Rail Abandonments." *I.C.C. Practitioners' Journal* 41 (July–August 1974): 553–73.

4854. Altazan, John E. "Economic Aspects of Restriction of Entry into the Motor Carrier Industry with Special Reference to Interstate Commerce Commission Policy." Ph.D. dissertation, University of Illinois, 1954. 295 p.

4855. Ames, H. C. "Can We Improve Present Procedure before Commission's Board of Suspension?" *I.C.C. Practitioners' Journal* 18 (November 1950): 107–08.

4856. Ames, H. C. "The Gwynne Bill. H. R. 2657." *I.C.C. Practitioners' Journal* 15 (March 1948): 443–65.

4857. Ames, H. C. "Is the Interstate Commerce Commission to Lose Control over Its Personnel and Procedure?" *I.C.C. Practitioners' Journal* 12 (February 1945): 445–49.

4858. Anderson, Eugene D. "Extra-Territorial Jurisdiction and the Interstate Commerce Commission." *I.C.C. Practitioners' Journal* 30 (February 1963): 569–80.

4859. Annable, J. E. "ICC, the IBT, and the Cartelization of the American Trucking Industry." *Quarterly Review of Economics and Business* 13 (Summer 1973): 33–47.

4860. "Antitrust and Motor Carriers: ICC Use of Clayton Act Section 7 to Prevent an Involuntary Takeover." *Transportation Law Journal* 8 (1976): 273–91.

4861. Arnburg, David, and Eule, Norman L. "Interstate Commerce Commission: The ICC and the NEPA." *George Washington Law Review* 41 (May 1973): 824–40.

4862. Arpaia, Anthony F. "Brass Tacks of the ICC Administrative Problem." *Public Utilities Fortnightly* 65 (March 1960): 433–42.

4863. Arpaia, Anthony F. "The Common Problems of Common Carriers." *I.C.C. Practitioners' Journal* 24 (October 1956): 14–21.

4864. Arpaia, Anthony F. "Criticism of the Commission and Its Work; Address." *I.C.C. Practitioners' Journal* 20 (December 1952): 203–08.

4865. Arpaia, Anthony F. "A Screened Assault on the Independence of the Interstate Commerce Commission." *I.C.C. Practitioners' Journal* 23 (October 1955): 4–10.

4866. Axelrod, Bernard. "Railroad Regulation in Transition, 1897–1905: Walker D. Hines of the Railroads vs. Charles A. Prouty of the ICC." Ph.D. dissertation, Washington University, 1975. 310 p.

4867. Baker, D. W., and Greene, R. A. "Commercial Zones and Terminal Areas: History, Development, Expansion, Deregulation." *Transportation Law Journal* 171 (1978): 171–200.

4868. Barke, Richard P. "Economic and Political Determinants of Regulatory Decisions: The Interstate Commerce Commission and Railroad Abandonments." Ph.D. dissertation, University of Rochester, 1980. 247 p.

4869. Barnard G. M. "Administrative Agencies—The Interstate Commerce Commission." *I.C.C. Practitioners' Journal* 13 (May 1946): 732–34.

4870. Barrett, C. "Public Interest and the Adversary System." *I.C.C. Practitioners' Journal* 42 (November–December 1974): 42–52.

4871. Barrett, C. "Regulation—The Wind of Change." *I.C.C. Practitioners' Journal* 42 (July–August 1975): 560–71.

4872. Bishop, David W. "Railroad Decisions of the Interstate Commerce Commission, 1887–1950: Their Guiding Principles." Ph.D. dissertation, Catholic University of America, 1962. 193 p.

4873. Blaine, J. C. D. "The Role of the ICC in the Administration of the National Transportation Policy." *North Carolina Law Review* 44 (February 1966): 357–79.

4874. Bleakney, Robert G. "The Interstate Commerce Commission." *Boston College Industrial and Commercial Law Review* 11 (May 1970): 785–803.

4875. Blum, Walter J. "The Interstate Commerce Commission as Lawmaker: The Development of Standards for Modification of Railroad Securities." *University of Chicago Law Review* 27 (Summer 1960): 603–60.

4876. Bober, G. M. "Elimination of Gateways in Section 5(2) and 212(b) Proceedings." *Transportation Law Journal* 9 (1977): 257–71.

4877. Boyer, K. D. "Equalizing Discrimination and Cartel Pricing in Transport Rate Regulation." *Journal of Political Economy* 89 (April 1981): 270–86.

4878. Brook, Elizabeth C. "The Struggle for the Adoption of the Interstate Commerce Commission, 1872–1877." Ph.D. dissertation, University of Chicago, 1925. 1923 p.

4879. Brown, Corman E. "The Interstate Commerce Commission and Monopoly—A Study of the Commission's Powers and Duties in the Antitrust Field." *I.C.C. Practitioners' Journal* 29 (February 1962): 596–604.

4880. Bunting, James W. "The Distance Principle in Railroad Rate Making (An Evaluation Based upon Studies and Findings of the Interstate Commerce Commission)." Ph.D. dissertation, University of Pennsylvania, 1946. 259 p.

4881. Bush, William L. "The Year in Review." *I.C.C. Practitioners' Journal* 32 (June 1965): 764–70.

4882. Chandler, George M. "Convenience and Necessity: Motor Carrier Licensing by the Interstate Commerce Commission." *Ohio State Law Journal* 28 (Summer 1967): 379–401.

4883. Cimokowski, Edwin W. "Government Transportation Audit before and after Amendment of Section 16(3) of I.C.C. Act and Related Provisions of Law." *I.C.C. Practitioners' Journal* 27 (February 1960): 473–84.

4884. Clark, Jere W. "Commodity Flow Interconnections within the United States as Reflected in the Carload Waybill Analyses of the Interstate Commerce Commission 1949–1950." Ph.D. dissertation, University of Virginia, 1953. 165 p.

4885. Clarke, Owen. "The Relationship between the Interstate Commerce Commission and Congress." *I.C.C. Practitioners' Journal* 24 (June 1957): 988–94.

4886. Conant, Michael. "The Administrative Conference of the United States: Recommendations for the Interstate Commerce Commission." *ICC Practitioners' Journal* 31 (June 1964): 993–1003.

4887. Corber, Robert J. "Regulatory Reform—Seeking the Least Circuitous Route to the Public Interest." *I.C.C. Practitioners' Journal* 42 (July–August 1975): 600–05.

4888. Corsi, T. M. "Policy of the ICC in Trucking Merger, Control, and Acquisition of Certificate Cases, 1965–1972." *I.C.C. Practitioners' Journal* 43 (November–December 1975): 24–38.

4889. Costello, C. D. "Unity through Diversity: An Historical Perspective of the Association of ICC Practitioners." *I.C.C. Practitioners' Journal* 49 (November/December 1981): 51–75.

4890. Curry, R. G. "Bills in Congress Sponsored by American Bar Association Seek to Prevent Nonlawyers from Practicing before the Interstate Commerce Commission." *I.C.C. Practitioners' Journal* 14 (March 1947): 491–507.

4891. Curry, R. G. "Looking Forward with the Interstate Commerce Commission." *I.C.C. Practitioner's Journal* 12 (September 1945): 1113–16.

4892. Curry, R. G. "Proposed Legislation Imperils Long Established and Highly Important Statutory Procedure for Review of I.C.C." *I.C.C. Practitioners' Journal* 14 (February 1947): 380–400.

4893. Curry, R. G. "Serious Disability of Interstate Commerce Commission in Shortage of Stenographic Services." *I.C.C. Practitioners' Journal* 14 (December 1946): 228–29.

4894. Davis, G. M., and Dillard, J. E. "Growth and Structural Changes in Class One Motor Carriers: An Empirical Analysis." *I.C.C. Practitioners' Journal* 48 (July/August 1981): 543–59.

4895. "Discriminatory Freight Rates; Implications of the Interstate Commerce Commission's Regulatory Powers." *University of Chicago Law Review* 15 (Autumn 1947): 177–88.

4896. Dixon, Robert G. "Civil Rights in Transportation and the ICC." *George Washington Law Review* 31 (October 1962): 198–241.

4897. Eads, George C. "Railroad Diversification: Where Lies the Public Interest?" *Bell Journal of Economics and Management Science* 5 (Autumn 1974): 595–613.

4898. Eckhardt, R. C. "Market Dominance in the Staggers Act." *I.C.C. Practitioners' Journal* 48 (September/October 1981): 662–86.

4899. Emmons, O. N. "Inside I.C.C." *I.C.C. Practitioners' Journal* 20 (May 1953): 729–34.

4900. "Environmental Law: NEPA and ICC Rate Suspensions." *Wisconsin Law Review* 1974 (1974): 600–12.

4901. Erenbert, M., and Kasson, B. M. "Case-In-Chief: Reform as yet Unfulfilled." *Transportation Law Journal* 9 (1977): 37–52.

4902. Falk, M. J., and Chais, R. I. "Applicability of Section 1 (18) of the Interstate Commerce Act to Rail Line Construction in Western Coal Regions." *I.C.C. Practitioners' Journal* 45 (January–February 1978): 175–94.

4903. "Federal Supervision of Railroad Passenger Service: The Sunset Case, Dawn of a New Era or Monument to the Old?" *Duke Law Journal* 1970 (June 1970): 529–71.

4904. Fine, J. "Presumptions in Motor Carrier Cases before the Interstate Commerce Commission." *I.C.C. Practitioners' Journal* 20 (September 1953): 950–56.

4905. Fishwick, John P. "The ICC's Regulation of Rail-Motor Competition: A Study in Administrative Lag." *Virginia Law Review* 41 (June 1955): 559–80.

4906. Flood, Kenneth U. "Research in Transportation Sources and Procedure." *I.C.C. Practitioners' Journal* 27 (March 1960): 7–46.

4907. Fort, J. C. "Who May Maintain Suits to Set Aside Orders of the Interstate Commerce Commission." *I.C.C. Practitioners' Journal* 12 (May 1945): 792–809.

4908. "Forum on I.C.C. Practice and Procedure." *I.C.C. Practitioners' Journal* 22 (June 1955): 866–84.

4909. Frankfurter, Felix. "Remarks on Occassion of Exercises in Observance of the 75th Anniversary of the Interstate Commerce Commission." *I.C.C. Practitioners' Journal* 30 (November 1962): 153–59.

4910. Franzen, D. E. "Enforcing a Cartel: A Study of the ICC and the Motor Carrier Industry." *Southwestern University Law Review* 11 (1979): 597–639.

4911. Freas, Howard G. "Interstate Commerce Commission: Organization of Divisions and Boards and Assignment of Work, Business and Functions." *I.C.C. Practitioners' Journal* 25 (March 1958): 1–23.

4912. Freas, Howard G. "Ratemaking Powers of the Interstate Commerce Commission." *George Washington Law Review* 31 (October 1962): 54–84.

4913. Freas, Howard G. "Revised Qualifications Standards for Admission to Pracrtice of Non-Lawyers." *I.C.C. Practitioners' Journal* 22 (February 1955): 404–09.

4914. Freas, Howard G. "Statement before the Special Subcommittee on Legislative and Foreign Commerce, House of Representatives." *I.C.C. Practitioners' Journal* 25 (February 1958): 500–12.

4915. Frew, James R. "Existence of Monopoly Profits in the Motor Carrier Industry." *Journal of Law and Economics* 24 (October 1981): 289–315.

4916. "Functions and Activities of the Interstate Commerce Commission." *I.C.C. Practitioners' Journal* 24 (March 1957): 591–609.

4917. Garson, H. Neil. "Remarks." *I.C.C. Practitioners' Journal* 35 (September–October 1968): 945–51.

4918. Ginnane, Robert W. "The Work of the General Counsel's Office." *I.C.C. Practitioners' Journal* 23 (June 1956): 880–84.

4919. Goff, Abe M. "The Role of the Interstate Commerce Commission as to Developments in Transportation." *I.C.C. Practitioners' Journal* 31 (May 1964): 887–92.

4920. Guandolo. J. "Role of the Interstate Commerce Commission in the 1980's." *American Economic Review; Papers and Proceedings* 71 (May 1981): 116–21.

4921. Guelzo, Carl M. "The Interstate Commerce Commission and Common Sense." *I.C.C. Practitioners' Journal* 25 (January 1958): 388–94.

4922. Harbeson, Robert W. "Transport Regulation: A Centennial Evaluation." *ICC Practitioners' Journal* 39 (July/August 1972): 628–37.

4923. Harmon, George M. "The Interstate Commerce Act and Pipe Line Consent Decree as Public Policy Devices for Regulating Oil Pipe Lines: A Study of Business Administration in a Particular Situation as it was Affected by Government Policy and Action." D.B.A. dissertation, Harvard University, 1963. 460 p.

4924. "Hearings on Bills Relating to Review of Interstate Commerce Commission Decisions: The Maris Bill." *I.C.C. Practitioners' Journal* 14 (March 1947): 541–68.

4925. Hillyer, C. R. "An Independent Commission." *I.C.C. Practitioners' Journal* 15 (April 1948): 584–601.

4926. Hillyer, C. R. "Power of the Interstate Commerce Commission to Require Railroads to Shorthaul Themselves." *I.C.C. Practitioners' Journal* 13 (April 1946): 595–601.

4927. Hillyer, F. C.; McFarland, W.; and Hillyer, C. R. "A Manual of Practice and Procedure before the Interstate Commerce Commission." *I.C.C. Practitioners' Journal* 12 (January 1945): 273–350.

4928. Hilton, George W. "The Consistency of the Interstate Commerce Act." *Journal of Law and Economics* 9 (October 1966): 87–113.

4929. Hilton, George W. "The Hosner Report: A Decennial Evaluation." *I.C.C. Practitioners' Journal* 36 (March–April 1969): 1470–86.

4930. Hitchcock, C. F. "Regulatory Reform in the Intercity Bus Industry." *University of Michigan Journal of Law Reform* 15 (Fall 1981): 1–44.

4931. Hoogenboom, Ari, and Hoogenboom, Olive. *A History of the ICC: From Panacea to Palliative.* New York: Norton, 1976. 207 p.

4932. "House Judiciary Committee Reports Bills Changing Method of Review of I.C.C. Orders and Establishing Uniform Procedure for Convening Special District Courts." *I.C.C. Practitioners' Journal* 15 (April 1948): 533–55.

4933. Huntington, Samuel P. "Marasmus of the ICC: The Commission, the Railroads, and the Public Interest." *Yale Law Journal* 61 (April 1952): 467–509.

4934. Huntington, Samuel P.; Williams, G. Dickerman; and Morgan, Charles S. "The ICC Re-Examined: A Colloquy." *Yale Law Journal* 63 (1953): 44–63.

4935. Hutchinson, Everett. "Assistance Available to Practitioners and the Public." *I.C.C. Practitioners' Journal* 27 (October 1959): 32–35.

4936. Hutchinson, Everett. "ICC Organization and Procedure." *George Washington Law Review* 31 (October 1962): 29–36.

4937. Hutchinson, Everett. "Improving Commission Organization and Procedure—Some New Developments." *I.C.C. Practitioners' Journal* 32 (December 1964): 134–38.

4938. Hutchinson, Everett. "Time Element in Commission Procedure." *I.C.C. Practitioners' Journal* 24 (June 1957): 1000–03.

4939. "ICC Jurisdiction of Great Lakes Rail-Water Competition." *Cleveland State Law Review* 19 (May 1970): 407–19.

4940. "ICC Regulation: The Economics of Motor Carriage." *Stanford Law Review* 19 (November 1966): 217–31.

4941. "ICC's Power to Replace SEC in Regulating Securities Issues of Holding Company Upheld." *Columbia Law Review* 58 (January 1958): 115–18.

4942. "Impact of Proposed Administrative Code upon Interstate Commerce Commission, Its Practice and Its Practitioners." *I.C.C. Practitioners' Journal* 23 (November 1955): 1–14.

4943. "Initial Rate Filings for Common Carrier Pipelines—An Exercise in Sisyphean Labor." *Houston Law Review* 15 (January 1978): 331–55.

4944. "International Freight—Railroads—Interstate Commerce Commission Has Power to Regulate Joint Through Rate of United States and Canadian Carriers." *Texas International Law Forum* 3 (Summer 1967): 393–401.

4945. "Interstate Commerce Commission." *I.C.C. Practitioners' Journal* 24 (November 1956): 1–16.

4946. "Interstate Commerce Commission and the Motor Carrier Industry—Examining the Trend toward Deregulation." *Utah Law Review* 1975 (Fall 1975): 709–25.

4947. "The Interstate Commerce Commission Documents and Records Its Major Inservice Training Courses, Conducted Particularly for the Benefit of Its Examiners." *I.C.C. Practitioners' Journal* 14 (April 1947): 630–36.

4948. "Interstate Commerce Commission, Organization Division and Assignment of Work, Business and Functions of the Interstate Commerce Commission under the Reorganization Effective July 1, 1942, as Amended, Brought up to Date by Association of ICC Practitioners, May 1, 1945." *I.C.C. Practitioners' Journal* 12 (May 1945): 822–37.

4949. "Interstate Commerce Commission—Sixtieth Annual Report to Congress, November 2, 1946." *I.C.C. Practitioners' Journal* 14 (January 1947): 336–47.

4950. "Interstate Commerce—ICC Recognizes Certification and Complaint Procedures as Alternative Remedies for Inadequate Service by Existing Carriers." *University of Pennsylvania Law* 110 (December 1961): 286–92.

4951. "Is the ICC Bureau of Valuation in Jeopardy?" *I.C.C. Practitioners' Journal* 12 (June 1945): 968–1003.

4952. James, L. G. "Rebating on the High Seas." *I.C.C. Practitioners' Journal* 47 (January/February 1980): 174–93.

4953. Johnson, James C., and Whiteside, T. C. "Professor Ripley Revisited: A Current Analysis of Railroad Mergers." *I.C.C. Practitioners' Journal* 42 (May–June 1975): 410–52.

4954. Johnson, W. H. "Railroad Revitalization and Regulatory Reform Act of 1976." *I.C.C. Practitioners' Journal* 45 (November/December 1977): 27–49.

4955. Jones, Alan. "Thomas M. Cooley and the Interstate Commerce Commission: Continuity and Change in the Doctrine of Equal Rights." *Political Science Quarterly* 81 (December 1966): 602–23.

4956. Jones, William H. "ICC Collision: Regulation Debate May Produce Challenge to Agency Survival." *Washington Post* (January 26, 1975): p. C-I.

4957. Kahn, Fritz R. "Abolition of the Trucking Exemption: Pros and Cons." *American Bar Association Antitrust Law Journal* 47 (January/February 1980): 154–61.

4958. Kahn, Fritz R. "NEPA and the ICC." *I.C.C. Practitioners' Journal* 41 (January–February 1974): 204–14.

4959. Kahn, Fritz R. "Reorganization of the ICC—1961." *I.C.C. Practitioners' Journal* 29 (February 1962): 586–95.

4960. Knudson, James K. "Remarks on Behalf of the Commission's Bar on the Occasion of the 75th Anniversary of the Interstate Commerce Commission." *I.C.C. Practitioners' Journal* 30 (November 1962): 181–90.

4961. Korbel, Herbert J. "The Interstate Commerce Commission and Monopoly—A Study of the Commission's Powers and Duties in the Antitrust Field: The Commission and Railroad Unifications—From Unrestrained Competition to Regulated Monopoly." *I.C.C. Practitioners' Journal* 29 (December 1961): 318–29.

4962. LaRoe, Wilbur. "Administrative Side of the Interstate Commerce Commission." *I.C.C. Practitioners' Journal* 18 (November 1950): 113–16.

4963. LaRoe, Wilbur. "Regulation as Part of the Democratic Process." *I.C.C. Practitioners' Journal* 24 (April 1957): 721–25.

4964. LaRoe, Wilbur. "The Reorganization Plan—A Devastating Blow." *I.C.C. Practitioners' Journal* 17 (March 1950): 455–57.

4965. LaRoe, Wilbur. "This is War!" *I.C.C. Practitioners' Journal* 23 (November 1955): 123–31.

4966. Layne, A. Alvis. "Discovery Procedures in Proceedings before the Interstate Commerce Commission." *I.C.C. Practitioners' Journal* 32 (June 1965): 782–88.

4967. "Lea Resolution Response by Former Commissioner B. H. Meyer, Makes Interesting Recommendation, Including Suggested Panel from Which ICC Appointments Should Be Made." *I.C.C. Practitioners' Journal* 13 (April 1946): 618–30.

4968. Lee, R. C. "Maritime Commission Practice and Procedure as Compared with Practice and Procedure before the ICC." *I.C.C. Practitioners' Journal* 16 (June 1949): 865–72.

4969. Leland, D. "Emergence of Competition as a Factor in Motor Common Carrier Licensing." *I.C.C. Practitioners' Journal* 46 (November–December 1978): 56–63.

4970. Levin, R. C. "Railroad Rates, Profitability, and Welfare under Deregulation." *Bell Journal of Economics and Management Science* 12 (Spring 1981): 1–26.

4971. Levin, R. C. "Railroad Regulation, Deregulation, and Workable Competition." *American Economic Review; Papers and Proceedings* 71 (May 1981): 394–98.

4972. Levy, R. H. "Practice before the Interstate Commerce Commission." *Chicago Bar Record* 36 (February 1955): 207–12.

4973. MacAvoy, Paul W. *The Economic Effects of Regulation: The Trunk-Line Railroad Cartels and the Interstate Commerce Commission before 1900.* Cambridge, MA: MIT Press, 1965. 275 p.

4974. Macdonald, D. G. "'Behind the Iron Curtain': A Panel." *I.C.C. Practitioners' Journal* 27 (September 1960): 1074–99.

4975. McCarthy, J. J. "Dormancy, Past and Present: Or, 'I Shot an Arrow in the Air. . ..'" *I.C.C. Practitioners' Journal* 44 (July/August 1977): 569–90.

4976. McCoy, H. D. "Communications Act Amendments, 1952 Certain Aspects of Interest to ICC." *I.C.C. Practitioners' Journal* 20 (October 1952): 8–21.

4977. McCoy, H. D. "Revision of the Rules of Practice (Ex Parte No. 55)." *I.C.C. Practitioners' Journal* 23 (November 1955): 125–32.

4978. McFarland, W. "Practice and Procedure before the Commission." *I.C.C. Practitioners' Journal* 16 (March 1949): 537–54.

4979. McGrath, J. H. "Relation of Department of Justice to the Interstate Commerce Commission: Address." *I.C.C. Practitioners' Journal* 18 (November 1950): 83–89.

4980. Mapes, P. A. "Competition between Railroads and Water Carriers: A Comparison of the Regulatory and Antitrust Approaches and a Proposal for Reform." *University of Pittsburgh Law Review* 39 (Summer 1978): 653–705.

4981. Meyer, B. H. "Memorandum to Practitioners Relating to the Organization of the Interstate Commerce Commission." *I.C.C. Practitioners' Journal* 12 (December 1947): 232–33.

4982. Miller, Clarence A. "The Interstate Commerce Commission—Past and Present." *I.C.C. Practitioners Journal* 13 (June 1946): 799–804.

4983. Miller, Clarence A. *The Lives of the Interstate Commerce Commissioners and the Commission's Secretaries.* Washington, DC: Association of Interstate Commerce Commission Practitioners, 1946. 175 p.

4984. Mills, S. N. "Bureau of Safety, Interstate Commerce Commission." *I.C.C. Practitioners' Journal* 17 (February 1950): 379–92.

4985. Minor, Robert W. "A First Quarterly Report as a Member of the Interstate Commerce Commission." *I.C.C. Practitioners' Journal* 23 (June 1956): 860–67.

4986. Minsker, Judith E. "The Regulation of Carrier Securities: Section 20a of the Interstate Commerce Act." *I.C.C. Practitioners' Journal* 39 (May–June 1972): 525–39.

4987. Mohundro, O. L. "Improvements in Procedure before the Commission." *I.C.C. Practitioners' Journal* 20 (November 1952): 75–81.

4988. Momkus, E. J. "Impact of the National Environmental Policy Act on the Procedures of the Interstate Commerce Commission." *Transportation Law Journal* 9 (1977): 237–55.

4989. Moore, Thomas G. "The Beneficiaries of Trucking Regulation." *Policy Studies* 3 (1979): 157–73.

4990. Morash, E. A. "Regulatory Policy and Industry Structure: The Case of Interstate Household Goods Carriers." *Land Economics* 57 (November 1981): 544–57.

4991. Morgan, Charles S. "Critique of 'The Marasmus of the ICC: The Commission, the Railroads and the Public Interest.'" *Yale Law Journal* 62 (January 1953): 171–225.

4992. Mullen, F. E. "Modern ICC Procedure." *I.C.C. Practitioners' Journal* 22 (December 1954): 203–05.

4993. Murphy, Rupert L. "Commission Rules of Practice—Why They Should Be Followed." *I.C.C. Practitioners' Journal* 40 (November–December 1972): 7–13.

4994. Murphy, Rupert L. "Informational Activities of the Interstate Commerce Commission and the Role of Practitioners in the Decisional Process." *I.C.C. Practitioners' Journal* 30 (December 1962): 281–86.

4995. Murphy, Rupert L. "Regulation in Transition: Recent Changes in Commission's Internal Organization." *I.C.C. Practitioners' Journal* 29 (December 1961): 297–311.

4996. Murphy, Rupert L. "The Transportation Industry's Role as a Public Utility." *I.C.C. Practitioners' Journal* 37 (September–October 1970): 935–42.

4997. Murphy, Rupert L. "The Transportation Profession." *I.C.C. Practitioners' Journal* 33 (April 1966): 571–76.

4998. Nash, Gerald D. "Origins of the Interstate Commerce Act of 1887. *Pennsylvania History* 24 (1957): 181–90.

4999. Norton, Hugh S. "Economics and Economists in the Interstate Commerce Commission." *I.C.C. Practitioners' Journal* 36 (May–June 1969): 1646–53.

5000. Ogborn, M. J. "Impact of Deregulation of the Trucking Industry." *Memphis State University Law Review* 10 (Fall 1979): 1–36.

5001. Olmsted, Harry J. "Interstate Commerce Commission Policy in Regard to Railroad Use of Trucks in Line-Haul Service: A Critical Analysis." Ph.D. dissertation, University of Arkansas, 1961. 268 p.

5002. O'Neal A. D. "Interstate Commerce Commission Procedures." *I.C.C. Practitioners' Journal* 44 (September/October 1977): 730–37.

5003. O'Neal, A. D., and Schwartzbert, S. D. "Financial Disclosure—A Tool for Public Analysis." *Transportation Law Journal* 6 (January 1974): 1–9.

5004. O'Neill, P. L. "Competition Policy and Regulation: The Case of Motor Carrier Protest Standards." *I.C.C. Practitioners' Journal* 45 (July/August 1978): 569–89.

5005. O'Neill, P. L. "Implementation of Complex Remedial Regulations: The ICC Gateway Elimination Policy." *I.C.C. Practitioners' Journal* 43 (July/August 1976): 601–13.

5006. O'Neill, T. S. "Jurisdictional Conflicts between the Federal Maritime Commission and the Interstate Commerce Commission." *Maritime Lawyer* (Spring 1981): 51–75.

5007. "Organization of Divisions and Assignment of Work, Business and Functions of the Interstate Commerce Commissions under the Reorganization Effective July 1, 1942, as Amended." *I.C.C. Practitioners Journal* 17 (June 1950): 818–33.

5008. "Organization of Divisions and Assignment of Work, Business and Functions . . . under the Reorganization Effective July 1, 1942, as Amended." *I.C.C. Practitioners' Journal* 16 (October 1948): 24–40.

5009. "Organization of Divisions and Assignment of Work of the Interstate Commerce Commission and Organizational Chart (Revised to January 1, 1959)." *I.C.C. Practitioners' Journal* 26 (May 1959): 1–18.

5010. "Organization of Divisions and Boards and Assignment of Work, Business and Functions of the Interstate Commerce Commission." *I.C.C. Practitioners' Journal* 22 (March 1955): 516–34.

5011. "Original-Cost Concepts of the ICC in Motor-Carrier Accounting." *Harvard Law Review* 60 (November 1946): 118–23.

5012. "Outline of Study Course in Practice and Procedure before the Interstate Commerce Commission." *I.C.C. Practitioners' Journal* 26 (June 1959): 1–24.

5013. "An Outline of a Study Course in Practice and Procedure before the Interstate Commerce Commission: Second and Revised Edition, 1948." *I.C.C. Practitioners' Journal* 16 (November 1948): 5–37.

5014. "Panel Discussion: Education for Practice before the Interstate Commerce Commission." *I.C.C. Practitioners' Journal* 32 (December 1964): 141–62.

5015. Payne, J. S. "Bills in Congress Proposing Changes in Procedure for Review of Orders of the Interstate Commerce Commission." *I.C.C. Practitioners' Journal* 13 (February 1946): 355–62.

5016. "Power of ICC to Limit Carriers' Right to Add to Equipment by Lease." *University of Pennsylvania Law Review* 101 (October 1952): 155–60.

5017. "Power of Interstate Commerce Commission to Set Intrastate Rates." *Northwestern University Law Review* 54 (March–April 1959): 87–98.

5018. "Practitioners Appeal Ruling on Board of Suspension and Fourth Section Board Status." *I.C.C. Practitioners' Journal* 22 (December 1954): 206–11.

5019. Purcell, Edward A. "Ideas and Interests: Businessmen and the Interstate Commerce Act." *Journal of American History* 54 (December 1967): 561–78.

5020. "Railroad Reorganization—Equipment Trustee May Respossess Rolling Stock Essential to Railroad Operation without ICC Permission." *Harvard Law Review* 68 (April 1955): 1083–84.

5021. Ray, Ron. "ICC Practitioner." *I.C.C. Practitioners' Journal* 33 (March 1966): 498–503.

5022. "Regulation of Private Carrier Leasing Motor Equipment—Denial of Injunctive Relief." *Iowa Law Review* 37 (Summer 1952): 595–600.

5023. Rinteln, Victor A. von. "Hearing Examiner Recruitment and the Government Lawyer." *I.C.C. Practitioners' Journal* 35 (November–December 1967): 7–24.

5024. Roberts, G. "Search and Seizure by Authorized Interstate Commerce Commission Personnel of Common Carrier Records and Documents." *I.C.C. Practitioners' Journal* 47 (May/June 1980): 410–26.

5025. Rose, Joseph R. "Federal Regulation of Motor Vehicle Leasing Arrangements." *I.C.C. Practitioners' Journal* 45 (May/June 1978): 479–90.

5026. Rose, Warren. "What Single Improvement of the Interstate Commerce Act Is Most Needed?" *I.C.C. Practitioners' Journal* 32 (September 1965): 896–909.

5027. Schack, E. J. "Recent Decisions of the Interstate Commerce Commission." *Transportation Law Journal* 10 (1978): 1–14.

5028. Schenker, Eric. "The Rate-Making Powers of the ICC." *Public Utilities Fortnightly* 65 (May 1960): 649–59.

5029. Schrag, A. "Competing Modes of Transportation and the ICC." *University of Pennsylvania Law Review* 94 (July 1946): 378–99.

5030. Shiriak, B. D. "The Interstate Commerce Commission's Inattention to Captive Shippers." *Public Utilities Fortnightly* 112 (August 18, 1983): 15–19.

5031. Silver, B. S. "ICC Extension Hearings—A Newer Method for Larger Cases." *I.C.C. Practitioners' Journal* 45 (November/December 1977): 58–69.

5032. Sims, Joe. "Inedible Tallow, the Maximum Charges Rule, and Other Fables: Motor Carrier Regulation by the ICC." *Transportation Law Journal* 10 (1978): 55–66.

5033. Singer, Charles D. "Practice of Non-Lawyers before the Interstate Commerce Commission." *Federal Bar Journal* 15 (April–June 1955): 177–85.

5034. "Sixty-First Annual Report of the Interstate Commerce Commission to Congress Made Public." *I.C.C. Practitioners' Journal* 15 (February 1948): 387–402.

5035. "Sixty-Second Annual Report of Interstate Commerce Commission to Congress." *I.C.C. Practitioners' Journal* 16 (February 1949): 405–28.

5036. Skowronek, S. "National Railroad Regulation and the Problem of State-Building: Interests and Institutions in Late Nineteenth-Century America." *Politics and Society* 10 (1981): 225–50.

5037. Snitow, M. S. "Finding and Using the Expanded New York City Commercial Zone." *I.C.C. Practitioners' Journal* 45 (November–December 1977): 50–67.

5038. Spencer, H. E. "4-R Act, the New Rules of Practice, and Regulatory Lag: What Is Missing?" *I.C.C. Practitioners' Journal* 44 (March/April 1977): 319–26.

5039. Spychalsk, J. C. "Antitrust Standards and Railway Freight Pricing: New Round in an Old Debate." *American Economic Review; Papers and Proceedings* 71 (May 1981): 104–09.

5040. Stafford, George M. "The Interstate Commerce Commission and the Consumer." *Transportation Law Journal* 4 (January 1972): 1–9.

5041. Stephens, Harold M. *Administrative Tribunals and the Rules of Evidence.* Cambridge, MA: Harvard University Press, 1933. 128 p.

5042. Stephenson, F. J. "Transport Deregulation—The Air Freight Forwarder Experience." *I.C.C. Practitioners' Journal* 43 (November–December 1975): 39–55.

5043. "Suggested Revisions of the General Rules of Practice." *I.C.C. Practitioners' Journal* 28 (September 1961): 1220–28.

5044. "Supreme Court Decisions Important to the Interstate Commerce Commission." *I.C.C. Practitioners' Journal* 18 (May 1951): 3–62.

5045. "Survey of Organization and Operations of the Interstate Commerce Commission." *I.C.C. Practitioners' Journal* 20 (February 1953): 358–408.

5046. Taff, Charles A. *Operating Rights of Motor Carriers; Interstate Commerce Commission Policy Regarding Property Carriers.* Dubuque, IA: W. C. Brown Co., 1953. 251 p.

5047. Tally, J. O. "The Supreme Court, the Interstate Commerce Commission and the Freight Rate Battle." *North Carolina Law Review* 25 (February 1947): 172–91.

5048. "Teamsters, Truckers, and the ICC: A Political and Economic Analysis of Motor Carrier Deregulation." *Harvard Journal on Legislation* 17 (Winter 1980): 123–51.

5049. Thomas, Starr. "The American Bar Association's Legislative Proposals as They Affect the Interstate Commerce Commission and Its Practitioners." *I.C.C. Practitioners' Journal* 24 (September 1957): 1129–41.

5050. Thoms, William E., and Laird, Michael J. "Derailing the Passenger." *I.C.C. Practitioners' Journal* 36 (November–December 1968): 1118–34.

5051. Thomson, J. W. "Railroad Regulation—A Perspective." *I.C.C. Practitioners' Journal* 42 (July–August 1975): 588–99.

5052. Tierney, Paul J. "The Commission and Innovations in Ratemaking." *I.C.C. Practitioners' Journal* 32 (June 1965): 776–81.

5053. Tierney, Paul J. "Interstate Commerce Commission Reorganization." *I.C.C. Practitioners' Journal* 33 (February 1966): 406–10.

5054. Tierney, Paul J. "Remarks." *I.C.C. Practitioners' Journal* 34 (September–October 1967): 910–15.

5055. Tierney, Paul J. "Remarks." *I.C.C. Practitioners' Journal* 35 (September–October 1968): 931–37.

5056. Towle, William H. "Appeal of ICC Suspension Orders." *I.C.C. Practitioners' Journal* 35 (January–February 1968): 220–34.

5057. "Transportation—Interstate Commerce Act—ICC Has Plenary and Exclusive Jurisdiction over Joint through Routes between Outlying Possessions or Territories and the United States." *Vanderbilt Journal of Transportation Law* 13 (Fall 1980): 885–94.

5058. Tucker, William H. "A Day's Work." *I.C.C. Practitioners' Journal* 32 (May 1965): 669–75.

5059. Tucker, William H. "The Interstate Commerce Commission Hearing Examiner Corps." *I.C.C. Practitioners' Journal* 34 (July–August 1967): 709–13.

5060. Tucker, William H. "Renovating the Decisional Process in an Independent Regulatory Commission." *I.C.C. Practitioners' Journal* 35 (January–February 1968): 207–19.

5061. Tuggle, K. H. "Status of Federal Hearing Examiners." *I.C.C. Practitioners' Journal* 22 (November 1954): 129–34.

5062. Turney, J. R. "Current Problems of the Profession and the Association; Address." *I.C.C. Practitioners' Journal* 18 (March 1951): 473–80.

5063. Ulen, Thomas S. "Cartels and Regulation: Late Nineteenth Century Railroad Collusion and the Creation of the Interstate Commerce Commission." Ph.D. dissertation, Stanford University, 1979. 423 p.

5064. Ulen, Thomas S. "Market for Regulation: The ICC from 1887 to 1920." *American Economic Review* 70 (May 1980): 306–10.

5065. Wagner, W. H. "Future of the Interstate Commerce Commission and Its Examiners?" *I.C.C. Practitioners' Journal* 19 (December 1951): 271–77.

5066. Webb, Charles A. "How the Commission Decides Its Cases." *I.C.C. Practitioners' Journal* 34 (January–February 1967): 247–52.

5067. Webb, Charles A. "Reflection on the Report of Nader's Raiders." *I.C.C. Practitioners' Journal* 37 (September–October 1970): 943–48.

5068. Weiner, George T. "Piggyback and the Interstate Commerce Commission." Ph.D. dissertation, Massachusetts Institute of Technology, 1962.

5069. Weisser, John F. "Recommendations of the Administrative Conference of the United States—To What Extent Should They Be Adopted by the Interstate Commerce Commission?" *I.C.C. Practitioners' Journal* 31 (May 1964): 893–901.

5070. Whitesel, Theodore L. "The Jurisdiction of the Federal Power Commission over Interstate Commerce in Electricity and Natural Gas." Ph.D. dissertation, University of Illinois, 1952. 1308 p.

5071. Williams, Ernest W. "The ICC and the Regulation of Intercarrier Competition." *Harvard Law Review* 63 (June 1950): 1349–72.

5072. Williams, Ernest W. "The Regulation of Rail-motor Rate Competition by the Interstate Commerce Commission." Ph.D. dissertation, Columbia University, 1951. 252 p.

5073. Winston, C. "Welfare Effects of ICC Rate Regulation Revisited." *Bell Journal of Economics and Management Science* 12 (Spring 1981): 232–44.

5074. Wood, F. L. "Practice and Procedure under the Hobbs Act." *I.C.C. Practitioners' Journal* 42 (May–June 1975): 406–18.

5075. Wooldridge, W. C. "Arbitral Function of Railroad Regulation." *American Bar Association Journal* 66 (October 1980): 1238–42.

5076. "'Write' to Argue: Modified Procedure in ICC Motor Carrier Cases." *Transportation Law Journal* 6 (January 1974): 11–30.

5077. Zerbe, Richard O. "Costs and Benefits of Early Regulation of the Railroads." *Bell Journal of Economics and Management Science* 11 (Spring 1980): 343–50.

5078. Zoll, E. J. "The Administrative Procedure Act and How It Affects the Interstate Commerce Commission." *I.C.C. Practitioners' Journal* 13 (May 1946): 677–84.

NATIONAL LABOR RELATIONS BOARD

5079. "A Look at the Revolving NLRB Policies Governing Union Representation Election Campaigns." *Wake Forest Law Review* 19 (June 1983): 417–40.

5080. "An Analysis of the NLRB's Role Organizing Southern Labor, 1935–1941." *Rocky Mountain Social Science Journal* 2 (March 1965): 108–09.

5081. Baird, James. "Lockout Law: The Supreme Court and the NLRB." *George Washington Law Review* 38 (March 1970): 396–430.

5082. Band, Richard E. "War on Business; Growing Federal Regulation and Racism." *American Opinion* 17 (February 1974): 23–36.

5083. Bok, Derekm C. "The Regulation of Campaign Tactics in Representation Elections under the National Labor Relations Act." *Harvard Law Review* 78 (November 1964): 38–141.

5084. Brotman, Billie A. "A Comparative Analysis of National Labor Relations Board and Private Sector Arbitration Decisions." Ph.D. dissertation, University of Notre Dame, 1978. 227 p.

5085. Capozzola, John M. "The New York City Regional Office of the National Labor Relations Board: A Study of Field-Headquarters Relationships." Ph.D. dissertation, Pennsylvania State University, 1964. 363 p.

5086. DeLorme, C. D. "NLRB Voting on Important Unfair Labor Practices Decisions: 1955–1975. *American Business Law Journal* 16 (Fall 1978): 223–29.

5087. Dooley, Mary L. "The Role of the National Labor Relations Board and Courts in Collective Bargaining." Ph.D. dissertation, University of Wisconsin, 1957. 260 p.

5088. Dotson, D. L. "Processing Cases at the NLRB." *Labor Law Journal* 35 (January 1984): 3–9.

5089. Drotning, John. "NLRB Remedies for Election Misconduct: An Analysis of Election Outcomes and Their Determinants." *Journal of Business* 40 (April 1967): 137–48.

5090. Fanning, J. H. "Labor Relations in a Period of Inflation and Recession: Policies of the NLRB." *Labor Law Journal* 26 (August 1975): 534–40.

5091. Fanning, J. H. "National Labor Relations Act and the Role of the NLRB." *Labor Law Journal* 29 (November 1978): 683–89.

5092. Fanning, J. H. "We Are Forty—Where Do We Go?" *Labor Law Journal* 27 (January 1976): 3–10.

5093. Gabriel, Ronald L. "A Critical Evaluation of the Role and Functions of the General Counsel of the National Labor Relations Board in the Investigation and Prosecution of Unfair Labor Practice Charges, August 22, 1947 to June 25, 1971." Ph.D. dissertation, American University, 1974. 236 p.

5094. Gabriel, Ronald L. "Role of the NLRB General Counsel." *Labor Law Journal* 26 (February 1975): 79–87.

5095. Garvey, D. B. "Prehearing Discovery in NLRB Proceedings." *Labor Law Journal* 26 (November 1975): 710–23.

5096. Gibson, R. F. "Can the NLRB Meet Today's Challenges?" *Industry Week* 182 (August 5, 1974): 26–31.

5097. "Gissel Bargaining Orders: Circuit Courts Struggle to Limit NLRB Abuse." *Washington and Lee Law Review* 40 (Fall 1983): 1661–84.

5098. Gould, R. D., and Goldstein, A. S. "*NLRB v. Iron Workers Local Union no. 103*: A Case Analysis." *Labor Law Journal* 30 (February 1979): 76–83.

5099. Handberg, R. "Supreme Court and the NLRB." *Labor Law Journal* 26 (November 1975): 737–39.

5100. Harter, L. G. "Are They Employees or Independent Contractors?" *Labor Law Journal* 29 (December 1978): 779–85.

5101. Heacock, Ronald C. "Private Influence and the National Labor Relations Board." Ph.D. dissertation, Michigan State University, 1983. 245 p.

5102. Heindenreich, Charles W. "An Analysis of Administrative Authority as Exercised by the National Labor Relations Board." Ph.D. dissertation, University of Minnesota, 1968.

5103. Hill, Herbert. "Black Labor, the NLRB, and the Developing Law of Equal Employment Opportunity." *Labor Law Journal* 26 (April 1975): 207–23.

5104. Hordes, Donald B. "Pre-Emption of State Labor Regulations Collaterally in Conflict with the National Labor Relations Act." *George Washington Law Review* 37 (October 1968): 132–52.

5105. Hough, Robbin R. "The National Labor Relations Board under the Taft-Hartley Act: A Quantitative Study." Ph.D. dissertation, Massachusetts Institute of Technology, 1963. 154 p.

5106. Imberman, W. "How Expensive Is an NLRB Election?" *Michigan State University Business Topics* 23 (Summer 1975): 13–18.

5107. Janofsky, L. S., and Peterson, A. C. "Exercise of Unreviewed Adminstrative Discretion to Reverse the US Supreme Court: Ponsford Brothers." *Labor Law Journal* 25 (December 1974): 729–35.

5108. Meinhart, Wayne A. "The Public Policy Implications of National Labor Relations Board and Court Decisions Interpreting the Unfair Labor Practices of Management 1955–60." Ph.D. dissertation, University of Illinois at Urbana-Champaign, 1964. 378 p.

5109. Miller, E. B. "Tangled Path to an Administrative Judgeship." *Labor Law Journal* 25 (January 1974): 3–11.

5110. Millis, Harry A., and Brown, Emily C. *From the Wagner Act to Taft-Hartley; A Study of National Labor Policy and Labor Relations.* Chicago: University of Chicago Press, 1950. 723 p.

5111. Morales, Gerard. "Presumption of Union's Majority Status in NLRB Cases." *Labor Law Journal* 29 (May 1978): 309–15.

5112. Morris, C. J. "National Labor Relations Board: It's Future." *Labor Law Journal* 26 (June 1975): 334–44.

5113. Murphy, B. S. "NLRB in Its Fortieth Year." *Labor Law Journal* 26 (September 1975): 551–58.

5114. Naffziger, F. J. "NLRB Attitude on Discrimination and the Judicial Response." *Labor Law Journal* 26 (January 1975): 21–32.

5115. Nash, P. G. "Board Referral to Arbitration and *Alexander v. Gardner-Denver.* Some Preliminary Observations." *Labor Law Journal* 25 (May 1974): 259–69.

5116. Nelson, W. B. "Clearfield Medical Services Case: Effectuating the Policies of the Act or Shortsighted, Pettifogging Insistence upon Litigation?" *Labor Law Journal* 29 (October 1978): 643–48.

5117. Penello, J. A. "NLRB's Misplaced Priorities." *Labor Law Journal* 30 (January 1979): 3–9.

5118. Penington, Ralph A. "The National Labor Relations Board: Three Decades of Operations." Ph.D. dissertation, Purdue University, 1968. 249 p.

5119. Pichler, J. A., and Fitch, H. G. "And Women Must Weep: The NLRB as Film Critic." *Industrial and Labor Relations Review* 28 (April 1975): 395–410.

5120. Posten, R. "Rise in NLRB Election Delays: Measuring Business New Resistance." *Monthly Labor Review* 102 (February 1979): 38–40.

5121. "Recent NLRB Rulings." *Monthly Labor Review* 107 (March 1984): 57–58.

5122. Roomkin, M., and Abrams, R. I. "Using Behavioral Evidence in NLRB Regulation: A Proposal." *Harvard Law Review* 90 (May 1977): 1441–74.

5123. Ross, Philip. "The National Labor Relations Board." *Current History* 49 (August 1965): 77–81, 114.

5124. Samoff, B. L. "Appointing NLRB Regional Directors." *Labor Law Journal* 26 (September 1975): 570–78.

5125. Samoff, B. L. "What Lies Ahead for the NLRB?" *Labor Law Journal* 25 (July 1974): 408–17.

5126. Scher, Seymour. "The National Labor Relations Board and Congress: A Study of Legislative Control of Regulatory Activity." Ph.D. dissertation, University of Chicago, 1957.

5127. Schwartz, S. J. "The National Labor Relations Board and the Duty of Fair Representation." *Labor Law Journal* 34 (December 1983): 781–89.

5128. Silverman, C. S. "Case for the National Labor Relations Board's Use of Rulemaking in Asserting Jurisdiction." *Labor Law Journal* 25 (October 1974): 607–17.

5129. Skotzko, E. "NLRB's Deference to Arbitration." *Monthly Labor Review* 97 (December 1974): 65–67.

5130. Taylor, Benjamin J. "An Evaluation of the National Labor Relations Board in the Administration of the Taft-Hartley Act in Indiana." Ph.D. dissertation, Indiana University, 1966. 194 p.

5131. Thompson, F., and Pollitt, D. H. "Oversight Hearings of the NLRB: A Preliminary Report." *Labor Law Journal* 27 (September 1976): 539–47.

5132. Truesdale, J. C. "From General Shoe to General Knit: A Return to Hollywood Ceramics." *Labor Law Journal* 30 (February 1979): 67–75.

5133. "Union Fines and the NLRB." *Monthly Labor Review* 96 (August 1973): 79–83.

5134. Walther, P. D. "Board's Place at the Bargaining Table." *Labor Law Journal* 28 (March 1977): 131–41.

5135. Weinberg, P. J. "Bargaining Units in Banking." *Bankers Magazine* 159 (Spring 1976): 73–80.

5136. Wilson, Harry O. "The Trial Examiner and Administrative Procedure in the National Labor Relations Board." Ph.D. dissertation, Northwestern University, 1946. 600 p.

5137. Winfrey, John C. "The Appropriate Bargaining Unit Decisions of the National Labor Relations Board: A Study of Evolving Administrative Policy and Its Bargaining Power Relationships and Bargaining Unit Structure." Ph.D. dissertation, Duke University, 1965. 377 p.

5138. Witney, Fred. "Wartime Experiences of the National Labor Relations Board." Ph.D. dissertation, University of Illinois at Urbana-Champaign, 1947. 428 p.

5139. Zagoria, S. "Some Reflections on the NLRB." *American Federationist* 82 (February 1975): 23–25.

NUCLEAR REGULATORY COMMISSION

5140. "The AEC Amendment: Temporary Licensing of Nuclear Reactors." *Harvard Journal on Legislation* 10 (February 1973): 236–55.

5141. "AEC Rulemaking and Public Participation." *Georgetown Law Journal* 62 (July 1974): 1737–51.

5142. "AEC Seeks Data on Local Units." *National Civic Review* 48 (February 1959): 102.

5143. "Atomic Energy Commission's ECCS Rulemaking." *Atomic Energy Law Journal* 16 (Spring 1974): 42–90.

5144. Bauser, M. A. "Development of Rulemaking within the Atomic Energy Commission: The Nuclear Regulatory Commission's Valuable Legacy." *Administrative Law Review* 27 (Spring 1975): 165–84.

5145. Bechhoefer, B. G. "Antitrust Powers of the AEC." *Prospectus* 3 (May 1970): 257.

5146. Berman, William H., and Hydeman, Lee M. *The Atomic Energy Commission and Regulating Nuclear Facilities.* Ann Arbor, MI: University of Michigan Law School, 1961. 336 p.

5147. Bieber, J. *"Calvert Cliffs' Coordinating Committee v. AEC* (449 F 2d 1109): The AEC Learns the True Meaning of the National Environmental Policy Act of 1969." *Environmental Law* 3 (Summer 1973): 316–33.

5148. Boskey, Bennett. "Antitrust Enforcement by the Atomic Energy Commission." *American Bar Association Antitrust Law Journal* 19 (1961): 399–406.

5149. Brebbia, J. H. "Antitrust Problems in the Licensing and Permit Authority of the United States Nuclear Regulatory Commission." *Mercer Law Review* 26 (Spring 1975): 749–94.

5150. Brewer, Thomas L. "The International Atomic Energy Agency." *Armed Forces and Society* 4 (Winter 1978): 207–26.

5151. Bromwich, D. "High Standard of Dying." *Dissent* 26 (Summer 1979): 271–74.

5152. Bronstein, Daniel A. "The AEC Decision-Making Process and the Environment: A Case Study of the Calvert Cliffs Nuclear Power Plant." *Ecology Law Quarterly* 1 (Fall 1971): 689–725.

5153. Bupp, Irvin C. "Priorities in Nuclear Technology: Program Prosperity and Decay in the United States Atomic Energy Commission, 1956–1971." Ph.D. dissertation, Harvard University, 1972.

5154. Burg, R. C., and Gantt, P. H. "Atomic Energy Commission Board of Contract Appeals—An Experiment in Government Contract Disputes." *Public Contract Law Journal* 6 (January 1974): 167–200.

5155. Caruso, Lawrence R. "Contracting with the Atomic Energy Commission." *Atomic Energy Law Journal* 4 (Winter 1962): 339–69.

5156. Cohen, Linda R. "Innovation and Atomic Energy: Nuclear Power Regulation, 1966-Present." *Law and Contemporary Problems* 43 (1979): 67–97.

5157. Davis, Kenneth C. "Dueprocessitis in the Atomic Energy Commission." *American Bar Association Journal* 47 (August 1961): 782–85.

5158. Davis, T. P. "Citizen's Guide to Intervention in Nuclear Power Plant Siting: A Blueprint for Alice in Nuclear Wonderland." *Environmental Law* 6 (Spring 1976): 621–74.

5159. Dignan, T. G. "Recent Amendments and Interpretations of the AEC Rules of Practice—A Solution to Delay?" *Atomic Energy Law Journal* 16 (Spring 1974): 3–41.

5160. Doub, William O. "The Right to be Heard—Laying It on the Line." *Atomic Energy Law Journal* 13 (Fall 1971): 211–24.

5161. England, W. T. "Part 25 Amendments to AEC's Information Control Regulations Authorizing Private Use of Classified AEC Enrichment Technology for Commercial Purposes." *Atomic Energy Law Journal* 15 (Fall 1973): 194–213.

5162. "Environmental Law: Public Participation in the Environmental Impact Statement Process." *Minnesota Law Review* 61 (January 1977): 363–81.

5163. Freeman, George C. "The AEC's Recent Experiment in 'Evidentiary' Rule Making." *Business Lawyer* 28 (January 1973): 663–82.

5164. Grainey, M. W. "Nuclear Reactor Regulation: Practice and Procedure before the Nuclear Regulatory Commission." *Gonzaga Law Review* 11 (Spring 1976): 809–37.

5165. Grammer, E. J. "Uranium Mill Tailings Radiation Control Act of 1978 and NRC's Agreement State Program." *Natural Resources Lawyer* 13 (1981): 469–522.

5166. Green Harold P. "The Joint Committee on Atomic Energy: A Model for Legislative Reform?" *George Washington Law Review* 32 (June 1964): 932–46.

5177. Henderson, G. B. "Nuclear Choice: Are Health and Safety Issues Pre-Empted?" *Boston College Environmental Affairs Law Review* 8 (1980): 821–72.

5178. "Increasing Citizen Participation in AEC Proceedings by Expanding Social Impact Considerations: The Maine Yankee Decision." *George Washington Law Review* 42 (August 1974): 1062–88.

5169. Jacks, W. T. "Public and the Peaceful Atom: Participation in AEC Regulatory Proceedings." *Texas Law Review* 52 (March 1974): 466–525.

5170. Johnson, D. B. "Some Problems of Cost-Plus Contracts." *Public Administration Review* 19 (Fall 1959): 219–26.

5171. Johnson, W. E. "AEC Uranium Policies." *Energy Law Journal* 12 (Fall 1970): 263–65.

5172. "Judicial Review of Federal Environmental Decision-Making: NRC Regulation of Nuclear Waste Management and Disposal." *Texas Law Review* 58 (February 1980): 355–91.

5173. "Judicial Review of Generic Rulemaking: The Experience of the Nuclear Regulatory Commission." *Georgetown Law Journal* 65 (June 1977): 1295–323.

5174. Klein, Jeffrey S. "The Nuclear Regulatory Bureaucracy." *Society* 18 (July/August 1981): 50–56.

5175. Lang, Herbert H. "Uranium Mining and the AEC: The Birth Pangs of a New Industry." *Business History Review* 36 (Autumn 1962): 325–33.

5176. Leopold, Richard W. "Historians and the Federal Government: Historical Advisory Committees: State, Defense, and the Atomic Energy Commission." *Pacific Historical Review* 44 (August 1975): 373–85.

5177. Lieberman, J. "Generic Hearings: Preparation for the Future." *Atomic Energy Law Journal* 16 (Summer 1974): 141–74.

5178. Lowenstein, Robert M. "The Need for Separation of the AEC's Functions." *Atomic Energy Law Journal* 13 (Fall 1971): 282–89.

5179. Malsch, M. G. "Costs, Benefits, and Alternatives in AEC's NEPA Process—AEC's Policies and Procedures." *Atomic Energy Law Journal* 15 (Fall 1973): 214–24.

5180. McCaffree, K. M. "Collective Bargaining in Atomic-Energy Construction." *Journal of Political Economy* 65 (August 1957): 322–37.

5181. Neel, James N. "The Atomic Energy Commission's Federal-State Program and Its Impact on the Utilization of Nuclear Materials in Kentucky." *Atomic Energy Law Journal* 6 (Fall 1964): 274–87.

5182. Nelson, Curtis A. "Compliance with Atomic Energy Commission Regulations." *Texas Law Review* 34 (June 1956): 862–66.

5183. Newman, J. R. "Atomic Energy Industry: An Experiment in Hybridization." *Yale Law Journal* 60 (December 1951): 1263–394.

5184. Niehoff, R. O. "Lyman S. Moore's Contribution to Housing and Atomic Energy." *Public Administration Review* 13 (1953): 163–65.

5185. Niehoff, R. O. "Organization and Administration of the United States Atomic Energy Commission." *Public Adminstration Review* 8 (1948): 91–102.

5186. Nigre, F. A. "Lilienthal Case." *Southwestern Social Science Quarterly* 40 (September 1959): 147–58.

5187. Northrop, R. M. "Changing Role of the Atomic Energy Commission in Atomic Power Development." *Law and Contemporary Problems* 21 (Winter 1956): 14–37.

5188. "NRC Antitrust Review of Nuclear Power." *University of Illinois Law Forum* 23 (1980): 1011–47.

5189. "Nuclear Accidents: Judicial Review of the NRC's Duty to Issue a Health Warning." *Fordham Urban Law Journal* 9 (1980/81): 353–84.

5190. O'Brien, John N. "The Conflict Between Civil Liberties and Nuclear Energy Safeguards: An Analysis of Current and Prospective Federal Regulation." Ph.D. dissertation, Syracuse University, 1977. 295 p.

5191. "Opportunities for Improving AEC's Administration of Agreements with States Regulating Users of Radioactive Materials. *Atomic Energy Law Journal* 15 (Summer 1973): 63–131.

5192. Plaine, Herzel H. E. "The Rules of Practice of the Atomic Energy Commission." *Texas Law Review* 34 (June 1956): 801–41.

5193. Price, H. L. "Current Approach to Licensing Nuclear Power Plants." *Atomic Energy Law Journal* 15 (Winter 1974): 227–37.

5194. "Procurement Policies and Powers of the Atomic Energy Commission." *Wyoming Law Journal* 9 (Spring 1955): 199–214.

5195. Ramey, James T. "The AEC Regulatory Program-Current Status, Future Trends." *North Carolina Law Review* 45 (February 1967): 323–39.

5196. Ramey, James T. "Economy in Government Contracting—Atomic Energy Commission Experience." *Law and Contemporary Problems* 29 (Spring 1964): 380–89.

5197. Ramey, James T. "The Role of Planning in the Atomic Energy Program." *George Washington Law Review* 36 (July 1968): 1060–78.

5198. Reis, Robert I. "Environmental Activism: Thermal Pollution—AEC and State Jurisdictional Considerations." *Boston College Environmental Affairs Law Review* 13 (March 1972): 633–84.

5199. Rowden, Marcus A. "Licensing of Nuclear Power Plants—Reforming the Patchwork Process." *Regulation* 2 (January/February 1978): 40–47.

5200. Schlesinger, James R. "Expectations and Responsibilities of the Nuclear Industry." *Atomic Energy Law Journal* 13 (Fall 1971): 197–210.

5201. Sekuler, S. N., and McCullough, J. J. "Litigating Nuclear Waste Disposal Issues before the NRC: A Fable of Our Time." *Tulsa Law Journal* 15 (Spring 1980): 413–42.

5202. Shapar, H. K. "Licensing of Nuclear Power Reactors in the United States—New Developments." *Atomic Energy Law Journal* 15 (Fall 1973): 135–54.

5203. "*Sholly v. United States Nuclear Regulatory Commission* (651 F 2d 780): The Agency's Statutory Duty to Provide a Hearing." *Mercer Law Review* 33 (Spring 1982): 935–47.

5204. Stein, B. A. "Which Road to Power?" *Trial* 10 (January 1974): 10.

5205. Strauss, P. L. "NRC Role and Plant Siting." *Journal of Contemporary Law* 4 (Winter 1977): 96–108.

5206. Temples, J. R. "Nuclear Regulatory Commission and the Politics of Regulatory Reform: Since Three Mile Island." *Public Administration Review* 42 (July/August 1982): 355–62.

5207. Thomas, M. "Appropriation Control and the Atomic Energy Program." *Western Political Quarterly* 9 (September 1956): 713–24.

5208. Tourtellotte, J. R. "Nuclear Licensing Litigation: Come on in the Quagmire Is Fine." *Administrative Law Review* 33 (Fall 1981): 367–92.

5209. Trubek, D. M. "Allocating the Burden of Environmental Uncertainty: The NRC Interprets NEPA's Substantive Mandate." *Wisconsin Law Review* 1977 (1977): 747–76.

5210. "Unresolved Safety Issues in Nuclear Power Plant Licensing: Reasonable Assurance of Safety or Nuclear Shell Game?" *Columbia Journal of Environmental Law* 7 (Fall 1980): 99–119.

5211. Zimmerman, John J. "Alternatives to Proposed Actions under NEPA: The AEC Response after Calvert Cliffs." *Atomic Energy Law Journal* 14 (Winter 1973): 265–313.

SECURITIES AND EXCHANGE COMMISSION

5212. Adler, T. "Amending the Foreign Corrupt Practices Act of 1977: A Step toward Clarification and Consolidation." *Journal of Criminal Law and Criminology* 73 (Winter 1983): 1740–73.

5213. "Administrative Law—Agency Order without a Hearing—The Allegation that a Securities and Exchange Commission Order Issued without a Hearing and Temporarily Suspending an Exemption from Registration of Certain Securities Deprives the Complainant of a Substantial Going Business Does Not State a Cause of Action." *University of Pittsburgh Law Review* 23 (June 1962): 1010–12.

5214. "Administrative Law—Hearings on Voluntary Plans for Simplifications under the Holding Company Act." *University of Pennsylvania Law Review* 95 (March 1947): 551–53.

5215. "Administrative Law—Powers of Agencies—Right of Registrant to Withdraw Registration Statement Filed with the Securities and Exchange Commission." *Michigan Law Review* 58 (March 1960): 780–82.

5216. "Ancillary Relief in SEC Injunction Suits for Violation of Rule 10b-5." *Harvard Law Review* 79 (January 1966): 656–71.

5217. Andre, T. J. "Collateral Consequences of SEC Injunctive Relief: Mild Prophylactic or Perpetual Hazard?" *University of Illinois Law Review* 1981 (1981): 625–70.

5218. "Antitrust Law—Presence of SEC Review Power Exempts Stock Exchange Fixed Minimum Brokerage Commission Rate System from the Operation of the Antitrust Laws." *Seton Hall Law Review* 6 (Winter 1975): 336–55.

5219. "Applicability of Corporate Charter Provisions in Readjustments under the Holding Company Act." *Yale Law Journal* 56 (September 1947): 1420–29.

5220. Aranow, Edward R., and Einhorn, Herbert A. "Corporate Proxy Contests: Enforcement of SEC Proxy Rules by the Commission and Private Parities." *New York University Law Review* 31 (May 1956): 875–93.

5221. Armstrong, J. Sinclair. "Congress and the Securities and Exchange Commission." *Virginia Law Review* 45 (October 1959): 795–816.

5222. Armstrong, J. Sinclair. "Current Developments at the Securities and Exchange Commission." *Business Lawyer* 12 (November 1956): 12–25.

5223. Armstrong, J. Sinclair. "Regulation of Proxy Contests by the SEC." *Virginia Law Review* 42 (December 1956): 1075–85.

5224. Armstrong, J. Sinclair. "The Role of the Securities and Exhange Commission in Proxy Contests of Listed Companies." *Business Lawyer* 11 (November 1955): 110–22.

5225. Atkeson, T. "Foreign Corrupt Practices Act of 1977: An International Application of SEC's Corporate Governance Reforms." *International Law* 12 (Fall 1978): 703–20.

5226. "Attorney Discipline by the SEC: 2(e) or not 2(e)?" *New England Law Review* 17 (1981–1982): 1267–308.

5227. "Attorney Liability under SEC Rule 2(E): A New Standard?" *Texas Tech Law Review* 11 (Fall 1979): 83–111.

5228. "Attorney Responsibility and Carter: Under SEC Rule 2(e): The Powers that be and the Fear of the Flock." *Southwestern Law Journal* 36 (September 1982): 897–924.

5229. Baird, Robert S. "Prospective Interpretative Rule-Making by the Securities and Exchange Commission under the Securities Act of 1933 and the Securities Exchange Act of 1934." *Business Lawyer* 25 (July 1970): 1581–616.

5230. Barr, Andrew, and Koch, Elmer C. "Accounting and the SEC." *George Washington Law Review* 28 (October 1959): 176–93.

5231. Barth, J. R., and Cordes, Joseph J. "Optimal Financial Disclosure with and without SEC Regulation." *Quarterly Review of Economics and Business* 20 (Spring 1980): 30–40.

5232. "Before Going Public: Federal Tax and SEC Consideration." *University of Florida Law Review* 19 (Spring 1967): 679–700.

5233. Benston, George J. "Appraisal of the Costs and Benefits of Government-Required Disclosure: SEC and FTC Requirements." *Law and Contemporary Problems* 41 (Summer 1977): 30–62.

5234. Benston, George J. "Required Disclosure and the Stock Market: An Evaluation of the Securities Exchange Act of 1934." *American Economic Review* 63 (March 1973): 132–55.

5235. Bialkin, K. J., and Grienenberger, W. F. "Summary of the Meeting between Members of the Securities and Exchange Commission and Representatives of the Federal Regulation of Securites Committee. Washington, D.C.—January 2, 1975." *Business Lawyer* 30 (July 1975): 1341–48.

5236. Boynton, Elwood D. "The Development of Government Regulation of the Securities Business: 1930–1960." Ph.D. dissertation, New York University, 1972. 203 p.

5237. Brenner, E. H. "Selected Jury Instruction Forms in an SEC Criminal Case." *Federal Rules Decision* 41 (December 1966): 93.

5238. "Bribes, Kickbacks, and Political Contributions in Foreign Countries—The Nature and Scope of the Securities and Exchange Commission's Power to Regulate and Control American Corporate Behavior." *Wisconsin Law Review* 1976 (1976): 1231–68.

5239. Brodsky, R. E., and Pickholz, M. G. "Assessment of Collateral Estoppel and SEC Enforcement Proceedings after *Parklane Hosiery Co. v. Shore* (99 Sup Ct 645)." *American University Law Review* 28 (Fall 1978): 37–62.

5240. "Broker Silence and Rule 10b-5: Expanding the Duty to Disclose." *Yale Law Journal* 71 (March 1962): 736–47.

5241. "Burden of Proof in SEC Disciplinary Proceedings: Preponderance and Beyond." *Fordham Law Review* 49 (March 1981): 642–60.

5242. Buri, James E. "The Role of the Regulations of the Securities and Exchange Commission as a Means to Strengthen Federal Policy Regarding Conglomerate Mergers." Ph.D. dissertation, University of Notre Dame, 1979. 214 p.

5243. Burton, John C. "Bank Reserves, Disclosure, and the SEC." *Bankers Magazine* 158 (Summer 1975): 50–56.

5244. Calkins, Francis J. "The Securities and Exchange Commission and Corporate Reorganization." Ph.D. dissertation, Northwestern University, 1947. 249 p.

5245. Cary, W. L. "Administrative Agencies and the Securities and Exchange Commission." *Law and Contemporary Problems* 29 (Summer 1964): 653–62.

5246. Cary, William L. "A Review of the Work of the Securities and Exchange Commission—1962–4." *Record of the Association of the Bar of the City of New York* 19 (November 1964): 458–69.

5247. Casey, W. J. "SEC and the Bankers." *Journal of Commercial Bank Lending* 54 (May 1972): 3–9.

5248. Casey, William J. "The SEC's Strategy for Increasing Investor Confidence in the Integrity of Our Capital Markets." *Business Lawyer* 28 (January 1973): 537–43.

5249. Chatov, Robert. "The Collapse of Corporate Financial Standards Regulation: A Study of SEC—Account Interaction." Ph.D. dissertation, University of California, Berkeley, 1973. 577 p.

5250. Clusserath, Thomas M. "The Amended Stockholder Proposal Rule: A Decade Later." *Notre Dame Lawyer* 40 (December 1964): 13–51.

5251. Cohen, Manuel F. "The SEC and Proxy Contests." *Federal Bar Journal* 20 (Spring 1960): 91–110.

5252. Cohen, Manuel F., and Rabin, J. J. "Broker-Dealer Seller Practice Standards: The Importance of Administrative Adjudication in Their Development." *Law and Contemporary Problems* 29 (Summer 1964): 691–727.

5253. "Commingled Civil and Criminal Proceedings: A Peek at Constitutional Limitations and a Poke at the SEC." *George Washington Law Review* 34 (March 1966): 527–39.

5254. Cook, G. Bradford. "SEC and Banks." *Banking Law Journal* 89 (June 1972): 499–513.

5255. Corotto, A. F., and Picard, I. H. "Business Reorganizations under the Bankruptcy Reform Act of 1978—A New Approach to Investor Protections and the Role of the SEC." *DePaul Law Review* 28 (Summer 1979): 961–1006.

5256. "Corporation—Securities Regulation—Violation of Proxy Regulations Gives Private Right of Action but Federal Courts are Limited Regarding Remedy." *Villanova Law Review* 7 (Fall 1961): 125–30.

5257. "Corporations—Insider Transaction—An Officer Selling Stock Acquired from a Corporation in Settlement of a Debt 'Previously Contracted' Need Only Display Subjective Good Faith to be Exempt from Shortswing Liability of Section 16(b) of the Securities Exchange Act of 1934." *University of Pittsburgh Law Review* 23 (June 1962): 1020–24.

5258. Cunningham, J. O. "Environmental Disclosure in Corporate Reporting." *Boston College Environmental Affairs Law Review* 8 (1980): 541–91.

5259. "Current Problems in Securities Regulation." *Michigan Law Review* 62 (February 1964): 680–751.

5260. Dawidoff, Donald J. "The Power of the Securities and Exchange Commission to Require Stock Exchanges to Discipline Members." *Fordham Law Review* 41 (March 1973): 549–68.

5261. Deaktor, D. B. "Integration of Securities Offerings." *University of Florida Law Review* 31 (Spring 1979): 465–550.

5262. DeBedts, R. F. "First Chairmen of the Securities and Exchange Commission: Successful Ambassadors of the New Deal to Wall Street." *American Journal of Economics and Sociology* 23 (April 1964): 165–78.

5263. Delaney, E. T. "Whys and Wherefores of Investment Letters." *Fordham Law Review* 30 (December 1961): 267–73.

5264. "Denying Retroactive Effect to Invalidation of Administrative Rules." *Stanford Law Review* 12 (July 1960): 826–31.

5265. Deutsch, Irwin F. "SEC Powers of Exemption and Unlisted Trading Privileges." *Business Lawyer* 20 (January 1965): 287–91.

5266. "Disclosure of Corporate Payments and Practices: Conduct Regulation through the Federal Securities Laws." *Brooklyn Law Review* 43 (Spring 1977): 681–745.

5267. "Disqualification of SEC Commissioners Appointed from the Staff: Amos Treat, R. A. Holman, and the Threat to Expertise: SEC Law." *Cornell Law Quarterly* 49 (Winter 1964): 257–73.

5268. Dodd, E. M. "The United States Securities and Exchange Commission: 1942–1946." *Modern Law Review* 10 (July 1947): 255–75.

5269. Dolin, M. F. "SEC Rule 2(e) after Carter-Johnson: Toward a Reconciliation of Purpose and Scope." *Securities Regulation Law Journal* 9 (Winter 1982): 331–73.

5270. "Due Process of Law—Participation in Adjudicatory Proceedings and Commission Rulings by a Commissioner Who Has Been a Member of the Investigative Staff During Part of the Time That the Case Was Being Investigated is a Violation of Due Process without any Showing of Personal Bias or Prejudice." *Georgetown Law Journal* 51 (Fall 1962): 186–91.

5271. "Equitable Remedies in SEC Enforcement Actions." *University of Pennnsylvania Law Review* 123 (May 1975): 1188–216.

5272. "Ethical Investor and the SEC: Conflict over the Proper Scope of the Shareholder's Role in the Corporation." *Journal of Corporate Law* 2 (Fall 1976): 115–61.

5273. "The Expanding Jurisdiction of the Securities and Exchange Commission: Variable Annuities and Bank Collective Investment Funds." *Michigan Law Review* 62 (June 1964): 1398–412.

5274. "Fairness and New Asset Valuation in Mergers under the Investment Company Act: *Collins v. SEC* (532 F 2d 584)." *Columbia Law Review* 76 (December 1976): 1332–53.

5275. Flowers, Theodore W. "SEC Investigations: A Current Appraisal." *Pennsylvania Bar Association Quarterly* 43 (June 1972): 521–37.

5276. Frankhauser, Mahlon M., and Belman, P. Dennis. "The Right to Information in the Administrative Process: A Look at the Securities and Exchange Commission." *Administrative Law Review* 18 (Winter–Spring 1966): 101–35.

5277. Freedman, D., and Tew, J. A. "Practice in Securities and Exchange Commission Investigatory and Quasi-Judicial Proceedings." *University of Miami Law Review* 27 (Fall–Winter 1972): 1–21.

5278. Freedman, M. H., and Sporkin, S. "Securities and Exchange Commission's Enforcement Process." *Washington and Lee Law Review* 38 (Summer 1981): 781–812.

5279. Freeman, Milton V. "A Private Practitioner's View of the Development of the Securities and Exchange Commission." *Cleveland Bar Association Journal* 31 (March 1960): 83, 94–99.

5280. Freund, C., and Greene, E. F. "Substance over Form S-14: A Proposal to Reform SEC Regulation of Negotiated Acquisitions." *Business Lawyer* 36 (July 1981): 1483–1536.

5281. Fridkis, Cliff, and Hunter, William J. "Securities and Exchange Commission: Anticompetitive Practices." *George Washington Law Review* 41 (May 1973): 860–79.

5282. Friend, Irwin, and Herman, Edward. "Professor Stigler on Securities Regulation: A Further Comment." *Journal of Business* 38 (January 1965): 106–10.

5283. Frolin, F. L. "Toward Corporate Environmental Disclosure: *NRDC v. SEC.*" *Environmental Affairs* 6 (1977): 155–77.

5284. Gadsby, Edward N. "Historical Development of the SEC—The Government View." *George Washington Law Review* 28 (October 1959): 6–17.

5285. Gadsby, Edward N. "The Securities Exchange Commission." *Boston College Industrial and Commercial Law Review* 11 (May 1970): 833–62.

5286. Garrett, R. "SEC Involvement in the Disclosure of Energy Reserves." *Oil and Gas Law and Taxation Institute* 27 (1976): 97–118.

5287. Garrett, R., and Weaver, W. B. "Securities and Exchange Commission and the Code." *Vanderbilt Law Review* 30 (April 1977): 441–63.

5288. Gilbert, Lewis D. "The Proxy Proposal Rule of the Securities and Exchange Commission." *University of Detroit Law Journal* 33 (January 1956): 191–212.

5289. Goldborough, G. J. "Preliminary Survey of Pending SEC—Otis Litigation—Effect of Regulation of Over-the-Counter Securities Transactions." *George Washington Law Review* 18 (June 1950): 510–40.

5290. Gourevitch, H. G. "Role of the SEC in Tax Matters." *New York University Institute on Federal Taxation* 33 (1975): 1317–63.

5291. Guinn, David M. "The Proposed Revision of the Federal Administrative Procedure Act and Its Effects on the Securities and Exchange Commission." *Arkansas Law Review* 22 (Fall 1968): 439–53.

5292. Hazen, T. L. "Administrative Enforcement: An Evaluation of the Securities and Exchange Commission's Use of Injunctions and Other Enforcement Methods." *Hastings Law Journal* 31 (November 1979): 427–72.

5293. Henderson, G. D., and Sommer, A. A. "Sensitive Corporate Payments: The SEC's Voluntary Disclosure Program." *Institute on Securities Regulation* 8 (1977): 423–51.

5294. Hodes, Scott. "Shelf Registration: The Dilemma of the Securities and Exchange Commission." *Virginia Law Review* 49 (October 1963): 1106–49.

5295. Hooton, M. E. "Role of the Securities and Exchange Commission under Chapter X, Chapter XI and Proposed Amendments to the Bankruptcy Act." *Boston College International and Comparative Law Review* 18 (March 1977): 427–65.

5296. Hopper, George W. "Securities and Exchange Commission as It Affects the General Practitioner." *University of Colorado Law Review* 36 (Fall 1963): 36–75.

5297. Horwitz, B., and Kolodny, R. "Line of Business Reporting and Security Prices: An Analysis of an SEC Disclosure Rule." *Bell Journal of Economics and Management Science* 8 (Spring 1977): 234–49.

5298. "Increased Control over Proxy Contests: The Proposed Amendment to Regulation X-14 of the Securities and Exchange Commission." *Georgetown Law Journal* 44 (January 1956): 285–303.

5299. "Injunctive Relief in SEC Civil Actions: The Scope of Judicial Discretion. *Columbia Journal of Law and Social Problems* 10 (Spring 1974): 328–69.

5300. "Insider Liability under Securities Exchange Act Rule 10b-5: The Cady, Roberts Doctrine." *University of Chicago Law Review* 30 (Autumn 1962): 121–70.

5301. "Invalidation of SEC Rule of Stock Options." *Southwestern Law Journal* 13 (Fall 1959): 545–48.

5302. "Investment Advisers and Disclosure of an Intent to Trade." *Yale Law Journal* 71 (June 1962): 1342–50.

5303. "Investment Company Automatically Reverts from ICC to SEC Control When It Divests Itself of Carriers." *Virginia Law Review* 42 (October 1956): 834–36.

5304. "Is the SEC the Appropriate Federal Agency for Policing Bribery of Foreign Nationals by Multi-national Public Corporations?" *Case Western Reserve Journal of International Law* 13 (Summer 1981): 517–40.

5305. Jacobs, A. S. "Judicial and Adminstrative Remedies Available to the SEC for Breaches of Rule 10b-5." *St. John's Law Review* 53 (Spring 1979): 397–465.

5306. Jarrell, Gregg A. "Economic Effects of Federal Regulation of the Market for New Security Issues." *Journal of Law and Economics* 24 (December 1981): 613–86.

5307. Jenkins, J. A. "Such Good Friends: The SEC and the Securities Lawyers." *Washington Monthly* 9 (February 1978): 53–57.

5308. Jennings, R. W. "Self-Regulation in the Securities Industry: The Role of the Securities and Exchange Commission." *Law and Contemporary Problems* 29 (Summer 1964): 663–90.

5309. "*Jerry T. O'Brien, Inc. v. SEC*: Does the Target of an SEC Investigation have the Right to Notice of Third Party Subpoenas?" *Notre Dame Law Review* 59 (1984): 733–53.

5310. Johnson, N. S. "Dynamics of SEC Rule 2(e): A Crisis for the Bar." *Utah Law Review* 1975 (Fall 1975): 629–61.

5311. Joseph, Michael. "Civil Liability under Rule 10b-5: Judicial Revision of Legislative Intent? D. S. Ruder: A Reply." *Northwestern University Law Review* 59 (May–June 1964): 171–84.

5312. "Judicial Approval of Retroactive Orders of the SEC." *Illinois Law Review* 42 (January–Feburary 1948): 828–32.

5313. Karmel, Roberta S. "Delicate Assignment: The Regulation of Accountants by the SEC." *New York University Law Review* 56 (November/December 1981): 959–77.

5314. Katskee, M. R. "Calculus of Corporate Reorganization Chapter X v. XI and the Role of the SEC Assessed." *Reference Journal* 45 (Spring 1971): 171–75.

5315. Kelleher, J. J. "Scourging the Moneylenders from the Temple: The SEC, Rule 2(e) and the Lawyers." *San Diego Law Review* 17 (July 1980): 801–56.

5316. Kelly, Richard S., and Green, Harry. "Application of Section 16(b) of the Securities and Exchange Act of 1934 to Insiders' Transactions under Employee Stock Option Plans." *Business Lawyer* 17 (January 1962): 402–09.

5317. Kemp, Paul J. "Disciplinary Proceedings by the SEC against Attorneys." *Cleveland-Marshall Law Review* 14 (January 1965): 23–43.

5318. Knorr, John C. "An Appraisal of the Securities and Exchange Commission's Regulation of the New York Stock Exchange Specialist." D.B.A. dissertation, Arizona State University, 1975. 134 p.

5319. Kosek, R. "Professional Responsibility of Accountants and Lawyers before the Securities and Exchange Commission." *Law Library Journal* 72 (Summer 1979): 453–69.

5320. Kripke, Homer. "SEC, Corporate Governance, and the Real Issues." *Business Lawyer* 36 (January 1981): 173–206.

5321. Lacy, R. B. "Adverse Publicity and SEC Enforcement Procedure." *Fordham Law Review* 46 (December 1977): 435–58.

5322. Lalle, A. Wayne, and Morland, John C. "*SEC v. Continental Tobacco Co.* and SEC Proposed Rule 146 As Attempts to Define a Private Offering: The Insecure Exemption from Registration under the Securities Act of 1933." *George Washington Law Review* 41 (March 1973): 582–603.

5323. Lamden, Charles W. "The Securities and Exchange Commission: A Case Study in the Use of Accounting as an Instrument of Public Policy." Ph.D. dissertation, University of California, Berkeley, 1949. 418 p.

5324. Levine, T. A. "SEC Enforcement." *Institute on Securities Regulation* 12 (1981): 245–51.

5325. Levine, T. A.; Ferrara, R. C.; and Moylan, J. J. "Administrative Proceedings under the Securities Exchange Act of 1934." *Mercer Law Review* 25 (Spring 1974): 671–725.

5326. Levy, A. "Role of the Securities and Exchange Commission and the Judicial Functions under the Bankruptcy Reform Act of 1978." *American Bankruptcy Law Journal* 54 (Winter 1980): 29–43.

5327. Liebtag, Bill. "1984 SEC Conference: Self-Regulation Viewed against 'Changing Mood' in the Enforcement Division." *Journal of Accountancy* 157 (March 1984): 42–45, 48–52.

5328. "Limited Waiver of the Attorney-Client Privilege upon Voluntary Disclosure to the SEC." *Fordham Law Review* 50 (April 1982): 963–88.

5329. Lipman, F. D. "SEC's Reluctant Police Force: A New Role for Lawyers." *New York University Law Review* 49 (October 1974): 437–77.

5330. Lockhart, W. J. "SEC No-Action Letters: Informal Advice as a Discretionary Administrative Clearance." *Law and Contemporary Problems* 37 (Winter 1972): 95–134.

5331. Longstreth, B. "The SEC's Role in Financial Disclosure." *Journal of Accounting, Auditing and Finance* 7 (Winter 1984): 110–22.

5332. "Longstreth Study Suggests Reduced SEC Role in Bankruptcy Cases." *Journal of Accountancy* 157 (February 1984): 14.

5333. Loomis, Philip A. "Recent Activity at the Securities and Exchange Commission." *Northwestern University Law Review* 61 (November–December 1966): 677–86.

5334. Loomis, Philip A. "The SEC as Amicus Curiae in Shareholder Litigation—A Reply." *American Bar Association Journal* 52 (August 1966): 749–53.

5335. Loss, L. "The SEC and the Broker-Dealer." *Vanderbilt Law Review* 1 (June 1948): 516–30.

5336. Lothian, J. R. "Role of Government in the Securities Market." *University of Miami Law Review* 33 (September 1979): 1587–96.

5337. Lowenfels, Lewis D. "Scienter or Negligence Required for SEC Injunctions under Section 10(b) and Rule 10b-5: A Fascinating Paradox." *Business Law* 33 (January 1978): 789–809.

5338. Lowenfels, Lewis D. "SEC 'No-Action' Letters: Some Problems and Suggested Approaches." *Columbia Law Review* 71 (November 1971): 1256–79.

5339. Manko, J. M. "Environmental Disclosure—*SEC v. NEPA.*" *Business Law* 31 (July 1976): 1907–19.

5340. Martin, Charles L. "An Empirical Analysis of the Practicality of the Security and Exchange Commission's Replacement Cost Disclosure Requirements." D.B.A. dissertation, George Washington University, 1981. 239 p.

5341. Mathews, Arthur F. "Criminal Prosecutions under the Federal Securities Laws and Related Statutes: The Nature and Development of SEC Criminal Cases." *George Washington Law Review* 39 (July 1971): 901–70.

5342. Mathews, Arthur F. "Litigation and Settlement of SEC Administrative Enforcement Proceedings." *Catholic University Law Review* 219 (Winter 1980): 215–312.

5343. Mathews, Arthur F. "Litigating and Settling SEC Administrative Disciplinary Proceedings." *Litigation* 5 (Spring 1979): 30–34.

5344. Mathews, Arthur F. "SEC and Civil Infunctions: It's Time to Give the Commission an Administrative Cease and Desist Remedy." *Securities Regulation Law Journal* 6 (Winter 1979): 345–56.

5345. Mathews, Arthur F. "SEC Injunctive Proceedings against Attorneys." *Business Lawyer* 36 (July 1981): 1819–29.

5346. Mazo, M. E. "Antitrust Courts Versus the SEC: A Functional Allocation of Decisionmaking Roles." *Harvard Journal on Legislation* 12 (December 1974): 63–110.

5347. McQuillen, Charles D. "Evaluation of Regulation A of the Federal Securities Act of 1933." Ph.D. dissertation, University of Florida, 1969. 324 p.

5348. Meeker, Thomas G. "SEC Legal Assistance Available to the General Practitioner." *Practical Lawyer* 3 (October 1957): 42–49.

5349. Merrifield, L. B. "Investigations by the Securities and Exchange Commission." *Business Law* 32 (July 1977): 1583–631.

5350. Miller, Roger L. "Government Regulation of Corporate Financing with Particular Reference to Authority of the Securities and Exchange Commission under the Public Utility Holding Company Act." Ph.D. dissertation, University of Illinois, 1966. 481 p.

5351. Modigliani, F., and Pogue, G. A. "Alternative Investment Performance Fee Arrangements and Implications for SEC Regulatory Policy." *Bell Journal of Economics and Management Science* 6 (Spring 1975): 127–60.

5352. "*Natural Resources Defense Council, Inc. v. SEC* (432 F Supp 1190): Environmental Disclosure under the Federal Securities Laws." *New England Law Review* 13 (Winter 1978): 523–49.

5353. "*NRDC v. SEC* (606 F 2d 1031): A Question of Judicial Review." *Columbia Journal of Environmental Law* 6 (Spring 1980): 217–42.

5354. Orrick, Andrew D. "Organization, Procedures and Practices of the Securities and Exchange Commission." *George Washington Law Review* 29 (October 1959): 50–85.

5355. Orrick, Andrew D. "The Revised Proxy Rules of the Securities and Exchange Commission." *Business Lawyer* 11 (April 1956): 32–36.

5356. "Parallel Proceedings: The Impact of *SEC v. Dresser Industries, Inc.* (628 F 2d 1368)." *Washington and Lee Law Review* 138 (Summer 1981): 1075–96.

5357. Parlin, G. S., and Everett, E. "Stabilization of Security Prices." *Columbia Law Review* 49 (May 1949): 607–27.

5358. Parrish, Michael E. "Securities Regulation and the New Deal." Ed.D. dissertation, Yale University, 1968. 299 p.

5359. Pashkoff, L. E. "Obtaining Immunity in Securities and Exchange Commission Investigations." *Securities Regulation Law Journal* 5 (Summer 1977): 165–79.

5360. Pines, J. A. "Securities and Exchange Commission and Accounting Principles." *Law and Contemporary Problems* 30 (Autumn 1965): 727–51.

5361. Plum, M. "The SEC Liaison Committee." *Financial Analysts Journal* 39 (November–December 1983): 6.

5362. Posner, Daniel B. "Developments in Federal Securities Regulation." *Business Lawyer* 18 (July–November 1963): 931–59.

5363. Posner, Daniel B. "Developments in Federal Securities Regulation." *Business Lawyer* 22 (April 1967): 645–80.

5364. "Protections Afforded Defendant during Parallel Civil and Criminal Proceedings: *SEC v. Dresser Industries, Inc. Alabama Law Review* 32 (Fall 1980): 231–50.

5365. Purcell, G. "Structure and Functions of the Securities and Exchange Commission." *Federal Bar Journal* 6 (April 1945): 241–52.

5366. Purcell, G.; Foster, R. S.; and Hill, A. "Enforcing the Accountability of Corporate Management and Related Activities of the SEC." *Virginia Law Review* 32 (April 1946): 497–554.

5367. Putnam, Karl B. "An Empirical Evaluation of the Association of Recent Changes in the Securities' Regulatory Environment with the Predictive Ability of Quarterly Earnings." Ph.D. dissertation, Oklahoma State University, 1980. 106 p.

5368. Raaf, Daniel W. "Treatment of Security Holders and Financial Standards Employed by the Securities and Exchange Commission under Section 11 (B) of the Public Utility Holding Company Act of 1935." Ph.D. dissertation, Brown University, 1953.

5369. "Reassessing the Validity of SEC Rule 2(e) Discipline of Accountants." *Boston University Law Review* 59 (November 1979): 968–91.

5370. "Recent Developments in Securities Regulation: A Panel." *Columbia Law Review* 63 (May 1963): 856–72.

5371. "Recent Judicial Extensions of SEC Rule 10b–5." *Columbia Law Review* 63 (May 1963): 934–44.

5372. Reese, Peter A. K. "Securities Legislation of 1960." *Business Lawyer* 17 (January–April 1962): 661–76.

5373. Regis, G. E. "Disappointment for Shareholders." *Business and Society Review* 5 (Fall 1977): 76–77.

5374. "Regulation of Business—SEC Rule X-10B-5—Recovery of Corporation Fradulently Induced to Issue Shares (*Hooper v. Mountain States Sec. Corp.* 282 F 2d 195)." *Michigan Law Review* 59 (June 1961): 1267–70.

5375. "Regulation of Business-Securities Act of 1933—SEC Loses Fight to Regulate Variable Annuity." *Michigan Law Review* 56 (February 1958): 656–59.

5376. "Relationship of SEC to Qualified Employee Plans." *Real Property, Probate and Trust Journal* 2 (Winter 1967): 570–77.

5377. "Report of the Disclosure Advisory Committee." *Institute on Securities Regulation* 9 (1978): 357–59.

5378. Riccio, W. H., et al. "The Securities and Exchange Commission and Small Business: An Overview of an Administrative Response to the Capital Needs of Small Business." *New England Law Review* 18 (1982/1983): 841–81.

5379. "The Role of the SEC in Corporate Reorganizations under the Bankruptcy Act." *University of Illinois Law Forum* 1958 (Winter 1958): 631–45.

5380. "Role of the SEC in Tax Matters." *New York University Institute on Federal Taxation* 33 (1975): 1397–409.

5381. "The Role of the Securities and Exchange Commission under Section 16(b)." *Virginia Law Review* 52 (May 1966): 668–89.

5382. Ruder, David S. "Civil Liability under Rule 10b–5: Judicial Revision of Legislative Intent?" *Northwestern University Law Review* 57 (January–February 1963): 627–86.

5383. "Rule 10b–5—Insider Transactions by Brokers (Cady, Roberts & Co. SEC Securities Exchange Act Release No. 6668—Nov. 8, 1961—)." *University of Miami Law Review* 16 (Spring 1962): 474–77.

5384. Sargeant, J. C. "SEC and the Individual Investor: Restoring His Confidence in the Market." *Virginia Law Review* 60 (April 1974): 553–87.

5385. Schafer, Eldon L. "Securities Regulation of Unlisted Companies." Ph.D. dissertation, University of Nebraska, 1963. 272 p.

5386. Scheiner, J. H., and Morse, W. J. "Impact of SEC Replacement Cost Reporting Requirements: An Analysis." *Quarterly Review of Economics and Business* 19 (Spring 1979): 141–52.

5387. Schneider, Carl W. "Nits, Grits, and Soft Information in SEC Filings." *University of Pennsylvania Law Review* 121 (December 1972): 254–305.

5388. Schoeffler, Charlton G. "A Study of the Influence of the Securities and Exchange Commission on the Development of Accounting." Ph.D. dissertation, University of Illinois, 1960. 374 p.

5389. Schwartz, D. E., and Weiss, E. J. "Assessment of the SEC Shareholder Proposal Rule." *Georgetown Law Journal* 65 (February 1977): 635–90.

5390. Schwert, George W. "Public Regulation of National Securities Exchanges: A Test of the Capture Hypothesis." Ph.D. dissertation, University of Chicago, 1975.

5391. Schwert, George W. "Public Regulation of National Securities Exchanges: A Test of the Capture Hypothesis." *Bell Journal of Economics and Management Science* 8 (Spring 1977): 128–50.

5392. "Scienter in SEC Injunctive Proceedings." *Washington and Lee Law Review* 38 (Summer 1981): 917–36.

5393. "Scope of Review or Standard of Proof—Judicial Control of SEC Sanctions." *Harvard Law Review* 93 (June 1980): 1845–57.

5394. Seamons, Q. F. "SEC and Corporate Governance." *Chicago Bar Record* 60 (March/April 1979): 262–71.

5395. Sebring, H. Orvel. "Log Jam on the Potomac—The Current Delay Problem of the SEC." *Business Lawyer* 15 (July 1960): 921–30.

5396. "SEC—A Close-up: A Panel." *Business Lawyer* 29 (November 1973): 269–309.

5397. "SEC Action against Fraudulent Purchasers of Securities." *Harvard Law Review* 59 (May 1946): 769–80.

5398. "SEC and Allowances in Corporate Reorganization." *Georgetown Law Journal* 42 (March 1954): 420–46.

5399. "SEC and Court-Appointed Directors: Time to Tailor the Director to Fit the Suit." *Washington University Law Quarterly* 60 (Summer 1982): 507–36.

5400. "The SEC and the Problem of Corporate Fiduciary Responsibility and Reorganization Plans." *George Washington Law Review* 18 (June 1950): 492–97.

5401. "SEC as Environmentalist: The Reluctant Champion." *Notre Dame Lawyer* 53 (June 1978): 985–1002.

5402. "SEC Control of Fees and Expenses in Reorganizations under the Public Utility Holding Company Act." *Harvard Law Review* 68 (June 1955): 1409–22.

5403. "SEC Disciplinary Proceedings against Accountants—A Study in Unbridled Discretion." *Administrative Law Review* 27 (Summer 1975): 255–74.

5404. "SEC Disciplinary Proceedings against Attorneys under Rule 2(e)." *Michigan Law Review* 79 (May 1981): 1270–89.

5405. "SEC Enforcement of the Rule 10b-5 Duty to Disclose Material Information—Remedies and the Texas Gulf Sulphur Case." *Michigan Law Review* 65 (March 1967): 944–67.

5406. "SEC Intervention in Corporate Rehabilitation." *Nebraska Law Review* 56 (1977): 635–58.

5407. "SEC—Regulation as a Pervasive Regulatory Scheme—Implied Repeal of the Antitrust Laws with Respect to National Securities Exchanges and the NASD." *Fordham Law Review* 44 (November 1975): 355–72.

5408. "SEC Rule 10b-5 Invoked to Suspend Broker Who Failed to Disclose inside Information When Selling on National Exchange." *Columbia Law Review* 62 (April 1962): 735–41.

5409. "SEC Rule X-10B-5 as a Weapon against the Stock Swindle (*Hooper v. Mountain States Sec. Corp.* 282 F 2d 195)." *Washington and Lee Law Review* 18 (Fall 1961): 253–59.

5410. "SEC Rulemaking Authority and the Protection of Investors: A Comment on the Proposed 'Going Private' Rules." *Indiana Law Journal* 51 (Winter 1976): 433–56.

5411. "*SEC v. National Securities Inc.* 387 F 2d 25." *American University Law Review* 17 (June 1968): 554–61.

5412. "SEC's Power to Exempt from Insider Liability Limited." *Columbia Law Review* 57 (December 1957): 1177–81.

5413. "The SEC's Spy System: Monitoring Computers and Fielding Tips." *Business Week* (April 23, 198): 29–30.

5414. "Section 3(a) (10) of the Securities Act of 1933—*SEC v. Blinder Robinson & Co* (511 F Supp 799)—Proposed Standards for Fairness Hearings." *New England Law Review* 17 (1981–1982): 1397–418.

5415. "Securities Acts—In General—Failure of Broker-Dealer to Disclose Insider Information Violates Antifraud Provisions of the Federal Securities Acts." *Harvard Law Review* 75 (May 1962): 1449–51.

5416. "Securities and Exchange Commission: An Introduction to the Enforcement of the Criminal Provisions of the Federal Securities Laws." *American Criminal Law Review* 17 (Summer 1979): 121–51.

5417. "Securities and Exchange Commission Regulation of Proxy Contests." *Harvard Law Review* 69 (June 1956): 1462–76.

5418. "Securities Exchange Act of 1934: Private Investor has Private Right of Action under Section 14(a) (*Dann v. Studebaker-Packard Corp.* 288 F 2d 201)." *Duke Law Journal* 1962 (Winter 1962): 151–62.

5419. "Securities Regulation—Administrative Agency—Burden of Proof in Administrative Disciplinary Proceedings—In an Adjudicatory Proceeding before the Securities and Exchange Commission, 'Preponderance of the Evidence' Is the Proper Standard of Proof in Determining Whether the Antifraud Provisions of the Federal Securities Laws Have Been Violated." *University of Cincinnati Law Review* 50 (1981): 664–75.

5420. "Securities Regulation—Adminstrative Agency—Burden of Proof in Administrative Disciplinary Proceedings—The Securities and Exchange Commission Must Use the 'Clear and Convincing Evidence' Standard in Administrative Enforcement Proceedings Involving Alleged Violations of Antifraud Sections Which Carry the Risk of Severe Sanctions." *University of Cincinnati Law Review* 47 (1978): 147–54.

5421. "Securities Regulation and Antitrust Laws—Implied Repeal of the Antitrust Laws with Respect to Practices of the Securities Industry—Active SEC Review or Pervasive Regulatory Scheme Sufficient to Imply Immunity." *Loyola University Law Review* (LA) 9 (December 1975): 226–50.

5422. "Securities Regulation: Exemption of Short Term Profits from Recovery under Section 16 (b)." *Duke Law Journal* 1962 (Autumn 1962): 589–94.

5423. "Securities Regulation—Federal Anti-Fraud Provisions—Applicability of Inside Responsibility to Broker in Possession of Insider Corporate Information." *Michigan Law Review* 60 (March 1962): 651–55.

5424. "Securities Regulation—Liability of Insiders—Broker who Obtained Unsolicited Inside Information from Partner-Corporate Director and Sold the Corporation's Nationally Listed Security without Disclosing the Unpublicized Data is Subject to Liability under the Securities Acts of 1933 and 1934." *Virginia Law Review* 48 (March 1962): 398–404.

5425. "Securities Regulation—The Appropriate Remedy for Breach of SEC Settlement Agreement." *Temple Law Quarterly* 51 (1978): 127–38.

5426. Shefsky, L. E. "Publicly Offered Shelters: Can the SEC and IRS be Served?" *Taxes* 53 (September 1975): 516–33.

5427. Shipley, Carl L. "The SEC's Amicus Curiae Aid to Plaintiffs in Mutual Fund Litigation." *American Bar Association Journal* 52 (April 1966): 337–41.

5428. Shipley, Carl L. "The SEC's Expanding Definition of a Security." *New York State Bar Journal* 37 (December 1965): 521–28.

5429. Sierck, A. W. "When the SEC Wants to Talk with Your Client: A Brief Survey of the Scope, Procedures and Consequences of a Formal SEC Investigation." *Law Notes* 12 (Spring 1976): 25–31.

5430. Sierck, A. W., and Watson, K. S. "Post-Watergate Business Conduct: What Role for the SEC?" *Business Lawyer* 31 (January 1976): 721–26.

5431. Silberman, S. J. "Proxy Contests—Clearing Proxy Materials (and Preproxy Materials) at the SEC." *Institute on Securities Regulation* 10 (1979): 215–230.

5432. Sommer, A. A. "Impact of the SEC on Corporate Governance." *Law and Contemporary Problems* 41 (Summer 1977): 115–45.

5433. Sommer, A. A. "Therapeutic Disclosure." *Securities Regulation Law Journal* 4 (Autumn 1976): 263–75.

5434. Solomon, Kenneth I. "Pro Forma Statements, Projections and the SEC." *Business Lawyer* 24 (June 1969): 389–407.

5435. Sprokin, S., and Freedman, M. H. "Securities and Exchange Commission's Enforcement Program: A Debate on the Enforcement Process." *Washington and Lee Law Review* 38 (Summer 1981): 781–812.

5436. Srodes, J. "All Aboard the Money-Go-Round." *Far Eastern Economic Review* 94 (December 24, 1976): 12–13.

5437. Steinberg, M. I. "SEC and Other Permanent Injunctions—Standards for Their Imposition, Modification, and Dissolution." *Cornell Law Review* 66 (November 1980): 27–73.

5438. Steinberg, M. I. "*Steadman v. SEC* (101 S Ct 999)—Its Implications and Significance." *Delaware Journal of Corporate Law* 6 (1981): 1–15.

5439. Stern, R. L. "SEC Action against Fraudulent Purchasers of Securites." *Harvard Law Review* 59 (May 1946): 769–80.

5440. Stern, R. L. "SEC and the Public Utility Holding Company Act." *Harvard Law Review* 59 (July 1946): 925–45.

5441. Stevenson, J. R. "SEC and International Law." *American Journal of International Law* 63 (April 1969): 278–84.

5442. Stevenson, R. B. "SEC and Foreign Bribery." *Business Law* 32 (November 1976): 53–73.

5443. Stevenson, R. B. "SEC and the New Disclosure." *Cornell Law Review* 62 (November 1976): 50–93.

5444. Stigler, George J. "Public Regulation of the Securities Markets." *Journal of Business* 37 (April 1964): 117–42.

5445. "Summary and Successive Suspension of Trading under the Exchange Act of 1934: The Constitution, the Congress and the SEC." *Catholic University Law Review* 18 (Fall 1968): 57–79.

5446. Thomas, B. S. "The Internationalization of the World's Capital Markets—Can the SEC Help Shape the Future?" *Private Investors Abroad* (1982): 83–97.

5447. Thomforde, F. H. "Exemptions from SEC Registration for Small Businesses." *Tennessee Law Review* 47 (Autumn 1979): 3–46.

5448. Thomforde, F. H. "Negotiating Administrative Settlements in SEC Broker-Dealer Disciplinary Proceedings." *New York University Law Review* 52 (May 1977): 237–81.

5449. Thomforde, F. H. "Patterns of Disparity in SEC Administrative Sanctioning Practice." *Tennessee Law Review* 42 (Spring 1975): 465–525.

5450. Tigue, J. J. "Protecting the Client: Mandated Disclosure under SEC and Other Regulatory Agencies' Rules versus Appropriate Nondisclosure to IRS." *New York University Institute on Federal Taxation* 35 (1977): 263–300.

5451. Timbers, William H. "SEC Litigation—Before the Commission and the Courts." *Record* 13 (May 1958): 286–302.

5452. Timbers, William H. "Some Practical Aspects: The SEC and the Federal Judiciary." *American Bar Association Journal* 41 (December 1955): 1136–41.

5453. Timbers, William H., and Garfinkel, Barry H. "Examination of the Commission's Adjudicatory Process: Some Suggestions." *Virginia Law Review* 45 (October 1959): 817–30.

5454. "Toward Corporate Environmental Disclosure: NRDC v. SEC (*Natural Resources Defense Council, Inc. v. SEC.* 432 F Supp 1190)." *Environmental Affairs* 6 (1977): 155–77.

5455. "Trading by Management in Securities of the Corporation during Reorganization." *University of Pennsylvania Law Review* 96 (March 1948): 586–89.

5456. Treadway, J. C. "SEC Enforcement Techniques: Expanding and Exotic Forms of Ancilliary Relief." *Washington and Lee Law Review* 32 (Summer 1975): 637–79.

5457. Trump, Guy W. "The Impact of the Securities and Exchange Commission on Corporate Reorganizations under Chapter X of the National Bankruptcy Act." Ph.D. dissertation, University of Iowa, 1951.

5458. "'Underwriter' Concept of Securities Act Extended to Pledgee (*SEC v. Guild Films Co.* 279 F 2d 485)." *Stanford Law Review* 13 (May 1961): 652–56.

5459. Vinikoor, M. "The Securities Exchange Commission and Proxy Regulation." *Temple Law Quarterly* 21 (April 1948): 406–17.

5460. Von Mehren, R. B., and McCarroll, J. C. "Proxy Rules: A Case Study in the Administrative Process." *Law and Contemporary Problems* 29 (Summer 1964): 728–48.

5461. Welch, Francis X. "Functions of the Federal Power Commission in Relation to the Securities and Exchange Commission." *George Washington Law Review* 14 (December 1945): 81–95.

5462. Werner, W. "Adventure in Social Control of Finance: The National Market System for Securities." *Columbia Law Review* 75 (November 1975): 1233–98.

5463. Wheat, Francis M. "The Disclosure Policy Study of the SEC." *Business Lawyer* 24 (November 1968): 33–42.

5464. Whittington, William E. "The Influence of the United States Securities and Exchange Commission upon the Practice of Auditing." Ph.D. dissertation, University of Illinois, 1957, 197 p.

5465. Wilsey, Harry L. "The Securities and Exchange Commission." Ph.D. dissertation, Cornell University, 1954.

5466. Winter, R. H. "Representing Witnesses in SEC Formal Investigations." *Litigation* 5 (Spring 1979): 24–27.

5467. Wolff, Elliot R. "Comparative Federal Regulation of the Commodities Exchanges and the National Securities Exchanges." *George Washington Law Review* 38 (December 1969): 223–64.

5468. Wolfson, Nicholas. "Critique of the Securities and Exchange Commission." *Emory Law Journal* 30 (Winter 1981): 119–67.

5469. Woodside, Bryan D. "Development of SEC Practices in Processing Registration Statements and Proxy Statements." *Business Lawyer* 24 (January 1969): 375–88.

5470. Woodside, Bryan D. "Resume of the Report of the Special Study of Securities Markets and the Commission's Legislative Proposals." *Business Lawyer* 19 (January 1964): 463–79.

VI. Reference Works

RESEARCH GUIDES

5471. Caiden, Gerald E., et al. *American Public Administration: A Bibliographical Guide to the Literature.* New York: Garland, 1983. 201 p.
This up-to-date guide helps students find reference materials, indexes and leading journals on American public administration and affairs. It covers such areas as public finance, education, urban affairs and American government.

5472. Campbell, Malcolm F. *Business Information Services: Some Aspects of Structure, Organization and Problems.* 2d ed. London: Clive Bingley Ltd., 1981. 179 p.
This concise guide includes thirteen bibliographic essays. It is especially good for identifying information about company and market information.

5473. Daniells, Lorna M., comp. *Business Information Sources.* Rev. ed. Berkeley, CA: University of California Press, 1985. 673 p.
This is the best guide on sources of information in business. It is divided into twenty-one chapters and covers all aspects of business comprehensively.

5474. Larson, Henrietta M. *Guide to Business History.* Cambridge, MA: Harvard University Press, 1948. 1181 p.
Although this guide is somewhat out of date, it is still indispensible for locating information on business history, biographical studies, and histories of businesses and industries.

5475. Ryans, Cynthia C. *International Business Reference Sources.* Lexington, MA: Lexington Books, 1983. 195 p.
This bibliography is the most up-to-date for locating information about companies doing business abroad. It covers government documents, loose-leaf services, journals and other standard reference works.

5476. *Sources of Information in the Social Sciences: A Guide to the Literature.* 2d ed. comp. by Carl White and associates. Chicago: American Library Association, 1973. 703 p.
This is an excellent basic guide to sources of information in the social sciences. It is divided into the eight social sciences and provides annotations of reference works plus a list of important books.

DICTIONARIES

5477. Ammer, Christine, and Ammer, Dean S. *Dictionary of Business and Economics.* Rev. ed. New York: Free Press, 1984. 507 p.
This comprehensive dictionary provides clear and easy to understand definitions. It also provides examples of terms.

5478. Berman, Ben. *The Dictionary of Business and Credit Terms.* New York: National Association of Credit Managers, 1983. 206 p.
This dictionary is designed for use in the business office. It includes definitions of the most commonly used legal and business terms.

5479. Black, Henry C. *Black's Law Dictionary.* 5th ed. St. Paul, MN: West, 1979. 11,511 p.
This is the standard reference source for finding definitions in the fields of American and British law and jurisprudence.

5480. Brownstone, David M., and Franck, Irene M. *The VNR Investor's Dictionary.* New York: Van Nostrand Reinhold, 1981. 326 p.
This specialized dictionary provides definitions for terms used in investments and related businesses. It also includes examples of usage.

5481. Cooper, W. W., and Ijiri, Yuji, eds. *Kohler's Dictionary for Accountants.* 6th ed. Englewood Cliffs, NJ: Prentice-Hall, 1983. 574 p.
While this dictionary specializes in providing accounting definitions, it also covers other areas such as auditing, finance, taxes, statistics, law and information systems.

5482. Davids, Lewis E. *Dictionary of Banking and Finance.* Totowa, NJ: Littlefield, Adams, 1978. 229 p.
This is an excellent desk dictionary. The definitions are concise and clear.

5483. Davids, Lewis E. *Dictionary of Insurance.* 6th rev. ed. Totowa, NJ: Rowman and Allanheld, 1983. 338 p.
This dictionary provides definitions of terms in insurance and related fields. This dictionary is designed for the layman.

5484. Green, Thomas E.; Osler, Robert W.; and Bickley, John S., eds. *Glossary of Insurance Terms.* Santa Monica, CA: Merritt Co., 1980. 234 p.
This dictionary covers insurance terms. It is especially useful for finding out about acronyms and abbreviations.

5485. Greenwald, Douglas, et al. *McGraw-Hill Dictionary of Modern Economics.* 3d ed. New York: McGraw-Hill, 1983. 632 p.
This is one of the best overall dictionaries in the field of economics. It is well written and covers a variety of theories, terms, phrases and techniques.

5486. Johannsen, Hano, and Page, G. Terry. *The International Dictionary of Business.* Englewood Cliffs, NJ: Prentice-Hall, 1981. 376 p.
This dictionary includes over 5,000 entries covering all aspects of business and management. This dictionary is different in that it also includes a great deal of data.

5487. Moffat, Donald W., ed. *Concise Desk Book of Business Finance.* Englewood Cliffs, NJ: Prentice-Hall, 1975. 387 p.
This is a standard dictionary for terms, concepts and theories used in the field of finance.

5488. Moffat, Donald W. *Economics Dictionary.* 2d ed. New York: Elsevier, 1983. 331 p.
This is a basic economics dictionary intended to be clear and understandable by the layman. Its easy-to-understand-style is its strength.

5489. Pearce, David W., ed. *The Dictionary of Modern Economics.* Rev. ed. Cambridge, MA: MIT Press, 1983. 481 p.
This dictionary was designed for students. It also includes entries on economists and organizations.

5490. Rice, Michael D. *The Prentice-Hall Dictionary of Business, Finance and Law.* Englewood Cliffs, NJ: Prentice-Hall, 1983. 362 p.
This dictionary includes a good mixture of terms from both business and law, including finance and government abbreviations and agencies.

5491. Rosenberg, Jerry M. *Dictionary of Banking and Finance.* New York: Wiley, 1982. 690 p.
This comprehensive dictionary includes over 10,000 terms in banking and finance. This dictionary also contains a great deal of data and can be used as a concise statistical handbook as well.

5492. Rosenberg, Jerry M. *Dictionary of Business and Management.* 2d ed. New York: Wiley, 1983. 631 p.
This extensive dictionary includes over 10,000 terms in the fields of business and management. Like his other dictionary, this one also includes extensive data.

5493. Ross, Martin J., and Ross, Jeffrey S. *New Encyclopedic Dictionary of Business Law—With Forms.* 2d ed. Englewood Cliffs, NJ: Prentice-Hall, 1981. 349 p.
This dictionary is primarily useful for the nonlawyer who wants definitions of business legal terms and phrases.

5494. Ryder, F. R., and Jenkins, D. B., eds. *Thomson's Dictionary of Banking.* 12th ed. London: Pitman, 1974. 669 p.
This dictionary includes entries that range from a single sentence to many pages. This dictionary has a strong British focus and is not as useful for American terms.

5495. U.S. Social and Economic Statistics Administration, Department of Commerce. *Dictionary of Economic and Statistical Terms.* 2d ed. Washington, DC: U.S. Government Printing Office, 1973. 83 p.
This dictionary is designed for individuals using the statistics in the *Survey of Current Business and Business Conditions Digest.*

5496. Walmsley, Julian. *A Dictionary of International Finance.* Westport, CT: Greenwood Press, 1979. 270 p.
This dictionary provides clear and concise definitions for terms on international economic, banking, trade and business.

ENCYCLOPEDIAS

5497. Blume, Marshall E., and Friedman, Jack P., eds. *Encyclopedia of Investments.* Boston: Warren, Gorham and Lamont, 1982. 11,041 p.
This comprehensive encyclopedia provides information on all aspects of investment instruments, including market funds, stocks, real estate, bonds, etc.

5498. *Encyclopedia of Accounting Systems.* Rev. and enl. ed. Englewood Cliffs, NJ: Prentice-Hall, 1976. 3 vol.
This encyclopedia is designed for the working accountant. It provides information on accounting in over seventy businesses and industries, including banking, investment, utilities, etc.

5499. *Encyclopedia of Associations.* Detroit, MI: Gale Research Co., 1986. 5 vol.
This comprehensive encyclopedia is most useful in identifying U.S. national organizations and providing background information on each.

5500. *Encyclopedia of Business Information Sources.* 5th ed. Detroit, MI: Gale Research Co., 1983. 728 p.
This encyclopedia is more of a research guide than it is a true encyclopedia. It provides listings of information sources by subject and industries.

5501. *Encyclopedia of Information Systems and Services.* 5th ed. Detroit, MI: Gale Research Co., 1982. 1242 p.
This encyclopedia is the most comprehensive guide to data-base producers, online vendors, bibliographic utilities and fee-based information services. It includes information on numerous services directly related to business.

5502. *Exporters' Encyclopedia.* New York: Dun and Bradstreet International, 1985. 1 vol.
This is a comprehensive world-marketing reference guide. It includes information on markets, organizations, international legal terms as well as specific information on each country.

5503. Greenwald, Douglas, ed. *Encyclopedia of Economics.* New York: McGraw-Hill, 1982. 1070 p.
This is an excellent one-volume encyclopedia of economics. It provides over 300 in-depth definitions of the most important economic concepts and terms.

5504. Munn, Glen G. *Encyclopedia of Banking and Finance.* 8th ed. rev. Boston: Bankers Publishing Co., 1983. 1024 p.
This one-volume encyclopedia includes over 4000 entries on all areas of finance and banking.

5505. *The New Encyclopedia of Stock Market Techniques.* Larchmont, NY: Investors Intelligence, 1983. 1 vol.
This specialized encyclopedia is a survey of methods and techniques used by traders and investors in the field.

5506. Prentice-Hall, Inc. *Accountant's Encyclopedia.* Englewood Cliffs, NJ: Prentice-Hall, 1981. 2 vol.
This encyclopedia is a practical guide to accounting. It is more of a technical guide providing information on how to prepare reports, statements, etc.

5507. Prentice-Hall, Inc. *Corporate Treasurer's and Controller's Encyclopedia.* Englewood Cliffs, NJ: Prentice-Hall, 1975. 2 vol.
This is another technical encyclopedia designed for controllers and treasures. It provides information on such topics as inventories, payroll, cost accounting, etc.

5508. Sills, David, ed. *International Encyclopedia of the Social Sciences.* New York: Macmillan, 1979. 18 vol.
This is the best encyclopedia on the social sciences. Entries are generally several pages in length and include useful bibliographies. It includes information on both topics and individuals.

5509. Thorndike, David. *Thorndike Encyclopedia of Banking and Financial Tables.* Rev. ed. Boston: Warren, Gorham and Lamont, 1980. 1 vol.
This encyclopedia specializes in providing tables in the areas of banking and finance, including data on such topics as interest and saving, bonds, real estate, mortgage loans, etc. This work is more of a statistical handbook than it is an encyclopedia.

HANDBOOKS

5510. Altman, Edward I. *Financial Handbook.* 5th ed. New York: Wiley, 1981. 1 vol.
This handbook is the best work of its kind on banking, money and all aspects of finance. This work also includes numerous bibliographical references.

5511. Arbuckle, J. Gordon, et al. *Environmental Law Handbook.* Bethesda, MD: Government Institutes, 1978. 560 p.
This standard guide to environmental law is heavily footnoted and includes extensive appendices of documents and statutes.

5512. Arkin, Herbert. *Handbook of Sampling for Auditing and Accounting.* 3d ed. New York: McGraw-Hill, 1984. 526 p.
This handbook is a compilation of statistical techniques and methodologies used in auditing and accounting.

5513. Baughn, William H., and Mandich, Donald R., eds. *The International Banking Handbook.* Homewood, IL: Dow Jones-Irwin, 1983. 853 p.
This handbook is an excellent overall survey of international banking. It includes fifty-one chapters on topics such as foreign exchanges, legal and regulatory matters, credits and markets.

5514. Baughn, William H., and Walker, Charles E., eds. *The Bankers' Handbook.* Rev. ed. Homewood, IL: Dow Jones-Irwin, 1978. 1205 p.
This handbook includes essays on eighty-seven topics dealing with all aspects of banking, including credit, regulations, management and systems and control.

5515. Beutel, Frederick K. *Bank Officer's Handbook of Commercial Banking Law.* 4th ed. Boston: Warren, Gorham and Lamont, 1974. 403 p.
This handbook is especially useful for its nontechnical coverage of legal terms and phrases used in banking law.

5516. Black, Homer A., and Edwards, James D., eds. *The Managerial and Cost Accountant's Handbook.* Homewood, IL: Dow Jones-Irwin, 1979. 1297 p.
This handbook includes forty-two chapters focusing on the practical aspects of cost accounting. It covers topics such as methodology, managerial accounting, economic entities, etc.

5517. Blensly, Douglas L., and Plank, Tom M. *Accounting Desk Book.* 7th ed. Englewood Cliffs, NJ: Institute for Business Planning, 1983. 472 p.
This concise reference work provides information on accounting, taxes and management. It is an excellent desk-top reference work.

5518. Brauns, Robert A. W., and Slater, Sarah W., eds. *Bankers Desk Reference.* Boston: Warren, Gorham and Lamont, 1978. 1 vol.
This is an excellent one-volume handbook on banking. It includes chapters on consumerism, government regulations, state laws and the reserve system.

5519. Buge, Edward W. *Business Financing Handbook.* Englewood Cliffs, NJ: Prentice-Hall, 1982. 431 p.
This handbook is intended for the layman and provides easy and clear information. It also includes numerous exhibits, tables and illustrative materials.

5520. Burton, John C.; Palmer, Russell E.; and Kay, Robert S., eds. *Handbook of Accounting and Auditing.* Boston: Warren, Gorham and Lamont, 1981. 1 vol.
This handbook is a scholarly volume including forty-nine chapters on various aspects of accounting and auditing. It includes chapters on the legal environment and regulatory matters.

5521. Cashin, James A., ed. *Handbook for Auditing.* New York: McGraw-Hill, 1971. 1 vol.
This handbook covers all aspects of auditing, especially new techniques and procedures. Almost all of the chapters include bibliographies.

5522. Castle, Gray; Cushman, Robert F.; and Kensicki, Peter R., eds. *The Business Insurance Handbook.* Homewood, IL: Dow Jones-Irwin, 1981. 753 p.
This handbook is especially useful for information regarding the legal aspects of the real estate industry, including regulatory matters.

5523. Cleverley, William O., ed. *Handbook of Health Care Accounting and Finance.* Rockville, MD: Aspen Systems Corporation, 1982. 2 vols.
This handbook includes sixty-six chapters on accounting and finance in the health care industry. It is an especially good source for information on government regulation in this industry.

5524. *The Corporation Manual.* New York: United States Corporation Co., 1985. 2 vols.
This annual publication provides information regarding the statutory provisions relating to the regulation and taxation of domestic and foreign corporations.

5525. Darst, David M. *The Handbook of the Bond and Money Markets.* New York: McGraw-Hill, 1981. 461 p.
This handbook was designed for both the professional and the layman. It includes an excellent account of the federal reserve system.

5526. Davidson, Disney, and Weil, Roman L., eds. *Handbook of Cost Accounting.* New York: McGraw-Hill, 1978. 1 vol.
This handbook includes twenty-seven chapters covering all aspects of cost accounting. It contains information such as how cost accounting relates to regulatory matters.

5527. Davidson, Sidney, and Weil, Roman L., eds. *Handbook of Modern Accounting.* 3d ed. New York: McGraw-Hill, 1983. 1 vol.
This handbook is a good introductory guide to accounting. It includes forty-two chapters, each containing a short bibliography.

5528. Davis, F. T. *Business Acquisitions Desk Book.* 2d ed. Englewood Cliffs, NJ: Institute for Business Planning, 1981. 414 p.
This handbook specializes on the topic of acquisitions. It provides in-depth coverage of securities, tax and regulatory laws.

5529. Dominguez, George. *Government Relations: A Handbook for Developing and Conducting the Company Program.* New York: Wiley, 1982. 415 p.
This handbook provides information regarding the various relationships between businesses and government, including regulatory procedures and the legal environment.

5530. *Donnelly SEC Handbook.* Chicago: Donnelly and Sons, 1982. 2 vol.
This handbook is a compilation of laws, rules and forms under the Securities Act of 1933, Securities Exchange Act of 1934 and the Public Utility Holding Act.

5531. Fabozzi, Frank J., and Zarb, Frank G., eds. *Handbook of Financial Markets: Securities, Options, Futures.* Homewood, IL: Dow Jones-Irwin, 1981. 794 p.
This handbook focuses on all types of financial markets. It is especially useful for information regarding securities regulations and other forms of market regulation in general.

5532. George, Abraham M., and Giddy, Ian H., eds. *International Finance Handbook.* New York: Wiley, 1983. 2 vols.
This comprehensive handbook provides information regarding the practice of international finance. This is an excellent source for information regarding trade regulation.

5533. Gladstone, David J. *Venture Capital Handbook.* Reston, VA: Reston Publishing Co., 1983. 402 p.
This guide to how to raise venture capital includes important information about government regulations, programs and opportunities.

5534. Goodman, Sam R., and Reece, James S., eds. *Controller's Handbook.* Homewood, IL: Dow Jones-Irwin, 1978. 1253 p.
This comprehensive handbook includes forty-six chapters on topics such as budgeting, performance and expenditures. It also contains information regarding the regulation of financial procedures.

5535. Gotthilf, Daniel L. *Treasurer's and Controller's Desk Book.* Englewood Cliffs, NJ: Prentice-Hall, 1977. 511 p.
This handbook includes extensive exhibits, charts, graphs and illustrative materials. It is a concise and handy source for quick information on the legal environment in which treasurers and controllers work.

5536. Gregg, Davis W., and Lucas Vane B., eds. *Life and Health Insurance Handbook.* 3d ed. Homewood, IL: Dow Jones-Irwin, 1973. 1336 p.
This handbook on the insurance industry covers such topics as pensions, estate planning, government benefits, etc. This is a good source for information regarding government regulation of this industry.

5537. Heller, Pauline B. *Handbook of Federal Bank Holding Company Law.* New York: Law Journal Press, 1976. 413 p.
This handbook is the only one of its kind. It provides extensive material on bank holding company law, regulations and judicial interpretations and rulings.

5538. Holzman, Robert S. *Dun and Bradstreet's Handbook of Executive Tax Management.* New York: T. Y. Crowell, 1974. 372 p.
The aim of this handbook is to give managers the information they need about tax regulations to make business decisions.

5539. Kaufman, Perry J. *Handbook of Futures Markets: Commodity, Financial, Stock Index, Options.* New York: Wiley, 1984. 1 vol.
This comprehensive handbook specializes on futures markets, including their organizations and operations. This work also details the regulation of futures markets.

5540. Lee, Steven J., and Colman, Robert D., eds. *Handbook of Mergers, Acquisitions and Buyouts.* Englewood Cliffs, NJ: Prentice-Hall, 1981. 747 p.
This merger handbook includes thirty-nine chapters on all aspects of buyouts, acquisitions and mergers. It includes information on antitrust, securities regulation and state laws.

5541. Levine, Sumner N., ed. *Dow Jones-Irwin Business and Investment Almanac.* Homewood, IL: Dow Jones-Irwin, 1982. 577 p.
This almanac is largely a compilation of data, including industrial surveys, business and economic indicators. This work also includes SEC corporate filings and other data useful to the study of government and industry.

5542. Levine, Sumner N., ed. *The Investment Manager's Handbook.* Homewood, IL: Dow Jones-Irwin, 1980. 1037 p.
Intended for investment managers, this volume includes thirty-eight chapters on topics such as stock market indexes, money market funds and management. It includes an excellent section on regulatory politics.

5543. Maffry, Ann D. *Foreign Commerce Handbook.* 17th ed. Washington, DC: International Division, Chamber of Commerce of the United States, 1981. 274 p.
This reference book lists the major international and national organizations that provide international business services. The work also includes an extensive bibliography of books, articles and reports on the subject.

5544. Makridakis, Spyros, and Wheelwright, Steven C., eds. *The Handbook of Forecasting: A Manager's Guide.* New York: Wiley, 1982. 620 p.
This specialized handbook covers all aspects of forecasting, including approaches, applications, roles of and management. It also discusses the political and regulatory aspects of forecasting.

5545. Metzger, Norman, ed. *Handbook of Health Care Human Resources Management.* Rockville, MD: Aspen Systems Corporation, 1981. 903 p.
This handbook includes seventy-one articles on health care resources. Most important to the subject of regulation are the sections on labor relations and employees.

5546. Pierce, Phyllis S., ed. *Dow Jones Investor's Handbook.* Homewood, IL: Dow Jones-Irwin. (Annual)
This volume is a useful compilation of daily and historical data on stock prices. It is particularly useful for data on transportation and utility stocks.

5547. Prentice-Hall, Inc. *Federal Tax Handbook.* Englewood Cliffs, NJ: Prentice-Hall. (Annual)
This is a comprehensive guide to tax preparations for businesses and industries.

5548. Rao, Dileep. *Handbook of Business Finance and Capital Sources.* 2d ed. New York: AMACOM, 1982. 606 p.
This volume is both a sourcebook and directory of capital sources, including banks and venture capital companies.

5549. Redding, Harold T., and Knoght, Guyon H. *The Dun and Bradstreet Handbook of Credits and Collections.* New York: T. Y. Crowell, 1974. 352 p.
This guide to credit management includes sections on credit systems, credit informations and the laws and regulations affecting this industry.

5550. Rogers, William J. *Handbook on Environmental Law.* St. Paul, MN: West, 1977. 956 p.
This is an excellent introductory textbook designed for law students. It provides extensive coverage of environmental regulations.

5551. Rothstein, Nancy H., and Little, James M., eds. *The Handbook of Financial Futures: A Guide for Investors and Professional Financial Managers.* New York: McGraw-Hill, 1984. 638 p.
This comprehensive handbook is designed for both the layman and the expert. It analyses such topics as futures markets, speculation and regulatory implications.

5552. Scharf, Charles A. *Acquisitions, Mergers, Sales and Takeovers: A Handbook with Forms.* Englewood Cliffs, NJ: Prentice-Hall, 1971. 332 p.
This specialized handbook is a guide to acquiring and merging business. It gives detailed analyses of rules, regulations and legislation regarding mergers.

5553. Seidler, Lee J., and Carmichael, D. R. *Accountant's Handbook.* 6th ed. New York: Wiley, 1981. 2 vols.
This is the most comprehensive handbook on accounting. It includes forty-five chapters, each with a bibliography. There are several chapters related to regulatory aspects of accounting.

5554. Standard and Poor's Corp. *Analyst's Handbook.* New York: Standard and Poor's Corp. (Annual)
This handbook is chiefly a compilation of composite corporate per share data. It includes data on sales, profits, earnings and prices for seventy-two industries.

5555. Sweeny, H. W. Allen, and Rachlin, Robert. *Handbook of Budgeting.* New York: Wiley, 1981. 778 p.
This handbook of budgeting includes twenty-six chapters on such topics as concepts, applications and techniques. The volume also discusses budgeting in relation to regulatory processes.

5556. Troy, Leo. *Almanac of Business and Industrial Financial Ratios.* Englewood Cliffs, NJ: Prentice-Hall. (Annual)
This handbook provides financial and operating ratios for approximately 150 industries.

5557. Walter, Ingo, and Murray, Tracy, eds. *Handbook of International Business.* New York: Wiley, 1982. 1 vol.
This handbook includes forty-two chapters covering topics such as international marketing, trade, finance and management. It is especially useful for its coverage of the legal aspects of international business.

5558. Weston, J. Fred, and Goudzwaard, Maurice B., eds. *Treasurer's Handbook.* Homewood, IL: Dow Jones-Irwin, 1976. 1181 p.
This volume includes thirty-five chapters covering the role and work of corporate treasurers. It is particularly useful for finding information regarding corporate responsibilities under the law.

DIRECTORIES

5559. *Book of the States.* Lexington, KY: Council of State Governments. (Biennial)
This volume details the structure, operations and financial working of state government. It includes a directory of state elective officials and administrative officials.

5560. *Business Organizations and Agencies Directory.* 2d ed. Detroit, MI: Gale Research Co., 1984. 1371 p.
This work is a directory of major business and trade organizations. It also includes government agencies, labor unions, convention centers, publishers, research centers and data services.

5561. *Conservation Directory.* Washington, DC: National Wildlife Federation, 1979. 1 vol.
This directory is a compilation of organizations, citizens' groups and agencies, arranged by states, that are concerned with natural resource use and management.

5562. *Consumer Protection Directory.* Chicago: Marquis Who's Who, Inc., 1975. 1 vol.
This directory covers all levels of government in both the United States and Canada dealing with consumerism.

5563. Corporate Data Exchange, Inc. *CDE Stock Ownership Directory: Banking and Finance,* New York: CDE, 1980. 245 p.
This directory of 153 banking and financial companies provides the names and information of principal stockholders.

5564. *Directory of Business and Financial Services.* 8th ed. New York: Special Libraries Association, 1984. 189 p.
This directory supplies information for over 1,000 economic, business and financial services published serially. It also includes information on over eighty online services.

5565. *Directory of Corporate Affiliations.* Skokie, IL: National Register Publishing Co. (Annual)
This directory provides information for over 4,000 parent companies. The directory supplies data about sales, number of employees, corporate officers and subsidiaries.

5566. *Directory of Corporate Financing.* New York: Dealer's Digest. (Semiannual)
This specialized directory reports security offerings. The information is arranged alphabetically by issuer with information regarding the date, amount and underwriter.

5567. *Directory of Directories.* Detroit, MI: Gale Research Co. (Biennial)
This directory is extremely comprehensive, including over 6,000 citations. It covers such directories as buyer's guides, professional directories and advertising directories.

5568. *Directory of Federal Regulatory Agencies.* St. Louis, MO: Center for the Study of American Business, Washington University, 1978. 69 p.
This directory provides a listing for federal agencies, including their legislative authority, areas of regulatory activity and organization.

5569. *Directory of Municipal Bond Dealers of the United States.* New York: Bond Buyer. (Semiannual)
This is directory of bond dealers, lawyers and municipal consultants.

5570. *Directory of State Environmental Agencies.* Chicago: American Bar Association, Section of General Practice and Young Lawyers Division, 1985. 273 p.
This directory provides a listing of the states' major environmental regulatory agencies, including a description of the agencies' duties and the statutory authority under which they operate.

5571. *Directory of United States Importers.* New York: Chamber of Commerce. (Biennial)
This directory lists, state by state, over 25,000 importers. It provides information regarding the type of business, customhouse broker, port of entry and address.

5572. *Directory of Wall Street Research.* Rye, NY: Nelson Publications. (Annual)
This directory lists Wall Street research analysts. This volume also includes a catalog of over 10,000 research reports, many of which are on regulation.

5573. *Directory of Online Databases.* Santa Monica, CA: Cuadra Associates, Inc. (Quarterly)
This directory lists online databases, including both bibliographic and numerical databases. It provides the name of the vendor, coverage, time span covered and cost.

5574. *Dun's Marketing Services. America's Corporate Families: The Billion Dollar Directory.* Parsippany, NJ: Dun's. (Annual)
This directory lists over 2,500 of the largest companies. It provides information on subsidiaries, officers, sales, number of employees and chief executives.

5575. *Electronic News Financial Fact Book and Directory.* New York: Fairchild Publications. (Annual)
This directory specializes in electronic companies, giving the names of officers, subsidiaries, sales, earning, number of employees and other related information.

5576. *Federal Regulatory Directory.* Washington, DC: Congressional Quarterly Inc. (Annual)
This directory is a guide to federal regulatory activity including extensive profiles of regulatory agencies, including information resources, organization, and a listing for all agencies with rule making power.

5577. *Foundation Directory.* New York: Foundation Center. (Biennial)
This directory lists foundations, state by state, which have assets over $1 million. It provides information about donors, activities, officers and directories, and grants.

5578. *Guide to American Directories.* Coral Springs, FL: B. Klein Publications. (Biennial)
This is a directory of directories in the areas of industry, commerce, and the professions. It includes information on over 7,000 major directories.

5579. *Guide to World Commodity Markets.* 3d ed. New York: Nichols Publishing Co., 1982. 393 p.
This directory lists commodity exchanges and markets throughout the world. It also includes a country by country listing of commodity statistics for the major commodities.

5580. *Information Industry Market Place.* New York: R.R. Bowker. (Annual)
This is a directory of information services which are machine readable, including online databases. It is especially good for identifying services in the area of business.

5581. *Insurance Almanac.* Englewood, NJ: Underwriter Printing and Publishing Co. (Annual)
This is a directory of insurance companies. It gives data on the history of the company, officers and statistics.

5582. *The Insurance Directory and Year Book.* Brentwood, Middlesex, England: Buckley Press Ltd. (Annual)
This directory provides information about insurance companies in the United Kingdom.

5583. *Million Dollar Directory.* Parsippany, NJ: Dunn's, 3 vols. (Annual)
This directory provides information for over 120,000 businesses. It includes such information as officers, number of employees, stock exchange abbreviation, etc. There is a geographic index and SIC index.

5584. National Association of Mutual Savings Banks. *Directory and Guide to the Mutual Savings Banks of the United States.* New York: The Association. (Annual)
This is a complete directory of mutual saving banking, providing the types of accounts, interest rates and reserves.

5585. *National Trade and Professional Associations of the United States.* Washington, DC: Columbia Books, Inc. (Annual)
This is an alphabetical listing of approximately 6,000 trade associations, organizations, societies and unions. It provides information about the association's officers, membership, activities and history.

5586. *Rand McNally International Bankers Directory.* Chicago: Rand McNally. 4 vols. (Semiannual)
This directory includes both a geographical listing of U.S. banks as well as a section on the 100 largest world banks. The directory also includes banking associations.

5587. *Research Centers Directory.* Detroit, MI: Gale Research Co. (Annual)
This directory lists over 6,000 research centers, institutes, foundations and university centers in the United States. It is particularly useful for finding out about centers that do research on regulation.

5588. *Standard and Poor's Register of Corporations, Directors and Executives.* New York: Standard and Poor's Corp. 3 vols. (Annual)
The first volume is an alphabetical listing of over 40,000 companies, including the standard information. The second volume is a listing of directors and executives. The third volume is an index volume, including indexes by location and SIC code.

5589. *Standard Directory of Advertisers.* Skokie, IL: National Register Publishing Co. (Annual)
This directory includes over 17,000 companies that advertize nationally. The directory is arranged by industry and includes an alphabetical index of companies.

5590. *Thomas Register of American Manufacturers and Thomas Register Catalog File.* New York: Thomas Publishing Co. 17 vols. (Annual)
This directory is a comprehensive directory to industries and businesses.

5591. *U.S. Industrial Directory.* Stamford, CT: Cahners Publishing Co. 4 vols. (Annual)
This directory is very similar to Thomas' but not nearly as comprehensive. It includes a telephone/address directory, list of companies arranged by industry and catalog of literature, such as brochures, catalogs, etc.

5592. *Washington Information Directory.* Washington, DC: Congressional Quarterly, Inc. (Annual)
This annual directory is a guide to information sources in the executive branch, Congress, and private organizations in the Washington area.

5593. *Who Owns Whom: North America.* London: Dun and Bradstreet. (Annual)
This directory lists U.S. companies and their subsidiaries. The companies also are indexed by subsidiaries.

5594. *World Aviation Directory.* Washington, DC: Ziff-Davis Publishing Co. (Semiannual)
Issued twice yearly, this includes sections on federal, state, and local government and information on the aviation industry, both domestic and international.

BIOGRAPHICAL DIRECTORIES

5595. *American Men and Women of Science: Economics.* New York: R. R. Bowker, 1974. 636 p.
This volume contains in-depth biographies of American economists up to the 1970s.

5596. *American Men and Women of Science: The Social and Behavioral Sciences.* 13th ed. New York: R. R. Bowker, 1978. 1545 p.
This volume contains in-depth biographies of American social scientists. It is arranged by discipline.

5597. *The Corporate Finance Bluebook.* New York: K. Zehring. (Annual)
This directory provides biographical and corporate information for over 2,000 managers in the field of finance.

5598. *Directory of U.S. Banking Executives.* New York: American Banker, 1980. 824 p.
This biographical directory provides brief biographical and corporate information for American bankers.

5599. *Federal Executive Telephone Directory.* Washington, DC: Carroll Publishing Co. (Annual)
This is an alphabetical listing of all executive managers in cabinet departments and major administrative agencies with a cross reference to the organization and title.

5600. *Federal Yellow Book.* Washington, DC: The Washington Monitor. (Annual)
This is a looseleaf directory of key staff people in the White House, the executive office of the President, and federal departments and agencies, listed by organization, including titles, names, addresses and telephone numbers. This directory is kept up to date by replacement pages issued throughout the year.

5601. Ingham, John W. *Biographical Dictionary of American Business Leaders.* Westport, CT: Greenwood Press, 1983. 4 vols.
This set provides in-depth biographies of 835 American businessmen from colonial times to the present.

5602. *Standard and Poor's Security Dealers of North America.* New York: Standard and Poor's Corp. (Semiannual)
This is a biographical directory of brokers, dealers and other individuals related to the securities industry.

5603. *Who's Who in America.* Chicago: Marquis Who's Who. 2 vols. (Biennial)
This is a general who's who. It provides brief biographical information.

5604. *Who's Who in Finance and Industry.* Chicago: Marquis Who's Who. (Biennial)
This biographical directory focuses on businessmen in the areas of finance and industry.

5605. *Who's Who in the Securities Industry.* Chicago: Economist Publishing Co. (Annual)
This is another biographical directory of individuals working in the securities industry. It includes pictures of each individual.

BIBLIOGRAPHIES

5606. Aggarwal, Raj. *The Literature of International Business Finance.* New York: Praeger, 1984. 297 p.
This is a comprehensive bibliography of over 3,600 citations on all aspects of international finance. It includes citations dealing with international regulatory activities.

5607. American Council of Life Insurance. *A List of Worthwhile Life and Health Insurance Books.* New York: ACLI and the Health Insurance Institute. (Annual)
This is an excellent place to start a search for citations to materials dealing with the health insurance business. Entries are annotated and arranged by subject.

5608. *Bibliographic Guide to Business and Economics.* Boston: G. K. Hall. (Annual)
This is a comprehensive listing of materials in the fields of economics and business which have been cataloged by the Library of Congress and the New York Public Library. It is arranged by author, title and subject.

5609. Brealey, Richard A., and Pyle, Connie, comps. *A Bibliography of Finance and Investment.* Cambridge, MA: MIT Press, 1973. 361 p.
This bibliography of over 3,600 citations to books, articles and dissertations focuses on corporate finance and the securities industry.

5610. Brooke, Michael Z.; Black, Mary; and Nevil, Paul. *International Business Bibliography.* New York: Garland, 1977. 480 p.
This bibliography includes citations to books and articles on all aspects of international business. It is arranged by author and includes a subject index.

5611. Chicago Board of Trade. *Commodity Futures Trading: A Bibliography.* Chicago: Board of Trade. (Annual)
This continuing bibliography includes books and articles arranged by topic. The beginning volume covered the years 1967–1974.

5612. *Corporate and Industry Research Reports.* Eastchester, NY: JA Micropublishing, Inc., 1983-.
This is a microfiche collection of over 13,000 research reports on industries and corporations. It is a complete text collection plus printed guide.

5613. Haikalis, Peter D. *Real Estate: A Bibliography of the Monographic Literature.* Westport, CT: Greenwood Press, 1983. 317 p.
This is a basic bibliography of books on land use, housing, investment and real estate business. It includes a section on the legal regulations of real estate.

5614. Hills, William G., et al. *Administration and Management: A Selected and Annotated Bibliography.* Norman, OK: University of Oklahoma Press, 1975. 182 p.
This bibliography includes citations to material relevant to both public administration and business management. It is particularly useful in the area of administrative processes and law.

5615. *Insurance Society of New York. Books in Insurance: Property, Liability, Marine, Surety.* 10th ed. New York: Insurance Society, 1980. 21 p.
This is a highly selected annotated bibliography of books and articles on the insurance industry.

5616. Jones, Donald G., and Troy, Helen. *A Bibliography of Business Ethics, 1976–1980.* Charlottesville, VA: University Press of Virginia, 1982. 220 p.
This bibliography includes citations to books and articles on business ethics, including such topics as corporate responsibility and accountability.

5617. Lister, Roger, and Lister, Eva, comps. *Annotated Bibliography of Corporate Finance.* Toronto, Ontario: Macmillan of Canada, 1979. 240 p.
This classified bibliography includes citations to material on all aspects of both theoretical and practical finance. It includes an author and subject index.

5618. Lovett, Robert W. *American Economic and Business History Information Sources.* Detroit, MI: Gale Research Co., 1971. 323 p.
This annotated bibliography includes citations to all aspects of American economic and business history, including agriculture, technology, labor and individual industry histories.

5619. *Mergers and Acquisitions: A Comprehensive Bibliography.* McLean, VA: Mergers and Acquisitions, 1972. 223 p.
Though outdated now, this is a comprehensive bibliography on mergers and acquisitions. It is arranged in a classified format by topic and includes country and industry indexes.

5620. Mints, Frederic E. *Bibliography of Internal Auditing, 1969–1979.* Altamonte Springs, FL: Institute of Internal Auditors, 1981. 204 p.
This is a selected bibliography of books and articles covering the literature of internal auditing, including legal and regulatory aspects.

5621. National Association of Accountants. *The Bookshelf.* New York: The Association, 1982. 83 p.
This is a basic bibliography of books and journals on accounting. The bibliography is designed to serve as a basic reading source list for accountants.

5622. *Occupational Safety and Health: A Bibliography.* Washington, DC: U.S. Department of Labor, 1977. 37 p.
This is a compilation of various sources dealing with occupational safety and health and is geared toward employers, employees and the public.

5623. Price Waterhouse and Company. *Basic Accounting Library.* New York: Price Waterhouse, 1980. 9 p.
This is a basic reading list of materials in accounting, recommending the best journals and reference works.

5624. Society of Industrial Realtors. *Industrial Real Estate: An Annotated Bibliography.* Washington, DC: Society of Industrial Realtors, 1982. 34 p.
This is a highly selective bibliography of articles, reports and books on the topic of industrial real estate.

SOURCEBOOKS

5625. Berg, Richard K., and Klotzman, Stephen H. *An Interpretative Guide to the Government in the Sunshine Act.* Washington, DC: U.S. Government Printing Office, 1978. 134 p.
This work presents an examination of the questions which have arisen or will most likely arise under the open meeting provision of the Act.

5626. *The Corporate Finance Sourcebook.* New York: K. Zehring. 1 vol. (Annual)
This sourcebook is essentially a directory of firms that are sources for corporate financing, including capital lenders, commercial lenders, banks, pensions, brokers and securities firms.

5627. Crane, Donald P., and Jones, William A. *The Public Manager's Guide.* Washington, DC: Bureau of National Affairs, 1982. 287 p.
This sourcebook is designed as a practical guide for managers. After each chapter there is a list of further readings, journals, reference works and associations.

5628. Federal Home Loan Bank Board. *Savings and Home Financing Source Book.* Washington, DC: Federal Home Loan Bank Board. (Annual)
This sourcebook is essentially a statistical compendium for the saving and loan industry.

5629. Hancock, William A. *Executive's Guide to Business Law.* New York: McGraw-Hill, 1979. 1 vol.
This sourcebook contains sixty-one chapters on all aspects of business law. It includes chapters on trade regulation, securities law, warranty and liability and environmental regulations.

5630. Malawer, Stuart S. *Federal Regulation of International Business.* Washington, DC: National Chamber Foundation, 1981. 2 vols.
This is a sourcebook of treaties, legislation, regulations, cases and secondary sources dealing with international business. It is arranged by subject.

5631. *Merger and Acquisition Sourcebook.* Santa Barbara, CA: Quality Services, Co. (Annual)
This sourcebook is essentially an inventory of merger activity during the previous year. It includes a listing of mergers, terminations and firms specializing in mergers and statistics.

5632. Michael, James R., ed. *Working on the System: A Comprehensive Manual for Citizen Access to Federal Agencies.* New York: Ralph Nader's Center for Study of Responsive Law, 1974. 950 p.
This is guidebook for citizen participation in the federal regulatory process. It includes chapters on FTC, ICC, FCC, AEC, FPC, CAB, FDA, NHTSA, IRS, EPA, OSHA and CPSC.

5633. *Television Factbook.* Washington, DC: Television Digest, Inc. (Annual)
This publication is in two volumes and gives listings and current information for U.S. and Canadian television stations.

5634. *Washington Researchers.* Washington, DC: Washington Researchers, 1983, 521 p.

This sourcebook is a directory of organizations, associations and agencies that provide information of private and public companies. It covers such sources as libraries, databases, federal, state and local sources, and private information vendors and brokers.

5635. Wasserman, Paul, and Memmerling, Diane. *Commodity Prices.* Detroit, MI: Gale Research Co., 1974. 200 p.

Though out of date, this sourcebook lists the wholesale and retail quotations for more than 5,000 products.

YEARBOOKS

5636. *Bankers' Almanac and Year Book.* London: T. Skinner. (Annual)

This yearbook includes a listing of all British and international banks. It also includes information and statistics on currencies of the world.

5637. *Broadcasting Yearbook.* Washington, DC: Broadcasting Publications, Inc. (Annual)

This book gives a complete listing of all aspects of broadcasting, including full listings for every radio and TV station in the U.S.

5638. *Oil and Gas International Year Book.* Harlow, Essex, England: Longman. (Annual)

This yearbook contains textual information and statistical data for all major world oil and gas companies.

5639. *Securities Industry Yearbook.* New York: Securities Industry Association. (Annual)

This yearbook provides a listing of all SIA members. It also includes basic statistics about the security industry and a ranked list of firms.

5640. *Yearbook on Corporate Mergers, Joint Ventures and Corporate Policy.* Ipswich, MA: Cambridge Corporation. (Annual)

This yearbook lists mergers for the previous year by industry. There is also a section summarizing the major events and trends of the year.

CASEBOOKS

5641. Davis, Kenneth C. *Administrative Law of the Seventies.* Rochester, NY: Lawyers Co-operative Publishing Co., 1976. 280 p.

This work is a supplement to Davis' *Administrative Law Treatise.*

5642. Davis, Kenneth C. *Administrative Law Treatise.* St. Paul, MN: West, 1958. 4 vols.

This is the standard legal treatise for the treatment of this subject area.

5643. Lowenfeld, Andreas F. *Aviation Law: Cases and Materials.* Albany, NY: Matthew Bender, 1981. 1 vol.

This book includes chapters on the regulation of domestic and international air transportation. A separate documents supplement includes over forty domestic and international documents.

5644. Schwartz, Bernard. *Economic Regulation of Business and Industry: A Legislative History of U.S. Regulatory Agencies.* New York: Chelsea Publishers, 1973. 5 vols.

This work is part of the *Statutory History of the United States* series. It has chapters on the ICC, FTC, FPC, FCC, SEC, NLRB, CAB and FAA.

CITATORS

5645. *Shepard's Acts and Cases by Popular Names: Federal and State.* Colorado Springs, CO: Shepard's Citations, 1968–.
Federal statutes are often referred to by their popular names. This service lists statutes in alphabetical order by popular name and cites their location in the *Statutes at Large* and *United States Code.* It provides the same access for state acts. Federal cases referred to by popular names can be accessed by using the section that refers you to the *United States Supreme Court Reports.*

5646. *Shepard's Federal Labor Law Citations.* Colorado Springs, CO: Shepard's Citations, Inc., 1959–.
Published with bimonthly cumulative supplements, the set consists of a case edition and a statute edition. The case edition covers federal labor law decisions as reported in the federal court system, Supreme Court decisions, the *Federal Reporter* and the *Federal Supplement.* Articles in labor relations periodicals and law journals are included.

5647. *Shepard's Federal Tax Locator.* Colorado Springs, CO: Shepard's Citations, Inc., 1974–.
This is a comprehensive subject index to all the current sources of law relating to federal taxation. It covers laws, rules and regulations; rulings, bulletins and other releases; cases; and tax services.

5648. *Shepard's United States Administrative Citations.* Colorado Springs, CO: Shepard's Citations, Inc., 1967–.
This lists all the decisions of federal agencies, boards and commissions published in the agencies' own indexes and digests. It also includes citations to articles in law journals and various other reporting series. Some of the more important indexes for particular agencies are identified in the following source.

5649. *Shepard's United States Citations: Statute Edition.* Colorado Springs, CO: Shepard's Citations, Inc. 1955–.
By providing citations to earlier and later statutes and cases as well as other legal sources, this work allows one to determine the validity of an act or judicial decision. A student or researcher can determine the current status of a decision or act by identifying which amendments, other enactments or legal decisions have affected a particular statute or decision.

FINANCIAL SERVICES

5650. American Stock Exchange. *Stocks and Bonds.* New York: F. E. Fitch. (Annual)
This volume provides ticker symbol, option symbol, par value and CUSIP number for each company on the AMEX.

5651. *Bank and Quotation Record.* New York: National News Service. (Monthly)
This service provides a monthly summary of price ranges for stocks and bonds listed on the American and New York stock exchanges as well as other exchanges.

5652. *Commercial and Financial Chronicle.* New York: National News Service. (Weekly)
This service provides daily stock prices and trading statistics on the NYSE, AMEX, Midwest, Pacific, Philadelphia exchanges.

5653. *Moody's Bond Record: Corporates, Convertibles, Governments, Municipals, Commercial Paper Ratings, Preferred Stock Ratings.* New York: Moody's Investors Service. (Monthly)
This service provides the call price, interest dates, price range, yield to maturity and Moody's ratings.

5654. *Moody's Handbook of Common Stocks.* New York: Moody's Investors Service. (Quarterly)

This handbook provides price charts and financial statistics for over 900 stocks. The data includes capitalization, quarterly earnings, dividends and institutional holdings.

5655. *Moody's Investors Fact Sheets: Industry Review.* New York: Moody's Investors Service. 1 vol. (Loose leaf)

This service provides a ranked list of companies in 140 industry groups according to key financial, operating and investment indicators. Over 4,000 companies are covered.

5656. *Moody's Manuals.* New York: Moody's Investors Service. 7 vols. (Annual with weekly supplements)

This series consists of seven manuals:
Moody's Bank and Finance Manual
Moody's Industrial Manual
Moody's International Manual
Moody's Municipal and Government Manual
Moody's OTC Industrial Manual
Moody's Public Utilities Manual
Moody's Transportation Manual
Moody's Complete Corporate Index
These are the most important services for finding up-to-date information on industries.

5657. Standard and Poor's Corp. *Corporation Records.* New York: Standard and Poor's Corp. 7 vols.

This loose-leaf service covers capitalization, corporate background, officers and directors, stock data and earnings, and finances for the corporations listed.

5658. Standard and Poor's Corp. *Industry Surveys.* New York: Standard and Poor's Corp. (Annual)

This is an important source for basic data on thirty-three industries, with financial comparisons of the companies in each industry. For each industry there is a basic analysis. It includes information on revenue, income and profitability for over 1,000 companies in each industry.

5659. Standard and Poor's Corp. *Security Price Index Record.* New York: Standard and Poor's Corp. (Annual)

This volume includes weekly indexes on over 100 industries for a ten-year period, daily indexes for industrials, railroads, public utilities, and the composite 500 stocks, since 1928, daily NYSE sales since 1918 and Dow Jones averages since 1903.

5660. Standard and Poor's Corp. *Standard Corporation Descriptions.* New York: Standard and Poor's Corp. 6 vols. (Annual)

This loose-leaf service is comparable to Moody's covering companies having listed and unlisted securities. It includes a well-indexed *Daily News Section.*

5661. Standard and Poor's Corp. *Stock Reports.* New York: Standard and Poor's Corp. (Semiweekly)

These loose-leaf services are:
Standard ASE Stock Reports
Standard NYSE Stock Reports
Standard OTC Stock Reports
They include a short company report providing information on recent developments and changes.

5662. Standard and Poor's Corp. *Trendline Stock Chart Services.* New York: Standard and Poor's Corp.

Three publications comprise this charting service: *Daily Action Stock Charts* (weekly), showing daily trends for the past nine months, *Current Market Perspectives* (monthly), giving weekly price/volume charts on some 14,000 traded stocks. *OTC Chart Manual* (bimonthly) charting over 800 traded OTC stocks.

5663. *Value Line Investment Survey.* New York: A. Bernhard and Co. (Weekly)
This loose-leaf service reports on 1,700 companies in about 100 industries. The information is reviewed, industry by industry, on a continuing basis so the information on each company is revised every three months.

REPORTERS

5664. *Administrative Law.* Washington, DC: Pike and Fischer.
This is a service in twenty-three volumes plus a four-volume Digest and loose-leaf Desk Book. This service covers court and administrative decisions. The Desk Book provides the rules of practice of the major administrative agencies.

5665. Bureau of National Affairs.
The Bureau of National Affairs reports and interprets the decisions of federal authorities in the fields of business regulation, labor relations, and consumer and environmental protection. Full texts are provided for administrative actions, decisions, opinions, rulings, policy-statements and other political outputs. Some of the reporters are:
Antitrust and Trade Regulation Report
Criminal Law Reporter
Daily Labor Report
Daily Tax Report
Energy Users Report
Environmental Reporter
Foreign Imports and Exchange Controls
Government Employee Relations Report
International Trade Reporter and the Common Market
Labor Relations Reporter
Media Law Reporter
Occupational Safety and Health Reporter
Securities Regulation and Law Report
Union Labor Report
Washington Financial Reports

5666. Commerce Clearing House.
Numerous series of law reports, issued with varying frequency, provide the text of statutory laws and administrative and judicial decisions relating to atomic energy, aviation, banking, transportation, labor relations, business, trade and taxation. Some of the reports are:
Atomic Energy Law Reports
Aviation Law Reports
Consumer Product Safety Guide
Corporations Law Guide
Employment Safety and Health Guide
Federal Banking Law Reports
Federal Carrier Reports
Federal Energy Regulatory Commission Reports
Federal Securities Law Reports
Food, Drug, Cosmetic Law Reports
Labor Law Reports
Labor Arbitration Awards
Nuclear Regulation Reports
Standard Federal Tax Reports
Stock Exchange Guides
Trade Regulation Reports
Utilities Law Reporter

5667. *Federal Tax Regulations.* St. Paul, MN: West, 1954–.
This reference work is issued in two volumes each year. It provides the full text of the rules and regulations promulgated by the Treasury Department in respect to income, estate and gift taxes.

5668. Prentice-Hall.
These reporter sets, issued in loose-leaf format, provide up-to-date coverage of legislative, judicial and administrative authorities relating to banking, labor relations and business. Some of the major reporters are:
American Labor Arbitration
Control of Banking
Consumer Product Law
Consumer Energy Law
Federal Regulatory Week Controls
Federal Taxes
Securities Regulation
State and Local Taxes

5669. *United States Law Week.* Washington, DC: Bureau of National Affairs, 1931–.
This periodical service includes important sections on the Supreme Court. It has four indexes: the Topical Index; the Table of Cases; the Docket No. Table; and the Proceedings Section. In addition to containing the full text of all decisions, it also has a number of useful sections, including (1) cases filed last week; (2) summary of cases filed recently; (3) journal of proceedings; (4) summary of orders; (5) arguments before the Court; (6) argued cases awaiting decisions; (7) review of the Court's work; and (8) review of the Court's docket.

STATISTICAL COMPENDIA

5670. *Aerospace Facts and Figures.* New York: Aviation Week and Space Technology. (Annual)
This volume includes statistical data on the U.S. aerospace industry, including the production of planes, missile and space craft.

5671. American Financial Services Association. *Finance Facts Yearbook.* Washington, DC: American Financial Services Association. (Annual)
This data compilation provides statistics on consumers, including their income, spending, finance and credit.

5672. American Gas Association. *Gas Facts: A Statistical Record of the Gas Utility Industry.* Arlington, VA: American Gas Association. (Annual)
This is a comprehensive statistical compendium on the gas industry, including data on prices, supplies, reserves, consumption and distribution.

5673. American Petroleum Institute. *Basic Petroleum Data Book: Petroleum Industry Statistics.* Washington, DC: American Petroleum Industry. (3/yr)
This volume provides detailed data on the petroleum industry, including statistics on reserves, consumption, drilling, prices and imports and exports.

5674. *American Statistics Index.* Washington, DC: Congressional Information Service. (Monthly)
This is a comprehensive index and abstracting service of data contained in U.S. government publications. It is the best index for identifying government statistics on regulatory activities.

5675. American Stock Exchange. *AMEX Statistical Review.* New York: American Stock Exchange. (Annual)
This is a statistical overview of AMEX, including companies listed, stock trading, market indexes and membership.

5676. Balachandran, M. *A Guide to Trade and Securities Statistics.* Ann Arbor, MI: Pierian Press, 1977. 185 p.

This is a subject and keyword index to statistical data on the trade and securities industry. It indexes over thirty publications containing statistical data.

5677. Bankers Trust Company. *Credit and Capital Markets.* New York: Bankers Trust Company. (Annual)

This volume includes data on funds raised and supplied for numerous kinds of capital markets, including investment funds, government securities, bonds, state and local funds and stocks.

5678. Chicago Board Options Exchange. *Market Statistics.* Chicago: Chicago Board Options Exchange. (Annual)

This is a statistical summary and review of the past year's activity on the Chicago Board.

5679. Commodity Exchange, Inc. *Statistical Yearbook.* New York: Commodity Exchange. (Annual)

This volume is a statistical summary and survey of the past year's trading on the COMEX, including trading in gold, silver, treasury bills and notes.

5680. *CRB Futures Chart Service.* Jersey City, NJ: Commodity Research Bureau. (Weekly)

This statistical service charts the most actively traded commodities. It also includes price charts and trend analyses.

5681. *Directory of Industry Data Sources.* Belmont, CA: Information Access Co. 5 vols. (Annual)

This is a guide to statistical data on industries in the U.S., Canada and Western Europe. It provides descriptions of banking reports, forecasts, market reports, journals, books, yearbooks, handbooks and other sources of data.

5682. Electronic Industries Association. *Electronic Market Data Book.* Washington, DC: Electronic Industries Association. (Annual)

This is the standard statistical volume focusing on the electronics industry, including both consumer and industrial electronics.

5683. Frank, Natalie D., and Ganly, John V. *Data Sources for Business and Market Analysis.* 3d ed. Metuchen, NJ: Scarecrow Press, 1983. 470 p.

This is a detailed guide to statistical data contained in government documents, journals, directories and statistical serials. It is arranged by source with an additional subject index.

5684. New York Stock Exchange. *Fact Book.* New York: New York Stock Exchange. (Annual)

This is a concise statistical summary and overview of the activities of NYSE for the previous year. It also includes historical data going back to 1939.

5685. Public Securities Association. *Statistical Yearbook of Municipal Finance.* New York: Public Securities Association. (Annual)

This is the standard source for statistical data about regional, state and municipal bonds and securities.

5686. *Sources of Insurance Statistics.* Rev. ed. New York: Special Libraries Association, 1965. 191 p.

This is the best guide to sources of data on all kinds of insurance. It indexes data contained in journals and reference works.

5687. Standard and Poor's Corp. *Security Owner's Stock Guide.* New York: Standard and Poor's Corp. (Monthly)

This is a concise compendium of data on approximately 5,000 preferred stocks, including S and P ratings of earnings, dividends and prices.

5688. *Standard Rate & Data Service: Business Publication Rates and Data.* Skokie, IL: Standard Rate and Data Service. (Monthly)
This is a guide to subscription and advertising rates for trade journals. It is arranged by industry. It is also useful as a guide to journals by industry.

5689. *Statistical Reference Index.* Washington, DC: Congressional Information Service. (Monthly)
This is the most comprehensive index to statistical data published in the private sector. It indexes data published by banks, trade organizations and associations, research institutes, state agencies and business groups.

5690. U.S. Bureau of the Census. *Census of Manufactures.* Washington, DC: U.S. Government Printing Office. (Quinquennial)
This is the most detailed data on industries in the U.S. It includes data on plants, equipment, expenditures, machinery and new additions to industries.

5691. U.S. Bureau of the Census. *Census of Transportation.* Washington, DC: U.S. Government Printing Office. (Quinquennial)
This is a comprehensive statistical summary of the use and operation of both private and commercial cars and trucks. It is especially useful for data relating to the regulation of trucking and carriers.

5692. U.S. Bureau of the Census. *Current Industrial Reports.* Series M-28A: Inorganic Chemicals. Washington, DC: U.S. Government Printing Office. (Monthly)
This volume provides data for many products which are regulated, including fuels, pharmaceutical supplies and fertilizers.

5693. U.S. Bureau of Labor Statistics. *CPI Detailed Report.* Washington, DC: U.S. Government Printing Office. (Monthly)
This statistical series provides specific data on various categories of the Consumer Price Index, including food, housing, fuel, clothing, health care and goods.

5694. U.S. Civil Aeronautics Board. *Handbook of Airline Statistics.* Washington, DC: U.S. Government Printing Office. (Biennial)
This is a general statistical summary of financial statistics and traffic for individual carriers.

5695. U.S. Department of Transportation. Research and Special Programs Administration. *National Transportation Statistics.* Cambridge, MA: U.S. Department of Transportation. (Annual)
This is a compendium of data taken from several government sources. It includes data on various kinds of transportation and cargo operations regulated by state and federal agencies.

5696. U.S. Federal Aviation Administration. *FAA Statistical Handbook of Aviation.* Washington, DC: U.S. Government Printing Office. (Annual)
This is a comprehensive statistical summary and overview of aviation activities during the past year.

5697. U.S. Industry and Trade Administration. *Measuring Markets: A Guide to the Use of Federal and State Statistical Data.* Washington, DC: U.S. Government Printing Office, 1979. 101 p.
This is a guide to sources of data, both state and federal, for basic economic categories, including employment, taxes, income, sale, population, etc.

5698. United States League of Savings Institutions. *Savings Institutions Sourcebook.* Chicago: United States League of Savings Institutions. (Annual)
This is a concise statistical handbook of data on the saving industry. It includes data on savings, housing, loans, lending, etc. It contains a section on new regulatory changes.

DOCUMENTS

5699. *Administrative Conference of the United States, Annual Report.* Washington, DC: U.S. Government Printing Office. (Annual)
The Administrative Conference has the authority to recommend changes in administrative procedures and works to have departments and agencies adopt its recommendations.

5700. Androit, John L. *U.S. Government Serials and Periodicals.* McLean, VA: Documents Index, 1964. 2 vols.
These volumes cover current serials and periodicals of the various government agencies located in the Washington, DC area. The judicial and legislative branches of the government are also covered. In the section covering Congress, material issued by the various committees is listed.

5701. *Annual Report of the Board of Governors of the Federal Reserve System.* Washington, DC: Division of Administrative Services, Board of Governors of the Federal Reserve System. (Annual)
As required by the Federal Reserve Act, the annual report covers the operations of the Board.

5702. *Civil Aeronautics Board Decisions.* Washington, DC: U.S. Government Printing Office, 1938–.
The decisions of this board regulate airline routes, freight rates, and passenger fares, and approves or disapproves proposed agreements and corporate relationships between air carriers.

5703. *Code of Federal Regulations.* Washington, DC: U.S. Government Printing Office, 1938–.
The *Federal Register* is codified in the *Code of Federal Regulations.* It includes executive orders, proclamations and administrative regulations.

5704. *Codification of Presidential Proclamations and Executive Orders.* Washington, DC: U.S. Government Printing Office, 1977. 1 vol.
The text of presidential proclamations and executive orders can be found in convenient form in this official reference publication. Each codified document is assigned to one of the fifty chapters representing broad subject areas similar to the title designations in the *Code of Federal Regulations* of the *United States Code.*

5705. *Congressional Index.* Washington, DC: Commerce Clearing House, 1937/38–.
This weekly publication indexes congressional bills and resolutions and lists their current status. It is designed to enable the user to follow the progress of legislation from initial introduction to final disposition. A section on voting records reports all roll-call votes. Vetoes and subsequent congressional actions are recorded. The guide provides a sequential history of legislation and is a good tool for following a bill through Congress.

5706. *CIS/Index: Congressional Information Service/Index to Publications of the United States Congress.* Washington, DC: Congressional Information Service, 1970–.
An inclusive monthly index to all congressional publications, this abstracts all forms of publications emanating from the legislative process. Materials are indexed by subject, names, committees, bill numbers, report numbers, document numbers, and names of committee chairpersons. The *CIS/INDEX* abstracts of reports, hearings and other congressional documents saves the researcher time, and many check it first when tracing legislation. There are quarterly cumulative indexes and the *CIS/ANNUAL* is issued at the end of the year. There is also the *CIS Five-Year Cumulative Index, 1970–1974* and the *Four-Year Cumulative Index, 1975–1978.* A guide to using *CIS/INDEX* and *Abstracts,* the *CIS/INDEX User Handbook,* is available in most libraries that subscribe to *CIS/INDEX* or can be obtained from the Congressional Information Service. A CIS/INDEX database is also available on-line through ORBIT (System Development Corporation) for computer searching.

5707. *The Costs of Government Regulation of Business.* Washington, DC: U.S. Government Printing Office, 1978. 97 p.
This study was prepared for the Joint Economic Committee of the U.S. Congress by Murray L. Weidenbaum. The study was for use in evaluating the impact of federal rules and regulations on private businesses and industry.

5708. *Decisions of Federal Administrative Agencies and of Federal Courts in Agency Cases, Prior to 1958.* Westport, CT: Redgrave Information Resources Corp. 1972. 1 vol.
This work includes the administrative decisions, findings, orders and reports of the U.S. Bureau of Labor Statistics, U.S. Civil Aeronautics Board, U.S. Federal Communications Commission, U.S. Federal Power Commission, U.S. Federal Trade Commission, U.S. Immigration and Naturalization Service, U.S. National Labor Board, U.S. National Labor Relations Board and the U.S. Securities and Exchange Commission.

5709. *Economic Indicators.* Washington, DC: U.S. Government Printing Office. (Monthly)
Prepared by the President's Council of Economic Advisers, this publication contains charts and statistics on factors affecting the nation's economy, including business activity, prices and business sales. A supplement contains selected charts and historical tables, along with a description of the limitations, and uses of each indicator.

5710. *Economic Report of the President.* Washington, DC: U.S. Government Printing Office. (Annual)
The Council of Economic Advisers assists and advises the President in the preparation of this report as well as do members of the cabinet and heads of independent agencies. The reports survey the economic situation of the country and make recommendations for the coming year.

5711. *Environmental Quality: Annual Report of the Council on Environmental Quality.* Washington, DC: U.S. Government Printing Office. (Annual)
This annual report discusses the regulatory, statutory and judicial achievements made and the present status of the country in environmental concerns.

5712. *Federal Communications Commission Reports.* Washington, DC: U.S. Government Printing Office, 1934–.
The reports and orders of this commission regulate radio, television and cable communication. The commission also sets rates for interstate and international communication.

5713. *Federal Maritime Commission Decisions.* Washington, DC: U.S. Government Printing Office, 1917–.
The reports of this commission regulate shipping, rates and waterway transportation.

5714. *Federal Power Commission Reports, Opinions and Decisions.* Washington, DC: U.S. Government Printing Office, 1931–.
The commission regulates rates and practices in the interstate transmission of electric energy and regulates the transportation and sale of natural gas.

5715. *Federal Register.* Washington, DC: U.S. Government Printing Office, 1936–.
The first section of the *Federal Register* includes executive orders, proclamations and other presidential materials—memoranda from the President to the heads of departments or agencies, directives for officials, letters and reorganization plans for agencies. New Federal Advisory Committees are also recorded. Notices of each meeting of advisory bodies are published.

5716. *The Federal Register: What It Is and How to Use It: A Guide for the User of the Federal Register—Code of Federal Regulations System.* Washington, DC: U.S. Government Printing Office, 1980. 97 p.
This guide explains the *Federal Register* and the *Code of Federal Regulations.* It contains dozens of illustrations depicting all of the relevant parts of the two publications.

5717. *Federal Regulatory Programs and Activities.* Washington, DC: General Accounting Office, 1978. 231 p.

This report is an inventory of federal regulatory programs and activities by agency and authorizing legislation. It identifies federal agencies with regulatory activities. These agencies are classified by areas, such as energy, natural resources and environment. The agencies have also been classified by type of regulatory activity and degree of regulation.

5718. *Federal Trade Commission Decisions.* Washington, DC: U.S. Government Printing Office, 1915–.

This commission administers laws preventing advertising misrepresentation, unfair competition, false packaging and mislabelling of products, price discrimination, credit gouging and antitrust violations.

5719. *GPO Sales Publications Reference File.* Washington, DC: U.S. Government Printing Office, 1977–.

The *Publications Reference File* is a "Documents in Print," for it catalogs all federal publications currently sold by the Superintendent of Documents. Documents are arranged by subjects, titles, agency, series and report numbers, key words, authors, stock numbers, and SUDOCS classification numbers. The PRF is issued on 48X microfiche and is available to depository libraries. The PRF is easy to use and is the first place to look to identify new or recent documents.

5720. *Index to the Code of Federal Regulations.* Bethesda, MD: Congressional Information Service, 1977–.

The detailed subject index allows a search of all fifty titles at once. The researcher can search a general or a specific subject and be referred to all the relevant parts and subparts. There are two geographical indexes. The first indexes regulations regarding political jurisdictions (states, counties, and cities). The second cites properties administered by the federal government (parks, military bases, etc.). There are also two other indexes that can save time if a citation is already known. A list of descriptive headings is assigned to each part of the code. A list of reserved headings indicates which parts of the code have been designated reserved, either for future use or because they are no longer in use.

5721. *Interstate Commerce Commission Reports.* Washington, DC: U.S. Government Printing Office, 1887–.

This commission regulates interstate surface transportation, freight forwarders, oil pipelines and express companies. Regulation is exercised by certification of carriers, rate-fixing, and the approval or disapproval of mergers.

5722. *Monthly Catalog of United States Government Publications.* Washington, DC: U.S. Government Printing Office, 1895–.

An important index for identifying many congressional publications, it is especially useful for finding committee hearings and reports. The *Monthly Catalog* has a subject index as well as an index arranged by government author. Carrollton Press has published a *Cumulative Subject Index to the Monthly Catalog of U.S. Government Publications, 1900–1971.*

5723. *National Labor Relations Board Decisions and Orders.* Washington, DC: U.S. Government Printing Office, 1935–.

The decisions and orders of this board prevent and remedy unfair labor practices by employers and labor unions.

5724. Nelson, Dalmas H. *Administrative Agencies of the USA: Their Decisions and Authority.* Detroit, MI: Wayne State University Press, 1964. 341 p.

This book provides a description of administrative orders by subject and includes a table of cases and bibliography.

5725. *Publications Catalog.* Washington, DC: U.S. Government Printing Office. (Annual)

This is the annual list of publications for the Department of Commerce. It identifies reports and data on a broad range of economic and business topics. It is arranged by organization and has a subject index.

5726. *Public Papers of the Presidents of the United States.* Washington, DC: U.S. National Archives and Records Administration, 1958–.
Materials in this annual publication are arranged in chronological order with a subject index. It contains texts of President's Messages to Congress, public addresses, messages to heads of state, released statements on various subjects and news conferences.

5727. *Report to the President and the Attorney General of the National Commission for the Review of Antitrust Laws and Procedures.* Washington, DC: U.S. Government Printing Office, 1979. 2 vols.
This report makes recommendations for reform on numerous antitrust topics.

5728. *Securities and Exchange Commission Decisions and Reports.* Washington, DC: U.S. Government Printing Office, 1934–.
The decisions of this commission regulate the operation of stock markets securities dealers and investment firms.

5729. *Study on Federal Regulation.* Washington, DC: U.S. Government Printing Office, 1975. 6 vol.
This study of federal regulation was conducted by the staff of the Senate Committee on Government Affairs in 1975. Six volumes have been published. The six are: Volume I, The Regulatory Appointments Process; Volume II, Congressional Oversight of Regulatory Agencies; Volume III, Public Participation in Regulatory Agency Proceedings; Volume IV, Delay in the Regulatory Process; Volume V, Regulatory Organization; Volume VI, Framework for Regulation.

5730. *Supreme Court Reporter.* St. Paul, MN: West, 1883–.
This is a nongovernmental publication containing annotated reports and indexes of case names. It includes some material not covered in the *United States Reports*, such as opinions of justices in chambers.

5731. *United States Code.* Washington, DC: U.S. Government Printing Office, 1926–.
The *Code* is a compilation of all federal laws in force, arranged by subject under fifty "titles." The index volume contains a table of all title and chapter headings and a subject index to all sections. The Office of the Federal Register has published two useful guides for learning how to use the *Statutes* and *Code: How to Find U.S. Statutes and U.S. Code Citations* and *The Federal Register: What It Is and How to Use It; A Guide for the User of the Federal Register-Code of Federal Regulations System.*

5732. *United States Code Annotated.* St. Paul, MN: West, 1927–.
Although this set reprints the *United States Code*, the statutes are accompanied by extensive annotations, legal notes and analytic comments on the specific statute and its legislative history. This supplemental material is invaluable for anyone interested in researching the original intent and later interpretation of the statute.

5733. *United States Code Congressional and Administrative News.* St. Paul, MN: West, 1939–.
This monthly service reprints the full text of all public laws and reproduces the *U.S. Statutes at Large.* It includes selected presidential messages, executive orders and proclamations, listed by number, date and subject. It also reprints selected House and Senate documents. In addition, this service provides seven tables on the status of legislation. One of the tables provides a complete legislative history of all bills passed as law.

5734. *United States Code Service.* Rochester, NY: Lawyers Cooperative Publishing Co., 1972–.
This service is similar to the above item. It reprints the *United States Code* and includes annotations, notes and legislative histories. One of the volumes, the *U.S. Code Guide,* is especially useful for relating the code to several other reference tools, including the *United States Supreme Court Reports, Lawyers' Edition* and *American Jurisprudence.*

5735. *United States Government Manual.* Washington, DC: U.S. Government Printing Office, 1935–.

This annual publication is the official handbook of the federal government. It gives information on the agencies and departments of all three branches of government, as well as on quasi-official agencies, international organizations and boards, committees and commissions. Programs and activities of these agencies are described. This manual includes a section summarizing the duties and functions of the executive branch. There is a separate name index and a subject index. Its earlier title was *U.S. Government Organization Manual.*

5736. *United States Reports.* Washington, DC: U.S. Government Printing Office, 1790–.

The *Reports* contain the official text of all opinions of the Supreme Court.

5737. *United States Statutes at Large.* Washington, DC: U.S. Government Printing Office, 1789–.

This is a compilation of public and private laws. There are some presidential materials included, such as a list of proclamations, full texts of these proclamations and a list of reorganization plans. A subject index to these materials is provided.

5738. *United States Supreme Court Reports: Lawyers' Edition.* Rochester, NY: Lawyers Cooperative Publishing Co., 1790–.

While all other casebooks contain the official reports, this service also contains numerous per curiam decisions not found elsewhere and individually summarizes the majority and dissenting opinions and counsel briefs. The Index to Annotations leads one to the legal notes provided for each case.

5739. *Weekly Compilation of Presidential Documents.* Washington, DC: U.S. Government Printing Office, 1965–.

Published every Monday, this work covers the previous week. It contains texts of messages to the Congress (budget, economic, and State of the Union Addresses), texts of proclamations and executive orders, and transcripts of presidential news conferences. It also provides presidential speeches, statements, letters, remarks of welcome to foreign leaders, and similar materials made in public in the form of White House Press Releases. Letters, memos and reports to the President from cabinet members and other officials released by the White House Press Office are included. This provides an up-to-date source for presidential policies and activities. There is an index of contents and a cumulative index to prior issues. There are semiannual and annual indexes as well.

INDEXES

5740. *ABA Banking Literature Index.* Washington, DC: American Bankers Association. (Monthly)

This is an index to the literature of banking. It covers over 170 journals in the fields of banking, law, accounting and management.

5741. *ABC POL SCI: A Bibliography of Contents: Political Science and Government.* Santa Barbara, CA: ABC-Clio. (Monthly)

This lists and indexes tables of contents from approximately 300 selected journals, both U.S. and foreign. This bibliography is especially useful for finding very recent articles on regulation and subjects related to political science.

5742. *Accountants' Index.* New York: American Institute of Certified Public Accountants. (Quarterly)

A comprehensive index to English-language books, documents and articles on accounting and related fields of auditing, data processing, financial reporting and management, investments and securities.

5743. *Annual Legal Bibliography.* Cambridge, MA: Harvard University Law School, Library. (Annual)
This is a bibliography covering books and articles acquired by the Harvard University Law School Library. The entries are classified in the following groups: common law, civil law and other jurisdictions, private international law, and public international law. The entries are not annotated. This bibliography provides excellent coverage of administrative law and presidential relations with the Congress and Supreme Court.

5744. *Applied Science and Technology Index.* New York: H. W. Wilson (Monthly)
This is an index to over 300 journals in the fields of aeronautics, chemistry, computer technology, construction, energy research, engineering, food industry, geology, metallurgy, minerology, oceanography, petroleum and gas, physics, plastics, textile industry and transportation. It is especially useful for finding industry reactions to regulatory proposals.

5745. *Business Index.* Los Altos, CA: Information Access Co. (Monthly)
This index consists of a monthly microfilm reel inserted into a viewer. It indexes articles by subject and name in about 650 periodicals. Included are articles in *Barron's*, the *Wall Street Journal* and the business section of *The New York Times.*

5746. *Business International Index.* New York: Business International Corp. (Quarterly)
This index of BIC publications covers their periodicals, research reports and reference services in the field of international business. It includes information on countries, companies and subjects.

5747. *Business Periodicals Index.* New York: H. W. Wilson. (Quarterly)
This work indexes articles occurring in English-language business periodicals published in the United States. It covers accounting, advertising, finance, labor, management, public administration and general business.

5748. *Contents of Current Legal Periodicals.* Los Angeles: Law Publications. (Monthly)
Tables of contents are provided for legal journals in this work. The articles are also indexed by subject. The virtue of this service is the currency of its indexing. It is most useful for finding recent legal studies on regulation.

5749. *Current Law Index.* Menlo Park, CA: Information Access Corp. (Monthly)
This index covers legal periodicals and newspapers. Its microfilm counterpart, *Legal Resource Index*, cumulates the information found in the paper copy. It also indexes books and documents. These two indexes provide extensive coverage of the regulation and related topics. While mostly reviewed in connection with legal issues, they should be consulted regardless of the subject.

5750. *Energy Index.* New York: Environment Information Center. (Annual)
This is a comprehensive index to energy literature.

5751. *Federal Tax Articles.* Chicago: Commerce Clearing House. (Monthly)
This loose-leaf service describes tax articles that have appeared in tax, law, accounting and business journals. It is arranged by Internal Revenue Code section, with author index and subject index.

5752. *Humanities Index.* New York: H. W. Wilson. (Quarterly)
This cumulative index to English-language journals in the humanities indexes articles by author and subject. Covering the major journals in history, it is an excellent resource for locating citations related to the history of regulatory politics.

5753. *Index of Economic Articles in Journals and Collective Volumes.* Homewood, IL: Irwin. (Annual)
A classified index of English-language articles in major professional economics journals and in collective volumes. The first seven volumes are for the years 1886–1965. It also includes an author index.

5754. *Index to Federal Tax Articles.* Boston: Warren, Gorham and Lamont. (Quarterly)
This is an index to articles on federal income taxes that appear in legal, tax, accounting and economic journals. It includes an author index and list of journals covered.

5755. *Index to Legal Periodicals.* New York: H. W. Wilson. (Monthly)
This work indexes articles appearing in legal periodicals of the U.S., Canada, Great Britain, Northern Ireland, Australia and New Zealand. Articles are indexed by author, subject and cases. This is another legal index that should be used in almost every search on regulation. Because it is the oldest legal index, it can serve as a tool for historical research as well.

5756. *Index to Periodical Articles Related to Law.* Dobbs Ferry, NY: Glanville Publications. (Quarterly)
This indexes, by author and subject, articles found in journals published by law schools, lawyers' associations and law institutes. It contains some citations relevant to the study of the presidency, but it should be used only after consulting the other legal indexes.

5757. *International Bibliography of Political Science.* Chicago: Aldine Publishing Co. (Annual)
This bibliography lists books, articles, reports and other research publications. The entries are classified under six sections: political science, political thought, government and public administration, governmental process, international relations and area studies. Entries are selected from over 2,000 journals. This is another source for foreign-language materials on regulation. It also includes many English-language citations as well.

5758. *International Political Science Abstracts.* Oxford: Basil Blackwell. (Bimonthly)
This work abstracts articles published in 600 English-language and foreign-language political science journals. The abstracts for the English-language journals appear in English; the foreign-language articles are abstracted in French. This is the best source for finding foreign-language articles about regulation.

5759. *Journal of Economic Literature.* Nashville, TN: American Economic Association. (Quarterly)
Each issue includes an annotated list of new books classified by subject; a subject index of articles in current periodicals and selected abstracts of some articles arranged by subject.

5760. *Legal Resource Index.* Menlo Park, CA: Information Access Corp. (Monthly)
This is a monthly cumulating COM index. It indexes 660 law journals and five law newspapers.

5761. *Life Insurance Index.* Ann Arbor, MI: University Microfilms International. (Quarterly)
This is an index to life insurance articles appearing in about fifty journals. The subject section contains short summaries describing each article.

5762. *Management Contents.* Northbrook, IL: Management Contents. (Biweekly)
This index reproduces the tables of contents for over 300 journals. There is a subject index in each issue.

5763. *Monthly Digest of Legal Articles.* Greenville, NY: Research and Documentation Corp. (Monthly)
This service is most useful for finding recent journal literature on regulation.

5764. *Predicasts F and S Index of Corporate Change.* Cleveland, OH: Predicasts, Inc. (Quarterly)
This is an index to information in newspapers and periodicals on mergers, acquisitions and other corporate changes.

5765. *Predicasts F and S Index Europe* and *Predicasts F and S Index International (F and S).* Cleveland, OH: Predicasts, Inc. (Monthly)
These are companion indexes to the below index, covering articles on foreign companies and industries. They are similar in format except that these indexes have a section arranging the articles by region and country.

5766. *Predicasts F and S Index United States (F and S).* Cleveland, OH: Predicasts, Inc. (Weekly)
This is an index to information about U.S. products and industries. It indexes over 750 business, industrial and financial journals.

5767. *Property and Liability Insurance Index.* Ann Arbor, MI: University Microfilms International. (Quarterly)
A companion to the *Life Insurance Index*, this index covers property and liability insurance articles in about fifty journals. It also contains short summaries with each entry.

5768. *Public Affairs Information Service Bulletin.* New York: The Service. (Weekly)
This is a weekly subject guide to the field of American politics in general, indexing government publications, books and periodical literature. It includes citations to many hearings. Additionally, it indexes the *National Journal, CQ Weekly Report, Congressional Digest* and selections from the *Weekly Compilation of Presidential Documents.* All of these journals are invaluable guides to studying regulation on a current basis. A fifteen-volume *Cumulative Subject Index to the P.A.I.S. Annual Bulletins, 1915-1974* has been published by Carrollton Press. *P.A.I.S.* is cumulated quarterly and annually.

5769. *Sage Public Administration Abstracts.* Beverly Hills, CA: Sage Publications. (Quarterly)
This work abstracts articles selected from approximately 200 English-language journals as well as books, pamphlets and government publications dealing with public administration. This service should be consulted when searching for information related to policy analysis, public management, bureaucratic studies and federal programs.

5770. *Sage Urban Studies Abstracts.* Beverly Hills, CA: Sage Publications. (Quarterly)
This index includes books, articles, pamphlets and government documents on urban studies. Each issue is arranged in twenty-three subtopics under general headings such as urban research, land use and urban affairs.

5771. *Social Sciences Citation Index.* Philadelphia, PA: Institute for Science Information. (3/yr)
Items appearing in the *SSCI* have been cited in footnotes or bibliographies in the social sciences. These works include books, journal articles, dissertations, reports, proceedings, etc. There are four separate indexes: a source (author) index, a citation index, a corporate index and the Permuterm subject index. Though difficult to use, it does have several unique features useful for studying regulation. The corporate index enables the researcher to identify publications issued by particular organizations. The source and citation indexes allow the user to identify the works of a particular scholar who has written extensively on regulation and to identify other researchers who have cited their writings.

5772. *Social Sciences Index.* New York: H. W. Wilson. (Quarterly)
This work indexes articles found in about 150 social sciences journals. It covers all of the major journals in political science as well as the other social sciences and should be used for all studies of regulation, regardless of the topic.

5773. *United States Political Science Documents.* Pittsburgh, PA: University Center for International Studies, University of Pittsburgh. (Annual)
This work indexes and abstracts about 120 political science journals and appears annually in two volumes. The first volume contains indexes by the author, subject, geographic area, proper name and journal title. The second volume abstracts the articles indexed in volume one. This is another index that should be used for studying regulation, regardless of the topic. Because it indexes many of the new journals in political science, it covers journals not indexed elsewhere.

5774. *Writings on American History: A Subject Bibliography of Articles.* Millwood, NY: KTO Press. (Annual)

This is a bibliography of journal articles published on American history from approximately 500 periodicals. The entries are arranged chronologically, geographically and by subject. There is an author index but no subject index. It includes journals from political science, economics and other social sciences. Though most researchers do not think of using this index unless they are looking for citations to history journals, it usually contains many useful citations on regulation.

DATABASES

5775. ABI/INFORM. Louisville, KY: Data Courier, 1971–.

This database covers approximately 550 English-language journals in the areas of accounting, finance, management and production.

5776. AMERICA: HISTORY AND LIFE. Santa Barbara, CA: ABC-Clio, 1964–.

This reference, available both in hardcover and online through DIALOG, provides comprehensive coverage of all areas of U.S. history, international relations, and politics and government. This is the best database for finding articles dealing with the history of regulatory agencies and politics.

5777. CONGRESSIONAL RECORD ABSTRACTS. Washington, DC: Capitol Services, Inc., 1976–.

This contains abstracts of items appearing in the *Congressional Record.* It covers bills, resolutions, committee and sub-committee reports, public laws, executive communications, speeches and inserted materials.

5778. ECONOMIC LITERATURE INDEX. Nashville, TN: American Economic Association, 1984–.

This is an online bibliographical database corresponding to the *Index of Economic Articles in Journals and Collective Volumes* and *The Journal of Economic Literature.*

5779. FEDERAL INDEX. Washington, DC: Capitol Services, Inc., 1976–.

This indexes the *Washington Post, Congressional Record, Federal Register,* presidential documents and other federal documents, including rules, regulations, bills, speeches, hearings, roll calls, reports, vetoes, court decisions and executive orders. It is the best single source for finding information about the federal government. Because it indexes a wide scope of legislative and executive documents, it is extremely useful for researching regulatory politics.

5780. FEDERAL REGISTER ABSTRACTS. Washington, DC: Capitol Services, Inc., 1977–.

This database abstracts materials in the *Federal Register.* It covers government regulations, proposed rules, and legal notices, such as presidential proclamations, executive orders and presidential determinations. For anyone studying regulatory agencies, this is indispensable, for it is an excellent index to administrative law in general.

5781. GPO MONTHLY CATALOG. Washington, DC: U.S. Government Printing Office, 1976–.

This contains records of reports, studies, etc., issued by all U.S. federal government agencies, including Senate and House hearings, and is useful for finding documents issued through the Office of the President and the Executive Office. While it is better suited for finding documents issued by departments of the executive branch, it can also be used in compiling a legislative history.

5782. GPO PUBLICATIONS REFERENCE FILE. Washington, DC: U.S. Government Printing Office, 1971–.

Essentially an online version of the *GPO Sales Publications Reference File* described above, this is best suited for finding citations to new publications, especially those that have not yet been cited in the *Monthly Catalog* or for determining whether a particular document is still available for purchase.

5783. HISTORICAL ABSTRACTS. Santa Barbara, CA: ABC-Clio, 1964–.
This reference is a guide to the literature of world history and the related social sciences and humanities. It contains article abstracts and annotations from more than 2,000 journals published worldwide. *Historical Abstracts'* database contains approximately 145,000 records, and approximately 15,000 new bibliographic records are added to the database each year. Covers the historical period from 1450 to the present.

5784. LEGAL RESOURCE INDEX. Menlo Park, CA: Information Access Corporation, 1980–.
This database provides the best overall coverage to legal materials, for it indexes over 660 law journals, five law newspapers, legal monographs and government publications from the Library of Congress MARC database. It can be used for researching almost any topic related to regulation.

5785. LEXIS. Dayton, OH: Mead Data Central, Inc., 1973–.
This system searches through legal documents to retrieve needed information. Using a LEXIS terminal and telephone, text is retrieved from a computer storing the documents in Dayton, Ohio. You can use this system to find citations to several different perspectives on the presidency, including legal analyses of policies, administrative decision making and regulatory politics.

5786. MAGAZINE INDEX. Menlo Park, CA: Information Access Corporation, 1976–.
This database indexes articles from over 370 general magazines and provides good coverage of current affairs. While not as extensive in scope as the previous two, this resource is useful for researching headline stories about regulation and current issues and controversies surrounding regulation.

5787. MANAGEMENT CONTENTS. Management Contents, 1974–.
This database indexes and abstracts articles in over 700 English-language business journals, proceedings and books.

5788. NATIONAL NEWSPAPER INDEX. Menlo Park, CA: Information Access Corporation, 1979–.
This indexes the *Christian Science Monitor, The New York Times* and *The Wall Street Journal.* It covers all items except weather charts, stock market tables, crossword puzzles and horoscopes. It provides good coverage of government relations and is especially useful for finding articles related to regulatory affairs.

5789. NEWSEARCH. Menlo Park, CA: Information Access Corporation, 1978–.
This is a daily index of more than 2,000 news stories, information articles and book reviews from over 1,400 newspapers, magazines and periodicals. It indexes articles for the current month. At the end of the month the magazine article data is transferred to the MAGAZINE INDEX, and the newspaper data is transferred to the NATIONAL NEWSPAPER INDEX. NEWSEARCH is another excellent source for keeping up to date on regulation.

5790. PAIS INTERNATIONAL. New York: PAIS, Inc., 1976–.
Each year approximately 25,000 citations found in over 1,200 journals and over 800 books, pamphlets, government documents and agency reports are added to this database. It covers all fields of the social sciences—political science, public administration, international relations, law and public policy—and is useful not only for finding materials related to current events, but for doing research on specific topics as well. Because it indexes books, documents and articles from journals (such as the *CQ Weekly Report* and the *National Journal*), a search can yield a wide variety of citations to both primary and secondary sources.

5791. SOCIAL SCISEARCH. Philadelphia, PA: The Institute for Scientific Information, 1972–.
This covers all areas of the social and behavioral sciences. Entries are chosen from the 1,000 most important social science journals, as well as from 2,200 others in the natural, physical and biomedical sciences. Its scope, in terms of both the number of journals and disciplines covered, is larger than any other database, and it provides citations to almost any facet of regulatory studies.

5792. USPSD. Pittsburgh, PA: University of Pittsburgh Press, 1975–.
Articles from approximately 120 major political science journals published in the U.S. are abstracted and indexed. This database can be best used to find citations from the major journals in the field of political science. It is also the best for identifying articles on regulation from the growing number of policy studies journals.

5793. WESTLAW. St. Paul, MN: West, 1978–.
All recent U.S. state and federal court decisions are abstracted in this database. It covers judicial decision making and the court system and can be used most effectively to find citations related to the interpretation of public laws and regulatory decisions.

NEWSPAPERS

5794. *Legal Times of Washington.* Washington, DC: Legal Times of Washington, 1978–.
A weekly newspaper which includes in-depth analyses of new legislation and regulations and articles of general regulatory interest.

5795. *Market Chronicle.* New York: W. B. Dana Co., 1967–.
This newspaper covers securities markets. It includes short articles on financial affairs and companies, current OTC bid/ask stock prices and OTC stock price indexes.

5796. *National Law Journal.* New York: New York Law Publishing Company, 1978–.
A weekly newspaper geared toward the legal profession.

5797. *New York Times Index.* New York: The New York Times, 1913–.
A highly detailed index, arranged alphabetically. Articles and news from *The Times* can also be accessed online in the *National Newspaper Index.*

5798. *Wall Street Journal.* New York: Dow Jones and Co., 1958–.
This is the most important financial and business newspaper in the U.S. It is particularly good for its reporting of regulatory matters.

5799. *Wall Street Journal Index.* New York: Dow Jones and Co., 1958–.
This index is in two parts: corporate news and general news. Indexing is based on the Eastern Edition.

JOURNALS

5800. *ABA Banking Journal.* New York: Simmons-Boardman Publishing Corp. (Monthly)
Official ABA publication which provides information on banking trends, techniques and services.

5801. *Accounting Review.* Sarasota, FL: American Accounting Association. (Quarterly)
A professional journal devoted to accounting research.

5802. *Across the Board.* New York: Conference Board. (11/yr)
This journal provides coverage of new industrial technologies, business regulation and economic development.

5803. *Administrative Law Review.* Chicago: Administrative Law Section, American Bar Association. (3/yr)
Aspects of administrative law and procedure are featured. Includes articles on government agencies.

5804. *American Banker.* New York: American Banker, Inc. (5/wk)
Banking developments, legislation, monetary affairs, bank stock quotations and bank rankings are among the areas covered in this periodical.

5805. *American Business Law Journal.* Atlanta, GA: American Business Law Association. (3/yr)
Contains scholarly articles and book reviews on business and corporate jurisprudence.

5806. *American Economic Review.* Evanston, IL: Northwestern University, American Economic Association. (5/yr)
A journal which covers business regulations, antitrust law and economic theory, among other related areas.

5807. *Antitrust Law Journal.* Chicago: American Bar Association, Section of Antitrust Law. (3–4/yr)
This publication features in-depth articles by antitrust scholars and practitioners as well as textual accounts of (ABA Antitrust Section) panel meetings.

5808. *Bankers Magazine.* Boston: Warren, Gorham and Lamont. (Bimonthly)
Banking and money management are featured topics in this journal. Includes book reviews.

5809. *Banking Law Journal.* Boston: Warren, Gorham and Lamont. (10/yr)
A scholarly publication which contains articles on financial law and regulation as well as abstracts of essays appearing in other banking periodicals.

5810. *Barron's.* New York: Dow Jones and Co. (Weekly)
A "national business and financial weekly" which provides coverage of industry and corporate developments for investors.

5811. *Business and Professional Ethics Journal.* Troy, NY: Rensselaer Polytechnic Institute. (Quarterly)
A journal devoted to the study of the ethical issues and problems faced by the business and professional community.

5812. *Business Economics.* Cleveland, OH: National Association of Business Economics. (Quarterly)
A scholarly journal with articles on new developments and research trends in economic theory.

5813. *Business History Review.* Boston: Harvard University, Graduate School of Business Adminstration. (Quarterly)
A journal of industry, management, economic and corporate history.

5814. *Business International.* New York: Business International Corporation. (Weekly)
A weekly newsletter which appraises multinational business executives and managers of financial, legal and political developments throughout the world.

5815. *Business Lawyer.* Chicago: Section of Corporation, Banking and Business Law, American Bar Association. (Quarterly)
A periodical devoted to the legal aspects of business and finance.

5816. *Business Week.* New York: McGraw-Hill. (Weekly)
A leading weekly news magazine which covers a wide range of events and issues of interest to managers, investors and businessmen.

5817. *Columbia Journal of World Business.* New York: Columbia University Graduate School of Business. (Quarterly)
A quarterly publication with articles on current trends and developments in international business.

5818. *Congressional Quarterly Weekly Report.* Washington, DC: Congressional Quarterly, Inc. (Weekly)
A weekly summary of pending federal legislation and congressional news.

5819. *Corporation Law Review.* Boston: Warren, Gorham and Lamont. (Quarterly)
A quarterly review devoted to those legal and tax developments of interest to business executives.

5820. *CPA Journal.* New York: New York State Society of Certified Public Accountants. (Monthly)
The official organ of the New York State Society of Public Accountants with articles on financial accounting, auditing and taxation.

5821. *Dun's Business Month.* New York: Dun and Bradstreet. (Monthly)
A popular magazine with financial, industry and corporate information for managers, investors and executives.

5822. *Economic History Review.* Cumbria, UK: T. Wilson and Sons. (Quarterly)
A scholarly journal which features in-depth articles on Western European economic thought and history.

5823. *Federal Communications Bar Journal.* Washington, DC: Federal Communications Bar Association. (Quarterly)
A quarterly review of trends and developments in communications law.

5824. *Federal Reserve Bulletin.* Washington, DC: Division of Administrative Services, Board of Governors of the Federal Reserve System. (Monthly)
A monthly summary of the board's reports, statistical compilations and regulatory interpretations.

5825. *Financial Analysis Journal.* New York: Financial Analysts Federation. (Bimonthly)
A leading publication for investment managers and securities analysts.

5826. *Food-Drug-Cosmetic Law Journal.* Chicago: Commerce Clearing House. (Monthly)
A periodical reporting legal developments which affect the food, drug and cosmetic industries.

5827. *Forbes.* New York. (Biweekly)
A popular magazine with articles on industrial, corporate and financial topics.

5828. *Fortune.* New York: Time Inc. (Biweekly)
A leading journal which covers business and economic developments.

5829. *I.C.C. Practitioners' Journal.* Washington, DC: Association of Interstate Commerce Commission Practitioners. (10/yr)
A monthly digest of ICC decisions and relevant judicial interpretations.

5830. *Industry Week.* Cleveland, OH: Penton Publishing Co. (Biweekly)
This periodical features articles on business and industrial developments.

5831. *International Management.* London: McGraw-Hill International Publications Co. (Monthly)
A serial with concise articles on worldwide managerial trends.

5832. *Journal of Accountancy.* New York: American Institute of Certified Public Accountants. (Monthly)
Current issues and topics in financial accounting are covered in this monthly professional publication.

5833. *Journal of Accounting, Auditing and Finance.* Boston: Warren, Gorham and Lamont. (Quarterly)
Issues and topics of interest to corporate and professional accountants are features in this periodical.

5834. *Journal of Accounting Research.* Chicago: Institute of Professional Accounting, Graduate School of Business. University of Chicago. (Semiannual)
A semiannual journal with scholarly articles on accounting theory.

5835. *The Journal of Air Law and Commerce.* Dallas, TX: Southern Methodist Law School. (Quarterly)
This quarterly publication includes book reviews and articles on legislation and judicial decisions currently having an impact on the air transportation industry.

5836. *Journal of Bank Research.* Park Ridge, IL: Bank Administration Institute. (Quarterly)
A quarterly publication of research papers devoted to the study of bank accounting and finance.

5837. *Journal of Broadcasting.* Washington, DC: Association for Professional Broadcasting Education. (Quarterly)
Periodical with scholarly articles and book reviews on current trends and issues in the media.

5838. *Journal of Business.* Chicago: University of Chicago Press. (Quarterly)
An academic journal with articles on economic and market theory.

5839. *Journal of Business Ethics.* Boston, MA: D. Reidel Publishing Co. (Quarterly)
A publication with articles devoted to the study of ethical and moral business practice.

5840. *Journal of Business Finance and Accounting.* Oxford: B. Blackwell. (Quarterly)
This leading publication features analyses of financial problems and issues.

5841. *Journal of Economic History.* Raleigh, NC: North Carolina State University. (Quarterly)
An academic quarterly published by the Economic History Association.

5842. *Journal of Environmental Economics and Management.* New York: Academic Press. (Quarterly)
The problems of environmental and resource management are covered in this quarterly publication.

5843. *Journal of Finance.* New York: American Finance Association. (5/yr)
A leading journal featuring articles on a wide variety of financial topics. Book reviews are provided in four of the five annual issues.

5844. *Journal of Futures Markets.* New York: Wiley. (Quarterly)
A periodical with articles of interest for futures analysts.

5845. *Journal of International Business Studies.* Newark, NJ: Academy of International Business and Rutgers Graduate School of Business Administration. (Quarterly)
A publication with scholarly articles on international business research.

5846. *Journal of International Economics.* Amsterdam, Netherlands: North Holland Publishing Co. (Quarterly)
A journal which contains articles on trade deficits and surpluses.

5847. *Journal of Law and Economics.* Chicago: University of Chicago Law School. (Annual)
This annual publication is devoted to the economic impact of the law.

5848. *Journal of Money, Credit and Banking.* Columbus, OH: Ohio State University Press. (Quarterly)
A serial with articles on research on monetary exchange and policy.

5849. *Journal of Policy Analysis and Management.* New York: Wiley. (Quarterly)
A periodical which is devoted to the study of public sector administration and policy formation.

5850. *Journal of Risk and Insurance.* Bloomington, IL: American Risk and Insurance Association. (Quarterly)
A quarterly which covers a wide range of issues in actuarial science.

5851. *Journal of Taxation.* Boston: Warren, Gorham and Lamont. (Monthly)
This periodical surveys recent legal decisions and commission rulings which have an impact on tax accountancy.

5852. *Journal of World Trade Law.* Twickenham, Middlesex, England. (6/yr)
International trade policies are covered in this research periodical.

5853. *The Kiplinger Washington Letter.* Washington, DC: Kiplinger. (Weekly)
This serial summarizes congressional and bureaucratic developments of interest to investors and businessmen.

5854. *Law and Policy in International Business.* Washington, DC: Georgetown University Law Center. (Quarterly)
The legal aspects of international business are featured in this academic journal.

5855. *Management International Review.* Wiesbaden, Germany: Th. Gabler GmbH. (Quarterly)
A quarterly journal of management and international business.

5856. *Mergers and Acquisitions.* Philadelphia, PA: Information for Industry. (Quarterly)
A journal which covers the financial terms and agreements of recent U.S. corporate mergers, acquisitions and joint ventures.

5857. *Money.* Los Angeles: Time Inc. (Monthly)
A popular magazine which provides advice for individuals and families on financial and investment topics.

5858. *Multinational Business.* London: Economist Intelligence Unit. (Quarterly)
A quarterly journal with articles on international management, investment and finance.

5859. *National Public Accountant.* Alexandria, VA: National Society of Public Accountants. (Monthly)
The official publication of the National Society of Public Accountants with articles on a broad range of accounting subjects.

5860. *National Tax Journal.* Columbus, OH: National Tax Association/Tax Institute of America. (Quarterly)
This joint publication of the National Tax Association and the Tax Institute of America contains articles on the many aspects of federal taxation.

5861. *Nation's Business.* Washington, DC: Chamber of Commerce of the United States. (Monthly)
A monthly publication of the U.S. Chamber of Commerce which reports on trends and developments in the private sector.

5862. *Public Administration Review.* Washington, DC: American Society for Public Administration. (Bimonthly)
A leading academic journal which covers the theory and practice of public administration.

5863. *Public Utility Fortnightly.* Washington, DC: Public Utilities Reports. (Biweekly)
A biweekly summary of legislative, bureaucratic and legal developments for public utility managers.

5864. *Regulation: The AEI Journal on Government and Society.* Washington, DC: American Enterprise Institute. (Bimonthly)
Regulatory policy and development are the focus of this bimonthly periodical.

5865. *Securities Law Review.* New York: Clark Boardman. (Annual)
The legal aspects of securities trading law are included in this research journal.

5866. *Securities Regulation Law Journal.* Boston: Warren, Gorham and Lamont. (Quarterly)
Legal decisions which have an impact on securities regulation are analyzed in this serial.

5867. *Tax Management International Journal.* Washington, DC: Tax Management, Inc. (Monthly)
Multinational business and economic development are the focus of this monthly journal.

5868. *Taxes.* Chicago: Commerce Clearing House. (Monthly)
Recent developments associated with federal and state taxation are featured in this monthly publication.

5869. *Transportation Law Journal.* Denver, CO: University of Denver, College of Law. (Semiannual)
A professional publication with research articles on the legal and regulatory aspects of the transportation industry.

5870. *West Federal Case News.* St. Paul, MN: West. (Weekly)
Summaries of important federal and state court decisions are provided in this weekly newsletter.

Author Index

Numbers refer to citation numbers, not page numbers.

Title Index

Numbers refer to citation numbers, not page numbers.

Subject Index

Numbers refer to citation numbers, not page numbers.